# Universal '40s Monsters
# A Critical Commentary

John T. Soister, Henry Nicolella
Harry H Long, Darío Lavia

BearManor
Media

Orlando, Florida

Published in the USA by
BearManor Media
1317 Edgewater Dr. #110
Orlando, FL 32804
www.BearManorMedia.com

Softcover Edition
ISBN: 978-1-62933-692-3

Printed in the United States of America

**Universal 40s Monsters; A Critical Commentary** is dedicated to:


"To John Cosari – For the 50 years of friendship and those back issues of *Famous Monsters*." (Bill)

"Dziękuję i pozdrawiam również SWOJĄ żonę!! Szczepan" (Steve)

"A la memoria de mi padre, Oscar Lavia." (Darío)

"For Arlene. If there's a heaven, there are horror films on the big screen and cats in her lap. RIP, dear separated-at-birth sister." (Harry)

"To my mother. You said I would never make a dime from my horror hobby. And you were right, Ma, but it's been a lot of fun." (Henry)

"For Nancy, who – in 38+ years of marriage – has never understood what a grown man sees in old horror movies like these. Thanks for seeing *me* in a loving and supportive light." (John)

# Table of Contents

Introduction and Acknowledgments -                                          xi

*1940 -*
The Invisible Man Returns (12 January) -                                     1
Black Friday (12 April) -                                                   15
The House of the Seven Gables (12 April) -                                  27
Enemy Agent (19 April) -                                                    41
The Mummy's Hand (20 September) -                                           47
The Invisible Woman (27 December) -                                         63

*1941 -*
Man-made monster (28 March) -                                               73
Horror Island (28 March) -                                                  91
The Black Cat (2 May) -                                                    103
Cracked Nuts (1 July) -                                                    119
Hold That Ghost (8 August) -                                              129
A Dangerous Game (22 August) -                                            139
The Wolf Man (12 December) -                                              147

*1942 -*
Sealed Lips (2 January) -                                                 163
The Mad Doctor of Market Street (27 February) -                          173
The Ghost of Frankenstein (13 March) -                                   183
Mystery of Marie Roget (3 April) -                                       199
The Strange Case of Doctor Rx (17 April) -                               213
Invisible Agent (31 July) -                                              225
Sherlock Holmes and the Voice of Terror (18 September) -                 237
Destination Unknown (9 October) -                                        247
The Mummy's Tomb (23 October) -                                          255
Night Monster (23 October) -                                             267
Nightmare (13 November) -                                                281
Sherlock Holmes and the Secret Weapon (25 December) -                    291

*1943 -*
Frankenstein Meets the Wolf Man (5 March) -                              299
Sherlock Holmes in Washington (30 April) -                               317
Captive Wild Woman (4 June) -                                            325
Phantom of the Opera (27 August) -                                       341
Sherlock Holmes Faces Death (17 September) -                             361
Flesh and Fantasy (29 October) -                                         369
Son of Dracula (5 November) -                                            385
The Mad Ghoul (12 November) -                                            399
Calling Dr. Death (17 December) -                                        411

*1944 -*
The Spider Woman (21 January) -                                          421
Weird Woman (14 April) -                                                  429
The Scarlet Claw (26 May) -                                              441

The Invisible Man's Revenge (9 June) -        449
Ghost Catchers (16 June) -                    459
Jungle Woman (7 July) -                        467
The Mummy's Ghost (7 July) -                   475
The Pearl of Death (22 September) -            485
The Climax (20 October) -                      493
Dead Man's Eyes (10 November) -                503
Murder in the Blue Room (1 December) -         511
House of Frankenstein (15 December) -          519
Destiny (22 December) -                        537
The Mummy's Curse (22 December) -              547

*1945* -
The House of Fear (16 March) -                 557
That's the Spirit (1 June) -                   565
The Frozen Ghost (29 June) -                   579
The Jungle Captive (29 June) -                 591
The Woman in Green (27 July) -                 599
Strange Confession (5 October) -               605
Pursuit to Algiers (26 October) -              613
House of Dracula (7 December) -                619
Pillow of Death (14 December) -                635

*1946* -
Terror by Night (1 February) -                 643
The Spider Woman Strikes Back (22 March) -     649
House of Horrors (26 March) -                  655
She-Wolf of London (17 May) -                  667
The Cat Creeps (17 May) -                      679
Dressed to Kill (7 June) -                     689
Danger Woman (12 July) -                       695
The Time of Their Lives (16 August) -          703
The Brute Man (1 October) -                    711

*1948* -
Abbott and Costello Meet Frankenstein (15 June) -   721

*Afterword* -                                  737

*End Notes* -                                  739

*Bibliography* -                               749

*Index* -                                      755

# NOTA BENE

"Pay no attention to the man behind the curtain!" boomed the all-powerful Wizard of Oz.

But attention must be paid to Bill Chase, our own man behind the drapery. Bill has contributed to all our projects over the years, starting with our silent horror/fantasy/sci-fi encyclopedia back in 2007. Thanks to Lantern and other online sources, material on that era is much more accessible today, but back then, reviews and articles were not that easy to find. It took five years for that book to be completed and it would have taken twice as long without Bill's research. Bill, the Pride of the Cleveland Public Library, was able to rustle up obscure articles, books, pictures and all sorts of gems relevant to pursuing info on so many little-known films.

He continued to lend his help (and his humor) to our subsequent efforts – whether we acted alone or as a duo – on Paul Wegener, offbeat thrillers, Frank Wisbar, and now, on our current run-down on Universal in the forties.

And he hasn't only lent a hand to us. Pick up just about any book on Universal horror and you'll probably find his name listed on the acknowledgments page.

Thanks, Bill, for your generosity, help... and patience. Beware, as we will no doubt be calling upon you again to lurk about the library stacks, to dust off more ancient tomes, to unearth documents of indeterminate origin (but of incredible value) in our never-ending crusade to generate some kind of interest in films that were meant to be seen once and then forgotten.

*—Henry and John*

# Introduction and Acknowledgments

It's been a while – 20 years, in fact – since I commented on Universal's horror, science fiction, & "twisted mystery" films from the 1930s. Back then, some of my essays in **Of Gods and Monsters** were praised while others were pooh-poohed, and I couldn't have been happier, as it proved to me that there were still fans of the "oldies" out there and that their opinions – no matter what they were - were as strong as ever. I had sort of planned on doing a '40s Universal follow-up soon thereafter, but a series of projects with a number of absolutely great collaborators followed instead: the late JoAnna Jones (née Wioskowski) partnered with me to do a paean to our favorite actor, and thus, **Claude Rains: A Comprehensive Illustrated Reference**, and we did so with Jessica Rains's blessing, as well as her foreword and photographs. Conrad Veidt biographer Pat Wilks Battle contributed to **Conrad Veidt on Screen**, as did Henry Nicolella, who would prove to be not only a dear friend, but also the most consistent of colleagues.

Somehow, I pulled off **Up from the Vault: Rare Thrillers from the '20s and '30s** on my own, but my next project brought together a group of gents who devoted *years* to chronicling the run of **American Silent Horror, Science Fiction and Fantasy Feature Films, 1913-1929**: Henry, Harry H Long, Steve Joyce, and Bill Chase. This two-volume, 800+-page-long encyclopedia attempted to list and comment on every film that fit the titular criteria. (We did receive a few comments from folks disappointed with how we had omitted foreign-made films, serials, and short subjects, but come on, guys… look at the *title*! Other folks were unhappy with what they perceived were snarky comments interspersed here and there amidst what they felt should have been a "highly academic" treatment. Well, they were spot on, but all the snarkiness was limited to *my* commentaries, as my share of the pictures to be covered – said shares were fairly and honorably distributed among us – included some of the worst stinkers and most misleading titles in film history.

And just a tad more on "snark." I'd be willing to bet a brass farthing - I loaded up on those guys just before the bottom fell out - that most genre fans are genre fans because they perceive the films, plays, books, etc. *to be fun*. When we were still of grammar-school age, some of the guys in my old neighborhood and I started a monster club right after "Shock Theater" debuted back in the mid-'50s. We adored those films – most of them were totally unexpected manna from heaven – yet we celebrated what we took to be the high points, full-throatedly critiqued most of the monster-centric footage, and snarked the bejesus out of things that even we seven- and eight-year-olds had little patience for. (Intriguingly, we didn't snark the series' non-horror entries, if only because the plot tip-offs in the *TV Guide* assured us that they weren't worth our time.) Thus, methinks there are any number of approaches to scrutinizing pictures with titles like *The Mummy's Ghost* and *Cracked Nuts*, and one such approach may well include the use of a semi-respectful tongue in cheek. (We demurred from considering herein how the removal of the stake from Dracula's heart in *House of Frankenstein* restored not only the undead count, but also his centuries-old, doubtlessly quite ripe soup and fish. Or how, logically, it would be quite impossible for almost any of our favorite monsters to catch a victim unawares, given that not one of the critters whose careers we have supported over the decades has even once wrestled with soap and water.) And allow me to throw down the gauntlet and defy anyone *not* to snarkify – not even a tad - when he/she has frittered away a good chunk of the day hoping that a Steenbeck-screening of a 1917 featurette entitled *Vengeance of the Dead* would justify one's time and merit inclusion in one's current project; in this case, the Silent Features encyclopedia mentioned above. First off, I reveled in the discovery of that title (*Hey!* Titles don't get much better than *that*); then I rejoiced at finding that – subject to a six-hour round-trip drive - I had access to the print; and then I snarked a bit [okay; a *good* bit] upon discovering that the enticingly named four-reeler centers on lawyers screwing around with a last will and testament.

Anyhow, Henry and I then teamed up again for **Many Selves: The Horror and Fantasy Films of Paul Wegener**. There was – and is – a ton of literature out there on Herr Wegener, but most of it is in German, so we decided to craft some commentary on the screen's first horror star, concentrating on him while in his element. In the midst of it all, I was surprised to find that Paul Wegener's son – Dr. Peter Wegener –

had been living for some years in Branford, Connecticut, presumably not far (Branford is *not* a big city) from where my wife and I were raising our three kids. Dr. Wegener and I corresponded for a short while and then I was stunned to learn of his passing. More recently, Hank (that's Henry, to his fans and friends) and I revisited some films that hadn't received that much attention when or since they were released, in **Down from the Attic**. (A tentative title for a future volume of same might be "Out of the Garage, from behind that Box of Christmas Decorations.")

Thanks – and a tip of the Soister hat (any Jimmy Hatlo fans out there?) - to amazing make-up/SPFX artist, Tom Burman, for actually taking the time to cogitate with us over his dad's contributions to the "Frankenstein" series. And, if I might, a moment of solemn yelling and carrying on in memory of the aforementioned JoAnna Jones, whose incredible creativity, generosity, and enthusiasm made our book on Claude Rains a comprehensive and valuable work. I was blessed to work with her. Also helping variously and enormously on these sundry projects were folks like Michaela Krause, Olaf Brill, Bob Dickson, Susan Duic, Tessa Forbes, Mary Corliss, the late John Parnum, the late Alan Levine, Vivienne Phillips, Arndt Pawelczik, Gary Rhodes, Werner Mohr, Kristen Dewey, Hans Wollstein, Bill Kaffenberger, André Stratmann, the late Richard Bojarski, Xochitl and Rogelio Agrasánchez, George Chastain, Cortlandt Hull, Scott Essman, and dozens of others who remain in our hearts and for whom we are eternally grateful.

The book at hand – filled with (hopefully) insightful opinion and commentary, but (fairly) low on snark – is a celebration for me. Not only is the band (Henry, Harry, Steve, and Bill) back together, but we've added the talent and generosity of Darío Lavia, author, film historian, and webmaster of www.Cinefania.com, which is quite a site for genre-hungry eyes. Perhaps the most dedicated of Universal fans in South America, Argentine Darío is also the creator of **Los Breviarios de Cinefania**, a series of pocket-sized books devoted to both "The Titans of Horror" (like Chaney, Lugosi, Karloff, et al) and "The Icons of Horror" (Dracula, Frankenstein, Jekyll and Hyde, et al, with the added bonus of having our own Steve Joyce pen the introduction to the volume on Stevenson's diametrically-opposed duo). For some years now, Henry has both done himself proud and fandom a great favor via insightful articles in *Castle of Frankenstein*, *Scary Monsters*, and *Van Helsing's Journal*; most recently, he penned the most excellent of biographies of Frank Wisbar (1). Harry, too, has been active in spreading the word hither, thither and yon, most notably in *Film Score Monthly*, *Filmfax*, *Outré*, *Video Watchdog*, *Little Shoppe of Horrors*, and *Classic Images*. Harry was also the long-time editor of *Scarlet, the Film Magazine* and *Van Helsing's Journal*.

Henry, Harry, Darío, and I have taken on the writing assignments herein, while the other lads are doing the heavy-lifting research-wise, providing illustrations, applying necessary technology, and the like. Each of us four scribes has his own style, and – to be honest – said styles may be seen to shift a tad this way or that, depending on the particular film we're scrutinizing. We've not attempted to ape the stylistics of our fellow authors/writers/historians, etc. in the field, and things like precise revenue figures and the minutiae of interrelationships of the personae involved in the production of these films is not our end here. (Interviews, of course, are the sole provenance of Mr. Thomas Weaver.)

Our beautiful cover art is the work of the über-talented Avril Aguire Aguire, architect, illustrator, and teacher at the National Autonomous University of Mexico. For more examples of Avril's brilliant work, please visit http://www.linkedin.com/in/arq-diana-avril-aguirre. The splendid piece that graces our back cover is due to the genius of Cortlandt Hull, whose "Witch's Dungeon Classic Movie Museum" - a remarkable experience akin to (and every bit as outstanding as) a visit to Madame Tussaud's in London (or anywhere!) – was begun by the spectacularly accomplished artist whilst still a teenager! For the Classic Monster fan, a junket to the Bristol, Connecticut Horror Haven is akin to a pilgrimage to Jerusalem or El Camino de Santiago. Many thanks to the Witch's Dungeon Classic Movie Museum for a good number of the photos and posters found throughout the book. More on Cortlandt and his museum may be found at www.preservehollywood.org. Both of these phenomenal artists may be followed on Facebook.

Many other of the photos that illustrate our essays are courtesy of George Chastain, artist, film buff, and collector extraordinaire. George is also the curator of a fantastic online site yclept "The Mad Monster Lab," an amazing trip back in time to the wonderful world of TV Horror Hosts (with sections on M.T. Graves and Zacherley especially notable), horror-film thesps, "Frankenstein University," and so much more! George – who moderates the site as his alter-ego, "E-gor" (viz. www.egorschamber.com) – has a portfolio of his work up for examination there, and – Boy! - would that the Fates had allowed George and Universal at its horror height to have worked together! Herr Chastain is also on Facebook.

Our Argentine colleague, Darío Lavia, also contributed a batch of photos from the pictures discussed herein. (The young fellow is a never-ending source of wisdom and opinion and visual evidence that backs up said wisdom and opinion!) ¡Muchísimas gracias, hermano! We're grateful, too, to Hans Wollstein – author (**Strangers in Hollywood** [1994], **Vixens, Floozies and Molls** [1999]), film reviewer, and former associate editor of the All Movie Guide – for lending us publicity shots and "alternate world" promotional artwork for classic films that never saw the carbon arc. Tak for din venlighed, Hans!

And, in need of a still that would capture the essence of Boris Karloff's character going to great lengths to do some drawing, we turned to Dr. Macro's High Quality Movie Scans. Thank you, Dr. Macro, for providing our image of a profoundly impatient Dr. Niemann.

Several of the essays which bear my name have been reprinted from the late and lamented *Cult Movies* magazine, wherein they appeared about 20 or so years ago; I have updated them and can honestly say they still reflect my feelings on those films. Many thanks to Mr. Buddy Barnett for granting me entrée into the world of opinionated so-and-sos in the first place.

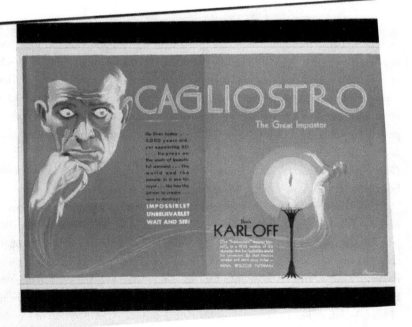

It didn't take long for Nina Wilcox Putnam and Richard Schayer's treatment, "Cagliostro," to become Karl Freund's haunting *The Mummy* (1932), with Boris Karloff a smash as Im-Ho-Tep, long-suffering lover *par excellence*. Less than a decade later, though, it would be the perpetual predator Kharis wielding *The Mummy's Hand*, as that film's original trailer made it clear that the "New" Universal required a new mummy.

As I wrote in my introduction to **Of Gods and Monsters**, I'm a commentator: someone who offers his viewpoints on something in order to get the ball rolling toward a meaningful (and fun) debate. So, too, are my collaborators herein. Albeit it's highly unlikely that you're reading this book without being familiar with the bulk of these films, for most of them we have included synopses; some we've stuck right at the beginning of our essays; others – apologies for the Rodgers and Hammerstein paraphrase - have got to be carefully sought; still others may be abbreviated in a nod to this era of "Spoiler Alert!" Our observations on the 1940s Universal genre output have the basic-titles-list in common with other books on the same theme (with a few additions), but we're hoping to add to the literature on those pictures, and not merely repeat it. We have sought to mention the effects of World War II on a number of these films, as well as on the studio itself, but again, the history of the era is not our main concern.

In order to be a member of the "Fellowship of This Here Thing," a film has to have been a Universal production (Duh!) made in the '40s and either a) have been aired on the original "Shock Theater," b) been aired on the follow-up, "Son of Shock," or c) have contained an element of horror, science fiction, or "twisted mystery." Thus, we included the Basil Rathbone/Nigel Bruce "Sherlock Holmes" series which – more often than not – had a villain(ess) who bordered on the colorfully psychotic. Thus, we passed on serials, Maria Montez/Jon Hall epics (despite exotic and intriguing near-mythological settings), and we reined in our critical horses with 1948's *Abbott and Costello Meet Frankenstein*, as that was the last of Universal's treatments of its "classic" horrors."

Our overly meticulous parsing of the studio product – to which we refer a couple more times herein, especially in discussions of those films whose "Shock" participation puzzled and annoyed us when we were lads – is reflected somewhat in the title of our book. Mostly, we're celebrating the return of our favorite monsters, whether they were revivified by new interpreters or not. (Of course, they were; only the Wolf Man – who hadn't so much as let out a yelp in the previous decade – would be the sole provenance of his originator. For a chapterful on his British forbear – the *WereWolf* of London – please check out the aforementioned **Of Gods and Monsters**.) While we're up for making points and pointing fingers at the "Inner Sanctum" films or the pictures that celebrated the Great Consulting Detective and his amanuensis, it was the classic monsters that spawned and held our interest over the decades.

Other than ...*Meet Frankenstein*, our coverage ends with 1946's *The Brute Man*, the last Rondo Hatton/"Creeper" film to be produced by the studio (albeit it was sold to and released by PRC), and the last of Universal's non-comedic horror "series."(2) On the 20 July of that year, Universal merged with International Pictures, and Universal-International Pictures – under the leadership of William Goetz, a son-in-law to Louis B. Mayer – renounced chapterplays, horror pictures, and "B"-pictures in general, while announcing to the film world that the new entity would involve itself (almost) solely with prestige productions. Many studies of the Universal horror output and horror films as a genre aver that the market for such products dried up after the war, causing a shift to *films noir*, described by many as atmospheric *psychological* horror stories. While the shift in dynamic may be so, Gary Rhodes – one of our absolutely favorite film historians – draws our attention to the fact that, even in that last half of the decade, there was no dearth of horror pictures on screens throughout the USA.

For example... [there were] twenty-five horror movies starring Bela Lugosi. Twenty-five, all in the space of three years, even though Lugosi made only one new serious horror movie (*Scared to Death*) and only one horror comedy (*Abbott and Costello Meet Frankenstein*) during the second half of the decade. In other word, none of these twenty-five Lugosi movies at movie theaters were new; they were all reissues. The back catalogs of studios like Universal and Monogram saturated theaters with old horror movies to the extent that they generally satisfied whatever demand existed for them, cheaply and efficiently. Put another way, why hire an actor like Bela Lugosi and produce a new horror film when an old one would literally fill the bill? (3)

Dr. Rhodes also points out that, after the mid-'40s, there were no more pictures featuring Universal's classic monsters, save for the above-cited Abbott and Costello classic which received mostly very positive reviews. He then goes on to posit – quite persuasively – that...

...as a result of such reactions, Universal-International planned more Abbott and Costello comedies (including the film that became *Abbott and Costello Meet the Killer, Boris Karloff* [Charles Barton, 1949]), but not any horror films featuring Dracula, the Wolf Man, and Frankenstein's monster. The studio abandoned the old monsters, another apparent sign that the horror movie was under siege in the late 1940s, even if its decline did not begin until 1947. (4)

Nonetheless, a number of new horror films were released by various studios in 1947, 1948, and 1949, just none – the Abbott and Costello pictures excepted - from Universal-International.

In previous tomes (**Up from the Vault, Down from the Attic**), we tried to "preview" each of the films covered here in the introduction. Just too many to do so, this time 'round. Still, we can break them down into categories. First off, we have what are probably the most popular of the lot: the "classic monster continuations." Among those returning would be Frankenstein's Monster, albeit no longer impersonated by the gentle Brit who had essayed the role for Universal in 1931. Indications of any sort of personality not fueled by violence had likewise been left in the previous decade, as the Monster – now pretty much the henchman and secondary character Karloff had foretold in his last turn in 1939 – would be lab material for any number of poor family relations or medical types who just could not be dissuaded from wanting to see the fearsome giant "at the height of his powers."

Back, too, was the Invisible Man; more properly – as we argue in the body of the essays herein – *an* Invisible Man. Again, apparently the need for transparency – or the drive to restore visibility to the already transparent - ran in the veins of almost anyone bearing the name Griffin. *In medias res*, we were given .... *errrrr*.... a glimpse of an heroic Griffin, who assumed the mantle of invisibility to save America from her Axis foes, and a quite lovely distaff non-Griffin, who answered a newspaper ad on the subject pretty much as a lark. Thankfully – for those genre-lovers who wanted their "heroes" to be anything other than heroic – yet another Griffin would cap off the series on an end-note of revenge.

**Albeit shot during rehearsal for the CBS (radio) broadcast of *The Hands of Mr. Ottormole* (1948), with a bit of imagination this might well be irrefutable evidence of Claude Rains tutoring Vincent Price on how to *sound* invisible.**

A Mummy also was resurrected come the new decade. Not the mystical Im-ho-tep who had pined for his Anck-es-en-amon in 1932, but the perennially pissed-off Kharis, whose drive to throttle those who defiled the tomb of his Ananka managed to defile both space and time in the course of four "B"-features. Dracula returned, too... sort of. Was this "Alucard" really the count himself, cloaked (Sorry!) in the most ridiculously transparent (apologies to the Messrs. Griffin) sobriquet imaginable? Or was he, in fact, truly the direct offspring of the original Voivode from Transylvania? If so, his acquired command of English was remarkable, to say the least; not a hint of the pronunciation (or delivery) made famous by his father. When Dracula, too, was reduced to secondary-cast status in the first of the *House* features, we were left to determine whether he was, indeed, *he* – What was the deal with this "Baron Latos" baloney? Why yet another alias? - or was he perhaps the "son" of the chap in the previous picture who had lost a bit of weight but retained his matinee-idol mustache? Come the second *House* adventure, we had no doubt with whom we were dealing, albeit the old darling now confessed to being weary of the whole business.

One of Universal's biggest budget projects of the decade was the 1943 reworking of *The Phantom of the Opera*. In exchange for subtracting the definite article from the 1925 title, the studio went for the gold and shot the musical extravaganza in Technicolor. A "super-jewel" if there ever was one, the reimagining included a faceful of acid – make-up genius Jack P. Pierce was given no option to offer an original concept – an indecisive take on the relationship between Opera Ghost and student, and a more dramatically satisfying plunge of the chandelier. Still, genre mavens moaned over the plethora of singing, the fairly tepid denouement, and the fact that the actor playing the title role was billed third, under a 19-year-old soprano and the "Singing Capon." Planned as a semi-sequel to *Phantom* was *The Climax*, yet another Technicolor sojourn throughout the studio's "Phantom stage." Any number of adjustable spanners were dropped into the works, though, and what emerged was essentially a second film featuring Susanna Foster trying to sing like the diva she was whilst navigating her way around another lunatic.

In addition to the sundry "returns," some new grotesques made their debuts. Lon Chaney's Wolf Man was popular-isimo from his inception, and his tormented lycanthrope – the only classic Universal monster to have but one interpreter - would return time and again, seeking peace while rending throats. On the female side, in addition to the "she-wolf" who prowled the streets of London, we were witness to a sort of instantaneous – and absurd – chemical evolution wherein apes would transform into gorgeous (if otherwise fairly blah!) young women; the originator of that role would last for but two of the three pictures dedicated to the character. The '40s *did* allow the fair sex to come into their own, as it were, and whether they were captive (but wild!), known for their viridescent garb, or just plain weird, it was a joy to see them getting something along the lines of equal time. (Only the bean-counters could comment on equal pay.) Acromegaly victim Rondo Hatton would find a niche in the studio's Horror Hall of Fame, although only within the last two years of his life. Whether playing the "Hoxton Creeper" in *The Pearl of Death*, the descriptor-less Creeper in *House of Horrors*, or the "Hal Moffat" Creeper in the posthumously released *The Brute Man*, Hatton's contribution to the genre was a result of his personal tragedy, and not due to any literary or cinematic forbear.

A brace of series was introduced: Sherlock Holmes mysteries and the "Inner Sanctum" thrillers. The former – of which *The Pearl of Death* was an entry – became a Universal property in 1942 when, per one interpretation, Basil Rathbone's agent (5) argued against having the Great Consulting Detective's adventures locked into 20th Century Fox's idea of the Victorian Era:

The very conditions in Europe (war, bombings, modern espionage) which had made the turn-of-the-century Holmes of the misty Fox films seem so hopelessly dated and out of place were to provide the cases for the new, 1940s Holmes! It seemed to Rathbone – who had never played the detective except against a hansom-cab-and-gaslight backdrop – a refreshing concept indeed... Basil Rathbone and Nigel Bruce signed with Universal Pictures. Quick to exploit crises torn out of wartime headlines, the studio was to call the first film *Sherlock Holmes Saves London.*

The "Inner Sanctum" series consisted of nail-biters that may have born the "I.S." trademark, but which were original mysteries wherein Lon Chaney was given the chance to wear suits and ties, eschew grunting and snarling for fairly decent dialogue, furrow his brow, and take turns being the alleged perpetrator and the near-victim. Only a couple of the films came anywhere close to having genuine horrific elements, and the majority of criticism of the series almost from Day One could be expressed in a single adjective: tepid.

Taking inventory of its '40s genre titles, one might easily come to the opinion that the studio was responsible for more housing than was Levittown, New York, come the '50s. The earliest to be erected was Hawthorne's *Shanty of the Seven Gables*; this, of course, was all she built until the middle of Advent 1945, when the *Fireside of Frankenstein* was followed (in fairly short order) by *The Flophouse of Fear*, the *Domicile of Dracula*, and the *Habitation of Horrors*. While this titling trend did foreshadow a number of thrillers centered around a specific location – *House of Wax* (1953), *House on Haunted Hill* (1959), *House of Usher* (1960), and *House of Dark Shadows* (1970), to name but a few – the cinema would never again offer such a concentrated spate of unmarketable real estate to the public.

Along with the aforementioned, the studio's genre (and quasi-genre) output until 1946 also featured a goodly number of miscellaneous malefactors: Mad Ghouls (despite a singular title, a sort-of-second emerged at the picture's end), Mad Doctors (fairly ubiquitous albeit with unique hang-ups), Spider Women (two archvillainesses who, while played by the same actress, were unrelated save for their love of arachnids), cats of black, claws of scarlet, etc., etc., etc.

Universal-International would pull the plug in 1946; 'twas not just a change in taste on the part of the audience, but also a change in investment policy in re: "B" films, and much of the studio's product had obviously devolved into same. The combination of 1948's "last hurrah" for the studio's classic grotesques (contractually obligated to confront Abbott and Costello, whose box office appeal was waning somewhat), the agreement to have Realart Pictures and Film Classics re-release the lion's share of the classic horror films in theaters everywhere, plus the introduction of Dracula and colleagues to the nascent TV generation assured the continuation of "the dynasty." Reimaginings courtesy of England's Hammer Films (et al), America's Allied Artists (and others), and Mexico's Cinematográfica Calderón S.A. (y otros) ginned up the ferocity a bit and the sensuality a bit more, while presenting still more monstrous relatives, offshoots, and variations. (In the interest of recalling Universal's main overseas markets during the '40s, we've added a few foreign-language versions of their contemporaneous publicity materials. Kind of neat...) Underneath it all - and serving as the foundation of the countless remakes "improved" by developing technology and a greater acceptance of nudity and violence – remain the iconic creatures adapted to the screen by the Laemmles and their successors during times of financial disaster and worldwide conflict.

Welcome to the World of Gods and Monsters, as imagined some 80 years ago!

*—John Soister*

# *The Invisible Man Returns* (1940)

Universal's "Great Horror Revival" of the 1940s actually began in January of 1939, when the Frankenstein Monster – his post-explosion treatment and therapy having been successful – arose from the comfort of his stone slab and began exploring the architectural wonder that bore his father's name. As it was Karloff's Monster who had followed Lugosi's Vampire into the hearts and minds of Great Depression audiences only months after the release of *Dracula* in mid-February 1931, it was only fitting that Boris and Bela would join forces to lead their fellow grotesques – and the genre, itself – back into theaters now filled with patrons seeking escape from the dread of what appeared to be impending (and inevitable) war. *Son of Frankenstein* was a resounding success – audiences were grateful for shudders that portended nothing more than a couple of sleepless nights, and Universal was grateful for the audiences – so it seemed reasonable to expect that the next move would be from Castle Frankenstein to Carfax Abbey to witness the imminent resurrection and subsequent predations of everyone's favorite thirsty count.

Alas! The King of the Vampires would have to wait until 1943 for his next cinematic gig, and how he must have felt, what with his being beaten back to the screen by the Mummy (and not the one he had rubbed box-office elbows with earlier, either!), the Phantom of the Opera, the Wolf Man, the Frankenstein Monster (again!) and Ygor (Are you kidding?), some sort of Man-Made Monster, the Wolf Man (also

1

again!), the Frankenstein Monster (for the third time!), a Wild Woman held Captive, and that second Mummy, once more. And, for the love of Mike, by the Invisible Man, an Invisible Woman, and even an Invisible "Agent."

To be fair to Count Dracula, his chagrin at coming in last may have been diminished a tad had he realized that – save for the Wolf Man and Ygor – not one of that '40s company bore the face of his original impersonator and not one of the horrific "reappearances" noted above featured the same actor twice. And - given his bandages, over-sized sunglasses, and total transparency - on the...errr...face of it, determining that the Invisible Man who returned was, in fact, an entirely different guy than the one who had expired in bed some seven years earlier was theoretically impossible. Granted, Claude Rains had gone on to diversify quite substantially since his sound-film debut back then, but he *was* "The Invisible Man," no? And even if we admit that we realize we're talking about the character and not the actor here, the title blatantly states that "The Invisible Man" is the returnee here, so our finding out that we're not about to... errr... not see Jack Griffin, but, rather, some nobody yclept Sir Geoffrey Radcliffe makes the more grammatically-anal among us a bit disconcerted.

Anyhow, with bits and pieces of some *Tower of London* interiors still on the back-lot – and having earlier bought the film rights to the character from Herbert George Wells - Universal determined that having a titled Brit take the heat (and the injection) might add a bit of fresh blood (and English box-office revenue) to the mix. With genuine-Brit Rains over at the Brothers Warner for the nonce, ersatz-Brit Vincent Price (late of both *The Private Lives of Elizabeth and Essex* and the aforementioned *Tower of London*) filled the bill quite nicely. Price's voice was as mellifluous and distinctive as was Rains' and, what with his standing 6'4" tall, there was zero need to place the Missouri-born Price on a box whilst interacting with his onscreen fellows. Another advantage to using Price as the protagonist was that he could facilitate for the rest of the cast and crew director Joe May's semi-incoherent instructions. As quoted in **Universal Horrors**, Price explained: "May was difficult to understand, as he spoke no English. I had something of a rapport with him because of my knowledge of German."(1)

The most intriguing idea raised by all this is the claim (promoted and supported by the advertising of the release and subsequent re-release[s] on VHS/DVD/Blu-Ray of all the '30 & '40s films + the '50s Creature trio) that the Invisible Man is one of Universal's "Classic Monsters." Really? Over the two decades or so that separated the character's initial adventures from his run-in with Abbott and Costello, the recipients of Jack Griffin's research had changed personage, motive, allegiance, and gender. We'd run the gamut from an appreciation of Wells's original (married, so to speak, with Philip Wylie's **The Murderer Invisible**) to a tale of anger and retribution (see: *The I.M.'s Revenge*) on the part of Robert Griffin, a psychopath in his own right who just happens to share coincidentally nomenclature with principals in the first two series' entries. Come on… is every Griffin a sucker for invisibility juice, the way every Frankenstein pines to see Uncle Heinrich's pride-and-joy at the peak of his powers? (Has any of this occurred to Seth MacFarlane?) All this, whilst we pause to consider the role of an unseen patriot in wartime and to picture – with our mind's eye - that naked lady running about, unnoticed, in our midst. Come the '50s, "The Invisible Man" became a hero (of sorts) on the small screen, battling spies and generic bad guys seeking to do… *well*… whatever it was they had planned to do. Classic figure? Perhaps. Monster? Uh-uh.

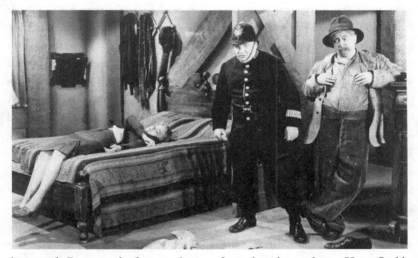

**Apparently Duocaine leads not only to madness, but also to clutter. Harry Stubbs is visibly upset with the slovenliness of the invisible Vincent Price, while Nan Grey is obviously beyond distressed. Forrester Harvey (right) eyes the abandoned garments with a keen and craving eye.**

Still, there *is* that moment late in *Returns* when a rain-soaked bobby speculates on the nature of the Invisible Man with his superior. "You'll know soon enough," advises his boss, "when he leaps on your back and starts sucking your blood." Now it takes a fairly awkward bit of ratiocination to lump the unseen Radcliffe in there with such feral types as the Werewolf (of London, natch) or Dracula (late of Carfax Abbey),

3

especially when the accounts of local boy Jack Griffin's misadventures had earlier filled the British press and neither gymnastic feats nor intimations of vampirism has figured into Griffin's megalomaniac delusions. But here, just after a series of off-camera transfusions from a batch of friendly collieries workers and just prior to the clench-and-close as the end-music swells, Dr. Frank realizes aloud that "The new blood itself is the antidote!" to all that went wrong with his pal. Perhaps *had* his older brother chomped down on an artery or two when those chuckle-headed townsfolk at Iping wouldn't give him a moment's peace, most – if not all - of the subsequent violence and destruction might not have taken place. Who can say for sure?

*The Invisible Man Returns* is the only picture in any of the runs of *any* of those "Classic Monsters" to acknowledge onscreen that it is a sequel. This confession undoubtedly was a requisite codicil to the paperwork that gave Universal the screen rights to Wells's transparent protagonist. That brief flash of a snapshot of Claude Rains in the Scotland Yard file on Jack Griffin also served to tie-in the current offering directly with the 1933 production, which had almost immediately been considered a masterpiece by everyone except for Mr. Wells, who reportedly was less than thrilled with the picture because the screenplay turned his protagonist "into a lunatic." The picture regurgitates a couple of bits from its 1933 *pater familias*. Like Dr. Frank's brother, Geoffrey Radcliffe goes unseen throughout the entire film and is restored to full opaqueness only at the denouement whilst abed, up to his chest in bedclothes. The unwrapping of the head (before a mirror) likewise had been done earlier, as is the scene in which the bandaged protagonist rather operatically foresees a despotic future for himself while in the company of the woman he loves. We note *en passant* that while Frank Griffin has *not* packed a false nose in the suitcase left for the fleeing (and buck-naked) Radcliffe, neither had he pack any undies. One can imagine well enough the suffering one must endure, battling the English countryside during a cold spell whilst nude, without having to deal with the chafing that needs occur when one's privates negotiate directly with the trousers of a tweed suit. That snippy attitude affected by Radcliffe fairly early on may not be due *entirely* to the invisibility solution.

The plot begins with an invisible Geoffrey Radcliffe escaping his prison cell to hunt down the man who had murdered his brother (Geoff himself is set to be executed for the crime) while trying mightily not to go mad *a la* the invisibility solution Dr. Frank Griffin has injected into him. Obviously as guilty as hell at first glance – without the savvy moviegoer even needing to know opportunity or motivation - is Richard Cobb, cousin to the Radcliffes and apparently heir to their "collieries" (*ahem...* coal mines and assorted buildings associated with them) should the brothers somehow be removed from the scene. Geoff chases after Willie Spears, a newly-minted (but perennially tipsy and wildly unqualified) foreman at the mines, rightly figuring Spears' promotion was given in exchange for keeping his mouth shut. Spears fingers Cobb as the murderer, and Geoff – having sequestered Spears – captures Cobb, whom he brings at gunpoint to be confronted by Spears. Cobb escapes and runs into the collieries, but he is fatally injured when, battling the invisible Geoff, he falls from atop a coal cart emptying its load; luckily, he confesses to the murder before expiring. Geoff, who was shot during the struggle with Cobb, is restored to visibility and Helen's embrace following a blood transfusion. Interspersed through all this are several scenes in which 1) Geoff's descent into madness and megalomania seems to be accelerating; 2) Scotland Yard's Inspector Sampson – armed with knowledge of the misadventures of Geoff's older brother and a cache of cigars - gets closer and closer to capturing the Invisible Man; 3) Frank Griffin putters around his lab, juggling test tubes, retorts and hypodermic needles as he works around the clock to find an antidote; and 4) legions of smartly-caped bobbies, hot on the case, are engulfed in smoke and rain. Again, while it's true that the basic plot of the picture (Invisible Man is chased by police, chaos ensues, he is shot and becomes visible again) and a good bit of filler (experimentation to find a way back, expressions of love and regret to the skirt, bad guy in roadster speeding off with unseen passenger) were first onscreen in 1933, there are enough new details to keep one's interest from flagging for the 81 minutes the picture is on.

At one point, for example, Frank reveals that all that awful business with his brother had occurred some nine years prior to the mishegas concerning Geoff and the murder accusation. Some of us might wonder why Frank – who had been sitting on the invisibility solution for darn near a decade – waited only until after he had injected his good friend with it to begin working seriously toward an antidote. We might regard as facile the notion that adding colored powder to blood drawn from Geoff's arm would make it visible but not affect adversely in any way the scientific conclusions to be drawn. We might tip our hat to blatant villain Cobb, who, having killed the lights in Spears' house, shouts that now *he* is just as invisible as Geoff, as the two begin to throw the furniture about. We doff said hat completely in respect for and admiration of the lyric scene in which Geoff addresses a scarecrow in a field while simultaneously dressing himself in its clothing and then bidding it *adieu*. And one final question: Following his massive blood transfusion (how did Frank Griffin gauge the precise amount of blood needed, anyhow?), Geoff takes a moment to gaze gratefully at his arm. Under "normal" conditions, can the Invisible Man see *himself*?

5

As had Claude Rains, Vincent Price demonstrated a good bit of self-effacement for the body of the picture in the interest of a dramatic bonus at its end: for Rains, the movie-going public's first glimpse at an actor who would captivate them for decades to come; for Price, an extended medium close-up that gave a much better look than audiences had been afforded via *Tower of London* or *Elisabeth and Essex* with their period hair appliances. The cinematic careers of both men would be lengthy and eclectic, yet each would be associated with a role or three in the genre we love so much. Whereas Rains had escaped from the Laemmles' ongoing series of moody atmospheric thrillers after *The Mystery of Edwin Drood* (1935), within a lustrum he was to be tapped as Sir John Talbot in *The Wolf Man* and later signed on to do the titular honors in the Technicolor *Phantom of the Opera* (1943). Other than the film at hand, only *The House of the Seven Gables* (1940) and his brief, comic cameo as the Invisible Man in *Abbott and Costello Meet Frankenstein* (1948) mark Price's collusion with this volume. With nearly three times the film credits of Rains, Price saw his involvement with the horror genre begin in earnest with 1953's *House of Wax*, pick up steam through the rest of that decade, and then come into its own – thanks mostly to Roger Corman – in the '60s. The actor does quite well here as the ever more unstable Radcliffe, and his towering above most of his fellow cast members adds more than a hint of the physical menace that would be compounded by transparency.

Among the last pictures that featured Sir Cedric Hardwicke before filming began on *Returns* were RKO's *The Hunchback of Notre Dame* and M-G-M's *On Borrowed Time* (both 1939). Sir Cedric was the villainous Frollo in the former and Death himself in the latter; little wonder the Worcestershire-born actor would be tapped to be the murderer of Sir Michael Radcliffe. Both the screenplay and the direction of *Returns* make it bloody obvious from the get-go that Roger Cobb is a creature of barely-concealed emotions, or that all of them are bad. Knighted in 1934 for his work on the British stage and screen (right between his appearances with Boris Karloff in *The Ghoul* and with Conrad Veidt in *Bella Donna* – both films being shot in Great Britain), Hardwicke as Cobb seems to be playing to the back row, as the dour expression on his face leaves little doubt as to where he stands in re: Nan Grey's Helen. The picture offers no plot surprises – does anyone *really* believe that Geoff Radcliffe and Helen Manson will not end up in each other's arms? – so with John Sutton's Frank Griffin the only other "main" character in the mix, Cobb's the man.

Unless you count 1939's *Wuthering Heights* (a toss-up at best), *Returns* is Cecil

Kellaway's first venture into the genre. His Inspector Sampson is Johnny-on-the-spot with his file on Jack Griffin - a "Maniac-Murderer" readeth the description - some stogies with which to spot the invisible one's outline, and more coppers than can be seen at the Policeman's Ball. Granted, the inspector is still under the impression that Geoffrey Radcliffe is as guilty as all get-out, but his putting two and two together *vis-à-vis* the escape from the prison cell in the twinkling of an eye is impressive. Nine years after most of Britain was befuddled by the very idea of an invisible man, the local representative of national law enforcement takes his existence just for starters. And although neither Sampson nor that army of police appears to be within earshot of Roger Cobb as he whispers his confession, the subsequent hospital-bed drama attests that they've taken the word of Frank and Helen as to Geoff's innocence, even though the entire movie is predicated on the fact that no one has taken anyone's word on Geoff's innocence at any time. While Kellaway brings his uniquely "semi-serious" take to the role, the gleeful resolve with which his character approaches the investigation is believable because of his certainty in the methodology he is following. There is more on Mr. Kellaway in the essay on *The Mummy's Hand*.

Alan Napier, whose most memorable role may have been that of Alfred, Bruce Wayne's butler and confidant, in the hit-'60s television series, *Batman*, offers a memorable job here, as well. Physically, his Willie Spears is a bit taller and a lot grimier than anyone else in the cast, while behaviorally he is just filled with himself, as the former night-watchman revels in his newfound title and status. The British Napier would go on to a long and varied career and took full advantage of the job opportunities offered later in life by the introduction of the boob tube, appearing in dozens of TV series (including *Thriller*, *The Twilight Zone*, *Night Gallery*, and *The Alfred Hitchcock Hour*) apart from his stint at "stately Wayne Manor."

Holdovers from *Tower of London* include John Sutton and Nan Grey (plus Price, of course, and contract players like Ivan Simpson, Ed Brady, Cyril Thornton, et al). Most genre aficionados immediately think of Grey as the soulful victim of Gloria Holden in *Dracula's Daughter* (1936), but the lovely Houston native had already wet her genre toes with an uncredited bit in the 1935 version of *The Great Impersonation*, and the Crime Club entries *The Black Doll* and *Danger on the Air* (both 1938). She and Vincent Price (and Cecil Kellaway and Alan Napier) would share the screen again in 1940's *The House of the Seven Gables*, but Grey would retire from the screen a year later, her last role coming in Columbia's rather exploitative *Under Age* (1941). Her Helen

Manson hasn't much to do but wring her hands and bite her lip, but Grey wrings and bites quite well. The only "flaw" in the portrayal is the actress's noticeable lack of any "Englishness" in her delivery; going up against that gang of "born-elsewheres" (besides the Britons listed above, Kellaway was from South Africa, Forrester Harvey from Ireland, Sutton from India [!], and Price… well, he was Vincent Price), her lack of "vocal lilt" sort of stands out.

The aforementioned Mr. Sutton – born in Rawalpindi of British parentage – had quite a number of "uncredits" before stepping into the shoes of Jack Griffin's younger (and taller) brother. The actor was in most of the Bulldog Drummond series, whether credited or "un-," and he, too, was in *The Private Lives of Elizabeth and Essex*, albeit without enjoying the sight of his name in the cast crawl. Sutton managed to avoid following *Returns* with an armful of other, similar films and spent most of the '40s making a name for himself at 20th Century Fox, usually in secondary roles. His Frank Griffin certainly goes through enough of the motions one would expect from a dedicated scientist under the most desperate of deadlines, although – even given the common elements of both "Invisible" pictures - it's a tad difficult picturing Frank and brother Jack sharing a crumpet together.

The film got some good press, perhaps a bit because the 1933 picture had made such a positive impression, but quite enough on its own merits. Philip K. Scheuer, writing in the 16 February 1940 edition of the *Los Angeles Times*, opined:

People who look askance at sequels may safely relax in the current instance, for this follow -up to the original production from the pen of H.G. Wells is, although the work of two other fellows, fully as amusing, unexpected and pulsating an affair. It will give you a delightfully jittery 81 ½ minutes As in the preceding film, no opportunity for imaginative humor has been neglected. The invisible one's passing-by is the occasion for all sorts of whimsical horseplay, to which the trick camera responds nobly.

Scheuer's colleague-in-criticism, Edwin Schallert, had recorded his approval in that paper more than a month earlier…

*The Invisible Man Returns* rates headline attention as an entertainment novelty. Portions of the picture may seem far-fetched and overly theatrical, but the technique is splendid, and the production keeps up its spell of excitement. It will take rating along with the first *Invisible Man*, which had Claude Rains is [sic] the 'unseen' personage of the plot, while James Whale directed…

10 January 1940

In the *Times* that was more familiar to folk on the East Coast, Frank S. Nugent mixed his opinion with a quite interesting fact:

Universal makes no peace offering, in the form of a credit, to Mr. Wells, for the non appearance of his disembodied semi-phantom. One Joe May is billed as author, and among his adapters we find the name of Cedric Belfrage, who once wrote, as though in prophecy, a tome called 'Away from It All, the Notebook of an Escapologist.' Ghostly, isn't it? ... Somehow, we were not as astonished as once we were... This camera hocus-pocus still has its fascination, of course but the script is annoyingly unoriginal... And for the sheer absurdity of the thing, we don't suppose there has ever been a sequence to match the one in which Sir Cedric is being hustled along by the collar, with a pistol prodding him in the back, and not a soul in sight (except Sir Cedric).

*The New York Times*, 16 January 1940

Belfrage, a socialist scribe who was co-founder of the *National Guardian* weekly newspaper, started his career as a part-time film critic for England's *Kinematograph Weekly* in 1924. Although his name will ring more bells for political activists than movie buffs, Belfrage occasionally helped vet scripts at Universal. It was probably not because of his activity at the Big U that he was deported from the United States in 1955.

Joe May and Kurt Siodmak shared the "original story" credit (Mr. Belfrage went uncredited) for *Returns* and, as noted above, there's not really all that much original about it. Still, reviewer Richard L. Coe, writing for the *Washington Post*, did note that "The present scenarists have created a background of realism and a story of *mere murder* [emphasis ours] as an accompaniment for the incredulous circumstances of the disembodied one" (3 February 1940). May, of course, also directed the project, and Siodmak, soon to be "Curt," reveled in reviving the notion that Jack Griffin's "Monocaine" (yclept "Duocaine" herein; after all, it *is* its second time around) would lead to madness. Much of Siodmak's published fiction and many of his screenplays dealt with abnormalities to and/or hyper-extensions of rationality and, with *Returns*, he was just getting his brain wet.

In his autobiography, **Wolf Man's Maker**, Siodmak speaks briefly of his contribution to the film:

*The Return of the Invisible Man* [sic] did not need much imagination. The subject of 'invisibility' was not new to me since my last novel written for the German market, *The Power in the Dark*, dealt with it. The theme of *The Return of the Invisible Man*

9

Thanks to John P. Fulton's visual magic, JoeMay's direction, and – mostly – the
still photographer's playing with available images, FrancesRobinson's Nurse, Cecil
Kellaway's Inspector Sampson, Nan Grey's Helen Manson, and a dozen or so of
Universal's most reliable extras stare directly *into* Vincent Price's Invisible Man.

was the seemingly inevitable corruption of power. The wish to be invisible is deeply ingrained in the human mind. To observe but not to be seen contains a temptation to misuse that potential... Since return was nominated for an Academy Award because of its special effects and was also a financial success, I had to write every one of Universal's 'Invisible' pictures. (2)

Well, other than 1944's *The Invisible Man's Revenge* and the 1951 pastiche, that is. Siodmak's German-language novel deals with a scientist who becomes transparent in order to commit acts of aggression/destruction against nations who are on the verge of starting a war between themselves in order to frighten them into different behaviors. Calling his book's theme "prophetic," the novelist claimed "The same thing on a small scale I used for my assignment," namely, *The Invisible Man Returns*. Perhaps that might have been Siodmak's original intention, but Geoffrey Radcliffe indulges in megalomaniac blather only whilst at table with Dr. Griffin and Helen Manson; otherwise – despite his fear of succumbing to the mental lure of Duocaine – he stays pretty close to the road to revenge on Richard Cobb. Academically, at least, it might prove quite interesting to see the extent to which screenplay-collaborator, Lester K. Cole, may have altered Siodmak's thematic diminution so as to give us the picture we have today.

Joe May (like Kurt Siodmak) had emigrated from The Fatherland to the USA, although May hopped about Europe first before settling into the Hollywood lifestyle. Signing up with Universal in 1939, May quickly demonstrated the kind of flair he had shown during the Silent Era was just what the studio was looking for: he helmed *The House of Fear* (1939), *Returns*, and *The House of the Seven Gables* back-to-back-to-back. His vision in *Returns* was nothing extraordinary, but – as may be seen in Richard Coe's comment, above – most audiences (and critics) of the time were more than willing to accept a fairly mundane Whodunit when spiced with a bit of exotica. May's poor English and authoritarian manner with his coworkers did not lead to an extended contract with Universal, though, and the Vienna-born director ended his film career a few years later at Monogram. More on May will be found in our essay on *House of the Seven Gables*.

First of those "classic monster" movies to hit the screen after the '30s called it quits, *The Invisible Man Returns* reworked the original formula to its credit. A bit of head-scratching here and there – Whatever happened to the contents of your stomach taking a while to invisible-ize? Or why would a research scientist who works with guinea pigs have a couple of sets of manacles lying around the house? – but that comes with sequel territory, no? Best of the more serious of the invisible follow-ups, the picture boasts more advanced SPFX than the original – check out the *inside* of the bandaged head or the bit where Cecil Kellaway's cigar smoke does its job – and an equally strong cast. Even if *The* Invisible Man didn't make it back a second time, his gauze and goggles were worn (and his clothes tossed about the floor) by a worthy "understudy."

*The Invisible Man Returns –*
12 January 1920 – 81 minutes (ST)

**CAST**: Sir Cedric Hardwicke as Richard Cobb; Vincent Price as Sir Geoffrey Radcliffe; Nan Grey as Helen Manson; John Sutton as Dr. Frank Griffin; Cecil Kellaway as Inspector Sampson; Alan Napier as Willie Spears; Forrester Harvey as Ben Jenkins; Harry Stubbs as Constable Tewksberry; Frances Robinson as Nurse; Ivan Simpson as Cotton; Edward Fielding as Prison Governor; Leland Hodgson as Chauffeur; Mary Gordon as Cook; Billy Bevan as a Warden; Bruce Lester as Chaplain; Matthew Boulton, Frank Hill, Cyril Thornton and Ed Brady as Policemen; Paul England and Raoul Freeman as Detectives; Dave Thursby as Bob; Louise Brien as Dr. Griffin's Secretary; Rex Evans as Constable Briggs; Frank Hagney as Bill; Jimmy Aubrey and Colin Kenny as Plainclothesmen; George Hyde, George Kirby, George Lloyd, Edmund MacDonald, Harry Cording, Ellis Irving, Dennis Tankard, Chet Brandenburg as Miners; with Mary Field, Stanley Blystone, Charles Brokaw, William Newall, Sidney Grayler, Boyd Irwin, Berry Hayes, Frank Colleti

**CREDITS**: Director: Joe May; Associate Producer: Ken Goldsmith; Screenplay: Lester K. Cole and Kurt Siodmak; Original Story: Joe May, Kurt Siodmak and Cedric Belfrage (uncredited); Based on characters and situations from *The Invisible Man* by H.G. Wells; Director of Photography: Milton Krasner; Art Director: Jack Otterson; Associate Art Director: Martin Obzina: Special Photographic Effects: John P. Fulton, Cleo E. Baker (uncredited); Special Effects: David S. Horsley (uncredited); Film Editor: Frank Gross; Assistant Director: Phil Karlstein [Karlson]; Set Designer: Russell A. Gausman; Music Score H.J. [Hans] Salter and Frank Skinner; Musical Director: Charles Previn; Sound Supervisor: Bernard B. Brown; Technician: William Hedgecock; Gowns by Vera West

**Shock Theater** Catalog No. 711: "A whole city cried stop him, but how can you stop something you can't see? Don't miss the sensational 'The Invisible Man Returns,' the *Shock* feature film presentation starring Vincent Price and Sir Cedric Hardwicke on this channel (day) at (time).

-*JTS*

# *Black Friday* (1940)

*Synopsis*: As he heads off to the electric chair. Dr. Ernest Sovac hands a reporter his medical diary. We flash back to the past and witness Sovac and his daughter Jean taking the doctor's friend, George Kingsley – a college professor in the town of Newcastle - to the train station. As Kingsley steps out of the car, gunfire is heard, and two cars – the occupants of which are shooting at each other – careen around a corner. The car driven by gangster Red Cannon hits the professor before crashing, and the men in the second car – gangsters Eric Marnay, Frank Miller, William Kane, and Louis Devore – take all this in and speed away.

To save his dying friend, Sovac transplants part of Cannon's brain into Kingsley's skull, an operation as dangerous as it is illegal. Kingsley rallies while Cannon dies. Discovering that the dead gangster had stashed away a half-million dollars not long before the car crash, Sovac decides to reengage Cannon's brain in order to track down the money. Telling Kingsley that a junket to New York City will do him a world of good, Sovac takes his recovering friend to a couple of Cannon's haunts: the hotel where he had hidden from the cops and the nightclub where his old girlfriend, Sunny Rogers, is a singer. It's not long before the extant part of Red Cannon's brain begins to exert its influence; when the gangster Kane passes by Kingsley's table, the professor is suddenly stricken with a horrific headache. As Kingsley sleeps back at the hotel, Sovac attempts to communicate with what's left of Cannon's consciousness by repeating his name. After some heightened mood music and mental images of the men from that second car, Kingsley – rather, Red Cannon – awakes! Sovac clues Cannon in on his plan, but the revivified gangster lams it when Sovac is distracted. While making his way through the city that night, Cannon comes upon Devore and strangles him.

15

The next morning, it seems that Kingsley has "reappeared." Not for long, though, as a siren in the night transforms the professor back into the gangster. After choking the life from Kane – another of the men in that second car – Cannon visits Sunny at her apartment. Angry at the intrusion of a man she perceives to be a stranger, Sunny becomes stunned with disbelief as the man demonstrates knowledge of every nook and cranny of her apartment. Later, Marnay and Miller follow Cannon – who has been betrayed to them by Sunny – to the control room of the city reservoir to retrieve his half-million dollars. Confronted by his enemies, Cannon strangles Miller while Marnay grabs the money box and makes for Sunny's apartment, where Cannon catches up with him. After Marnay is shoved into a broom closet and left to suffocate, Cannon throttles his treacherous ex-moll, grabs his cash, and then hales a cab to the airport. Falling asleep in the cab, the fleeing gangster awakens once again as Kingsley and changes course for the hotel, where he heads into his bedroom and collapses onto his bed. Sovac, having opened the box, is quite satisfied with its contents.

Back in Newcastle, all appears to be back to normal until a siren upsets Kingsley while he is teaching class, and the personality switch begins yet again. To the resurgent Cannon, it seems that the ghosts off his strangulation victims are rising from among the students in the room; he's out of there in a hurry. The bad news for Sovac is that the gangster heads to the doctor's home and attacks Jean. Sovac, carrying a gun, shoots Cannon before any harm comes to Sovac's daughter. As he expires, Cannon fades back into Kingsley.

We are in the present once again, wherein Sovac is executed in the electric chair as the reporter finishes reading his diary. As a final nod to the physician's inner angels, we note that the last page of his diary mentions his hope that someone better balanced than he can use his discoveries to aid humanity.

Excepting *Gift of Gab*, *Black Friday* is the least of the Universal Karloff/Lugosi chillers, a status at once deserved and lamentable. Set in a milieu in which neither horror star felt much at ease – the world of gangsters, molls, and dirty double-crossers – the picture tries to meld elements of *Frankenstein*, *Doctor Jekyll and Mr. Hyde*, and *Svengali* with Curt Siodmak's first cinematic shot at (literally) messing with somebody's mind.(1) The dramatic pivot on which the film turns is the melding of the personality of milquetoast college professor, George Kingsley, with that of vicious and violent gangster, Red Cannon, and whatever success the film enjoyed stems mainly from Stanley Ridges' fine performance. That someone named Stanley Ridges would snatch the brass ring away from Boris Karloff and/or Bela Lugosi has always been a matter of not so *sotto voce* muttering, and the failure of the two leading bogeys to share so much as a moment together onscreen has also contributed to the picture's generally being regarded as a profound disappointment. For a science-fiction thriller singularly bereft of sputtering Strickfadenations, *Black Friday* did have its sideshow attraction, though: a well-hyped, behind-the-scenes bout with hypnosis, deigned to augment the already baroque stylistics of Bela Lugosi.

For Bela, Universal's having revivified the "monster movie" with 1939's *Son of Frankenstein* was a godsend. The studio – and Bela – had basically created the sound horror film for American moviegoers with 1931's *Dracula*, and Lugosi continued to play a critical role in the development of that genre, both for the Laemmles and their sundry competitors. For a good five years or so following the vampire classic, everything was rosy. In fact, as quoted by Lugosi biographer Arthur Lennig, the actor was looking forward to quite a stretch of easy sledding:

Every year a number of films with fantastic or supernatural characters are made, and will, it seems, continue to be made, whatever may happen to the horror 'cycle' of pictures. I have deliberately specialized in such characters – and I firmly believe that there will be suitable roles for me for a long time to come. (2)

The Laemmles' loss of Universal to J. Cheever Cowdin and the Standard Capital Corporation *and* the British horror ban are dealt with in detail by both Lennig and Gary Don Rhodes, whose requisite biographies may be found in the bibliography. Both factors led to the production of those "films with fantastic or supernatural characters" coming to an abrupt halt in 1936, with Bela's last film for Universal the blah *Postal Inspector*, a dreary drama in which the actor portrayed a nightclub owner forced by circumstances to heist a small fortune, only to be undone by the dedicated folk who toil to deliver our correspondence. Between that omega and the alpha that *Son of Frankenstein* betokened in January 1939, Sam Katzman's serial, *Shadow of Chinatown*, and the vigorous Republic chapterplay, *S.O.S. Coast Guard*, marked Lugosi's only film appearances in over two years. The former was shot in roughly two weeks in the fall of 1936, and the latter - in which Bela's plans were undone by the dedicated folk who toil to protect our coasts – provided him with a similar stretch of employment in mid-1937. Thus, the second "Frankenstein" sequel was something of a second coming for Bela, who would find small parts at 20th Century Fox (*The Gorilla*) and M-G-M (*Ninotchka*), rather more screen time at RKO (in *The Saint's Double Trouble*), and leading roles both at the "new" Universal (the 12-chapter *The Phantom Creeps*) and in England, where he got to play two characters in *Dark Eyes of London*. Thence, to the film at hand.

For Boris Karloff, the second sequel - his third jaunt in full Pierce-ian regalia -

would be his last, as he envisioned his Monster heading down the slippery slope to mediocrity. Boris's last Universal feature before said farewell for a bit was 1937's *Night Key*, in which – gray of mustache and woolly of hair – the actor essayed a grandfatherly inventor of burglar alarms. (Take *that*, claimants that "there's nothing new under the sun!") Earlier that year, he had starred as an operatic baritone (singing dubbed by Tudor Williams) suspected of murder in Fox's *Charlie Chan at the Opera*, and in October 1938, Boris himself took on the mantle of an Asian sleuth in Monogram's *Mr. Wong, Detective*, the first of six features based on the stories by Hugh Wiley. Since 1936's *The Invisible Ray* – the last pairing of the Masters of Horror at Universal City until *Black Friday* - Karloff had drawn paychecks at Warner Bros. (*The Walking Dead*, 1936; *West of Shanghai*, 1937; *The Invisible Menace*, 1938; and *British Intelligence*, 1940), Gaumont-British (*The Man Who Lived Again*, 1936), Grand National (*Juggernaut*, 1936), and Columbia (*The Man They Could Not Hang*, 1939) – all in addition to the titles mentioned above, plus that second sequel *and Tower of London* over at J. Cheever Cowdin's newly configured Universal. Per the empirical evidence, the British horror ban had had less financial effect on the gentle Briton from Camberwell than on his Hungarian sometimes-partner-in-crime. Still, without Bela, *Black Friday* would have been just another Boris Karloff/Mad Doctor feature, and, God knows, there would soon be enough of those around. It was Bela, of course – much more than his British "rival" – who got screwed due to the casting changes promulgated in pre-production; following *Dracula*, when did the Hungarian ever see a Universal feature film through to its conclusion without some compromise as to prestige, billing, or money, or without being slated to appear opposite the contemptible Karloff? Sure, all that nonsense about being hypnotized on the set got his picture in the paper, but it was still poor consolation for the loss of a major role because that English tea-swiller had reportedly demurred from attempting the part of Red Cannon.

In an interview with Tom Weaver for *Fangoria* magazine some years back, Curt Siodmak - who co-wrote *Friday*'s screenplay with Eric Taylor – offered a smug, condescending account of his own genius and everyone else's shortcomings. He maintained that the complexity of the role had intimidated the cautious Karloff, a puzzling (and downright insulting) statement in light of Boris's splendidly conceived portrayal of the twins, Gregor and Anton, in Columbia's atmospheric *The Black Room*, in 1935. The actor's ability to delineate the differences between the brothers through subtle shifts in posture and carriage, demeanor, and vocal quality – and his masterful creation of yet a third personality, Gregor *as* Anton – seem to indicate that Siodmak's account of the casting change was just another of his facile, unsubstantiated attacks on artists whose ascension to that Higher Plane had left them incapable of rebuttal.

(Whatever value Siodmak's recollections may have for current film scholarship must be carefully weighed against the late writer's alarming tendency to bad-mouth virtually everyone with whom he had worked. The quotes which pepper **Universal Horrors** and the body of Siodmak's own **Wolf Man's Maker** leave one with the image of a disgruntled old man whose efforts at building his own mythos are dependent to a large extent upon his success at assailing the myths of others, chiefly that of his brother, Robert. I'm of a mind to ignore altogether any statements he had made concerning his former colleagues and to reduce by half his claims to personal brilliance.)

**Awareness of Red Cannon's return seems to have driven Sunny Rogers (Anne Nagel) to drink, yet she and the rather disheveled Eric Marnay (Bela) pause to consider the icebox as the perfect hiding spot for the strongbox containing Red's ill-begotten gains.**

Nonetheless, when Stanley Ridges was brought in to assume the personages of Professor Kingsley/Red Cannon, both Boris and Bela took a step down. The move put Karloff into the role of Dr. Ernest Sovac, a fanatical researcher for whom Red Cannon's hidden loot could open many doors and - in the original scheme of things - the part to be enacted by Lugosi. Arthur Lennig poses an interesting theory that goes Siodmak's targeting Karloff one better:

Under his gentle, polite façade, Karloff was a sharp negotiator; knowing he had clout at the studio, he was perhaps not beyond enjoying some revenge on the imperious actor who a few months before bragged that his Ygor had stolen *Son of Frankenstein*. Could it be possible that Karloff rejected the role of the professor/ gangster not because he was afraid to play it, but because doing so would prevent Lugosi as the doctor from committing acting theft again, as Bela had done as Dr. Vollin in *The Raven*, and as Ygor? (3)

No matter which theory one chooses to believe, the casting ultimately stuck Lugosi in the closet, the door to which Ridges had not only closed, but buttressed shut. After Ridges and Karloff had divided the plums, there were really no sizable male parts left; the sundry minions of law and order were basically interchangeable, and only Red Cannon could tell the gangsters one from another without a scorecard.

Bela became Eric Marnay, a grasping thug who stood apart from his lawless cronies chiefly because of his Hungarian accent. The bland, non-sensational nature of the gangster worked against the actor's flamboyant personality: forced to soft peddle his innate tendency to take center stage, Lugosi lost his edge, and his performance was largely a waste of time. Bela biographer Robert Cremer posits that the actor's playing along with the alleged hypnotically-enhanced suffocation scene – the subject of so much publicity and so many contradictory accounts – might well have brought him more professional pride than the sum total of Eric Marnay's screen time.(4) God knows the "death by closet" scene was trimmed before release to the point of being almost negligible. Anyone interested in studying this supposed highlight of Bela's performance should peruse the film's *trailer* and pass on the feature itself. The studio would deny Bela the chance to don his iconic cloak again until the "New" Universal morphed into Universal-International late in the decade.

For Boris, the avaricious brain specialist was another in the familiar line of mad medical types he had lined up at Columbia. As did most of those patented medicos, Ernest Sovac takes advantage of one of fate's crueler quirks to indulge in a little experimental surgical procedure which saves the life of his colleague and is performed out of concern, compassion, and nobility. That music changes quickly enough; any and all thought of Kingsley's subsequent recovery is forgotten as Sovac opts to exercise a little mind control to try and discover from what's left of Red Cannon just where the gangster had hidden his swagger. This sort of formula – mixing the "mad" scientist's misplaced idealism with crasser instincts – also permeated the actor's Columbia canon and would pop up again when Karloff's sole Monogram horror film – *The Ape* – was released some five months after *Black Friday*. The Svengali-like influence that Sovac wields over Kingsley/Cannon adds a bit more body to the mixture, but not enough to elevate the character – and the performance – above the level found in *The Man They Could Not Hang*, *The Man with Nine Lives*, or *Before I Hang*.

Stanley Ridges' turn as Professor Kingsley/Red Cannon was a comparative *tour de force*. The awkwardness of that phrase is intentional; while Ridges clearly walks away with the acting honors, he hasn't a lot of competition. As stated above, only the dual role he enacts and the part of Dr. Sovac have any meat at all to them. Who in blazes remembers which petty crook gets strangled where, and who – save for a handful of supporting-player spotters (like myself) – even gives a second glance at those uniformed cops, plainclothes dicks, prison officials, hired help, or over-age students who fill out the movie? The only reason we pay the slightest bit of attention to Eric Marnay is because that's our boy, Bela, up there. Had the role been played by, say, Warren Hymer, Marnay would have blended into the wallpaper along with all the others. It's not hard to find the North Star when the rest of the night sky offers nary a twinkle.

This is not to say that Ridges does not deserve the good press he has received over the years; the actor is thoroughly adept, and both of the personalities he enacts are strongly representative of their respective types (absent-minded professor and hard-boiled crime boss) without ever getting within hailing distance of broad caricature. It is his talent – and not some quality inherent in the Siodmak and Taylor screenplay – that empowers us to make the enormous suspension of disbelief required to swallow the mental metamorphosis of Kingsley (an elderly man of average stature) into Cannon (the same man, sans *pince-nez*), enabling the newly-emerged criminal to choke the hell out of a half-dozen palookas, all of whom are bigger or younger (or both!) than he.

The Hampshire-born Ridges had been a familiar figure on the British stage before crossing the Atlantic and working his way onto the American screen. His played his first major film role while Claude Rains was playing his second – in 1934's *Crime without Passion* – and, by the time *Black Friday* was in production, Ridges had been enjoying an enviable reputation as a dependable character actor. His extensive background in the legitimate theater led to his ability to do a credible "American" (among other accents), and this knack gave his Red Cannon a bit of assumed verisimilitude that Karloff either could not or would not duplicate.

(Apart from his early sound work in films like *Scarface* or *Night World* or his later, Native-American roles in *Unconquered* or *Tap Roots*, Boris never expended a great deal of effort in trying to sound like anyone other than Boris Karloff. While the Briton's mellifluous voice has always been an integral part of his tremendous

21

charm, it might be argued that his unwillingness to attempt to alter his trademark tones denied him several opportunities for more mainstream work. If Sir Anthony Hopkins could be the chilling Hannibal Lector at one moment and a believable Richard Nixon the next, Boris Karloff could have accomplished very nearly the same thing had he allowed himself to be push the envelope vocally. Lugosi, with a voice as unique and immediately recognizable as that of his British "rival," would have been twice challenged to assume a different vocal pattern: adjustment in tone and pronunciation in one's *second* language would require both an extreme comfort level in that language and a fairly substantial awareness of subtle cultural variations. The only departure from the "norm" might be heard in Bela's dialog as Dr. Dearborn in 1939's *The Dark Eyes of London*, which, of course, was dubbed by Londoner O.B. Clarence. Bela's successful assumption of the über-Karloff role of Jonathan Brewster in mid '40s to mid-'50s stage performances of *Arsenic and Old Lace* required only the explanation that he had dispatched certain folks because they told him that he looked "like Bela Lugosi." [As for *sounding* like him…] Still, Bela's distinctive voice played as important a role in establishing his public persona as did his kabuki gestures and trademark facial expressions, so any attempt at diverting from that course would have been profoundly counterproductive.)

**It took a while – although not quite as long as it did for the Realart re-release to hit the screen – but Red Cannon (Stanley Ridges) *did* finally catch up with Sunny and Eric.**

Contributing to the madness were the two Annes: Nagel and Gwynne. Bostonian Nagel spent the better part of her first few years in film as an uncredited teenager before landing a Warners' contract and appearing in such disparate stuff as *China Clipper*, *The King of Hockey* (both 1936), and *The Devil's Saddle Legion* (1937). The early '40s saw her in a batch of Universal genre titles including a brace of "Green Hornet" serials in 1940, *The Invisible Woman* that same year, *Man-Made-Monster* the year after, and *Sealed Lips* and *The Mad Doctor of Market Street* (both 1942). As the decade progressed, she appeared more frequently in uncredited bits (including 1949's *Mighty Joe Young*) and – having purportedly descended into alcoholism – died way too young (at age 50) in 1966. *Black Friday* marks Nagel's first credited genre portrayal (she *did* have another of those sans-credit appearances in 1939's *The Witness Vanishes*, last of the studio's "Crime Club" series), and the lady's Sunny Rogers is no lady.

On the other hand, Anne Gwynne's Jean Sovac is the closest thing we have to an angel without wings. Also present in 1940's chapterplay, *The Green Hornet* (albeit as a face without a onscreen cast mention), she, too, graduated to many of Universal's '40s thrillers, seemingly appearing in every title that Anne Nagel (or Evelyn Ankers) passed on. She went from *Black Friday* to *The Black Cat* (1941), and thence to *The Strange Case of Doctor Rx* (1942), *Weird Woman* (1944), *Murder in the Blue Room*, and *House of Frankenstein* (both 1944). As with so many contract players (and stars!) of the war-torn (yet fickle) '40s, Gwynne saw her concentration move from the big to the small screen come the '50s. Still, one of her last films was 1958's mind-blowing *Teenage Monster*, in which she was top-billed. The beautiful Texan retired from the industry in 1970, and passed away in 2003.

*Black Friday* is a study in obsession. To wit: Sovac is driven by friendship and his basic humanity to perform what amounts to an illegal operation, and then by greed and selfishness to manipulate whatever part of Red Cannon survived the procedure into divulging the hiding place of Red's ill-gotten gains. The reincarnated Cannon is a one-man whirlwind, bent on avenging himself on his former enemies for rubbing him out, and on Sunny (Anne Nagel), his former moll, for setting him up. Marnay and the other inept members of his gang are frantic to locate the half-million dollars and to be rid once again of their nemesis. And – to return to a previous mention - screenwriter Kurt [Curt] Siodmak revealed *his* preoccupation with the undetermined potential of the human brain for the first time in his career at the studio.

From the moment that Robert Florey introduced that business about the abnormal brain in his developing screenplay for the 1931 *Frankenstein*, horror and science-fiction pictures had found it almost next to impossible to work their chilling magic without some kind of tie-in – either overt or intimated – with the seat of consciousness and reason. It figures that this early account of personality transference would have come from a European; dualism (body and soul), psychic influence, mental control, spiritual invasiveness, and other related themes had made their cinematic debuts years before the filming of *Black Friday*, chiefly in the studios that dotted Berlin and its environs. Most of the German classics of the '10s and '20s – Expressionistic and otherwise – had drawn upon Teutonic or Hebraic Ur-legends or moody Romantic/Victorian literature (including Stoker's and Stevenson's genre masterpieces) as fuel for their passionate fires. Tempered by the theatrical influence of Max Reinhardt and other eccentric contemporary geniuses, these source materials became splendidly visual studies in which physical abnormality represented one's intellectual, emotional, and/or psychological aberration: *Nosferatu, Der Student von Prag*, and *Der Golem* became (and remain) powerful demonstrations of how there is no greater horror than man at his worst.

After the arrival of sound – but prior to Siodmak's moving the brain to the center ring – there had been attempts to situate the more pervasive elements of one's personality in sundry other areas. Borrowing once again from the German (1925's *Orlacs Hände*), M-G-M and "Papa" Karl Freund strove to convince Depression-Era audiences that a pair of severed hands could retain their original owner's idiosyncrasies and wrest behavioral control from any corpus at all (*Mad Love*, 1935) or, indeed, no corpus whatsoever (*The Beast with Five Fingers*, 1946). Earlier, Charles Laughton's Dr. Moreau (*Island of Lost Souls*, 1932) had demonstrated that creative vivisection – the actual reshaping of the bodily form through radical surgery – would influence animals to think and behave as men. And even when dealing with an entirely "complete" (albeit deceased) human being, viewers and Edmund Gwenn discovered that personality had a more elusive, spiritual quality that defied scientific analysis and which transcended scientific accomplishment (*The Walking Dead*, 1936).

With the exception of his contributions to the "Invisible Man" series, wherein the key element was transparency of the body, Siodmak's genre work made straight for the brain, as his stories – either as originally conceived or as subsequently filmed – depended heavily on the concepts of personality change, transference, or control. It should be sufficient to note here that the writer's fascination with said concepts, as well as his insistence on dragging in bandaged crania and jarfuls of brains wherever even remotely feasible, enjoyed varying degrees of success. As the "40s progressed, and the '50s – the beginning of the Era of Atomic-Age Science Fiction – dawned, old Curt would still be going to the skull... *errrr*... the well in order to work his by-then fairly predictable magic.

Albeit heralded as a "New Universal Picture," *Black Friday*'s critical reception was "mixed." The *Washington Post*'s movie critic, Nelson B. Bell, didn't have to get into much detail when the headline to his piece read "'House of the Seven Gables', 'Black Friday' Run Up Three Hours of Turgid Drama" (14 March 1940). The 23 March 1940 number of *The Christian Science Monitor* was a bit more charitable, opining: "Film based on a fantastic premise but provided with sufficient technical skill to provide entertainment of the horror school for those who appreciate it." And John L. Scott, commenting on the picture in the 19 April 1940 issue of the *Los Angeles Times*, was totally underwhelming in his enthusiasm: "*Black Friday* has an eerie premise... [Plot recap] There are loopholes of various kinds in *Black Friday*, but the shocker fans probably won't care." The *Box Office Digest* (5 March 1940) spent more of its brief coverage mulling over the cast, rather than the story:

[Stanley] Ridge [sic] is a discovery who will be heard from on the screen. Karloff is adequate, while Lugosi is wasted. We only hope the unimportant role in which he is seen will not disappoint some of the ticket buyers. Supporting cast is okay, with Anne Nagel handling the principal feminine burdens, while a newcomer, Anne Gwynne, shows excellent promise for the future in a less important role.

The notice paid to the film in the May 1940 edition of *Hollywood* magazine was pretty much confined to a plot synopsis, but the anonymous reviewer did close with a question about the special effects...

Why and how [Stanley Ridges'] hair changes from grey to black in these swift moments of transformation is not explained, but only a very petty and captious critic would bother about a little detail like that.

... while "Motion Picture Reviews" – a section of the monthly magazine published by the Women's University Club (Los Angeles branch) – topped off *its* story summary with a brace of caveats with respect to the possible screening of *Black Friday* to those not quite covered by the term "adult": "Adolescents (12-16) – Morbid and ethically confusing; Children (8-12) – Impossible"

Still, both *The Hollywood Reporter* (29 February 1940) and *Variety* (13 March 1940) were of a different mind, with the *Reporter* reporting...

*Black Friday* is a highly imaginative story, quite off the beaten track of the usual Universal-Karloff horror pictures. It is not exactly a show for kids, but will give adults, who like their murder and suspense in large doses, general satisfaction.

... and the "Bible of Show Business" gushing...

Equaling, if not surpassing Universal's best efforts as a maker of chiller fare, *Black Friday* should ring the B.O. bell in those situations catering to the blood curdling type of entertainment.

Really? How quickly they forget.

*Black Friday* – 12 April 1940 – 70 minutes (SoS)

**CAST**: Boris Karloff as Dr. Ernest Sovac; Bela Lugosi as Eric Marnay; Stanley Ridges as George Kingsley/Red Cannon; Anne Nagel as Sunny Rogers; Anne Gwynne as Jean Sovac; Virginia Brissac as Margaret Kingsley; Edmund MacDonald as Frank Miller; Paul Fix as William Kane; Murray Alper as the Bellhop; Jack Mulhall as the Bartender; Joe King as the Chief of Police; John Kelly as Taxi Driver; James Craig as Reporter; Jerry Marlowe as the Clerk; Edward McWade as Newspaper File Attendant; Eddie Dunn as Detective Farnow; Emmett Vogan as Detective Carpenter; Edward Earle as Detective; Kerman Cripps as Detective; Edwin Stanley as Dr. Warner; Frank Sheridan as the Chaplain; Harry Hayden as Prison Doctor; Dave Oliver, Harry Tenbrook as Cab Drivers; Raymond Bailey as Louis Devore; Ellen Lowe as Maid; Franco Corsaro as Headwaiter; Frank Jaquet as Fat Man at Bar; Dave Willock, Tommy Conolon, Wallace Reid, Jr. as Students; William Ruhl as Man; Victor Zimmerman as G-Man; Jessie Arnold as Nurse; Doris Borodin as Nurse

**CREDITS**: Director: Arthur Lubin; Associate Producer: Bert Kelly; Screenplay by Curt Siodmak and Eric Taylor; Cinematographer: Elwood Brendell; Art Director: Jack Otterson; Associate Art Director: Harold MacArthur; Musical Director: Hans J. Salter; Makeup: Jack P. Pierce; Gowns: Vera West; Set Decorations: Russell A. Gausman; Sound Supervisor: Bernard B. Brown; Technician: Charles Carroll; Special Effects: John P. Fulton; Editor: Philip Cahn

*- JTS*

# *The House of the Seven Gables* (1940)

*Synopsis*: A written prologue tells the grim origin of the House of Seven Gables. During the time of the Salem witch hunts, the ruthless Colonel Pyncheon coveted some land owned by the simple carpenter Matthew Maule and, when Maule refused to sell, the Colonel had him railroaded to the gallows on a charge of witchcraft. Before being hanged, Maule uttered a curse on Pyncheon, proclaiming that "God will give you blood to drink!" Pyncheon built his great house on Maule's land but on the day it was completed, the Colonel was found dead in his study, blood on his lips.

160 years later, Gerald, the current head of the Pyncheon clan, is reluctantly considering selling Seven Gables to pay off the family's debts. His youngest son, Clifford, heartily approves and wants to use the money to marry his distant cousin Hepzibah and move to New York to continue his career as a songwriter. The eldest son Jaffrey is aghast at the idea as he believes old family lore that a valuable land claim deed and gold are hidden somewhere in the house. He also gives credence to Maule's curse. When Gerald changes his mind about selling, he and Clifford have a furious argument that is overhead by neighbors. Gerald has a fatal stroke and collapses, hitting his head on a desk in the process. Jaffrey accuses Clifford of murder.

A biased judge and jurors who don't approve of Clifford's free-spirited ways find him guilty of murder and the young man is sentenced to life imprisonment. Jaffrey's plans to tear down the house in his search for treasure are thwarted when it is discovered the house has been left to Hepzibah. She orders Jaffrey out and becomes a recluse although she works tirelessly to free Clifford.

20 years pass. Hepzibah is bitter and withdrawn, but her life is brightened by the arrival of her pretty young cousin Phoebe. Jaffrey has become a judge but crooked

business dealings supplement his income. In jail Clifford is joined by none other than young Matthew Maule, descendant of the ill-fated carpenter. Maule is an abolitionist and is serving a brief sentence for inciting to riot. The two become friends, laugh about the curse, and concoct a plan to set things right. Upon his release, Maule, using the name Holgrave, becomes a boarder at Seven Gables. He and Phoebe fall in love. The governor commutes Clifford's sentence and he is free, but is still deprived of his civil rights. He is reunited with Hepzibah but does not confide in her. Holgrave plants an article in the local newspaper claiming that Clifford, during his imprisonment, had studied old documents that prove treasure is hidden in Seven Gables. This piques Jaffrey's interest, although he has his hands full trying to placate Deacon Foster who has secretly loaned Jaffrey money Foster had embezzled from the Quakers abolitionist group, funds that Jaffrey has invested in a slave ship.

Clifford confronts Jaffrey at Seven Gables and tells him he can have the house if he signs a document saying he was mistaken about how his father died. Jaffrey refuses and promises to have Clifford sent to an insane asylum if he doesn't tell him the whereabouts of the treasure. Deacon Foster arrives just ahead of the abolitionists and, realizing now that he will be disgraced, shoots himself; Hepzibah accuses Jaffrey of his murder. As the abolitionists knock on the door, Jaffrey becomes frantic and signs the paper. He then has a stroke and dies. Holgrave reveals his true identity to Phoebe and the two are married in a double ceremony with Clifford and Hepzibah. All four depart and we see a "For Sale" sign in front of the House of the Seven Gables.

> You remember it. You read it in high school. You had to. It was on the required reading list. It was about the elderly spinster and her graying brother who lived in the house with seven gables. And it was perhaps the dullest, driest, most uninspiring book on the English teacher's shelf.
> Frederick Othman, *Washington Post*, 12 January 1940

Mr. Othman should have counted his blessings; a few decades later **House of the Seven Gables** was replaced by **Silas Marner** on many high-school reading lists. Mr. Othman went on to note that "You can't get much excitement into a brother's high regard for his sister" so Universal turned them into cousins and "younged them up" but "suffered qualms of conscience" that led them into taking pains to create the original look of the house that inspired Hawthorne's story.

While Nathaniel Hawthorne's contributions to the silver screen don't measure up to those of his contemporary, Edgar Allan Poe, a number of the gloomy New

Englander's stories were turned into movies. His **The Scarlet Letter** went before the cameras a number of times, displaying varied length and quality in such productions as the Kalem short in 1908, the sublime 1926 Victor Seastrom version that starred Lillian Gish, and the ridiculous 1995 fiasco with Demi Moore. Hawthorne's short satire, "Feathertop," in which a scarecrow given life by a witch, was both turned into a Broadway play, *The Scarecrow,* and adapted several times in the Silent Era, most notably as *Puritan Passions* (1922).

The first version of *The House of the Seven Gables* ran one reel and was directed by J. Searle Dawley for Edison in 1910. The movie starred Mary Fuller, who would go on to play Elizabeth in Edison's *Frankenstein* that same year. *House* is lost, but a detailed plot description can be found in a couple of the trade papers of the day. A number of incidents taken from the novel are included, the curse is *real*, and Matthew Maule's ghost makes a couple of appearances.. *The Nickelodeon* thought the whole project a bad idea:

> The novel has a ponderous ethical structure which a few short scenes done in pantomime cannot hope to indicate and without this the mere story amounts to very little. The mere story is all that lay at the producers' disposal, and they have presented it with good pictorial effect, even suggesting some of the spiritual overtones but the piece is, dramatically speaking, unimpressive
> 1 November 1910

*Moving Picture World* (29 October 1910) found the film to be ambitious but with so many subtitles that the reviewer noticed that the audience was bored and one viewer even dozed off (and this during a film that probably ran no more than 12 minutes!). And when the film played in Salem, audiences there were put off by the historical inaccuracy of Maule being burned at the stake rather than hanged, the usual punishment for suspected witches in America. The 12 June 1920 issue of *Visual Education* noted a reissue of a five-reel *House of the Seven Gables* released through Beseler Films; I suspect this is an error as I can find no other mention of this version. Beseler specialized in non-theatrical films and focused mainly on nature movies, travelogues, documentaries on manufacturing, and so on. Since they did occasionally release - or reissue - films based on literary classics, they might well have done so at some point with the one-reel Edison movie. In April 1935 announcements appeared in the trade papers that the newly-formed Republic Pictures was planning to film

*House of the Seven Gables* with veteran director Reginald Baker at the helm, but nothing came of it.

Come fall of 1939, the trades reported that Universal had taken *House of the Seven Gables* "off the shelves" for spring production (whether said shelves were to be found in the public library or in Universal's vault of unrealized projects is not stated). In spite of another announcement that Universal had "purchased" the rights to the book, Hawthorne's work was in the public domain and hence especially attractive to the penny-pinching studio. A "heavy budget" was promised, but if anyone involved in the project had any notion that the film would be an expensive M-G-M Classic-Comic-Book-style adaptation, they quickly found out otherwise as the picture went into production in late December with a "B"-movie budget of $152,625 (it ended up running $9,000 over budget) and a capable but hardly stellar cast. The second great horror cycle was in full swing, kicked off by *Son of Frankenstein* and the reissues of *Dracula* and *Frankenstein* and, since Hawthorne's book had some spooky elements, the film was sold along those lines. In case there was any doubt, it was to be paired with the Karloff-Lugosi thriller, *Black Friday*. As late as the 29 December 1939, Robert Cummings was announced as "the probable lead" for the film, but on the very next day Cummings, having fallen ill, was replaced by Vincent Price. Cummings would probably have been less hammy than Price as Clifford, but it's not likely he would have been able to match Price's evil, hysterical laughter as he's dragged away from the courtroom after reminding Jaffrey that he's inherited the Maule curse as well as the house. Margaret Lindsay did a screen test for the role of Hepzibah on the 17 December, and Universal was apparently so impressed with her performance that they subsequently offered her a five-year contract. *House's* script was done by Lester Cole, who had come to Universal with the film's producer Bert Kelly. Cole had a reputation as a script doctor, though Universal wasn't happy at meeting his price of $600 a week; he was also a card-carrying communist and one of the founders of the Screen Writer's Guild in 1935. It was Cole's attempt to unionize readers at M-G-M that got him blacklisted at that studio. Later he became one of the "Hollywood Ten," writers who were jailed for refusing to cooperate with the House on Un-American Activities, and he was subsequently blacklisted altogether by Hollywood. Cole's list of screen credits is not particularly impressive and, in his autobiography, **Hollywood Red,** he denies accusations by right-wingers that he propagandized for communism in his screenplays:

The truth is that if anyone were foolish enough to try something that silly it would immediately be discovered and eliminated. The other truth is that 'politics' are expressed in every film. Any escapist 'entertainment' is political to the degree that it denies existing social realities... My politics, pro-union and pro-socialist were never 'injected' into film, yet I believe often the feelings were represented in attitudes of the characters. (1)

Of course, it should be remembered that in those days merely supporting progressive causes like the New Deal was enough to have conservatives cry "Red!" Cole was particularly proud of turning Hawthorne's Holgrave into an abolitionist. In the book, Holgrave has some unconventional ideas - like Hawthorne, he spent some time in a commune - but in the film, he's an activist who is jailed simply for exercising his right of free speech to promote the abolitionist cause. Cole claims Universal was particularly unhappy about this, fearing a Southern backlash. Hollywood was indeed very reluctant to offend white Southern audiences with that particular subject, though *Souls at Sea* (1937) has Gary Cooper as an abolitionist who pretends to be a slave trader, and it even has a scene aboard a slave ship where the slaves kill the brutal captain, all of which seems far more radical than anything in Cole's script. The South isn't mentioned at all in *House*, and by making Jaffrey - a Yankee businessman - complicit in the slave trade, there would seem to be little cause for objections south of the Mason-Dixon line. Nevertheless, Cole deserves some props for bringing the subject up at all and in a sympathetic way, especially when you consider that a film like *Santa Fe Trail* - released the same year as *House* - equivocates about both the Civil War and slavery, and depicts John Brown as a madman and a villain. Cole's script certainly extols personal freedom and opposes stuffy, repressive traditionalism, but this is hardly exclusive to left-wing propaganda. New York is praised as a bastion of progress (in an anachronistic and unintentionally funny line, Price gushes over the tall buildings there that "even scrape the sky") while Boston is dismissed as "provincial" (perhaps Cole never forgave them for executing Sacco and Vanzetti). Lawrence Raw, in his book **Adapting Nathaniel Hawthorne to the Screen** (2008), claims that Cole and director Joe May made the film as an anti-Nazi, anti-isolationism message. If so, it took the message 68 years to be delivered as no contemporary critic saw anything like that in the movie. After the film's release, Cole was surprised at the critical reaction:

To our astonishment, no critic had apparently read the book - either before or after seeing the film. No reviews that I saw remarked upon the changes from the original. So much for critical scholarship. (2)

Apparently, Cole didn't seek out too many reviews, as his changing Clifford and Hepzibah from siblings to lovers was noted by several critics. A change that reviewers often *did* fail to note was that Cole completely eliminated the suggestions

31

of the supernatural found throughout Hawthorne's book, hints that probably drew Universal to the novel as a potential horror tale in the first place. Hawthorne has these intimations float "like a mist" above the characters and suggests that the official and rational history of events may not tell the whole story. Even though Matthew Maule was condemned to death to glut the greed of one man, Hawthorne frequently refers to him as the "old wizard." It is also suggested that Maule had the ability to mesmerize and that this trait was passed down to his descendants, one of whom mesmerized Alice Pyncheon and had her commit embarrassing acts under his spell, inadvertently causing her death. (After Alice dies, legend has it that her ghost haunts Seven Gables and plays the harpsichord. This is mentioned several times in the novel and sometimes people think they actually hear her playing.) As Holgrave also has this power to mesmerize, the curse might be linked to an inherited tendency to apoplexy among the Pyncheon men; perhaps that's simply the method by which the curse is enacted.

The family legend about a land claim turns out to be true, and the deed is found in a secret panel behind the sinister portrait of Col. Pyncheon. In the film, the curse is just the result of the never-ending acquisitiveness of the Pyncheon family. "High blood pressure and thin-veined aristocracy!" Clifford snarls after pointing out to his father how all their ancestors put money before honor. (Vincent Price's Clifford Pyncheon going from one family portrait to another is a bit like the scene in 1960's *House of Usher*, wherein his Roderick Usher does much the same thing, although without the hysteria.) Clifford dismisses stories of the treasure and family deed, and scoffs at the legends of hidden staircases and secret panels. The only character to believe in the curse is Jaffrey and even *that* conceit is unconvincing given that he's played by George Sanders with his usual cynical persona. Jaffrey's death scene might suggest something supernatural as he seems to be reacting to some unseen menace, but then he yells "Don't let them in!" referring to the abolitionists. And he's certainly overreacting greatly in assuming that he'll be lynched by a bunch of Quakers who don't even know about his part in the deacon's fraud. Cole's treatment does give a nod to one of Hawthorne's themes: how the sins of the fathers are visited on the sons with the weight of history bearing down relentlessly on them. Jaffrey's accusing Clifford of murder in order to acquire the house is really no different than Col. Pyncheon's framing Matthew Maule. It's only when this second injustice is finally answered for, and a Maule and a Pyncheon marry, that the moral order of things rent by Col. Pyncheon's greed can be restored.

In the film, Seven Gables is left to the realtors while the two couples merrily go their way, Price perhaps to Tin Pan Alley; still, in the book there's an unspoken irony when the characters discover they have inherited Judge Pyncheon's *other* great house and make that their destination. But is that house any less the product of the tainted Pyncheon legacy than Seven Gables? While Hawthorne also suggests that Holgrave has lost interest in his radical ideas about property and tradition, that's too cynical for the movie, with its emphasis on the pure love of Clifford and Hepzibah and how they've been driven apart by treachery and a hypocritical community too eager to believe the worst.

The publicity department sometimes ignored the fact that Cole and Joe May really didn't deliver a horror film. The fact that the movie played at the Rialto - *the* showcase for blood and thunder - caused the *New York Times* critic to warn that people expecting stronger stuff were bound to be disappointed. Some ads for the film depicted a giant skeletal hand reaching out for Price and Margaret Lindsay. When the movie played at the Eckel Theater in Syracuse, New York, exhibitors offered $10 to any couple who would sit alone at midnight in total darkness in an empty theater and watch the double bill of *House* and *Black Friday*. There were no takers, perhaps indicating the Depression was finally over. Reviews for *The House of the Seven Gables* were mixed. B.R. Crisler of *The New York Times* criticized the film's "slow, heavily mannered pace" and was unimpressed with the leads:

> As the sorely oppressed lovers, Vincent Price and Margaret Lindsay perform in the perfect lavender-and-old lace tradition, with much sighing and misting of eyes. Offers dreary and slightly stale fare.
>
> 15 April 1940

The critic for the 1940 edition of *The Movies and the People Who Make Them* had a different opinion:

> This adaptation of Nathaniel Hawthorne's American classic rises well above the entertainment level which its modest cast and moderate budget might indicate to those who prejudge movies by their marquee splurges. The novel itself is essentially a melodramatic piece given distinction by the manner in which it is presented, by the insight given to its characters and by the atmospheric overtones which permeate every page. The film follows that formula very competently. It is an out and out melodrama but it gives thoughtful attention to development of character and its careful period settings and photography with low tone lighting achieve both strict realism and impressive mood.

Nelson Bell of the *Washington Post* much preferred *House* to its Karloff-Lugosi co-feature:

> There are of course overtones of mystery and tragedy in this classic tale but they are given admirable plausibility by a cast of excellent selection…There has been no attempt here to place *House of the Seven Gables* in the cycle of horror pictures. It is on the contrary played with earnestness and sincerity and a fine eye to realism. Mr. Sanders, whom we applauded for efficient work in *Green Hell*, the season's worst picture, again adds to the impressiveness of his stature as an actor of more than ordinary versatility. The others in the cast effectively match Mr. Sanders' skill.
>
> 14 March 1940

Still, John Scott of the *Los Angeles Times* had some good things to say about the film:

> There are various clever touches in the picture which was directed by Joe May. Perhaps performances are pretty melodramatic, especially those of Vincent Price and Gilbert Emery in earlier reels. Price improves with 'age.' George Sanders, the villain this time, gives a fine performance as Jaffrey. Margaret Lindsay turns in an excellent account of Hepzibah, her transition from gay youth to taciturn spinsterhood being accomplished successfully.
>
> 19 April 1940

But the 22 March 1940 edition of *The Christian Science Monitor* thought the actors were not up to the task:

The sets and atmospheric effects are the most authentic part of the film. But the acting is less satisfactory. Modern men and women, with modern voices, modern ways and modern motions are attired in fancy dress costumes to represent New England of a vanished age. It might do well enough for a pageant. For anything as intimate as a motion picture, *House* is moderate entertainment for those who have forgotten or have not experienced the quality that is Hawthorne. Gilbert Emery stands out as the one player who seems to come nearest to grasping the idea of the original story.

Bert Harlen of *The Hollywood Spectator* agreed:

The house of the seven gables has been created with charm and yet an effective somber mood as well as historical value... The story is worthy not only of better adaptation and directorial handling but also of better casting. As Hepzibah, who grows into an embittered old maid, shut off from the community she hates, alone in the big house, Margaret Lindsay works hard to realize something from an assignment of manifest possibilities. Now and then there are flashes of creative insight but by and large Miss Lindsay does not rise above being only a competent stock actress. Which is regrettable. I have liked her in lighter things. George Sanders' performance seems but a display of mechanics. Vincent Price plays much of the time as though he were performing in a municipal auditorium.

15 March 1940

**"Millions have thrilled to this great love story! Now millions more will be enraptured as an immortal romance surges to soul-stirring reality!" Or so said some of the ads for the film. Universal then hedged its bets by sometimes promoting *Seven Gables* as a horror film and co-billing it with *Black Friday*.**

The world premiere of the film took place at the Paramount Theater in Salem, Massachusetts on the 19 March 1940, with the profits donated to a settlement program for Polish immigrant children run by the charitable foundation that had purchased and restored Seven Gables. The house, located at 115 Darby Street, did not actually have seven gables in Hawthorne's day, but his cousin - who owned the house - told the author that it once had. Much of the publicity for the film centered on Margaret Lindsay and her transformation from vivacious young girl to reclusive spinster. An article in the June 1940 *Hollywood Magazine* - it also managed to put in a plug for various beauty products - focused on how this illusion was accomplished. In addition to wearing her hair pulled back to give her a severe look, Lindsay did not wear rouge, lipstick, or any cosmetics. A grey-white shade of powder was applied to her skin and lips to give it a dull, colorless look, while alternating light and dark foundation cream under her eyes gave the impression of crow's feet. Perhaps no small part of the change comes from Lindsay's overly girlish mannerisms in her scenes as the young Hepzibah: she's all curtsies and giggles and mooning with adoring eyes over Clifford. This *is* a bit cloying, but it provides a strong contrast to Hepzibah in middle age where's she's exchanged frilly dresses for black cotton. Lindsay also did a good job making the tone of her voice cold, stern, and unemotional as the older Hepzibah.

Less was done to give the illusion of aging for Vincent Price since he only sports some gray at the temples and a bit of five-o'clock shadow. At the end, when Cecil Kellaway as the kindly lawyer sends the reunited couple off, he remarks how he sees them as they were when young, which would not take a great deal of imagination in Price's case. At least Price's performance is appropriately more restrained at this point, though he hardly convinces as a man who's spent 20 years behind bars; still, the scene where he sees Hepzibah for the first time since his imprisonment is nicely understated. Perhaps the film's best scene is when Lindsay runs from window to window throughout the house and slams them shut and closes the shutters, defiantly isolating herself from the society that has unjustly taken away her lover; she identifies with him by imprisoning herself. In an interview, Lindsay told how she had to psych herself up to appear breathless and exhausted after closing the last shutter. The mostly good notices Lindsay received for *House* didn't do a great deal for her career which, in the '30s, consisted mostly of 2nd-feature fodder with the occasional "A" (*Jezebel*, *G–Men*). After leaving Universal, she became a regular in the Columbia "Ellery Queen" series.

Art director Jack Otterson is best remembered by horror buffs for the eccentric, Expressionist sets of *Son of Frankenstein*. He shows much more restraint here and creates a realistic, stately old mansion, solemn but hardly foreboding, all appropriate given the tone of the film. Otterson went to Salem to view the house of seven gables and came back with measurements, drawings, and photographs on which to base the set. I didn't find Frank Skinner's music for the film particularly memorable, but it was nominated for an Academy Award (it lost to Disney's *Pinocchio*; Werner R. Heymann's score for *One Million B.C.* was also in the running). Skinner also wrote the song "The Color of Your Eyes," warbled in the movie by Vincent Price. Price, a dabbler in Gilbert and Sullivan and a glee-club member at Yale (his alma mater), wisely did not pursue a musical career. In a mostly favorable review of the film in the 1 January 1940 edition of the *Los Angeles Times*, Philip Scheuer noted the following:

Despite the New England locale, this picture savors of the foreign, possibly because its director was Joe May, once of Germany. The same technique to which one owes various clever camera touches, is responsible unfortunately for certain melodramatic exaggerations of performance which, particularly in the first half, remind one of an older, hammier era.

Joe May was a major figure in the German Silent Era. He did a series of detective films in the '10s, but later switched to epic, multiple-part exotic thrillers like *Mistress of the World* (1919) and *The Indian Tomb* (1921), both starring his wife, the former opera singer, Mia May. In *Tomb*, alternately fascinating and campy, Mia May exhibits all the sexual magic of Margaret Dumont, but the film contains a memorable Conrad Veidt performance and the magnificent sets one associates with Joe May's films of that era. Nonetheless, May's career suffered several setbacks in the mid-'20s - especially when his *The Farmer from Texas* proved to be a huge flop - but he made a comeback with two of his best films, *Homecoming* (1928) and *Asphalt* (1929), realistic dramas quite in contrast to his earlier work. When sound came in, May did another about-face and switched to musical comedy. However, once the Nazis came to power, May, who was Jewish, fled with Mia first to France and then to England, and ultimately settled in America. There he directed Gloria Swanson in *Music in the Air* (1934) which had the participation of two other German exiles, Billy Wilder and Erich Pommer. The *New York Times* critic approved, but the film still tanked at the box office. May's next picture, *Confession* (1937), finished off his career as an "A-director. The story had been done in 1935 as *Mazurka* with Pola Negri, and Joe May liked the original so much he decided to duplicate it shot by shot. He studied the earlier film through a movieola, ran the film on the set so the actors could copy the performances of their German counterparts exactly, and even used a stopwatch to make sure the different sequences in the American film were exactly the same length as in the German. Naturally, this

37

bizarre approach slowed things down considerably and made for a very unhappy shoot. At one point the star, Kay Francis, had an argument with May over a line of dialogue. Kay wanted to say "I won't" and May insisted on "I can't" and when an exasperated Kay asked what the difference was, May responded "It's the difference between you and a good actress."(3) When Basil Rathbone, playing the villain, gets shot and falls down the stairs, May refused to hire a stunt double, and Rathbone was obliged to take the plummet himself ten times (Fritz Lang did something like this to Peter Lorre in *M*; Lorre forever hated Lang's guts as a result).

Kay Francis fans think *Confession* is one of her best performances, but whether it's because of May or in spite of him is the subject of debate. Universal then hired May for their "B"-movie unit. It's surprising that a man with such exacting methods was able to accommodate his style to the quick shoots and low budgets of these modest features, but he succeeded in doing so, no doubt in part because he realized he had no other options open to him. Vincent Price had a few memories of May when they first worked together on *The Invisible Man Returns*:

> He was very difficult, mainly because he didn't speak English. He'd try to give me a direction and I'd say 'For God's sake, Joe, tell me in German because I can get along better with you in German than I can in English!' I don't think anyone in the cast understood a word he said! (4)

Lester Cole claimed he was assigned as dialogue director for *House of the Seven Gables* because Joe May had made "only one film in this country and it was felt that his command of English had not been yet been established."(5) This was, of course, inaccurate as May had already done five Hollywood films prior to *House* and had not been assigned a dialogue director for any of them. May *did* have a very thick accent though his autocratic ways were probably an equal handicap. George Sanders hated May, but Alan Napier, who plays Fuller the mailman in *House*, had worked with May in *The Invisible Man Returns*, and the two had become friends after initially exchanging insults on the set.

May then found himself having to contend with the Dead End Kids/Little Tough Guys in a couple of films, no doubt a trying experience. Evelyn Ankers, who played in *Hit the Road*, recalled that the professional urchins had no use for the German director:

> It was very hard on poor Joe May, who was very conscientious and

> trying to do a good job. He came to me once and begged me to talk to
> the boys, who wouldn't stop clowning and get to work. Mr. May pleaded
> with them to be serious; they just ignored him. I went back to the set
> with him and gave them a good, stern bawling out. (6)

No doubt May was tempted to imitate the response of his German colleague, E.A. Dupont, who slapped one of the Dead End Ends for mocking his accent during the filming of *Hell's Kitchen*. (Dupont was fired as a result.) May ended his film career with a minor comedy, *Johnny Doesn't Live Here Anymore* (1944). He might not have won any popularity contests with American actors and crews, but he was well liked by other émigrés like Hedy Lamar, Otto Preminger, Robert Siodmak, and Walter Reisch, who pitched in to help May open a Viennese restaurant, "The Blue Danube" (it closed after just a few months, as May apparently insisted on telling his customers what to order). After that, May was financially dependent on the kindness of his German friends and the European Film Fund which was designed to help refugees.

Joe May gives *House* an appropriately gloomy atmosphere that is a bit reminiscent of the 1925 German film, *Chronicles of Grey House*, another tale of family division that spans generations and revolves around an old family estate and has suggestions of the supernatural. Since Cole's script had drained the story of uncanny undertones, May didn't go in for the long shadows and low-key lighting that would have given the film more of a macabre feel. Some of the editing is clever enough: the back and forth between the townspeople about the sale of Seven Gables ("It used to be that the Postal Service was the fastest way of spreading the news," grumbles the mailman), the transitions showing the house falling into disrepair, and the passing of time being indicated by the letters Clifford sends to Hepzibah.

The actors all have their moments, though it's hard to take likable lug Dick Foran seriously as an abolitionist zealot, and Miles Mander is such a bundle of nerves as Deacon Foster that it's surprising his fellow Quakers don't catch on that something is amiss much sooner. Alan Napier's Mr. Fuller seems to fit into the period better than any of the other actors. Fans of Universal horror will no doubt spot Edgar Norton, Harry Cording, and Michael Mark in small roles. Vincent Price played the villain in a very loose adaptation of the novel that is one of the three episodes of 1963's *Twice-Told Tales*, and Hawthorne's story then returned in an obscure 1967 film that seems to have completely disappeared.

The novel - no doubt because it required only one set and a small cast - became a favorite of '50s TV anthology shows. One surprisingly good version was done in

1960 - as an episode of *Shirley Temple's Storybook* – and boasted a particularly good cast: Jonathan Harris (Judge Pyncheon), Martin Landau (Clifford; true to the novel's depiction of him as a mere ghost of a man), Agnes Moorehead (Hepzibah), Robert Culp (Holgrave), and John Abbott (Uncle Venner), with Temple taking the part of Phoebe. In a mere 50 minutes, this adaptation was closer to Hawthorne - and far spookier - than the 1940 film.

*The House of the Seven Gables* - 12 April 1940 - 89 minutes

**CAST:** George Sanders as Jaffrey Pyncheon; Margaret Lindsay as Hepzibah Pyncheon; Vincent Price as Clifford Pyncheon; Dick Foran as Matthew Maule (aka Holgrave); Nan Grey as Phoebe Pyncheon; Cecil Kellaway as Philip Barton; Alan Napier as Fuller; Gilbert Emery as Gerald Pyncheon; Miles Mander as Deacon Foster; Charles Trowbridge as the Judge; Edgar Norton as Phineas Weed; Harry Woods as Wainwright; Hugh Sothern as Rev. Smith; Myra McKinney as Mrs. Reynold; Harry Cording as Mr. Hawkins; with Margaret Fealy, Caroline Cook, Jane K. Loofbourro, Marty Faust, Murdock McQuarrie, Kernan Cripps, Colin Kenny, Robert Dudley, Jack C. Smith, Ruth Rickaby, P.J. Kelly, Sybil Harris, Leigh De Lacy, Lori Ranson, Ed Brady, Hal Budlong, Ellis Irving, Michael Mark, Etta McDaniel, Claire Whitney

**CREDITS:** Director: Joe May; Assistant Director: Phil Karlsen; Script: Lester Cole, Harold Greene; Based on the eponymous 1851 novel by Nathaniel Hawthorne; Producer: Burt Kelly; Photography: Milton Krasner; Art Director Jack Otterson; Assistant Art Director: Richard H. Riedel; Editing: Frank Gross; Set Decoration: R.A. Gausman; Costumes: Vera West; Musical Score: Frank Skinner; Conductor: Charles Previn; Sound: Bernard B. Brown; Sound Technician: William Hedgcock; Dialogue Director: Lester Cole

*–HN*

# *Enemy Agent* (1940)

*Synopsis*: Someone has been secretly photographing plans and such of the Flying Fortress and its bombsights at Fulton Aircraft, an American aircraft factory, and despite the onsite investigations by FBI agent Gordon, Jimmy Saunders is accused of being the spy. In reality, Jimmy has been set up by Dr. Jeffrey Arnold, local businessman, *bon vivant*, and leader of the spy ring, who has had his man Lester Taylor plant a camera/watch in Jimmy's locker at the factory. Jimmy denies the accusation, and there is no real proof against him so he is not jailed for long; nevertheless, he is treated everywhere with contempt by the local citizenry and is unable to find another job due to the suspicion that still hangs over his head. In the interim, we see Arnold in the company of restaurant hostess Irene Hunter, apparently just another of the many women attracted to the man of means.

During all this, Jimmy has himself become suspicious of Taylor, who has given him a lead on a job in Kansas City, which he has written on the back of an envelope that bears a questionable inscription. Jimmy breaks into Taylor's apartment where he finds a bank book and the stolen plans, irrefutable proof that Taylor was the one doing the camera work earlier. He is discovered in the apartment, though and, following a bit of a chase, is arrested and jailed once again – this time for burglary. While behind bars, Jimmy is visited by his girlfriend, Peggy, in whom he confides that he has hidden a photo he took in Taylor's apartment and papers that will prove his innocence. Peggy tells this to Irene – with whom she works at a local restaurant - and Irene finds the photo in Jimmy's car.

A bit later, Jimmy is once again released from jail, only to be immediately kidnapped by Dr. Arnold and taken to the spy's mansion/hideout, where he is to be "questioned" about the location of the papers taken from Taylor's desk. Before this gets serious though, a group of drunken frat boys is admitted by happenstance to Arnold's house where, after some supposed liquor-induced acrobatics, they reveal themselves to be G-men – as does Irene - and the spies are arrested.

Introducing our entry on 1942's *Destination Unknown* is our explanation for including that film in a tome that deals mostly with tales of the grotesque and supernatural. The rationale unloaded there applies also to this film, to *Danger Woman*, and to several other decidedly un-grotesque and non-supernatural pictures that were part of the original 1957 "Shock Theater" package. The long and the short and the tall of it all is that these films – and the others – were meant to *shock* you and not necessarily frighten you. Considering the sacrifices made, hardships endured, and horrors faced by those whom Tom Brokaw and others call the "Greatest Generation," the "shocking" elements of *Enemy Agent et al* are woefully small. Nonetheless..

Even the owners and managers of the airplane factory wherein we open aren't really shocked that there's a spy in their midst. They're a tad disappointed it's taking FBI mole Gordon as long as it is to find out who it is; if he'd only vary the timing of his occasional excursions into the locker room, he'd definitely stumble onto the villain's identity more quickly. But young Jimmy Saunders is shocked when he's told that *he* has been named as the eponymous enemy agent and upset when he learns that the community will have no more of his secreting film cells hither, thither and yon. What's shocking to us – until we remember that when the picture was released, we weren't actually at war with anyone – is the fairly casual condemnation of Jimmy by the businesses in the community, all of whom seem to have taken the tack of Jerry Seinfeld's much later "Soup Nazi": "No jobs for you!"

Despite the country's official policy of non-intervention in re: Hitler's movements throughout Eastern Europe, many Americans felt that it was only a question of time before they had to take action against the Third Reich. With the wisdom of hind-sight we have learned that their fears were legitimate and were – in many instances – realized, via both programs of spying and intimidation, these last in American neighborhoods populated largely by recent emigrants from the very lands where Hitler's thugs had come to power. *You* may be here, the message came across, but most of your family are still in the Old Country, and their safety may well rely upon your nonintervention. Message apart, *Enemy Agent* is little more than a programmer meant – I suppose – to alert Americans to threats around and about them here in the good old USA, not unlike our post-9/11 campaign to make us aware of packages left wherever or suspicious activity in public places. The film hasn't much action, Jack Carson and his pseudo-shnockered, highly acrobatic G-men at the climax notwithstanding. The sets – interiors and exteriors – are stock, the direction is adequate, and the acting, serviceable.

At the helm of the unexciting project was Lew Landers, who – after directing such memorable genre serials as *The Vanishing Shadow* (1934) and features such as *The Raven* (1935) (1) for Universal under his birth name, Lewis Friedlander – went on to well over a baker's- dozen-dozen films of varying quality and interest. Those pictures relevant to our proclivities include *The Boogie Man Will Get You* (1942), *The Return of the Vampire* (1943), and *The Ghost that Walks Alone* (1944) for Columbia, *The Mask of Dijon* (1946) for P.R.C., and *Seven Keys to Baldpate* (1947) for R.K.O. Nonetheless, the film at hand marks his only "Shock Theater" entry other than the aforementioned Karloff-Lugosi classic of the earlier decade. The title of his 1948 film-*noir*ish thriller, *Inner Sanctum*, leads one's mental processes directly to Universal's eponymous series covered throughout this book, but 'twas an unrelated, 62-minute-long programmer from a certain M.R.S. Productions that was released into theaters everywhere two weeks before Halloween 1948 (and pretty much into the abyss thereafter). Landers was the epitome of the journeyman director, and his last film – released posthumously in May 1963 – was Bern-Field Productions' *Terrified*, a haunted house chiller starring horror immortal, Rod (*Black Zoo*, *The Crawling Hand*) Lauren.

Robert Armstrong is, of course, *persona multa grata* to us genre fans for his appearance(s) in all three giant ape movies: *King Kong* and *Son of Kong*, both 1933, and – following about 100 non- simian-oriented pictures - 1949's *Mighty Joe Young*. Our concentrating on his Carl Denham(s) and Max O'Hara, though, might cause us to lose sight of his other genre contributions which, surprisingly, were but two: RKO's *The Most Dangerous Game* (1932) and *The Mad Ghoul* (1943) are the only ones to fill the bill that interests us most. Like many of his contemporaries, Armstrong moved to TV come the '50s, and it's likely that most mainstream film fans would best recognize him from his small-screen credits. His Agent Gordon may not be the sharpest knife in the drawer here, but – as is so often the case with "B"s and lesser efforts – the fault lies mainly in the mundane level of the script and not with the thespians.

Helen Vinson (Agent Irene Hunter) could trace her genre *bona fides* back to the original Broadway production of *Death Takes a Holiday*, wherein she and Phillip Merrivale created the roles that Evelyn Venable and Fredric March would bring to the screen. The Beaumont (Texas) native dipped her toe in cinematic genre waters with 1935's *Transatlantic Tunnel* and then with 1944's *The Lady and the Monster*, although she would probably have argued that her sundry appearances opposite the likes of Cooper, Cagney, Raft, Muni, Bogart, Veidt, *et al* merited more attention than the titles we cited. Her portrayal herein is quite good, giving no indication that Dr. Arnold's latest squeeze is a Fed until the rather improbable denouement.

**Although the picture itself undoubtedly reflected the increasing fears of the pre-Pearl Harbor American public, its title card was still pretty much par for the formulaic course. The savvy fan could readily match the faces with the names, except for the curve thrown in the case of Jack La Rue, who was replaced in the artwork by the infinitely lovelier Marjorie Reynolds.**

Marjorie Reynolds' Peggy is the vehicle via which the necessary info is got from the accused (her boyfriend, Jimmy, even if on the bounce) to the government (Irene, the first object of Jimmy's admiration), and the lovely Idahoan does the job without a false step. There's more on Miss Reynolds in our essay on *The Time of Their Lives*, but we ought to note that both she and Miss Vinson shared the screen with Boris Karloff; the former in 1940's "Mr. Wong" mystery, *Doomed to Die*, and the latter in 1934's *Gift of Gab* (featuring a cameo by Bela as well as Boris.)

By far the most interesting of the actors herein is Richard Cromwell (born Leroy Melvin Radabaugh) as the much put-upon Jimmy Saunders. Cromwell's pre-cinematic career still found him dabbling in the Arts, as he was a God's-honest painter who soon had a pretty respectable Hollywood clientele. Come the '30s, and the now-novice actor won the lead in the eponymous sound remake of D.W. Griffith's *Tol'able David*. His film career lasted but a decade and a half, with the young thesp

44

getting a title role only once more, in the 1942 indie programmer, *Baby Face Morgan*, a substantial slide downward from the "A" production that had essentially marked his motion picture debut. *Enemy Agent* his only "genre" effort (thanks again to the woefully defined *shock* in "Shock Theater"), and the California-born Cromwell went on to sign up for the Coast Guard during the Second World War. Upon his return, he became romantically involved with Angela Lansbury, and the couple wed in September 1945. They were divorced not quite a year later, when it devolved that – like so many others in the performing arts – Cromwell was homosexual. His Jimmy Saunders is hetero-isimo in *Agent*, as he quickly moves past undercover agent Irene Hunter to settle on a cute waitress working in the same eatery. Albeit his character swiftly descends into depression and alcoholism due to the ragged treatment he gets from his neighborhood American society, Cromwell doesn't go overboard and play to the balcony.

*Motion Picture Daily* (9 April 1940) found the film to be "60 minutes of action suspense and comedy," while *Film Daily* (out on the 26 April) shrugged, feeling the picture was "O.K. as nabe fare." Still, that review went a bit further and mentioned the whys and wherefores of the film:

There is nothing new or novel about the situations in the picture, but they are held together. Exhibitors don't have much in the way of marquee names, but but with worldwide conditions currently highlighting war and spies the picture should lend itself to exploitation on this score.

We may look back with a sort of "Duh!" reaction, but the isolationist policy of the Congress kept FDR from involving further our military until the 8 December of the following year. While it took more than slipping a film negative into someone's shoe to get things moving, the sense of unease that many Americans felt was born out here and by other films of the kind. *Motion Picture Herald* hit the nail on the head when reviewer V.K. opined that "Universal's 'Enemy Agent' affords opportunity for topical exploitation campaigns." *Harrison's Reports*, sharing the same publication date (13 April 1940), weighed in with:

A fair program espionage melodrama. The plot is familiar and, as in most pictures of this type, slightly far-fetched. Yet it has some ingredients for mass appeal, such as fast action and suspense, as well as an incidental romance.

We've come a long way when it comes to "fast action and suspense" and *Enemy Agent* really hasn't any moments in which we might regard as a "shock," but the picture does offer a glimpse at the studied paranoia the country felt at the outset of the madness in Europe and elsewhere.

*Enemy Agent* – 19 April 1940 – 64 minutes (ST)

**CAST**: Richard Cromwell as Jimmy Saunders; Helen Vinson as Irene Hunter; Robert Armstrong as Gordon; Marjorie Reynolds as Peggy O'Reilly; Vinton Hayworth (as Jack Arnold) as Lester Taylor; Russell Hicks as Lyman Scott; Philip Dorn as Dr. Jeffrey Arnold; Jack LaRue as Alex; Bradley Paige as Francis; Abner Biberman as Boronoff; Luis Alberni as A. Calteroni; Jack Carson as Ralph; Milburn Stone as Meeker; uncredited performances by Eddie Acuff and James Craig as Federal Agents, Ernie Adams as Janitor, Polly Bailey as Woman, Lloyd Ingraham as Barber, Brooks Benedict as Headwaiter

**CREDITS**: Director: Lew Landers; Producer: Ben Pivar; Cinematographer: Jerome Ash; Screenplay: Edmund L. Hartmann and Sam Robins; Original Story: Sam Robins; Film Editor: Ted J. Kent; Art Director: Jack Otterson; Set Decoration: Russell A. Gausman; Gowns: Vera West; Associate Art Director: Harold H. MacArthur; Sound Supervisor: Bernard B. Brown; Technician: William Fox; Musical Director: Hans J. Salter

*Shock Theater* Catalog No. 703: "They risked their lives to save their country. See Robert Armstrong, Richard Cromwell, and Helen Vinson in Enemy Agent," the feature film presentation on *Shock* over this channel (day), (date), at (time). It's a sensational expose of spies in action and the G-Men who fight to stop them."

*- JTS*

# *The Mummy's Hand* (1940)

*Synopsis*: In what is basically a prologue to the story, Professor Andoheb junkets to a Temple of Karnak in time to be appointed High Priest by his predecessor, who expires shortly after explaining about tana leaves. The fluid of three leaves keeps the mummy of Kharis – a prince of the Royal House who had been buried alive three thousand years earlier for trying to revive his dead lover, the princess Ananka – in a life-like state, and the fluid of nine gives him motion. But never should Kharis be given the fluid of more than nine leaves, or he would become "an uncontrollable monster." Kharis's mission – the reason he has been attended to by the priests of Karnak over the ensuing millennia – is to slay all those who would defile Ananka's tomb.

Hanging about a Cairo street bazaar – waiting to head back to the United States – are acclaimed archaeologist, Steve Banning, and his sidekick, Babe Jenson. Steve buys a broken vase from a vendor and he and Babe make for the Cairo Museum, where their claim that the vase gives clues to the tomb of Ananka is shared by senior archaeologist, Dr. Petrie. The excitement of the three men is not shared by Dr. Petrie's colleague, who turns out to be Andoheb. Despite being told by Andoheb that the vase is a fake and that that two previous expeditions in search of Ananka's tomb had disappeared without a trace, Steve and Babe decide to find funding and pursue the lead on the vase. Petrie obtains a permit to dig throughout Egypt, and Steve and Babe convince stage magician, The Great Solvani, to front the money necessary for the expedition. Before long, Steve, Babe, Dr. Petrie, Solvani, and the magician's daughter, Marta, are encamped in the Egyptian desert.

The first things discovered are the remains of a Dr. Gustavson and his wife, whose expedition had disappeared two years earlier. A premature dynamite explosion leads to a rock slide which uncovers a cartouche leading to the entrance to "an unholy tomb." As the men dig their way in, Andoheb watches from above. Inside the tomb, an upright sarcophagus is opened to reveal the mummy of Kharis. Dr. Petrie remarks that the mummy is in "the finest state of preservation" he's ever seen. That night, as jackals howl and the full moon rises, Andoheb appears out of nowhere and brings Petrie over to examine the now-supine Kharis. After the fluid of nine tana leaves has been dribbled onto his lips, Kharis arises and strangles Petrie.

Andoheb instructs his henchman – who had been following Steve and the others since the purchase of the vase in the Cairo bazaar – to plant vials of tana-leaf fluid in the tents of the unbelievers, as Kharis will seek out the fluid and do in the infidels. While Kharis is sent out on his mission, Marta interprets the hieroglyph on the vase as the route to Ananka's tomb, and the group begins to investigate. A huge jar that had been filled with tana leaves is now found to be empty, and, in one of the tents, Kharis dispatches Ali, the foreman of the native crew that has fled the forbidden tomb. Steve sends Marta and Solvani off to get some sleep after the magician finds Ali's body, and Kharis, entering their tent soon after, nearly strangles Solvani and carries off Marta.

Frantic, Steve and Babe split up – Babe heading around to the other side of the hill and Steve back into Kharis's tomb – looking for the path the mummy has taken. Kharis brings Marta into an enormous room that contains Ananka's sarcophagus, places the woman on a sacrificial altar, and then is sent out again by the high priest. Andoheb announces that he has decided to inject Marta and himself with the tana-leaf fluid so that they might spend eternity together. Babe's discovery of the enormous steps leading up to the temple brings Andoheb out to confront him, and the high priest is killed in an exchange of gunfire.

Kharis has returned to the temple and Marta warns Steve not to let the mummy near the brewing tana-leaf liquid. Tossing Steve out of his way, Kharis makes for the brew, but Babe knocks the cup from its hands with a well-placed bullet and, when Kharis creeps to the floor to drink, Steve uses the flaming brazier to set the mummy afire. The next scene finds the four Americans happy, healthy, and on their way back to the States.

Re-imagining a concept or an image or a product that has already made an impact or accumulated a following is always something of a risky business. "New Coke" didn't make the hoped-for impression on fans of the old stuff, for example, and some current market surveys maintain that – barring the introduction of solar power – there's not much left in the way of true innovation, cellphone-wise, to excite those who queue up annually to get the absolute latest means of ignoring the people around them. Hell,

48

my fellow sexagenarians who are still collecting comic books are grumbling that it will be a while yet before the verdict is in on the "transgendering" of the Norse God of Thunder.

Both the acquisition of the Marvel Universe (wherein Thor is still Chris Hemsworth – at least as I write this) by the Disney Corporation and the subsuming of the D.C. superhero stable into the corporate legacy of the brothers Warner have heralded a renaissance, if you will, for those titans who have entertained the masses via the printed page since the days of *Action Comics* No. 1 in 1938 or *Marvel Comics* No. 1 in 1939. Owning the rights to the characters means that one can virtually do whatever one wants with them. Thus, Ben Affleck's "Batman" (2016) was quite a departure from that of Michael Keaton (1989), who bore little resemblance to the Caped Crusader of Adam West (1966), who was, in turn, light years removed from *his* cowled ancestors, Lewis Wilson (1943) and Robert Lowery (1949). (In a nod to Cicero, I will forgo even mentioning *The Lego Batman Movie* of early 2017.)

The characters most recognizably branded with the Universal logo are, of course, its monsters. Dracula, Frankenstein, The Mummy: these grotesques first achieved international popularity in the early '30s features that made Universal a stand-out, even as every other studio in Hollywood jumped on the resultant bandwagon and sought to duplicate the success. The studio *did* have superheroes of its own – Buck Rogers, Flash Gordon, the Green Hornet – but these were celebrated solely in its serials, and thus relegated to a couple of reels every week as addenda to the picture(s) for which the audience paid cash. The iconic monsters – Dracula, Frankenstein, The Mummy – are the true immortals, having enjoyed reincarnations by the heirs and the heirs of the heirs of the Laemmles (and many others!) since the '40s. In addition, there have been notable versions/variations on these "themes" (e.g. 1999's *The Mummy* [and sequels] with Brendan Fraser; *The Wolfman*, 2010, with Benicio del Toro) released by the studio at various points throughout the years prior to it announcing its "Dark Universe."

The first re-imagining of the iconic monsters that was to have been part of the "Dark Universe" brand was 2014's *Dracula Untold*, a Universal co-production (with four other companies) that proved to be a critical wash. The CGI-heavy world of Dracula as the real-life Vlad Tepes was, well... so tepid that the inauguration of the "Dark Universe" was put off until the June 2017 release of *The Mummy*, wherein none other than Tom Cruise was tapped to do the archaeologizing. Nevertheless, the box office take on this latest *Mummy* – the bandages therein were wound 'round the lovely figure of Algerian actress, Sophia Boutella – apparently didn't quite cover the notes;

still, with the titles of the remakes already in the pipeline (*The Invisible Man, Bride of Frankenstein, Creature from the Black Lagoon*, etc.), the die was apparently cast.

As to the earlier re-imaginings... Although beaten to neighborhood theaters everywhere by *The Invisible Man Returns*, the 1940 reappearance of The Mummy – okay; of *a* Mummy - found fans who were still intrigued by the character's exotic nature, and who eagerly plunked down their nickels and dimes for a return trip to what passed for Egypt. Worldwide press coverage of Howard Carter's discovery of the remarkably not-despoiled tomb of Tutankhamen back in 1922 had led to an immediate fascination with culture and mores of the ancient kingdoms, and the coincidental deaths of a handful of those who had entered the tomb with Carter within a decade of the opening had contributed to the popular notion that Tut's tomb had borne a curse. Come 1932, and the disparate "elements" found at Universal (the ever more popular Boris Karloff; the veteran genre director and cinematographer Karl Freund; the incredible wizardry of Jack P. Pierce and John P. Fulton) melded with the most profound of universal experiences (love and death), the widespread belief in reincarnation, and the ongoing infatuation with all things Egyptian. Toss in essence of the 1931 *Dracula* – the vision of playwright/screenwriter John L. Balderston would be shared by both films - and the resultant picture was an eerie sensation. Come 1940, Imhotep and his Ankh-es-en-amon were replaced by Kharis and his Ananka. Whereas the terror wrought by Imhotep had been palpable yet understated - all violence was committed off-screen – Kharis wasted little time in making *his* lovelorn, linen-wrapped Romeo highly physical and literally in your face. And while the new decade may have found Universal unable to afford the production values Junior Laemmle had okayed in 1932, if nothing else *The Mummy's Hand* was a damned sight faster and more furious than its predecessor.

Some years back, I collected 16mm prints of the Universal horror classics, the great (and not-so-great) horror and science fiction films from the '20s through the '60s (inclusive!), the most self-maligned of Jack Benny's features, and virtually everything I could get my hands on with Buster Keaton, the Marx Brothers, and Laurel and/or Hardy. A few weeks after I'd finally gotten an original on *The Mummy's Hand* (we're talking 1978 here), artist and founding member of the international Laurel and Hardy fan club, the "Sons of the Desert," Al Kilgore, admitted to me that he had seen the film when it was first released and it had scared the "living hell" out of him. I found that somewhat hard to believe, but he swore that he and half the theater had jumped a couple of feet in the air when Tom Tyler sat up and choked the bejesus out of Charles Trowbridge. Everyone, he explained, had been primed for another tale of revivification and rejuvenation *a la* the original Karloff film, and the sight of that bandaged, black-eyed horror reaching out to force death down your throat was an unexpected and "nerve blasting" experience. A decade or so later, I picked up a copy of Leslie Halliwell's volume, **The Dead That Walk**, and read how...

...many people remember it as the most frightening film they have ever seen, even though the British censor saw no reason to give it anything stronger than an 'A' certificate, which meant that children of any age could get in to see it if accompanied by an adult. (1)

That so many folks, under such a variety of circumstances, had had such powerful memories of the impact of *The Mummy's Hand* was news to me; I've never known of anyone who has felt even remotely the same way about the Chaney sequels.

If anything, *Hand* ought to be considered apart from said sequels. It is, after all, the series' Act One, wherein the *dramatis personae* are identified, the necessary exposition is given, and the rules of engagement are drawn. The similarities between Griffin Jay's original story and the Karloff classic are reinforced by the use of footage from the earlier film, wherein – due to monetary constraints and if only in long shots – Karloff's Imhotep and Zita Johann's reincarnation of Anhk-es-en-amon are meant to be taken for Kharis and Ananka. Props and scenery likewise can be traced back to Papa Freund's moody mummy masterpiece, as well as to James Whale's loopy Incan bomb, *Green Hell*, which Universal had released in January of that same year. Jay and Martin Shane's screenplay introduces the concept of "tana leaves," perhaps the most inexpensive and least visually impressive means of maintaining eternal life ever recorded onscreen. *Hand* is also the only film in the series to have been helmed by Christy Cabanne, a veteran of the Silent Era and perhaps best known as a director of horse operas; this may serve to explain that spunky, if gratuitous barroom-brawl scene in downtown Cairo. Despite his reputation, though, Cabanne - and cinematographer Woody Bredell – at times achieved an atmosphere that none of the three sequels could match.

Anyhow, there's little doubt that the fabled revival showings of *Dracula* and *Frankenstein* at Los Angeles' Regina Theater in 1938 helped re-whet the appetites of Universal horror fans, but there's no record (that we could find, at any rate) of Karloff's *The Mummy* – or, except for RKO's *Son of Kong*, any of the other early-'30s titles - being similarly feted on the big screen. Thus, we assume that the folks who flocked to see *The Mummy's Hand* had only their memories of the 1932 feature to fall back on, the essence of which mattered not at all. Although Egyptians of a certain bygone era were apparently prone – upon revivification - to operatic emotions, the various hows and whys of our two protagonists' renewed existence were somewhat different. Whereas the earlier mummy had wanted nothing so much as to once again put his arms around his lady fair, the 1940 iteration just wanted everyone to leave his girlfriend the hell alone and would kill to do so. Whereas Imhotep (a high priest) could thank the aforementioned Scroll of Thoth for that sparkle in his eye, Kharis (a prince of the Royal House) was given the gift of locomotion by those bloody tana leaves. Whereas Karloff's ancient lover worked alone, Tyler's had a coterie of horny high priests who kept his lips wet and his anger piqued. Whereas the ultimate irony of *The Mummy* had the reincarnated gal for whom the titular grotesque had the hots speaking the words that returned him to dust, *The Mummy's Hand* eschewed irony and had a flaming brazier – and not his flame's brassiere – leading to the hots and the dust.

**Archaeology made easy: pith helmets, crow bars, the casually dropped outer sarcophagus lid, and an ancient vase, ignored and obviously of little value. L–R: Charles Trowbridge, Tom Tyler, Dick Foran, Wallace Ford, Cecil Kellaway, Peggy Moran.**

What gives rise to this comparison is Universal's decision to abandon the "mythos" established in its first mummy movie and create an entirely different scenario. Although the studio's personifications of the Frankenstein Monster and Count Dracula returned to the screen time and again, their back-stories and personae went essentially unchanged, no matter who portrayed the characters at any given moment. There may have been a busload of medical types yclept Frankenstein, but everyone and everything could be traced back to Colin Clive's primogenitor, and the Monster – save for his going woolly in 1939 – apparently owned but one suit of clothes. Dracula – who also wore naught save for his soup and fish – gained and lost a bit of weight, occasionally sported a mustache, had an accent that came and went, retrieved the top hat he had briefly worn while ambling through downtown London earlier, but nonetheless remained the off-kilter count from Transylvania. Granted, when Lawrence Talbot finally showed up on the screen (in 1941), his alter ego was a darned sight more feral than his British predecessor's had been, but Henry Hull was a Were*wolf*, whereas Lon Chaney was a Wolf *Man*, so we still have an out: we are (obviously) dealing with two different species here. Still – even after Sir John Talbot had pretty much tattooed his head with that silver pentagram cane – son Lawrence returned with pre-history intact for four more pictures.

So why two different mummies? It's not like we're involved with vampirism or lycanthropy or the awesome power of electricity. Imhotep and Kharis; well, to paraphrase the Sayer of the Law, "Were they not men?" Why did Universal not just pick up where the 1932 classic left off? Imhotep *was* reduced to dust, granted, but Frankenstein's Monster had been blown to atoms at the end of *Bride*, only to end up none the worse for wear in *Son*, even sporting a new shirt and with his hair restored to its original luster. Nor, apparently, was there ever be a problem with Dracula showing up time and again after he had been staked or sunlighted or whatever. When Tom Tyler's fairly youthful Kharis was still breathing and plotting and scheming within feet of his princess's coffin, he matched up decently to footage of Karloff from the earlier picture, so why not just continue with the charade? (We demur, however, from commenting on how – during Eduardo Cianelli's narrated flashback - the size and design of Ananka's burial chamber doesn't quite jive with the same site when the footage was of an identical sarcophagus containing Ankh-es-en-amon.)

Did Imhotep's descendants threaten litigation?

No matter. Jack Otterson's art direction and Russell A. Gausman's sets are as memorable as anything the actors or director or scenarists bring to the party. That secret Karnak sect that George Zucco would steadfastly support through this and two of the following sequels is apparently so secret that it assiduously avoids the quite substantial Temple complex that actually *does* stand at Karnak. In its stead, the sect has apparently built an impressive sacrificial altar with all sorts of connecting passageways and staircases on (or, rather, *in*) the Hill of the Seven Jackals, a spot not yet overwhelmed by tourists. We pause to note that the impressive facial statuary

53

atop the great stone steps on the far side of said hill (which no one in the Banning expedition thought to check out early on) is conceptually more Incan than Egyptian, but the picture found its way to the screen at a time when few Americans traveled abroad terribly much.

Despite the fact that, in flashback, Kharis is espied kneeling in front of it alongside Ananka's sarcophagus, the Scroll of Thoth was abjured by Griffin Jay and Maxwell Shane in favor of the aforementioned tana leaves, thus causing the persnickety viewer to rationalize: "Hmmmm… Maybe without a tongue, Kharis could not articulate the words on the Scroll of Thoth and thus was compelled to fall back on Plan B." If Kharis ever gets his lips around more than nine leaves, he will become an uncontrollable monster, we semi-quote Cianelli and then Zucco. But with Kharis already up and shuffling about - having done away with Dr. Petrie after a nine-leaf infusion - Andoheb still has his grungy henchman plant vials containing tana-leaf fluid all over the place, so what must one think? Can the mummy ingest vast quantities of the stuff without that uncontrollable side effect as long as he waits a few minutes between doses? We even accept that Kharis somehow understands Andoheb's rather stilted, English-language instruction in re: the vials – princes of the Royal House must have received quite an education way back when – and his pace *does* pick up a bit after throttling Ali and downing the contents of the latest one he has found…

But at what point does the knocking back of X-number of tana leaves kick Kharis's libido into high gear, what with his carrying off the only girl within miles of the place, sans specific instruction from Andoheb? We've zero indication that anyone trundling in and about the Seven Jackals' Hill has any awareness whatsoever of the reincarnation factor on which *The Mummy* had turned, so – other than the fact that the monsters are always looking to run off with pretty girls – what's up with Marta Solvani? Kharis rather unceremoniously dumps her on the altar, not ten yards from what we assume is his honey's casket, and then is sent on his way (he doesn't so much as look back or mime a sigh) so that Andoheb can reveal for the first time the raging hormones of the Karnak contingent. And when Kharis *does* return to the altar – shooed out of the temple by Andoheb, the mummy slowly takes a circuitous route and ends up back where he started - he makes a beeline for that flaming brazier; only Steve's moving directly into his path causes Kharis to so much as acknowledge his presence. Apparently – despite his stated mission to kill those who defile Ananka's tomb – Kharis's number-one focus is on how to get his fix before the full moon wanes and he's slipped back into his original packaging.

Top-billed in the film is Dick Foran, and the big fella just exudes boy-next-door charm. Having started his career as a radio crooner, Foran made his move into the movies (as "Nick" Foran) alongside Shirley Temple in 1934's *Stand Up and Cheer* and spent the next couple of years winning accolades as "The Singing Cowboy." His vocal talents soon took a back place to his thespic ability, though, and the New Jerseyan rubbed onscreen elbows with Claude Rains in every one of the *Four Daughters/Mothers/Wives* features and with Vincent Price and George Sanders in *The House of the Seven Gables*. As Steve Banning, he is a credible blend of scientific know-how and common sense, even if we're not sure whether dropping the hieroglyph-heavy lid to the outer box containing a sarcophagus to the ground and then walking all over it is SOP for well-established archaeologists. Then, too, we're at a bit of a loss as to how he has managed some of his major accomplishments in the company of Babe Jenson.

Banning's buddy on the Ananka expedition is played by British-born Wallace Ford, one of Hollywood's best-liked character men. Ford was something of a genre veteran by the time *Hand* went before the camera: during the previous decade – when he had been the leading man in any number of potboilers and whodunits – he had matched wits with Bela Lugosi in both Columbia's *Night of Terror* (1933) and Monogram's *The Mysterious Mr. Wong* (1935). Earlier, he had also been the nominal lead in Tod Browning's wild, unsettling *Freaks* (1932) over at M-G-M. Whether the hero or the hero's best pal, Ford came across as brash (without being obnoxious), wary (without being cowardly), and totally dependable when the chips are down. And, despite being required by the script to display a near-obsession with "Poopsie" (a dancing doll he has purchased at that Cairo bazaar), Ford demonstrates those qualities once again here.

Peggy Moran and perennial pixie Cecil Kellaway make quite a team, too. Miss Moran's participation in Universal's slick '40s product was curtailed when she married Henry Koster, one of the crowd of German émigrés beckoned to Hollywood by the Laemmles in the mid '30s. Per her obituary in the 31 October 2002 edition of the *Los Angeles Times*,

'He asked me to give up my career,' she told *The Times* in 2000, 'but he promised he'd put me in every movie he made from then on.' He did -- sort of. Koster had a bust made of Moran's head, and the bust appeared in all of his films made after their marriage.

(Thus, Miss Moran's presumed fate as Mrs. Banning in *The Mummy's Tomb* was safely thwarted.) Both here and in *Horror Island* – where she again played opposite Dick Foran – she essayed a savvy and cynical young woman. That she managed to pull off a couple of potentially hard-edged characters without yielding an inch of her femininity was a measure of her talent and personality.

**Somehow, Miss Moran's scribbled "Best Wishes" doesn't quite jive with her alarmed study in this advert. If nothing else, by being elsewhere during its filming, the Iowa-born actress managed to evade Kharis's grasp in *The Mummy's Tomb*, and her marriage to Henry Koster saved her from the subsequent sequels, as well.**

Everybody's favorite Irishman, Cecil Kellaway was born in Cape Town, South Africa, and got his cinematic feet wet in Australia. Following a featured role in William Wyler's *Wuthering Heights* (1939), the actor graced more "B"-product than "A"-, yet among his more than 140 film credits are titles – like *Brother Orchid* (1940) and *I Married a Witch* (1942) – whose contemporary charm and subsequent popularity had nothing to do with budgets. Here, his Solvani is a magical pixie, and Kellaway's chemistry with Peggy Moran – a familial relationship that parallels the amicable one of Foran and Ford, with ties to Brooklyn underlying everyone – beautifully contrasts with the unholy bond(s) existing among Kharis, Andoheb, and the passive Ananka. While *The Mummy's Hand* may be nestled in the lower end of the list of Kellaway's accomplishments (his name is misspelled in the opening credits), the film gave the actor an early opportunity to demonstrate his charisma and to establish his "brand."

Many of the old(er) commentaries I've read about Tom Tyler's Kharis make mention of the ex-cowboy star's bout with arthritis; all he had to do was slightly exaggerate his condition, these critics proclaimed, and – Voila! – instant Mummy. Baloney! This wholesale dismissal of the actor's willful contribution to the role is distressing. Tyler's Kharis has a baleful, genuinely frightening presence due to any number of factors – arthritis not being one of them – that were not or could not be duplicated when Chaney submitted to the gauze for the sequels. Perhaps it was the novelty of the situation – the Karloffian mummy-in-motion was evidenced only in bits and pieces – or the relative restraint with which Christy Cabanne used the Mummy, or even Tyler's lean, mean bearing. A plus often given the portrayal is the optical eradication of Kharis's eyes in several close-ups, a move that has the undead prince glaring daggers with black pools of nothingness. In what may seem like a contradiction in terms, Tyler's lack of mimed reactions to instructions or *ad hoc* situations makes his Kharis far more implacable and unnerving than Chaney's, who would mug, shrug, and/or wiggle at the slightest provocation in an effort to "act" while a mute prisoner to the gauze. And how would someone burdened with progressive arthritis manage to fight evil so physically in Republic's *The Adventures of Captain Marvel* (1941) and Columbia's *The Phantom* (1943)?

Still, I'm not certain why Tyler wasn't tapped for *The Mummy's Tomb*, first of the three sequels. Maybe once in the rig had been enough for him; maybe his essaying the handsome and manly Captain Marvel for the Republic serial a few months after creating the character of Kharis for *Hand* convinced him that he didn't need Jack Pierce to make him marketable. Maybe the eight features in which he did appear in 1942 – oaters, all – found him much more comfortable on horseback than in sarcophagi. Most likely, his casting would have run contrary to Universal's insistence on debuting and exploiting "The Screen's Master Character Creator" in a lengthy series of grotesque and mostly derivative make-ups.

In Kharis, the Mummy persona which had been so carefully delineated by Freund and Karloff almost a decade earlier was now reduced to a combination kidnapper/

hit man. Kharis would have no resilient alter-ego to mastermind the events leading to death and destruction, as Imhotep had as the "cleaned up" Ardath Bey. Wisely, Griffin Jay (who wrote the original story) split the character into separate entities and, henceforth, the movers and shakers in the ongoing saga would be the high priests of Karnak. These would prove lustful and ultimately inept, but although the sacerdotal line supposedly extended back as far as did the misguided Prince of the Royal House himself, never would there be a zealot so glib or so gleeful in his chosen line of work as George Zucco's Andoheb. Wily, deceitful, and not a little bit oily, Andoheb manipulates Kharis with the same certainty with which Zucco steals the picture. Zucco's high priest does have his gentle and solicitous side: he addresses Eduardo Cianelli's ancient as "father" and tenders a tentative touch to the old man's arm. More frequently, though, he's cheerfully coldblooded. While it may have been a dramatic convention for Andoheb to fall for Marta Solvani (thus triggering a pattern which almost every successive high priest will follow), Zucco imbues the lunatic "courtship" with a tad of pathos and a whole lot of technique. Of the handful of Karnak acolytes we have on view throughout the '40s Mummy series, only John Carradine comes close to shaving the ham with anything like the zest and the expertise of old George.

With the Kharis/Ananka saga taking the occasional left-hand turn over the course of four pictures with an aggregate running time of a shade more than four hours (*Hand* clocks in longest at one hour, seven minutes), we might question what particular appeal the plight of the two lovers had to the ancient gods of Egypt. Why, out of the innumerable tombs which pocked the Valley of the Kings or Queens (or the Hill of the Seven Jackals), did Isis, Osiris, and Amon-Ra – whose anger can shatter the world! - chose to station an undead watchdog (and a host of medallion-wearing enablers) here? One might also question the incredible string of bad luck experienced by King Amenophis: of all the pharaohs of all the dynasties in the Twin Kingdom, only Amenophis had two daughters (Ankh-es-en-amon and Ananka) who were snatched from him by untimely death. And only he had two frustrated, potential sons-in-law (Imhotep and Kharis) whom he was forced to order buried alive for their sacrilegious attempts at recalling said daughters from the underworld. Talk about not catching a break!

Contemporary critical commentary didn't bother much with silliness such as this, but opted to opine on the merits of spending the money to see the mummy. The 25 September 1940 *Variety* cut to the chase:

> With at least a nod at its Boris Karloff picture of seven years ago, *The Mummy*, Universal has whipped up another little pseudo-chiller for the

same trade. It's calling this one *The Mummy's Hand* and it's transparently just a road company edition. This time the embalmed menace is played by Tom Tyler. It's all strictly for the lesser duals.

The silliness the review didn't bother with was the fact that – having been buried alive – Tom Tyler's menace had *not* been embalmed. (Two points for us!) The Bible of Show Business may have felt that Cecil Kellaway and Wallace Ford were the "only ones achieving conviction," but the brief critique did mention an aspect of the picture that may be surprising to those of us who have viewed the film only on 16mm or TV: "Apparently with the idea of throwing the creeps into the audience, the sequences taking place in the excavations into early Egyptian remains are shown in green-tinted film." Wow! Live and learn!

Assigned to cover *Hand*'s 20 September New York premiere, *The New York Times* critic T.S. took a wry approach...

> The Rialto marquee holds that Frankenstein was just a lollipop compared to the mummy. It's not far wrong at that Once or twice [Peggy] Moran makes a grimace – as if she had caught an unpleasant odor – and screams. Otherwise every one [sic] seems remarkably casual. If they don't seem to worry, why should we? Frightening or funny, take your choice.

... while on the West Coast, G.K. - the *Los Angeles Times'* reviewer - commented after the picture's trade screening:

> One of those grisly spine-ticklers with comedy trimmings is *The Mummy's Hand*. The thrill job is done by Tom Tyler as the mummy and George Zucco as a sinister priest, while the running humor obbligato is furnished by Wallace Ford as a wise-cracking explorer of Egyptian tombs, also by Cecil Kellaway as a magician... The picture is really one of the best of its kind, and fans who love to quiver will get a big kick out of it.

In closing, Mr. K. commended the Messrs. Ford, Kellaway and Tyler once again, confessed that he found Dick Foran to be "adequate," and praised "the others" as being "all good."

I have to take a moment to note that – with *The Mummy's Hand* – we begin an experience in which time and space have no meaning. Literally. Assuming that the adventure under discussion was meant to be fairly contemporaneous with the film's release date – other than the purloined/adapted flashback footage, there is no indication we are dealing with a "period picture" here – the three Chaney sequels play havoc with temporal/spatial continuity for no other (apparent) reason than total indifference. By the time the "saga" had wrapped (with 1944's thus-blessedly-welcomed *The Mummy's Curse*), we were given to understand that about a half-century has passed since Eduardo Cianelli trembled his way through the tana-leaf blarney; that would have placed the action in the last installment somewhere in the 1990s. Why the delay? Recruitment problems with the Karnak/Arkam Team? Funding dry up? No matter... the mundane sameness of the surroundings and accouterments just offered proof that Universal was – at that point – unwilling/unable/oblivious to match up the supposed ongoing time-frame by depicting their forward-looking views of the America of the future; flash*backs* – not flash-forwards – were the basic stuff of the Kharis canon. We'll deal with these ludicrous bits in our essays on the rest of the series, but for those of us who just cannot get enough of the studio's Mummy muck-ups, please refer to Dan Mankowski's droll yet rich recounting of same ("Mummies for Dummies") in issue 34 of *Cult Movies* magazine.

*The Mummy's Hand* no longer has the power to frighten that it once had, but it hasn't lost its power to fascinate. The Mummy was the first of the '30s "Big Three" to be accorded a bit of '40s verve and polish and, in this initial outing, the results were admirable. Sure, the $80,000 budget hampered things a bit, necessitating not only some expository swipes from the earlier film, but also a shot of a wolf (from one of Christy Cabanne's Westerns?) filling in for a jackal and that (archaeologically sacrilegious) explosion that literally opens the door to the action. The wisdom of keeping the bandaged menace off-screen for a good bit of the story would be abandoned in subsequent installments, giving the one-note goblin far too much opportunity to wear out his welcome. But here the novelty of the theme combined with an excellent cast and an on-target production staff produce a tight and fast-moving film. The picture held its own with any of Universal's comparable genre efforts during the war years, and it still holds up well today.

*The Mummy's Hand* – 20 September 1940 – 67 minutes (ST)

**CAST**: Dick Foran as Steve Banning; Peggy Moran as Marta Solvani; Wallace Ford as Babe Jenson; Eduardo Cianelli as the High Priest; George Zucco as Professor Andoheb; Cecil Kellaway as The Great Solvani (Tim Sullivan); Charles Trowbridge as Dr. Petrie; Tom Tyler as Kharis; Siegfried Arno as the Beggar; Eddie Foster as the Egyptian; Harry Stubbs as the Bartender; Michael Mark as the Bazaar Owner; Mara Tartar as Girl; Leon Belasco as Ali; Frank Lackteen, Murdock MacQuarrie as Priests; Jerry Frank, Kenneth Terrell as Thugs

**CREDITS**: Director: Christy Cabanne; Producer: Ben Pivar; Screenplay: Griffin Jay & Maxwell Shane; Original Story: Griffin Jay; Director of Photography: Elwood Bredell; Film Editor: Philip Cahn; Art Director: Jack Otterson; Associate Art Director: Ralph M. DeLacy; Music: Frank Skinner & Hans J. Salter; Musical Director: Charles Previn; Assistant Director: Vaughn Paul; Set Decorator: Russell A. Gausman; Sound Supervisor: Bernard B. Brown; Technician: Charles Carroll; Makeup: Jack P. Pierce; Gowns: Vera West

*Shock Theater* Catalog No. 720: "'All who enter are doomed' was the curse of Ananka's tomb, yet they dared enter to solve a terror ridden secret 3000 years old. See Dick Foran in 'The Mummy's Hand' on *Shock* on channel at (time), (day)."

*–JTS*

# *The Invisible Woman* (1940)

With the Invisible Man having returned - over-budget, but still profitable - earlier that same year, the powers that were put their heads together and decided that the time was right for an Invisible Woman to... *errrr*...make an appearance. When the word got out that, maybe in *this* film, someone's cigar smoke might produce an outline that would raise an appreciative eyebrow or two, the audiences were pre-sold. (There was some cigar*ette* smoke this time 'round, but 'twas puffed *by* the amazing transparent woman and targeted no one.) There would be none of that monocaine or duocaine or third-time's-the-charm-ocaine that led to megalomania or madness. No siree, Bob! The thought of some gorgeous gal (leads in stuff like this were never anything but gorgeous) bouncing around in the altogether (they weren't going to start in with "invisible clothes," were they?) would definitely get one's blood pressure moving, but the only violence such antics might portend would be a chaste slap in the face or, perhaps, a well-placed kick to the posterior. With *Captive Wild Woman* still more than couple of years off and *Dracula's Daughter* almost a lustrum in the past, there was no current effort at making the fair sex fearsome.

While James Whale's trendsetting venture had had more than its share of sardonic humor, *The Invisible Man Returns* had been more than a trifle grim, so this project would be a much-needed comic take on invisibility. Claude Rains had remained a virtually unknown commodity for most of the original picture – his 1920 British silent, *Build Thy House*, had done zip to establish him in the cinema – but the young Vincent Price at least had had some name/face recognition prior to the denouement of *his* gauzy goings-on, thanks to his Universal contract. If there was to be any zest in the concept at this juncture, *la femme invisible* would have to be a well-known (and

63

*beeyootiful*) commodity before the transparency was called to a halt and she, too, was nestled safely under some bedclothes.

The off-kilter treatment here was the brainchild of Kurt (later, Curt) Siodmak, who had earlier conspired with Joe May on the screenplay for *Returns*. Both men again read the tea leaves accurately and sold the original story for *Woman* to Universal; Robert Lees, Frederic I. Rinaldo, and Gertrude Purcell then rearranged for the tale for filmability. Replacing May behind the megaphone on this third "Invisible" film would be A. Edward ("Eddie") Sutherland, a one-time Keystone Kop and favored director of W.C. Fields, Stan Laurel, and Oliver Hardy. The British-born Sutherland had had some experience with the horror/mystery/science-fiction genre prior to accepting the assignment at hand: he had helmed both *Secrets of the French Police* for RKO in 1932 and *Murders in the Zoo* for Paramount in 1933, and had appeared onscreen, thesping like crazy, in William Desmond Taylor's *The Witching Hour* (1921). Still, there wasn't to be much of the horror/mystery/science-fiction genre's more serious side in this picture, even with hypodermic needles, flashing lights, and mechanical cacophony.

**While the '30s saw both *Bride of Frankenstein* and *Dracula's Daughter*, the actresses portraying those titular characters did not see top billing. That changed come the '40s – at least for Virginia Bruce.**

The lovely, Minnesota-born Virginia Bruce was tapped to go clothes-less but unseen after Margaret Sullavan – an equally lovely Virginian with only the most tenuous of ties to the supernatural: see 1935's *The Good Fairy* or 1938's *The Shopworn Angel* – flew the contractual coop after considering the project to be beneath her. Bruce, a sloe-eyed lass who had appeared in a brace of Lon Chaney Sr. remakes (*The Miracle Man* and *Kongo*, both 1932), who had essayed the title role in 1934's *Jane Eyre* (albeit for Monogram), and who would – some years down the road – get stuck (along with *Son of Dracula* alumni, Robert Paige and Samuel S. Hinds) in Abbott & Costello's *Pardon My Sarong*, was perfect for the role. Beautiful, tenacious, and possessed of a sense of humor that was definitely not exploited in stuff like *Arsène Lupin Returns* (1938) or *Flight Angels* (1940), Bruce hit just the right notes as Kitty Carroll, fashion model and guinea pig to John Barrymore.

John Barrymore's Professor Gibbs is a long-time scientific quack who has somehow invented an "invisibility machine." When Kitty, a model at the Continental Dress Company, answers his newspaper ad, she is his first (and only) subject, and all appears to go well (no insanity, no egomania, no cheap jokes about nudity), although the state of invisibility is only temporary, and the use of alcohol brings on unexpected results. Kitty first uses her lack of visibility to land a trio of well-placed butt-kicks on the aptly-named Mr. Growley, the ill-tempered boss of the bevy of young Continental Dress Company models, and the frightened Growley soon changes his tune for the better. She is then introduced by Gibbs to Dick Russell, a playboy who can't help but gradually find the invisible woman attractive, despite the sarcastic give-and-take in which the two indulge. When Kitty is once again a sight for sore eyes, she sweeps Russell off his feet.

Meanwhile, a trio of fumbling thieves steals the invisibility machine for their crime boss, Blackie Cole, who plans to render himself invisible so as to end his exile in Mexico [!?] and head home. Unfortunately, the machine worketh not, so Blackie has Gibbs and Kitty kidnapped, intending to force the operational secret from them. Russell and his long-suffering butler, George, ride to the rescue, and with the help of the newly re-invisible Kitty, put the bad guys out of business. In a cute addendum to the main story, Kitty and Dick – now happily married and possessed of an heir – watch as their son begins to dematerialize before their eyes. The culprit? Rubbing alcohol.

The most astonishing element in the picture is the Great Profile – John Barrymore – here, about a year and a half prior to his all-too-soon demise. My colleagues and I have written elsewhere about Barrymore at his cinematic peak, just prior to his assuming the mantle of the Great Dane, Hamlet, and setting the theatrical bar higher than most of his successors could ever hope to reach. (1) It's tough to determine just when the actor shrugged and decided that making a quick buck was easier and more desirable than acting and making folks gape with wonder. His assuming a recurring role that was more window-dressing than germane drama in the "Bulldog Drummond" series might have tipped audiences to the change in philosophy. Still, Barrymore's last few film roles (and this is his antepenultimate venture) were marked by his all but winking at the seat-holders, an action that he would never have dreamed of doing a decade or so earlier. That having been writ, he *is* funny as the madcap inventor of the apparatus that will lead to chuckles rather than chills, given the studio and the preceding entries in this particular series.

*The New York Times*, in fact, felt that The Great Profile was the whole show here:

> Perhaps the maddest jape to have arrived hereabouts recently is *The Invisible Woman*, currently causing eye strain at the Rialto. It is silly, banal and repetitious; it is essentially a two-reel comedy with elephantiasis and full of the trick disappearances and materializations that seemed new when *Topper* first came out. The script is as creaky as a two-wheeled cart and were it not for the fact that John Barrymore is taking a rid [sic] in it we hate to think what *The Invisible Woman* might have turned out to be. But Mr. Barrymore takes to this trash as if he were to the manner born. He gives a performance that lampoons all actors, but especially his brother Lionel, who would be perfectly within his rights to sue John as an impostor and a plagiarist. As a crafty old scientist, full of formulas for making people invisible, he gives a ludicrous portrait of dementia. He is arch and gleeful by turns; he gropes with his hands, he blows in his cheeks and makes mirthful clucking sounds.
>
> 9 January 1941

By 1940, Barrymore was something of a drunken joke in Hollywood. There were times, though, when that joke may have turned sour and his being "arch and gleeful by turns" was not at all amusing. Siodmak – responsible for the original story here with fellow German immigrant, Joe May - has written that working with Barrymore at this point in the actor's life was not all fun and games:

The director, Edward Sutherland, had to devise methods to make Barrymore remember his lines, since his love for alcohol had greatly impaired his memory. Sutherland had John walk up and down a staircase, where he read his dialog displayed on the banister. He had to be hung up on wires, to prevent him from swaying out of close-ups. (2)

Kudos, then, to Eddie Sutherland, as Barrymore's performance belies all the trouble the actor may have caused during production.

The supporting cast of *The Invisible Woman* is probably one of the best of the early '40s, populated by some of the era's most beloved – and seemingly ubiquitous – character people. John Howard *was* Captain Hugh C. "Bulldog" Drummond in those late '30s series entries that featured Barrymore. More the leading man than the amigo for much of his career, the Ohio-born actor had made his genre debut in the classic *Lost Horizon* (1937) and had returned to the fold with Paramount's *The Mad Doctor*, which had been shot before but released after *The Invisible Woman*. (Howard revisited the thriller world – twice – in Richard Oswald's *Isle of Missing Men* and Fox's wonderful werewolf-chiller, *The Undying Monster* [both 1942].) Come the '50s, Howard devoted most of the rest of his career – nearly 30 years' worth – to the small screen.

**Margaret Hamilton – who would always be identified with her role as the "Wicked Witch of the West" – puts the eye on John Barrymore – who would forever be known as "The Great Profile."**

67

Here we also have Maria Montez, in her second feature since emigrating to the USA and not quite on the cusp of the Technicolor adventures over which she would briefly reign starting in 1942. Also, in the year-and-a-bit since the release of *The Wizard of Oz* in August of 1939 and the start of production for *Invisible* at Universal, Margaret Hamilton had appeared in a half-dozen pictures at five different studios; had worked in musicals, comedies, pastiches, romances, and crime dramas; and had supported everyone from the Dead End Kids and the team of Mickey Rooney and Judy Garland, to W.C. Fields and Buster Keaton. She, too, along with Charlie Ruggles, Donald MacBride, Shemp Howard, Thurston Hall, et al had created/would go on to create comic personae that would span the decades and survive to this day in the minds and hearts of vintage movie and TV fans everywhere. And for those very same fans, Mary Gordon *is* forever Mrs. Hudson.

This move to devisibilizing a woman rather than yet another guy with anger issues - less than a year after Vincent Price had weathered that storm - signaled a move toward greater female representation in the thrillers-end of the market. This comic treatment was the first and only entry in the "do not take seriously" vein; come 1942, and the aforementioned Maria Montez was tapped to play the eponymous Marie Roget in *The Mystery of....* Then opened the sluice gates: the following year, Acquanetta – the "Venezuelan Volcano" to Montez's "Caribbean Cyclone" – was the *Captive Wild Woman*; Louise Albritton's "heroine" made Lon Chaney's Count Alucard seem like a nursery-schoolmate in *Son of Dracula*; Gale Sondergaard introduced the character of the *Spider Woman* into the Rathbone/Bruce canon in January of '44; and Evelyn Ankers finally got her shot at giving someone *else* such a shot as the titular *Weird Woman*, the second entry in the newly-minted "Inner Sanctum" series. By midyear, both Acquanetta and Ankers would go on to grace the wretched hour-long sequel, *Jungle Woman* - the "Gorilla Girl" of the earlier film's publicity campaign was now "Paula, the Ape Woman" (something, I guess, of a promotion) - but the Venezuelan Volcano was replaced by Dubliner Vicki Lane for the series' windup, *The Jungle Captive*, in 1945. The Great Consulting Detective would then have to deal with *The Woman in Green*, the Spider Woman would strike back in early 1946, and everything wrapped with *The She-Wolf of London*, later that same year. Woof! Universal's women had come into their own - at least until the War had ended, our guys had come home from overseas, and the horror genre was supplanted by *Films Noir*, with the action centered more on erotica and less on exotica.

Effects wizard John P. Fulton was in charge of the "now you see it, now you don't" end of *The Invisible Woman*, as he had been for the '33 Rains/Whale classic, Vincent

Price's turn, and every genre film cranked out by Universal in the '30s and '40s that featured the word "Invisible" in the title. He was assisted by Roswell A. Hoffmann in the area of "optical photography," a line of work that has us wondering what other sort of photography we have been missing out on. Uncredited here, as he was for 1933's *The Invisible Man* and would be for 1942's *The Invisible Agent* and the 1951 *Abbott and Costello Meet...* epic, Hoffmann came into his own – with a screen credit for his optical magic! – when Universal-International went all-out science fiction in the mid-'50s with titles like *This Island Earth* (1955), *The Incredible Shrinking Man*, and *The Land Unknown* (both 1957). Until that point, the self-effacing technician usually received a paycheck – but no screen mention – as a second camera operator. In the film at hand, the optical and/or special photographic effects in evidence are pretty much standard or perhaps even a tad *below* previous outings – per **Universal Horrors**, John Howard groused about having to work at being convincing while playing "opposite nobody" – and in the scene in which Kitty gives Mr. Growley what for, the invisible Virginia Bruce's shadow may be seen on the wall. "Walt," writing in the 1 January 1941 *Variety*, had no such quibble, though.

**John Howard – who had recently played Bulldog Drummond opposite the Phyllis Clavering of Louise Campbell or Heather Angel for over a half-dozen pictures – now groused that he had to use his imagination whilst playing opposite "nobody." At least he could enjoy the stills "with" Virginia Bruce he could paste into his scrapbook.**

Picture is a novelty freak, played in broadest farce, with plenty of audience interest generated in the weird happenings, and will clock good biz in the regular runs generally Stunts of an invisible person walking in and out of rooms, through doors, and conking others over the head is [sic] played to the utmost and with satisfactory audience reaction... Trick photography has the invisible form of Miss Bruce walking around in visible clothes, but with head, arms and legs transparent. Weirdness of the situations are [sic] always played for the broadest farce and dramatics are subdued in hitting for the comedy angles of the picture.

Given the total comfort that today's studios feel in cranking out instances of mass destruction (usually *a la* CGI), individually-oriented mindless violence (*Saw* anything recently?), nudity (in part or in whole), mental illness in any and all of its forms, etc., it's almost charming to read of the efforts taken a lifetime ago to avoid presenting anything onscreen that might cause offense. Take the critique from *Box Office Digest* as an example:

Essentially, of course, the outstanding element of the picture is the fascinating technical work that gives us an invisible character, possible of introduction into all sorts of situations. You have seen it as horrifics, and in the Roach treatment for *Topper*. But the writers got a bolt of inspiration in this one, when they disclose to us that Barrymore, eccentric scientist, can only make his experimental victim – Virginia Bruce – invisible when she is in the nude. It sounds crude putting it that bluntly, so let's hasten to add that while this basic theme, of Virginia in the altogether running around the action, adds the spice to all her scenes, particularly with John Howard, there is keen taste shown in keeping dialogue and situation on a plane without the slightest offense.

30 December 1940

Reviewer Vance King, in the 31 December 1940 edition of *Motion Picture Daily*, took the time to spell this out.

The picture is also noteworthy for the appearance, or non-appearance, for the first time on the screen of 'invisible nudity,' the model first being required to divest her clothes behind a screen before the machine begins to operate. For most of the following sequences of invisibility, she is presumed not to be dressed.

"First time," my sainted grandmother! Although both Claude Rains and Vincent Price had pretty much explained in a variety of ways in their respective films the fact that they were also in the buff whilst unseen, no one saw fit to raise the issue until Virginia Bruce dropped her dress onto the floor in late December, 1940. In his memoir, Siodmak remarked on Bruce's supposedly being in the nude:

I told Fulton that she went into a bathtub, and all one could see was the imprint of her invisible body in the water. She was soaping her long slim legs, which made them appear, then her face. I tried to make her upper body visible, which would have made the picture X-rated. I even talked that scene over with her. Virginia, a fetching blonde, proud of her good looks, would have been game, but not the Hays Office, which controlled the morals of motion pictures. (3)

The invisibility conceit would once again introduce an "horrific" with 1944's *The Invisible Man's Revenge,* but only after being utilized as a weapon with which the Allies would fight the Axis in *Invisible Agent* (1942). Obviously, neither treatment would be played for laughs. While the transparent Kitty *does* have her revenge on Growley in *The Invisible Woman,* in December of 1940 there was still no reason to anticipate utilizing an invisibility machine (or whatever) to fend off America's enemies. Eddie Sutherland's picture was made strictly for laughs, and whether they were due to plot situations or comic characterizations, laughs were forthcoming. Pratfalls were to be had from Charlie Ruggles and Shemp Howard, while the male rump – and not the much-anticipated female derriere - was highlighted through that trio of love-taps Growley got from "his conscience" and a succession of butt-to-the-camera crouches effected by Howard and Edward Brophy.

The odd "person" out in a series of films built around men and their sundry propensities, *The Invisible Woman* is still well worth the 70 minutes it takes to reveal how the fair sex would deal with conditions that men found alarming or dangerous.

*The Invisible Woman* – 27 December 1940 – 70 minutes
CAST: Virginia Bruce as Kitty Carroll; John Barrymore as Professor Gibbs; John Howard as Dick Russell; Charlie Ruggles as George; Oscar Homolka as Blackie Cole; Edward Brophy as Bill; Donald MacBride as Foghorn; Charles Lane as Growley; Thurston Hall as John Hudson; Margaret Hamilton as Mrs. Jackson; Mary Gordon as Mrs. Bates; Anne Nagel as Jean; Maria Montez as Marie; Shemp Howard as

Hammerhead/Frankie; Kathryn Adams as Peggy; Kitty O'Neill as Mrs. Patton; Eddie Conrad as Hernandez; Kay Leslie as Model; Kay Linaker and Sarah Edwards as Fashion Show Buyers; with Harry C. Bradley and Kernan Cripps

**CREDITS**: Director: A. Edward Sutherland; Associate Producer: Burt Kelly; Screenplay: Robert Lees, Frederic I. Rinaldo, & Gertrude Purcell; Original Story: Kurt Siodmak & Joe May; Suggested by the character created by H.G. Wells; Director of Photography: Elwood Bredell; Special Photographic Effects: John P. Fulton; Art Editor: Jack Otterson; Associate Art Director: Richard H. Riedel; Film Editor: Frank Gross; Musical Director: Charles Previn; Sound Supervisor: Bernard B. Brown; Technician: Joe Lapis; Set Decoration: Russell A. Gausman; Assistant Director: Joseph McDonough; Gowns: Vera West.

*-JTS*

# Man-Made Monster (1941)

Having rediscovered box-office gold from horror movies, the execs at the New Universal also determined that they need not invest in big budgets for same and, after *The House of Seven Gables* (1940), they would approve only a few genre productions with an "A"-budget. They also rifled through existing projects, both filmed and unfilmed, to satisfy renewed audience appetites for shudder-producing productions – and hopefully to do so on the cheap. Not quite Monogram cheap, mind you, but hardly "A"-budget and decidedly designed for double-bill play. As with any/all of the major studios (Universal was still considered a minor major at the time and would continue to be so designated until the '50s), standing sets contributed to an illusion of polish – for their living mummy reboot, a slightly revamped temple set, left over from James Whale's *Green Hell* (1940), made the film look costlier than it actually was. Likewise the plantation-house exterior, built for a silent production of *Uncle Tom's Cabin* (1927) – and seen in productions as late as *This Island Earth* (1955) – served to boost the look of *Man-Made Monster*.

Universal also saved on some of the movie's below-the-line costs by dusting off an old project that would have teamed Boris Karloff as the victim of mad scientist Bela Lugosi's experiments. They were hedging their bets; sequels to the Frankenstein and Invisible Man movies, an adaptation of a classic novel (which, if push came to shove, could arguably not have been tagged a horror film), and a reboot of the Mummy character had marked the output thus far. All had a built-in box-office appeal... Triple

*M* would feature a wholly original monster character so the budget would be shaved to the bone. A short story, yclept "The Electric Man," had been purchased back in the day for horror's equivalent of Astaire and Rogers, but *The Man in the Cab*, as it was to have been titled, was never made because it was felt there were too many resemblances to *The Invisible Ray* (1936). Retrieved from limbo, it became the basis for a script by the film's director, George Waggner, writing under the pseudonym Joseph West. During production, per the **AFI Catalog**, it was known as *The Mysterious Dr. R*, *The Mysterious Dr. X* (titles that Universal would later sort of combine for another feature – nothing, but nothing went to waste at Universal), *The Electric Man*, and *The Human Robot*. Realart would later reissue the movie under still another title, *The Atomic Monster*. Waggner would find himself with more horror assignments at the studio (albeit *Man-Made Monster* is more science fiction than horror) courtesy a new seven-year contract offered on the basis of his work here, and the film would establish a new horror star for the new decade – and one with a bankable name.

When a bus crashes into an electric tower, all the passengers are killed save for Dan McCormick, aka Dynamo Dan the Electrical Man (Lon Chaney, Jr.), whose sideshow act involves such tricks as sticking his finger into a light socket. Newspaper coverage of the accident and its sole survivor catches the attention of electro-biologist Dr. Lawrence (Samuel S. Hinds), who persuades Dan to submit himself to being studied, the better to understand why he has built up an immunity to both alternating and direct current. Lawrence's associate, the insufficiently hinged Dr. Rigas (Lionel Atwill), is pursuing a peculiar line of research; he's convinced he can create "a race of superior Men," who have no will of their own and who need only electricity for nourishment. Precisely what the benefits of this transformation might be are pretty vague; perhaps, like Dr. Von Altermann's creations in 1943's *Revenge of the Zombies*, they can be sent off to wage our wars for us or be our slaves. In any event, Rigas takes advantage of Lawrence's absence at a convention to change Dan into just such a being. When his experiment is discovered, Rigas orders Dan – now a glowing creature whose very touch is deadly and who needs to wear a protective rubber suit to keep the electricity from draining away – to kill the kindly Lawrence and to confess to the deed. Despite the efforts of Lawrence's niece, June Meredith (Anne Gwynne), and her fiance, reporter Mark Adams (Frank Albertson), to prove otherwise, Dan is found guilty and sentenced to the electric chair. Rather than killing him, the voltage reinvigorates Dan who then escapes from prison and heads back to Lawrence's house, killing the warden and a luckless hayride driver along the way. Meanwhile. June is poking about the laboratory for evidence that will exonerate Dan (rather late in the day) when she is discovered by Rigas and threatened with being turned into an Electrical Woman.

(NB: Because we were dubious, we Googled electro-biology and it is indeed a branch of science. "1 a. The physical phenomena arising from the behavior of electrons and protons that is caused by the attraction of particles with opposite charges and the repulsion of particles with the same charge. b. The physical science of such phenomena. 2. Electric current used or regarded as a source of power." So there. Who says you can't learn stuff by reading about monster movies? Though quite what is has to do with the goings-on here is anybody's guess.)

Shot in three weeks for an estimated $86,000 (according to Wikipedia), the finished product was one of Big U's least expensive films of the year; per Richard Harland Smith on the TCM website, sequences were truncated or even eliminated during production to shave costs. None if it looks hurried or slapdash, though – the opening scale-model sequence of the bus crash engineered by John Fulton's team is pretty impressive, and Waggner not only keeps things moving at a fast clip – the better to get past the plot holes – he also finds more interesting camera set-ups than is his wont. He's abetted in the latter by cinematographer Elwood Bredell (surely one of the unsung heroes of '40s U horror). The way Atwill and Hinds are lit as Rigas and Lawrence debate the merits of the former's experiments tells you instantly who's the good guy and who's the bad guy. Not that we need further clarification, because Rigas is played by Lionel Atwill at his craziest, grinning wolfishly with his electric-lightbulb eyes at full wattage. Accused by Lawrence that he's not in his right mind, Rigas readily admits, "I *am* mad. But so was Galileo..." and offers a list of scientists who went beyond the established boundaries of their time. He'll gleefully confess to being off his rocker a couple more times during the film as well.

And there is where the film's weakness lies; it's pretty much a nothing burger. We know practically from the get-go that Rigas is the villain and that Dan will become his victim. There's no dramatic tension because we can easily predict the ending wherein Dan will turn on his tormentor (whether it makes sense or not) before meeting his own demise; this is tragedy of the prefabricated kind. There's little to be mined in terms of subtext, though one can speculate whether the set-up of a man being dragged into a tragic situation by a foreigner (Rigas just isn't a good, healthy American name, is it?) was a reflection of then-popular sentiment about how the U.S. was being "dragged into" World War II by foreigners who couldn't defeat the Axis powers without help. (Attitudes toward the war would largely change after the attack on Pearl Harbor – which came about after the film's release – though not about how our country had

75

been forced into the conflict.) To a great degree, Universal's monsters of the '40s were not self-determining, but rather, created by and often the tool of evil foreigners (see *The Mad Ghoul* [1944], all the Kharis films, and most of the Frankenstein monster entries from 1939's *Son of Frankenstein* on, for starters). It's no wonder the studio couldn't quite figure out what to do with Count Dracula; the character that started it all was given only one solo sequel before being dumped into the monster rallies. That guy wasn't about to take orders from anyone.

*Man-made monster* isn't just a simple story simply told, it's also simplistic; characters are one-dimensional. Dan is a likable lug (a type at which Chaney excelled); Lawrence is kindly; Rigas is diabolically insane, etc., etc. Lawrence's niece (Anne Nagel) and her reporter fiance (Frank Albertson) are stock characters and hardly essential to the plot. Their only function is to serve as surrogates for the audience and to express concern for Dan while doing almost nothing to help him; neither of them experiences a personality change during the course of the story. Dan is transformed from robust young man to a voltage-addicted zombie in the twinkling of an eye (the film isn't clear as to how long Lawrence has been away at his convention, but such things rarely last longer than a week), yet no one seems to be more than mildly concerned over Dan's rapid and radical decline. Well, almost no one. Corky the dog (Corky), who seems to belong to no one in the Lawrence household, is distressed every time Rigas takes Dan into the laboratory. Waggner wisely gives the little pooch the film's penultimate image as he mournfully lays his head over his lifeless friend.

While most who think of U horror in the '40s as chronicling the ongoing adventures of the Frankenstein monster, Count Dracula, the Wolf Man, and Kharis the mummy, the studio also turned out a healthy number of one-offs (or, at any rate, productions that didn't warrant follow-ups). *Man-made monster* is one of the least of them, but hardly the worst. As with all, it offers a solid cast of contract players (and in the case of Chaney the younger, a contract player-to-be). Technically it is a slick, well-made film. And it is fun if not particularly scary – but then it would be difficult to qualify any of this group of films as scary to anyone who had already experienced puberty.

Top-billed Lionel Atwill (1885-1946) was born in England to a wealthy family; while he had trained as an architect, his attention turned to the stage. After debuting at London's Garrick Theater at the age of 20, he was frequently seen on West End stages, often in the plays of Henrik Ibsen. He emigrated to the U.S. in 1915 and between then and 1931 appeared in 25 plays, while dabbling in film on the side (including some Vitaphone short subjects that could take advantage of his marvelous voice).

76

Atwill's first significant role came in 1932 (*The Silent Witness* aka *The Verdict*) and, that same year, he had his first brush with genre in *Doctor X*. The following year brought even more horror assignments with *The Vampire Bat*, *Mystery of the Wax Museum*, *Murders in the Zoo*, *The Sphinx*, and *Secret of the Blue Room* (his first genre assignment for Big U). Other than Universal, the studios involved therein were Majestic, Warner Bros., Paramount, and Monogram; Atwill was clearly freelancing successfully. His other genre assignments in the 1930s were *The Man Who Reclaimed His Head* (1934), *Mark of the Vampire* (1935), *Son of Frankenstein* (1939) - where he memorably jams a fistful of darts into his false arm and goes toe-to-toe in intense acting with Basil Rathbone - *The Hound of the Baskervilles*, and *The Gorilla* (both 1939). He deserves his top billing here in *Man-Made Monster* as he handily walks off with the show.

Although Atwill is known primarily as a horror actor, his films were quite varied during the '30s and early '40s. Interspersed with the horrors are turns, generally villainous, in *The Song of Songs* (1933), James Whale's *One More River*, *The Age of Innocence* (both 1934), von Sternberg's *The Devil is a Woman*, Michael Curtiz's *Captain Blood* (both 1935), *The Great Garrick* (1937), *The Great Waltz* (1938), and *The Three Musketeers* (1939). He would deliciously send himself up in Ernst Lubitsch's *To Be or Not to Be* (1942), playing a ham actor, but the rest of the '40s - until his death - would be spent in genre offerings and even on Poverty Row, which he'd avoided since his early days. *Man-made monster* would be followed by *The Mad Doctor of Market Street*, The *Ghost of Frankenstein* (where he essentially repeats his duplicitous Triple M characterization), *The Strange Case of Doctor Rx* (all 1942), the Dead End Kids and Little Tough Guys serial *Junior G-Men of the Air* (1942), *Cairo*, *Night Monster*, *Sherlock Holmes and the Secret Weapon* (all 1942), *Frankenstein Meets the Wolf Man* (1943), the Republic serial *Captain America* (1943), *House of Frankenstein* (1944), *Fog Island* (1945) for PRC, *House of Dracula* (1945) and *Genius at Work* (1946) at RKO with Bela Lugosi. Atwill was at work on the Universal serial *Lost City of the Jungle* (1946) when he died. His death from a heart attack might be chalked up to the stress of legal battles, possibly exacerbated by the death of his son John in combat in 1941 at much the same time his troubles began.

The reason for Atwill's career going up in smoke is the notorious Christmas party he threw shortly after *Man-Made Monster* wrapped. It was purportedly an orgy where pornographic films were shown and a rape allegedly occurred. Atwill was not charged for any of this (though adult films were quite illegal at the time). Rather he was convicted of perjury because he lied under oath to protect the identities of the guests as his get-together. The decision was later overturned, but the damage to

Atwill's career could not be undone. Most studios except Universal blackballed him; he would comment that, without paying assignments from them he'd have been "one dead egg." Whether or not one considers him a pervert, the actor left behind a body of excellent work in a variety of films; 77 of them all told.

Spilling ink on the career of Lon Chaney, Jr. (born Creighton Tull Chaney, 1906–1973) – as he is billed here for the first and last time in a Universal horror film – seems like a case of sending coals to Newcastle. Is there anyone reading this tome who isn't broadly aware of the man's resume? He joined his parents onstage in their vaudeville act at the tender age of six months old and, despite that, the elder Chaney was reportedly adamant that his son not pursue a show-biz career. The younger Lon avoided going into the movies (though he did work in theater) until after his father's death in 1930. He at first appeared under his own name, but he was getting nowhere fast until a producer insisted on the "Lon Chaney, Jr." billing for publicity impact. Chaney saw the value but always hated the name change, and he insisted on the "Junior" being dropped as soon as he had the clout to force the issue (those of a certain age might recall a *Castle of Frankenstein* interview where he became quite tetchy over being referred to in the diminutive). His taking the lead in *The Shadow of Silk Lennox* (1935) brought him some notice, but it wasn't until his portrayal of Lennie in *Of Mice and Men* (1939) that he was finally able to get past bit parts and uncredited appearances. His only genre titles prior to signing on with Universal are the Republic serial *Undersea Kingdom* (1936) and *One Million BC* for Hal Roach Studios (1940).

That would change once Universal signed him to a contract after *Man–Made Monster*. While there would also be a goodly number of Westerns at the studio, the New Universal proclaimed him "The Screen's New Character Creator," bumped Dick Foran from the title role in *The Wolf Man* (1941; see essay) and gave it to Chaney, and started the process that would ultimately have him portray all of the studio's classical quartet of monsters – the only actor to do so (somehow, he never got to be invisible). When the studio decided to eliminate all B-pictures, Chaney started freelancing (memorably sending up his Lennie characterization in the Bob Hope vehicle, *My Favorite Brunette*, 1947). He returned to the studio, now called Universal-International after the latter bought out the former, to reprise his Larry Talbot character for *Abbott and Costello Meet Frankenstein* (1948).

From the '50s on Chaney would vacillate between the big and small screens, and on the latter he portrayed the Frankenstein monster in episodes of *The Colgate Comedy Hour* (1951) and *Tales of Tomorrow* (1952). He was reportedly drunk and befuddled for the that show and gave a disastrous performance on a live broadcast (preserved for posterity courtesy of kinescope), mistaking it for a dress rehearsal. (In later years he was known to warn directors to get everything out of him by noon.) He still got work – a great deal of work – but it was generally in small roles or at independent studios. He appeared in *Bride of the Gorilla* (1951), *The Black Castle* (1952), *Manfish, Indestructible Man, The Black Sleep* (all 1956), *The Cyclops* (1957), TV's *13 Demon Street, The Alligator People* (both 1959), *La casa de terror* (1960), where he portrayed a mummy that revives and transforms into a werewolf, *The Haunted Palace* (1963), *Witchcraft* (1964), *House of the Black Death* (1965), *Gallery of Horror, Hillbillies in a Haunted House, Spider Baby* (all 1967), and *Dracula vs Frankenstein* (1971). He again played a werewolf when he teamed up with Karloff and Peter Lorre for an episode of *Route 66* entitled "Lizard's Leg and Owlet's Wing." Cast members of *Spider Baby*, interviewed for the Blu Ray release of the film, reported that Chaney "snacked" all day on oranges that had been injected with vodka. It is not surprising then that, when Prince Sirki came calling, the actor succumbed to liver failure and beriberi (a disease causing heart failure and caused by a severe lack of vitamin B1).

**Although as Akhoba he had stood up to monsters for Hal Roach Studios in 1940's *One Million B.C.*, it was for Universal that Lon first *became* a monster. Before electrocuting anyone, his Dynamo Dan would always reminisce about "the one that got away."**

Lon the younger may not have been a great - or even a very good – actor, and he was always acutely aware of living in his paterfamilias's shadow; having to assume the same name and in effect to cash in on dad's fame to establish his own cannot have helped. His alcoholism was hardly unique among Hollywood players who worked in the film colony during a period when heavy drinking was the norm. His range may have been limited, but as long as he was cast as the affable lug, he could turn in an acceptable performance. As Dynamo Dan he is quite good, and his line delivery is breezily natural, with nary a trace of reading his lines (as in *Son of Dracula* or the "Inner Sanctum" entries, where defining his performances as awkward would be a kindness). He may, however, have been the perfect horror star for the first half of the '40s, and the films that were produced during that period, portraying your basic nice-guy-tragically-drawn-into-forces-that-he-doesn't-understand and that are beyond his control.

Lovely Anne Nagel (1915-1966) did not have a happy life. Her mother and father pushed for her to become a nun, and she was in a preparatory school designed for that end when she began doing some modeling, work that sparked an interest in theatricals and making films. Her mother's second husband was a Technicolor expert (of the early two-strip kind) at Tiffany Studios, a studio that was not one of the majors but, at least until the Sound Era, was not of the Monogram or Mascot stripe, either. (James Whale's first feature assignment, 1930's *Journey's End*, was a Tiffany production, and James Cruze and John Stahl spent time there. Later, less ambitious productions such as 1931's *Drums of Jeopardy* and 1932's *The Death Kiss* would predominate). After some experimental short subjects directed by her step-father, she graduated to features and, when Tiffany closed its door in 1932, she landed a contract with Warner Bros. There she met and married her first husband, Ross Alexander, whose 1937 suicide – reportedly due to his inability to come to terms with his homosexuality – deeply affected her, may have marked the beginning of her life going downhill, and may possibly have led to her reported alcoholism. Nagel made no horror flicks at Warners, but did appear in a couple of mysteries including one Perry Mason entry, *The Case of the Stuttering Bishop* (1937).

Exposure to the genre would come with the move to Universal; shortly after her arrival, she found herself in serials, thrillers, and W. C. Fields' surreal masterpiece, *Never Give a Sucker an Even Break* (1941). For more on Nagel's Universal years, see the essay on *Black Friday* (1940). She left Universal in 1942 and freelanced, albeit not very successfully, stopping by PRC for *The Mad Monster* (1942) and at Columbia for the post-Larry Darmour serial, *The Secret Code*, the same year. By the time *Mighty Joe Young* was in production (1949), she was but an uncredited extra in the bar scene and had been reduced to doing that two years earlier. Even television – the financial salvation of many a less than "A"-list player – didn't offer much work, and she reportedly died penniless. Her looks and her talent should have resulted in a happier outcome. She did a commendable job in *Man-Made Monster*, *The Mad Monster*, and the late Ken Hanke, writing of her performance in Asheville, NC's *Mountain Express* in 2010, maintained that that she made a "surprisingly intelligent lady in distress… who could make the dumbest line sound pretty smart…" though he also noted, "… it's just not wise to find yourself alone with a madman and tactlessly point out that he's nuts."

Best remembered by film buffs as the illness-feigning playwright in the Marx Brothers' *Room Service* (1938), Frank Albertson (born Francis Healy Albertson, 1909-1964) was most often a supporting player who had the occasional lead in B-productions. Entering the industry as a prop boy, he gradually switched over to acting with 1923's *The Covered Wagon*. The wise-cracking but basically nice guy he plays here was his stock in trade, and besides the film under discussion, his genre credits include the certifiably oddball *Just Imagine* (1930), *A Connecticut Yankee* (1931), *It's a Wonderful Life* (1946), and – jumping ahead a bit – Hitchcock's *Psycho* (1960). Never idle for long, he moved on to television when the studio system started being dismantled; he added a *Tales of Tomorrow* and a *Thriller* to his CV, but these would prove to be his only other genre credits out of 129 big and small screen appearances (with three Oscar nominations for Best Supporting Actor).

Samuel S. Hinds (1875-1948) was a lawyer until the stock-market crash led him to switch from amateur theatrics to professional pursuit. At the tender age of 54 he started racking up credits in a late-in-life career that would ultimately include over 200 films, in which he usually was seen as a kindly authority figure (i.e., the other studios' answer to M-G-M's Lewis Stone). On the rare occasions he turned out to be the villain, and it came as a real surprise to the audience. He followed an early uncredited bit as a banquet guest in *Murders in the Zoo* with *Gabriel Over the White House*, *Deluge* (both 1933), *The Raven* (1935), *Night Key* (1937), *Hellzapoppin'* (1941), *The Strange Case of Doctor Rx* (1942), *Son of Dracula* (1943), *Jungle Woman* (1944), *It's a Wonderful Life* (1946), and *The Boy with Green Hair* (1948). He complemented his film appearances with stage work at the renowned Pasadena Playhouse and stayed occupied right up until his death.

And that brings us to Corky (birth and death dates unknown), the adorable canine who plays Corky the Dog. The little fella has quite the resume, stretching from 1934 to 1953 (at which time he was certainly getting on in dog years), when he played the family pooch on *Make Room for Daddy*. Corky may not be as renowned as Asta (Skippy), but he's the real heart of the film, and he even gets his own leitmotif, suggesting that Musical Director Hans J. Salter saw him as a major character. Corky's initial playfulness with Dan, followed by his reluctance to approach him – sensing his touch will be lethal – is a marker of Dan's humanity and its deterioration. In fact, the pup is aware that something is amiss long before the humans, even though the decline must be quite sudden. The image of Corky as he lies down over the corpse of his friend may not be the film's final image, but it's the one that lingers in the memory. *Night Life of the Gods* (1935) and the Joe E. Brown vehicle, *When's Your Birthday?* (1937) are the closest things to Corky's genre credits beyond *Man-made monster*, but he also appeared in *Garden of Allah* and *Theodora Goes Wild* (both 1936), *My Favorite Wife* (1940), *It Happened on Fifth Avenue* (1947), and *Criss Cross* (1948).

George Waggner (1894-1984) – who sometimes insisted on being billed as "george waGGner" – started out in Hollywood in 1932 as a writer, added directing to his portfolio in 1938 and producing three years later. *Man-made monster* was his first shot at directing a horror movie after a slate of Westerns and mysteries, and within the same year he would add *Horror Island* and *The Wolf Man*. While he would produce several more U horrors – *The Ghost of Frankenstein* (1942), *Frankenstein Meets the Wolf Man* (1943), *Phantom of the Opera* (1943), and *The Climax* (1944) – as well as the deliciously nutty *Cobra Woman* (1944), which comes *this close* to being worthy of consideration here, his only other directing credit of the films we are scrutinizing in this tome is *The Climax* (1944). His first horror is the most visually stylish of the quartet – check out the scene where Dan throttles Dr. Lawrence; Chaney's body blocks Hinds and the two move to screen right, camera following so that machinery further blocks the view and the violence is inferred rather than graphically displayed.

Prior to joining Universal in the late '30s, Waggner was employed by Poverty Row studios or the "B"-units of the lower-tier majors. Shunting him to the studios' horror films - along with hiring producer Ben Pivar (see *Horror Island*) and such quickie directors as Christy Cabanne, Reginald Le Borg, and William Nigh – was a clear sign that Universal, with a few notable exceptions, was no longer going to treat its horrors as prestige productions. Waggner may have been the recipient of a new contract following *M-MM*, but it was apparently not re-upped after Universal terminated its "B"-program. Within a few years he would be writing and directing for television – possibly the medium he was born for - including a number of Warner Bros. series such as *Cheyenne* and *77 Sunset Strip*. Genre assignments included several episodes of *The Veil*, seven episodes of *The Man from U.N.C.L.E.*, and ten episodes of *Batman*.

The short story that served as the basis for *Man-made monster* was written by *New York Daily Mirror* reporters Harry Essex, Sid Schwartz, and Len Golos, and was purchased by Universal for $3300 in 1935. It took six years for the trio to get their onscreen credit, and only Essex (1910-1997) - billed here as H. J. Essex - did further business with Hollywood. He became a busy story-man and scenarist, but it was not until a tad over a decade later that he returned to genre with the screenplay (from a Ray Bradbury story) for *It Came from Outer Space* (1953) and followed it a year later with the script for *The Creature from the Black Lagoon*. Essex became heavily involved in TV in the latter half of the '50s, but he returned to big screen genre with *Octaman* (1971) - essentially a retread of his *Black Lagoon* script - and *The Cremators* (1972). His final script, in 1996, was for the TV movie *It Came from Outer Space II*.

Elwood "Woody" Bredell (1902-1969) seems to have alternated with George Robinson in lighting the Universal horrors of the 1940s. Both men were experts at deploying dense shadows for maximum atmospheric effect, and Bredell also excelled at lush color, as may be found in his post-Universal assignment, *Adventures of Don Juan* (1948). After his first assignment for Tiffany Studios in 1927, he was absent from Hollywood for a decade; 1937 marked his first work for the "New" Universal and his first horror was *Black Friday* (1940). This was followed by the horrors, nigh-horrors and horror comedies *The Mummy's Hand, The Invisible Woman* (1940), *Horror Island, Hold That Ghost* (1942), *The Ghost of Frankenstein, The Strange Case of Doctor Rx, The Mystery of Marie Roget*, and *Sherlock Holmes and the Voice of Terror* (1942). During the '40s horror binge, he also lit *Hellzapoppin'* (1941), Robert Siodmak's noirs *Phantom Lady* (1944) and *The Killers* (1946), and *Lady on a Train* (1945). For *Man-made monster* Bredell gives each of the principals a distinct lighting for their close-ups: Rigas's round face is a sharp contrast between bright highlights and inky shadows; Lawrence's craggy features have smoother, less contrasted lighting; and June is a study in soft chiaroscuro that emphasizes Nagel's enormous, liquid eyes.

The Doctors Lawrence and Rigas have a laboratory as chock full of Kenneth Strickfaden (1896-1984) equipment as anything owned by any of the Frankensteins or by those who foolishly attempted to follow in their footsteps. Strickfaden was an electrician and set designer who in his spare time tinkered up eccentric machines that didn't do much but that looked awfully cool doing it. First seen onscreen in *Frankenstein* (James Whale, 1931), his gizmos would be rented so frequently by Universal that it seemed there was the equivalent of an Acme company catering to loony scientists, all of whom needed the same equipment. His work for Universal (where he was never once credited) scarcely needs cataloging here. Other studios used

83

his equipment for *Murder at Dawn* and *The Mask of Fu Manchu* (both 1932), wherein Strickfaden - in an unconvincing mask - stood in for star Boris Karloff who was understandably reluctant to perform a high voltage stunt. These were followed by the serials *The Vanishing Shadow* (1934), *The Lost City* (1935, where he receives a rare onscreen credit), *The Amazing Exploits of the Clutching Hand* (1936), and *The Shadow* (1940). His www.IMDb.com filmography is woefully incomplete, as it doesn't list M-G-M's *Fu Manchu* film or any of the post-*Bride* Frankensteins. Additionally we've spotted what looks like Strickfaden doohickies in some Republic serials and at least one of Bela Lugosi's Monogram Nines. Among his later films were *Monstrosity* (1963), an episode of *The Munsters* TV series (1966), *Games* (1967), *Dracula vs Frankenstein* (1971), and *Blackenstein* (1973). Mel Brooks' *Young Frankenstein* (1974) brought Strickfaden some late-in-the-day fame courtesy of publicity that noted how that film made use of the old Frankenstein equipment. *Man-made monster* offers several scenes that are the most lavish displays of his whatsits set to music since *Bride of Frankenstein* (1936), even "borrowing" a few shots from *Bride* even though the *M-MM* mad lab has no evidence of a stone wall behind them.

The music is courtesy Hans J. Salter (1896-1994) – billed here as H. J. Salter – whose credit as Musical Director suggests this is one of his "Salterized" scores, meaning it is mostly cobbled together from cues written for other films to shave dollars from the budget; Charles Henderson, Charles Previn, and Frank Skinner crafted some of the music Salter wove into this score. The main title is cribbed from *The Invisible Man Returns*, but some of it is surely original, such as Corky's "theme" and the deranged composition for strings and xylophone that plays every time Rigas starts flipping breakers, fiddling with switches, and twirling rheostats. The Viennese-born musician was music director of the Berlin State Opera and head of the music department at Ufa before emigrating to the U.S. in 1937 (becoming a citizen five years later). His first work on a Universal horror was 1939's *Son of Frankenstein* where (uncredited) he orchestrated Frank Skinner's compositions. The two would often work in tandem on later scores such as *The Invisible Man Returns* (1940) and *The Wolf Man* (1941), one napping while the other worked at the piano. The reason for this, as well as for Salterizing, was to turn out the reams of music the studio demanded on impossibly short deadlines. Salter would remain at the studio for nearly 30 years (until 1964), so a tally of all his horror and sci-fi scores (sometimes his only contribution being stock music) would take up a ridiculous amount of space here. But the depth as well as the breadth of his contribution to the U horrors of the '40s cannot be overstated. Producers, directors and actors came and went, but Salter was always there.

Reviews for *Man-made monster* may not have been glowing, but the trade assessments were more positive than one might expect. "FANTASTIC THRILLER IS EXPLOITABLE" reads the headline for the *Independent Exhibitors Film Bulletin*, which goes on to say:

> More fantastic than frightening 'Man-made monster' is, neverthe-less, made-to-order for the insatiable horror fans. The incredible adven-tures of the electrically-immune man will have a fascination for thrill addicts and the youngsters. Discriminating elders will scoff at the yarn. Lon Chaney, Jr's characterization is no 'King Kong' or 'Frankenstein,' but it is, at least, something new in the way of screen shockers. This is ripe for exploitation in the cheaper action houses...
>
> Lon Chaney, Jr. is not yet ready to take his late father's place as the screen's premiere 'horror' actor but he does impart some sympathy to the sketchily-written role of the helpless giant. Lionel Atwill is excellent as the crazed scientist. Samuel S. Hinds is convincing as his normal medical partner. The slight romantic interest is ably supplied by Anne Nagel as Hinds' daughter [sic], and Frank Albertson, as a reporter... The special effects are effectively photographed.
>
> Leyendecker, *Independent Exhibitors Film Bulletin*, 5 April 1941

> Although the theme of this picture is somewhat preposterous, delving into the weird results of the experiments of a crack-brained scientist, the picture has its moments of excitement and suspense for the run-of-the-mine film fans, who do not ask too many questions of their screen diet, as long as it is filling... George Waggner, who directed, contrived to keep the film moving with reasonable skill... The film reaches a far-fetched but novel climax...
>
> Charles S. Aaronson, *Motion Picture Daily*, 15 March 1941

> AUDIENCE SLANT: (Adult) For the dyed-in-the-wool horror fans, this will probably be intriguing. For others, it won't.
>
> BOX-OFFICE SLANT: Satisfactory, where they like horror pictures.
>
> A highly fantastic plot, the like of which has seldom been equaled is the highlight of this picture in which Chaney, while supposedly charged

with electricity walks about like a glow worm with a halo. It is all very ridiculous even to a horror fan, but the latter are probably so inured to improbabilities that they can take it. Romance has been dragged in by the heels to make it slightly more palatable, but the picture as a whole is second-rate and suitable only as the second half of a double feature bill."
*Showman's Trade Review*, 22 March 1941

*The New York Times'* critic offered his typical dismissive review (with every conceivable word-play on electricity), but a writer for *The Washington Post* offered a surprisingly positive reaction as did the reviewer for the *Los Angeles Times* though he (she?) had some reservations.

... this latest of Frankenstein brain-brats, which was wired into the Rialto yesterday, is perhaps the most high-flown scientific marvel since Ben Franklin hoisted his kite... What Dan can't do when under the influence of a couple of straight slugs of 'juice' is simply nobody's business... Silly? Of course he's silly, and the picture is low-grade shocker fare. But what a killer he is when 'lit'! And he's always good for a laugh.
Bosley Crowther, *The New York Times*, 19 March 1941

'Man-made monster' a Film of High Voltage
The leaping horrors of 'Man-made monster' are authentic as well as dynamic. There's something about the jittering flight of huge electrical bolts that scarifies the modern mind, fully aware of their deadliness... Not a speck of meanness attaches to this star monstrosity. But villainy underlined with insanity is the portion of Lionel Atwill, creator of the electric catastrophe. Chaney appears as a big, good-natured lug... Strictly speaking Chaney doesn't get much of a chance to act except in his early happy-go-lucky moments. But he's a figure of fright in the latter sequences with a drawn and oddly withered visage. Lionel Atwill manages to be repulsive with practically no visible effort... Like most of the recent horror pictures 'Man-Made Monster' is paced unevenly, lacks the saving relief of laughs. But its big moments are hard to top.
Mary Harris, *The Washington Post*, 26 April 1941

If people don't shiver, however, they will laugh, for there's a lot of absurdity in the way the halo-crowned youth plows about grabbing at folks... Wonder is Lon Chaney Jr. is going to follow in the footsteps of his dad by playing such roles as that of the electric youth. At least better vehicles should be found for him. Ann [sic] Nagle and Frank Albertson, too, are wasted in such films. Lionel Atwill brings sinister notes to his playing of the mad doctor.

G. K., *Los Angeles Times*, 22 March 1941

The production is viewed very kindly today.

A prime example of Universal's B-picture unit at its peak, Man-made monster is among the finest of the studio's second-echelon horror product.

Hal Erickson, *AllMovie.com*

Man-Made Monster was one of two collaborations between Lon Chaney, Jr. and director/writer (and sometime producer) George Waggner. Where most directors would be hampered by Chaney's limited acting range, Waggner manages to play to the star's greatest strength – his earnestness – and effectively glossed over his limitations, and evoked audience sympathy for the actor and the character that he plays. That's essential in a film as fast-paced as this one, and it's one of the major reasons why Man-Made Monster has endured in popularity across the decades... Waggner and Chaney would pull off a similar trick with The Wolf Man, except that the latter was inherently a more profound film that required more effort from viewers (and, admittedly, gave more in the way of chills, as well) – Man-Made Monster, by contrast, was just plain fun.

Bruce Eder, *AllMovie.com*

Every aspect of Man-made monster is perfect for what it sets out to be. The film looks and feels solid. The photography is moody and atmospheric. Hans J. Salter's musical score—most of which would appear again in other movies if it hadn't already—gave the film a tremendous boost. The characters are all sketched in with remarkable precision, even though there's not much time for characterization in a 59-minute movie. Yet—partly due to shrewd casting—they all seem real, or at least as real as they need to be. The film milks Chaney's naturally sympathetic

"big lug without much brains" persona very effectively, and wisely gives Lionel Atwill free rein to make his mad doctor as mad as they come.
Ken Hanke, Ashville, NC *Mountain Xpress*, 14 September 2010

*Man-made monster* - 28 March 1941 - 59 minutes (ST)

**CAST:** Lionel Atwill as Dr. Paul Rigas; Lon Chaney Jr. as Dan McCormick; Anne Nagel as June Lawrence; Frank Albertson as Mark Adams; Samuel S. Hinds as Dr. John Lawrence; William Davidson as District Attorney Ralph B. Stanley; Ben Taggart as Detective Sergeant Regan; Connie Bergen as Nurse); Ivan Miller as Doctor; Chester Gan as Wong; George Meader as Dr. Bruno; Frank O'Connor as Police Detective; John Dilson as Medical Examiner; Byron Foulger as Alienist #2; Following are uncredited: Jessie Arnold as Mrs. Frank Davis; James Blaine as Charlie, a Prison Guard; Gary Breckner as Radio Announcer; Corky as Corky the Dog; Lowell Drew as Jury Foreman; John Ellis as Assistant District Attorney; Douglas Evans as Police Radio Announcer; Jack Gardner as Reporter; William Hall as Mike the Dynamo Operator; Russell Hicks as Prison Warden Harris; Wright Kramer as Judge; Tom Quinn as Police Detective; Bob Reeves as Prison Guard; Mel Ruick as Defense Attorney; Francis Sayles as Frank Davis; Paul Scott as Prison Chaplain; David Sharpe as Hay Wagon Passenger; Victor Zimmerman as Dynamo Operator #2

**CREDITS:** Director: George Waggner; Associate Producer: Jack Bernhard; Writers: Harry Essex, Sid Schwartz, Len Golos (story "The Electric Man"); Screenplay: George Waggner (as Joseph West); Director of Photography Elwood Bredell; Film Editor: Arthur Hilton; Art Directors: Jack Otterson, Harold H. MacArthur; Set Decoration: Russell A. Gausman; Costume Design (Gowns): Vera West; Make-up: Jack P. Pierce; Sound Supervisor: Bernard B. Brown; Sound Technician: Charles Carroll; Special Effects: John P. Fulton (uncredited); Stunts: Bob Reeves, David Sharpe (uncredited); Musical Director: Hans J. Salter; Composer, stock music: Charles Henderson, (uncredited); Orchestrator: Charles Previn (uncredited); Composer, additional music: Frank Skinner (uncredited)

**Shock Theater** Catalog No. 716: "His strength was that of a dozen men. His slightest touch meant death. Super-Science let loose a titanic terror upon a trembling world. Don't fail to see Lon Chaney in 'The [sic] Man-made monster' on *Shock*'s full-length feature coming your way on channel___, (day), at (time)."

*- HHL*

# *Horror Island* (1941)

*Synopsis:* Bankrupt entrepreneur Bill Martin and his partner Stuff are constantly dodging bill collectors while Martin tries to come up with million-dollar ideas (such as canned condensed stuffing for turkeys). They rescue Tobias Clump - aka The Skipper - from an attack by The Phantom and find out he has a treasure map for an island Martin has inherited. Informed by map expert Prof. Quinley that it's a fake – "... one of the most skillfully made imitations I've ever seen" – Martin decides to stage treasure-hunting tours to the island and its "haunted" castle. The initial group includes his cousin George, who has offered to buy the island, a process server trying to halt the enterprise on the grounds of false advertising, a gangster and his moll fleeing the law, and Wendy Creighton – whom Martin has "met cute" courtesy an auto accident – and her perpetually snoozing boyfriend, Thurman.

The trip to the island is somewhat impeded by an exploding package and a magnet in the compass, but eventually the party reaches the fog-enshrouded island and the castle (Universal's familiar castle/lower level, albeit slightly altered and surprisingly not festooned with cobwebs), supposedly deserted for ages. Stuff stages some haunting effects while The Skipper searches for hidden rooms, but The Phantom has somehow preceded the assemblage and adds his own stunts. He creeps through a secret doorway and menaces Wendy, and then commandeers a PA system to exhort the group to

"Leave the castle! Leave the castle!" And then the murders start. The gangster is killed whilst trying to steal the boat (which for good measure then disappears, stranding the party *a la* Agatha Christie) and use it to escape U.S. Authorities, and Cousin George also falls victim. The Phantom is then impaled by an arrow shot from a mechanical crossbow wielded by a suit of armor. It is at first assumed he's fallen victim to one of his own traps, but it soon becomes apparent that the real killer is still very much in attendance.

We have already noted that horror films from all studios had a major resurgence in the '40s courtesy of the re-release of *Dracula* and *Frankenstein* (both 1931) and the subsequent box-office success of 1939's *Son of Frankenstein*. But thanks to two Bob Hope vehicles at Paramount - *The Cat and the Canary* (1939, originally a Universal property) and *The Ghost Breakers* (1940) - horror comedies had also become popular. Even Monogram tried to hop on the bandwagon, suggesting that exhibitors promote 1941's *King of the Zombies* along the same lines as the Paramount productions, if only based on the contribution of Mantan Moreland, who was, it must be admitted, funnier than Henry Victor. Universal - never one to eschew pouncing on some other studio's idea - brought forth *The Black Cat* (1941) in emulation of a certain feline-and-fowl film, and the little fun flick under discussion that aped *Ghost Breakers*. Oddly, Universal's trailer (or, rather, the Realart reissue trailer that survives) for the film suggested a straight-out horror thriller with only a touch of comic relief.

The parallels to *Ghost Breakers* are fairly obvious: for starters, an island with a haunted castle and a hidden treasure. But the film also repeats some plot points from *The Mummy's Hand* (1940): Foran and Moran back together again, Fuzzy Knight subs for Wallace Ford, a partial map is replaced by a potsherd, and a pirate's treasure fills in for a princess' tomb. (Universal so liked the set-up that it was essentially called back for 1954's *The Creature from the Black Lagoon*.) Now, whether Carrillo or Catlett stands in Cecil Kellaway, or whether Van Dolsen replaces Tom Tyler or Sigfried Arno is strictly up to the viewer. This breezy comedy with thriller relief certainly replaces *Hand*'s creepy horror with comic highlights - and it's genuinely funny, unlike the belabored antics of *The Black Cat*. Maurice Tombragel and Victor McLeod's script (based on the story "South Seas Terror" by Alex Gottlieb) offers little new in the way of plot, but the dialogue is rich with witty rejoinders. Ongoing fun is milked from the Skipper's broken English - possibly un-PC nowadays, but nonetheless amusing - as when he urges repairing to the island "the sooner the quicker." Our favorite quip, however, might be Thurman's query, "If I take an aspirin, will you go away?"

**No big stars, but a likable cast filled with familiar faces. (And even if their names weren't listed "above the title," for once, their faces were.)**

The script keeps the action moving, particularly once the scene shifts to the island. Characters are sent running for one reason or another from one locale to another within the castle (for once, enough rooms are seen to create the impression this really *is* a castle). Red herrings and misdirection are splendidly plentiful; only those mindful of the resemblance to *The Mummy's Hand* will guess the true killer before he is revealed. The romantic relationship between Bill and Wendy (who initially doesn't much care for Bill) is credibly developed even if their characters - indeed *all* the characters - are strictly stock. The production assembled a gaggle of dependable comic performers (Knight, Carrillo, Catlett, Adrian, Cavanaugh) to do justice to the clever script, and the "straight" characters are also perfectly cast. In short, this is a little gem of a flick that's more fun than a firkin of simians. As is often the case with Universal horror in the '40s, it's the minor entries that are the most satisfyingly realized and arguably the most interesting.

Singer Dick Foran (1910–1979) was initially tapped by Warner Bros. to star in Westerns and occasionally appear in supporting roles (where he might croon a tune or two) before moving to Universal. The studio apparently decided to groom him for horror stardom beginning with *Horror Island*, but his last genre credit for a long time in his lengthy career was 1942's *The Mummy's Tomb*, the follow-up to 1940's *The Mummy's Hand*. Peggy Moran (née Mary Jeanette Moran, 1918–2002) skipped repeating her role of Marta Banning (née Solvani) in that sequel and thus avoided becoming one of Universal's interchangeable (but agreeable) clutch of "B"-horror heroines. Her marriage to producer/director Henry Koster may have helped, and she ended her film career a few years after the wedding. More on both performers can be found in our entry on *Hand*.

Fuzzy Knight (born John Forest Knight, 1909–1976), he of the (also un-PC) comic stutter, is best remembered as the comic relief in a long list of Westerns and, by those of a certain age, in support of Buster Crabbe in TV's *Captain Gallant of the Foreign Legion* where he played... (wait for it)... Pvt. Fuzzy Knight. His CV is so varied, though, that it even includes several Mae West vehicles and work in "A"- and "B"-pictures for nearly every studio in Hollywood (possibly *every* studio) from M-G-M to Republic. In nearly 200 big- and small-screen appearances, *Horror Island* is his sole genre credit (unless one counts his appearance in an episode of TV's *Batman* [1966] shortly before his retirement).

Leo Carrillo (1881–1961) is also best remembered by those of a certain age as Pancho, the English-mangling comic companion to Duncan Renaldo's *The Cisco Kid* on '50s television, and a few low-budget features that preceded it. The actor's film career started during the late Silent Era and included dramatic as well as comic roles, usually of some undetermined Latino or Spanish ethnicity. Carrillo was one of California's old Spanish families - he claimed to trace his lineage back to the Conquistadors – and had what is reported to be a distinguished career on Broadway before going Hollywood. *Horror Island* was his first and only brush with genre, aside from the even more comedic Olsen and Johnson feature, *Ghost Catchers* (1944). California's Leo Carrillo State Park is named for him, as is the state's Leo Carrillo Beach, so it should come as no surprise that he served on the State Park and Recreation Commission.

John Eldridge (1904–1961) had his first of well over 200 movie and TV appearances in 1934, when he landed a contract with Warner Bros. after appearing on Broadway. He was generally cast as ineffectual types and even villains by that studio, which gave him his first genre assignment in *Sh! The Octopus* (1937). The same year he appeared as suspicious Cousin George in *Horror Island*, Eldridge was also cast in *The Black Cat*, and more on him may be found in our essay on that film.

Usually bespectacled onscreen, Hobart Cavanaugh (1886–1950) specialized in worried, nervous, downtrodden types, but he could also do a credible turn as the sneaky minion to the sinister main villain. Under contract to Warner Bros. from 1933 (starting with an uncredited role in *Gold Diggers of...* ) to 1938, the Virginia City native - already a frequent loan-out from WB - subsequently freelanced quite successfully. He portrayed Petty Louie opposite Boris Karloff in *Night Key* (1937) and had a minor role in Joe May's *The House of Fear* (1939 – a remake of Paul Leni's 1929 *The Last Warning*) before his *Island* sojourn. The actor would appear in the Sherlock Holmes entry, *The House of Fear* (1945 – Universal was never a studio to waste anything, including titles) and *The Spider Woman Strikes Back* (1946).

Blowhards were the specialty of Walter Catlett (1889–1960), whose entry into films was preceded by performances in both vaudeville and opera. His first film appearances were back in the Silent Era, but he made his genre debut here (as did most of this cast, amazingly enough) and wouldn't come near *le fantastique* again until Joseph Losey's allegorical *The Boy with Green Hair* (1948). Catlett's best-remembered turns may be *Bringing Up Baby* (1938) and *Yankee Doodle Dandy* (1942), and while TV took up most of his time in the '50s, he did finish out with a trio of big-budget films, including William Wyler's *Friendly Persuasion* (1956). He worked up to the end, passing away shortly after completing his scenes for *Beau James* (1957).

Hawk-faced Ralf Harolde (born Ralph Harold Wigger, 1899–1974) was almost certain to be typecast as a nogoodnik due to his lean and hungry visage; he's the Prosecutor in *A Tale of Two Cities* (1935) and the (uncredited) creep who shanghais John Garfield in *The Sea Wolf* (1941). The '40s found him in many *noirs* (a natural home for the actor) and even some serials, but his only other genre appearance is in Republic's *The Phantom Speaks* (1945), wherein Stanley Ridges essentially repeats his *Black Friday* characterization.

Iris Adrian (1912–1994), who portrayed a long succession of sexy-but-sharp-tongued waitresses, chorus girls, streetwalkers, molls – "dames" if you like – for over 40 years, almost always stole her scenes, and she does so here in a nifty exchange with Catlett. Even when she wasn't appearing in comedies and musicals (her natural milieu), her roles were generally comedic. Her first feature-film credit came in 1935, although her celluloid career had gotten its start in 1928. Frank Strayer's *Murder at Glen Athol* (1936) for Invincible was her first thriller, and it served as proof that she would work both for the best and the least regarded of studios in the course of her career. The neglected *Fingers at the Window* would follow *Horror Island* by a year, and that was followed by Fritz Lang's *The Woman in the Window* and Edgar G. Ulmer's *Bluebeard* (both 1944). The actress went uncredited in *Mighty Joe Young* (1949) – as she often did – and didn't visit the genre again until TV appearances on *Alfred Hitchcock*

*Presents* and *The Munsters*. (A 1978 episode of *The Love Boat* - entitled "Ship of Ghouls" and costarring Vincent Price – [surprisingly] doesn't qualify as a genre effort.) Adrian succumbed to complications of a broken hip suffered in the 1994 Northridge (California) earthquake.

Foy Van Dolsen (1911–1990) – and yes, Virginia, there really was a Foy Van Dolsen; the name wasn't just a Universal concoction to disguise The Phantom's identity – appeared in only a dozen films between 1936 and 1941. The Hoosier thesp doesn't do much in his only genre appearance, but his cape flourishes are second only to Bela Lugosi's.

Lewis Howard (1919–1951) also had a brief film career, lasting from 1939 (Hollywood's Greatest Year, so they say) until 1950, the year before his death at the age of 32. Howard made his first appearances in a pair of Deanna Durbin musicals for Universal and would be with the studio through *Hellzapoppin'* (1941). An uncredited role in *My Sister Eileen* at Columbia preceded his landing at M-G-M for a trio of pictures - interrupted by his stint in the Army - and then to Republic, and then to something yclept Symphony Films (playing Moussorgsky in a Tchaikovsky biopic with almost no name actors). Thence... well, a once-promising career continued to fizzle and his last three roles, each a year apart, were cameos and/or uncredited bits. Despondent, Howard committed suicide in most bizarre fashion; he went to a shooting gallery and, after taking out several clay pigeons, he tossed aside some pieces of paper that turned out to be his farewell note and instructions for his funeral. He then put the gun muzzle to his chin and pulled the trigger. But this ghastly public act wasn't quite the end; the bullet didn't do the intended job, and it's reported he besought onlookers to finish him. Mercifully, Howard died some hours later in a Manhattan hospital. His deliciously droll portrait of ennui in his only genre role is something to be treasured, and the tragedy is that his career didn't give more opportunities in all sorts of films.

By 1941, producer Ben Pivar (1901–1963) was apparently becoming a valued commodity at Universal to judge by the title card that announces this is "A Ben Pivar Production," as if such a commodity was something to brag about. (Given that, to our knowledge, this lavish acknowledgment was never repeated suggests it was not.) It may have been that the studio was impressed by his ability to craft an entire – and enjoyable – feature such as *Zanzibar* (1940) almost entirely from footage of earlier films (here, 1931's *East of Borneo* and 1934's *Beast of Borneo*). Many of his horror films are composed of a great deal of re-purposed footage, but *Horror Island* at least is mostly original (albeit we have our doubts about the sea journey sequence). Nonetheless, the cast and the restriction to a handful of locales tip off the thrifty approach. Beginning as an editor during the late Silent Era, Pivar started his producing career at Columbia in 1931 with a Spanish-language version of *The Criminal Code*, directed by Phil Rosen (only one of the Poverty Row directors Pivar would rely on during his stint at Universal). Columbia at the time was still struggling to transition from minor to major and, aside from Frank Capra's productions, was producing little that was held in high (or even medium) regard. Work at various low-level studios, including Republic and some most folks have never heard of, followed until he took up residence at Universal in 1937.

Pivar's output was varied (and would remain so) until he was given his first shot at a horror movie with *The Mummy's Hand* (a film containing quite a few flashbacks – and even props – from the Karl Freund original). *Horror Island* was next, followed by *The Mummy's Tomb* (1942 – whose first 20 minutes are flashbacks), *Captive Wild Woman* (1942 – with footage from an earlier Clyde Beatty film incorporated), *The Mad Ghoul* (1943), *Calling Dr. Death* (1943 – the first of six "Inner Sanctum" flicks built around Lon Chaney), *Weird Woman, Jungle Woman, The Mummy's Ghost, Dead Man's Eyes, The Mummy's Curse* (all 1944), *Strange Confession* (a remake of *The Man Who Reclaimed His Head*), *Pillow of Death* (both 1945), *House of Horrors, She-Wolf of London* and *The Brute Man* (all 1946). He was "dormant" until 1948 when he executive-produced three movies for Bernard Small Productions including *The Creeper*, about a completely unhinged scientist who transforms himself into a catlike creature. He re-emerged in 1953 as producer of several episodes over five years of a TV series yclept *Confidential File*. The titles of three of the episodes – "Are Homosexuals Criminals?" "Homosexuals Who Stalk and Molest Children" and "Homosexuals and the Problems They Present" – suggest that the series was more horrifying than any of Pivar's movies. Well, it *was* a different time.

Most of the praise due goes to the film's trio of writers, none of whom have the expected plethora of horror credits. Born in what is now the Ukraine, Alex Gottlieb (1908–1988) got his showbiz start writing gags for the radio shows of Eddie Cantor and Al Jolson; he then moved into screenwriting, first at Republic and later at Universal. His more-or-less genre credits prior to *Horror Island* were *Mystery of the White Room* (1939; a "Crime Club" entry) and *Dark Streets of Cairo* (1940), a title horror fans might want to seek out for the cast (Ralph Byrd, George Zucco, Sig Arno, Lloyd Corrigan, Henry Brandon, Nestor Paiva). In addition, he contributed to *Hellzapoppin'* (1941) afterward and supplied the story – uncredited - for the certifiably crackpot *The Strange Case of Doctor Rx* (1942). Gottlieb's most notable work at Universal was producing the screen efforts of Abbott and Costello, including their first, *Buck Privates* (1941), which was a huge hit for the studio on a comparatively minor investment. The picture's success made him a valuable studio asset, and he would go on to produce a number of the duo's flicks for Big U and, later, their TV show. That led him into a very busy time working for the small screen, which occupied him totally for the rest of his career.

Maurice Tombragel (1913–2000) got his first screenwriting credit at Universal in 1949 and *Horror Island* is the closest he came to genre for many years. He scripted a number of mysteries - including entries in the "Boston Blackie" and "Lone Wolf" series - and lots of Westerns, but his only other horror was *The Creeper* (1948), where he again worked with Ben Pivar. Victor McCleod (1903–1982) has a resume stuffed with work for Walter Lantz's animated short subjects (yes, even Woody Woodpecker), starting in 1933. His first feature credit was in 1940 and post-*Horror Island* he got to write even longer-form genre (if only two reels at a time) with Columbia's cut-rate serials, *Batman* and *The Phantom* (both 1943). (We will leave it to others to ponder the implications or ramifications or whatever of a writer of cartoon shorts scripting the live-action, episodic adaptations of comic-strip and -book characters.) Unsurprisingly he was employed exclusively in television sitcoms and variety shows from the mid-'50s to 1967.

Contemporary reviews were mostly (and unsurprisingly) not very favorable.

> They're playing at ghosts again at the Rialto, and the name of the game this time is 'Horror Island.' It resembles nothing so much as the initiation ceremonies of a small-town chapter of Shriners or Elks; it is also suitable for kiddies' birthday parties and church socials. It's all very simple. Take one leader dressed in a pirate's costume (otherwise Leo Carrillo), an assorted group of neophytes and a fog-bound old castle (any parlor will do), where all the rooms are secreted behind sliding panels, bookcases, etc. Make believe that there's a chest of treasure stored away in some subterranean vault, and then have everyone creep about in the dark shouting 'Boo!' It's not much fun nor very frightening, but it's innocent and any one can play.

T.S., *The New York Times*, 31 March 1941

But that was mild disdain, considering the following.

> 'Horror Island' is a fourth rate, low-budget mystery-and-adventure flapdoodle, poorly written, sloppily produced and directed... The

Alex Gottlieb story is a ridiculous olla-podrida of hoke, romance and claptrap... There is no concern for the plausible nor the consistent... About the only virtue of 'Horror Island' is that it's short, 61 minutes.

    Char, *Variety*, Wednesday, 2 April 1941

But not all writers found the film to be "olla-podrida" ("a highly spiced Spanish-style stew containing a mixture of meat and vegetables" or "any miscellaneous assortment or collection" – yes, we looked it up).

    'Horror Island' is a gasp-getter and will doubtless please fans who go for the spine- chillers, for it abounds in clutching hands, secret doorways, and a lot of new thrill stunts such as suits of armor that shoot arrows, dropping hatchets and such... and you will never guess whodunit.

    Anonymous, *Los Angeles Times*, 27 March 1942

'HORROR ISLAND' QUICKIE FOR JUVE AND ACTION AUDIENCES - This is a minor entry from Universal that will do adequate service for juvenile and action audiences. The story is not quite as "horrible" as the title would indicate, but there are a few spine-tingling moments, some of the dialogue is good and suspense is maintained by George Waggner's direction.

    HANNA (Hollywood), *Film Bulletin*, 5 April 1941

Contemporary film writers seem more inclined to accept *Horror Island* for what it is – an enjoyable bit of mystery-thriller fluff. An anonymous and undated review/ synopsis on Rotten Tomatoes stated:

It has been alleged that Horror Island was the least expensive of Universal's 1940s horror films. While it certainly looks that way, it remains an enjoyable outing from fade-in to fade-out. In the tradition of 'Ten Little Indians', a group of disparate types are lured to a supposedly haunted mansion on a remote island... Of the stellar all-character-actor cast, Iris Adrian shines as a leather-lunged blonde, alternating between wisecracks and shivers throughout the film's brisk 61 minutes.

And that same web page has a link that leads to this opinion by one of his generation's foremost writers on genre films.

The movie year of 1941 was probably the best one that director George Waggner — a solid craftsman, if not a particularly inspired one — ever had. In rapid succession, he knocked out Horror Island, Man-made monster, and The Wolf Man. There's no doubt that the last in the list is his best known, but in all honesty, I'll take Man-made monster over it any day of the week. That, of course, leaves Horror Island the odd film out. It always tends to get lost in the shuffle and that's too bad because this little 60-minute thriller is solid and a lot of fun. (It may be more fun than The Wolf Man.)

> ... Atmosphere makes up for much, as does the Hans Salter score, a
> clever script with bright dialogue and a first-rate cast.
> Ken Hanke, [Ashville] *Mountain Xpress*, 25 September 2012

Hanke added in the publication's online comments section, "Say what you will about these little movies, audiences do indeed seem to love them. That's kind of re- markable for 70-year-old pictures that no one thought much about at the time."

We couldn't have said it better.


*Horror Island* – 28 March 1941 – 60 minutes (ST)

**CAST:** Dick Foran as Bill Martin; Leo Carrillo as Tobias Clump; Peggy Moran as Wendy Creighton; Fuzzy Knight as Stuff Oliver; John Eldredge as Cousin George; Lewis Howard as Thurman Coldwater; Hobart Cavanaugh as Professor Jasper Quinley; Walter Catlett as Sergeant McGoon; Ralf Harolde as Rod Grady; Iris Adrian as Arleen Grady; Foy Van Dolsen as The Phantom; Emmett Vogan as The Stranger; Following are uncredited: Robert Barron as Wreck Spectator; Ted Billings as Wreck Spectator; Eddy Chandler as Police Officer; Don Dillaway as Sailor; Walter Tetley as Delivery Boy

**CREDITS:** Producer: Ben Pivar; Associate Producer: Jack Bernhard; Director: George Waggner; Script: Maurice Tombragel; Screenplay: Victor McCleod; Story: Alex Gottlieb; Musical Direction: Hans J. Salter (as H. J. Salter), Charles Henderson, Charles Previn, Frank Skinner; Director of Photography: Elwood Bredell; Film Editing: Otto Ludwig; Art Direction: Martin Obzina and Jack Otterson; Set Decoration: Russell A. Gausman (as R.A. Gausman); Gowns: Vera West; Sound Supervisor: Bernard B. Brown

**Shock Theater** Catalog No. 708: "Tragedy instead of treasure as adventurers seek to find buried pirate loot on eerie 'Horror Island.' See it on *Shock* this (day), (date), at (time), on this channel. Don't miss this fast-moving, spine-tingling feature film."

*- HHL*

## *The Black Cat* (1941)

*Synopsis:* Aged and wheelchair-bound Henrietta Winslow, who adores felines so much her isolated mansion and its extensive grounds are home to dozens and dozens of the critters, has survived another health crisis to the less-than-relief of her heirs, all of whom would like to get their hands on her fortune. Son-in-law Montague Hartley has even jumped the gun and summoned A. Gilmore "Gil" Smith to the estate with an offer from a wealthy buyer; tagging along is Mr. Penny who wants to scoop up the antiques and *objets d'art.* The heirs – daughter Myrna Hartley, her step-son Richard, granddaughter Elaine, other granddaughter Margaret, and grandson Stanley (whose surname sounds like Graybill in the dialogue but is Borden in the onscreen credits) – all have their reasons for wanting the old darling's moolah. Henrietta throws a monkey wrench into their greedy plans not only by not dying but by revealing the terms of her will: While she gives them all generous bequests, no one will receive a penny until housekeeper Miss Abigail and all the cats are deceased.

Not long after she escapes a poisoning attempt, Henrietta is done in with a knitting needle in what is presumed to be an accident (we, the viewers, know differently, and Gil has suspicions). Later Abigail is found hanged in her locked bedroom, but no one save Gil thinks that murder is afoot, though Mr. Penny, bumbling about through various disguised portals (including a revolving love-seat) and hidden passages, thinks "something very strange is going on." Gil points out that the splinters on the rope from the closet door are pointing in the wrong direction for suicide; Abby has been hoisted up onto the door and thus murdered. As in any good Old Dark House movie (or even this one), a number of false scares fills time as suspicions fall on Eduardo. Myrna even claims an attempt on her life by the grounds (and cats) keeper.

No, it isn't Edgar G. Ulmer's 1934 *The Black Cat*, nor even an inferior remake of same, even if it does include Bela Lugosi in the cast. Fie on Universal for re-using the title of that kinky/quirky classic, and shame on them for even pretending this opus has anything to do with Edgar Allan Poe, but let's try to set all that aside and approach the film for what it is: a minor comedy/thriller with a better cast and direction than it deserves. (Strangely, Universal promoted it as an outright horror; the trailer claimed "You'll forget you ever saw 'Frankenstein' or 'Dracula.'" Riiiight.) It isn't terribly good by any means – and it has numerous sequences that just don't make a lick of sense – but neither is it as bad as its detractors suggest. Now it's only supposition, mind you, but this writer suspects that Universal regretted selling the rights to *The Cat and the Canary* – which under the direction of Paul Leni is one of the jewels of its silent horrors – to Paramount, which made it into an *über*-successful vehicle for Bob Hope and Paulette Goddard, so it was decided to craft a very, *very* similar production. This relatives-gathered-for-the-reading-of-the-will-in-a-creepy-old-house has the dearly one not yet departed, though, and the house is more lavish than creepy, despite a plenitude of secret passageways.

*The Black Cat* is nowhere near an adaptation of the Poe story (except for a reference toward the very end, where a hidden body is revealed by the yowling titular feline), nor is it really a horror movie. It's an "Old Dark House" mystery (in a rather brightly lit mansion) replete with clutching hands appearing from behind draperies and a black-caped-and-cowled figure doing mysterious things. There are some horrific moments and a lot of comedy (possibly too much depending on your tolerance for Hugh Herbert, who is at his most annoying here – and that assessment is coming from a fan, mind you). The dim-witted, clumsy hero (Broderick Crawford), besotted with the lovely heiress (Anne Gwynne) and trying to protect her, is clearly patterned on *Cat and the Canary* (not only the Hope/Goddard production, but also Leni's silent and the play that inspired them both). To top things off, Gale Sondergaard all but repeats her "Miss Lu" characterization from Elliot Nugent's production. Surprisingly it took four (count 'em, four) writers to script this clone, all of them, apparently, with a tin ear for comic dialogue.

And as it obviously was a case of gathering the contract players, putting them through their paces on standing sets, and getting it in the can in a couple weeks (reportedly February 24 – March 10), the film didn't likely cost the studio very much – www.IMDb.com estimates $176,000, which is approximately a third of the estimated budget (per Wikipedia) for *Son of Frankenstein*. (A quick note about standing sets, a concept that Universal pioneered in the early silent days: Fans of the studio's horrors will recognize immediately the interior of Henrietta's mansion. While it is often asserted that the set was built for *The Wolf Man*, here it is months before that production even went before the cameras. In fact it can be seen two years earlier in *The Invisible Man Returns*. We have not been able to determine if it was built for that film – which notoriously went over-budget – or a still earlier one. In any event it would see heavy exposure – though modified over the years – in what at least seems like every other Universal "B"-horror, and who knows what else.)

*The Black Cat* looks fantastic, thanks to director Albert S. Rogell's conspiring with cinematographer Stanley Cortez on striking angles and compositions, and the latter providing some wonderfully atmospheric lighting effects. If the quartet of writers couldn't come up with much in the way of a compelling murder mystery, at least they created one in which the identity of the killer comes as a genuine surprise (and, courtesy of a terrific trick effect from John P. Fulton, a fiery demise for same). But, as is the case with much of the studio's horror output during the decade, the chief reason to pay any attention to this production is the cast. What fun there is to be had comes from their performances.

As the hero who's forever charging off when he thinks something nasty is afoot and then generally tripping over his own feet (or, courtesy his stunt double, tumbling off a balcony), Broderick Crawford (1911-1986) is a hoot. The actor is usually remembered as a tough guy, but his comedic chops are on display is several films, including *Seven Sinners* (1940) and *Born Yesterday* (1950). *Black Cat* was his only horror film during his stay at Universal or anywhere else for a long time. His chief claim to genre fame (if it can be called that) at the time was his being Lon Chaney's drinking and brawling buddy, and their trashing their dressing rooms. (Chaney's digs were subsequently given to Evelyn Ankers, reportedly causing the lasting enmity between the two.) Of interest to trivia buffs is that Chaney played the part of Lennie Small in 1939's *Of Mice and Men*, the role that Crawford created on Broadway. (Is it too much trivia to add that George S. Kaufman, the director of that stage production, caught a late-in-the-run performance and was so perturbed by Crawford's emendations to the role that he sent a telegram backstage that read, "Am watching from the back row. Wish you were here."?)

As with many not-quite-"A"-list actors of the Golden Age, Crawford saw his career falter in the '50s. While he was already accepting TV assignments by 1951, his working in films – usually in supporting roles - still predominated until he took the lead in the ultra-cheap *Highway Patrol* series. He returned to big-screen genre products with the 1966 Amicus production, *The Vulture*, and then *Terror in the*

*Wax Museum* (1973, with a roster of "Golden Age" horror actors), and then back to the boob-tube with TV movies *The Phantom of Hollywood* (1974) and *Look What's Happened to Rosemary's Baby* (1976). Crawford's final genre film – and final film – had him providing the (uncredited) voice of the computer in *The Creature Wasn't Nice* (1983). Appearances on TV series such as *The Man from U.N.C.L.E.* and *Land of the Giants* completed his sojourns into the fantastic.

Anne Gwynne (1918-2003) alternated with Evelyn Ankers in scream-queen roles in Big U's '40s horrors. While possibly not the greatest actress ever to appear on the silver screen, she makes the awkward dialogue of this film feel natural while effecting some extreme mood swings; on her lips the sub-par comedic lines take on a nigh Shavian ring. This suggests she had the talent to achieve stardom (she certainly had the looks – she was one of the top five pinups of World War II), but she never rose above the second ranks. Her chillers started in 1940 with *Black Friday* and there's more on her there.

Top-billed Basil Rathbone (1892-1967) scarcely needs any introduction to classic horror fans. Even before he made his first horror film (1939's *Son of Frankenstein*), he was generally cast as unpleasant characters in productions such as *Anna Karenina*, *Captain Blood* (both 1935), and *Night of Terror* (1937), though he was occasionally the hero, such as his turn as Philo Vance (to this writer's thinking, the definitive portrayal) in *The Bishop Murder Case* (1930). He is also regarded by many as still the definitive screen Sherlock Holmes, a role he was so familiar with by the time of *The Black Cat* that Crawford's Gil has a laugh line referring to it. Rathbone is covered in more detail in the entries on the Sherlock Holmes films.

Second-billed Hugh Herbert (1885-1952) came to films from the stage (in addition to performing, he wrote 150+ plays and sketches). He began appearing in the movies in 1927, but his best remembered body of work is as dim-witted, eccentric, and generally exasperating types in the '30s Busby Berkeley musicals for the brothers Warner. He is memorable as the Secretary of the Treasury trying to overthrow president W. C. Fields in the surreal satire, *Million Dollar Legs* (1932). His seven screenwriting credits include dialogue for *The Great Gabbo* (1929); taken from a Ben Hecht story, the film has Erich von Stroheim as an insane ventriloquist. His first onscreen chiller credit was 1937's *Sh! The Octopus*; four years would pass between that film and this one, his only other genre appearance. Herbert could be very funny given the right material, but he isn't given it here; the tea scene with Sondergaard is particularly cringe-inducing. Daffy Duck's "Woo-Hoo" cry is said to have been inspired by Herbert's trademark exclamation.

Bela Lugosi (1882-1958) gets fourth billing because Universal knew the value of his name, but he has very little screen time and even less dialogue. Mostly he is reduced to peering around doorjambs and through windows and ornamental grills (there is one nifty dissolve from his distinctive eyes to a car's headlights). Few things are more depressing than seeing this actor reduced to dashing about in the rain, crying "Kitty, kitty, kitty," trying to round up cats. While his screen time may be limited (and even demeaning), the publicity department shot a wealth of backstage stills of him to hype the flick. Aside from repeating his role of Ygor in *The Ghost of Frankenstein* (1942), the bosses at Big U played out his contract with nothing roles while cashing in on his name's marquee value. Although it seems unlikely any readers of this book are unfamiliar with his life and career, more can be found elsewhere between these covers.

Possibly the most unlikely member of any cast of any Universal horror is Gladys Cooper (1888-1971). The British-born actress was considered so photogenic at an early age that she started modeling when she was six. Her stage career started in 1905 and by 1911 she was receiving kudos for her performance in a London stage production of *The Importance of Being Ernest*. Her first motion picture came along in 1913 although she continued to concentrate on the stage for many years. Her first U.S. film was Alfred Hitchcock's production of *Rebecca* (1940) for David O. Selznick; this and similarly high-budgeted films – like Warner Bros.' *Now Voyager*, wherein she notably portrayed Bette Davis's domineering mother - bracketed *Black Cat*. Though only in her 50s at the time, she was perennially cast as stern old women, so perhaps she took on the role of the emotionally frail and insecure Myrna as a change of pace (it certainly doesn't appear likely that she was a Universal contractee). She didn't return to *le fantastique* until 1947 and *The Bishop's Wife*; that, an appearance on *The Outer Limits* and several on *The Twilight Zone* complete her genre CV. Dame Gladys continued working right up until her death, of pneumonia, in November 1971.

Gale Sondergaard (1899-1985) is the great, glamorous gorgon of horror films - of many types, actually - beginning with her first onscreen appearance in *Anthony Adverse* in 1936, for which she won the very first Academy Award for Best Supporting Actress. While she did occasionally portray sympathetic characters (as in 1937's *The Life of Emile Zola* and 1946's *Anna and the King of Siam*), she is better known for her sly, slinky, and sinister portrayals (which she could also send up, as she does here). The aforementioned *The Cat and the Canary* marked her first foray into the world of fantasy; it would be followed by *The Blue Bird* (1940), *The Spider Woman* (aka *Sherlock Holmes vs same*, 1943), *The Invisible Man's Revenge*, *The Climax* (both 1944), and *The Spider Woman Strikes Back* (1946). She was off the screen for almost two decades following 1949, the year her husband, director Herbert Biberman, became one of the "Hollywood Ten" and was jailed as a result of the infamous HUAC Hollywood hearings. Sondergaard refused to testify and was blacklisted. Man and wife both finally returned to work in 1969 (despite the "Have you left no sense of decency?" moment courtesy of Joseph N. Welch, the blacklist lasted that long for some folk) with the controversial *Slaves*, which he directed and in which she acted. Most of her following roles were on the small screen and included an episode of *Night Gallery* and Curtis Harrington's TV movie, *The Cat Creature* (1973). Her final film was *Echoes* (1983), about a man dreaming that his unborn twin wants to kill him; it reportedly makes *The Black Cat* look like *Wild Strawberries*.

As Henrietta, Cecilia Loftus (1876-1943) is so adorable - peering owlishly through her coke-bottle glasses - that her murder is the most shocking thing in the film. The Scottish-born actress started on stage back in 1893 as an actress, singer, music-hall performer, and mimic. A trip to Hollywood with a Shakespearean company two years later led to her decision to stay, although she had also established herself on the Broadway stage. She was arrested in 1922 for possession of morphine, and her death from a heart attack some 20 years later was reportedly due to her addiction to painkillers and alcohol. Loftus's first film appearance was in 1913 in *A Lady of Quality* (which was directed by J. Searle Dawley who, three years earlier, had directed *Frankenstein* for the Edison company). Aside from *The Blue Bird* - appearing again with Sondergaard and playing Shirley Temple's granny - *Black Cat* is her only genre appearance, although for what it's worth, she *did* play a character yclept "Sara Frankenstein" in the Deanna Durbin feature, *It's a Date* (1940).

In 1946 Claire Dodd (née Dorothy Ann Dodd, 1908-1973) was coming to the end of a film career that had started in 1930; early appearances included a stint as a Goldwyn Girl and many uncredited roles alternated with bit parts until she departed Paramount for Warner Bros. in 1933. Semi-genre appearances started with *Secret of the Chateau* (1934), two turns as Della Street in Warners' Perry Mason series, and *Charlie Chan in Honolulu* (1938), by which time she was freelancing. After *Black Cat* she would appear in *The Mad Doctor of Market Street* (1942) and complete two more films that same year before retiring. She was usually cast as conniving women; her normally aloof demeanor didn't allow her to be cast as sweet heroines, as she simply came off as too cynically cerebral. She reportedly loathed the Hollywood system and was probably all too happy to put it behind her after her second marriage.

John Eldredge is dealt with in the essay on *Horror Island*. Like Dodd, he hasn't much to do here, so that leaves us with Alan Ladd (1913-1964) just before he'd achieve stardom in *This Gun for Hire* (1942). Ladd had been making films for a decade by the time of *Black* Cat, with many appearances via a slew of uncredited bits, and quite possibly (it has never been verified) had stomped about a bit as one of the beast men in *Island of Lost Souls* (1932). His size and coloring were considered unsuitable for films at that time and so, while he *did* have some credited small roles, he still appeared without credit – as one of the reporters – in *Citizen Kane*, made the same year as *Black Cat*. Once he had established himself as a tough guy, he parlayed his stardom into other kinds of roles, including playing the title characters in *The Great Gatsby* (1949) and *Shane* (1953). Needless to say, Ladd never appeared in another horror film.

Producer Burt Kelly (1898-1983), like Ben Pivar (see: *Horror Island*), was a recruit from Poverty Row and independent productions – a sure sign the New Universal was not regarding their fantastic films as Super Jewels after lavishing "A"-budgets on the films that signaled the return of horror, 1939's *Son of Frankenstein* (which reportedly was initially planned for Technicolor) and 1940's *The Invisible Man Returns*. Pivar was one of the founders of K.B.S. Productions, whose rather ambitious slate included *A Study in Scarlet* and *Deluge* (both 1933). After a stint at Republic, he joined Universal and produced *The House of Seven Gables, Black Friday, The Invisible Woman* (all 1940), and *Hold That Ghost* (1941). He later moved over to Columbia where he handled the "Blondie" films and some of that studio's "B"-mysteries.

Director Albert S. Rogell (1901-1988) became involved in the movies while still a teenager and was tutored in every aspect of them during a stint with the now-forgotten George Loane Tucker company. It was producer Sol Lesser, however, who gave him his first shot at directing with a series of shorts beginning in 1921; he graduated to features two years later. Rogell was exceptionally prolific during the Silent Era (an even dozen films in 1927 alone) and perhaps the speed at which he worked is what relegated him to "B"-pictures. Action (including Westerns) and mysteries were his forte, and *Black Cat* is his only horror film (the excruciatingly horrible *Li'l Abner*, which he directed just before *Cat*, does not count). This is somewhat of a pity because his handling of the film's violent content – Abigail's hanging depicted by a shadow on the wall and the attack on Elaine suggested by a quick cut from a raised hand to a reflection in a mirror of her falling onto the floor – gives evidence that he could have brought flair to genre assignments. *Black Cat* may not be well written, but it is very well directed.

Four writers are credited for the script, though whether they collaborated or it was passed from hand to hand for additions is unknown; given the sometimes baffling sequences, the latter seems likely. Robert Lees (1912-2004) previously wrote *The*

*Invisible Woman* (1940) and would work on *Hold that Ghost* (1941) for Abbott and Costello. He'd also do script duty on the team's ... *Meet Frankenstein* (1948) and ... *Meet the Invisible Man* (1951), and several other of the duo's features. During his TV years, he'd write for *Alfred Hitchcock Presents*, *The Green Hornet*, *Land of the Giants*, and *The New Scooby and Scrappy-Doo Show*. Frederic T. Rinaldo (1913-1992) also worked on *Invisible Woman*, *Hold that Ghost*, ...*Meet Frankenstein* and ...*Meet the Invisible Man* and other A&C features. Eric Taylor (1897-1952) had a beefier genre resume with *The Lady in the Morgue* (1938), a number of "Ellery Queen" and "Crime Doctor" mysteries, *Black Friday* (1940), *The Ghost of Frankenstein* (original story, 1942), *Phantom of the Opera*, *Son if Dracula* (both 1943), and *The Spider Woman Strikes Back* (1946). For RKO he would script some "Dick Tracy" productions, including ...*Meets Gruesome* , which pitted Ralph Byrd against Boris Karloff (and featured Anne Gwynne!). Robert Neville (??-??) has no other genre credits in his very brief CV, and nothing is apparently known about him other than those assignments.

**The black cat and the inimitable Bela; what else can we say? Typical of Universal's waste of Lugosi during the forties.**

If Gladys Cooper is a surprising presence in the production then so, at first glance, is Stanley Cortez (nee Stanislaus Krantz, 1908-1997) who, the very next year, was tapped by Orson Welles to photograph *The Magnificent Ambersons*. (It is reported that it was his work on *Black Cat* that prompted the hire.) After working as a still photographer's assistant in Manhattan, he took the opportunity to work with Gloria Swanson's production company and then freelanced (as an assistant) until signing on with Universal in 1936 for the standard seven-year contract. As part of their "B"-unit he photographed *The Black Doll* and *Lady in the Morgue* (both 1938) and a slew of other "B"-productions of various stripes before being assigned to *Cat*. The cost overruns on *Ambersons* were blamed partly on his elaborate set-ups (such as the famous staircase scene), and his career suffered (as did Welles's, for that matter), and the rest of his professional life would find him bouncing between some pretty execrable low-budget productions and an occasional quality outing. He returned to Universal in 1943 for *Flesh and Fantasy*, and his other genre and nigh-genre films include *The Neanderthal Man* (1953), *The Night of the Hunter* (1955), *The Angry Red Planet* (1959), *Dinosaurus!* (1960), *The Madmen of Mandoras* (1963), *The Ghost in the Invisible Bikini*, *The Navy vs the Night Monsters* (both 1966), and *Scream, Evelyn, Scream!* (1970). We'd be remiss if we didn't also cite some other notable productions scattered amid these catchpenny efforts: *Since You Went Away* (1944), Fritz Lang's *Secret Beyond the Door* (1947), *The Man on the Eiffel Tower* (1950), *The Three Faces of Eve* (1957), *Back Street* (1961), *Shock Corridor* (1963), *The Naked Kiss* (1964), *The Bridge at Remagen* (1969), and, albeit uncredited for some reason, he worked on *Chinatown* (1974). Another bit of trivia: Cortez's brother, Jacob, changed his name to Ricardo Cortez, the better to cash in on the Latin Lover craze in Hollywood of the Silent Era after Rudolph Valentino's stardom. Stanislaus liked the sound of his sibling's new cognomen and altered his own birth name.

Given the stylish gowns worn by the women in the opening section of the film, the exquisite negligees in the final segment and the smart suits in between, perhaps we should devote some ink here to Vera West (1898-1947 – some sources list 1900 for her natal year). While her onscreen credit was invariably for "Gowns," she was Universal's chief costume designer for nearly two decades, responsible for the men's attire (no matter how off-the-rack it may have looked) as well as the women's. That means she was likely responsible for Wolf Frankenstein's nifty two-shade jacket and the Monster's furry vest in *Son of Frankenstein* (1939), the latter's initial black tee-shirt and suit look as well as his bride's bed-sheet wedding dress with opera-glove bandages (possibly with James Whale's input – no costume sketches survive). And negligees, of course; acres and acres of negligees worn in the Laemmle-era and New-Universal horrors (did any of those monsters ever carry off a heroine not so attired?). But she was also responsible for the period attire for the likes of Whale's *Showboat* (1936) and for *My Little Chickadee* (1940) – yes, West wore West in the wild west. She created all the over-the-top Maria Montez outfits for those daffy Technicolor extravaganzas and the more subdued wardrobe for Alfred Hitchcock's *Shadow of a Doubt* (1943). Some sources aver that she only designed the women's apparel in the films while others state she at least selected the men's outfits or directed their design. For someone who spent almost 20 years in the studio system, there is much that is murky about the lady. Reams have been written about other studio costume designers, but almost nothing about Vera West.

Her couture career began at a Manhattan salon from which she departed (rather abruptly it would seem – but more on that in a bit) and ended up at Big U. Per the IMDb, that was in 1924, but other online sources place her arrival in 1927 or '28. We prefer the latter for strictly emotional reasons as it would mean her first assignment would have been Paul Leni's *The Man Who Laughs*, which also marked the beginning of Jack P. Pierce's tenure with the studio. (History does sometimes provide such satisfactory coincidences; in any event it is her first onscreen credit.) The reasons for her relocation to the opposite coast are unknown, but it appears she committed a transgression of some kind and it may have followed her. Speculation that it may have been a crime seems unlikely because she worked under her own name with an onscreen credit in hundreds of movies; she was hardly hiding from the law, but it seems she did have something she felt needed to be kept a secret. She left Universal in 1947, just about the same time the studio ditched its "B"-productions (and Jack Pierce), and designed a collection for a Beverly Wilshire Hotel dress shop.

And then, a day after her birthday that year, she was found dead, floating in her swimming pool, by a resident of the guest house (Robert L. "Bob" Landry, who took the first photos of Pearl Harbor mere hours after the Japanese attack). She left two notes, one of which said, "The fortune teller told me there was only one way to duck the blackmail I've paid for twenty-three years... death." Why she was being blackmailed and who the blackmailer was – or her fortune teller for that matter – was never determined. *The New York Times* reported that police were investigating the death (leading some to speculate it was a murder), but after that... silence. Her businessman husband was away at the time, and he disappeared from history shortly afterward, but not before having all the buildings on the property razed. Grief? Guilt? Again from the *NYT* of 30 June, 1947:

112

Film costumer Vera West died in her swimming pool at 5119 Bluebell Ave. over the weekend. She suffered from marital difficulties, but the blackmail to which she alluded in her suicide note was, according to husband Jack C. West, a figment of her imagination. Mr. West claims he was staying at the Beverly Hills Hotel when his wife took her unfortunate dip, following a bad argument, and in anticipation of Mrs. West's consultation with a divorce attorney. Assistant county autopsy surgeon Dr. Marvin Goodwin's initial report was of asphyxia, probably due to drowning, but Dr. Frederick Newbarr, his superior, is refusing to sign a death certificate until additional tests are performed.

Presumably the autopsy confirmed the initial suspicion, but no further news reports were made. Per several web sites (with no attribution of sources), Mr. West stated through his attorney that he was familiar with his wife's finances, and there had been no blackmail payments. Also per these web sites (and equally unattributed), some friends averred that Vera claimed feelings of depression, though actress Ella Raines – another friend who had worked with her on Robert Siodmak's *Phantom Lady* (1944) – said she behaved as though she hadn't a care in the world. West's passing is as shrouded in mystery as her early life – even her actual birth date and her maiden name are unknown. But, oh, those horror duds.

We'd also be remiss if we didn't pay a bit of attention to Universal's special effects maestro, John P. Fulton (1902-1966). His likely most famous trick effect – and arguably most spectacular – was parting the Red Sea for Cecil B. De Mille. Nonetheless, decades before that he had made Claude Rains invisible (as he did later to Vincent Price, Virginia Bruce, and Jon Hall, garnering three Oscar nominations along the way for the trick work in the sequels), provided the matte work for the trip through Borgo Pass, and personally built – and rigged for destruction – the models for the watchtower in *Bride of Frankenstein* (1935) and the castles in *The Ghost of Frankenstein* (1942) and *Frankenstein Meets the Wolf Man* (1943). He blacked out Tom Tyler's eyes, gave both Boris Karloff and Lon Chaney, Jr. a pulsating glow, and allowed the vampires in *Son of Dracula* (1943) to transport themselves as an eerie mist. And who can forget the amazing sequence in *Bride of Frankenstein* where Dr. Pretorious reveals his miniature *homunculi* or Henry Hull's transformation into *Werewolf of London* (1935)? Hull's stroll behind the pillars - involving multiple traveling mattes – was a far more involved piece of work than the dissolves used for Larry Talbot. Fulton's work for Universal often went without an onscreen credit, but as head of the studio's effects department, he was ultimately responsible for all things "special."

In *The Black Cat*, *Fulton* supplied a fiery finale for the killer that is damned impressive for the pre-CGI era. Fulton's father, who painted theater backdrops, was vehemently against his son having anything to do with the movie business, but John quit his job as a surveyor to become an assistant cameraman for D. W. Griffith after watching said director at work. He then moved to the now forgotten Frank D. Williams Studio, apparently Hollywood's first enterprise devoted to special effects, where he learned about composites and traveling mattes. His experimentation with these techniques led to his being hired by Universal where he contributed at least a little something to all of the Universal horror titles of the Laemmle and New Universal periods. He also contributed notable trick effects such as the title sequence for *My Man Godfrey*, with its transition from a miniature Manhattan (with the cast and crew credits in lights) to a live-action shot of William Powell, and W. C. Fields' fall from an airplane onto a trampoline in *Never Give a Sucker an Even Break* (1941). His contributions to the horrors may have lasted only a few minutes in each, but they lent an illusion of a higher budgetary level than they possessed. (Ironically, he was forever at war with the studio over insufficient money.)

Fulton, too, departed Universal at the time of the ownership change, when International seemingly did a purge of all the old-order personnel. Still, he reportedly left of his own free will, when Samuel Goldwyn dangled the promise of feature-film directing. His time with Goldwyn's company brought him his first Academy Award (for 1945's *Wonder Man*, made on loan-out before he signed with the independent producer) but no directorial assignments, so he first joined Walter Wanger at Eagle-Lion (and even went unemployed for a time) before landing at Paramount, where he took over their effects unit after the death of Gordon Jennings in 1953. His post-Universal genre work includes *The Bishop's Wife* (1947), *Conquest of Space* (1955), *The Space Children, Colossus of New York, I Married a Monster from Outer Space* (all 1958), and, after he was let go from Paramount (when they disbanded their effects unit) and was again a freelancer, *The Bamboo Saucer* (1968), for which he also came up with the story. It was to be one of the last of his more than 250 films.

Reviews for *The Black Cat* were mixed; some saw it as the fluff it was (and more than which it never pretended to be). "Combination of Chills, Thrills and Farce is a Happy One..." reads the headline for one review.

> All the best mystery props known to the film business have been whipped out for this story, and in addition, a nice flavoring of farce is worked in for good measure, with the result as a whole turning out as entertaining screen fare... The cast is fine, the horror element in the story

is sufficient, with a full complement of secret passages, yowling cats and sinister characters and the direction in fine... things happen fast and furiously with plenty of chills and lots of laughs...

Anonymous, *Film Daily*, 28 April 1941

This production of "The Black Cat" has all the essentials of thrilling mystery plus a few extras which collectively make for an excitingly good time for mystery lovers. Under Albert S. Rogell's direction, the mystery is baffling to the very end, when the identity of the killer is divulged. In the events leading up to the climax, he has intermingled suspense with comedy and the combination works out very well... Hugh Herbert handles the comedy and deflates the tension in a manner which drew many chuckles from the patrons at the Rialto on Broadway.

G., *Motion Picture Daily*, 28 April 1941

Others were more disparaging, in keeping with the low regard in which horror films were held at the time.

There is about as much difference between the Alhambra's new shriek-and-squeal melodrama and Edgar Allen [sic] Poe's classic story which suggested it as there is between a one-inch firecracker and a Fourth of July skyrocket... Although the atmosphere seems creepy, the thrills are tamed somewhat by the routine plot and by the horseplay borrowed from "The Cat and the Canary." It is silly stuff made fairly amusing by Hugh Herbert... All the members of Universal's shock-and-hokum stock company do some daffy cutting up... You will hardly recognize Bela Lugosi, the mad, bearded gardener and keeper of the cats. Broderick Crawford dives into every slapstick farce every time he sees a shadow. It is rather a surprise to find Gale Sondergaard and Gladys Cooper capering in the crematory...

G.C. P., *Cleveland Plain Dealer*, 4 July 1941

A fair murder-mystery melodrama, with comedy. It is somewhat slow getting started, as a matter of fact, it is not until the closing scenes when the murderer's identity becomes known and the heroine's life is in endangered that the action is really exciting. Up until that point, the plot is developed in a routine fashion; and, in spite of the fact that the customary tricks to create an eerie atmosphere are employed, the picture is seldom "spine-chilling." Hugh Herbert provokes laughter by his familiar brand of comedy.

*Harrison's Reports*, 3 May 1941

And lest you think (as this writer did) that Hugh Herbert's comedy in this endeavor just didn't age well, Char, in a plot-heavy review for *Variety* on 4 February, 1941, termed Herbert "only meagerly funny" and didn't think much of the rest of the film, particularly the writing:

Like so many other B's of late, 'The Black Cat' is way down the alphabetical scale... Horror subject has been poorly written by no less than four scenarists and loosely produced by Burt Kelly, a pretty old hand in the B-making ranks. A large and capable cast tries to pull a wagon with traces made of string thus they can't be blamed for getting nowhere.

A short story by Edgar Allan Poe caused the picture to be made. Poe may not be so much at fault, however, as those who took his yarn in hand, moulded [sic] it into a 70-minute bore and are now seeking an indulgent market for the finished work. Although four writers were required, the combined talent of all has produced very little. Among other things the dialogue is trite. Result at comedy is even less than that...

The reputation of *The Black Cat* has not increased over the decades. While it has some moments it is decidedly a minor entry among Universal's mostly minor contributions to genre in the '40s. The following online post is probably representative of how the film is viewed .

... merely another 'Old Dark House' murder-mystery... The unfunny comedy relief is supplied by Hugh Herbert, while the remainder of the stalwart cast maintain interest throughout, despite a severely dragging middle in which virtually nothing of interest happens, one red herring topping another. The young Broderick Crawford is certainly likable, and pairs nicely with lovely Anne Gwynne, but top-billed Basil Rathbone is reduced to playing a weaselly scoundrel… One of the nicer aspects of the film is that the titular black cat actually becomes the hero during the admittedly thrilling climax, first alerting Crawford to his girl's danger, then causing the killer's demise.

Kevin Olzak on *IMDb*

*The Black Cat* – 2 May 1941 – 70 minutes

**CAST:** Basil Rathbone as Montague Hartley; Hugh Herbert as Mr. Penny; Broderick Crawford as Hubert A. Gilmore 'Gil' Smith; Bela Lugosi as Eduardo Vigos; Anne Gwynne as Elaine Winslow; Gladys Cooper as Myrna Hartley; Gale Sondergaard as Abigail Doone; Cecilia Loftus as Henrietta Winslow; Claire Dodd as Margaret Gordon; John Eldredge as Stanley Borden; Alan Ladd as Richard Hartley; Following were uncredited: Erville Alderson as Doctor Williams; Harry C. Bradley as Coroner; Jack Cheatham as 1st Moving Man; Edgar Sherrod as Minister

**CREDITS:** Producer: Burt Kelly; Director: Albert S. Rogell; Writers: Robert Lees, Robert Neville, Frederic I. Rinaldo, Eric Taylor; Cinematography: Stanley Cortez; Film Editor: Ted J. Kent; Art Director: Jack Otterson; Set Decorations: Russell A. Gausman; Gowns: Vera West; Assistant Director: Howard Christie; Special Photographic Effects: John P. Fulton; Musical Director: Hans J. Salter (as H.J. Salter); Stock Music Composers: Salter, Ralph Freed, Charles Henderson, Charles Previn (uncredited)

*- HHL*

# *Cracked Nuts* (1941)

*Synopsis*: Larry Trent, citizen of Oswego Falls, has won the $5000 grand prize in the Refrigerall radio show's slogan contest ("If's it a Refrigerall refrigerator, it refrigerates!"). The money, Larry states, will enable him to marry his sweetheart, Sharon Knight, who works in New York City as secretary to James Mitchell, a patent attorney. At the same time, Mitchell is being conned by Boris Kabikoff, who hope to have the attorney finance "Ivan the Robot," a mechanical shell occupied by Kabikoff's stooge, Eddie, who has an obsession with blondes. Adding to the madness is the presence of McAneny – the divorce lawyer for Mitchell's ex-wife – who is threatening to jail Mitchell if he doesn't come across with an overdue alimony payment within the next 24 hours. Into this mishegas steps Larry, who has come to propose to Sharon.

Mitchell and Kabikoff learn of Larry's $5000 winnings and - determined to bilk him of the money – they talk him into "investing" his windfall for a ten-percent ownership of the mechanical man. Tucking $2000 of the winnings into a bank account, Mitchell and Kabikoff repair for the attorney's home, where Eddie, done up in his apparatus as Ivan, spots Ethel (Mitchell's ex-wife – and a blonde) attempting to sneak into the house.

The following day, McAneny announces that he has attached the two grand Mitchell and Kabikoff had deposited, so the two men decide to relieve Larry of the balance of his winnings as a further "investment." Shortly thereafter, Sharon shows Larry a telegram that has arrived for Mitchell – a wire she has not shown her boss. From the Imperial Research Corporation, the telegram advises Mitchell that Kabikoff – a former employee – has made off with the corporation's incomplete robot and warns that Imperial will file an injunction should anyone try to patent the invention. An idea occurs to Larry who returns to Oswego Falls after telling Sharon not to show the telegram to Mitchell or to anyone. In the interim, "Ivan the Robot" is doing chores around the Mitchell house for Chloe the maid and, at one point, dresses as a ghost to frighten Burgess the butler. When Chloe sees her boss place Larry's remaining cash in his safe, Chloe calls Ethel to advise her of same and, later that night, Ethel breaks into the house – and the safe – to retrieve the cash.

Come the dawn and Larry returns to the City with his buddies Sylvanus Boogle and Wilfred Smun – the latter, the mayor of Oswego – and he introduces his two friends as millionaires looking to invest in Ivan the Robot. The only condition for their investing is that there be no one else involved, so Mitchell and Kabikoff convince Ethel to return all of Larry's money so that the moneyed newcomers might feel comfortable in investing a good deal more. That night, Larry ruefully allows himself to be bought out, but "Ivan" - blond-crazed as always – breaks into a department store to make off with a blond clothing dummy. Things come to a head as Benson the butler shows up and exposes Kabikoff, Eddie/Ivan leads the police on a merry car chase, and Larry and Sharon – accompanied by their two "millionaire" friends – take off for the peace and quiet of Oswego Falls.

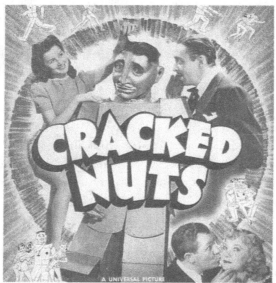

RKO's 1931 comedy of the same name featured Wheeler and Woolsey and some brief footage of pre-*Frankenstein* Boris Karloff. Universal's "take" had a boatload of comics, a faux mechanical man, and a non-*Frankenstein* Boris Kabikoff.

A silly, cheap little comedy – and intended to be nothing more than that – *Cracked Nuts* merits inclusion herein due solely to its faux mechanical man. Not to opine too strongly, but back in the '20s, when the Laemmles coded the financial investment in their products as ranging from "Red Feather" (the least expensive) to "Super Jewel" (the extreme other end of the fiscal spectrum), *Cracked Nuts* might well have been considered a "Pink Feather." "Ivan the Robot" (again, the *raison d'être* for this chapter) is notable for two reasons (both slight), neither of which has anything to do with the other. First off, having Ivan's head mirror the rather eccentric visage of Russian comic Mischa Auer intimates a bond between said pseudo-automaton and his creator, Auer's character, Boris Kabikoff. ("I breathed the very like of Boris Kabikoff into his body," Auer declaims at one point.) While entries in the '30s Frankenstein canon brought intriguing double meanings to the titles **Bride** *of Frankenstein* and **Son** *of Frankenstein* in terms of Henry Frankenstein's family and the trappings in which the Monster found itself, there was never any suggestion of any sort of relationship – physical, psychic, or otherwise - between Colin Clive's maddest of doctors and Boris Karloff's tormented creature. Here, we have not only a fairly juvenile play on words – can Boris Kabikoff not be the most obvious of comic tributes? - but also a blatantly transparent tie between con man and con-structed man. In his review of the film for *The New York Times* (23 March 1941), critic Douglas W. Churchill dwelt for a bit on this situation:

> Not satisfied with the startling qualities of Mischa Auer, Universal has constructed a mechanical man in the image of the actor with his peculiarities intensified. The robot's name is Ivan, and when Ivan sees a blonde his eyes, which have electric lights in them, flash on and off. This improvement on the human form was built in the mechanical shops at a cost of $845 for use in 'Cracked Nuts.'

The second is that Ivan is played by *two* actors: Shemp Howard gets the credit when Ivan is temporarily deprived of his headpiece or the character Eddie is espied totally sans metal-work, while London-born Ernie Stanton is saddled with the lion's share of the action whenever the "robot's" head is rooted firmly to its shoulders. Fun fact: Stanton, whose film career was mostly comprised of uncredited bits (*Adventures of Robin Hood* [1938], *The Wolf Man* [1940], and *The Ghost of Frankenstein* [1942] comprised the "noncredits" which would interest us most), is accorded a wink and a nod in the film's press-book...

121

Although [Ernie] Stanton is a well-known stage and screen personality, he is invisible to the audience throughout the entire action of 'Cracked Nuts.' He is the man inside the robot, around which so much of the film's hilarity is motivated.

... while Howard – who appeared in well over a dozen Universal features during the decade, including *The Invisible Woman* (1940), *Hold That Ghost* (1941), and *The Strange Case of Dr. Rx* (1942), all of which are dealt with in these pages – receives nary a mention therein. (We give Shemp his due in our essay on *Doctor Rx*.) In his review for *The Times*, Mr. Churchill thought it worthwhile to give brief mention to Stanton's *bona fides*:

> Ivan is actuated by Ernie Stanton, who did a music hall routine in vaudeville for years. He gets $200 a week for wearing Ivan, who is exceedingly uncomfortable. The robot consists of seven pieces – two legs, two torso pieces, two arms and a head. Ivan is bolted on Stanton and His clothes are so arranged that when he starts to disrobe the machinery that supposedly operates him is exposed. Ivan has so intrigued the local correspondents that the studio says they plan on giving him (and Stanton) feature billing on the title.

Intriguingly, while Stanton got that bit of exposure in the film's press-book and his name *did* make it to the opening cast scrawl (behind Shemp's, but before Ivan the Robot's), he is not credited with playing Ivan; Shemp *is* listed as playing "Eddie." Nor can Stanton be found in the press-book's "official" cast listing, where even Shemp's name goes missing, as neither character – Ivan or Eddie – is on the list as printed in the studio's official publicity publication. Go figure. (Compounding the misdemeanor, in *his* review of the film – for the 18 July 1941 edition of the *Los Angeles Times* – critic G.K. offered that "'Cracked Nuts' might well be called 'the adventures of a robot,' so very extensively is that comedy concerned with the comic manner in which Shemp Howard, who plays the 'innerds' [sic] of a phony robot, pursues blonds." Really? Did G.K. not have access to a press-book?)

As for those who *did* make it in both spots... In addition to his turn as Boris Kabikoff, Mischa Auer had already appeared as Boris Kalenkhov in Frank Capra's *You Can't Take It with You* (1938), as Boris Bebenko in Charles Lamont's *Unexpected Father*, and as Boris Callahan in George Marshall's classic, *Destry Rides Again* (the latter two, both 1939). Post-*Cracked Nuts* Borises would include 1944's *Up in Mabel's Room*, the 1958 French/Italian production, *Tabarin*, and an episode of the mid-'60s French TV anthology, *Le train bleu s'arrete 13 fois* (*The Blue Train Stops 13 Times*). There's more on the "Mad Russian" in our essay on *Hold That Ghost* (1941).

Una Merkel's experiences in Hollywood began in 1928, when she served as Lilian Gish's stand- in during the filming of *The Wind*. Unlike so many of her contemporaries, Miss Merkel did not then appear in a passel of uncredited parts, but moved immediately to smaller and featured roles, of which *The Bat Whispers* (1930), the 1931 *Maltese Falcon*, *On Borrowed Time* (1939), and *The Mad Doctor of Market Street* are of especial interest to us. While fairly early TV (like *The Monkey's Paw* episode on the – *ahem!* - well-remembered TV series, *Your Jeweler's Showcase* [1953] and *The Secret of the Red Room* on the rather more memorable *Climax!* [1957]) offered the end-all to her genre roles, the vivacious actress had become quite well known for her interactions with some of the medium's best comics, like Harold Lloyd (1934's *The Cat's-Paw*), W.C. Fields (*The Bank Dick*, 1940), Bing Crosby & Bob Hope (1941's *The Road to Zanzibar*), Kenny Delmar's Senator Claghorn (1947's *It's a Joke, Son*), and William Bendix (1950's *Kill the Umpire*). It was for fare like this – rather than for dreck like *Cracked Nuts* – that Miss Merkel was awarded a star on Hollywood's Walk of Fame in 1960. Still, the pert actress did win accolades from the *Los Angeles Times's* G.K., who opined "Una Merkel, of the crinkly eyes and trembly voice, is again proving herself one of Hollywood's ace comediennes, and pretty, too, with her new blond hair." Retiring from the industry in the late '60s, the Covington (Kentucky) native passed away in Los Angeles in January 1986.

Stu Erwin is probably best remembered by folks of a certain age as the lead in his eponymous TV show, which ran from 1950 until 1955, as well as for his performances in well over two dozen other TV series in the ten years that followed. Like Una Merkel, Erwin started his film career in 1928 (with *Mother Knows Best*), but – our present object of scrutiny apart – really never appeared in genre fare. It's hardly speaking ill of Erwin (or any of the cast, really) when one opines that neither his appearance herein – nor those of any of the others – impacted their career advancement to any appreciable degree. Also probably better remember for the boob tube rather than the big screen is William Frawley, always and everywhere celebrated as Fred Mertz on nearly a decade's worth of *I Love Lucy* and *The Lucy-Desi Comedy Hour*. Still – as with Stu – William doesn't make much of an impression here, either. Frawley, who got his cinematic feet wet in 1916 (in Arthur Maude's *Lord Loveland Discovers America*), opted to go the Vaudeville route with his brother until returning to film for good (after a few late-'20s shorts) in 1933. The Iowa-born actor graced the genre with 1934's *The Witching Hour* and 1951's *Abbott and Costello Meet the Invisible Man*. Betwixt those two features were about 100 pictures that gave Frawley the opportunity to portray everything from the sublime to the ridiculous. Fun Fact: In *Cracked Nuts*, Frawley's onscreen wife is named "Ethel."

Offsetting the fairly unfunny comedy of the first cast are the fairly funny – but what would a couple of decades later be considered racist – comedy portrayals of Hattie Noel and Mantan Moreland. Noel - whose character (Chloe, the maid) addresses Ivan as "Mr. Frankentin" - has her big moment in a scene in which Moreland (as Burgess the butler) is *of course* shooting craps with another African-American character. After a series of rather dull verbal interchanges between the two domestics ("Who dat?" "Who say 'who dat?' when I say 'who dat'?"), we watch as the robot is covered with a sheet (!) - setting up the classic stereotypical scene of a black man terrified by a ghost. The bit also includes the given that Burgess – like any black male – will whip out a straight razor with which to defend himself. Miss Noel's cinematic career was brief, lasting under a decade with (per IMDb.com) 18 appearances – mostly as domestics – with half of those uncredited. Given the narrow parameters of her role herein, though, Miss Noel is no better or worse than anyone else.

Mantan Moreland, of course, is another story altogether. Like Miss Noel a Louisiana native, Moreland saw his career span four decades, as the comedian appeared onstage, in radio, and in well over a hundred films, although – again like Miss Noel – a good number of those were in uncredited bits. The comedian – born Jesse James Brodnax on the 3 September 1903 – went on to be one of the most popular African-American comics in the '30s and '40s, along with folks like Spencer Williams, Willie Best, and Eddie "Rochester" Anderson. Arguably, Moreland's most famous role was as Birmingham Brown – Charlie Chan's Man Friday – during the last lustrum of the Chinese detective's movie series. His role in *Cracked Nuts* was a near parallel to his role (again, with an alliterative name – Jefferson Jackson) in Monogram's *King of the Zombies*, which had preceded *Nuts* into local theaters everywhere by a couple of months. No stranger to the genre – *The Strange Case of Doctor Rx* (see essay), *Mexican Spitfire Sees a Ghost*, *Phantom Killer*, and *Revenge of the Zombies* all were graced by his presence within only two years – Moreland would be a welcome addition to all types of films throughout the sound cinema's first two decades.

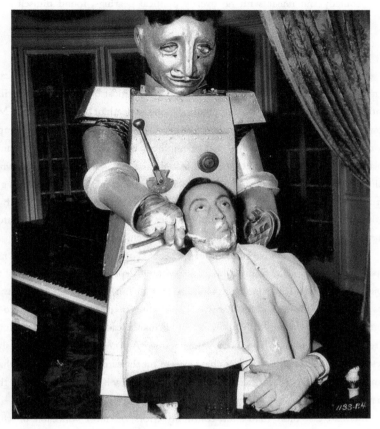

**Despite some rather obvious impairments to his vision, Ivan wields that straight razor with aplomb. Cinematic conventions of the time saw Mantan Moreland's character likewise adept with a razor, albeit with different intent and stylistics.**

Come the '50s, though... well, per biographer Michael H. Price:

> A great deal of purposefully applied laughter had yielded to anger and sorrow during the immediate postwar 1950s as black America began to cast itself in a grimmer light of social upheaval. Even the blues became an endangered idiom for a long while, there, falsely stigmatized by its perception as a throwback to primitivism and the plantation mentality of subservience. And Mantan Moreland, whose career hinged upon both

comedy and music with no overtly political bearings, found himself
thwarted at precisely the time that his star should have been gaining
further momentum.(1)

Humor that had been "acceptable," if not downright adored earlier now became
seen as demeaning and offensive. Still, many fans and most of his fellow comedians
continued to appreciate his brand of hijinks. Upon the death of his older brother, Moe
Howard – along with Larry Fine - sought to have Moreland replace the late Shemp as
the third Stooge; Moe maintained that Shemp had even recommended that Mantan
replace him "if the need should ever, God forbid, arise" (2), only to be voted down by
Columbia Pictures. Come the late '60s and early '70s, the comic found work with a bit
in the Lon Chaney indie, *Spider Baby* (1967), Melvin Van Peebles' comedic study on
bigotry, *Watermelon Man* (1970), and appearances in a number of TV series. Mantan
Moreland died of a cerebral hemorrhage in late September 1973.

Even if one were to give out handfuls of benefits of doubts, it would still be nigh
impossible to come away from *Cracked Nuts* without deploring the cheesiness of the
project. With Eddie labeled a "hyperblondiac by Babikoff," we can understand Ivan's
eyes lighting up whenever a lady whose hair is a lighter shade of pale wanders into the
room. Still, what is *wrong* with Eddie, when his mania leads him to snatch a blond-
haired *mannequin* from a department store window? A dummy? Really? Obviously, it
does set off the least impressive car chase ever to hit the screen, but the notion that a
human being would risk incarceration to snatch a dummy is more unbelievable than
the rest of the film.

There are also more than a few continuity errors, the most noticeable of which
is Ivan's toupee disappearing *sans raison* moments after the hirsute mechanism is
spotted when Ethel breaks into her husband's safe. There *are* grin-inducing bits - like
Mitchell's apartment house being tagged the "Venus de Milo Arms" - while, when
viewed with Millennium-age perspectives, the sight of Burgess the butler turning
white from fright (he's locked in the trunk of Eddie's car) may induce rather more
of a grimace than a grin. Offending the auditory nerves is a brief scene in which
Shemp Howard's voice is heard – poorly and obviously dubbed – whilst Ivan stands
motionless in a corner. Just that once could they not have rerecorded the voice for the
sake of credibility?

Of all the reviews we checked, only the *Los Angeles Times*' G.K. felt the hour-
long effort was worth his time: "There is altogether a lusty spontaneity about the
picture that is delightful. The 'name' cast does its job thoroughly, leaving no laugh-

stone unturned." The 26 July 1941 *Showmen's Trade* critique was less positive - "... flat as a pancake, due mostly to a script which lacks just about everything that goes into entertainment." - while the *Motion Picture Herald*, which saw print the same day, added fuel to the fire:

There is little in this number to engage interest save the names of the cast, a group of accomplished comedians who struggle without success to put humour into situations and dialogue which do not warrant the effort... Direction by Edward Cline and production by Joseph G. Sanford do not cope with the inadequacy of story material which is the film's basic fault. Result of their efforts is at best a picture in the 'filler' category.

A couple of days earlier – on the 22 July – the *Hollywood Review* assessment had also placed the blame squarely on the absence of funniness: "This comedy of gags and gadgets furnishes less in the way of humor than is promised by the names in its cast... Director Edward Cline doesn't have much to work with except talent handicapped by lack of material."

Considering that the script was the brainchild of silent-comedy specialist W. Scott (*Charlie Chan at the Opera, Ghost of Frankenstein*) Darling and Erna Lazarus, it just goes to show you that not every ball can be hit out of the park.

*Cracked Nuts* – July 1941 – 61 minutes

**CAST**: Stu Erwin as Lawrence Trent; Una Merkel as Sharon Knight; Mischa Auer as Boris Kabikoff; William Frawley as James Mitchell; Astrid Allwyn as Ethel Mitchell; Mantan Moreland as Burgess; Hattie Noel as Chloe; Shemp Howard as Eddie; Ernie Stanton as Ivan; Francis Pierlot as Mayor Wilfred Smun; Will Wright as Sylvanus Boogle; Emmett Vogan as Attorney McEneny; Tom Hanlon as Dixon, the Radio Announcer; Pat O'Malley as 1st Officer; with Bobby Barber, Billy Bletcher, Milton Parsons, Lyle Clement, Dorothy Darrell, Hal K. Dawson, Marion Martin, Pierre Watkin, Janet Warren

**CREDITS**: Director: Edward Cline; Associate Producer: Joseph G. Sanford; Screenplay: Erna Lazarus, W. Scott Darling; Cinematographer: Charles Van Enger; Film Editor: Milton Carruth; Art Director: Jack Otterson; Associate Art Director: Harold H. MacArthur; Set Decoration: R.A. Gausman; Sound Supervisor: Bernard B. Brown; Sound Technician: Jess Moulin; Musical Director: Hans J. Salter; Gowns: Vera West

*-JTS*

# *Hold That Ghost* (1941)

Come the new decade, America was finding comic relief in a host of new comedians, both on the radio and onscreen. Sure, Charlie Chaplin was still around; the Little Tramp had just melded his signature Silent Era character with *der Führer*, but the humor to be found in the resultant *The Great Dictator* is, for the most part, still achieved mutely and via mime, and not dialog; still, the most memorable bit of verbiage is the barber's mind-blowing speech on democracy. Buster Keaton – the Great Stone Face – was reduced to a series of low-budget shorts over at Columbia when he wasn't limited to guest appearances in someone else's feature films. Pretty much ditto with the sad clown, Harry Langdon, who career – and life – came to an abrupt close following a cerebral hemorrhage a few days before Christmas in 1944. Laurel and Hardy were still making movies fairly regularly until mid-decade, but their heyday at the Roach Studios was behind them, and – again, for the most part – the pictures they made for Fox and/or M-G-M were but pale shadows of their '20s and '30s classics.

Ole Olsen and Chic Johnson had come into *their* own a couple of years before the '30s called it quits when their theatrical revue, *Hellzapoppin*, opened at New York's 46th Street Theater in September 1938 and was still on Broadway (albeit at the Winter Garden) 1400 performances later. Universal filmed the long-running hysteria in 1941, but – despite its title – the picture doesn't contain enough genre elements to be commented on herein (please *do* see our essay on O&J's *Ghost Catchers*). The Marx Brothers, too, had a couple of films in their future, but nothing as memorable as the men had conceived and executed a lustrum or so earlier. Harold Lloyd's *The Sin of Harold Diddlebock* (1947) was both the popular silent comic's only '40s onscreen role *and* his last film appearance anywhere. Those other brothers – the Ritzes – moved over to Universal in 1940, but their feature-film output likewise died on the vine with *Never a Dull Moment*, released a few days before Thanksgiving in 1943.

In 1940, W.C. Fields had a trio of masterpieces ahead of him (all for Universal) – *My Little Chickadee*, *The Bank Dick* (both 1940), and *Never Give a Sucker an Even Break* (1941) – before moving onto lesser titles, guest appearances, and – on Christmas Day, 1946 – passing away far too soon. Larry Semon, Fatty Arbuckle, and the lion's share of those men (and women) who had brought great relief during the Silent Era and the ongoing malaise of the Great Depression had likewise passed on to their reward. It wasn't until after VJ Day in 1945 that Ethelbert "Muggs" McGinnis and the rest of the East Side Kids morphed into Terence Aloysius "Slip" Mahoney and the Bowery Boys, with the whole *mishegas* taking on a more humorous slant. (The sudden shift in characters and interpretations was due to Sam Katzman refusing to double Gorcey's salary, which, in turn, led to Gorcey and his agent, Jan Grippo, forming their own production company; thus were the subsequent 40+ "Bowery Boys" programmers born.)

What with the vagaries of space and time and the changing needs and tastes of American audiences, what Universal hoped for – Heck! What *every* studio hoped for – was a comedy team or headliner who could consistently bring laughs (and revenue) back into the system during the war years and beyond. To cut to the chase, Bud Abbott and Lou Costello – late of Atlantic City's Steel Pier – were given their cinematic "try out" in support of Alan Jones, Nancy Kelly, and Robert Cummings in Universal's *One Night in the Tropics* (1940). Costello – who had had a decent number of movie uncredits during the Silent Era (including an appearance as an extra in Laurel and Hardy's *The Battle of the Century*, 1927) – had first met Bud Abbott at the outset of 1933 at Minsky's, where each was working with another partner. Within three years they had found each other professionally and the rest, as they say, is hysteria. The boys' subsequent vaudeville, Broadway, radio, and television successes are cataloged in any of dozens of books on the team (please see our bibliography for a few), as are the first two comedies – wartime paeans both – that saw them in the driver's seat: *Buck Privates* and *In the Navy* (both 1941). *Hold That Ghost* (also 1941) was the team's third "solo" effort, and it was followed that same year by *Keep 'Em Flying*, the boys' nod to the Army Air Corps. "Haunted House" comedies being one of the movies' most popular genres, making one in the midst (as it were) of their service films offered very little risk.

While that release order is, in fact, totally accurate, *Hold That Ghost* was technically the *second* A&C film, going into production after *Buck Privates*. Both the unexpected box-office success of that first effort, plus the enormous popularity of service films at the outset of the '40s (even *before* the bombing of Pearl Harbor), led the studio to put *Ghost* on hold while *In the Navy* was quickly planned and produced. This move led to *Ghost*'s being revised to include the Andrews Sisters and Ted Lewis along with an opening sequence that both tipped the cognoscenti to the film's denouement and led to some fairly peculiar narrative developments. More below.

Plot-wise, there's not much ink to spill. Having failed miserably as waiters at a swanky nightclub, gas jockeys Chuck and Ferdinand (Bud and Lou) inherit gangster Moose Matson's Forester's Club - a dive thought to be the final resting place of Moose's accrued loot - after it is found that they had unknowingly satisfied a very odd codicil in the gangster's will which leaves all of his property to whoever is with him when he died. They are later dropped off – and abandoned – at said dive together with gangster Charlie Smith, academic nerd Dr. Jackson, gorgeous Norma Lind, and radio "sound effect," Camille Brewster. The boys then participate in an hour or so's worth of timeless haunted-house shtick, during which Smith is killed by yet another gangster whilst searching for the Moose's money; his body is thereafter found hither, thither and yon in the club, and Ferdy finally finds the much-sought-after cash in – *naturalmente* – a moose head hanging on the wall. This is followed by a lengthy chase after which the gangsters who had likewise been hunting for the loot are made to flee the environs when Ferdy displays his own gift at sound effects: he imitates a police-car siren. All ends up grandly after Dr. Jackson determines that the "waters" in the vicinity are health-inducing, and – with Moose's ill-gotten gains wisely spent - Chuck and Ferdy end up as the owners of a spiffy spa/resort. (We do have to wonder, though, how Chuck and Ferdy were permitted to keep the "ill-gotten gains"; would not restitution be demanded by those who had been cheated/robbed?)

As with Abbott and Costello films in general, the best moments in *Hold That Ghost* are the routines that Bud and Lou had perfected since meeting providentially in the mid-'30s, and which were still brand-spankin' new to the majority of movie-ticket holders. Costello's character - prone to taking literally almost everything articulated, especially by Abbott's character – demonstrates humor based on an almost infantile lack-of-command of language rather than on clever word-play. This sort of thing diminished somewhat for a while as their feature-film canon grew and their classic routines (like the "moving candle") were used with greater frequency, only to return with a vengeance come the '50s and the diminution of the team's powers. Said routines also provided the pivots around which the team's early '50s TV series centered. The earliest of the '40s A&C films featured musical interludes - in the boys' first three films, courtesy of the Andrews Sisters – which segments would bid *adieu* come 1942's *Who*

*Done It*). Still, the most creative dimension to the screenplays was the deft with which the old vaudeville shtick was massaged to fit the latest thematic classification (service comedy, western parody, fantasy, etc.). Inasmuch as the team would gain fame as the quintessential mix of impatient straight-man and childlike comic, the machinations set in motion at the Forester's club – revolving scenery, self-moving candles, and so forth – were among the best Bud and Lou would encounter in their film careers.

The film was to have been entitled "Oh, Charlie," per Ron Palumbo (1) a nod to the earliest ancestor of, among other things, the "moving candle" bit, yclept "Over the River, Charlie." (It may be argued that the early title was also something of a reference to the proposed ubiquitous presence of gangster Charlie Smith's cadaver following his murder in the furnace room. In the original script, the sight of Charlie's body falling out of a closet leads to the final musical number; per Palumbo, the revised script had the corpse sitting upright in the paddy wagon. From "Oh, Charlie!" it's not a long walk to Costello's constantly yelling out "Oh, Chuck!" to Abbott and how that metamorphosed into the repeated cry of "Oh, Chick!" in their 1948 classic in which the boys were pitted against Dracula, Frankenstein's Monster, et al. In the aforementioned TV series, Costello's frequent cry for help would, of course, be "Hey, Abbott!") Also mildly amusing is the conceit that not a one of the sundry gangsters so frantically seeking out Moose's stash could make the connection between the deceased mobster's nickname and the revelation that he had indeed hidden his ill-gotten gains "in his head," while Ferdy's penchant for anal language skills has him spot-on in pointing out the trophy on the wall some time before he gets his hand stuck therein.

The musical elements of the picture – provided by Ted Lewis and the Andrews Sisters – were afterthoughts, shot after post-production on *In the Navy*, when the Powers-That-Were determined that the female trio's presence had added exponentially to the popularity of the boys' first starring film, *Buck Privates*. As quoted by Scott Allen Nollen, Patty Andrews recalled that "The producers got a lot of resentment that we were originally excluded. Then they called us in from New York, and they stuck us in at the end of *Hold That Ghost*."(2) To accommodate the sudden presence of the sisters and Mr. Lewis and his coterie, that pre-get-the-plot-moving sequence in which Chuck and Ferdy are briefly seen working as "relief waiters" in a nightclub was inserted (The *Los Angeles Times* found said opening addition *meh*: "Abbott and Costello have their first adventure as waiters... and that sequence is just fair, for it drags"), with yet another nightclub scene – this one with the boys as co-owners – tacked onto the end. 'Twas the last appearance by Patty, Maxene and LaVerne in an Abbott and Costello film, and the only opportunity the "High Hat Tragedian of Song" had to ask "Is everybody happy?" in similar circumstances. (It may just be me, but I've even less patience with Ted Lewis's brand of "singing" than I have with El Brendel's style of comedy.)

Once you're in the know regarding the addition of the pre- and post-sequences, the construct becomes as clear as bottled water. Costello's character actually all but announces the Andrews Sisters before they hit the screen, and he goes on to deliver on a platter the revelation that, come the last reel, the boys will own a swanky nightclub of their own. We're a bit at sea with respect to Chuck and Ferdy's leaving the gas-station industry to pursue the almighty buck as relief waiters, especially when – once that late-in-the-day "prelude" has come and gone – we discover that the boys apparently *own* the gas station, evidence of which may be seen on the back of Costello's overalls and the sign on which Abbott is chalking up the latest sale in gasoline ("8 gallons for $1.00"). With the two sequences – restaurant & gas station – back to back, though, the repetition of some of the humor - Ferdy's clueless persistence in foisting "soup" on Thurston Hall's uncredited character and then pulling the same routine but with "oil" on William Davidson's Moose Matson - grows tedious. Still, the bloom wasn't yet off the rose – comedy-shtick-wise – and the sundry verbal and physical routines sparkle in their novelty.

**The essence of the comic genius as presented in the film: Lou Costello "matching wits" with Joan Davis, as a bogus bogeyman adds the ersatz-supernatural tinge to the proceedings. Nota bene: The lobby card is publicizing an "Eagle Lion re-release of a Realart picture!" Nothing in the movie itself is weirder than that!**

133

The first of the boys' genre features, *Hold That Ghost* is yet another of the fake supernatural offerings that were so popular during the Silent Era. With the arrival of *The Time of Their Lives*, though, Abbott and Costello would deal with a genuine other-worldly theme, and the soon-after introduction of the first – and best – of the "...*Meet*..." series would speak volumes as to the growing demand for interaction between the movies' most acclaimed comedy team and authentic science fiction/ horror personalities. Nonetheless, while *Ghost* marked the first of Evelyn Ankers "horror" pictures, the film did *not* mark the Scream Queen's first appearance with a "famed" comedy team. That honor – the term "comedy team" is here strictly *pro forma* - goes to Universal's *Hit the Road*, which starred the Dead End Kids (hardly the comedic force they would be once Leo Gorcey et al left the studio and started their own production company) and was released a couple of months before *Ghost* finally saw a screen in local theaters everywhere. The Chilean-born actress would go on to brighten a passel of Universal's '40s genre flicks, and thus the lovely lady's presence therein will be commented on throughout the book.

Richard Carlson already had one protoplasmic adventure under his belt before joining the present company: the previous year he had joined forces with Bob Hope and Paulette Goddard – themselves reuniting after battling the supernatural in 1939's *The Cat and the Canary* – in *The Ghost Breakers*. Mayhaps because of his real-life academic pursuits – the Minnesota-born Carlson held a Masters Degree in English - in both *Ghost* epics, his character was a professor. If nothing else – God knows his Doctor Jackson isn't of much use in the more physically demanding part of the scenario – the soft-spoken academic does provide the *raison d'être* for the spa-cum-nightclub that wraps the feature. Carlson, of course, would make more memorable inroads into the genre come the '50s, wherein he and Universal would create some science fiction classics (*It Came from Outer Space*, 1953, and *The Creature from the Black Lagoon*, 1954), while some of the competition signed on the amiable actor for a few worthy efforts of their own: *The Magnetic Monster*, *The Maze* (both 1953), and *Riders to the Stars* (1954).

Comedienne Joan Davis (born – I kid you not – *Madonna* Davis, at least per IMDb.com) was the eponymous star of *I Married Joan*, an early '50s TV series that I adored during my youth and still remember fondly today. Prior to *Ghost*, the actress had lent her talent to a couple of dozen films- mostly "B's," albeit 1938's *Sally, Irene and Mary* remains quite memorable – and afterwards, she was a regular on Rudy Vallee's radio show before ultimately landing her own shows (*Joanie's Tea Room* and *Joan Davis Time*) and appearing elsewhere on the air. Davis's Camille is the perfect counterpart to Costello's Ferdie, and the "dance" the two perform is one of the film's funniest moments. (Scott Allen Nollen reveals that Costello felt he was being "upstaged" by the amount of laughter the comedienne's dance movements generated, and that may explain – at least partially – why Davis wasn't brought back for the new closing scene at the night club.)

Most of the film's second cast are contract players who can be spotted in dozens of productions – by Universal and other companies – throughout the late '30s and '40s. Shemp Howard, Thurston Hall, Marc Lawrence, Mischa Auer, et al had been around for at least a dozen years (Hall for over 30!) by the time *Ghost* went in front of the cameras, and each was a familiar and welcome face to moviegoers.

Samuel Horowitz – aka Shemp Howard, one of the original Three Stooges – was replaced in that team by his brother Jerry (Curly) in 1933 when Shemp struck out on his own; he would return to the fold following Curly's stroke in 1947. In addition to his appearing repeatedly with his brother Moe and Larry Fine, Shemp was also to be seen in support of Abbott & Costello in *Buck Privates*, *In the Navy*, *It Ain't Hay*, and *Africa Screams*; of Bill Fields in *The Bank Dick*; of Olsen and Johnson in both *Hellzapoppin'* & *Crazy House*; and even of The Andrews Sisters (1944's *Moonlight and Cactus*) – all at Universal! For the record, his Universal '40s genre roles were as "Frankie" in *The Invisible Woman* and - intriguingly – as "Detective Sgt. Sweeney" in *The Strange Case of Doctor Rx*. The tallest of The Three Stooges (at a towering 5'7"), Howard passed away in November 1955.

Mischa Auer made his Hollywood debut in 1928's *Something Always Happens*, a Paramount four-reeler featuring Esther Ralston, Neil Hamilton and Sojin. From that fairly inauspicious beginning, the "Mad Russian" would go on to madly gracing films both in the USA and throughout Europe, and the pictures of his that would interest us most include the sci-fi musical *Just Imagine* (1930), *The Monster Walks* and *Sinister Hands* (both 1932), *The House of a Thousand Candles* (1936), and *Cracked Nuts* (1941), although mainstream fans probably remember him best as Kolenkhov in 1938's *You Can't Take It With You*, which copped the Oscars for best picture and director (Frank Capra). Auer's Gregory appears in the opening scene as a haughty maître d' as well as in the closing sequence wherein he is seen as a waiter in Chuck and Ferdy's club, sent there by the same employment agency responsible for the boys work as "relief waiters" at the outset. Auer could play "haughty" with the best of them, and his presence in both sequences highlights the sundry reversals of fortunes.

"Walt," in the 30 July 1941 issue of *Variety*, found said sequences of varying worth: Post-production insertion of musical and song interludes by Ted Lewis and

135

the Andrews Sisters gets the picture away to a flying start, but the finale with the entertainers on again is nothing more than an anti-climax.

Still, the critic's final assessment was that "[the] picture is a slam-bang and knockout comedy, silly and ridiculous, but a laugh-creator and audience-pleaser."

*Film Daily*, bearing the same release date as *Variety*, also found the picture an unqualified winner:

> Following the formula of the former A&C hits, with the sure-fire locale of a haunted tavern, and a rapid succession of those old-new burlesque routines, HTG is a cinch to please all those theater patrons who have become rabid A&C fans in the past few months... A plausible story, with Richard Carlson, Joan Davis and Evelyn Ankers to give it the 'straight' touch, and probably more mechanical contrivances than have been used in a half-dozen thrillers, is a perfect vehicle for the boys.

The August 1941 issue of *American Cinematographer* quite understandably looked at the comedy from a technical point of view, even noting that John Valentine had replaced Woody Bredell during the shooting of the added nightclub footage:

> The greater part of the action takes place in a haunted house, with the inevitable effect-lightings such a locale would inspire. [Woody] Bredell handles these very artistically, yet so skillfully that no comedy action is lost because of his pictorial shadowing – a more than praiseworthy achievement.... Valentine's contributions are excellently pictorial, and again he does wonders with the by no means photogenic Andrews Sisters – even better, in fact, than he did in their previous appearance in 'In the Navy.'
>
> The print previewed seemed, even for low-key effect-lightings, a trifle darker than was altogether pleasing. This was particularly true in the opening and closing sequences, in which the face-values were distinctly poor. It would seem that – especially in those sequences – the release-prints could to advantage be lightened by one or even two printer-lights.

"Hanna," reviewer in the 9 August 1941 *Film Bulletin*, though, separated the wheat from the chaff, even while praising the end-product:

> It is all as tawdry and hackneyed as can be, the production is cheap

and even careless – but the public will laugh like hell at the antics of A&C. To give the film some 'production values,' Universal tacked on two musical sequences featuring Ted Lewis and the Andrews Sisters. They are totally unnecessary!... Arthur Lubin, who delivered the previous A&C hits, has done a magnificent job of direction. It is not often that gags are so well planted and that business is made to account for so much humor.

The first of their features that relegated the musical sequences to the frame and allowed the body of the film to center on Abbott and Costello's characters, *Hold That Ghost* is funny, focused (mostly), and the first of a half-dozen of the team's encounters with the supernatural, even if the ghosts and what-not herein are faux. The sundry genre bits – like the moving candle – would come back to highlight (and not to haunt) their future Universal comedy thrillers.

*Hold That Ghost* – 6 August 1941 – 85 minutes

*CAST*: Bud Abbott as Chuck Murray; Lou Costello as Ferdinand Jones; Richard Carlson as Doctor Jackson; Evelyn Ankers as Norma Lind; Joan Davis as Camille Brewster; Mischa Auer as Gregory; Marc Lawrence as Charlie Smith; Shemp Howard as the Soda Jerk; Russell Hicks as Bannister; William Davidson as Moose Matson; Milton Parsons as Harry Hoskins; Frank Penny as Snake-Eyes; Nestor Paiva as Glum; Edgar Dearing as Irondome; Don Terry as the Strangler; Paul Fix as Lefty; Edward Pawley as High Collar; Howard Hickman as the Judge; Harry Hayden as Mr. Jenkins; Thurston Hall as Alderman; Janet Shaw as Alderman's Date; William Forrest as State Trooper; Paul Newlan as Big Fink; Joe LaCava as Little Fink; Ted Lewis and His Orchestra as Themselves; The Andrews Sisters as Themselves

**CREDITS**: Director: Arthur Lubin; Screenplay: Robert Lees, Frederic I. Rinaldo, John Grant; Original Story: Robert Lees, Frederic I. Rinaldo; Associate Producers: Burt Kelly, Glenn Tryon; Director of Photography (main story): Elwood Bredell; Cinematographer (musical sequences): John Valentine; Art Director: Jack Otterson; Associate Art Director: Harold M. MacArthur; Film Editor: Philip Cahn; Sound Supervisor: Bernard B. Brown; Technician: William Fox; Musical Director: Hans J. Salter; Musical Numbers Staged by: Nick Castle; Set Decorations: R.A. Gausman; Gowns by: Vera West

*- JTS*

# *A Dangerous Game* (1941)

*Synopsis*: Anne, a nurse at the Fleming Sanitarium, is puzzled by the behavior of the two main staff, Dr. Fleming and Dr. Robin. They are both dominated by a patient, Silas Briggs, who has recently inherited $250,000 in insurance money after the death of his uncle. The doctors also keep another patient, Olaf Anderson, isolated and under heavy sedation.

Two criminals, Bugs and Joe, arrive at the asylum in search of the $250,000 and hold staff and patients hostage, but Briggs has already hidden the satchel of money in the chimney. Dick, another hoodlum, gets the drop on Bugs and Joe, but then the trio join forces to try to find the loot. Three other criminals, one of them in drag, arrive at the asylum pretending to be Silas' relatives, and all the factions vie for supremacy. In the course of all this back-and-forth, Dr. Robin drops dead – poisoned - and Dr. Fleming soon meets the same fate.

Dick reveals himself as a detective and deduces that Briggs killed both physicians after murdering the uncle. Briggs is an imposter who schemed with the doctors to collect the insurance money while Olaf Anderson, the real Briggs, was kept under sedation. Briggs used tiddlywinks to launch poison capsules into his victims' drinks. "Anderson" recovers sufficiently to throw "Briggs" to his death over the staircase railing. Andy, Dick's helper who has been posing as a male nurse in the asylum, has found the money, but a fan blows all the loose bills into the air, and the detectives use a vacuum cleaner to try to collect them.

No relation to the famous, nearly identically titled, and much filmed Richard McConnell short story, "The Most Dangerous Game," *A Dangerous Game* is hands down the worst film covered in this volume. It's basically a slapstick one-reeler tortured into feature length while remaining painfully unfunny, the sort of movie where you feel sorry for the actors who are trapped in it but who are doing their best in spite of hopeless odds.

*A Dangerous Game* was part of a series of 14 films made between 1939 and 1941 that co-starred Richard Arlen and Andy Devine. Arlen - stalwart, manly, and likable - did the heroics while the increasingly rotund Devine provided the intentional comedy. The series, which began with *Mutiny on the Blackhawk*, was built around whatever stock footage Universal had on hand; thus, *Mutiny* incorporated scenes from Universal's big-budgeted *Sutter's Gold* (1936) and the 1933 German epic, *The Rebel*. Thanks to the magic of rear projection and a seemingly inexhaustible supply of said stock footage, Arlen and Devine would find themselves as wildcatters, race drivers, steel workers, stuntmen, and adventurers of every description.(1) Ben Pivar produced all these epics, most of which were directed by either Christy Cabanne or John Rawlins.

*A Dangerous Game* doesn't really fit the pattern outlined above. There's no stock footage and only one primary set: the hall of the asylum with a large, winding staircase. (Devine slides down the banister a couple of times accompanied by goofy sound effects. Pretty hilarious, eh?) It's unclear why Pivar and company deviated from the established norm to this degree. In his indispensable tome, *B Movies*, Don Miller speculates that the film made have been inspired by Jonathan Lattimore's *Murder in the Madhouse*, wherein hard-drinking detective Bill Crane has himself committed to an asylum to solve a crime. Universal had already done three films based on Lattimore's detective as part of its "Crime Club" series: *The Westland Case* (1937), *The Lady in the Morgue,* and *The Last Warning* (both 1938).

Insane asylums as a setting for crime turn up every so often in thrillers. *Return of the Terror* (1934), for example, takes place in a mental institution, but - as in *A Dangerous Game* - its inmates are mostly harmless eccentrics who are played for laughs. Madmen are considerably more dangerous in *Behind Locked Doors* (1948), wherein Richard Carlson - a reporter who also commits himself in order to uncover a criminal - faces a murderous Tor Johnson and, in *Shock Corridor* (1963), journalist Peter Breck, on a similar errand, ends up going nuts himself. Nothing that dramatic happens in *A Dangerous Game* (though the viewer might feel his own mind slipping while enduring the endless chase after the satchel), but the two doctors turning out to be conspirators is pretty much in keeping with the growing '40s movie trend of viewing psychiatrists as sinister. Technically, the phony Briggs *is* crazy, but here his madness seems a mere cover for criminality. Other inmates at the Fleming Sanitarium include the elfin-faced Mr. Whipple and the love-starved Mrs. Hubbard, who has a

140

crush on Andy. Her reaction when she finds out he was only *pretending* to be a nurse provides a slightly off-color moment.

While many whodunits suffer from strained plot developments that don't stand up to scrutiny, *A Dangerous Game* doesn't even pretend to play fair. After Doc Robin is killed, Anne confesses that *she* did it, claiming that he stole the institution away from her father. Little note is taken of this outburst, and it is never referred to again! Though this is supposed to be a comedy thriller, there is little emphasis on the latter. Typical of the strained humor is the sequence wherein one of the crooks is strapped into Andy's corny Rube Goldberg-like lie-detector machine. His fibs cause a power blackout resulting in the aforementioned silly chase scene wherein one character emerges from a room, is pulled back inside by another who then exits, and is yanked inside by someone else who is promptly hauled back in by a different party and so on and on, *ad nauseam*. A cartoon would have been subtler (or at least shorter).

**Jean Brooks looks more like a traditional starlet than she did in her best film, *The 7th Victim*, wherein she sported a black Cleopatra wig that made her resemble Morticia from *The Addams Family*. Andy Devine, on the other, hand, is always recognizable as Andy Devine.**

The film's working title was initially *Who Killed Cock Robin?*, but that was quickly changed to *Who Killed Doc Robin?*(2) Editing on the film was completed in October of 1940, but it was not released in New York until March 1941. Universal no doubt realized it had a real stinker on its hands, especially after the terrible reviews came out. The 22 March 1941 edition of *Independent Exhibitors Film Bulletin* summed it up accurately:

> Hitting a new low for absurdity in a feature produce *A Dangerous Game* is, without a doubt, the weakest of the Arlen-Devine vehicles to date. Mere slapstick without being funny. Probably realizing that this wacky number will do much to wean away the Arlen-Devine following, Universal has set back the film's release date to August 22. A wiser move would be to shelve it permanently. The climax is a surprise-as well as a relief-to bored patrons. Director John Rawlins must have been looking the other way during filming.

Indeed, though filmed before the Arlen-Devine *Men of the Timberland, Mutiny in the Artic,* and *Raiders of the Desert, A Dangerous Game* was not released until after those three hit the theaters, thus becoming the swan song for the Arlen-Devine pastiches.

Other reviews were equally contemptuous:

> *A Dangerous Game* is murder. Intended as a comedy-thriller, it's neither comic nor thrilling. It is undoubtedly one of the most strenuous and absurd farce attempts in years. But for all its frantic, deafening slapstick, it remains stubbornly humorless. If there is such a thing as a Class D picture this is it. Juve audiences may laugh at it but anyone over the age of twelve will get the fidgets... What it's all about, no one will ever know. But there's endless rushing up and down until it finally sprawls flat on its embarrassed little puss. Apparently, all the minor character comics in Hollywood are in it. They don't look too happy about it. But then who would?
> Hobe, *Variety,* 5 March 1941

> Another in the series of so-called adventures teaming Richard Arlen and Andy Devine, the film is an out-and-out farce with little to recommend it other than double bill addicts in the lesser situation. It is

composed largely of slapstick excitement and rarely rises above that level. A satirical yarn poking fun at the eerie type of detective-murder mystery, the story lacks the touch of subtle cleverness which is a necessary ingredient for films of this kind.

Charles S. Arronson, *Motion Picture Daily*, 6 March 1941

There's not much to recommend in this farce. An attempt is made to strike a serious note, involving a murder mystery. But it is difficult for one to take it seriously, since much of the incidents are handled in a slapstick manner. One or two situations provoke laughter; aside from that, the action is tiresome, since noise and silliness have been substituted for real comedy.

*Harrison's Reports*, 15 March 1941

The Grey Lady's T.M.P. was equally unamused as he wrote in his 4 March 1941 review:

A crack brained murder mystery which falls to come off as either comedy or mystery. A labored piece of nonsense. *A Dangerous Game*, which has no less than four authors, is a cinematic nightmare that is always silly but never even passably funny.

The vacuum-cleaner finale may have been a last-minute addition, at least according to co-star Richard Arlen's comments in the 9 November 1940 issue of *Boxoffice*:

So the studio said they wanted to finish my picture 'A Dangerous Game.' They wanted to introduce a new scene in it. A vacuum cleaner catches my tie and chokes me to death! I spent the last night there on the floor with a floor cleaner on my neck, with sound effects… Eeeeek!

Arlen, of course, was not Hoovered to death but left Universal to do more "B"-movies at Pine-Thomas and Republic. Action films had been Arlen's bread-and-butter all his career. He developed a love of flying as a pilot in the Royal Canadian Air Force during the Great War, and this served him in good stead when he tested for a part in William Wellman's *Wings* in 1927. Wellman asked Arlen if he could act, and he replied "Not worth a damn." But he *could* fly, so Wellman guided him through a dramatic scene so effectively that Arlen was never even conscious that the camera was rolling. The results were satisfactory, and Arlen, whose career at Paramount had consisted of bits and small parts, became one of the three stars of the first film to garner an Academy Award. A very limited actor, he nonetheless projected a natural affability that - along with his athleticism - kept him in starring roles during his subsequent years at Paramount. Genre fans remember him best as Parker, the hero of *Island of Lost Souls*, although, as Philip K. Scheuer noted in his review of that film, the character "at times shows such indecision of thought and action that he appears not quite bright." Arlen was cast against type as the scientist who falls under the spell of an evil brain in *The Lady and the Monster* (1944), a loose adaptation of Curt Siodmak's novel, *Donovan's Brain*. To indicate the malice of his possessed character, Arlen scowls a lot and lets low-key lighting do the rest.

The late '40s saw the end of Arlen's career as a leading man, but he soldiered on in a variety of smaller roles in films ranging in quality from the excellent political drama *The Best Man* (1964) to the execrable *The Crawling Hand* (1963). In between films, he did lots of television work as well as summer stock.

Jean Brooks' career was less happy. Her portrayal of Jacqueline, the morbid and doomed sister of the heroine of Val Lewton's *The 7th Victim*, is memorable, but no particular notice was taken of her performance at the time. It should be recalled that while Lewton's films are revered nowadays, most of them were dismissed by contemporary critics (the *Los Angeles Times* reviewer Edwin Schallert wrote that *Cat People* was less engrossing than its co-feature *The Gorilla Man*!). Brooks, then working the name Jeanne Kelly, had been under contract to Universal, where she worked primarily in "B"-pictures. In addition to *A Dangerous Game*, she also appeared in another Arlen-Devine potboiler, *The Devil's Pipeline*. Possibilities looked up for Brooks when she signed at RKO where she played Kiki the vivacious, funny heroine in *The Leopard Man* and did several episodes of the Falcon series with Tom Conway, as well as *The 7th Victim*. Unfortunately, the actress shared some of Jacqueline's self-destructiveness and struggled with an alcohol problem that ultimately led to her death in 1963, many years after her movie career had fizzled and she had been forgotten. Film historians Doug McClelland and Greg Mank later stirred up some interest in Brooks. As far as her performance in *A Dangerous Game* goes, she comes off no better or worse than the rest of the cast.

Rudolph Anders (Dr. Fleming) gets to play his part straight and is professional enough not to look embarrassed by all the nonsense. Anders left Nazi Germany in the early '30s but, as tensions between the United States and Germany increased at the end of the decade, he temporarily used the name Robert O. Davis on stage and screen; he is so billed in *A Dangerous Game*. It made little difference; because he had a Teutonic accent, he was repeatedly cast as Nazis. In the '50s he turned up in a number of horror cheapies: he's the mad Nazi scientist who creates the *She Demons* (1958), he donates his eyes to the Monster in *Frankenstein 1970* (1958), and he's again a scientist (twice, in fact), having to deal with *The Phantom from Space* (1953) and *The Snow Creature* (1954). On the stage, he received good notices playing Anne Frank's father in a Palm Springs production of *The Diary of Anne Frank*.

Cinematographer Stanley Cortez was given little opportunity to demonstrate his talent in *A Dangerous Game* save for a shadowy tracking shot to the asylum that gets the film off to a promising start. The rest of the time his camera just watches - no doubt wearily - as the actors chase each other around the madhouse. As far as director John Rawlins goes, lower-berth features were pretty much his level of competence, though he was occasionally allowed to helm a couple of higher-budgeted Universal extravaganzas like *Sudan* (1945) and *Arabian Nights* (1942). There's coverage on Andy Devine in our essay on *That's the Spirit*.

While even a misfire like *Sh! The Octopus* has its following (and both of us fans know who we are), it's as hard now as it was in 1941 to find any love for *A Dangerous Game*.

*A Dangerous Game* - 22 August 1941 - 61 minutes (ST)

**CAST**: Richard Arlen as Dick; Andy Devine as Andy; Jean Brooks (as Jeanne Kelly) as Anne; Edward Brophy as Bugs; Marc Lawrence as Joe; Robert O. Davis as Dr. Fleming; Richard Carle as Aunt Agatha (aka "Moose Face" Hogan); Andrew Tombs as Silas; Tom Dugan as Clem; Vince Barnett as Ephraim; Robert O. Davis (Rudolph Anders) as Dr. Fleming; Mira McKinney as Mrs. Hubbard; Richard Kean as Whipple; Irving Mitchell as Dr. Robin; George Pembroke as Olaf Anderson.

**CREDITS**: Director: John Rawlins; Assistant Director: Charles Gould; Dialogue Director Maurice Wright; Producer: Ben Pivar; Original Story by Larry Rhine, Ben Chapman; Screenplay by Larry Rhine, Ben Chapman, Maxwell Shane; Cinematographer: Stanley Cortez; Art Directors: Jack Otterson, Harold MacArthur; Film Editor: Ray Curtiss; Set Director: Russell A. Gausman; Costumes: Vera West; Music: H.J. Salter; Sound: Bernard Brown

*Shock Theater* Catalog No. 698: "A missing fortune leads to murder in a sanitarium in

'A Dangerous Game,' the full-length feature film thriller presented on *Shock* over this channel (day), (date) at (time). Richard Arlen stars as the detective who has to solve the mystery. Andy Devine is his partner. Don't miss this tense mystery."

*- HN*

# *The Wolf Man* (1941)

Having rediscovered horror with *Son of Frankenstein* (1939), the newest owners of Universal were probably tickled to acquire a new horror star – and one with a familiar name as well (no matter how assumed) – who, as a contract player, was likely cheaper than either Karloff or Lugosi (though the latter was always to be had at bargain basement prices). Lon Chaney – the "Jr." having been dropped by the time of *The Wolf Man*(1) - had proved adequate as the title role in *Man-made monster* (1941), so the studio opted to take the first step in what would ultimately have him portraying their classic quartet of monsters. The character of the Wolf Man was ostensibly new, but the film built around him owed more to John Colton's script for Stuart Walker's *Werewolf of London* (1935) than some - including *Wolf Man*-scripter Curt Siodmak - would have cared to admit.

The story arc is certainly very similar. Larry Talbot (Chaney) returns to his small Welsh hometown (unnamed here – for that matter even references to Wales were omitted in the finished film – but designated Llanwelly in the sequel) following the death of his brother, John. He has been in the United States due to some never-explained estrangement with his father, Sir John (Claude Rains). This seems to be as much due to the Talbot inheritance tradition, where the eldest son gets everything, as to some discomfort between the two. Through his dad's telescope he spies Gwen Conliffe (Evelyn Ankers) in her bedroom and visits her in her father's (J. M. Kerrigan) antique shop, where he awkwardly tries putting the make on her before buying a cane with a silver head in the shape of a wolf and pentagram. The design prompts Gwen to utter the ancient couplet (invented by Siodmak),

"Even a man who is pure in heart and says his prayers by night /
May become a wolf when the wolfbane blooms and the autumn moon is bright."

Larry presses Gwen to walk with him after the shop closes; even though she turns him down she meets him that night, but invites her friend Jenny (Fay Helm) to accompany them. The trio ends up at a gypsy encampment and decides to have their fortunes told. Only Jenny gets a sit-down with Bela (Bela Lugosi) before he sees a pentagram appear in her hand and insists that she leave. She does, only to find herself pursued and attacked by a wolf, which Larry kills with his walking stick; Jenny, however, has died as a result of the attack. When Colonel Montford (Ralph Bellamy) and Dr, Lloyd (Warren William) investigate, they find the body of Bela, but no wolf. Larry insists he killed a wolf, but when he goes to show them the bite he got during the altercation, he discovers it has mysteriously healed completely overnight. More gypsies arrive to celebrate Bela's death (they believe he's gone on to a better place and so rejoice) and a sort of carnival is set up. Here Larry learns from Bela's mother, Maleva (Maria Ouspenskaya) that Bela was a werewolf and, having been bitten and survived, Larry is now one as well.

The notion that "werewolfery" – as Dr. Yogami had termed it almost a decade earlier – can be transferred from one infected person to another is but one idea lifted from *Werewolf of London*; it is not part of non-cinematic werewolf lore. Another parallel with the earlier picture is Talbot being bitten by a foreigner while visiting another country; Henry Hull's Wilfred Glendon had the same experience. The carnage of the '40s lycanthrope is less extensive than that of his predecessor, though: he claims a gravedigger on the night of his first transformation (played by the same actor – Tom Stevenson – who portrayed a grave*robber* in the next entry), gets caught in a bear trap (and is changed back to human form by Maleva) on his second, and is killed before he can savage Gwen on the third (or maybe still the second – the chronology is a tad unclear). Yes, Larry Talbot's trip home is of very brief duration.

*The Wolf Man* has always been more popular than the subtler and more complex *Werewolf of London* – at least with a certain demographic – and possibly for that very reason. There may however be deeper reasons, and they are probably not something the film's makers deliberately intended. Most of us horror fans – and let's be clear that we are a predominantly male group – discovered this film during our pubescent years. Despite his age, Larry Talbot is awkward with women; his pick-up lines are some of the lamest ever recorded on film. At one point, he tosses pebbles at Gwen's window to attract her attention – can any action more "teenager" be imagined? Then, too, he is suddenly plagued with overpowering urges and hair growing in previously glabrous areas; a more pointed allegory of puberty – when boys are experiencing body changes and spontaneous erections and are trying to figure out how to interact with the opposite sex – there never was. Possibly some of this was intentional. Talbot the younger always announces himself as Lawrence while his father and other refers to him with the diminutive Larry. And the otherwise apparently original score lifts the puppy-dog cue from *Man-made monster* when Larry takes to the telescope. And the phallic implications of that device scarcely need be commented on at... *errr*... length.

**Lon Chaney and Maria Ouspenskaya. The diminutive Russian actress was as comfortable around this Universal hellion as she was in more prestigious pictures, like *Love Affair* (1939) and *King's Row* (1942). The next time she and Lon the Lycanthrope would cross paths (*Frankenstein Meets the Wolf Man*, 1943), her mystic influence on the hirsute horror – and her screen time – would be substantially reduced.**

More intriguing to this writer is that, as David Skal points out in his requisite tome, **The Monster Show**, *The Wolf Man* – along with many Universal horrors of the 1940s - is really set in some "Neverland" where World War II is not going full tilt. Admittedly the picture's time period is not specific, much like James Whale's two Frankenstein films or, for that matter, any and all of the Frankenstein films that followed. The Llanwelly citizenry dress in 1940s attire and Larry is shown arriving in an automobile, a late '30s or early '40s model that is seen again when he and his father attend church. A somewhat earlier-vintage car is glimpsed through the aforementioned telescope (in what might be footage cribbed from an earlier film). Nevertheless, when he spies on the town and Gwen in her bedroom (a bit of voyeurism apparently less icky in 1941 than now... or is this another clue to his immaturity?), a horse and carriage can be seen traversing the street. Still, most everyone save the gypsy Maleva seems to walk everywhere – they must be an incredibly fit lot. No one uses a telephone (though one would appear in the sequel), and even though the action is set in the United Kingdom, there's not even a mention of the German bombardment of Britain or a suggestion that Larry's transoceanic crossing from the former colonies, whether by water or air, would have been perilous.

Yet, in an odd, subtextual way, the worldwide conflict is reflected. Consider that Larry is an émigré Brit who has made his life in the United States. He not only returns across the Pond for reasons not of his own making, but his curse is inflicted upon him by a foreigner who, in fact, is not even a native of the land Larry is visiting. Similarly, the United States was dragged into war – unexpectedly and somewhat against the will of its citizens – by the Japanese attack on Pearl Harbor. Now that may be a bit much to lay on the movie, considering it was written well in advance of that event, but it *was* released less than a week afterward, which might explain why it did so well at the box office. Audiences may not have realized why it resonated so, but the parallels are certainly there. Perhaps Siodmak was subconsciously prescient...? No, that's being too generous to the guy.

One measure of the film's box-office success may be seen in Universal's reviving the Larry Talbot character three more times before all "B"-programming was dropped by executive decision. *The Wolf Man* was also credited with inspiring RKO's *Cat People* (1942), although Val Lewton and Jacques Tourneur's treatment made ambiguous the question as to whether or not their lead character actually turned into an animal. (Ironically, according to Siodmak, that same ambiguity was the approach *he* had wanted for the picture that was to have originally been entitled *Destiny*.) And that same year, 20th Century Fox - a studio not much noted for its horrors - brought forth *The Undying Monster*, directed by the underrated John Brahm. There was no vagueness about lycanthropy therein; in fact, there's a nifty dissolve from werewolf to human at the end, with the character clinging to a cliff before plunging to his death. (So much for being "undying"...) The film even included its own "ancient" rhyme addressing lycanthropy.

And then there was a neat little opus yclept *The Return of the Vampire* hailing

150

from Columbia in 1943, directed by Lew Landers and written by frequent Universal scripter, Griffin Jay. That studio, valuing Lugosi as more than just a name on the poster, cast him as the titular Armand Tesla (Count Dracula in all but name) and gave him a werewolf lackey. A year later Columbia followed with *Cry of the Werewolf*, also scripted by Jay. Previously all but ignored on the silver screen, werewolves (and werethings) were suddenly legion.

The Wolf Man is a wholly original character, one of the few Universal monsters (along with the Mummy and the Creature from the Black Lagoon) that have no textual basis. There had been werewolf novels, such as Guy Endore's novel, **The Werewolf of Paris** (the studio acquired the movie rights back in 1935 as a precaution) and the penny dreadful, **Wagner the Werewolf**, but none of them served as the basis for *The Wolf Man*. Siodmak borrowed bits and pieces from old legends and elsewhere: most cultures have some version of the shape-shifter myth that has witches, warlocks or shamans transforming into animals, usually by donning their skins at any time they choose. As stated above, the idea of a werewolf bite infecting the recipient was lifted from *Werewolf of London*, as well as something of its "full moon" invention. In *The Wolf Man*, though, it's not clear that the moon triggers Bela's or Larry's transformation; the blooming of wolfbane gets more emphasis as a trigger. The doggerel's reference to "the autumn moon" suggests the metamorphosis is annual (significantly, during hunting season), rather than monthly, and there is not a single insert of the full moon in the cloudy night sky to be found in this picture. And as for werewolves being done in only by silver bullets (or knives or bludgeons), that is a wholly-Siodmak invention that the writer admitted he got from listening to radio broadcasts of *The Lone Ranger*. Still, this has not prevented it from making its way into nearly every werewolf film that has come along since (along with the full-moon connection that Universal liked so much that the studio incorporated it into their Kharis outings).

Last-minute revisions to Siodmak's script resulted in some intriguing moves: Initially, Larry – *not* slated to be played by Chaney, but rather by Dick Foran – was to be a visiting engineer come to repair Sir John's telescope. Other conceits are more puzzling, such as that protective charm that Maleva gives to Larry, which he promptly passes on to Gwen. One wonders why the old gypsy didn't give such an item to her own son; in any case it doesn't prevent Gwen from being attacked in the finale. And how, when Larry, in lupine form, gets caught in a bear-trap, is Maleva able to change him back to human form? Is she a gypsy, or a witch? (She *is* referred to as an "old witch" in the dialogue.) Also, one can't help but be a bit puzzled about Gwen's abrupt decision to abandon her fiancé (Patric Knowles) and run off with Larry. As the film

151

runs a brisk 70 minutes, these things are scarcely notable (save to us monster movie fans who watch these productions again and again), but for the most part, Siodmak's script can only be charitably termed serviceable. Nonetheless, Maleva's eulogy to her son…

> The way you walked was thorny through no fault of your own. But as the rain enters the soil, the river enters the sea, so tears run to a predestined end. Your suffering is over, Bela, my son. Now you will find peace.

…*is* poetry of the highest order. Siodmak must have realized he'd spun gold with this because he repeats it twice with minor variations (and diminishing results).

Other perplexities are probably not of Siodmak's doing. Why does Bela transform into a wolf – barely glimpsed, but clearly running on all fours – rather than the biped hybrid that Larry becomes? (Did Bela merely get a nibble rather than a full bite?) And also on the subject of his transmutation, why does Larry don – or acquire as part of the change – what appear to be garage-mechanic duds for his hirsute rampages? This might be the place to acknowledge the work of Universal's makeup maestro, Jack Pierce. The Wolf Man is one of his most iconic creations, even if some have compared the look as more akin to a wild boar than a wolf. Syndicated columnist Harrison Carroll paid a visit to the set on the day Rains and Chaney filmed their climactic battle and reported on it in the 24 November 1941 installment of his "Hollywood Behind the Scenes." Ever the prankster, Chaney came from Pierce's makeup labors and crept up on Carroll from behind, surprising the writer by applying claws to his neck. Carroll notes it took four hours to apply the hair, rubber snout and furry appendages, and reports that Chaney groused "… Dick Foran said… it would take even longer to make me look handsome."

The makeup, according to several sources, was revived from Pierce's planned look for Henry Hull in *Werewolf of London*, which was rejected by the actor. (Per his nephew Cortlandt, Hull argued that, as his Wilfred Glendon was recognized by other characters after the full moon had wrought its evil magic, the planned makeup was too extreme.) Possibly because of the swift shooting schedule, only Larry's feet are shown in the man-to-werewolf conversion (lap dissolves from hairy legs to furrier, wolf-ier boots), though we twice see him revert to human form. Was it easier and quicker to *remove* the makeup for the lap dissolves? Robin Coons, the film reviewer for a local (West Virginia) newspaper in the early '40s, tied this together somewhat:

That 'wolfman' face Jack Pierce has been creating for six years... has finally found a wearer. It's Lon Chaney Jr. in the picture *Destiny*. But George Waggner, the director, is approaching this tale of werewolfery with an emphasis on psychological aspects rather than on the old horror technique. You'll see Chaney as the wolf only three or four times, and then he'll be half-hidden in shadow. This may be the first concrete effect of the Spencer Tracy 'Jekyll and Hyde' which went Freudian instead of whole-hog horrific.

*Bluefield* [WV] *Daily Telegraph*, 7 December 1941

*The Washington Post* on the 23 November 1941 had a round-up on films about to play D.C. theaters that appears to be comprised of press-book photo cuts and one article, sans byline and therefore probably a product of the Universal publicity department. Only weeks before the film's opening, it is still referred to as *Destiny*, with the article entitled "Old Fashioned Wolves Featured in This Horror Film." It tries to have it both ways, initially stating that "Lycanthropy is a disease akin to schizophrenia which causes a person to believe he is a wolf," and then saying that Waggner's picture... "will attempt to prove that a man bitten by a werewolf becomes a werewolf." Yet later it reverts and states "... Lon Chaney, jr. [sic], imagines he is a wolf..." It closes asserting that "[Jack Pierce] makes Chaney look so much like a wolf that the real one Pierce used as a model slunk into the corner of his cage when he spied a broad shouldered wolf that spoke like a man and smoked cigarettes."

Hands up, everyone who believes Pierce kept a live wolf in his workshop while designing the film's monster makeup (especially considering Ellis Burman reportedly sculpted the snout, as well as the wolf and pentagram cane).

"Functional" is the best description of George Waggner's direction. The film's lavish, fairy-tale look owes more to its art direction and cinematography (and the makeup of course) - not to mention a thrilling score by Frank Skinner and Hans J. Salter, whose contribution goes uncredited – than to Waggner's talent. (Still, check out the visible ceilings in the Conliffe emporium; a possible influence of *Citizen Kane*?) To be fair, no matter its glossiness, the film - unlike most of the productions of the Laemmle era at Universal (the deliciously nutty 1935 *The Raven* being a major exception) – was never intended as more than a programmer. When Junior was head of production, the goal was the creation of quality, artistic horror pictures, although making a profit was certainly desired; however, under this latest regime at Big U, money was the prime consideration. We have found several, surely unintended subtexts (noted previously) in *The Wolf Man*, but they are nothing as compared to the deliberate ones running through *Werewolf of London*, wherein the evocation of Oscar Wilde's "The Ballad of Reading Gaol" – in which the British writer avers "Each man kills the thing he loves." – says much. And Chaney, while still an affable screen presence, is nowhere near as accomplished an actor as Henry Hull. He may be okay in the first part of the film, but he is not up to the demands of the latter portion, wherein his agony at the realization of his curse just comes across as overdone whining. Rains commands all their scenes together – hell, even Ankers does so – and Chaney's depiction of grief and anguish over Bela's coffin is just embarrassing. (Contrast this to Oliver Reed's depiction of torment in Terence Fisher's 1961 *The Curse of the Werewolf*.)

Universal may have imposed a tight "B" (well maybe "B+") budget of $180,000 and a relatively short shooting schedule on *The Wolf Man* (September 8 – November 25, 1942, per IMDb, but far shorter according to other sources), but it scarcely shows thanks to the company's extensive back lot and standing sets. Talbot Hall, the village streets and even the Conliffe establishment are all repurposed from earlier productions. Sets as old as The Court of Miracles and the titular cathedral from Chaney's father's 1923 *The Hunchback of Notre Dame* make return appearances. (Needless to say they also show up again and again in the films considered here.) The seemingly extensive forest was achieved by placing individual tree units on casters that were moved into various configurations (low-lying fog obscuring the wheels). Waggner's most interesting compositions (abetted by cinematographer Joseph Valentine) are to be found in the forest, though he also makes decent use of the Talbot-castle downstairs as well. The film boasts a cast lineup that is unrivaled by any other U horror of the decade (and arguably of any horror from any studio up till that time). The studio was so proud of it they revived a 1930s tradition of presenting them in the opening credits via clips from the film with their names superimposed. What can't be said is that the film itself makes very good use of them; Bellamy and Knowles in particular have roles that are barely there and could have been played by any Universal contract players. Their names on the poster helped build the impression this was a major production.

Aside from Chaney, the only actors with significant screen time are Claude Rains (borrowed from Warner Bros.) and Evelyn Ankers. Rains (1889-1967) made one silent film in 1920 before appearing (or, more precisely, *not* appearing) in arguably his most famous role, the title character of James Whale's *The Invisible Man* (1933). Though never considered a horror star thanks to a varied choice of roles, he nevertheless racked up a significant number of genre appearances. *The Man Who Reclaimed His Head* (1934) and *The Mystery of Edwin Drood* (1935) followed at Universal before he left the studio. *The Clairvoyant* (1935), co-starring Fay Wray, was made for Gainsborough in his home country of Britain. Thence, Rains didn't return to fantastic films until *Here Comes Mr. Jordan* (1941) and *The Wolf Man*, but these were followed by *Phantom of the Opera* (1943), Arch Oboler's *Strange Holiday* (1945), *Angel on My Shoulder* (1946), the horrendous remake of *The Lost World* (1960), and the poverty-stricken *Battle of the Worlds* (1961). Among the multitude of his television appearances are the TV movies *The Pied Piper of Hamelin* (1957) and *Shangri-La* (1960), in which he played the High Lama. Rains was highly regarded by his fellow actors, including Bette Davis, who could be very critical of her costars (her public comments on Miriam Hopkins and Joan Crawford are masterpieces of vitriol).

Evelyn Ankers (1918-1985) was the quintessential Universal scream queen of the '40s (though some might nominate Anne Gwynne) and a better actress than is usually acknowledged. Her earliest film appearances were uncredited bits in Alexander Korda productions. With the war in Europe and the bombing of Britain escalating, she relocated to the U.S. and snagged a contract with Universal. Her first role there was in the Abbot and Costello feature, *Hold That Ghost* (1941), quickly followed by *The Wolf Man*. After that came roles in *The Ghost of Frankenstein* (1942), *Captive Wild Woman*, *The Mad Ghoul*, *Son of Dracula* (all 1943), *Weird Woman*, *Jungle Woman*, *The Invisible Man's Revenge* (all 1944) and *The Frozen Ghost* (1945). She also appeared in two Sherlock Holmes entries, *Sherlock Holmes and the Voice of Terror* (1942) and *The Pearl of Death* (1944). When Big U ditched "B"-films, she left the studio to freelance at 20th Century Fox, Columbia, and even lowly PRC. Married to "B"-movie stud-muffin Richard Denning (who became a staple of Universal's genre productions in the 1950s) in 1942, Ankers was mostly employed in TV in the 50s until her retirement in 1958. She made one last feature appearance two years later in Denning's *No Greater Love* before hanging it up completely. When her hubby had an ongoing role as the governor on *Hawaii 5-0*, she was invited to play his wife, but she declined. (For more on Ankers, see the entry on *The Mad Ghoul*.)

Warren William (1894-1948) was a dependable leading man at Warner Bros., particularly in the pre-code era when he often gave the impression he thought he was John Barrymore. He portrayed Perry Mason in a quartet of screwball adaptations of Erle Stanley Gardner's lawyer-sleuth mysteries. Both Philo Vance (once) and The Lone Wolf (multiple times) were amongst his other detective portrayals. *The Wolf Man* was William's only pure genre credit, but he did make *Strange Illusion* for director Edgar G. Ulmer in 1945; this oddball, modern-dress rethinking of *Hamlet* needs to be seen to be disbelieved.

Known primarily as the perpetual guy-who-doesn't-get-the-gal (at least until he played Franklin Delano Roosevelt), Ralph Bellamy (1904-1991) also made relatively few genre features: *The Ghost of Frankenstein* (1942), where he *did* get the girl, was his only other U-horror. Television would increasingly dominate his resume, beginning in 1949 with the leading role in the long-running series, *Man Against Crime*. *Sunrise at Campobello* (1960) – wherein he reprised the role he played on the Broadway stage – offered his only return to the big screen until 1968, when he appeared as the duplicitous doctor in Roman Polanski's *Rosemary's Baby*. Of possible genre qualification are *Oh, God!* (1977) and *Amazon Women of the Moon* (1987) which interspersed his very busy TV schedule (hell, he even did a *Love Boat!*). His most prestigious work in his final years was to reprise his FDR impersonation in Dan Curtis' two mammoth mini-series *The Winds of War* and *War and Remembrance* (1983 and 1988-89). Bellamy was so well regarded by his peers he was awarded an Honorary Oscar in 1987 "for his contributions to the acting profession."

A rather curious poster of the reissue which seems to be advertising the film as a psycho pic rather than a horror movie. Note bats and a gallows in the framed picture.

156

Late of M-G-M and Warner Bros. - where he partnered with drinking buddy Errol Flynn on a couple films, most famously, 1938's *The Adventures of Robin Hood* - Patric Knowles (1911-1995) also lost his genre cherry on *The Wolf Man*. His other genre credits while a Universal contractee would include *The Strange Case of Dr. Rx*, *Mystery of Marie Roget* (both 1942) and *Frankenstein Meets the Wolf Man* (1943), all of which offered him significantly meatier roles. Never quite an "A"-lister, he too would increasingly turn to television after the 1940s. There would be a few major features interspersed, including *Auntie Mame* (1958), but his only other genre credits are *From the Earth to the Moon* (also 1958) and the back-to-back-made cheapies, *Terror in the Wax Museum* and *Arnold* (both 1973), which were his final credits out of well over 100 screen appearances. Perhaps equally impressive - given the Hollywood marriage-go-round - was that Knowles was married to his wife, the former Enid Percival, for 60 years (from 1935 until his death).

There is only a handful of genre credits in the relatively short Hollywood career of Maria Ouspenskaya (1876-1949), and two of them were in werewolf films. After *The Wolf Man* she made *Mystery of Marie Roget* (1942), repeated her role as Maleva in *Frankenstein Meets the Wolf Man* (1943), and thesped against a guy in a loin cloth in *Tarzan and the Amazons* (1945). Formerly of the Moscow Art Theatre and a devotee of the Stanislavski "method" approach, she augmented her supporting roles in a slew of memorable "A" productions (and several "B"s) with coaching others in the craft of acting; it was to fund her school that she began making Hollywood films, beginning with *Dodsworth* (1936). She was reputed to have been a devotee of astrology, which dictated when she would appear before cameras, driving crews and casts nuts. It is said she was intensely disliked – her imperious demeanor left no doubt she thought any film work was slumming – but no one can deny her impressive screen portrayals and her dominating presence.

Still another newcomer to genre, Fay Helm (1909-2003) started out at Paramount where independent producer Budd Schulberg was grooming her for stardom until his mistress, Sylvia Sydney, saw her as too much of a rival and kiboshed the plan. She had several prominent supporting roles, including an ongoing role in Columbia's "Blondie" series, before landing at Universal where she was cast in several of their horror movies. Roles in *Night Monster* (1942), *Captive Wild Woman*, and *Calling Dr. Death* followed. (She also contributed a notable cameo to Robert Siodmak's underrated 1944 *noir*, *Phantom Lady*.) Helm's only other nigh-genre credit is *One Body Too Many* (1944). Frustrated by her inability to rise to leading-player status, she left films in 1946 to concentrate on her family. Her many remarkable performances make this a great pity.

The only genre regular in the cast is Bela Lugosi (1882-1956), whose film career had been iffy almost from its beginning. By the time of *The Wolf Man*, he had signed a non-exclusive contract with Universal that began with *Black Friday* (1940) and which allowed him to sign another multi-picture deal, with the notorious Sam Katzman, whose threadbare productions would be released through the Poverty Row studio, Monogram Pictures. One can only speculate if this latter arrangement provided little inducement to give Lugosi roles of any significant meat or screen time at Universal, save for his reprisal of Ygor in *The Ghost of Frankenstein* (1942). Even his signature role of Count Dracula was passed on to Chaney and John Carradine (assuming one accepts the theory that the characters they essayed were really Count Dracula – but more on that in the article on *House of Frankenstein*). His genre credits are likely too well known to need listing here; the shameful waste Universal made of his talent is in evidence throughout this book.

"And Lon Chaney" is how the actor was billed in many of his Universal films (including this one) and so it is that we finally get to the performer portraying the titular character. With *The Wolf Man*, Chaney began his run of playing all the Universal star monsters (though he would play only Talbot's alter-ego and the Mummy more than once). While his career is covered in detail in the essay on *Man-made monster*, we should note here that he again played a werewolf – or more accurately a mummy that comes to life and becomes a werewolf – in the 1959 Mexican film *La casa del terror* and again in the 1962 Halloween episode of *Route 66*, "Lizard's Leg and Owlet's Wing." (The latter also featured Boris Karloff in a poorly simplified version of his Frankenstein Monster makeup.) And of course Chaney got to play his "baby" in three serious sequels, *Frankenstein Meets the Wolf Man* (1943), *House of Frankenstein* (1944), and *House of Dracula* (1945) before the initial Abbott and Costello horror send-up that ended the career of Lawrence Talbot.

Producer/director George Waggner is likewise dealt with in *Man-made monster*, while scenarist Curt Siodmak receives attention in the article on *Black Friday*. *The Wolf Man*, just like all other Universal horrors, makes use of the studio's roster of contract players for minor roles and walk-ons; look fast and Gibson Gowland, Olaf Hytten, Harry Cording, Doris Lloyd, and (yes!) Ottola Nesmith can be glimpsed as the film unreels.

Reviews at the time were not always positive.

> Perhaps in deference to its Grade-B budget it has tried m to make
> a little go a long way, and it has concealed most of that little in a deep

layer of fog. And out of that fog, from time to time, Lon Chaney Jr. appears vaguely, bays hungrily and skis back into mufti. Offhand, though we never did get a really good look, we'd say that most of the budget was spent on Mr. Chaney's face... nobody is going to go on believing in werewolves... if the custodians of these legends don't tell them with a more convincing imaginative touch. And that is precisely where the wolf man is left without a paw to stand on; without any build-up by the scriptwriter or the director, he is sent onstage, where he looks a lot less terrifying and not nearly as funny as Mr. Disney's big bad wolf.

T. S., *The New York Times*, 22 December 1941

... a first-class example of spook-spoofing... Young Lon is still no great shakes as an actor, but if it comes to that, neither was Chaney, Sr... However the son does have the quality of sincerity... When he is bitten on the chest by a vicious wolf... he is as good as marked for the select and infamous company of Count Dracula, Bela Lugosi, et al. Indeed, it speedily turns out the wolf which bit him WAS Bela Lugosi. You can't top that for a piece of hard luck... Production is on the artistic side, the story being developed slowly but carefully and with an eye to logic.

Philip K. Scheuer, *Los Angeles Times*, 24 January 1942

About the only things "The Wolf Man" will do will make you wonder how a good cast, headed by Claude Rains and Maria Ouspenskaya, could be hurled into such a mess; how any money at all could be wasted on so impossible a script. In other word "The Wolf Man" is terrific, and we don't mean good.

Richard L. Coe, *The Washington Post*, 9 March 1942

Contemporary takes on the film are kinder; it has a 94% positive rating on Rotten Tomatoes, which site features the following breakout quotes:

*The Wolf Man* serves its horror straight. A very substantial cast undertakes to sell believably a tale of superstitious folklore.

Anonymous, *The Hollywood Reporter*, 7 April 2015

159

*The Wolf Man* is a compactly-knit tale of its kind, with good direction
and performances by an above par assemblage of players...
Anonymous, *Variety*, 8 October 2008

A stodgy Universal thriller from 1941, redeemed by a name-heavy
cast and by Lon Chaney Jr.'s lumbering, affable performance in the title
role.
Dave Kehr, *Chicago Reader*, 8 October 2008

This Universal classic not only established Lon Chaney Jr as a horror
star but also instigated most of the cinematic werewolf lore concerning
pentagrams, the Moon and the fatality of silver.
Alan Jones, *Radio Times*, 6 October 2013

*The Wolf Man* – 12 December 1941 – 70 minutes (ST)

**CAST**: Claude Rains as Sir John Talbot; Lon Chaney, Jr. as Lawrence Talbot/The
Wolf Man; Warren William as Dr, Lloyd; Ralph Bellamy as Captain Paul Montford;
Patric Knowles as Frank Andrews; Maria Ouspenskaya as Maleva; Bela Lugosi
as Bela; Evelyn Ankers as Gwen Conliffe; Fay Helm as Jenny Williams; Leyland
Hodgson as Kendall; Forrester Harvey as Victor Twiddle; J.M. Kerrigan as Charles
Conliffe; Doris Lloyd as Mrs. Williams; Olaf Hytten as Villager; Harry Stubbs as
Reverend Norman; Tom Stevenson as Richardson; Eric Wilton as Chauffeur; Harry
Cording as Wykes; Ernie Stanton as Phillips; Ottola Nesmith as Mrs. Bally; Connie
Leon as Mrs. Wykes; La Riana as Gypsy Dancer; with Carolyn Cooke, Margaret
Fealy, Jessie Arnold, Eddie Polo, Gibson Gowland.

**CREDITS**: Producer and Director: George Waggner; Original Screenplay: Curt
Siodmak; Director of Photography: Joseph Valentine; Special Effects: John P. Fulton;
Art Director: Jack Otterson; Associate Art Director: Robert Boyle; Film Editor: Ted
Kent; Musical Director: Charles Previn; Music: Hans J. Salter and Frank Skinner;
Assistant Director: Vernon Keays; Set Decorator: Russell A. Gausman; Director of
Sound: Bernard B. Brown; Technician: Joe Lapis;
Make-up: Jack P. Pierce; Gowns: Vera West

**Shock Theater** Catalog No. 744: "A night monster... prowling, killing, terrifying a countryside... Don't miss the Hollywood *Shock* dramatic feature-length sensation 'The Wolf Man' starring Lon Chaney and Ralph Bellamy on this channel (day) at (time)."

*- HHL*

# *Sealed Lips* (1942)

*Synopsis*: New York gangster Mike Rofano is nearing the end of a four-year prison sentence in California. When Rofano doesn't retaliate for an unsuccessful attempt on his life in the penitentiary mess hall, state investigator Gary Benson calls in his crack agent Lee Davis to express his growing doubts that it really is Rofano they have behind bars. The hitherto murderous criminal has become an expert gardener ('The only thing Mike Rofano ever planted is his rivals," cracks Benson) and an authority on flowers. Davis thinks his boss has lost his mind but visits Rofano in prison. The prisoner's mild and retiring manner is something of a surprise, but Davis is not convinced he isn't the notorious tough guy, especially as the prisoner's fingerprints match the only ones on record as being Rofano's. Nevertheless, Davis heads for New York to further investigate. Benson warns him that this must be done secretly as he fears adverse publicity if it becomes known the authorities were duped.

In the Big Apple, two thugs attempt to push Davis in front of an oncoming subway train, but it goes wrong and one of the crooks falls on the tracks instead. It's only much later that Davis realizes that he was the intended victim. Davis is assisted by "Lips" Haggarty, a deaf policeman who's an expert lip reader, and Lori, a reporter who senses something's up and doesn't buy Davis' story that he's just a writer looking for material. Davis promises her a big scoop if she keeps quiet.

Davis' investigation begins gathering steam and he discovers that the only time Rofano was fingerprinted was when he applied for a gun permit, an act suspicious in itself. Davis also learns that a man named Fred Morton was a dead ringer for Rofano and was nearly taken for a fatal ride by Rofano's enemies. However, Morton was later burned to death in a house fire so terrible that his remains could only be recognized by dental records.

Posing as an insurance agent, Davis visits Morton's mother and his wife, Mary. Mary seems a little nervous when he starts asking questions, but the mother is quite chatty and even shows Davis a botany book her son was writing. She lends him the book, and it is subsequently discovered that the prints on the book match those of the prisoner who is supposedly Rofano. The prints also match the gun-permit applicant.

Davis decides to visit Morton's dentist, Dr. Evans, and pretend to be a patient. He is surprised to find that Mary works there as a receptionist. Sitting in the dental chair, Davis is overpowered by Rofano's thugs and given a hefty dose of gas by Dr. Evans. Davis is taken to Rofano's hideout in the country, but Lori and the police are not far behind. Davis meets the real Rofano, and the whole plot is slowly revealed. Morton agreed to act as Davis' double in New York and apply for the gun permit. However, when Morton realized he was being used as an alibi to cover up murders, he balked. Rofano, seeking to escape increased police scrutiny in New York, decided to plead guilty to a minor charge in California. Morton agreed to take his place in prison on condition that he and his family would not be harmed and would be given new lives after the four years were up. At the house where he is being held, Davis tries to convince Mary that there's no way Rofano will let them live after her husband's release. Mary is too terrified to defy the gangster.

Rofano intends to fly by private plane to California to await Morton's imminent release and take his place and then attend a big coming-home party in New York. However, the police raid the house and free Davis who, with Lips and Lori, beat Rofano to the airport. Davis and Lips fly with Rofano and deliver him to the prison warden who is delighted to be able to issue the gangster a prison uniform and shave his beard.

However, the authorities are in a quandary. Breaking the news to the press would be bad enough, but they might not be able to hold Rofano or send him back to New York, as his lawyers will argue he was never actually convicted of anything since it was Morton at his trial. Morton admits that he doubled for Rofano while the gangster was eliminating a rival. Since he's willing to testify to that, Davis and Benson decide they will let Rofano return on his own to New York where he will be surprised to find himself indicted for murder. Rofano leaves the prison and is picked up by his men who think he's actually Morton despite his protests to the contrary. He is then taken for a final ride by his own thugs.

The authorities are saved from admitting their mistake and Davis placates Lori for her loss of a big scoop by proposing marriage.

Years ago, on the snowy streets of my hometown of Syracuse, numerous friends and acquaintances of mine told me they had spotted someone on the street who very much resembled me. My own cousin went up to speak to him and then realized her mistake. This went on for quite awhile though eventually the sightings ceased. I never got to lay eyes on the man myself, but perhaps it's just as well, as meeting your doppelganger is supposed to be a fatal encounter.

The notion that someone could have an exact double has intrigued any number of famous literary minds. We have Mark Twain's **The Prince and the Pauper,** Alexandre Dumas's **The Man in the Iron Mask,** Charles Dickens's **A Tale of Two Cities,** and Wilkie Collins's **The Woman in White,** to name just a few. An element of realism was added with Hitchcock's *The Wrong Man*, with the real culprit *resembling* Henry Fonda's innocent man enough to confuse eyewitnesses without his being a perfect match. In horror literature you have the sinister double who makes life miserable for his other self in tales like "William Wilson" and "The Student of Prague."

In the Silent Era, a direct biological link was added to the mix with numerous films dealing with twins, one good, the other often not. Such plots became very stale and died out in the Sound Era, although there was the occasional exception like Bette Davis's 1946 *A Stolen Life* (Davis later went back to the twin-sister shtick in 1964's *Dead Ringer*) and Karloff's *The Black Room* (1935). A more complex variation on this theme could be found in 1988's *Dead Ringers*.

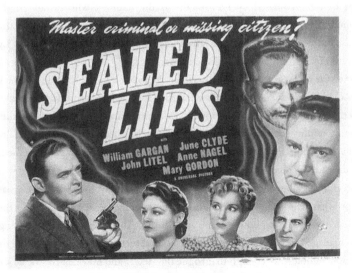

**Actually, John Litel plays 'em both.**

In connection with the release of *Sealed Lips*, Universal's publicity department released the following:

> Did Al Capone ever serve a sentence on Alcatraz or was the prisoner on the Rock an imposter? Long before the government obtained a conviction against Capone, the rumor was that the original Capone was dead, and that a double was taking his place.

Heaven only knows where Universal came up with this one. Presumably the double must have been a master of make-up as well in order to reproduce Capone's facial scars. And what exactly would be the point of someone willing to do time for a criminal who was already dead? No doubt it was the real Scarface in the brutal and dangerous Alcatraz, where he was nearly killed by a fellow prisoner, not in the mess hall, but rather in the shower.

Presumably, Mike Rofano is based to some degree on Capone, though less so than *Scarface*. John Litel's Rofano doesn't have the goombah accent or crudity of Paul Muni's gangster chief, but his flamboyance is no doubt meant to recall the celebrity status of Chicago's favorite bootlegger. Perhaps perversely, Litel makes the gangster almost likable, whereas his Morton comes off as stiff and mopey, a spineless fall guy. Litel, a veteran stage actor, was part of Warner's stock company in the '30s and is perhaps best remembered by horror fans as the scientist who brings child-killer Humphrey Bogart back to life in *The Return of Dr. X*. He played a wide variety of dramatic and comedic parts in the '40s and had a recurrent role as Jimmy Lydon's exasperated father in the Henry Aldrich series.

One year after *Sealed Lips*, Universal would go back to the "double" theme in *The Strange Death of Adolf Hitler*, wherein a hapless German bureaucrat (Ludwig Donath) is forced by the Gestapo to impersonate *der Führer*. *Strange Death* takes a different approach to telling the story than does *Sealed Lips* by making it the double's tale right from the first, though the ending is similar, with the "wrong" man getting killed. *Lips'* writer-director George Waggner could have done something akin to that with the Morton character, but instead presents his film as a kind of mystery. There's really no doubt as what it is going on; clips during the opening credits introducing the cast show that Litel is playing both Rofano and Morton. The real puzzle is unraveling how Rofano managed to pull all this off. The twists and turns of these revelations - though not always credible - are enough to intrigue the viewer and make up for the lack of the action one expects from gangster melodramas and George Waggner.

Stanley Cortez's photography - with a frequent use of Venetian-blind shadows (and their suggestion of bars) - captures the eye when the film threatens to get bogged down with too much gab. It's not clear what the title is supposed to mean or to whom it might refer: while Morton's lips *are* sealed, we also have a character named Lips (played by Ralf Harolde, for once on the right side of the law). A lip-reading, deaf detective is an unusual touch, though Lips' skills don't play a great part in the action. At one point he reads the lips of Rofano's crooked lawyer (played by that bane of widows and orphans, Charles Lane) while the shyster is in a phone booth. Later, when the police surround the house where Davis is being held, Lips uses a pair of binoculars to read Davis who illuminates his face with a flashlight. This scarcely seems necessary, as the police are going to raid the joint anyway; nonetheless, only a very few films where lip-reading plays any part at all (like *White Heat*) come to mind.

Other nontraditional touches - noted by at least one critic – give to the audience cops who *aren't* portrayed as dim-witted, clueless flatfoots, and the girl reporter who *doesn't* solve the mystery (although she does help out). The *pro forma* romance between detective and reporter is brisk and painless and doesn't slow down the story. Still another offbeat element is a villainous *dentist* (played by Russell Hicks): unique, I think, in vintage films. The scene where William Gargan is rendered unconscious by gas in the dentist's chair hardly ranks with the excruciating encounter between Dustin Hoffmann and Laurence Olivier in *Marathon* Man, but was likely a Hollywood first.

George Waggner was quite the multi-talented man, starting his career as a stunt rider and actor (an uncredited bit in 1932's *The Sign of the Cross* was his last film as a thesp), but later switching to songwriting ("Mary Lou, Mary Lou, Cross My Heart, I Love You") and scripting in the Sound Era. He did the music and story for 1933's *The Sweetheart of Sigma Chi* before embarking on a busy period of directing and writing, usually Westerns and action films. His sojourn at Universal during the '40s – when he directed, wrote, and produced - was likely his happiest period professionally. Critic Philip Scheuer was in awe of him:

> At the studio his pictures occupy a unique position somewhere between those juke-box 'soundies' and the top 'A's.' In fact one producer confided to me that Waggner's output spells the difference between 'an ordinary year and a successful one.' I myself have observed that he can take a 30-day potboiler, western, horror or whatnot and turn out a good solid job, endowing even the wildest action with a certain slick plausibility."

*Los Angeles Times*, 18 October 1942

Scheuer also noted that Waggner had kept "an inherited Irish sense of humor." The latter was on display when he was asked why *The Wolf Man*, which had a much more stellar cast than the typical Universal, had been tentatively titled *Destiny*, to which Waggner responded: "We had to tag the script *Destiny* to get actors to read it - actors who wouldn't take a look at one called *Wolf Man*."

**William Gargan is in for more than a check-up from dentist Russell Hicks and his gangster boss, Mike Rufano (John Litel), as Anne Nagel and two thugs look on. In George Waggner's *Man-made monster*, Hicks plays the warden who's zapped by Lon Chaney.**

William Gargan (Davis) was the perfect "B"-movie hero; stalwart, intelligent, good-looking and with plenty of blarney (but not so much as to become obnoxious, which was often the case with James Dunn). Gargan actually had some experience as a detective, though he was no threat to Sam Spade:

> I had a job once as an investigator. I was hired by a credit firm to trace 'skips' – debtors who disappear without paying their bills. Well, I once followed a man all over the state of New York - spent a lot of the firm's money and finally ran him to earth in a suburb of Albany. Then I wired the firm. I expected a raise - but I got fired, for I had been trailing the wrong man!
>
> *Hartford Daily Courant*, 3 March 1942

168

Though Gargan's movies were mostly lower tier, he did the occasional "A" like *I Wake Up Screaming*, the notorious *The Story of Temple Drake*, and *They Knew What They Wanted* (for which he received an Academy Award nomination as Best Supporting Actor.)

June Clyde, recently returned to Hollywood after some success on the stage in England, is fast-talking and funny as the intrepid girl reporter. Anne Nagel's portrayal of Mary Morton initially seems a bit ambiguous, and I half expected her to turn out to be on the Dark Side, but in the end, she's just a frightened but devoted spouse. Addison Richards (Benson) delivers his usual high-decibel performance.

Reviewers thought the film delivered the second-feature goods:

> Engrossing in its own right... If things sometimes move a little too quickly, if one or two parts are left out when the mechanism is put together again, one shouldn't complain. The cast wins it 'B' letter easily.
>
> S.L.S. *The Philadelphia Inquirer*, 29 January 1942

> A top flight supporting film that should please any type of audience. It's a fast-moving detective yarn with a swell story twist and holds one's interest from beginning to end. William Gargan turns in an outstanding performance as the sleuth aided by some nice work by June Clyde, John Litel, Anne Nagel and Ralf Harolde. George Waggner, serving as writer and director, delivers in an expert manner in both departments.
>
> *Showman's Trade Review*, 6 December 1941

The Bible of Show Biz concurred:

> *Sealed Lips* is a compact and entertaining B programmer that injects some fresh angles to the cop-chasing gangster formula. It's good meller entertainment to groove as above par supporter in the duals. Director-writer George Waggner swings his tale along at a consistently breezy pace in both departments, with sufficient touches of romance and excitement to hold interest. William Gargan clicks as the sleuth.
>
> *Variety*, 8 December 1941

Nonetheless, columnist Jimmy Fiedler, writing in the 2 December 1941 edition of the *Los Angeles Times*, was not impressed: "Gangland mystery that is neither too mysterious nor good." Still, it wowed an exhibitor in Marengo, Indiana:

"Excellent prison picture, fast moving, snappy dialogue, all together making up good entertainment. This picture had a great deal more entertainment than some of the big ones."

"Mae Tinee," writing for the 14 February 1942 edition of *The Chicago Tribune*, described the film as "a grim little gangster melodrama" that would please "folks who like this type of movie."

If "Mae" had attended the movie some ten days later, she might have had something else to write about. On February 24, audiences in a packed theater in the Loop were enjoying a double bill of *Sealed Lips* and *Hellzapoppin'*. The former film had barely begun when a shot and a scream were heard from the balcony. Most of the people who heard the noise assumed it was some sort of gimmick in the spirit of *Hellzapoppin'*. But it wasn't; a teenage girl had just been shot dead by her jealous boyfriend. The police surrounded the theater, but the manager did not want them to enter for fear of causing a panic among the 1000 or so patrons in attendance. They had an eyewitness description of the killer, so police simply waited for him to emerge. Incredibly, they allowed people to continue to go into the theater, including some who came not for the movie, but rather because of the rumor someone had been shot. At midnight, the police ran out of patience and entered the theater but, not surprisingly, the killer was long gone. The murderous boyfriend, having fled the picture palace, went on to attend another double feature, Hitchcock's *Suspicion* (appropriately enough) and *The Chocolate Soldier*. He was caught the next day and said he timed the shooting to coincide with the noisy mess-hall fight in *Sealed Lips*.

The perils of movie-going. And perhaps of seeing too many movies.

*Sealed Lips* - 2 January 1942 - 62 minutes (ST)

**CAST**: William Gargan as Lee Davis; June Clyde as Lois Grant; John Litel as Mike Rofano and Fred Morton; Anne Nagel as Mary Morton; Mary Gordon as Mrs. Morton; Ralf Harolde as Lips Haggarty; Joseph Crehan as Dugan; Addison Richards as Benson; Russell Hicks as Dr. Evans; Edward Stanley as Warden; Charles Lane as Immanuel "Manny" Dixon; with William Gould, Walter Sande, Joseph Downing, Paul Bryar, Russell Dix, John Dilson, Chuck Morrison, Walter Wills, Alan Bridge, Larry Kent, Eugene Jackson, Ray Spiker, Charles Sullivan, Eddie Hart, Charles Sherlock, Dale van Sickel, Kenneth Lundy

**CREDITS**: Director: George Waggner; Assistant Director: Stewart Webb; Producer:

Jack Bernhard; Writer: George Waggner; Photography: Stanley Cortez; Art Directors: Jack Otterson, Richard H. Riedel; Editor: Arthur Hilton; Set Decorator: R.A. Gausman; Costumes: Vera West; Music: H.J. Salter; Sound: Bernard Brown, Joseph Lapis

**Shock Theater** Catalog No. 732: "Terror builds a city of silence when men who wouldn't talk and women who dared not talk meet in the dramatic *Shock* feature film telecast on this channel (day) at (time)."

*- HN*

# *The Mad Doctor of Market Street* (1942)

*Synopsis*: Chemist Ralph Benson is conducting experiments in suspended animation. He believes that if a person suffering from a disease can be kept comatose, he can be successfully revived once a cure for his illness has been found. Saunders, a man desperate for money, accepts Benson's offer of $1000 to be a human guinea pig, but the drug-induced coma kills him. Benson flees from the police and boards a ship headed for New Zealand. A detective on his trail is also on the ship, but Benson throws him overboard. A fire causes the ship to sink but Benson, still hanging on to his medical kit, escapes in one of the lifeboats.

The lifeboat ends up on a tropical island. Along with Benson, other survivors include Patricia Wentworth and her ditzy Aunt Margaret; boxer Red Hogan; Jim the steward - who's also a doctor - and the ship's officer, the obnoxious and cowardly Dwight. A native tribe, mourning the death of Tanao, wife of Elan the chief, captures the castaways and are going to burn them alive when Benson, seeing that Tanao is not dead but in a coma, revives her with adrenaline. The natives then proclaim Benson to be the "God of Life." Benson decides to use his newfound status to continue his experiments, but will do so on his "more civilized" shipmates rather than the natives. He also forces Patricia to agree to marry him.

Benson uses his drug to put Jim in a state of suspended animation and successfully revives him later. However, Barab, a villager, catches Dwight attempting to escape in a canoe and, in the resulting struggle, both men are drowned. Barab's body is brought to Benson's hut, and Elan demands that Benson bring him back to life, giving him until dawn to do so. As the other castaways escape, Benson is thrown into the flames by the natives; the fire attracts a plane that has been searching for the castaways. The plane lands and rescues the group from the pursuing islanders.

The film encourages mis-seeing and pulls our focus away from the diegesis. The film induces a strange dissociated state in the spectator. Our mind starts to resemble a B picture as our thoughts grow asynchronously and we actively dub a new story over the one we are told.

Lance Duerfahrd on *The Mad Doctor of Market Street* (1)

"A crazed mind lusting for the terrible power of life!"
- Tagline for the film

This combination of mad-scientist thriller and jungle potboiler would likely be on the scrapheap of movie history had it not been directed by Joseph H. Lewis. Lewis started working in the Silent Era and did his apprenticeship as assistant cameraman, film editor, and assistant director before helming his first picture in 1937. Specializing in Westerns for a while, he earned the nickname "Wagon Wheel Joe" because of his fondness for shooting a scene through the spokes of a wagon wheel. He later said he did this not for any aesthetic reason, but to give the audience something to look at that would distract them from the triteness of the dialogue and the scene. Such was surely the case for his *Invisible Ghost* (1941), a film whose story is incoherent even for a Monogram horror movie. Lewis uses cinematic devices like shooting from the interior of a fireplace and moving the camera through cutaway walls, shots that would not stand out in a bigger-budgeted, more polished production, but which are conspicuous in a Poverty Row cheapie that would normally be filmed in a totally nondescript, by-the-numbers manner.

By the '40s, Lewis was working in a variety of genres, directing everything from comedies to war films to gangster melodramas. He didn't really attract any attention until two noteworthy "B" thrillers, *My Name is Julia Ross* (1945) and *So Dark the Night* (1946), but it was *Gun Crazy* (1950), a variation on the Bonnie and Clyde story, that became his most lasting success. It led to bigger productions; still, by the late '50s, Lewis - who had health problems - was working primarily in television.

As the *auteur* theory caught on, Lewis was rediscovered by film enthusiasts like Martin Scorsese and Jay Cocks, with the latter writing an article about him for the 12 May 1999 edition of *The New York Times* in which he extolled the director, mostly for his extraordinary contribution to *film noir* with *Gun Crazy*. *The Mad Doctor of Market Street* doesn't rate a mention therein, but die-hard *auteur*-ists to this day are still trying to make something out of that one. God knows, it isn't easy.

*The Mad Doctor of Market Street*, like many Universal "B" thrillers, starts off

174

promisingly with a gloomy atmospheric scene depicting Saunders' arrival to Benson's lab. There's a storm outside and the interior of the house is dark. Benson (Lionel Atwill) greets Saunders and – alas! - turns on the lights revealing a laboratory that looks like it was stocked from one those chemistry sets they used to sell to kids interested in science. No Ken Strickfaden electrical paraphernalia or bubbling vats from *Doctor X* in evidence anywhere; just a few random test tubes and beakers and a cage or two holding animals Benson has experimented on. What gives the sequence whatever *frisson* it has comes from Hardie Albright's performance as Saunders. In a few quick and efficient strokes, Hardie depicts a character at the end of his tether because of his poverty but still fearful of the bargain he has made with the doctor, whose assurances that all will be well fail to convince. There's a POV shot from Saunders' angle as Benson looms over him in close-up and reaches down with the drug-soaked cotton swab to put him to sleep. There are similar shots later, when Benson contemplates knocking Tanao out with a drugged flower and when he experiments on Jim (it must be a favorite Atwill conceit; it happens again when he puts Ygor under in *The Ghost of Frankenstein*).

**As the sun rises, Lionel Atwill fearfully awaits his doom.**

The subsequent shipboard sequence is pretty dismal. Una Merkel's daffy Aunt Margaret ("I love the Chinese - they're so Oriental") isn't as annoying as is Jim's attempt to romance Patricia (Claire Dodd, in one of her last film appearances). At one point he purposely collapses her deck chair with her in it while she's reading the

175

true-life nautical adventure, *Fifty South by Fifty South*. Somehow, she finds this boorish behavior irresistible. There's also a goofy subplot in which we learn that Margaret is headed for New Zealand to marry Sir Archie, whose disappearance during her previous visits suggests he's not very keen on the nuptials. Still, he offers a large reward when Margaret goes missing; (that's what the rescue pilots are after).

Benson's disguise consists only of his having shaved his beard, but the detective - who apparently learned police work from Inspector Lestrade - still isn't able to recognize him. (The disguise apparently also fooled whoever wrote the film's closing credits, as Atwill is listed as playing "Graham," the name Benson assumes for his escape.) The shots of the burning ship were obviously lifted from another film, and the action cuts quickly from the lifeboats to the castaways finding themselves on the island. After another abrupt jump, they are prisoners about to go the stake. "Say, are you on the level about giving us a jungle hotfoot?" asks Hogan (played by the perennially clueless Nat Pendleton). The scene where Tanao is "brought back to life" would be a bit more effective if there weren't a close-up of her showing her clearly breathing *before* Benson begins his ministrations. It would seem Elan and his tribesmen need an optometrist, and not a "God of Life."

Benson's being revered by the islanders because of his "miracles" is reminiscent of *West of Zanzibar* (1928), wherein magician Lon Chaney, as "Dead Legs" Flint, uses his vaudeville stage magic to convince the tribesmen that he has real supernatural powers. Unlike Benson, Flint does a Mr. Kurtz (*a la* "Heart of Darkness") and joins in the debasing rituals of the tribe. (In all fairness, Benson *does* submit to a native marriage ceremony.) Nonetheless, Flint also ends up in ashes when the disillusioned natives burn him alive. Benson's flock seems particularly hard to satisfy; they complain more than did the Israelites to Moses in the desert.

"What it lacks in story content is made up for by the tried and true hokum and one of the best pieces of overacting, by Lionel Atwill, ever seen on the screen" (*Showman's Trade Review*, 10 January 1942).

If Bela Lugosi has his "Monogram Nine," then *The Mad Doctor of Market Street* is Lionel Atwill's "Universal One," the only film at the Big U built entirely around his performance. After 1933's *Mystery of the Wax Museum*, Atwill was a contender for the title of the "new Lon Chaney." He talked about that in an interview in the 12 February 1933 edition of *The Los Angeles Times:*

Lon Chaney was a great movie actor. He was a specialist in certain roles. I never dreamed of following in his footsteps. But-if the movies want me to do so-all well and good... Give me a role in which the mental as well as the physical portrayal is important. Let me do a maniac, if you will, but let me express mentally as well as through physical make-up, the flare of a tortured soul, the cackling and diabolical fiendishness of a crazed man.

Atwill didn't become the new Lon Chaney; nor did anybody else. After his time as a "horror star" (*Doctor X, Murders in the Zoo, The Vampire Bat*), Atwill became a solid character actor in a number of important productions; by the '40s, though, he was enjoying considerably less prestige as a Universal contract player. He played burgomasters, police inspectors and red herrings, but he was the "star" only in *Mad Doctor of Market Street*. While Atwill is over the top here, he lacks conviction, a bit like Boris Karloff in *Frankenstein 1970*. In his Monogram movies, Bela played ape men and mad doctors as though he were doing Shakespeare; he never condescended to the material, however awful it was. Atwill isn't exactly kidding the script here, but he doesn't seem to think it deserves any special effort. Lugosi would have owned a line like "I shall be the greatest man ever to set foot on earth"; Atwill seems to want to get it out of his mouth as quickly as possible and move on to something else. His one effective moment is at the finale, where he realizes the dawn will spell his end and there's nothing he can do about it except play around with the test tubes, hands trembling, in a futile attempt to convince the natives he can do the impossible, but knowing he's just postponing the inevitable.

Benson's theories smack a bit of Karloff's Columbia mad doctor films - like *The Man They Could Not Hang* (1939), which contains a sequence with the police breaking in during an experiment in which the subject is dead, but could have been revived had not the law intervened at a crucial point. The difference here is that Saunders has died, not just gone into a coma as planned (it's never explained what went wrong; just one of those things, I guess). Karloff's medicos were sincere in their desire to help mankind, but Benson comes off as a crackpot (he is referred to as "a pseudo scientist" and a "so-called scientist") and an egomaniac. Nevertheless, his work isn't entirely bogus, as he does succeed in bringing Jim back from suspended animation. Jim is not too impressed with the novelty of Benson's ideas: "Several scientists have suspended life by freezing. People have been kept alive indefinitely that way." I'm not sure where Jim ran across such startling information; perhaps he had seen another Karloff film, *The Man with Nine Lives*. Cryonics anyone?

It's not clear whether Benson gets nuttier as the film goes on, or whether he's just forgotten that his experiments are about suspended animation and not raising people who are actually deceased. "I'll be able bring back people who have been dead for years," he exclaims at one point. There's also a moment of - likely unintentional - irreverence when Benson has the natives place the comatose Jim in a cave tomb and seal the entrance with rocks. Benson announces that he can keep him unconscious for "three days or more" before reviving him. The native chief, however, doesn't like playing Joseph of Arimathea and complains that it's bad luck to put someone in the ground. This is the beginning of Benson's downfall (no pun intended).

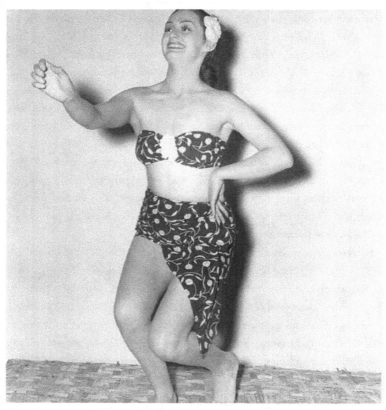

**Tani Marsh, a well-known Hawaiian dancer, posed for a *MDoMS* publicity shot or two, although she is barely glimpsed in the film. Marsh was much more conspicuous in the unforgettable *From Hell It Came* (1957), wherein she had a cat-fight with the villainess just before the latter was tossed into the quicksand by the mighty Tabonga.**

The chief is played by Noble Johnson, friend of Lon Chaney and minion to Fu-Manchu, Dr. Mirakle, Count Zaroff, and Imhotep. Johnson's complexion is lighter here than his Skull Island chief in *King Kong*, and he actually has relevant dialogue, unlike with his usual roles. The Missouri-born actor's only starring parts were for the Lincoln Film Company, established in 1915 by a group of black businessmen who wanted to make movies aimed at African-American audiences and to provide a positive picture of black Americans as an answer to films like *Birth of a Nation*. Noble's brother George stayed on as the guiding light of the company after Noble moved on to mainstream studios. Considering that his parts were often very brief or were even uncredited bits, Noble got his share of publicity. In the 2 January 1932 edition of the *Baltimore Afro American*, for example, the African-American press manifestly took pride in his career:

> Noble Johnson lives in Glendale, the exclusive section of the movie capital, has an ofay wife, makes money in real estate, was the first to break into the movies and played with such stars as Rudolph Valentino and others, has watched others come and go.

Johnson retired from the movies in 1950; no doubt his real estate investments had paid off.

As mentioned earlier, the best bit of acting in *Market Street* is done by Hardie Albright, who had a long and successful career on the stage as both thesp and playwright. His 1938 play, *All the Living*, set in a mental institution and based on a book entitled **I Knew 3000 Lunatics**, got an excellent review from Brooks Atkinson of *The New York Times*. Albright's performance as Hamlet drew glowing notices, and he also played in the Los Angeles stage production of the chiller, *The Double Door*. Hardie's film career was less distinguished, although genre fans no doubt recall *The 9th Guest* (1934) which anticipates Agatha Christies' **Ten Little Indians**. After World War II, Hardie became a drama coach and wrote books about acting.

Reviewers were not impressed with *The Mad Doctor of Market Street*.

> Although this is supposed to be in the thriller class, it is doubtful it will have a frightening effect on anyone. So ridiculous the story and so slow-moving is the action, that patrons will be bored instead of excited. There is nothing that the players can do to enliven the proceedings, for they are up against trite material and stilted dialogue. The romance is routine.

*Harrison's Reports*, 10 January 1942

This is an obvious job of padding to 60 minutes. Swell library ship footage only serves to make the plot more pallid by contrast. Pic is strictly a tail ender... Number of players are very capable but hampered by poor material... Lines and situations are often ludicrous. Add such stuff as a tribe of South Sea natives who at one moment can't talk English at all and a second later let out with a schoolboy's idea of how an Indian might talk. Director Joseph Lewis does a lot of slick piloting. His principal worry seems to have been how to make the film run 60 minutes but actually film runs pretty fast considering plot.

Herb, *Variety*, 7 January 1942

As a short cut to Bellevue, this corner unhesitatingly recommends "The Mad Doctor of Market Street"; he American Medical Association will no doubt be relieved to learn that the maniacal Dr. Benson finally, and by a plot route only a wise man could follow, was chucked into a South Sea Island stew pot to pay for his crimes in strict Hays Office tradition. Despite the fact that Lionel Atwill appeared in each sequence, the film seems to have been constructed from odd strips of celluloid on the cutting room floor. A mistake like that could happen, couldn't it?

T.S., *The New York Times*, 5 January 1942

*Motion Picture Herald* (10 January 1943) described the film as "thrills for the timid," while the reviewer for the 6 January 1942 *Motion Picture Daily* wrote that "par for the course about defines it." *The Los Angeles Times* dismissed it as a "phony chiller" and noted that "Incidentally, the camera has even succeeded in making Miss Dodd unattractive" (24 January 1942). The 10 January 1942 *Showman's Trade Review* opined that:

"it's the kind of melodrama that takes one back to the old silent days which should give an idea of what kind of screen fare to expect" but still allowed that "in spots it's thoroughly enjoyable with enough suspense here and there to satisfy the horror fans.

*The Mad Doctor of Market Street* was filmed in July of 1941 when it was then variously titled *Terror of the Islands* and *Terror of the South Seas*. It's not clear why

Universal waited until early 1942 to release it. Perhaps its short length and lack of star power made it problematic for a general run, and the studio was just looking for a stronger title to pair it with. *The Wolf Man*, released at the tail end of 1941, seemed a good choice, and the two frequently played together. The double bill played for four weeks at the Vogue Theater in Los Angeles, and when the duo proved a bit hit in Minneapolis as well, the pundits were surprised.

> Trade here is trying to figure out why in these days of war horrors the local film public has such a strong yen for horror films. 'The Wolf Man' and 'Mad Doctor of Market Street' combo hit the Loop March 13 and whammed 'em for an entire week at the Aster. Since then it has been cleaning up in the nabes at the same admission rate as downtown… Trade is puzzled and the only explanation advanced is that 'it must just be another one of those cycles.'
>
> *Variety*, 6 May 1942

*Market Street* was sometimes billed with *The Ghost of Frankenstein*. In Madison, Wisconsin, the movie was shown with *Among the Living* and *The Tell-Tale Heart*. Local reviewer Sterling Sorenson thought the film was a sequel to *The Mad Doctor*, but that it didn't "stack up to its forerunner." When the picture played in Sheboygan, Wisconsin, the other feature was, appropriately enough, *The Man Who Returned to Life*. No matter what it played with, *Mad Doctor of Market Street* was unlikely to have been the draw.

*The Mad Doctor of Market Street* - 27 February 1942 – 60/61 minutes

**CAST:** Una Merkel as Aunt Margaret; Lionel Atwill as Dr. Ralph Benson (aka Graham); Nat Pendleton as Ned Hogan; Claire Dodd as Patricia; Anne Nagel as Mrs. Saunders; Hardie Albright as William Saunders; Richard Davies as Jim; John Eldredge as Dwight; Ray Mala as Barab; Noble Johnson as Elan; Rosina Galli as Taneo; Al Kikume as Kalo; Milton Kibbee as Hadley; Byron Shores as Crandell; Tani Marsh as Tahitian dancer; Billy Bunkley; Bess Flowers as Lady.

**CREDITS:** Director: Joseph H. Lewis; Assistant Director: Melville Shyer; Producer: Paul Malvern; Screenplay: Al Martin; Photography: Jerome Ash; Art Direction:

Jack Otterson, Ralph M. DeLacy; Editor: Ralph Dixon; Set Decoration: Russell A. Gausman; Costumes: Vera West; Music: H.J. Salter; Sound: Bernard B. Brown, Jess Moulin

***Shock Theater*** Catalog No. 714 - "A fire at sea maroons a strange group on a savage-infested island. See this thrilling adventure in 'The Mad Doctor of Market Street.' It's another *Shock* feature film presentation on this channel (day), at (time). Lionel Atwill stars as a crazed scientist who believes he holds the secret of life."

*HN*

# *The Ghost of Frankenstein* (1942)

*Synopsis*: We open in the village of Frankenstein, as the villagers receive the mayor's permission to blow up the remains of Castle Frankenstein, which they see as the cause of all the misfortune that has befallen them. This proves to be harder than anticipated, for Ygor – the broken-necked, vengeful blacksmith from *Son of Frankenstein* – is not above tossing a few rocks at them from a parapet. Fleeing to the castle's nether-regions for safety, Ygor espies a hand sticking out of the now-hardened sulfur pit. Digging in, he is astonished to see that the hand belongs to the arm of the Frankenstein Monster who – albeit somewhat the worse for wear – is still alive. Freeing his "friend," Ygor leads the Monster off into the nearby woods.

A thunderstorm rises suddenly, and the Monster is struck by lightning; remarkably, rather than destroying him, the lightning restores his strength. Putting two and two together, Ygor leads his friend off to Vasaria, wherein dwells Dr. Ludwig Frankenstein, younger son of the mad scientist who first cried out, "It's alive!" Somehow, despite his bearing one of the most unique and infamous surnames in all of Germania, Ludwig has avoided being associated with his father's woeful experiments by everyone in the vicinity – and that includes his daughter, Elsa. While Ygor is putting the arm on Ludwig, the Monster has killed one of the locals and is now in police custody. Only after Ygor threatens to spill the beans about Ludwig's patronymic does the good doctor head down to the courthouse to see about the Monster. The Monster, possibly seeing a family resemblance and sensing an ally, is nonetheless enraged when Ludwig denies knowing anything about him, and bursting his chains, runs off to the hills again, accompanied by Ygor.

Come nightfall, the pair make for the castle Frankenstein, where the Monster tears through the doctor's laboratory in an effort to carry off Elsa, killing assistant Dr. Kettering in the process. Both Monster and Ygor are overcome by gas pumped in through the air ducts, and Ludwig – determined to disassemble the Monster piece by piece – asks Dr. Bohmer for advice and assistance. Bohmer talks Ludwig out of the dissection and suggests that the placement of a normal brain inside the Monster's body might result in a creature who is an actual boon to mankind. Seeing as he has Kettering's brain on hand, Ludwig agrees and prepares for the operation. Bohmer, looking to regain his professional reputation (tarnished by past experiments-gone-wrong), conspires with Ygor to place the *blacksmith's* brain in the Monster's skull instead of Kettering's. In the meanwhile, the Monster has kidnapped young Cloestine – a child who has acted in a friendly fashion toward him – and brings her to the laboratory, insisting that *her* brain go into his head. Ludwig straightens things out (in the course of which Ygor is crushed behind a sturdy door by his erstwhile "friend"), preps the Monster for the transplant, and then - unbeknownst to him – connects Ygor's brain to the Monster's circuitry, thanks to Bohmer.

Back at the village, everyone is frantic about the Monster having vanished and the sudden disappearance of Cloestine. As they prepare to storm the castle, Elsa's boyfriend, Erik Ernst, confers with Ludwig, who informs him that – the operation having been quite successful – the Monster's personality is now that of the gentle Dr. Kettering. All – except for Dr. Bohmer – are shocked when the Monster, now speaking with Ygor's voice, boasts that with his newly recovered strength he will rule the world! Moments later, though, the Monster is apparently going blind, due to incompatibility of blood types. While the angry mob breaks into the castle, the Monster, raging about the laboratory, sends Bohmer crashing to his death into an electric panel. Thrashing about wildly, he knocks chemicals onto the floor, where they combine to set the place afire. Erik and Elsa escape with their lives, but Ludwig and the Monster perish in the flames.

Much of the fun one has with Universal's Frankenstein series, of course, is to be found in marveling over nomenclature and inconsistencies.(1) The 1931 *Frankenstein* originally keyed in on the epic missteps taken by Colin Clive's Henry Frankenstein in an abandoned watchtower high in the hills above the village of Goldstadt. "Missteps" is a moral evaluation of Henry's purposeful experiments, which suffered also from muck-ups, like the breaking of the neck of the cadaver cut down from the gibbet, and the deceitful substitution by Fritz of an abnormal brain for the good one he dropped, having been startled by the dramatically inexplicable sounding of a gong at Goldstadt

Medical College. (Said college is doubtless part of the larger Goldstadt University from which Dr. Pretorius will admit to having been "booted" in *Bride*.) Lying somewhere between missteps and muck-ups are also mysteries, such as why Henry is disturbed when Dr. Waldman informs him that the brain Fritz – Dwight Frye, enacting his second straight tormented sidekick for Universal - had filched had belonged to a criminal, when the first place Frankenstein had ventured in search of a brain was the body of someone publicly hanged by the neck (and presumably not for acts of charity). Or what was the logic behind issuing the new creation a pair of black platform shoes? Were these – like what would become the Monster's trademark black suit – found in a cupboard someplace? Despite all this, we had our iconic "Frankenstein Monster."

Ya seen one, ya seen 'em all! Compare the elevated glances of the dramatic personae here to those of the cast on the title card from *Enemy Agent*. Whether depicting classic horrors or contemporary heroics, '40s Universal layouts seemed completely interchangeable. (Still, Ralph Bellamy and Evelyn Ankers *do* make a cute couple, no?)

With *Frankenstein* a hit, Junior Laemmle's production team had begun readying the world for *The Return of Frankenstein* - the sequel to the earlier sensation and the film that marked the reunion of James Whale and Mary Shelley's legacy – in 1933. Soon enough, the project was retitled *Bride of Frankenstein*, and it was bandied about by the publicity department that a "search" was underway for just the right actress to portray the titular bride. Although Colin Clive had reportedly been disappointed that his much-anticipated death scene at the end of the 1931 classic had been supplanted by Frederick Kerr's toast to an heir for the "House of Frankenstein" and the need for his character to survive to experiment another day, he was happy to be involved in the sequel, which would open with his Henry and the Elizabeth of... *ummm*... Mae Clarke? making good on the old baron's toast. Okay. While Clarke would soon appear again at Universal with the increasingly popular Boris Karloff (*Night World*, 1932), she was either unavailable, unwilling, or unasked to come to the signing of the pertinent contracts a couple of years later. For all the good-natured folderol of the supposed search for one bride or the other, there was little mystery as to with whom said "bride" would be paired. Only had Elizabeth's heart been used to power up the female creature the Monster would briefly woo – as plotted in the original script – would anyone have paid a brass farthing to witness the goings-on of Valerie Hobson.

Although little flower-tossing Maria had ended up in the drink as she was bonding with the Monster in the 1931 original, the next time the Monster was a total emotional mess had to be when O.P. Heggie's blind hermit sawed away at the "Ave Maria" in his cottage (a musical *hommage* to the Monster's first, inadvertent victim?). In fact, following the clever opening badinage between Byron and the Shelleys, *Bride* gets underway as Maria's dad, Hans (Reginald Barlow), spews righteous anger over his daughter's death, a moment that allows the audience to recall the scene in which Maria's dad, Ludwig (Michael Mark), had carried her lifeless body through the streets of Goldstadt in the earlier film. Hey, if Elizabeth can undergo such an amazing transformation (for the *better*, many argue), why not old Hans... errr... Ludwig?

And why can't the torch- and whip-wielding Fritz metamorphose into the near-imbecilic Karl, in what would be Dwight Frye's third straight take on a half-wit at Universal? (Please recall that Frye's appearance as a cogent, articulate reporter in Whale's *The Invisible Man* [1933] was uncredited.) In his seminal **It's Alive: The Classic Cinema Saga of Frankenstein**, film historian Gregory William Mank explains the hemi-demi-semi-nature of Frankenstein's latest assistant:

> To showcase Frye's talents at lunacy and comedy, Whale combined two separate roles of the original script: Karl, 'a bit of a village idiot,' quoth the script, and Fritz, the 'first ghoul' who assists Pretorius, into simply Karl, who became both a village idiot and a ghoul and one of Frye's most memorable performances.(2)

Frankenstein's Monster also became simply "Frankenstein" a lot sooner than it took the studio to acknowledge the maneuver via Basil Rathbone at the town railway station (please note: town also now apparently yclept "Frankenstein") four years later. No one (that I've ever met, at any rate) ever raised an eyebrow over Henry Frankenstein's having miraculously survived the climactic laboratory detonation that was set off by the jilted Monster (please ignore the long-shot to the contrary that somehow survived the final edit), or his subsequently making an honest woman of Elizabeth, or her bearing him a couple of sons, or his ending up a baron (the original script for the 1931 film had called for Frederick Kerr's character to die of shock, thus passing the title down to Henry), or even that the "Henry" of the first two features turned out to be the "Heinrich" of the third.

Come that third – the Whale-less *Son of Frankenstein* of 1939 – and we learn that Heinrich und Elizabeth had a son, Wolf, who at some point married a redhead named Elsa, moved to the USA to teach at an American college, and had his own son, Peter. (The order in which these events occurred is of no importance.) Unlike his dad and grandfather (called plain old "Baron Frankenstein" in the 1931 film), Wolf goes by *von* Frankenstein, which can be translated *of* or *from* Frankenstein. Per our colleague, film reviewer Hans Wollstein, there's a method to this morass:

If dear old Frederick Kerr's character *was* a baron, then his son's name should have been Heinrich, Baron von Frankenstein all along. Heinrich/Henry would have had his father's family surname – which might well have been Müller or Schmidt - when he was CREATED Baron Frankenstein, at which point the "von" would then have been applied when spelled out. The title would have been awarded by the emperor, Wilhelm I, or his chancellor, Prince von Bismarck, and it would be in evidence from the costumes and setting.

Thus, God only knows what the family name of the baron and his progeny and *their* issue was "in reality." If the men insisted on bearing the title that was evidently handed down from one generation to the next, they could wander about known only by it and their Christian name (Guten Tag! Ich bin Heinrich, Baron von Frankenstein!) Wolf either took a pass on the title (his brother, Ludwig – who gets embroiled in this mess in *Ghost* – didn't toss *his* being a baron in anyone's face, either) or adopted this short-cut en route to assimilating into the USA. A tempest in a teapot? Yessiree!, but we learn from that conductor's timely interruption of Wolf's diatribe that the eponymous terrain on which stand the family castle and old watch tower is a village large enough to be worthy of its own train station, grumbling populace, and hair-splitting Burgomeister: "We come to meet you, not to greet you!"

187

Again, there's that bit of nonsense about just who is being touted in the picture's title. Wolf is, of course, the son of Heinrich, "Maker of Monsters" (per the torch-inscribed snarl that someone managed to sneak in and scrawl onto his tomb); little Peter is the son of Wolf, and it is Peter's precarious position (under the platform-shoe'd foot of the Monster) that leads his father to finally do something more action-oriented than playing darts. As for the Monster... well, Ygor's intriguing insistence to Wolf that "Your father made him, and Heinrich Frankenstein was *your* father, too!" does little more than once again poke those viewers who had chuckled their way through the "Bride" kerfuffle some years earlier. (One of the kids with whom I formed a monster club a lifetime ago argued at the time – seriously, and not a little persuasively – that Karloff's Monster in *Son* **was** the offspring of Karloff's Monster from *Bride*, as the 1939 iteration was "not dressed" up in his trademark black suit, but instead "wore a sweatshirt." So how, my old friend continued, could *that* Monster – the one kicked into the sulfur pit whilst accoutered in something akin to what we would now call a "fleece" – be the same Monster who was resurrected from the pit in *The Ghost of Frankenstein*? We weren't familiar with technical terms like "continuity" in those days...)

Anyhow, with *The Ghost of Frankenstein* (why the "The" and why now?), we're back at it; the ambiguity has returned with this, the first '40s execution of a radically '30s concept. Ghost-wise, one might opt for the ethereal Sir Cedric Hardwicke (transparent of figure and naked of scalp as Henry/Heinrich) as he lays a guilt trip on the corporeal Sir Cedric Hardwicke (who is weighted down with hair appliances) as Ludwig (no "von") Frankenstein. Or one might take the low road and claim that Chaney's initial appearance onscreen as the Monster – covered with "dried sulfur" and as white as any flour-dredged apparition in a Mantan Moreland comedy – gave *him* dibs on the meaning behind the title. Discussions like this one are always fun, even if they seldom matter; as neat a shot as the erstwhile House That Carl Built took in 1942, it was the very "Frankenstein" franchise that was but a shade of its former self.

James Whale had bailed after the first sequel – and he hadn't much wanted to do *that* one until he was given assurance that his stylistic approach to the rest of Mary Shelley's screed would be welcomed - and *fama erat* it was he who had contrived to have the Monster blown to atoms to save himself (and others) the trouble of yet another follow-up. Karloff had jumped ship after the second sequel; in his opinion, his beloved Monster was rapidly becoming a stooge, a henchman. Although only three films – quality outings, all – had been made, Boris felt that the integrity of the original concept was being sacrificed to Mammon. The gentle Briton was enough of a realist to understand that the undying Monster's immortality was due to profitability, rather than to electricity or lightning, but enough of an idealist to quit while he – and his immortal alter-ego – was ahead of the game.

For a while, the actor had gone AWOL from the industry itself. While the boys at Universal's publicity department were stirring up enough pap on the impending production to keep the trades and the dailies happy, the Great White Way had taken Boris Karloff and all his boogeyman baggage to its heart. *Arsenic and Old Lace* proved to be everything for the '40s-vintage actor that *Frankenstein* had been for his younger self. Boris found that his reputation had preceded him, and that he could bring down the house night after night by chalking up his latest murder to the victim's unfortunate choice of words: "He said that I looked like Boris Karloff!" The word was out that the actor did not mind guying himself and was not at all upset about publicity pieces highlighting Jack Pierce's famed make-up, those asphalt-spreaders boots, and/or even the unseen five-pound steel "spine" that the first film's publicity campaign claimed was "the rod which conveys the current up to the Monster's brain."

Back at the studio, of course, the bullshit was flying fast and furious. A glance at the stuff that Universal's PR staff cranked out for *The Ghost of Frankenstein* makes one doubt – if not outright disbelieve – anything he/she has *ever* heard about *any* of these films. The baloney stretched from the news of the "search" (Zounds! *Déjà vu*, all over again!) for a successor to Karloff to Greg Mank's revelation of a "studio policy" that dictated which actors would always be seen in Frankenstein movies: uncredited, perhaps, but still Lawrence Grant's Burgomeister was back, as were Michael Mark and Lionel Belmore as town councillors [sic] (despite their having been killed by the Monster in *Son*), Dwight Frye as a villager, and even Colin Clive, via stock footage – he had died of a combination of tuberculosis and alcoholism some five years earlier – as Henry/Heinrich Frankenstein's younger/handsomer self.(3) In on the never-ending stream of absurdity came prefab and ludicrously headlined pressbook articles like "Lon Chaney Appears as Monster in Horror Film" (as opposed to his appearing as a monster in a comedy of manners or a Civil War drama). With the nonstop peddling of blarney such as this, one might readily have come to the conclusion that Universal not only thought ten or so to be the age of the average horror moviegoer, but also that ten might be on the high side of that movie fan's I.Q.

There's probably more truth to that than any of us would care to admit. How old were my colleagues and I – and I'd venture to ask the same of many of the readership – when we first fell under the spell cast by *Frankenstein*, *Dracula*, *The Mummy*, or any of the old horror movies we still embrace so passionately? The TV fodder introduced by "Shock Theater" or "Son of Shock" at the end of the '50s had, in the '30s, been pitched to grownups; they offered offbeat takes on adult themes - life after death, medical ethics, forbidden love, etc., etc., - and served them up in the company of grotesques perfectly capable of scaring the drawers off the patrons. Come the '40s, and half the population was either overseas fighting the war, or involved in the home front outfitting the war. No one needed "adult" themes shoved down his or her throat, even if they were couched in greasepaint and putty; wartime anxiety, death, and deprivation provided enough unwelcome fodder without any help from Hollywood. Moviegoers were looking for escapism, and the grownups *and the kids* sought a breather from Hitler and Hirohito in the company of Kharis and Frankenstein.

THE GHOST OF FRANKENSTEIN

With Castle Frankenstein having been destroyed by an outraged townspeople, Ygor and the Monster are forced to get their steps in by sauntering through Germania's most unkempt cemetery. No matter; within moments, a lightning bolt will regenerate the Monster, dry clean his only suit, and get him – and the plot – moving at a faster clip.

And *The Ghost of Frankenstein* didn't just fill the bill back in April of '42, it was – critics be damned – a hit. Wartime ticket-buyers were a different breed than the seat-warming populace looking for a bit of relief from the Great Depression. The formula for most "B"-movies (please, let's not get unrealistic about *Ghost*) seemed to be that mood was fine and the plot important, but pacing was everything. Especially in cases like this one – where most regular moviegoers knew the ongoing details of the story backwards, forwards, and inside out – the picture could forego footage usually devoted to exposition and cut right to the chase. (Would that the *Son of Dracula* crew had shared a beer with *Ghost of Frankenstein*'s.)

Many fans regard this picture as being the last "solo" appearance of the Monster. Heck, I maintain that that pitiable giant figure was never able to get by without his support system of mad scientists, deformed/demented assistants, and the like – all of whom would be in on the official count of monsters come the publicity campaigns for the *House*(s) *of Frankenstein* and *Dracula* a couple of years down the road. The box office receipts in 1931 had assured that Henry Frankenstein's problem child would become far too profitable for him to handle only once and far too risky for him to handle alone. Still, as the Monster returned for each successive misadventure, he became encumbered with extra weight that may have added dimension to the ongoing saga, but also robbed it of its innocence and purity.

*Ghost* was hardly a solo venture. Beginning with *Son of Frankenstein*, the Monster had been terrorizing the countryside, so to speak, under the influence of an evil genius – Ygor. In the first two films, Whale and Karloff crafted a Monster who was adept enough to tell right from wrong, to rescue an innocent from drowning after having inadvertently drowned another, to relish the moments of friendship and camaraderie with a person unable to judge a book by its cover, and so on and so forth. In *Son*, the Monster came to rely, almost blindly, on his broken-necked friend and to lash out at the most innocent of the assemblage (Peter) following Ygor's death. Here, Chaney's Monster - whose capacity for recognition (Ludwig at first, Cloestine later) is the most human of his virtues and for whom loyalty and friendship ultimately play no part – ignores, betrays, and finally kills his broken-necked comrade. With Lon under the makeup, no spark that might temper the supercharged Monster can be seen; none of the sensitivity of his predecessor – the originator of the role – survived the transition. While *Ghost*'s Monster latched onto a child, there was none of the childlike spark that permeated his predecessor's take on the role. Karloff, by far the more cerebral of the two actors, gave us presence; Chaney, by far the more physical of the two, gave us volume.

**Universal Horrors** does a grand job of summing up the early aberrations of the script which the eponymous **MagicImage Film Book** volume includes *in toto*, so there's little point into going into that here. Yet for all the effort at innovation – its new Monster, the new Frankensteins, and (save for the Messrs. Grant, Mark, Belmore, et al) the new villagers – *Ghost* is mired in a lot of same old same old.

Take the "fly in the ointment" wrinkle: from its inception, the cinematic Frankenstein success story included an element of surprise, both logical and unpredictable, which had led to a cocking up of the initial game plan. In 1931, the fly had been Fritz's sneaky-ass substitution of the abnormal brain for the good one; this, (we were told) led to the Monster's propensity to lash out violently whenever he was being whipped or seared with a torch. *Bride*'s fly was the woman; if the rallying cry of most men is "You can't live with them, and you can't live without them," just who did the Monster think *he* was? More importantly, why would Henry Frankenstein imagine even for a moment that an old queen like Pretorius could concoct a female who would soothe the Monster's troubled breast? In *Son*, Wolf (like the Monster) falls victim to Ygor's mind-games and the loopy grandeur of the family residence; the resultant misguided drive to restore his father's good name leads to his firing up the furnaces once again. (By comparison, the incredible 180 Frank Mannering pulls in 1943's *Frankenstein Meets the Wolf Man* is a total misfire. Even though his veins are completely free of Frankenstein blood, and he's strengthened by the resolve of yet another [and curvier] Elsa [who's standing *close* by his side], Mannering opts for the dark side only because, if *someone* doesn't do *something* fast, the bell will ring and the audience will have to go home.)

Here, we have more wrinkles than Ayesha after that second fire. The Monster's all for the transplant, but wants the brain of Cloestine (where *do* they get these names?) to sleep over forever. Ygor, the sly devil, plots to have his own noodle plopped into that square skull, as he can see where this would ease his way into prestige, power, and some real money. Dr. Bohmer, who at first doesn't seem to do much other than hang around in his smock and suffer Ludwig Frankenstein's thoughtless and insensitive comments, is lulled as much by a desire to marry his fist to Ludwig's stiff upper lip as he is by Ygor's silver tongue. Even with all this slumgullion boiling on the fire, one knows that the chances of Dr. Kettering's brain making it into the Monster's rigging start at zero and go down from there.

Another leftover from earlier installments has already been brought up for consideration: the Monster's best suit. This – the absence of which in *Son* had sent Boris Karloff into rounds of kvetching (about "furs and muck") that were not at all like him – was accepted with not so much as the blink of an eye upon its reappearance. Karloff had been right; the Monster's Sunday best was part of the larger picture, as closely interwoven in the Frankenstein mythos as the Wolf Man's work clothes and

Dracula's ever-crisp soup and fish were essential to their respective personas. The restoration of the basic black ensemble and its presence throughout the rest of the Universal canon only made the furry miscalculation in *Son* seem more of a head-scratcher than it had been originally.

Bela's Ygor is a sight for sore eyes. Happily, as resistant to small-arms fire as had been George Zucco's Andoheb, the remarkably resilient high priest in the Kharis series, Ygor is hale, hearty, and – if an apparent good scrubbing and the periodontal work is any indication – in *better* shape than he was in the earlier feature. Along with his appearance, Ygor's goals have been ratcheted up; ridding the village of old nuisances is no longer a pastime worthy of his attention. The crafty old blacksmith's master plan now encompasses taking over the entire country! While this might be biting off more than any one man (or Monster) can chew, Ygor's yodeling away that he now possesses "the strength of a hundred men" is a picture of megalomania unrivaled since Boris Karloff's less exuberant but equally daft claims in *Mask of Fu Manchu*.

(And yet you have to wonder if, indeed, the Monster *did* grow stronger with each successive picture. In the first, Heinrich and the elderly Dr. Waldman [along with a hypodermic needle and a bludgeon] managed to wrestle him to the floor. *Bride* witnessed him being tied down and carried off – semi-crucified - by a mere dozen or so yokels, while in *Son*, a bit of momentum behind a well-placed kick was all it took to topple the Monster from his pins. Still, this sudden blossoming of superhuman power in the Monster's mighty arms may exist only in Ygor's feverish [and transplanted] mind; the only other times we hear of such outlandish claims are in the excised scenes between a gabby Ygor-cum-Monster and Larry Talbot in *Ghost*'s own son, *Frankenstein Meets the Wolf Man*.)

*Ghost* marks the first time since *Frankenstein* that brains are bandied about like wholesale commodities, but the idea here seems particularly apt. You could watch any of Karloff's three performances and *see* his Monster turning over thoughts and ideas in his mind. Even in *Son* (wherein Ygor does most of the mental heavy-lifting for the pair), his acceding to his partner's decisions is *visible*. With the vintage-1942 Monster bearing inscrutable and near-frozen features, there is *very* little indication as to whether the lights are on upstairs and if, indeed, anyone is home. A new brain is clearly called for, but the plethora of available raw materials not only skirts the edge of risibility, but also foreshadows the "monster rally" sequels wherein frenetic brain-swapping would prove a plague on both houses.

So long as you don't require much humanity amid the horrors and can get past his perpetual squint and scowl, Lon Chaney is not *too* bad as the Monster. His attachment to Cloestine is obviously meant to reflect the Karloffian viewpoint where children were concerned, but no more perfect image of the depths to which this concept had sunk can be had than the still whereon a stiff-limbed Eddie Parker (doubling for Chaney), clutching a wooden stand-in for Janet Ann Gallow, has just sent a buttocks-grabbing stuntman plunging to his out-of-frame mats. The childlike confusion on the Monster's part that resulted in little Maria's being tossed into the river had given way to slick contrivance. And again, as Chaney's Monster offers no other sign of fidelity and is evidently capable of turning his rage toward anyone who stands in his way (including his old goombah, Ygor), no assurance is had that the brute might not dropkick the little girl 100 yards or so down the road if someone *else* were to become the apple of his eye. After all, Dr. Kettering is killed without so much as a second - or any – thought (although the impulsive action does free up a brain for future use); killing is what monsters do best, and Chaney's giant is – first, last, and always – a monster.

**"Blinded due to an unforeseen screw-up in the brain-transference operation, the Monster makes for the door. Had it not been for his slamming into that quaint bit of technology on the right, we might never have had *Frankenstein Meets the Wolf Man*."**

The rest of the *dramatis personae* are fine - they almost always are in the Frankenstein series. Sir Cedric Hardwicke's cool and imperturbable Ludwig is an interesting sibling to Basil Rathbone's near-frantic Wolf, albeit the latter's fairly

194

constant state of near-hysteria makes him much more a chip off the old Heinrich than his younger brother. Ralph Bellamy does better by Erik Ernst than he did by Captain Montford in *The Wolf Man*, but this may be due to W. Scott Darling and Eric Taylor's screenplay providing him with a more well-delineated part; said screenplay also gives the delectable Evelyn Ankers to him this time 'round. Miss Ankers, in a role that's essentially interchangeable with that of Gwen Conliffe in *The Wolf Man*, takes another step toward her accession of the title of '40s Scream Queen. And Lionel Atwill is as enjoyable in his quieter moments (as when he's glaring daggers while Ludwig runs off at the mouth at Bohmer's expense) as he is in his premature snarl of triumph in the last reel.

Having all but snatched *Son of Frankenstein* away from Boris and Basil a couple of years earlier, Bela's copping the honors in *Ghost* must have been a walk in the park for him. With Chaney portraying an unpredictable automaton, Bela runs the show, not realizing – until it's too late – that although the Monster can recognize Ludwig Frankenstein (whom he has never met), he will fail to consider Ygor's place in his heart while crushing the old boy behind the laboratory door. More so here than in *Son*, Lugosi's blacksmith has to shift gears constantly; here, he goes from being the guy in the driver's seat to the victim of his erstwhile friend's petulance before being back (albeit quite briefly) on top of the world. Performance-wise, Bela is in command every step of the way, and had Chaney happened to glance sideways even once through those slits he used for eyes, he'd have learned more in a moment from Lugosi than he'd cadged from Erle C. Kenton during the entire 25-day shoot.

Not up to the snuff introduced back in the '30s, *The Ghost of Frankenstein* was just fine, thank you, for the tastes of the next decade. Hans J. Salter's pulsating score keyed the film's more ominous moments, and both Woody Bredell and Milton Krasner performed the kind of visual magic in which Universal's cinematographers were known to excel. (If the puffs in their respective press-books were meant to be taken – *ahem!* – at face value, the 1931 Monster stood seven feet tall, while Chaney's goblin was merely six foot, nine. Nonetheless, this very minor discrepancy might explain why James Whale had Arthur Edeson's camera capture the Monster head-on, while Erle C. Kenton had Krasner and Bredell constantly aim the lens *up* at the shorter of the giants. The following year, George Robinson – tasked with making Lugosi's Monster as threatening as Eddie Parker's [or even Gil Perkins'] in *Frankenstein Meets the Wolf Man*, had to contend with changes in perspective in almost every scene.)

*The New York Times*'s Bosley Crowther – who never seemed to like much very much – ended his rather tepid review with an act of prognostication that was hardly a foregone conclusion in 1942:

> To be sure, the replenished monster is being consumed by fire when we see him last, but the thought that he may yet return for further adventures with his body and Lugosi's sconce fills us with mortal terror. That is the most fearful prospect which the picture manages to convey. 4 April, 1942

Richard L. Coe, assigned the picture as part of his responsibilities at *The Washington Post*, took a somewhat unusual approach to informing his readership of the film's story line:

> This morning we will discuss the love life of your old friend 'Frankenstein,' the monster who's assumed, in the course of years, the name of his creator. This titivating subject has been raised on the Pix screen of 'The Ghost of Frankenstein,' a yarn employing, uh, should we say, talents of Sir Cedric Hardwicke, Lon Chaney, Jr., Lionel Atwill, and Bela Lugosi. But, of course, by now you're palpitating for further details of this beguiling passion – what's she like, is she pretty, how big is she?

The "beguiling passion" mentioned in this 1 May 1942 appreciation of the picture turns out to be Janet Ann Gallow's Cloestine, and Coe - after averring that "Bela Lugosi becomes the town's philosopher, a sort of perverted Frank Craven" - concludes with "… there are other things you can read in this morning's paper, so we'll let you go now." Earlier that year, on the 25 March, the *Los Angeles Times'* Philip K. Scheuer tersely opined that "It's a spooky movie, all right, in the best Universal manner and fairly ingenious. At the close the monster goes down in flames again – but that doesn't fool us for a minute. He'll be back, girls; he'll be back. Grr." Yet another prediction, but one that was ultimately less impressive than Bosley Crowther's.

A fast paced, atmospheric romp through familiar countryside, *The Ghost of Frankenstein* might well be the next logical step to Boris Karloff's well-stated fear: the Monster as henchman. Pretty much a callow bully here, he had moved from a date that went tragically wrong to finding a homey with whom to hang to palling around with little kids, all the while being manipulated by those who claimed to act in his – and science's – best interests. No offense is intended in calling the picture an excellent journeyman effort, albeit the lack of a master's touch is obvious and lamentable. The Monster and the franchise could – and would - do worse.

*The Ghost of Frankenstein* – 13 March 1942 – 67 minutes (SoS)

**CAST**: Sir Cedric Hardwicke as Dr. Ludwig Frankenstein; Lon Chaney as The Monster; Ralph Bellamy as Erik Ernst; Lionel Atwill as Dr. Theodor Bohmer; Bela Lugosi as Ygor; Evelyn Ankers as Elsa Frankenstein; Janet Ann Gallow as Cloestine Hussman; Barton Yarborough as Dr. Kettering; Olaf Hytten as Hussman; Doris Lloyd as Martha; Leyland Hodgson as Chief Constable; Holmes Herbert as Magistrate; Lawrence Grant as Mayor; Brandon Hurst as Hans; Otto Hoffman & Dwight Frye as Villagers; Julius Tannen as Sektal; Lionel Belmore & Michael Mark as Councillors; Harry Cording as Frone; Dick Alexander as Vision; Ernie Stanton & George Eldredge as Constables; Jimmy Phillips as Indian; Eddie Parker – stunts

**CREDITS**: Producer: George Waggner; Director: Erle C. Kenton; Screenplay: W. Scott Darling; Original Story by Eric Taylor; Directors of Photography: Milton Krasner and Elwood Bredell; Art Director: Jack Otterson; Associate Art Director: Harold H. MacArthur; Film Editor: Ted Kent; Musical Director: Hans J. Salter; Set Decoration: Russell A. Gausman; Sound Director: Bernard B. Brown; Technician: Charles Carroll; Assistant Director: Charles S. Gould; Makeup: Jack P. Pierce; Gowns: Vera West

*- JTS*

# *Mystery of Marie Roget* (1942)

In the 1940s, Universal was mostly looking to its past for inspiration with regard to its horror product. The "Frankenstein" and "Dracula" movies were given new sequels; the mummy and werewolf characters were rethought (today we'd say "rebooted"), *The Phantom of the Opera* would have a remake that considerably reworked the particulars of Gaston Leroux's novel, and the sundry works (or, at any rate, the name) of Edgar A. Poe – as the nineteenth-century writer preferred signing his work – would be revisited. The studio had had some success with films purportedly based on his screeds (and had stirred up a bit of a hornet's nest with one of them), so they re-used the title of one (1941's *The Black Cat*) and tackled a follow-up to another. In printed form, "The Mystery of Marie Roget" has often been subtitled "a sequel to The Murders in the Rue Morgue," and Universal sorta-kinda treated this production as a sequel to their 1932 film. In that earlier production, Poe's reclusive amateur detective, C. Auguste Dupin, was a medical student named Pierre; here, he is 1) the chief medical officer of the Paris police, 2) named Paul, and 3) acknowledged as the person who solved the Rue Morgue murders. The heroine in both adventures is named Camille (who was a victim in Poe's "Murders"), and there are little nods both to Poe's initial Dupin story and Robert Florey's film throughout.

Poe's story, originally published in three parts in *Snowden's Ladies Companion*, was based on an actual murder case; indeed, it is apparently the first such fictional exploration of a real case. "Marie Roget," in fact, beat not only "The String of Pearls" to the punch by several years - assuming the Demon Barber was a real person, as has been alleged, and not just an urban legend or a completely fictional creation – but also all those "based on a true story" crime movies by a century and a half or so. In

199

1842, Mary Cecelia Rogers disappeared (and not for the first time), and her body was later found floating in the Hudson River (definitely for the first time). She had first vanished in 1838, returning (so to speak) without explanation a few days later. As she was renowned as the most beautiful cigar girl in Manhattan, both disappearances and the tragic result of the latter instance made for sensational newspaper copy. The coverage even reached to Baltimore, Maryland - where Poe was living at the time - and the writer became intrigued by the case. An alternate allegation exists in which the owner of the cigar store where Rogers worked - a prime suspect - had paid Poe to craft a narrative that exonerated him. One can certainly envision the perpetually insolvent writer pouncing on the opportunity to earn two paychecks for a single story. Somewhat bizarrely, even Poe himself has been accused as being the killer.

In any event, Poe decided to resurrect his reclusive, nocturnal detective, C. Auguste Dupin, and have him solve the case almost completely by extracting clues from the newspaper coverage (as Poe himself was doing). The scene was reset to France, and the decedent became Marie Roget, a perfume seller whose body is discovered in the Seine. The ending is a tad coy in that the concluding paragraphs are supposedly excised by the *Snowden's* editor, and no culprit is actually named. Yet Poe does point in the direction of a solution and, when a deathbed confession was made some years later (a botched abortion – referred to in those days as a "premature delivery" – was the cause), Poe's inferred deduction proved uncannily correct. The late-in-the-day admission notwithstanding, the case is still referred to as "Unsolved."

In Paul Malvern's production, Mamzelle Roget has become a popular musical performer at the "Comédie Français" (it would not do for Universal's rising star, top-billed Maria Montez, to be a mere purveyor of scent or, worse, cigars). At film's start, Mlle. Roget has been missing for ten days, and Beauvais (John Kitel), a naval official, is berating Prefect of Police Gobelin (Lloyd Corrigan) for not having found her. (Beauvais, it transpires, is a friend of the Roget family, but really has no official excuse for getting uppity with the constabulary.) Just then news arrives that a woman's body has been found on the banks of the Seine, and Gobelin and Beauvais – the latter is oddly reluctant - go off to inspect the body and possibly identify it. They are accompanied by chief medical officer, Paul Dupin (Patric Knowles).

It turns out the corpse's face has been torn off, as if by the claws of an animal, though in height and build the remains answer to the description of Marie. The policeman and the naval officer repair to the Roget household to inform Madame Roget (Maria Ouspenskaya) - who keeps a full-grown leopard as a pet - of her granddaughter's apparent demise. Just then Marie flounces in and blows off all attempts to explain her absence. (That her theater has been shut down for a week and a half is apparently of no concern to her, either.) Her sister Camille (Nell O'Day) is overjoyed to have her sister alive and well. Later Mme. Roget overhears Marie plotting with Camille's fiancé, Marcel (Edward Norris), to kill Camille at a party; she summons Dupin and offers to employ him to escort the young woman and prevent the murder; he demurs until he meets Camille. Of course, he is smitten, even though she may be the blandest and most perpetually upbeat heroine in the Universal canon. At the party, however, it is Marie who is assaulted, and murder is proved when her body, too, is later removed from the Seine, her face also disfigured. Mme. Roget insists the case remain uninvestigated (and the body not definitively identified), so Dupin and Gobelin must proceed looking into things *ex-oficio*; Dupin is convinced both deaths are linked and that Camille's life may also be in danger.

**Lloyd Corrigan as the bumbling police inspector plays comic foil to Patric Knowles' Dupin. At least he's an improvement over Bert Roach in *Murders in the Rue Morgue*. Still, we must ask... were the iconic detectives of the Victorian Age truly as omniscient as they were presented, or did they're being surrounded by fools and incompetents merely make them brilliant by comparison?**

While it considerably embroiders Poe's story – adding an initial death to Marie Roget's disappearance and further original plotting after the titular character is done in – this particular adaptation of the author's work nonetheless remains remarkably faithful to the original, unlike nearly every other movie purportedly based on Poe's work. There are some serious plot holes – Marie's initial absence is never explained - as indeed neither was Mary Rogers' - though within the larger plotting of a movie story it ought to have been given a rationale. Nor are we given the the reason for the killer's donning a cape and slouch hat *a la* The Shadow to assault Camille; apparently the garb was employed simply to delay the reveal. (Just why the wheelchair and double-cane-dependent Mme. Roget is continually mentioned as a suspect is a bafflement as well.) But the running time is so short and things move so briskly under Phil Rosen's direction, that most of these questions don't arise while one is viewing the film – except for essayists such as I, who watch the danged thing multiple times prior to writing about it. *Mystery of Marie Roget* is a better than adequate - though only by a smidge - mystery thriller.

The "hand cultivator" – as Gobelin describes the soil-breaking, forked gardening implement – as an implement of murder became something of a favorite in Universal's horror/mysteries of the period. It would reappear in both *The Scarlet Claw* (1944) and *She-Wolf of London* (1946), leading this writer to refer to the three films as "Universal's Garden Weasel Trilogy" in an online message-board post. Here, it is used post-mortem to disfigure and disguise the victims; in the others, it is the actual murder weapon. The script doesn't play completely fair with the viewer; way too much of Dupin's detecting is done off-screen, out of the sight of Gobelin and the viewer. Given that his superior is prone to dashing off to arrest someone (anyone!) at the drop of a suspicion, this might be SOP, but it also means the spectator is not allowed to participate in the guessing game. A properly crafted mystery has its clues out in plain sight and even displays the detective taking notice of them. To the script's credit, Dupin makes his deductions through ratiocination (and a midnight brain theft!) rather than guesswork. And his ultimate unmasking of the killer - by putting the heroine in mortal danger - is straight out of the "Sherlock Holmes" playbook. (Cue the chorus of voices pointing out that Poe and Dupin got there first and served as the model for Doyle and Holmes. Poe's Dupin, however, never resorted to that stunt.)

Several times, Dupin's actions also result in making his somewhat dim superior look like an even bigger fool than he is. Gobelin is, of course, the counterpart to the intellectually-challenged sidekick that Nigel Bruce's Dr. Watson became in the movies, but never was in Sir Arthur Conan Doyle's stories. Neither is Poe's unnamed literary narrator, for that matter; like Watson, he simply isn't as brilliant or observant as his friend. In the movies, though, it was easier for lazy writers to make the sleuth look smart by making his companion comically dim. Still, the portrayal here – which is not as annoying as Bruce's Watson – allows for several lovely exchanges between Gobelin and the sharp-tongued Mme. Roget, one of which ends with her memorable retort, "Go have yourself stuffed!" Despite that, one can't help but wonder how this nitwit rose to the position he holds.

*Mystery of Marie Roget* is one of the few Universal horrors of the '40s – or the '30s for that matter – to have a proper period setting (unlike the vague settings of the "Frankenstein" films), though it should be noted that 1889 is 40+ years removed from the actual crime or Poe's story. It does, however, allow for sets that, while they may have been left over from other productions, are not the ones familiar to so many of the other Universal horrors of the time, aside from the European streets complex. Director Phil Rosen makes good use of this permanent, still-standing, outdoor set (which dates at least as far back as 1923's *The Hunchback of Notre Dame*) for a sequence wherein Dupin engages in some "second story work," a frantic carriage pursuit (wherein different camera angles disguise the fact that the same streets are being driven over again and again), and an exciting, climactic rooftop chase. This last is one of several bits lifted from 1932's *The Murders in the Rue Morgue* to fill out a film that used up Poe's material by its halfway point. Another is the suspicion of an animal assailant: in this case, a leopard and not an ape. (There's also a morgue scene, all but duplicated from *Mystery of the Wax Museum*.) True, Dupin is still engaged in solving Marie's murder, but there's lots of business with Beauvais trying to impede the investigation, and Mme. Roget insisting that the murder not be looked into and solved. Come the plot's resolution, the first makes no sense and, as regards the latter – mustn't murders be scrutinized even if the family of the deceased objects? Everyone, even Camille (who might be hiding Marie's diary), seems to be hiding something or shielding someone.

The film does not move well. After an intriguing set-up, the film continues to the party whereat Dupin is to be Camille's protector; curiously, he spends little time with her, even repairing to the veranda for a cigar. Marie sings a song (Dorothy Triden dubbing Montez) that may allow for extra footage to showcase the soon-to-be Universal "Queen of Technicolor" exotica, but it stops things cold. The subsequent investigation plays out too leisurely. Dupin proves the first victim came from England by examining the contents of her stomach (beef – which, by the way, is not unknown in French diets), visiting a zoo, and discovering that Mme. Roget's leopard is now a resident; (don't blink or you'll miss Charles Middleton, Ming the Merciless himself, as the zoo keeper). Capping this all off is his strolling through the grounds of the estate where the party was held and promptly disappearing. It's all handled so languidly that the hour running-time seems longer by half. Some of this may be due to Knowles' restrained performance; he's a good actor, but it may not have been in him to own a movie dynamically the way, say, Basil Rathbone owned the "Sherlock Holmes" films.

Things don't really pick up again until the exciting climax when Dupin races to Camille's rescue; while this never ceases to be entertaining, it's never quite as engaging as it ought to be. Some online scribes have labeled the film a proto-*noir* because of its use of German Expressionist shadows, apparently not realizing that the look marked Universal horrors (and those from other studios) from the early '30s on. No, *Marie Roget* is your garden variety murder-mystery with a few – very few – horror accents. (If you want to credit a U-horror with being a *noir* precursor, it should be *Son of Dracula*, whose *femme fatale* makes a sap out of a guy to get an inheritance - courtesy of a murder - and the man she's really hot for prefigures Billy Wilder's *Double Indemnity* by a year.) The photography – both in composition and lighting – is one of the saving graces here. Note the visible ceilings in the Roget house, making the snug little abode feel even more claustrophobic while possibly harboring a secret. (While this *may* have been influenced by *Citizen Kane*, it should be pointed out that ceilings had been visible in films long before Orson Welles decided to use low-angled camera positions for his tyro feature.) Really impressive work is on view in the frequent and foggy night scenes; the work of Elwood Bredell (profiled in our essay on *Man-made monster*) is spectacular in those. If the film has horror atmosphere, it is his doing.

And, as usual, the cast makes it worth giving this flick at least one viewing. Patric Knowles makes a fine, sturdy Dupin in the third of his quartet of Universal horrors. (We realize neither this nor *The Strange Case of Doctor Rx* are truly horror films, but they were promoted as such.) The viewer is never in doubt that he will solve the conundrum, and he's sexy in that understated Code kind-of-way. He's treated at length in our essay on *The Wolf Man* as is Maria Ouspenskaya who, thanks to her appearances in a clutch of Universal chillers, might well be termed the "Grande Dame of 1940s Horror." Whether confined to a wheelchair or hobbling about on two canes, she's a formidable presence, and when she attacks the killer with one of those sticks upraised, you almost believe she'll prevail. Lloyd Corrigan gets his due as an actor in another lupine entry, *She-Wolf of London*, but it should be added that in the early '30s he was also active as a director and helmed the final Paramount "Fu Manchu" entry, *Daughter of the Dragon* (1931), the "Hildegarde Withers" mystery, *Murder on a Honeymoon* (1935), and the Boris Karloff feature, *Night Key* (1937). He was also, until 1939, a very busy screenwriter, and his output includes all three Paramount "Fu Manchu" features. Frank Reicher, the irrepressible skipper of the Skull Island expeditions - who here has a small but prominent role as a magistrate - is also covered elsewhere in this volume.

The rest of the cast is unique to Universal horrors, and lest you think that producer Paul Malvern (another enlistee from the Poverty Row studios for Big U's genre productions) was trying to distinguish the film from the rest of the studio's chillers - the better for it to serve as a launch for Maria Montez - bear in mind that Peggy Moran was initially cast but bumped from the role a mere two days before production began. La Montez was at the time not noted for her acting ability, but rather for the off-screen publicity she received for her looks. (She was once quoted as saying, "When I look at myself I am so beautiful I scream with joy.") She never would be noted for her thespic chops, and the best that can be said is that she was better than Acquanetta (but then, a wooden Indian had a broader acting range than Acquanetta). Montez (1912-1951) had teeny-tiny roles in a number of films, including *The Invisible Woman* (1940), prior to *Marie Roget*, but she soon was cast as the star of a series of Universal productions such as *Arabian Nights* (1942), *Ali Baba and the Forty Thieves*, and the certifiably daffy *Cobra Woman* (both 1944), usually with Jon Hall and Sabu in tow. (Given her newly found stardom, Universal would reissue *Marie Roget* a year later as *Phantom of Paris*, giving her more prominent billing.)

**Edward Norris and Maria Montez. Montez's role as a vain and imperious cabaret star couldn't have been much of a stretch for the tempestuous actress, who was just on the cusp of becoming Universal's Queen of Technicolor hokum.**

Montez's only other true brush with genre was 1949's *Siren of Atlantis*, the third adaptation of Pierre Benoit's **She**-like novel, **L'Atlantide**. (The film's production serves as the setting for Gore Vidal's novel, **Myron**, a sequel to his notorious **Myra Breckenridge**.) The actress was cut loose from Universal at least in part because audience taste was shifting to darker material after the end of WWII, and this independent production was a sign her career was in trouble; she would decamp to Europe for her remaining films. Maria Montez passed away at the age of 39, having drowned in her bath, possibly following a heart attack.

John Litel (1892-1972), suspicious as all get-out from the get-go here, was a Warner Bros. contract player during the '30s who had appeared in support of the likes of Bette Davis and Errol Flynn, and was featured as Nancy Drew's father; still, he didn't appear in any of the company's horror productions until *The Return of Dr. X* (1939). The same year as *Marie Roget* he made *Sealed Lips* and *Invisible Agent*. The '40s found him bouncing back and forth between Universal (*Murder in the Blue Room*, 1944) and Columbia, where he had recurring roles in the "Crime Doctor" films, and at Paramount, where he would be cast as Henry Aldrich's father throughout that series. Freelancing was good for Litel. In 1951, he showed up in *Flight to Mars* - a Monogram "Cinecolor" production (!) - and began dividing his time between the large and small screens, including a recurring role on the latter as The Governor in Disney's *Zorro*. His only genre appearance on television in a decade and a half was in *Voyage to the Bottom of the Sea*.

Fiancé Marcel was played by Philadelphia native Edward Norris (1911-2002), who got started in the film biz after a chance encounter with William Wellman resulted in being hired as Buddy Rogers' stunt double in *Wings*. After a stint on stage to better learn his craft, he had his first screen appearance in 1933, an uncredited bit in *Queen Christina*. His first genre appearance came two years later with another uncredited appearance ("Man Outside the Theater") in *Mad Love*. Louis B. Mayer initially planned to groom Norris for stardom, but ditched those plans after discovering Robert Taylor. Thankfully, by the release of Fox's *The Gorilla* (1939), his character bore a name. Still, Fox treated him no better than had M-G-M, and he took to the bottle. Despite a reputation for being difficult, he apparently cleaned up his act by 1941 and began freelancing successfully, with *The Man with Two Lives* – a sort of "Black Friday, reimagined" made in '42 for the inestimable A.W. Hackel Productions - his last genre title on the big screen. TV-wise, other than one entry in the 1956 series, *Strange Stories*, he had no more credits of interest to folks like us. Norris did make some canny investments and was able to retire from acting completely in 1963, devoting his time to his hobbies. Ann Sheridan was one of his five wives.

Director Phillip/Phil Rosen's (1881-1951) name is better known to fans of Monogram's "Charlie Chan" whodunits with Sidney Toler than it is to horror hounds; an even half-dozen appear on his CV. Russian-born Rosen began his film career in 1912 as a cinematographer for Edison before graduating to directing and, in that capacity, he worked for a variety of studios, both major and minor, directing some of the biggest stars of the silent period, including Rudolph Valentino in *The Young Rajah* and Wallace Reid in *Across the Continent* (both 1922). Come the talkies, he inexplicably was relegated to Poverty Row, along with a number of other directors who had been in demand before the introduction of the microphone. (A possible explanation was the studios' rush to sign on stage directors who were thought better equipped to handle the new demands of spoken dialogue. No one to our knowledge has investigated this phenomenon.)

Rosen's first brush with horror (if it can be termed that) saw him directing Bela Lugosi and The East Side Kids in *Spooks Run Wild* (1941). Two years after *Marie Roget*, he'd direct Lugosi again in the wonderfully loopy *Return of the Ape Man*. He moved over to television in 1951 and logged in a single episode of *Front Page Detective* before passing away that same year at the age of 63. On the personal side, his second marriage was to exotic (or should that be erotic?) dancer, Joyzelle Joyner (1905-1980), who may be best known for her attempt to seduce Frederic March in terpsichorean fashion in Cecil B. De Mille's *The Sign of the Cross* (1932). Sometimes billed merely as Joyzelle (and yes, that really is the name her parents gave her), she also undulated in *Just Imagine* (1930), *House of Mystery* (1934), and *Dante's Inferno* (1935). Her film career ended when the Production Code went into full force – surely not coincidentally.

The story and screenplay for *Charge of the Light Brigade* (1936) – which had Knowles in a featured role – might be regarded as the high point of Michel (sometimes billed as Michael) Jacoby's career insofar as credited prestige assignments go. Jacoby (1898-1970) also worked without credit on the same year's *The White Angel*, the Florence Nightingale biopic starring Kay Francis. Lesser assignments at lesser studios followed, including a Mr. Wong mystery, *Doomed to Die* (1940). The same year as *Marie Roget* he penned – or rather typed – the underrated *The Undying Monster* for Twentieth Century Fox. He added one more *fantastique* credit to his resume with *Face of Marble* (1946) and then, following a final screenplay for Monogram (taken from a George Waggner story), he disappeared from Hollywood. What he did for the next decade and a half is unknown.

Bosley Crowther's review in the *New York Times* of 5 May 1942 was headlined, "Why – Oh, Why?" and reeked of his usual disdain for chillers.

> Usually when murder is done in fiction, it is best to show some motive for the crime. But that very obvious essential is just one of the conventions which has been overlooked – at least so far as this spectator could fathom – in Universal's butchered retelling of Edgar Allan Poe's 'The Mystery of Marie Roget'... the conclusive fact of the matter is that this is a dreary, aimless film, devoid of logic or excitement or even a shadow of suspense. Vaguely it leaves an impression of wretched futility. Several fairly good actors have been buried beneath a molehill of dust.

It should be noted that yes, there is a motive for both the two murders and the attempted homicide, and this is plainly stated in the dialogue. But we suspect Mr. Crowther did not enter the Rialto intending to pay all that much attention to the "B" chiller about to unreel. Or mayhaps he expected a "Charlie Chan" or "Nick Charles"- style final monologue laying it all out. In any event the trades, as usual, were more inclined to deal with the production for what it was. All singled out Rosen for praise.

> Not too exciting in its overall setup, and lacking clarity in several spots, picture still retains sufficient melodrama and suspense to satisfy as supporter in the lower bookings. Maria Montez carries the title role as the hazily-identified siren... Phil Rosen steers the tale on a steady course despite the inadequacies of the script. Cast is above par for a low budget programmer... Corrigan is particularly effective as the jittery and generally-bewildered prefect of police, while Mme Ouspenskaya provides her usual polished performance.

Walt, *Variety*, 8 April 1942

The "Showbiz Bible" dubbed it a "Mildly interesting whodunit" in its Miniature Reviews.

> This Edgar Allen [sic] Poe tale has been fashioned into an engrossing film, one that should have a sizable audience waiting since the author's works have long been in the preferred list of mystery fans. The picture has been handled competently. Under the well-balanced

direction of Phil Rosen, the atmosphere of mystery is sustained until the end, and the few 'horror' phases of the story are carefully toned down. The performances are good and the settings are unusually impressive, for which credit goes to Jack Otterson.

Arneel, *Motion Picture Daily*, 3 April 1942

The credits are somewhat mysterious on this since it is called 'Edgar Allan Poe's Mystery of Marie Roget' yet Michel Jacoby is given credit for an original screenplay. Poe's story has been somewhat twisted and turned about but with it all, a good horror story is the result. Some of the action is not sufficiently explained to dovetail with the end but the horror fans won't mind that too much. Excellent performances are given by a cast worthy of better material... Direction has been smooth and well-handled to keep up the suspense.

Anonymous, *Showman's Trade Review*, 4 April 1942

While the anonymous author of this critique claims Poe's story was "twisted and turned about," he (she?) later confesses it has been some time since he/she has read it and has only dim memories thereof. The original, of course – like a good deal of the author's work – defies a strict adaptation, but pretty much everything in it reached the screen. Online comments reflect the latter-day appreciation of the film as good, if scarcely great, fun.

... The cast is interesting, though it's really hard to buy that Maria Montez (with a French accent) is the granddaughter of Maria Ouspenskaya (with a Maria Ouspenskaya accent). The latter is a suspect largely because she keeps a pet leopard (but, then, who doesn't?), and, for that matter, the daughter is also a suspect (that is, until she becomes a victim). The horror elements are the fact that it comes from a Poe story, the presence of the leopard, and the gruesomeness of the murders. For me, most of the enjoyment of the movie is just watching Maria Ouspenskaya act, even in a strange-looking wig.

Dave Sindelar, "Fantastic Movie Musings and Rambling"s

... The piece is only 61 minutes long but it's lean, mean and ready for anything. The rapid-fire editing of Milton Carruth is to be praised

209

because there isn't a down moment as we leap from location to location, scene to scene and revelation to revelation. It slows down somewhat in the aftermath of Marie's second disappearance, but soon ratchets back up to speed again, with what is as much a dry comedy as it is a mystery... as Dupin outstrips his friend, the Prefect of Police, who flusters gloriously. This double act was a joy to behold... Michel Jacoby's script throws no end of sparkling dialogue their way. 'I have an idea,' says Gobelin at one point, having finally figured out what Dupin has known all along. 'It's about time,' replies Dupin.

Hal C. F. Astell, "Apocalypse Later Film Reviews"

*Mystery of Marie Roget* – 3 April 1942 – 60 minutes

**CAST**: Patric Knowles as Dr. Paul Dupin; Maria Montez as Marie Roget; Maria Ouspenskaya as Mme. Roget; John Litel as Henri Beauvais; Edward Norris as Marcel Vigneaux; Lloyd Corrigan as Prefect of Police Gobelin; Nell O'Day as Camille Roget; Frank Reicher as The Magistrate; Clyde Fillmore as Mons. De Luc; Paul E. Burns as Gardner; Norma Drury as Madame De Luc); Charles Middleton as Curator; William Ruhl as Detective; Reed Hadley as Naval Officer; remainder of cast uncredited - Raymond Bailey as Gendarme; Joseph E. Bernard as Man; Paul Bryar as Detective; Caroline Frances Cooke as Woman; Lester Dorr as Subordinate to Prefect; Paul Dubov as Pierre, News Vendor; Jimmie Lucas as Parisian; Alphonse Martell as Vegetable Cart Driver; John Maxwell as Detective; Frank O'Connor as Man; Beatrice Roberts as Woman #2 Reading Newspaper; Francis Sayles as Parisian; Dorothy Triden as dubber of Marie's Singing Voice; Charles Wagenheim as Subordinate to Prefect

**CREDITS**: Associate Producer: Paul Malvern; Director: Phil Rosen (as Phillip Rosen); Screenplay: Michel Jacoby; Based on story by Edgar Allan Poe); Music: Hans J. Salter, Ralph Freed, Richard Hageman, Charles Previn, Frank Skinner, Franz Waxman (composers: stock music, uncredited); Cinematography: Elwood Bredell; Film Editor: Milton Carruth; Art Direction: Jack Otterson; Set Decoration: Russell A. Gausman (as R.A. Gausman); Costume Design: Vera West (Gowns), Makeup: Jack P. Pierce; Associate Art Director: Richard H. Riedel; Sound Director: Bernard B. Brown; Sound Technician: Robert Pritchard

**Shock Theater Catalog** No. 724 - "Is she a beautiful beast? Maddening with her soft caress – murdering with steel-clawed terror? Only Edgar Allan Poe could pen such a masterpiece of horror and thrills. See 'The Mystery of Marie Roget,' the full-length feature film on *Shock* (day), at (time) on this channel."

*- HHL*

# *The Strange Case of Doctor Rx* (1942)

*Synopsis*: Five men have been found dead with ropes around their necks – apparent suicides save for a note signed "Rx." All were known criminals who had been acquitted at trial. The police are stumped as to the identity of the vigilante and Captain Bill Hurd (Edmund MacDonald) entreats private detective Jerry Church (Patrick Knowles), recently returned from a year-long sojourn in South America, to help crack the case. Church demurs; he's had it with sleuthing and plans to join the family bond business in Boston. A check for 10k from Dudley Crispin (Samuel S. Hinds), with promise of another if the case is solved, changes his mind. Crispin was the defense attorney for several of the men killed by Dr. Rx (as the press has labeled the anonymous murderer) and fears ruin – as in no more clients if they continue being snuffed. And, lo, another one bites the dust immediately after a not-guilty verdict is handed in by the jury; the perp expires dramatically, apparently strangled, in full view of a crowded courtroom with an Rx note in his hand. Church receives warnings to drop the case but soldiers on despite the fact that his fiancée Kit (Anne Gwynne) - whom he has impulsively married – insists that he quit, although she was initially keen on the idea. The advisability of bowing out becomes apparent when Church is kidnapped by Dr. Rx, who plans on quashing Church's investigation by switching the detective's brain with that of the doctor's pet gorilla, Nbongo (Ray Corrigan).

Quite possibly the oddest of the Universal programmers that made their way into the "Shock Theater" package is this screwball comedy-cum-murder mystery with a hint of horror that frankly looks like a prank foisted on the Universal executives. And who would have expected such a lunatic romp from hack director, William (*The Mysterious Mr. Wong*) Nigh? Universal may have initiated the horror genre, but it was just as prone to borrowing ideas from other studios, in this case, M-G-M. Dr. Garth and his assistant, Janet, may have bickered in emulation of Nick and Nora Charles, but that was as nothing compared to the back-and-forth between Jerry and Kit Church here. The "Thin Man" series was still popular – having premiered in 1934, its last entry, *Song of the Thin Man*, wouldn't hit screens until 1947 - which might explain why the screwball elements are so prevalent. Then again, there might be another reason, but we'll get to that in due course.

As might be gathered from the opening precis, *The Strange Case of Doctor Rx* gets pretty danged outrageous - even veering into Curt Siodmak territory - before "The End" flashes onto the screen. (And you might be forgiven if the thought occurs that every other Universal title of the era somehow involved brain transplants. Here, at least, we aren't subject to witnessing Ray Corrigan morph into Acquanetta.) But the scenario gets so nutso and increasingly comedic from its sober start, where we see the shadow of a man hanged from his bedpost, that the introduction of a cranial operation by the hooded titular medico just doesn't seem all that wild.

Still, the most curious aspect of this film is that it plays like a later installment of a series that never was. Scenarist Clarence Upson Young (working with an Alex Gottlieb story) introduces characters with his typical economy, but he also brings them on the scene as though they should already be familiar to us. Just why Jerry Church has spent a year in South America is never explained, although his junket there does help him identify the poison used by Dr. Rx (presumably curare, but never identified as such). Just what is Hurd referring to when he asks Church to help him solve the serial killings, saying that the two of them should be "big enough to forget the past?" We never do find out what might have caused any enmity. And just why is Church so adamantly opposed to continued detecting? His Manhattan apartment is lavish enough to suggest he's been pretty danged successful at it; he even employs a valet (who else but Mantan Moreland?). When Church discovers that it is Kit who has placed a hidden microphone in his apartment (to get ideas for her mystery fiction), the dialogue plays out as though the viewer should be familiar with their history and why they broke off their engagement.

But quite how much of this mix and the deranged plot twists can be laid at Young's feet is an open question. Some may have come from Gottlieb's original story, while others may have resulted in the picture going into production without a finished script – as would Hal Wallis's *Casablanca* (1942) – a quite unusual circumstance at Universal. An article on the "Turner Classic Movie" website explain:

Anne Gwynne recalled working on *The Strange Case of Doctor Rx* in **It Came**

214

**from Weaver Five**, a collection of interviews by Tom Weaver, and said it was 'Fun, fun, fun. I loved working with Patric Knowles. So very tall and handsome. A Britisher and very nice – but married. He and I also worked together on *Sin Town* [1942].' Gwynne also confirmed the long-standing rumor that much of the movie was ad-libbed. 'Right, it was done off-the-cuff. I would go home at night and study my lines, only to arrive the next morning to learn that everything was thrown out! It didn't take me too many nights to know to just go home and relax – there was no telling what to expect the next day – but it was an anxious-to-get-the-studio feeling, that was for sure. Like in *The Black Cat* [1941], the ad-libs were used, only much more so. Each of us would suggest things, and the director, William Nigh, would use them. That was just great, an experience I never had before or since. Of course, as a result, there are some plot loopholes in the finished product, but who cares? It was an hour of laughs and chills, a real crowd-pleaser.'

It is perhaps due to the improvisational nature of its creation that *Doctor Rx* isn't a proper mystery. While the revelation of the killer *is* a true surprise, it's because the clues that Church discerns to surmise his (or maybe her) identity are not shared with the viewer. It even cheats when the murder weapon is clearly nowhere to be seen during the courtroom killing. (A properly constructed mystery will have all clues in plain sight so the viewer – or reader – can guess along with the detective.) It's possible, given that the script hadn't been completed when filming started, that no one involved knew the killer's identity until late in the shoot – just as no one involved knew whether Ilsa would end up with Rick or Victor in *Casablanca*. Crispin's brother (Paul Cavanagh) makes the initial outreach to Church, which puts him in the Most Unlikely category and therefore a possibility. And then there's second-billed Lionel Atwill - in coke bottle glasses as Dr. Fish - who's forever popping up suspiciously. And how about Hurd? He must be frustrated with crooks getting off scot free, and Church *does* seem reluctant to share his findings with the cop – he even sends him off on wild goose chases twice. First-time viewers might be well advised not to even try to determine the killer's identity and just settle in for a wild ride.

As my colleague John Soister points out in his observations on the film, the killer isn't the only one in the cast of characters to have a double identity; most of the principals have some sort of duality.

The Churches enjoy dual lives, as well, although detectives who were also members of the idle rich were, in the '30s and early '40s, as plentiful as cigarettes between the lips of onscreen characters. (Sleuths depicted in other media at the time also maintained healthy bank accounts; Bruce Wayne was in no way an outlier.) Kit's crime-oriented other self serves to balance her more domestic side; the repartee she enjoys with Captain Hurd and the pluck she demonstrates in having the police assist her in tailing her errant husband certainly belong to someone other than the typical wealthy house-frau. There are also there are hints that something is going on between John Crispin and his brother's wife – her rummaging through the desk, for example, or her surprise at John's arrival, or the pair's frantic need to talk in private – but these are merely blind alleys that lead to nothing other than a longer running time.

Gwynne and Knowles - who made the film while on furlough from the army - have terrific chemistry together, and that's a good part of what makes the film work. Gwynne especially deserves credit for making her emotional one-eighties credible. Knowles is convincing as a determined sleuth (something he'd repeat in the same year's *Mystery of Marie Roget*); he's covered in more detail in the essay on *The Wolf Man*. Gwynne is likewise treated more fully in another essay, in this case, *The Black Cat*. Atwill and Hinds get substantial coverage in the entry on *Man-made monster* (all 1941).

**Major the dog is eliminated as a suspect. Looking only slightly nonplussed by his demise are Anne Gwynne, Mona Barrie, Paul Cavanagh, Patric Knowles, Samuel S. Hinds, and Lyland Hodgson.**

Paul Cavanagh (1888-1964) just may have the most colorful pre-acting resume of any 1940s U-horror player: Cambridge educated, he was a barrister and a Royal Canadian Mountie (!) before he heard greasepaint calling to him. He made his first film in 1928, but the closest he came to genre before *Doctor Rx* was *The Kennel Murder Case* (1933) and *Tarzan and His Mate* (1934). Subsequently, he appeared in *The Scarlet Claw* (1944), *The Man in Half Moon Street*, *The House of Fear*, *The Woman in Green*, and *Club Havana* (all 1945; the latter film felt to be Edgar G. Ulmer's budget-edition of *Grand Hotel*). Fritz Lang's *Secret Beyond the Door* (1947), *Bride of the Gorilla*, *Son of Dr. Jekyll*, *The Strange Door* (all 1951), *House of Wax*, *Port Sinister* (both 1953), *The Man Who Turned to Stone*, *She Devil* (both 1957) and *The Four Skulls of Jonathan Drake* (1959) all followed. The 1950s saw him increasingly turning to television shows, including – appropriately enough – *Sgt. Preston of the Yukon*. If nothing else, Paul Cavanagh was one busy man.

The brief life – and resultant short film career – of Edmund MacDonald (1908-1951) included *The Invisible Man Returns* and *Black Friday* (both 1940) prior to *Doctor Rx*. He also graced *Whispering Ghosts* (1942), *Sherlock Holmes in Washington* (1943), and Ulmer's *Detour* (1945). It was said that MacDonald had a face for *noir*, and he appeared in more than a few. He died at age 43, his life was cut short by a stroke and a brain hemorrhage.

The comic relief – if you discount the bickering between the Churches – is supplied by Shemp Howard (née Samuel Horowitz, 1895-1955) as Hurd's assistant, Sergeant Sweeney, and the incomparable Mantan Moreland (1902-1973) as Jerry Church's valet. Brother to Moe and Curly, Shemp took the latter's place in their Columbia "Three Stooges" two-reelers when Curly took ill, but he had a healthy resume in feature films as well, beginning in 1930. He can be spotted in *Another Thin Man* (1939), *The Bank Dick*, *The Invisible Woman* (both 1940), *Hellzapoppin'* (1941), *Arabian Nights* (1942 – as Sinbad!), and a clutch of Abbott and Costello films. While amusing solo, here he's at his funniest in a crap-shooting scene with Moreland and not terribly amusing elsewhere.

Mantan Moreland had been an established star of black cinema for some while when he chose to spend at least half his time in the stereotypical servant roles available for African-Americans in Hollywood major. His Horatio is no more cowardly than most of the similar characters Moreland would portray in zombie epics or for Sidney Toler's or Roland Winters' Charlie Chan – he *is* confronted with genuine physical violence here – but he's definitely a lot less sharp. Between demeaning associative-memory gags and fourth-rate shtick with the usually (but not here) funny Shemp Howard, the black comedian is reduced to a brainless, pop-eyed sight gag: the climactic sight of the white-haired Horatio is at once a sigh of relief (the white guy wasn't hurt) and a casual dismissal (only the black guy took his knocks). If we compare

217

this with the denouement of *Cracked Nuts* – wherein Moreland visibly fades to near-Caucasian pallor – we see the undeniable elements of a cinematic (and social) trend. The incomparable Moreland is given his proper due in our essay on the latter film.

The viewer can only shake his/her head in amazement at the gorilla. No one would ever begrudge Crash Corrigan or Steve Calvert or George Barrows or whomever a pay check, but this insistence on dragging N'Bongo (1) out of the well-worn woodwork is a throwback, plain and simple. Sure, the '40s saw an ape or two here and there, but unless confined to the less demanding parameters of the serial (cf. Columbia's *The Monster and the Ape*, 1945) or a fairly upscale one-shot (1949's *Mighty Joe Young*), the simian population could usually rely only on Tarzan, Jungle Jim, or Bela Lugosi for steady employment. Perhaps at least in part due to RKO's 1949 "King Kong" reworking, something of a simian renaissance would occur in the '50s, with Bela and Ed Wood each contributing to perhaps less memorable, but definitely more unforgettable examples of ape *amor* (*Bela Lugosi Meets a Brooklyn Gorilla* and *The Bride and the Beast*, respectively). Nonetheless, Doctor Rx (and *The Monster and the Girl*'s George Zucco) probably found it lonely at the top of the previous decade's roster of respectable villains harboring frenetic gorillas.

The honor this time fell to physical culturist and athlete Ray Corrigan (born Raymond Benitz, 1902-1976), who was a Hollywood fitness instructor who started out doing bit roles in 1932; he's a gorilla in M-G-M's first two Tarzan movies and is one of the hawkmen – as well as Bongo the gorilla – in the 1936 Republic serial, *Darkest Africa*, a guard in 1936's *She*, and Apollo in the previous year's *Night Life of the Gods* (billed therein as Raymond Benard). His first starring role was in *Undersea Kingdom* (1936 was a very busy year for Corrigan), and he decided on his screen name from the character he played; his nickname of "Crash" came from his willingness to undertake dangerous stunts. That particular deliciously dotty Republic serial features a surely unintentional but nonetheless outrageous homoerotic moment when the muscular Corrigan - clad in fish-scale briefs and a winged helmet, and suggestively spread-eagle across the front of a military tank - is threatened with being crashed into a castle's gates. "Ram away!" he instructs the tank's driver (Lon Chaney, Jr.). Also in 1936 he took on a recurring role in 24 entries of Republic's "Three Mesquiteers" series. He left Republic over a salary dispute and went to Monogram for the copycat "Range Busters" series.

Corrigan first donned his own gorilla suit for *Hollywood Party* (1934) and quickly reprised the impersonation for the same year's *Murder in the Private Car*. Reportedly a heavy drinker, he may have found it easier to work in his gorilla costume than keep in tip-top shape, and it sometimes seems through the '40s that, if it wasn't Emil Van Horn in a simian suit, it was Corrigan. His impersonation of apes (and other creatures as noted) were to be found in *Flash Gordon* (1936, as the Orangapoid), *Round Up Time in Texas* (1937), *Three Texas Steers* (1939), *The Ape* (1940), *Dr. Renault's Secret* (1942), *Captive Wild Woman*, *The Phantom* (1943), *Nabonga*, *The Monster Maker*, *The Hairy Ape* (all 1944), *The Monster and the Ape* (where he also played the robot, thus negating any scene between the two title characters as depicted on the posters), *The White Gorilla*, *White Pongo* (all 1944), *Miraculous Journey*, *Unknown Island* (as one of the dinosaurs), and *Congo Bill* (all 1948). In 1948 Corrigan reportedly sold his gorilla suits to bartender Steve Calvert, and any gorilla credits following that year are probably Calvert's, even if they are listed in some Corrigan filmographies. He *is* wearing the suit – constructed over his long-johns by Paul Blaisdell - in *It! The Terror from Beyond Space*, his final film (1958). For additional income, the actor/impersonator operated "Corriganville," a faux Western town that was available for rent as a film location on weekdays and as a tourist attraction - with gunfights, saloon gals, and such - on weekends. It was just up the road from the Spahn Ranch, where Charles Manson and his followers would take up residence.

**Universal released a series of goofy publicity shots of Anne Gwynne posing with Nbongo the gorilla (Ray Corrigan) though, in the film, beauty and the beast have no scenes together.**

219

Director William Nigh (born Emil Kreuske, 1881-1955) directed the first of his 125 films in 1914, shortly after the film trust was broken up and U.S. producers were allowed to make films longer than a single reel. That's not quite the birth of American cinema, but it's.... *ummmmm*.... nigh close. Nigh had started out as an actor three years prior (36 credits by 1925), but moved into directing for Mack Sennett, which may explain the ad-lib comedic approach he was able to impart to this flick. (He also had 21 writing credits between 1913 and 1945.) From 1926 through 1929, he was employed at M-G-M during which time he directed Lon Chaney the elder in *Mr. Wu* (1927). For reasons that remain unknown, his career faltered with the coming of sound, and he wound up for the most part at the minor studios. (This was not uncommon; many Poverty Row studio directors - such as William Beaudine and Christy Cabanne - helmed prestigious projects in the Silent Era but moved to Gower Gulch afterwards.) He was at Monogram for 1934's *House of Mystery,* which was based on the same Adam Hull Shirk play that was purportedly the basis for Boris Karloff's *The Ape* (1940), which Nigh also directed. (One would be hard-pressed to discern much similarity between the two; chalk that up to Curt Siodmak throwing out everything in the latter opus save the idea of someone donning a gorilla skin to commit murder.)

Nigh directed Bela Lugosi in the delightfully loopy "Fu Manchu" knock-off, *The Mysterious Mr. Wong* (1934), and Karloff in *Mr. Wong, Detective* two years later, along with four follow-ups. Just prior to *Doctor Rx* he again directed Lugosi in the goofy Sam Katzman serial, *Black Dragons* (1942). He then briefly joined up at Universal, along with the veritable wave of "quickie" directors drawn to the studio after its decision to turn out bottom-of-the-bill "B"s as thriftily as possible. (We might well ask how ever did William Beaudine miss out on that move?) Nonetheless, Nigh was soon back with the independent producers (the short-lived Alexander-Stern Productions for starters) and would retire six years later without another horror in his varied resume.

Considering all the improvisation that occurred, it's anyone's guess as to how much of Alex Gottlieb's story or the screen adaptation by Clarence Upson Young (1895-1969) made it to the screen. But it should be noted that Young is also part of the team behind Universal's other highly original '40s horror, *Night Monster* (1942), so suspicion is high that some of his work is here as is some of Gottlieb's. Gottlieb worked on another successful blend of mystery and comedy with horror elements, *Horror Island* (1941), and he is covered in the entry on that film. Young's first script was *The Plot Thickens* (1936), one of RKO's "Hildegard Withers" murder mysteries; this one with ZaSu Pitts filling the schoolteacher-cum-sleuth's sensible shoes. The rest of his most active period was filled with a slew of Westerns, some action pictures, and several comic mysteries – a sub-genre into which *Doctor Rx* fits quite neatly. *Night Monster* was his only horror script – and it, too, is structured as a mystery. Despite its title, *The Ghost that Walks Alone* (1944) features no ghost or horror aspects, although it did star Arthur Lake, which is admittedly pretty horrifying. While there were two Westerns made from his stories in the late 1950s, his active scripting career ended in 1949.

The one mainstream review we uncovered didn't think much of the picture but at least conveyed its dismissal in a fashion as amusing as the film. As usual, it remained to the trades to treat the production for what it was: entertainment, not high art.

> Continuing its long research in morbid psychology, the Rialto is this week probing 'The Strange Case of Dr. Rx' in a spirit, mind you, not strictly scientific. At best it merely confirms the fact that mad doctors, mad scientists and mad inventors all have god-complexes and singularly murderous impulses. They like to scare daylights out of their intended victims by cackling balefully behind slitted hoods, by flourishing hypodermic needles and strange scalpels, or by remarking sotto voce with a nod to a larger-than-life ape bouncing up and down in his cage, 'He is stupid now, but after we transfer the brain....?' No wonder men's hair turns white in a matter of seconds. That is precisely what happens in 'The Strange Case of Dr. Rx,' and particularly to one Mantan Moreland as a dark-skinned and blandly inefficient houseboy who steals what little there is to steal in the picture... the new Rialto film is a collection of babbled clues, butlers at windows and gloomy manses, leers by Lionel Atwill and matrimonial badinage by Patric Knowles and Anne Gwynne – most of which is beside the point... Dr. Rx's case is quite familiar...
>
> T. B., *The New York Times*, 28 May 1942

> 'The Strange Case of Dr. Rx' is even stranger than is par for Universal horror films, although considerably less horrific. The ape, which is standard equipment for these numbers, makes its entry late in the picture, as does the idea of transferring a man's brain into the ape's cranium, but these matters are handled as incidents rather than prime factors this time... the whole matter becomes so perplexing that a sort of post-picture sequence is supplied in which the principals explain to

each other, and thus to the audience, just what happened and who made it happen... William Nigh... kept momentum at high pitch throughout.

Roscoe Williams, *Motion Picture Daily*, 30 March, 1942

## COMPLICATED MELODRAMA IS SCARY ENOUGH TO PUT IT OVER

Those who like to be puzzled when they go to the movies will get just what they want in 'The Strange Case of Dr. Rx.' The torturous course of the plot is so complicated and muddled that they'll be lucky if they can unravel the whole mess at all. Whether they do or don't won't matter very much because there is enough melodramatic ammunition thrown around to keep the works popping and the audience in suspense. The horror fans will gurgle happily when the villain is on the verge of arranging a brain-swapping act between the hero and a ferocious gorilla.

*The Film Daily*, 2 April 1942

Reflecting the fun that can be had from the best (and even less than best) of the entries from the second half of Universal's Golden Age is the following:

... more mystery than horror, though *Dr. Rx* is a mystery with horror trappings (movies with hooded scientists with electrical gizmos and a pet gorilla aren't quite your average mystery) and one horror star in Lionel Atwill (whose character name would give away his function) in what amounts to be a bit part... slick, fast and fun—not to mention sometimes funny... with not only Mantan Moreland (he steals the show), but also Shemp Howard on hand.

Ken Hanke, (Asheville) Mountain Xpress, 2 August 2011

*The Strange Case of Dr. Rx* – 17 April 1942 – 66 minutes

**CAST:** Patric Knowles as Private Detective Jerry Church; Lionel Atwill as Dr. Fish; Anne Gwynne as Kit Logan Church; Samuel S. Hinds as Dudley Crispin; Mona Barrie as Eileen Crispin; Shemp Howard as Det. Sgt. Sweeney; Paul Cavanagh as John Crispin; Edmund MacDonald as Det. Capt. Bill Hurd; Mantan Moreland as Horatio B. Fitz Washington; John Gallaudet as Ernie Paul; William Gould as District Attornry Mason; Leyland Hodgson as Thomas, the Butler; Following are uncredited:

Frank Austin as Jury Foreman; Gary Breckner as Radio Announcer; Paul Bryar as Bailiff; Eddy Chandler as Cop outside Church's apartment; Ray Corrigan as Nbongo the Gorilla; Boyd Davis as Police Commissioner; Drew Demorest as Club Waiter; Matty Fain as Anthony 'Tony' Zarini; Mary Gordon as Mrs. Scott; Harry Harvey as Nightclub Manager; Selmer Jackson as Judge; Jack Kennedy as Policeman; Joe Recht as First Newsboy; Jack C. Smith as Policeman; Leonard Sues as Second Newsboy; Jan Wiley as Lily; Victor Zimmerman as Kirk

**CREDITS**: Associate Producer: Jack Bernhard; Director: William Nigh; Screenplay: Clarence Upson Young: Original Story: Alex Gottlieb (uncredited); Musical Director: Hans J. Salter; Music: Hans J. Salter, Frank Skinner (uncredited); Composer/Stock Music: Ralph Freed (uncredited); Cinematography: Elwood Bredell (as Woody Bredell); Film Editing: Bernard W. Burton; Art Direction: Martin Obzina, Jack Otterson; Set Decoration: Russell A. Gausman (as R. A. Gausman); Sound Department: Bernard B. Brown (Sound Director), Charles Carroll (Sound Technician); Costumes and Wardrobe: Vera West

***Shock Theater*** Catalog No. 740: "He took the law into his own hands, was doomed by the justice for which he killed. Don't miss the thrills and suspense of 'The Strange Case of Doctor Rx.' It's another exciting feature film on *Shock*, and it's coming your way on this channel, (day), at (time). For tops in mystery films, see 'The Strange Case of Doctor Rx'."

*- HHL*

# *Invisible Agent* (1942)

Other than several entries in its updated Sherlock Holmes series, the studio's genre-arm offered no '40s feature film more directly connected with the War than *Invisible Agent*. Taking a break from acts of vengeance and/or megalomania, the "Invisible" run made the creative move of utilizing the Griffin-oriented propensity to have its hero become transparent in order to battle America's (and Britain's) greatest enemy since... *well...* since they fought each other during the American Revolution. As stipulated earlier in this book, H.G. Wells's tragic scientist went from a fairly faithful cinematic adaptation in 1933 to being a chap helped in being rendered unseen by said scientist's brother in order to clear himself of an accusation of murder, to a young model – of no apparent relation - doing the see-through thing in response to a newspaper ad, to the film at hand, wherein the titular character is the grandson of the eponymous protagonist of the original. (All those who are shocked and outraged, worry not! *An invisible man had his revenge in 1944*, and we've got the essay to prove it!)

Inasmuch as there's usually a war being waged somewhere at any given point, fictional treatments dealing with invisible armies, robot warriors, instantaneously-healing soldiers, immortal troops, and the like have always been popular. Getting the technological edge on the enemy is the aim of the scientific arms of both (or all, I guess) sides of a conflict, so the contemporaneous reaction to the news that the Luftwaffe had been *this close* to battling the Allied Air Forces with jet-propelled planes ran the gamut from open-mouthed admiration to appalled disbelief to outright horror. Whereas *our* know-how and tenacity were signs of our forthright commitment to regain the peace and maintain law and order in the world, *their* knowledge and drive were deplorable indications of the desire to foment chaos and crush humanity under

225

the heels of their jackboots. Naturally, both viewpoints pivoted per one's allegiance, so even the less physically outrageous aspects of a world war – like the clandestine choreography required to negotiate the slippery slope of espionage – were declared to be courageous or cowardly depending on the uniform one had doffed so as to move more easily among one's foes.... in some instances, actually *impersonating* them.

Thus, even as the War was raging, entertainment was being melded with propaganda – a procedure hardly unique to American cinema – and both Allied and Axis forces were tarred with brushes dipped in the most poisonous of paints by movie-makers working from ideologically opposite *Sitz im Leben*. Popular Hollywood conceits had *der Führer* and his under-staff made to look ridiculous – *a la* Charlie Chaplin as Adenoid Hynkel in 1940's *The Great Dictator* and Jack Benny as ham actor, Josef Tura ("So... They call me 'Concentration Camp Ehrhardt'?") in 1942's *To Be or Not to Be*. Making these portrayals all the more powerful was the fact that both were enacted by renowned Jewish comedians. (1) Equally popular-yet-ironic was the casting as high-ranking members of the Third Reich Germans, Austrians, and the like who had fled that regime for political or humanitarian reasons. Albert Bassermann and Conrad Veidt, for example – both Max Reinhardt alumni and husbands to Jewish wives – found their cinematic livelihoods tied to no little extent to their backgrounds and accents: 1942 saw Bassermann tapped to play a handful of nefarious Germans (including the evil sanatorium head, Dr. Storm, in Paramount's *Fly-By-Night*), and Veidt set to embody what came to be regarded as one of his signature roles: Major Strasser in Warner's *Casablanca*. When there were no authentic Germans to be had at the moment, Britons filled the goose-stepping need, as most American moviegoers of that generation found an English accent to be a believable stand-in for otherwise unintelligible mutterings *auf Deutsch*. And, on the rarest of occasions, even otherwise unexceptional American actors might be called on to pull the wool down over the eyes of their Axis enemies, as was Ralph Bellamy – as Baron von Ragenstein (a titled enemy agent) and Sir Edward Dominey (his non-Teutonic doppelgänger) - in Universal's *The Great Impersonation* (1942).

The star of Universal's *Invisible Agent* was hardly an "unexceptional" American actor. Born Charles Felix Locher in Fresno, California, Jon Hall was son to a Swiss inventor (who himself entered acting in his dotage) and a woman consistently described in print (without being named) as a "Tahitian princess." Having spent most of his youth in Tahiti, it must have seemed quite natural to the 20-year-old novice that one of his earliest cinematic "uncredits" was as a "Tahitian Native" in M-G-M's *Mutiny on the Bounty* (1935), the landmark film based on the novel by Charles Nordhoff and

James Norman Hall; the latter was the young actor's uncle, after whom he took his screen name. Hall's first major movie credit (as Charles Locher) saw him play opposite Warner Oland in *Charlie Chan in Shanghai* (1935), and – following a brace of indie programmers in which he was billed as "Lloyd Crane" - he metamorphosed into Jon Hall and spent the next couple of years starring in a string of romantic adventures set in his "old neighborhood": *The Hurricane* (1937), *South of Pago Pago* (1940), *Aloma of the South Seas* (1941), and *The Tuttles of Tahiti* (1942).

Come 1942, Hall not only dabbled in invisibility but also began to dabble in Maria Montez, as he and the "Queen of Technicolor" – usually in the company of Sabu and/or Turhan Bey – cornered the market on even more exotic romantic adventures set in the Middle East or the sub-continent. For the next lustrum, the Hall-Montez-Technicolor epics hit theaters everywhere every six to eight months or so, but starting in 1947, Technicolor gave way to Cinecolor, Universal gave way to Columbia (and other studios), and Hall – who would portray the screen's only Robin Hood to have most of his Merry Men go uncredited (1948's *The Prince of Thieves*) - would find his yet-to-come greatest renown as TV's *Ramar of the Jungle*. Like his father, Hall invented stuff in his spare time, and with his father, he invented the "Locher-Hall Telecurve Map," a device that showed both the distance and shortest air-path that exists between any two spots on Earth. Following his involvement (acting) in 1965's *The Beach Girls and the Monster* and (co-directing, albeit sans credit) in *The Navy vs. the Night Monsters* (1966), Hall retired from the screen. Later in his life – plagued by inoperable bladder cancer – he committed suicide (13 December 1979) and was buried next to his father in Forest Lawn Cemetery.

Hall's Frank Raymond (born Griffin) is the sort of earnest, affable, hard-working guy Americans have always liked to identify with, especially in times of strife. When visited by five foreign-types (3 Germans, 2 Japanese) in his printing shop, Frank manages not only to kill the lights and slug his way out, but also to snatch the invisibility formula right out from under their noses. Both Conrad Stauffer (Sir Cedric Hardwicke) and Baron Ikito (Peter Lorre) aver that Raymond is the grandson and namesake of John Sutton's *Frank* Griffin (and not Claude Rains's *Jack* Griffin), so we're dealing with *Duo*caine here (not that anyone is keeping count). Hence, it turns out that profound napping at inconvenient moments – rather than fits of narcissism and megalomania – is the side effect that manifests itself during the narrative. (The cynic in me wonders whether Sir Cedric Hardwicke's agent refused to answer the phone following this film and the earlier *Returns* when Universal announced that Jon

Hall would once again go unseen as yet another Griffin a couple of years later in *The I.M.'s Revenge.*)

Given that – apart from the comedic, distaff spin-off essayed by Virginia Bruce – *Agent* directly followed *Returns*, it's a bit odd that, what with all the Nazis and whoever puffing away on cigarettes to beat the band, John Fulton didn't engineer some sort of follow-up to Cecil Kellaway's cigar-smoke ploy. Come on... even when Hardwicke's office is afire and there's smoke up the wazoo almost everywhere, there's not the slightest indication of a Griffin outline to be found. Had Mr. Fulton forgotten about the clever effect he had pulled off a couple of years earlier? Or had the Powers That Were ixnayed on any additional expense, effects-wise, due to the War?

Speaking of the War, for a film released in July of 1942 to base its premise on a situation that preceded the 7 December 1941 might have struck some as peculiar. Raymond/Griffin refuses at first to share his grandfather's formula with anyone – even the USA – but this opening gambit takes place prior to the film's acknowledging the bombing of Pearl Harbor and subsequent disasters via a slew of newspaper headlines. Even so, afterwards, the stubborn printer will agree to the formula being applied only to himself, although he has zero experience either as a uniformed soldier or as an undercover agent. And the assemblage (just who are they, anyhow?) votes to go along, rather than cite the crucial need to protect the country's welfare and just seize the formula via eminent domain (or some such).

The film opens with the aforementioned five Nazis/Nipponese threatening to de-finger Frank Raymond/Griffin unless he comes across with his grandfather's transparency concoction. Escaping into the night, Frank is granted permission by the U.S. Dept. of Something or Another to parachute into Germany and retrieve classified information on Hitler's activities. With the help of cabinet/coffin-maker Albert Schmidt, Frank makes his way to Berlin where he hooks up (sort of) with the beautiful Maria Sorenson whilst demeaning via invisible hijinks Karl Heiser, one of the Third Reich's uniformed toadies. Heiser is further demeaned (and arrested) by Conrad Stauffer, a higher-ranking Nazi who works hand-in-hand with Baron Ikito, one of Japan's top spies.

Frank displays his manly phiz to Maria via a cold-cream treatment and the two fall for each other. While searching Stauffer's headquarters, Frank is (temporarily) held at bay, but he once again escapes, this time bearing a book that names all of the German/Japanese espionage agents in the USA. Although Albert Schmidt is detained after a phone call from Frank to Maria is traced to his digs, Frank frees Heiser from his jail cell after the Nazi reveals the what and when of Hitler's incipient plans to attack the USA. Not long after, though, Frank is captured (via a fish-net littered with fishhooks) and taken to the Japanese embassy. Maria shows up a bit later, and the two escape after truckloads of soldiers, summoned earlier by Stauffer, arrive and begin to clash with the Japanese. Baron Ikito stabs Stauffer and then commits seppuku, while Frank and Maria steal a German bomber and head toward England to advise the Allies of the imminent attack on New York. Their plane downed by anti-aircraft fire, the two parachute to safety and later, after Frank has somehow (he reveals it not) been restored to visibility, he and Maria – in reality, yclept Goodrich, an English agent – embrace and signal that all will soon be well.

The lovely Maria Sorenson/Goodrich was essayed by the lovely Ilona Massey (née Ilona Hajmássy) from Budapest who would, the following year, impersonate the lovely Baroness Elsa von Frankenstein in *Frankenstein Meets the Wolf Man*. The actress had made her entertainment debut as a singer – she was briefly a member of the Hungarian State Opera – and she sang onscreen opposite Nelson Eddy a couple of times, including *Balalaika* (1939, featuring Albert Bassermann as Ludwig von Beethoven), and also to the accompaniment of famed Spanish pianist, José Iturbi (in *Holiday in Mexico*, 1946). Somehow, she didn't sing - pretty much due to Vera Ellen's vocalizing and the Marx Brothers' being the Marx Brothers - in 1949's quasi-musical, *Love Happy*. Massey's Maria acts according to convention here, her feminine side almost immediately attracted to Griffin (and vice-versa) while her double-agent side proves heroic as she shoves the unconscious invisible man from the German bomber before the plane starts its descent to disaster. The silly side of things is hardly her fault; twice she's tossed over the shoulder of her transparent boyfriend and carried away from danger, an action that both stupidly exposes Griffin's otherwise unknown presence and diminishes Goodrich's professional and personal dignity.

Sir Cedric Hardwicke and Peter Lorre also pretty much play by the book, Nazi- and Nipponese-wise. Hardwicke intones his lines in standard Hardwickian fashion – no faux German accents for him – and Lorre here sounds pretty much like Lorre anywhere. Both villains are pretty laid back, although Stauffer does get agitated when Griffin begins to set his office afire and the guards posted outside can't seem to get the damned door unlocked. As this is a blatant feel-good propaganda film made in the midst of the Second World War, there is not the slightest hint that either Stauffer or Ikito or any of their compatriots or subordinates is anything other than a cold-blooded murderer. We witness the tenuous alliance between Germany and Japan fall apart – physically as well as symbolically - as Ikito stabs Stauffer and then himself (thumbs-up to Lorre for demonstrating he hadn't forgotten his faux *jiu jitsu* skills

229

from a lustrum's worth of Mr. Moto films and to Hardwicke's stunt double for turning a somersault worthy of the Olympic trials), while we watch Heiser being machine-gunned by soldiers wearing the same uniform as he. A tip of the *Stahlhelm* to J. Edward Bromberg's Heiser who credibly makes the transition from pseudo-comic foil at the outset of the film to whining prisoner halfway through to the picture of ambitious National Socialism moments before meeting his fate.

Mayhaps the 1943 Oscars reflected the fact that 1942 wasn't an especially big year for Special Photographic Effects, but it's tough to see how John P. Fulton could have been nominated for his work here. Fulton had likewise been nominated a year earlier for his Photographic Effects for 1940's *The Invisible Woman* (released in 1941), but he and his sound man (John Hall [!] for *Agent*, Bernard B. Brown for *Woman*) lost both times to Paramount and the team of Farciot Edouart and Gordon Jennings.(2) *Agent*'s effects were not up to the standards Fulton et al had established for previous "Invisible" epics, and none of the other sequels could hold a cigarette to his work in *Returns*. The sequence in which Jon Hall's presence is represented by a dress cap perched above a starched coat collar has to be seen to be disbelieved, and there is more than one other instance (the cold-cream application scene, for instance) where the vaguest of outlines of the actor's head may be espied. (Have to be honest; the miniature work in the film is likewise rather poor.)

**Not one of John P. Fulton's finest visual effects; still, this may have represented Vera West's only career opportunity at depicting invisibility!**

230

Story-wise, Curt (here, Curtis) Siodmak's original screenplay hadn't all that much originality to it, other than the concession the local War Board made to Griffin in allowing him – with no relevant background, training, or experience whatsoever – to make contact with (and thus endanger) the lives of Allied operatives in Germany. When Albert Basserman(n)'s Arnold Schmidt reveals his hands have been broken via Gestapo interrogation, we need only recall the succession of doors opening/closing within everyone's sight and the traceable phone call made from the woodworker's shop to Maria's Berlin digs to realize that apparently Griffin's common sense suffered greatly when his brain also became transparent. Then again, with most of the Nazis either flailing about ludicrously – the oafs that enter Stauffer's office to capture Griffin are positively simian-like - or doing operatically poor double-takes in the course of the picture, one might ask why it took the Invisible Agent almost 80 whole minutes to disrupt Hitler's plans for invading New York. American moviegoers must have come away from this film feeling that the average German soldier was fairly dim, easily incapacitated, and a ready target of the Luger or machine gun wielded by his superior officers, and that those superior officers were given to fits of desperation and betrayal.

Director Edwin L. Marin remains better known for films featuring Ann Sothern or Randolph Scott than for *The Invisible Agent*, but he did begin his work at the megaphone with *Dracula* alumni Bela Lugosi and Edward Van Sloan in *The Death Kiss* (1932). In addition, the New Jersey native's CV also includes mysteries of every stripe – including a couple of Philo Vances - some screwball comedies, and the Reginald Owen/Gene Lockhart rendition of Dickens's *A Christmas Carol* (1938), so Merin had gotten his feet wet in most genres at many studios prior to landing this assignment at Universal. What he ultimately may have added to Siodmak's script and Fulton's effects sequences was speed and efficiency; that plan to obtain the info on Hitler's big project may have been quite sketchy, but it was carried out without too much time being wasted on any save for the most rudimentary (and predictable) of character development.

Back in the day – when local press reflected local opinion and mores – *The Invisible Agent* won strong support from moviegoers (who doubtless hoped the Government was working on something like this) and multiple thumbs up from the paid opinionators. The 19 September 1942 edition of the *Cleveland Plain Dealer*, for example, held that:

The plot is filled with intrigue and excitement. The solution is satisfying... The lighting is unusually good, and the 'materialization' of the hero via cold cream is not the least among the picture's camera feats.

As for the *dramatis personae*, well...

> The cast is an unusually good one but, as is usually the case with these wilder action - melodramas, the pace is so furious it carries the players quite as much as they propel it... Director Edwin L. Marin's pace keeps the excitement high.

Not every media venue shared the *Plain Dealer*'s enthusiasm. The 7 August 1942 *Christian Science Monitor* didn't concentrate on pacing or excitement, but rather on what it perceived to be a very poor on the state of Western Civilization.

> The... film is wanting in inventiveness and taste. It plays the old tricks in inappropriate circumstances. Moreover, while presenting Nazi officials as brutes, it tries at the same time to make them figures of fun. It turns from scenes of torture to Keystone comedy. This treatment, in view of the present state of the world, is amazing in its callousness.

*The New York Times* – which had hit the streets the day before the *Monitor* – anticipated the scolding and took it much further:

> It is a shocking fact that in this fateful Summer Hollywood should have the temerity to offer American audiences such a film as 'Invisible Agent,' now at the Criterion. For it is as obvious a breach of taste as the screen has provided – and it has provided more than one example – in the past season. Out of the fanciful notion of placing an invisible spy in present-day Germany, the author has concocted an irresponsible tale that blithely mingles gauche attempts at comic satire with melodramatic sadism. In one scene it portrays the Gestapo bullies as so many Keystone Kops; in the next it reveals them torturing an old man whose hands they have broken... 'Invisible Agent' takes the ruinous point of view that maniacal brutes may be simultaneously shown as laughable dolts. It is as incredible as a joke told in a nightmare.

A month later, the *Washington Post* (11 September 1942) pretty much beat the same drum:

In view of current headlines and the President's warning of further sacrifices on the home front, it becomes increasingly difficult to pass off as 'entertainment' the kind of film which indulges in wishful thinking where our enemies are concerned.

Still, *Post* reviewer Ernest L. Schier did go on to allow that...

The one bright spot in viewing the melodramatic thriller was the attitude of the teen-age audience, composing most of the packed house, who laughed raucously at the unbelievable situations and refused to be taken in by the plot, which portrays the Germans and Japanese as blundering fools.

In his memoir (3), Curt Siodmak - "the author" of the "irresponsible tale" per *The New York Times* – took what was essentially the three papers' observations and attempted to reconfigure same into positive attributes:

Since [*The Invisible Man Returns*] was nominated for an Academy Award because of its special effects and was also a financial success, I had to write every one of Universal's 'Invisible' pictures. After a hiatus of years, I was assigned to write *The Invisible Agent*. To send an invisible spy to Nazi Germany during World War II was an obvious theme. Jon Hall played the transparent intruder, helped by the shapely Ilona Massey, a beautiful blonde Hungarian singer. The girl in the film, in love with Jon Hall, was never sure whether the invisible agent was hiding in her bedroom at night and did not dare to undress, jumping fully clothed into bed. The German background gave me an opportunity to turn that comedy into a strong propaganda film against the Nazis. It had some very grim scenes depicting the cruelty of the Nazis, even against each other.

Per the critiques above – pretty much representative of the opinion of the more influential press - the Axis Powers' cruelty to each other did little to counterbalance what was perceived of as ranging from inappropriate to appalling, except, of course, by the "teen-age audience." Still, those commentaries were writ by professional evaluators who either ignored or were ignorant of the fact that "the author" of the conceit they found to be so unsettling was himself a German émigré who had fled the Third Reich. Most audiences (including the "older" segments) found *Invisible Agent* to be ideologically upbeat, fast-moving – it takes the Axis search party a mere 30 seconds to report in to Hardwicke and Lorre that the invisibility drug is nowhere to be found in Griffin's print shop - and not terribly demanding attention-wise.

If nothing else, the film managed to do what had probably been thought of as impossible: transform one of Universal's classic '30s grotesques into a bona fide hero. While yet another Griffin is not *The* Invisible Man – obviously, there *is* no *The* Invisible Man - he is *an* Invisible Man, and that's just what the wartime moviegoers paid to.... *errrrr....* see.

*Invisible Agent* – 31 July 1942 – 79 minutes

**CAST**: Ilona Massey as Maria Sorenson/Maria Goodrich; John Hall as Frank Raymond/Frank Griffin; Peter Lorre as Baron Ikito; Sir Cedric Hardwicke as Conrad Stauffer; J. Edward Bromberg as Karl Heiser; Albert Basserman(n) as Arnold Schmidt; John Litel as John Gardiner; Holmes Herbert as Sir Alfred Spencer; Keye Luke as Surgeon; Philip Van Zandt as S.S. Officer; Matt Willis as Nazi Assassin; Mabel Concord as Maid; John Holland as Spencer's Secretary; Marty Faust as Killer; Alberto Morin as Free Frenchman; Wolfgang Zilzer as van Porten; Ferdinand Munier as Bartender; Eddie Dunn & Hans Schumm as S.S. Men; John Burton as R.A.F. Flier; Lee Tung-Foo as General Chin Lee; Milburn Stone as German Sergeant; Michael Visaroff as Verichen; Walter Tetley as Newsboy; Pat West as German Taxi Driver; Leslie Denison as British Radio Operator; William Ruhl and Otto Reichow as Gestapo Agents; Pat McVey as German; Wally Scott & Bobby Hale as English Tommies; Charles Flynn, Phil Warren, Paul Bryar and John Merton as German Soldiers; Lee Shumway as Brigadier General; Henry Zynder as Colonel Kelenski; Victor Zimmerman, Bill Pagan & Henry Gutterman as Storm Troopers; Lane Chandler, Duke York & Donald Curtis as German Sentries; Charles Regan as Ordinance Car Driver; Sven Hugo-Borg as German Captain; James Craven as Ship's Radio Man; Eddie Parker

**CREDITS**: A Frank Lloyd Production; Director: Edward L. Marin; Associate Producer: George Waggner; Original Screenplay: Curtis Siodmak; Suggested by the novel *The Invisible Man* by H.G. Wells; Director of Photography: Les White; Special Photographic Effects: John P. Fulton; Film Editor: Edward Curtiss; Art Director: Jack

Otterson; Associate Art Director: Robert Boyle; Assistant Director: Vernon Keays; Musical Director: Hans J. Salter; Set Decorator: Russell A. Gausman; Associate Set Director: Edward R. Robinson; Director of Sound: Bernard B. Brown; Technician: William Hedgecock; Gowns: Vera West

*-JTS*

# Sherlock Holmes and the Voice of Terror (1942)

In 1938, Sherlock Holmes was an almost forgotten figure to North American cinema inasmuch as his last adventure produced by an American studio had been the indie feature, *A Study in Scarlet* (1933), starring British ex-pat, Reginald Owen. While 1937 had seen the release of *Silver Blaze* - the last of a five-picture series starring another British Holmes impersonator, Arthur Wontner - the feature went unseen in the United States until 1941, when it was retitled *Murder at the Baskervilles* in an attempt at capitalizing on 20th Century-Fox's hit. Fox had acquired the rights to one of the most famous of Arthur Conan Doyle's novels, **The Hound of the Baskervilles**, due to the renewed interest in horror films, thanks largely to the 1938 Regina Theater triple-feature (*Dracula, Frankenstein, Son of Kong*) mentioned elsewhere in this volume. Fox lost no time in adapting the novel to the screen, and the finished product arrived at movie houses throughout the country by the end of March 1939. The tremendous success of the picture moved the studio to redouble its bet and a few months later marked the premiere of *The Adventures of Sherlock Holmes* (1939), which cemented the association of Basil Rathbone and Nigel Bruce as the immortal Holmes and Watson on the screen. At that point, planning to launch a series, Fox signed on to produce a Holmes feature film every year, but it ran up against the unusual stipulation of the representatives of the Conan Doyle heirs who demanded great literary fidelity in any subsequent movies.

The outbreak of the European War had imposed a standstill to Holmes on the screen although not to the negotiation table, where of the representatives of the Conan Doyle estate and interested studios continued to meet. Months after Arthur Wontner's last film arrived in the United States - when the poverty-stricken Astor

Pictures hoped against hope its release would cash in a bit on Fox's earlier success - it was reported that Warners had acquired "The Speckled Band," one of the 56 canonical stories to be brought to the screen with the Rathbone-Bruce duo under the direction of William Dieterle. The following month, it was revealed that the option had lapsed and that the film would not be made. Nonetheless, Rathbone and Bruce continued interpretations of Holmes and Watson fascinated audiences throughout the country via NBC's radiophonic waves in "The Adventures of Sherlock Holmes." Sponsors were fighting to get involved. And while the movies were continuing to go Holmes-less, the radio press chose their most popular participants – their "Champions of Champions" - and, according to the *Motion Picture Herald* article, "Champions of Radio Chosen by Editors" (21 December 1940), Basil Rathbone placed third in the popularity ratings of the "Film Players of the Air."

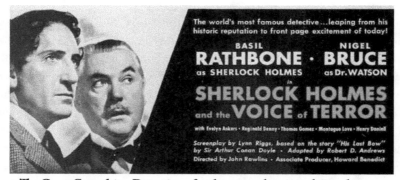

**The Great Consulting Detective – for the nonce, bearing a hairstyle more appropriate to the Roman Republic – and his Grand Deliberating Colleague, as featured in the *Film Daily* ad for this, the first of the Universal series.**

All of a sudden – and surprisingly – it was Universal who concluded an agreement, forking over $300,000 for the cinematic rights to 21 of the stories about the Great Consulting Detective. Denis, third son of Conan Doyle and attorney in charge of promoting his father's literary legacy, arranged a deal whereby Universal could offer three movies per year on condition that they extend it annually for up to a maximum of seven years. Of these first three films, two would be based on canonical stories and the third could be a new story especially written directly for the screen. In **Basil Rathbone: His Life and Films**, author Michael B. Druxman relates how producer Howard Benedict explained that "all the scripts for the pictures were our originals, being that we couldn't use more than one or two elements from Doyle's stories in each one."

The first film of the series would consist of an adaptation of "His Last Bow," a late work written by Conan Doyle in 1917 and with its background in the Great War. (1) Despite there being some very interesting characters to draw on in the body of canonical tales (Irene Adler, Moriarty, Colonel Sebastian Moran), this short story's chief antagonist is German agent Von Bork; however, in the film, he is no longer in the service of the Kaiser, but rather of the Swastika.

As an introduction, scenarists Lynn Riggs and John Bright redacted a text that might well have been taken from Vincent Starrett's **The Private Life of Sherlock Holmes**:

> Sherlock Holmes, the immortal character of fiction created by Sir Arthur Conan Doyle, is ageless, invincible and unchanging. In solving problems of the present day, he remains – as ever – the supreme master of deductive reasoning.

With this prologue, displayed in the film's first frames, Universal set the scene for its series in wartime and, attentive to the causes of success of the Fox films, highlighted the chemistry of the duo (which, per its literary source, was on a second level of importance, since the focus therein was on the crimes and the amazing tactics of Holmes). If the more squeamish moments for the civilian population of England had passed and the specter of an invasion receded day by day, the bombings and life at night in the anti-air attack refuges struck a nerve and an anxiety that this was intended to be reflected in the film's script, initially named *Sherlock Holmes Saves London*.

The BBC in London captures mysterious radio transmissions coming from Nazi Germany. In each message, the "Voice of Terror" announces a forthcoming terrorist act: the blowing up of a bridge, the setting afire of a factory, the derailment of a passenger train, etc. Each tragedy ends up happening just as the broadcast goes on air. Intrigued, the Defense Committee, presided over by Sir Evan Barham (Reginald Denny), sends for the great Sherlock Holmes to unravel the puzzle. "This isn't a case for a private detective. It's a matter of state," shout the other members of the committee, especially intelligence official, Sir Anthony (Henry Daniell, in typical suspicious role number one).

Holmes and Watson get involved in the matter and are put to work immediately although the first clue is a cadaver at the same 221b Baker Street: that of their street informant. They then descend into the underworld (metaphorically and literally) - to a seedy bar that operates in a cellar - where they meet Kitty (Evelyn Ankers), the girlfriend of the dead man, who becomes angered upon learning that the killers were Nazi conspirators. The dialog sequence between her and Holmes, presented via some touching and somber close-ups on the part of director John Rawlins, reaches some unusually dramatic levels for a Holmes film. And if nowadays we can readily perceive propaganda comments in every aspect of the story, upon our being transported back into the context of 1942 and keeping in mind the horror of the bombings of civilian targets, we can readily understand the emotion of Kitty's speech to the habitues of the bar:

> Help me or help the Nazis. Don't you know that all the crimes they commit are being blamed on you? For me, I'm British and I'm proud of it. Nobody is going to call me a Nazi and get away with it.

And in the face of the apathy and lack of confidence of her fellow countrymen, she takes on tones more appropriate to a Winston Churchill and demands:

> I'm not asking this for myself. England is at stake. Your England as much as anyone else's. About time to think about whose side we're on. There's only one side, England, no matter how high or how low we are. You, you, you, and you! We're all on the same team. We've all got the same goal: Victory!

The effect of her harangue is better than it would have been had the original conceit in the script – that Kitty was a prostitute – had been retained, but that had been removed in the first revision by those responsible members of the Production Code.

A little later, when Holmes is ambushed by the arrogant Meade (Thomas Gomez, with the Manual of Villainy in his pocket), the script gets complicated and the intrigue grows with the lack of the Committee's confidence in Holmes's methods, Kitty's attempt to infiltrate as an accomplice of Meade, and the suspicion that one of the members of the Committee may be a spy. Of course, the "Voice of Terror" might be a decoy, merely part of a much larger plan than the one Holmes intends to disrupt, with or without the Committee's help. The action doesn't stop and, despite the fact that the 65-minute-long running time seems quite brief, the film unfolds with a rhythm more appropriate to a serial, the genre in which Rawlins had made his name.

In an epilogue, the scenarists allowed themselves to quote some of the dialogue from the text of "His Last Bow," with Holmes alluding to a certain breeze coming from the East that will bring destruction and bitterness, but which will end up improving the lands "when the storm has cleared." The Apocalyptic (but hopeful) tone serves as an interesting twist on two different but perfectly cyclic moments in time in the history of the 20th Century: the two World Wars.

Taking a well-deserved break from interacting with werewolves and such in favor of interceding with indifferent/despairing countrymen and such herein is Evelyn Ankers as Kitty. The lovely Chilean-born actress would spend the lions' share of her career in the company of Universal's genre stars and character people, and there's a comprehensive listing of those sundry adventures in our *Wolf Man* essay. Another actress who would come to be associated with Universal was Hillary Brooke, perhaps best known to her more venerable fans as Abbott and Costello's friend and fellow renter in Sidney Fields's apartment house in the comics' eponymous '50s TV show. Brooke, born in decidedly less exotic surroundings than Ankers (Astoria, Queens, New York), started her career with a slew of uncredited bits (including Victor Fleming's *Dr. Jekyll and Mr. Hyde* in 1941, and her role as Jill, the British Army driver, here) before seeing her name – and that of her character, Sally Musgrave - onscreen in *Sherlock Holmes Faces Death*. More on the lovely Ms. Brooke may be found therein.

"SHERLOCK HOLMES AND THE VOICE OF TERROR"

**Holmes and Watson's first Universal adventure had them facing down the Third Reich *and* meeting the lovely Jill Grandis (Hillary Brooke, still pretty much in her "uncredited" days).**

The English cadences of Reginald Denny, the villain of our piece, were not affected, as the actor had been born – and, 75 years later, would die – in Richmond, Surrey, in England. Before opposing the Great Consulting Detective, Denny had spent a number of years – and eight features – as Bulldog Drummond ally, Algy Longworth, and although the actor's last feature film credit would be for the decidedly pop *Batman* in 1966, he had been thesping onscreen since 1915 (in Famous Players' *Niobe*); there were nearly 200 movie and television credits between the two. As the ersatz Sir Evan Barham (and the real-life Heinrich von Bock), Denny's depth of role is an easy match for Rathbone's, Bruce's, and everyone's, actually. While Denny would never match wits again with Universal's Holmes, he had once striven to match charisma with the Great Profile himself, when that heady gentleman had played the title role in Albert Parker's 1922 production of *Sherlock Holmes*.

New York City native, Thomas Gomez, made his screen debut in *Voice of Terror* and proceeded to play any number of of different types of roles, on the big- and small-screen for the next three decades, his career (and his life) ending only following a car accident in 1971. Like so many character people from the '30s and '40s, Gomez ended up spending most of his professional time working on guest appearances on TV shows. Still, his contributions to the genre, Universal-style, include 1944's *Phantom of the Opera* follow-up, *The Climax*, and an "Inner Sanctum" entry that same year, *Dead Man's Eyes*.

In retrospect, it's astounding that Glaswegian Mary Gordon received no screen credit here for her unforgettable debut as Holmes's long-suffering landlady, Mrs. Hudson. In films since 1925 – she was 43 years old when she first appeared onscreen, again uncredited, in Larry Semon's *The Dome Doctor* - she would work under her future film partner, Roy William Neill, for the first time in the 1926 crime film, *Black Paradise*. Loads of uncredited bits – usually as Mrs. This or Mrs. That, almost always a widow – followed until she received screen credit as the benign and infallibly concerned Mrs. Hudson by 20th Century-Fox for *The Hound of the Baskervilles*. She followed up in Fox's follow-up and continued in the role for Universal, occasionally without seeing her name in the cast crawl. Unlike most of her contemporaries, Miss Gordon did not segue into a long and profitable television career; one appearance – in a 1950 episode of *The Cisco Kid* – was plenty for her, and she left the industry "in pursuit of other things." Of particular relevance to us Universal genre fans is the knowledge that – the Holmes series apart – Miss Gordon was a frequent participant in the studio's horror and mystery films. A quick recap: *Frankenstein* ("mourner"/uncredited), 1931; *The Invisible Man* ("screaming woman"/uncredited), 1933; *Bride of Frankenstein* ("Hans's wife"), 1935; *The Invisible Man Returns* ("Cookie, the cook"/uncredited), 1939; *The Invisible Woman* ("Mrs. Bates"), 1940; *Sealed Lips* ("Mrs. Ann Morton"), 1942; *The Strange Case of Doctor Rx* ("Mrs. Scott"/uncredited), 1942; *The Mummy's Tomb* ("Jane Banning"), 1942; and *Strange Confession* ("Mrs. O'Connor"), 1945. Her presence – if not her name - onscreen for more than 300 productions, the wonderful Mary Gordon passed away after a long illness in 1963.

**German spy R.F. Meade (Thomas Gomez) will regret forming a relationship with Kitty (Evelyn Ankers), as the British barmaid will, in her own way, do as much to inspire her customers and fellow countrymen to fight the Nazi menace as would Winston Churchill.**

Although the characters and plots were updated by the House that Carl Built, the Baker Street *sanctum sanctorum* pretty much retained its original "flavor" whenever depicted during the series. Thus, most of the industry press spilled ink to warn of the change in time period but still welcomed *Voice of Terror* with thumbs up. *Variety* (9 September 1942) described it as "a well-packaged concoction of sleuthing, with suspense holding to a good level throughout. It's a strong programmer of type, and due for plenty of dating in the regular runs as a supporting number." The review also had some comments about the screenwriters, who "provide tight and crisp unfolding, which adds materially in maintaining audience interest in the proceedings."

For Vance King, Sherlock reviewer in the 9 September 1942 edition of *Motion Picture Daily*, it was a "highly acceptable entertainment with all the old flavor of Sir Arthur Conan Doyle's noted characters." This same King added, in the 12 September 1942 *Motion Picture Herald*, that "veteran Doyle fans will find the transformation of the period enjoyable; addicts of melodrama will find it more than adequate." (For all the hoopla over the "transformation of the period," when Holmes and Watson are ensconced in their Baker Street digs, it's virtually impossible to posit what year it is in the world outside the window; inside, we're still in Victorian England. If anything, Rathbone's new hairstyle – which would be abandoned come *Sherlock Holmes Faces Death* in September of 1943 – appears to be a remnant of that earlier era. There *is* a cute moment when Holmes is "tsk-tsk'd" from donning his deerstalker by Watson, who argues that Holmes "had promised" ostensibly to forego the fore-and-aft headgear during some prior and unrecorded conversation.)

*Showmen's Trade Review* (12 September 1942) observed that the producer "Howard Benedict has filled the picture with color and sets necessary for the realization of terror and feeling of the background." *Harrisons Reports* – bearing the same date of publication – considered it "a fairly good espionage melodrama," although that didn't stop him from remarking that "the story is a bit on the implausible side, but followers of mystery pictures should find it to their liking, since it keeps the head spy's identity concealed." Despite "the only reward Lynn Riggs, the author of the screenplay, has seen fit to offer the girl is death at the hands of one of the saboteurs," the critic at *Film Daily* (16 September 1942) wasn't moved, and he classified the picture as "a routine and undistinguished... melodrama." What we can appreciate nowadays is the reviewer stressing the picture *did* have "a fair amount of thrilling action and much speed, for which thanks, chiefly to the direction of John Rawlins." *Photoplay* (December 1942), which rated it as "pretty average fare," observed what at first glance might have been shocking to fans:

It was our idea the famous Conan Doyle character lived somewhere back in the nineties, gay or otherwise. Nevertheless and notwithstanding, we find the old boy, who must be getting along in years, with his inseparable pal, Doctor Watson... uncovering a Nazi radio nest and preventing all sorts of German invasions. My word, what an active bird, to be sure.

In addition to Tom Weaver's observation in his and the Brunas brothers' grand *Universal Horrors* of the similarities between the plot of *Voice of Terror* and the second remake of *The Great Impersonation* (1942) - also directed by Rawlins – with respect to the conceit of murdering "a titled Englishman and [replacing] him with a German who is his exact double," it is also a bit reminiscent of the infamous "Lord Haw Haw." For almost the entire duration of the war, from September 1939 until the end of May 1945, radio owners in Great Britain received bursts of war propaganda from Hamburg (these would reach the United States through short wave) from the broadcaster who, although baptized "Lord Haw Haw" by the press, was in fact a North American of Irish descent, William Joyce. Each one of his transmissions began with a call to attention: "Germany calling, Germany calling," not unlike the Voice of Terror's opening words: "Germany broadcasting, Germany broadcasting." In fact, as Amanda J. Field remarks in **England's Secret Weapon: The Wartime Films of Sherlock Holmes**, the first "working title" with which the project was known was *Sherlock Holmes vs. Lord Haw Haw*.

Current information usually attributes Holmes's contemporary ambiance at Universal to a studio marketing strategy, intended to lessen production costs and to attract the young(er) public. Nevertheless, one must take into account the course of action the Office of War Information, which – during the spring of 1942 – urged all the Hollywood studios that their new pictures have plots elements that draw the attention to the delicate situation of war in the Old World or in Oriental Asia. In this way, the War wasn't only present in the Holmes films, but also in those of Tarzan, Abbott & Costello, et al.

According to a 1964 interview, Rathbone himself commented that he had loved performing in this picture, and that in principle he liked the idea of updating the scripts as the dramas of the time appeared somewhat old-fashioned to him. More than the updated environment or the tenuous fidelity to the canonical stories, the most serious crime the series is accused of by its fans is that of presenting Watson as being reduced to a whipping boy, a bumbler who at times seems to border momentarily on idiocy. Naturally, arriving at a valid opinion one must enter the context of the time. In his unpublished memoirs (2), Nigel Bruce himself wrote that he saw the goal of his character as "introducing a little light relief. The doctor, as I played him, was a complete stooge for his brilliant friend and one whose intelligence was almost negligible."

This formula - a contemporaneous Holmes with a ridiculous hairstyle, diminished budgets which somehow did not produce "B"-film appearances – seemed to work better given wartime exigencies than had Fox's "A" features in 1939. As a result,

Rathbone, Bruce, and the sweet Mary Gordon (as the maternal Mrs. Hudson) spent the rest of the War embodying their characters in the subsequent series features that Universal would produce.

***Sherlock Holmes and the Voice of Terror*** – 18 September 1942 – 65 minutes

**CAST**: Basil Rathbone as Sherlock Holmes; Nigel Bruce as Doctor Watson; Evelyn Ankers as Kitty; Reginald Denny as Sir Evan Bartham; Thomas Gomez as Meade; Henry Daniell as Sir Anthony Lloyd; Montagu Love as Gen. Jerome Lawford; Hillary Brooke as Jill Grandis; Olaf Hytten as Sir Fabian Prentiss; Leyland Hodgson as Capt. Roland Shore; Mary Gordon as Mrs. Hudson; Arthur Blake as Crosbie; Harry Stubbs as Taxi Driver; Harry Cording as Camberwell; Donald Stuart as Grady; the voice of Edgar Barrier as the Voice of Terror

**CREDITS**: Director: John Rawlins; Producer: Howard Benedict; Screenplay: Lynn Riggs, John Bright; Adaptation: Robert D. Abrews; Original Story: "His Last Bow," by Sir Arthur Conan Doyle; Music: Frank Skinner; Musical Director: Charles Previn; Director of Photography: Elwood Bredell; Film Editor: Russell F. Schoengarth; Art Director: Jack Otterson; Set Decorator: Russell A. Gausman; Gowns: Vera West

*– DL*

# *Destination Unknown* (1942)

*Synopsis*: In Japanese-occupied Shanghai – following a montage of troops marching, planes flying, and bombs dropping – merchant Sun Wat Lin is gunned down by two Japanese soldiers. Before expiring, he hands off a small object to his servant, who, moments later, is stabbed by a man in a black hat and overcoat; the small object – which appears to be a clock – is removed from the dead servant's body.

Cut to a drunken Karl Renner, a German agent, attempting to put the moves on the lovely Elena Varnoff, an expatriate Russian beauty who manages to avoid his advances until he passes out. As she is searching his desk, though, the now conscious Renner attacks her, demanding to know for whom she works. Slugging him with a convenient desk-top statue, Elena makes good her escape. Heading over to the Japanese Military Headquarters, Varnoff asks what they would pay for the Saint Petersburg jewels. Told that the Japanese already have their eye on that prize, she leaves, bumps into an American in the street, and makes for her hotel, where the American – introducing himself as Briggs Hannon – starts to make small talk. Varnoff walks out on him, but he catches up to her in the street, once again fast-talks her, and they head off together in a cab.

In the interim, the Japanese have captured Renner, but - despite his being tortured - the German agent does not reveal the location of the jewels. Briggs and Elena arrive at Renner's home – Elena has a key – and they begin to search for clues to the whereabouts of the jewels. Briggs pockets a small clock, while maintaining that a picture hanging on the wall bears a clue to the location: an address in Peking. Elena's two henchmen, Victor and Wellington, relieve Briggs of the picture at gunpoint, and the two men and Elena depart, leaving the American behind.

247

Back at the hotel, Briggs discovers that Elena and her two aides intend to take a train to Peking, and he boards the same train. Coincidentally coming to share his compartment is Renner, seeking to capture the Russian and force her to return the little clock he believes she has stolen from him. Halfway to Peking, Elena and her two aides exit the train, hoping to throw Renner off their track. Renner leaves, too, & holds them at gunpoint. Fortunately, Briggs – who has also jumped the train – in turn holds Renner at gunpoint, and the German is tied up and stuffed into a nearby hut. The four uncertain allies then begin to walk toward Peking. They spend the night at the house of an amiable farmer, who provides them with horses; in the morning, the farmer and his family are killed by Japanese troops.

Briggs et al are picked up in a touring car by the secretary of a Chinese friend of Briggs after the horses are released. Staying the night at the "Chinese friend's" house, Elena finds that Briggs has flown the coop at some point and – courtesy of the secretary – learns about the value of the clock and that the American has taken same to Peking. Elena – now understood by all to be a Dutch agent hoping to use the jewels to pay for "a shipload of arms" - calls the Holland Legation in Peking and tells a Mr. Van Horn to have Briggs arrested for possessing false American papers. In Peking, Briggs - disguised as a Chinese farmer - meets up with curio dealer, Wing Fu, who knows the American as Terry Jordan, an heroic aviator. Fu shares with his friend a section of code that – together with the characters hidden within Renner's clock - will lead to the location of the St. Petersburg jewels. However, at that moment, three Dutch military personnel enter the shop, seize Briggs, and hustle him off to be "interviewed" by the monstrous Captain Muto of Japanese Military Intelligence.

Elena, Victor and Wellington soon discover Briggs's true identity, and – chastened – they set out to free him from the anticipated torture. Although a representative from the American Legation cannot convince Muto to release his American captive, the famous aviator pulls a fast one on his jailers and literally walks out of the building. Jumping into a car driven by Victor et al, Briggs leads Muto and his Japanese retinue on a merry chase, escaping when they shoot out the pursuing car's tires. Boarding a small plane, Briggs – let's call him Jordan now – and Elena, along with a heavy box of what we assume are the St. Petersburg jewels, fly to Chun King to pay for that shipload of arms and to find conjugal bliss. "God be with us, then," Elena says. "And with Chiang Kai-Shek and good people everywhere," adds Jordan.

First off, let us acknowledge upfront that had *Destination Unknown* not been a member of the original "Shock Theater" package, we would not be covering it (or a handful of other productions) here. As we have writ elsewhere – and as others have stated – the name of the TV series was "*Shock* Theater" and not "Monster Chiller Horror Theater" (apologies to SCTV, Count Floyd, Dr. Tongue, and Woody Tobias, Jr.), so not every film featured a grotesque. Hey, some of the wartime dramas that were included – like the film under discussion - didn't feature many elements reckoned to "shock," either. Virtually every entry in the 1957-1958 package – and there were 52 of them, one for every week of the year – was a Universal film, with most '30s or '40s monster pics, and the rest either purloined from the "Crime Club" run or patriotically-oriented offerings made during World War II. The subsequent package - "Son of Shock" - had but 20 films to offer; mayhaps the late '50s entree into the world of horror by Britain's Hammer Film Productions and the ever-increasing number of American-made science-fiction epics hitting movie theaters everywhere sucked the novelty out of the boob-tube's sequel series. Be that as it may, more than half of "Son's" films had been rendered by studios other than Universal.

As a kid, the *source* of the "monster movies" didn't matter to me at all. I was seven years old when "Shock Theater" debuted, and the series was my introduction to a world that – at that point - I hadn't imagined possible. It was as if the weirdest of heavens had descended on Brooklyn. By the time I had watched *Frankenstein* – okay; by the time I had watched up to Karloff's *entrance* in *Frankenstein* – I and a batch of my friends had started a monster club, and we would meet and talk about (and *draw!*) those classic monsters we had seen as well as fill each other in on movies we hadn't been allowed to stay up to watch, for one reason or another. Every once in a while, though, we'd pass on a picture when the *TV Guide*'s description failed to intrigue us, like *The Spy Ring,* or *Chinatown Squad...* or *Destination Unknown.*

Along with everybody else in Hollywood, in the early 1940s Universal saw it as its duty to produce – in addition to its revivified monstrous product - uplifting pictures that would encourage those on the home front to view the combat overseas in a more positive light. Films such as *Enemy Agent* (released in 1940, over a year-and-a-half before the USA reacted to Pearl Harbor) and *The Great Impersonation* (1942; the second enemy-agent-oriented remake of a silent drama, updated to deal with Nazis rather than the Kaiser's gang) (1) were meant to encourage audience members about the wisdom and might of their armed forces in part by depicting the country's foes as less intelligent/capable than we. The late-'50s contractual obligation between Universal and Screen Gems led to the inclusion of *Enemy Agent* in its "Shock Theater" bundling. For your more typical wartime/genre mix, please see the first three or four of the "Sherlock Holmes" pictures herein, or *Invisible Agent.*

*Destination Unknown* remains a horse of a different color, though. Set in Japanese-occupied China at a time that was probably intended to be contemporaneous with the film's release, the hero of the piece, Briggs Hannon, is in no way portrayed as any sort of American hero for most of the film's running time. Affable, wise-cracking William Gargan's character is certainly capable of talking/acting his way out of a mess, but until Olaf Hytten's Wing Fu spills the beans to Irene Hervey's Elena Varnoff that Hannon is really American flying ace, Terry Jordan, we're led to believe that we're dealing with a smooth talker who's only out to make a million or so bucks for himself. The revelation that Varnoff – supposedly a Russian expatriate likewise on the hunt for a secure future – is actually a Dutch patriot (sent by the Netherlands government of Java) likewise is meant to be something of a last-minute surprise. Sure, movie-house audiences in 1942 may well have suspected early on that the two leads would end up allies (in more ways than one) by the denouement, but all the talk of Holland and Chun King may have been obfuscated a bit by the ubiquity of Felix Basch's German spy, Karl Renner, and the alleged "inhumanity" of Turhan Bey's Captain Muto.

**We do not defer to the Screen Gems caption because we can do better, but because Screen Gems got it wrong: "William Gargan and Irene Hervey star in 'Destination Unknown' a story of the 'underground movement in war-torn Europe during World War II." Really? The film itself is set in Japanese-occupied China. Maybe this latter locale was a "Destination Unknown" to the Universal production staff!**

The production – like many of all studios' wartime efforts – was clearly shot on the lowest of possible budgets. When, for example, the four Peking-bound adventurers leap onto their steeds late in the game and *trot* off leisurely toward their destination, they're clearly horsing in front of a backdrop; ditto with a scene or two during the climactic Muto/heroes chase. Much of the film is bound to interiors (some quite fancy), standing sets, or back-lot acreage, a situation that reflects the wartime prohibition on the building of new sets or the use of any materials that might be better utilized by the armed forces. If nothing else, the film provided work for a good number of Asian thesps, even if – per the long-standing Hollywood practice up to that point (and beyond) – most of the featured roles (Captain Muto, Wing Fu, Colonel Suyakawa) were essayed by Occidentals.

William Gargan followed the usual path to stardom in the '30s & '40s: a few uncredited appearances early on, followed by some bits as the years rolled by, to featured/second cast roles, and thence to top- (or darned close to it) billing. Gargan was featured (or starred) in a few of the '30s Universal efforts that had at least a modicum of genre appeal - 1937's *Reported Missing*, 1938's *The Crime of Doctor Hallett*, 1939's *The House of Fear* – when not venturing elsewhere, like to M-G-M, with stuff like the decidedly non-genre *Joe and Ethel Turp Call on the President*; to 20th-Century Fox, with 1941's more-like-it *I Wake Up Screaming*; or even to Columbia, where he impersonated the detective-cum-mystery writer for a trio of that studio's "Ellery Queen" features. As Briggs Hannon/Terry Jordan, the actor brought his trademark affability - a quality earnestly sought after during the hyper-stressful '40s – as well as his capacity for assurance that almost always led his fellow *dramatis personae* (and audiences) to feel that there was nothing plot- or emotion-wise that Gargan's character could not readily handle. There's a bit more on the Brooklyn-born actor in our essay on *Sealed Lips*.

Irene Hervey's career path followed Gargan's, except her bits were fewer and her featured roles quicker to come down the pike; this may be due to the fact that the Venice (California) native had graduated from M-G-M's school of acting right into a studio contract. Hervey's Elena Varnoff is one of the few "ethnic" characters in *Destination Unknown* not to attempt an accent, albeit her being revealed as Dutch may have accounted for that; still, she *did* spend half the picture pretending to be from Russia, so her skipping from one to the other would probably have been a bit much. (The only Dutch character in the film to read his lines with the appropriate intonation and zest is the uncredited Frederick Vogeding – one of the three military officers sent by the Holland legation to snatch Briggs – and this is probably due to the man's actually having originated in the Netherlands.) Hervey and Gargan somehow keep their nearly incessant, arch back-and-forth from becoming intolerable due more to the force of their assumed personalities and one's curiosity as to where this is all leading rather than to the splendor of Lynn Riggs and John Meehan Jr's script. Like so many others of her vintage, the actress spent the lion's share of the '50s (and subsequent decades) adding a bit of class to a vast multitude of TV series.

Turhan Bey pops up hither, thither and yon in these pages, but the sight of the Austrian-born, Turkish heartthrob arrayed in Asian eye appurtenances as Captain Muto takes a moment to adjust to. Having been told of Muto's inhumanity, it's a bit of a dramatic disappointment for the viewer not to see the mad torturer at work; only Renner – the Nazi "ally" - gets a good going over (including whips to the soles of his feet & bamboo shoots under his fingernails), and that happens via shadow-play fairly early in the proceedings. As with most of the characters herein, Muto is stereotypical, but neither the 63-minute running-time nor the contemporaneous hatred for the Axis powers would have permitted a more nuanced portrayal. Bey, who had just come from sharing the screen with Irene Hervey in the Leo Carrillo/Andy Devine wartime epic, *Unseen Enemy*, would be back with that unlikely pair shortly in a tale of Nazis who have strayed as far from the European theater as possible, *Danger in the Pacific* (both 1942). *Destination Unknown* followed and then, in a move that is doubtless more to our liking, Bey ran across the parking lot to assume the role of another Bey – Mehemet – and swap out the congenial William Gargan for the equally amiable Dick Foran in *The Mummy's Tomb*.

As with most of the studio's war-themed programmers churned out during this first lustrum of the '40s, the rest of the cast is populated by Universal contract players, cinematic old-timers, and character actors of all sizes, stripes, and backgrounds. Genuine Russian import Sam Levene – due to be Broadway's original Nathan Detroit in *Guys and Dolls* – is Elena's right-hand man, Victor, and Brit Donald Stuart assumes his position (as "Wellington," no less) on the Dutch agent's left. The Cantonese Keye Luke fills the bill as Briggs' Chinese friend's nameless secretary/chauffeur, Glaswegian Olaf Hytten dons the robes of Wing Fu, and the Romanian Edward Colebrook impersonates Lieutenant Kawabe. Among the uncredited thesps filling in the background was a passel of Chinese and Chinese-American men (among them Paul Fung, Eddie Wong, Tom Yuen, and Victor Wong [memorable for also having played the uncredited Charlie-the-cook in *King Kong*], some of who were required to play the hated Japanese foe. Stuttgart-born Hans Schumm – who had come to America's shores in the late '20s already an established actor – may have gone sans credit here, but starred as the colorful principal villain ("The Mask") in Republic's serial, *Spy Smasher*, to be found on some of the same screens showing *Destination Unknown*.

While director Ray Taylor didn't helm those monster movies I came to know via the more "shocking" presentations on "Shock Theater," the man *was* responsible for a pile of Universal's silent & sound chapterplays, like *Clancy of the Mounted* and *The Phantom of the Air* (both starring Tom [Kharis] Tyler), as well as relevant non-Universal serials, like Sol Lesser's *The Return of Chandu* (with that Lugosi fellow), and – along with James W. Horne – Columbia's *The Spider's Web*. In all the man provided the vision displayed for 15 minutes or so every week in dozens of chapterplays, as well as a load of horse operas, including fairly lengthy runs starring either Johnny Mack Brown and Fuzzy Knight, or Lash LaRue and Fuzzy St. John. It may well be that *Destination Unknown* was either too brief or too "Eastern" for Taylor to adjust to, as not even the sequences on horseback or the grand finale's car chase are as exciting as one might hope.

Saddled with not-much-better-than-adequate photography by John W. Boyle (who *had* served as Director of Photography for the "Crime Club" entry, *Mystery of the White Room* [1939] and *had* been behind the camera for the 1941 classic, *Six Lessons from Madame La Zonga*), and a meandering story line by Lawrence Hazard and John H. Kafka (the scenarists are mentioned above), *Destination Unknown* is worth a look only for the charms of Mr. Gargan and Ms. Hervey. Or, perhaps, as an alternative to giving up candy during Lent.

***Destination Unknown*** - 9 October 1942 – 63 minutes (ST)

**CAST**: William Gargan as Briggs Hannon/Terry Jordan; Irene Hervey as Elena Varnoff; Sam Levene as Victor; Turhan Bey as Captain Muto; Keye Luke as Secretary; Felix Basch as Karl Renner; Donald Stuart as Wellington; Olaf Hytten as Wing Fu; Edward Colebrook as Lieut. Kawabe; Willie Fung as Farmer; Charles Lung as Col. Suyakawa; Herbert Hayes as Daniels, American Diplomat; with uncredited appearances by Edward Van Sloan as Dutch Legate; Frederick Vogeding as Dutch Officer; Luke Chan as Chinese Waiter; Hans Schumm as Muller; Paul Bryar and Harry Strang as German Henchmen; Jack Santos as Military Clerk; Tom Yuen as Sun Wat Lin; Spencer Chan as Chinese Servant; Grace Lem as Farmer's Wife; Paul Fung as Japanese Officer; Victor Wong as Train Man; Eddie Wong as Peasant; Frederick Giermann as Van Hoven; Colin Kenny as Hotel Clerk

**CREDITS**: Director: Ray Taylor; Associate Producer: Marshall Grant; Cinematographer: John W. Boyle; Original Story: Lawrence Hazard and John Kafka; Screenplay: Lynn Riggs and John Meehan, Jr.; Film Editor: Charles Maynard; Art Director: Jack Otterson; Set Decoration: Russell A. Gausman; Gowns: Vera West; Associate Art Director: Ralph M. DeLacy; Associate Set Decorator: Edward R. Robinson; Sound Supervisor: Bernard B. Brown; Sound Technician: Joe Lapis; Musical Director: H.J. Salter; Stock Music Composers (uncredited): Ralph Freed, Richard Hageman, Charles Previn, Hans J. Salter, Frank Skinner

*Shock Theater* Catalog No. 700: "Thrills in the Orient as spy battles spy in the exciting adventure 'Destination Unknown,' the *Shock* feature film presentation on this channel, (day), (date), (time). William Gargan and Irene Hervey are the co-stars who risk torture and death to discover the secret of a fortune in jewels. Here's tingling adventure on *Shock*."

*- JTS*

# *The Mummy's Tomb* (1942)

Although a distant cinematic relative of Wilfred Glendon's Werewolf of London, Lawrence Talbot's Wolf Man – also a hirsute predator who made his debut roaming the British Isles – was born and bred (and, ultimately, killed off) joined at whatever passed for a lupine hip with Lon Chaney, Jr. Snarling, howling, salivating, ripping, tearing, manhandling... the Wolf Man acted with feral instincts and reacted with bestial fury. Not much in the way of emotional growth or motivational change for him, other than that which came naturally.

Chaney's other grotesques – Dracula, the Frankenstein Monster, Kharis – weren't so much joined at his hip as they were affixed there through hip-replacement surgery. Sure, Chaney (he dropped the "Junior" after *Man-made monster*) wasn't Lugosi or Karloff – he wasn't even Tom Tyler – and he certainly wasn't responsible for the screenplays that played havoc with those classic monsters. He was merely a link in the continuity of the roles, a "space-saver" in familiar make-up who went through the scripted motions while the characters' personalities and motivations underwent a series of variations that took them ever farther from their original pictures.

Karloff's Monster, forever shunned and misunderstood, pitifully continued to seek out a friend – both via excellent mime and a shaky and uncertain voice – over the course of three exceptional features. Chaney's Monster – due either to Eric Taylor's original story, or W. Scott Darling's screenplay, or both – *killed* his best friend over a dispute on whose brain was going where. The throats of choice of Lugosi's Dracula belonged to beautiful women; Renfield, let us not forget, was targeted only when Dracula needed a wing-man. Chaney's vampire fed on an elderly cripple and a kid, and – while we assume that he'd have much preferred to dine regularly on lovelies like

Louise Albritton's Katherine Caldwell – his getting within munching distance of his "bride" was both a set-up and a scam, and he was the ultimate patsy.

Even his trio of turns as Kharis started off on a lower shelf than Tom Tyler's and kept going south (*literally*)! The Tyler epic – yclept *The Mummy's Hand* because, we suppose, 'twas his hand that kept the action going – provided the exposition: For whatever reason, the high priests of Karnak are adamant that no one will ever set foot in the tomb of the Princess Ananka, and they've kept Kharis ("a prince of the Royal House") on tana-leaf-fueled high alert for millennia, just to make sure nobody wanders in, either by accident or design. In the course of the narrative, Kharis throttles a couple of archaeologists and/or assistants who had found themselves on the wrong side of the doorway and then is burned to a crisp whilst lying prone, lapping up tana fluid like a dog.

Two years later, in *The Mummy's Tomb* (so-called, we hypothesize, because that's the destination to which Kharis seeks to return Ananka and the rest of the treasure; a coffin alone does not a tomb make), it's *30* years later! Said tomb is totally empty – even Ananka has been spirited away – save for George Zucco's Andoheb, who is apparently as indestructible as that very lengthy flight of stone steps he careered down some decades earlier. And despite his having had a flaming brazier dropped on his back, Kharis is also in great shape, save for burn marks on his obverse [?], some facial blotching and smudging, and his having lost the fingers on his right hand. (We note that Kharis had previously done in infidels and transgressors with his left *hand*, so we feel this last is no great loss.) Again, having waited t-h-i-r-t-y years, Andoheb hires (or ordains, or something) a certain young Mehemet Bey to schlep Kharis over to Mapleton, Massachusetts in order to dispatch any surviving members of the Banning expedition and to retrieve the princess and her paraphernalia.

Seemingly within moments (the film runneth but an hour, including the requisite replaying of footage from its immediate predecessor), that brace of Egyptians is in the New World and Kharis has done away with the now elderly Stephen Banning, his sister Jane (totally not fair!), and Babe Jenson, whose attempt at avoiding strangulation by changing his surname was in vain. Mehemet Bey – not only a heartthrob but also possessed of the knack of being in just the right spot whenever anyone utters a word to advance the plot – has had his eye on Isobel Evans, the girlfriend of the late Stephen Banning's son, John. (Shades of Andoheb and Marta Solvani!) Kharis is thus commanded to carry off the young beauty, but all comes to naught as the local police plug the high priest and Kharis is once again set afire.

If this were any genre other than our favorite, Andoheb would have arranged for a team of lawyers to hie to the Commonwealth of Massachusetts and horrors of another sort would have scurried about the screen. Still... thirty years! Perhaps it took the old boy and the chaps at Karnak three decades to save up for the steamship tickets (shipping Kharis overseas in a body bag rather than his original, opulent sarcophagus might have saved a few pounds of weight and a few dollars in fees; it's not like he was going to be put on display in the cemetery caretaker's opulent digs), or perhaps it took that long for them to convince the Mapleton boneyard to hire an unknown commodity from Africa rather than a local who was probably related to one or more of the occupants. These sticky bits apparently didn't bother original storyteller Neil P. Varnick (also responsible for the laying the ground floor of *Captive Wild Woman*), or to scenarists Griffin Jay and Henry Sucher, so our grousing about it now – several 30-years-later(s) later – isn't going to add a farthing or a featherweight to our discussion. (And let's be frank; had there been a dramatically viable reason for the decades-long hiatus between tana infusions, honesty – and a bit of mystery-oriented vocabulary - would have demanded the picture be named *The Mummy's Lacuna*.)

**Kharis has traveled through time and space to eradicate those who defiled Ananka's tomb... and to help Mehmet Bey put the moves on Elyse Knox's Isobel Evans. Over Chaney's left shoulder we can see what appears to be an obelisk. With more sensible packing habits, the Karnak crowd might have afforded this junket decades earlier.**

The picture is quite a departure from the fairly straightforward narrative of *The Mummy's Hand*, but it's not unusual for a sequel to mess around a bit with the original. Sure, we understand that here we have a sort of reverse-archaeological expedition: Kharis and Bey are looking to recover Ananka and all her possessions and do in the Bannings, and guided by Amon-Ra - whose anger can shatter the world! - they know (without benefit of maps or prep sessions) where everyone/thing is located. Still, as we noted in our essay on this epic's predecessor, here starts the rather grand number of inconsistencies and illogical moves that will pepper the rest of the series. The first couple of reels are dominated by flashback footage – replete with soundtrack, including the very first recitation of the tana-leaf rituals – plus some intermittent reflections by Banning pater, including one in which he admits he regrets not bringing the mummy (Kharis) back from Egypt with him. Why couldn't he? He and Babe snatched everything else in sight. Customs and Immigration complain of a foul odor?

When we finally do segue to "present day" Egypt, we again find ourselves in some tomb or other (Which? Where? Both from the earlier film had been emptied of everything save the walls, but this one's got yet another statue of Isis with a treasure-box beneath her feet) and face-to-face with George Zucco's Andoheb, who is now wearing Eduardo Cianelli's costume and hairpiece from *Hand*. (Was this due to budgetary concerns, or because of High-Priest-of-Karnak haberdashery traditions?) Andoheb tells Bey that Babe's bullet only "crushed my arm," yet we just saw in the flashback Babe fire three times into the guy, point-blank, after which he rolled about a half-mile down those Mayan steps. And despite our having heard Cianelli's old duck do the tana-leaf count with the much younger Andoheb only minutes earlier, we have to sit through recitation number two, after which Mehemet Bey is given a new targets list: Kharis is going to be rampaging through the backwoods of Massachusetts until "the last remaining member of the Banning family is destroyed."

Okay. We suspend our incredulity and buy into the fact that, somehow - during the Second World War - the International Order of High Priests of Karnak has managed to arrange for an Egyptian national to be hired on to oversee a small-town cemetery in New England. (In a later scene, we note how his terms of employment are apparently so generous as to allow him to bring a sarcophagus containing "a loved one" in with his baggage via a horse-drawn hearse.) We're aware of the time period because one of the newspapermen who invade Mapleton says he took that assignment rather than cover the "Russian Front." (Quick question: If we're now indisputably putzing about in the '40s, does that mean *The Mummy's Hand* took place in the '10s?) Now, the possibility of hiring anyone of Egyptian nationality to do menial work within the

United States at the time the picture was in post-production and about to be released would have been dubious at best, as Erwin Rommel and his Afrika Korps had most Egypt sewn up at that point. Still, we *are* talking a mummy movie here... Hey, if Stephen Banning can have an older sister who speaks with a Scots burr, why can't the town of Mapleton hire from outside its borders?

Chaney's Kharis makes his onscreen debut onboard the steamer headed to Massachusetts, and he takes his first step inside the mortuary not long thereafter. We see Bey roll out an Egyptian sarcophagus (presumably from one of the in-wall slots) – he's in shape, this newly-minted high priest, as he wields that sarcophagus lid as easily as Thor does his hammer – but we don't get to witness Kharis climb *out* of his box. (We didn't get to see Bela's Dracula exit his coffin, either. Might it be that the vintage Undead – despite their sundry powers and attributes – had lower-back problems that impacted their capacity to maneuver in/out of their caskets gracefully?) We hear another – although mercifully abbreviated – rendition of the tana-leaf greatest hit, but we don't get to watch Bey provide Kharis with victims' addresses or directions. Perhaps the scent of the Bannings fills Kharis's nose, so he doesn't need a GPS in this strange land. How, then, does he make a beeline for Isobel's house after Bey tells him to get moving and fetch the blonde bombshell back to the cemetery? (This latter bit of exposition – wherein Bey launches into some convoluted ratiocination to explain just why it is in Kharis's best interests that Bey canoodles with John Banning's fiancée – affords Chaney his only opportunity to act in the film... if, by acting, we mean shrugging, sulking, and then glaring menacingly.)

We watch Wallace Ford's Babe Jenson/Hanson affect a pince-nez with about as much credibility as the coroner displays when he pooh-poohs the "grayish" mark on Stephen's throat as if it has nothing whatsoever to do with evidence in a strangulation case. And why – when that barroom-full of reporters runs out to see the latest horror on High Street - does Babe decide that could not possibly involve the horror *he* has been blabbing about and instead takes the low road that leads him into Kharis's good arm? All that business with the kids in the jalopy and the old lady in the bed next to Harry Cording and farmer Glenn Strange and poor Jim What's-his-Name and those dogs, the first time 'round: shadows? Really? Is the full moon hovering five feet off the surface of the earth to allow some of those shadows to have their way?

I was impressed (I'll forego with the "we" here) to learn that Kharis's very bandages are imprinted with hieroglyphics linked to Ananka. Cut out his tongue, bury him alive, but don't give the guy a break on Ananka-guilt for three millennia? And wouldn't you think that of all those newspapers – that raft of local dailies and the New York heavy-hitter that had sent their ace reporters to cover the story from the most popular bar in Mapleton – *one* might have discovered the last name of "Jim," the aforementioned dog attendant who is felled by some sort of fear-induced paralysis before Kharis kicks schmutz in his face? And John Banning will later speak of the "dust mark" found on his Aunt Jane's throat *and Jim's*, albeit we had earlier witnessed Kharis just step around the latter without so much as lifting a menacing finger.

Why, with all the talk of a mummy loose in small-town America, does no one seem to be aware of the handsome and exotic foreigner overseeing the local cemetery until some old guy towards the end of the film – a deus-ex-machina if ever there was one – mention hearing quotes from the "Egyptian bible?" In a milieu where the populace runs to report *shadows* to the constabulary, you'd think an import from the Land of the Nile would be the talk of the town! You might also think that, with all the dragging of Kharis's bad leg to and fro the Banning house, one of the cops might have thought to follow that trail back to its source, no? I mean, with those wolves howling hither, thither, and yon, there must be *someone* out there with tracking instincts. And why, in the name of Amon-Ra – whose anger can shatter the world! – does Kharis carry Isobel *back* to the Banning house when Bey tells him to get her out of the way while he takes care of the fools?

Although it's always nice to see stock footage from the original *Frankenstein* (you don't think they went out and hired all those guys-in-hats to follow Kharis during the wrap-up, did you?), would a '40s-vintage sheriff, in arming his posse, hand out torches and clubs? Were all the available flashlights and pistols en route to the Russian Front? And, after all these years, I still don't understand why Chaney's Kharis didn't just make a rush for that pot of tana fluid as the film approached its end (as had Tyler's Kharis, at *his* film's action-climax) and just knock Bey the hell out of the way and drink that goblet of the stuff that was to make both Isobel and the horny high priest immortal for years to come.

*Sigh...* In addition to its allowing Kharis to meander down the street, over the river and through the woods, Griffin Jay and Henry Sucher's scenario is peppered with gems of dialogue that strike home the disparity that exists between natural and supernatural. As Mrs. Evans is tucking her daughter in bed – moments before a grumbling Kharis snatches her back out – Isobel asks her mom, "You've been very happy, haven't you, Mother?" an open invitation to share the joy both women feel about Isobel's incipient wedding to John Banning. Signaling the deep and intimate bond that runs between the two, Mom responds, "We'll talk about that later, dear." ??? Or did *none* of the men listening to the sheriff thunder "Men, the facts are here and we've got to face them. There's a creature who's been alive for 3000 years. And he's in this town!" question his sanity or not think to himself, "I'll have whatever he's been drinking?" A bit of a downer to realize that there could have been more of the same had there been fewer tana-leaf litanies in the course of the hour.

Elyse Knox's Isobel is a gorgeous wide-eyed innocent, just the sort of gal to sit enthralled at the sight of her honey playing checkers for hours with his dad. Ms. Knox spent much of the early '40s at Universal appearing with such disparate talents as Leo Carrillo and Andy Devine in *Top Sergeant* (1942), the Dead End Kids *and* the Little Tough Guys in *Keep 'Em Slugging* (1943; surely you remember Huntz Hall's signature role of "Pig?" or Gabriel Dell's - "String?"), and the Andrews Sisters in *Moonlight and Cactus* (1944). She settled in at Monogram later in the decade, where she co-starred with Leon Errol and Joe Kirkwood, Jr. in Monogram's "Joe Palooka" series, under the direction of Reginald Le Borg. The lovely ex-fashion model called it quits, cinematically speaking, in 1949 and retired to give birth to filmmaker Mark Harmon two years later.

The greater part of John Hubbard's acting career was spent on the small screen, but the Chicago-born thesp – who took the screen name of Anthony Allan for a handful of late-'30s films – came into his own during the war years. Having appeared opposite Chaney when he was still billed as "Junior" – the two were in support of Victor Mature in 1940's *One Million B.C.* – Hubbard's John Banning is fairly blasé about confronting Chaney's Kharis; for a look of total shock on his face, cf. the scene in which he gets the telegram calling him up to active service. This would be Hubbard's last encounter with the supernatural, but he did catch up with Elyse Knox again in 1948's *Joe Palooka in Fighting Mad*.

Neither Dick Foran nor Wallace Ford has that much to do here. Foran looks wistfully into the past for most of his footage, which is split between the "here and now" and the Ananka-tomb-raiding flashback from some 30 years earlier. He *does* switch from a happy-go-lucky visage to one mired in sort-of-horror when Lon stumbles across his bedroom floor, but the performance isn't much when compared with Ford's awkwardly fumbling with his pince-nez or pontificating from under his homburg. The two archaeological remnants – and Mary Gordon's totally innocent sister – don't have time enough to make an impression, given all the screen time devoted to close-ups of Turhan Bey.

A Turk born in Austria – Bey both debuted and signed off in Vienna – Turhan Selahattin Sahultavy burst onto the screen (as it were) in Warners' *Shadows on the Stairs* (1941) and first bumped into Maria Montez – with whom he (and Jon Hall)

261

helped create a cottage industry of semi-fantastic, exotic adventure movies - in his initial Universal feature, *Raiders of the Desert*, later that same year. The mustachioed heartthrob would appear in several more genre efforts, including *The Mad Ghoul* (1943), *The Climax* (1944), and *The Amazing Mr. X* (1948). As Mehemet Bey, Bey is adequate, but this meh! critique should be chalked up more to the fact that he is essentially playing a young(er) and more attractive Andoheb than George Zucco rather than to his not being equal to the challenge.

Was Zucco aware that he was to be Eduardo Cianelli's doppelgänger when he signed on for *Tomb*? Putting it charitably, Universal could have rerun Cianelli's footage – maybe blurred his face a bit or superimposed some obfuscating shadows – and saved themselves a couple of hundred bucks on George. A bit later into the film, we note that lots of men and women familiar to such as us populate Mapleton, including Harry Cording, a Brit who became one of the Big U's great bit players and second-shelf villains; Frank Reicher, Munich-born and, among many other offerings, *King Kong*'s Captain Englehorn; and Glenn Strange, future *Monstre de Frankenstein*, who hailed from the pre-United States New Mexico territory. All three chaps, plus a slew of other recognizable character folk (most of whom go uncredited) make a walk through Mapleton seem like a turn 'round the old neighborhood to fans of the studio and the genre.

Even though there is an apparently unlimited supply of ersatz-high priests on tap, there's only one Kharis, and Lon's Kharis is but a pale (although charred!) imitation of Tom Tyler's. Denied an effective facial makeup – Jack Pierce fabricated an over-the-head mask that would save time and money but would deny the Screen's Master Character Creator a chance to emote – Chaney's non-throttling footage limits him to being supine whilst swallowing, clumping his way through the woods and past jalopies, and reacting once or twice as operatically as if playing to the back row of the Met balcony. Having successfully essayed the studio's most successful Jekyll-Hyde variation ever the previous year in *The Wolf Man*, Chaney was doubtless less than thrilled to be stuck as a mute engine of destruction whose most powerful thespic moment was an over-the-top double-take – something akin to one of Sid Caesar's trademark moves – when informed that Mehemet Bey needed Kharis to be his wing man. As Don Smith stated in his 1996 biography of the actor, "Production stills indicate that Chaney's only pleasure during shooting was the tender moments spent with his dog Moose during takes." (1) Sadly, with one exception, the two sequels wouldn't give Lon as much to work with as he had here.

**One of the few "tender moments" allowed the murderous, vengeful "prince of the royal house." Obviously, Jack Pierce was unable to disguise Chaney's scent, thus allowing his dog "Moose" the chance to lay one on *The Mummy's Lips*.**

Critic TS, opining on the film for *The New York Times*'s 26 October 1942 edition, noted the gauze-wrapped lover's intriguing past:

In 1932 the Mummy was declared to be Boris Karloff; in 1940 and *The Mummy's Hand*, it was Tom Tyler. Now in *The Mummy's Tomb*, at the Rialto, it is Lon Chaney, Jr. Obviously, a couple of these boys are imposters… For all we know, he will bob up again as Bela Lugosi. No wonder the Mummy lasted for 3,000 years. In that tandem fashion, he may go on for another 3,000 – heaven forbid!

The *Motion Picture Herald* (16 October 1942) devoted most of its ink to a plot recap, but did admit (finally) that "The picture manages somehow to maintain a measure of plausibility and the audience should find it 'right in the groove'." The 19 October 1942 *Film Daily* felt that "In neighborhoods where screams and chills are considered valid entertainment, this production... should fill the bill nicely." As for the title character, though...

The mummy is played by Lon Chaney. It is a role that adds little to the young man's stature as an actor since it depends for its effectiveness upon make-up rather than acting ability. In fact, Chaney's own features are at no time discernible under the grotesque make-up required by the part.

Reporting from Hollywood on the 15 October, *Motion Picture Daily's* Roscoe Williams disagreed with the *Herald* ("It makes no pretense of plausibility, but cause and effect such as they are, do figure in the result") but not so much with *Film Daily*: "Lon Chaney, as the mummy, heavily made up and silent, returns to animation after 3,000 years..."

With virtually the only elements that had changed since the formula was introduced in *Hand* being the increase in the scope of the vengeance and its venue, *The Mummy's Tomb* didn't leave the viewer with a sense of dramatic progression so much as with a sense of inevitability. Maybe Bela didn't get *his* shot at shuffling bandaged-ly along otherwise-deserted American side-streets, but Lon's performance, that measure/ pretense of "plausibility," and moviegoers' continual exposure to studio propaganda on how the war was affecting virtually every element in the motion picture industry kept Kharis – and audiences – coming back for more.

*The Mummy's Tomb* – 23 October 1942 – 60 minutes (ST)

**CAST**: Lon Chaney as Kharis; Dick Foran as Stephen Banning; John Hubbard as Dr. John Banning; Elyse Knox as Isobel Evans; Wallace Ford as Babe Hanson; Turhan Bey as Mehemet Bey; George Zucco as Andoheb; Mary Gordon as Jane Banning; Cliff Clark as Sheriff; Virginia Brissac as Ella Evans; Paul E. Burns as Jim; Frank Reicher as Professor Matthew Norman; Eddy C. Waller as Chemist; Harry Cording as Vic; Myra McKinney as Vic's wife; John Rogers as Steward; Otto Hoffman as Caretaker; Emmett Vogan as Coroner; Fern Emmett as Laura; Janet Shaw as Girl; Dick Hogan as Boy; Bill Ruhl as Nick; Guy Usher as Doctor; Pat McVey as Jake Lovell; Jack Arnold as Reporter; Glenn Strange as Farmer; Rex Lease as Al; Grace Cunard as Farmer's wife; Lew Kelly as bartender; Eddie Parker as Chaney's stand-in; with Frank Darien, Charles Marsh, Walter Byron.

**CREDITS**: Director: Harold Young; Associate Producer: Ben Pivar; Screenplay: Griffin Jay & Henry Sucher; Original Story: Neil P. Varnick; Director of Photography:

George Robinson; Art Director: Jack Otterson; Associate Art Director: Ralph M. DeLacy; Film Editor: Milton Carruth; Musical Director: Hans J. Salter; Sound Director: Bernard B. Brown; Technician: William Schwartz; Set Decorator: Russell A. Gausman; Associate Set Decorator: Andrew J. Gilmore: Assistant Director: Charles S. Gould; Make-up: Jack P. Pierce; Gowns: Vera West

*Shock Theater* Catalog No. 721: "See Lon Chaney – the screen's sensational master of menace – as the monster that would not die on *Shock*'s feature film, 'The Mummy's Tomb,' (day), at (time), on channel... You won't want to miss seeing Kharis, the sacred living mummy that terrorized a town."
*- JTS*

# *Night Monster* (1942)

*Synopsis:* The film begins with housekeeper Sarah (Doris Lloyd) scrubbing away at the carpet. Margaret Ingston (Fay Helm) calls her out for doing a maid's job and informs her she knows Sarah wants to keep it a secret because the stubborn stain is blood. "The whole house reeks of it. The air is charged with death and hatred and something that's unclean!" It's a pretty operatic rant, but the underrated Helm has the chops to carry it off, and it announces from the get-go that this production is going to play out as full-throated melodrama. Margaret further informs Sarah that she has sent for a psychiatrist to determine if she is insane or just overwrought by an unspecified "something."

Millie (Janet Shaw), apparently the only maid in an enormous and therefore understaffed house, meanwhile is on the phone to the constable, also hinting vaguely at something unnatural going on in the mansion. Her connection is cut off by butler Rolf (Bela Lugosi), who warns her about using the phone for personal business and spreading rumors about her employers. She informs him he needn't terminate her because she's quitting. She gets a ride into town from slimy chauffeur Laurie (Leif Erickson), who loutishly tries to force his attentions on her after pulling over to the side of the road. She escapes a near rape and hitches a ride on the wagon of one of the locals. Laurie continues into town and picks up a trio of doctors – King, Timmons, and Phipps (Lionel Atwill, Frank Reicher and Francis Pierlot) who have been summoned to the Ingston estate. They had treated patriarch Kurt Ingston (Ralph Morgan), but their best efforts left the man a hopeless cripple. Only Timmons displays any sign of remorse; the others contend they did everything medical science could do.

Millie returns to the mansion to collect her belongings but is attacked on her way

267

back to town by someone (or something) that comes through a loudly creaking door in the wall to the estate. Dr. Lynn Harper (Irene Hervey) is also on her way to the Ingstons when her car breaks down; she gets a ride from Dick Baldwin (Don Porter), a mystery-novel writer who's a pal of Ingston and is thus also headed for the house. On arrival the doctors, the shrink, and the writer encounter Agor Singh (Nils Asther), an Eastern mystic whose practices fascinate Ingston. Finally, we also meet Ingston, a quadriplegic who must be carried downstairs to his wheelchair by the chauffeur. He informs his doctors he has summoned them to witness a demonstration by the yogi that Ingston contends will revolutionize medical thinking about lost limbs: they will emulate a lobster's ability to regrow its claw.

Way before the word "franchise" was appropriated to designate a series of movies, Universal was dedicated to the ongoing exploits of its star quartet: the Frankenstein monster, the Wolf Man, Count Dracula, and Kharis the Mummy. (The "Sherlock Holmes" and "Inner Sanctum" series also qualify for franchise designation – but then most studios had some sort of "B" offerings of the kind, whether it was "Road" flicks or "Charlie Chan" mysteries.) They also brought forth a batch of one-off horrors usually destined for the lower half of the double-bill in support of the big guns. Perhaps some of them were contemplated as a series if it seemed warranted (the Paula Dupree trilogy might easily have been a one-off; that it actually begot two sequels is a bit of a head-scratcher) while others clearly had no possible sequel potential. Some were gems. *Night Monster* is one of these and one of the best (maybe the *very* best) despite an unlikely director and a nearly fatal casting misjudgment.

All the action recounted above occurs within the first ten minutes or so of the film, and we have gone into detail to indicate how thoroughly but succinctly screenwriter Clarence Upson Young established the principal characters and the murderous menace involved. While we will not point them out here, the script has also dropped several clues in plain sight that solve the mystery in what is essentially an "Old Dark House" movie. The later demonstration by Singh – wherein he materializes a kneeling skeleton he states comes from a tomb in Thessaly, and it leaves a pool of blood behind – is a further clue. Shortly afterward, Dr. King, who has refused to witness Singh's psychic display, is murdered - throttled but with a pool of blood near him - and Timmons follows not much later in identical fashion. But who has killed them (not to mention Millie and another physician who shuffled off *his* mortal coil before the movie started)? Pools of blood were found there, too, plus enormous footprints. Who would have a motive aside from Ingston who, it transpires is not merely crippled, but also missing his arms and legs?

NIGHT MONSTER (1942)

The cast of characters offers lots of possibilities. Butler Rolf is often skulking about in the background; he terminates Millie's phone call to the sheriff and apparently (we are told but do not see) informs Millie's ride back to town that she's decided to stay the night, thus causing the luckless lass to head off on foot and meet her doom. Housekeeper Sarah is keeping a secret of some kind. She bosses about Ingston's sister Margaret, but is she physically strong enough to overpower several men? The same might apply to Margaret, but then she might be crazy, and it's said that the insane can be very powerful. Laurie is demonstrably muscular and he's totally pond scum. Would he be taking revenge for his master's condition (either under orders or on his own initiative) because of his devotion to his employer? If some of Universal's horror mysteries of the period suffer from a lack of suspects, the same cannot be said of *Night Monster*. The who- and how-dunit remain opaque to the end.

The atmosphere is thick and creepy. Singh's materialization in a dimly lit room is startling and unnerving – one of the most potent images in any Universal horror of the Laemmle or Standard Capital eras. The sight of one victim hanging in a closet is more graphic than you'd expect in a film of that era (how did the censors let them get away with that?). Equally gruesome is the scene where Ingston has his bedclothes drawn back to reveal his lack of legs and follows that by pulling a prosthetic mechanical arm from his sleeve – prefiguring a similar moment in William Wyler's *The Best Years of Our Lives* (1946) wherein Harold Russel disassembles himself at bedtime. Conversely, the foggy scene where Millie is murdered is potent more for what we don't witness than for what we do. The door to the estate creaks open ominously and the tree frogs stop their chatter with horrible suddenness... and that's it. The killing itself is indicated by an off-screen scream. Near film's end we get an indistinct glimpse of what emerges through the door, and what we are able to see of the misshapen thing through the fog is equally disturbing.

Aside from limiting the action almost entirely to the familiar mansion/castle set, re-purposing the Wolf Man's feet (worn differently), cribbing the conflagration footage from *The Ghost of Frankenstein* (1942), and compiling a score from existing cues courtesy of musical director H. J. Salter, the film's thrift is revealed by a cast drawn almost entirely from Universal's roster of contract players. But then, that's not a bad thing; this group may not in all cases be the best known "B"-listers of the '40s, but they're a solid and dependable lot. Lugosi gets top billing on screen and posters for a role that gives him a decent amount of screen time but little else. He may not have much dialogue, but he's often puttering around in the background and is given several close-up reaction shots; perhaps director Beebe was trying to build up his red-herring butler-did-it quotient. Or maybe Beebe, having worked with the actor on *The Phantom Creeps* (1940), just wanted to beef up his role. Lugosi was in an irreversible career down-slide, and if Universal (or anyone else for that matter) waved a paycheck, he had to grab for it. The '50s, of course, would bring even more dire circumstances. There's more on Lugosi in the essay on *The Wolf Man* (1941).

There's also more on Lionel Atwill in the entry on *Man-made monster* (1942). He's second-billed here but is the first doctor to get bumped off; not that any of the doctors gets much in the way of screen time, but what footage they do get gives each of them some very nice moments. The second medico to meet his maker is played by Munich-born Frank Reicher (1875-1965), survivor of two expeditions to Skull Island. Trained in Germany, he was successful enough on the New York stage to be beckoned to Hollywood in 1915 for the first of over 200 films. His genre and nigh-genre credits alone comprise *Rasputin and the Empress* (1932), his signature role of Capt. Englehorn in *King Kong*, reprised in *Son of Kong* (both 1933), *Return of the Terror* (1934), *Life Returns*, *The Florentine Dagger*, *Charlie Chan in Egypt*, *The Great Impersonation* (all 1935), *The Invisible Ray*, *The Devil Doll* (both 1936), *Night Key* (1937), *Mystery of the White Room* (1939), *Dr. Cyclops* (1940), *The Face Behind the Mask* (1941), *Mystery of Marie Roget* (1942), *The Mummy's Tomb* (1942) and *The Mummy's Ghost* (1944), *Captain America*, *House of Frankenstein* (both 1944), *The Strange Mr. Gregory* (1945), *Monsieur Verdoux*, *The Secret Life of Walter Mitty* (both 1947), and *Superman and the Mole Men* (1951), his final film. Judging by how he worked at multiple studios within any given year, he was quite successful at freelancing. He also directed 43 films, all but one in the Silent Era.

Third-billed Leif Erickson (born William Y. Wycliffe Anderson, 1911-1986) started his showbiz career as a big-band singer and trombonist with the Ted Fio Rito orchestra. It was in that capacity that he made his first film appearances, beginning in 1933, billed as Glenn (sometimes Glen) Erickson. From 1936 on, he began using Leif with various spellings of the surname. He's probably best remembered for playing Big John Cannon in the TV series *High Chapparal*. Unless one counts the sci-fi-ish *The Big Broadcast of 1936*, his first genre credit was *Night Monster*, and he had no brushes with it again until he played the dad-with-a-glowing-red-jewel-in-his-neck in *Invaders from Mars* (William Cameron Menzies, 1953). By the middle of the '50s, television increasingly offered work though he still managed roles in a healthy number of movies. His only other genre appearances were on the small screen in episodes of Alfred Hitchcock's half-hour and hour-long anthology shows, *The Sixth Sense*, *Night Gallery*, and *Project U.F.O.*

270

**Don Porter, Irene Hervey, and Leif Ericson in a rather stiff publicity pose. The film has a cast of characters that's unusually strong for a "B" picture.**

Irene Hervey (née Beulah Irene Herwick, 1909-1998) was trained at the M-G-M School of Acting and signed up there as a contract player in 1933. She followed then-husband Allen Jones to Universal in 1938 and remained there until 1943. Memorable in the Marlene Dietrich-Jimmy Stewart hit, *Destry Rides Again* (1939), she appeared that same year in *The House of Fear* – a remake of Paul Leni's 1929 *The Last Warning*. An auto accident kept Hervey off-screen for several years and, when she returned, it was in the role of Mrs. Peabody in 1948's *Mr. Peabody and the Mermaid*. From 1954 on, she was primarily engaged in television with only a smattering of film work; her longest run on the small screen was playing Aunt Meg on the *noirish Honey West* (1965-66). Hervey's final role came in the TV movie, *Goliath Awaits*, in the company of John Carradine and Christopher Lee. She is a remarkably strong woman in *Night Monster* - the sort of character rarely depicted in a Universal horror - and doesn't fall into the damsel-in- distress category until the climax.

Brother of the better known (and possibly more lucratively employed) Frank, Ralph Morgan (born Raphael Kuhner Wupperman, 1883-1956) came from a well-to-do family whose wealth came from Angostura Bitters. Morgan obtained a law degree, but acting onscreen instead of before a jury prevailed, and he made his first appearance in 1914 (following work on the Broadway stage starting in 1909). Nonetheless, he didn't dip his toe into the genre pool until the Sound Era. While Frank would mostly portray genial types (as in 1939's *The Wizard of Oz*), Ralph specialized in smooth villains. He portrayed Czar Nicholai in *Rasputin and the Empress* (1932) and the following year was seen in William Cameron Menzies' *Trick for Trick*. His first real genre role was playing the unknowing vampire in *Condemned to Live* (1935) for the Poverty Row company, Invincible Pictures; this was a sign of things to come, as the bulk of his genre work would be for indie studios. His next horror – really more a mystery despite the title – was *The Mad Doctor* (1940); the following year he put in time at Republic in the serial *Dick Tracy vs. Crime, Inc.* After *Night Monster* came *Weird Woman* (1944), followed the same year by *The Monster Maker* for PRC, the gonzo Columbia serial, *The Monster and the Ape* (1945), and *The Creeper* (1948). Despite seeming to appear in every other low-budget horror flick, Morgan had quite a few upper tier films in his CV, at least until the '40s: *Strange Interlude* (1932), *Magnificent Obsession* (1935), *Anthony Adverse* (1936), *The Life of Emile Zola* (1937), and *Wives Under Suspicion* (James Whale, 1938) to mention but a few. He was a founding member of the Screen Actors Guild, which issues an annual award in his honor.

Never an "A"-lister on the big screen, Don Porter (1912-1997) would achieve a modicum of fame on the tube. His first film role was in Universal's "Crime Club" entry, *Mystery of the White Room* (1939). *She-Wolf of London* (1946) would mark his only other contribution to Universal horror, the studio having kept him busy on a variety of other "B"-productions. Porter moved almost exclusively to television, starting out in 1953 as Ann Sothern's boss in her two series, which ended in 1961. He is also known for essaying the role of Gidget's father in *Gidget Goes to Rome* (1963) and the TV series that followed two years later. Small screen roles in *The Norliss Tapes* (1973), episodes of *The Six Million Dollar Man* and *The Bionic Woman*, and the TV movie, *The Ghosts of Buxley Hall* (1980), finish out his genre contributions.

Copenhagen-born Nils Asther (1897-1981) began his career in Europe during the Silent Era, working with Mauritz Stiller, Victor Sjöström, and Michael Curtiz (who was then still in Germany). He relocated to Hollywood in 1927 and his dishy looks resulted in his being cast as romantic leads opposite Pola Negri and Greta Garbo (with whom he reportedly fell deeply and unrequitedly in love – she rebuffed his marriage proposal). Despite his still having a thick accent, it wasn't the talkies that deep-sixed his career; rather, it was being blacklisted in 1934 for breaking a contract. Asther then decamped to England for several years, but his return to Tinseltown did not jump-start his career; by 1949 he was reportedly driving a truck to make ends meet. He had a bit role as a Martian in *A Trip to Mars* (1918) and appeared opposite the Man of a Thousand Faces in *Laugh, Clown, Laugh* (1928), but his few horror roles were initiated with *Night Monster*. That was succeeded by *Bluebeard* (Edgar G. Ulmer, 1944) at PRC, *The Man in Half Moon Street* (1945), *The Feathered Serpent* (1948) for Monogram, an uncredited role in DeMille's *Samson and Delilah* (1949), and the inevitable move to television in 1951. Before his fall, he'd work with the likes of Frank Capra (*The Bitter Tea of General Yen*, 1932) and James Whale (*By Candlelight*, 1933). His being cast as Agor Singh in the film under discussion has always been a bone of contention for some fans who feel the role should more properly have gone to Lugosi; the film has been unfairly disdained because of that. As the late Ken Hanke observed in the (Ashville) *Mountain Express*:

Lugosi gets a fair amount of screen time as the butler—and a few choice lines— but he really doesn't do anything other than stand around and be Lugosi. That might matter less if it weren't for the fact that there's the smaller—in terms of screen time— but juicier role of Agor Singh, an Eastern mystic, which is given to Nils Asther. Nothing against Asther, but Lugosi would have made the role into an indelible creation and it's hard to watch the film without being aware of that.

It falls to Fay Helm to give the most indelible performance here with two over-the-top monologues (o-t-t both in the writing and her appropriate delivery of them); Helm's career is covered in the essay on *The Wolf Man* (1941). Doris Lloyd (née Hessy Doris Lloyd, 1896-1986) is nearly as memorable as the dominating housekeeper who's secretly in love with Kurt Ingston. Born in Liverpool, she moved to Hollywood in 1925 after a number of appearances on the London stage. She had only intended to visit her sister, but decided to stay and began her film career the very same year. Lloyd nabbed two Best Supporting Actress nominations (1935's *Mutiny on the Bounty* and 1965's *The Sound of Music*) in a long list of film appearances that includes *The Blackbird* (1926) with the elder Chaney, *Disraeli* (1929) and *Old English* (1930) with George Arliss, *Waterloo Bridge* (James Whale, 1931), *Tarzan the Ape Man* (1932), as Nancy Sykes in Monogram's *Oliver Twist*, *A Study in Scarlet* (both 1933), *Dangerous Corner*, *The Man Who Reclaimed His Head* (both 1934), the "Crime Club" entry *The Black Doll* (1938), *Dr. Jekyll and Mr. Hyde*, *The Wolf Man* (both 1941), *The Ghost of Frankenstein* (1942), *Frankenstein Meets the Wolf Man*, *Flesh and Fantasy* (both 1943), *The Lodger*, *Phantom Lady*, *The Invisible Man's Revenge* (all 1944), *The House of Fear*, *Kitty*, *My Name is Julia Ross* (all 1945), *Tarzan and the Leopard Woman* (1946), *The Secret Life of Walter Mitty* (1947), the voice of the rose in Walt Disney's *Alice in Wonderland*, *The Son of Dr. Jekyll* (both 1951). Soon after, she focused mostly on television, including an episode of *One Step Beyond* and numerous appearances on *Alfred Hitchcock Presents*, *The Alfred Hitchcock Hour*, and *Thriller*. Lloyd's handful of '50s and '60s movies included

George Pal's *The Time Machine* and *Midnight Lace* (both 1960) and *Mary Poppins* (1964).

Francis Pierlot (1875-1955) came to Hollywood at the age of 64, hoping to make a few quick bucks before retiring. Instead he started a second career in the flickers that lasted 15 years, working right up to the end and racking up over 100 appearances in that span. He already had played a healthy number of small and sometimes uncredited parts by the time of *Night Monster*, though none was in horror movies. Pierlot's second genre appearance wouldn't be until 1945's Jack Benny fantasy, *The Horn Blows at Midnight*. The following year, though, he added *Dragonwyck*, *The Catman of Paris*, and Edgar G. Ulmer's *The Strange Woman* to his list of credits. An uncredited appearance in *The Man with a Cloak* (1951) marked his final genre role.

As the "corncrib constable," Robert Homans (1877-1847) is about as close as the film gets to comic relief. Cap Beggs doesn't so much bumble as simply be flabbergasted and stumped after he arrives at *chez* Ingston to investigate Millie's murder. Homans' almost 400 appearances - often as officers of the law and just as often without credit - began in 1927 and include D. W, Griffith's *Abraham Lincoln* (1930), *The Drums of Jeopardy*, *The Black Camel* (both 1931 and both with Warner Oland), *Mystery of the Wax Museum* (1933), *The Thin Man* (1934), *The Informer* (1935), *Charlie Chan at the Race Track* (1936), *Black Legion*, *Stella Dallas* (both 1937), *Hollywood Stadium Mystery*, *The Sisters* (both 1938), *Stagecoach* (1939), *The Grapes of Wrath* (1940), *The Maltese Falcon* (1941), *Fingers at the Window* (1942), all before appearing before Ford Beebe's camera. *Night Monster* was one of 19 films he made that year and the quantity was not unusual. Post-*Night Monster* his genre credits include *I Married a Witch* (also 1942), the Republic serial *G-Men vs. the Black Dragon* (1943), *It Happened Tomorrow*, another Republic serial, *Haunted Harbor*, *The Thin Man Goes Home*, *Destiny* (all 1944), *The Phantom Speaks*, *The Scarlet Clue* (1945) and *The Strange Love of Martha Ivers* (1946). The last was released after he'd retired to the Motion Picture Country House.

Janet Shaw (born Ellen Martha Clancy, 1919-2001) decided at the age of three that she would become an actress, having been influenced by the Douglas Fairbanks Sr.'s *Robin Hood* (1922). Her earliest screen appearances were under her own name, but when Jack Warner signed her in 1937, he gave her a *nom de cinema*. While at Warners she appeared in the Errol Flynn rendition of the Sherwood Forest legend and several Bette Davis vehicles. The seven-year Warner Bros. contract seems not to have lasted for the duration because, by 1940, she was showing up in films from M-G-M, Columbia, and Universal. Bracketing *Night Monster*, she had minor roles in *Hold That Ghost* (1941) and *The Mummy's Tomb* (1942). It seems more than unlikely that Universal would have borrowed her for these uncredited bits, so she was either freelancing or came under contract to the studio. Her other genre credits are *The Scarlet Clue* (1945), *House of Horrors, Dark Alibi* (both 1946) and – maybe, her participation has not been verified – *Prehistoric Women* (1950). Leonard Kohl interview with Ford Beebe, Jr. revealed, on the "Scarlet Street" for a, that Alfred Hitchcock screened *Night Monster* to evaluate Shaw's performance because he was considering her for *Shadow of a Doubt* (1943). He did indeed cast her in what may be her best-remembered role of waitress Louise Finch; this, unfortunately, did nothing for her career, and she went back to uncredited bits. Hitchcock also expressed his astonishment that Beebe, Sr. had shot the film in just under a fortnight.

**The picture's biggest disappointment is that the "monster" proves not to be very terrifying after such an intense build-up. Perhaps the producers should have looked to the Moon Killer from *Doctor X* for inspiration.**

But Ford Beebe (1888-1978) knew how to make them fast. He had started out directing shorts, but by 1931 had graduated to serials with *The Vanishing Legion* for Mascot. He remained there until that studio's serial producer, Barney Sarecky, was positioned to replace Henry MacRae in the shakeup that followed the Laemmles' loss of their studio; Sarecky took Beebe and those Mascot personnel who didn't end up at Republic – after it had absorbed Mascot – over to Universal. Chapterplays were always made inexpensively, which meant that - among other economies - they had short shooting schedules; thus, their three+ hours of celluloid were exposed at breakneck speed. (In light of this, 13 days for a one-hour film must have seemed downright luxurious.) Except for the many Western-themed productions, most serials had some element of science fiction to them, and the most overt of Beebe's (with or without an assortment of co-directors) were *Flash Gordon's Trip to Mars* (1938), *Buck Rogers* (1939), *The Phantom Creeps* (1940), *The Green Hornet, Flash Gordon Conquers the Universe*, and *The Green Hornet Strikes Again* (all 1940). After *Smilin' Jack* (1942), the studio execs moved Beebe over to feature films and production duties. In 1944 he directed *The Invisible Man's Revenge* and *Enter Arsène Lupin*. When Universal chose to end its "B"-productions and recapture its status as a major studio, Beebe decamped to Monogram (soon to be Allied Artists) where he took charge of the "Bomba, the Jungle Boy" series, the entries of which he frequently wrote as well as produced. In the end, his resume included 127 writing credits, with only slightly more than 100 for directing. He'd finish his career manning the megaphone on six episodes of *The Adventures of Champion* (1955).

Oh… and Cyril Delevanti (1887-1975) who plays gatekeeper Torque – another suspicious character – was Beebe's father-in-law. His 163 (usually brief) roles on large and small screens include the genre productions *Buck Rogers* (1939), *Frankenstein Meets the Wolf Man* (as doomed grave-robber Fred Jolly), *Phantom of the Opera, Son of Dracula* (all 1943), *The Lodger, Phantom Lady, The Invisible Man's Revenge* (all 1944), *The Jade Mask, House of Fear* (both 1945), *The Phantom of 42nd Street, The Shanghai Cobra* (also 1945), *The Shadow Returns*, the serial *Lost City of the Jungle, Dressed to Kill* (all 1946), *Monsieur Verdoux, Lured* (both 1947), multiple appearances on *Science Fiction Theater*, an episode of *The Adventures of Superman, Sabu and the Magic Ring* (1957), one episode of *One Step Beyond*, several of *Alfred Hitchcock Presents*, an episode of *Thriller*, multiple *The Twilight Zone* episodes, *Dead Ringer, Mary Poppins* (both 1964), a *Voyage to the Bottom of the Sea* appearance, *Crowhaven Farm* (1970), *Bedknobs and Broomsticks* (1971), a role on *Night Gallery*, and *Soylent Green* (1973). Outside the genre realm he is particularly memorable as the aged poet, Nonno, in *The Night of the Iguana* (1964).

That *Night Monster* is the most unusual and original of Universal's '40s horrors does reflect a slight debt to 1933's *Doctor X*. In the main, though, the picture is the grand result of Clarence Upson Young's amazing script. There's more on the man in the essay on *The Strange Case of Doctor Rx* (1942), but for this production, let's note again the economical way in which he introduces a relatively large cast of characters, broadly establishes their personalities, suggests the film's menace, and even drops all the clues necessary to unraveling the mystery within the film's opening minutes.

Cinematographer Charles Van Enger (1890-1980) was an old hand at lighting movies, having started in 1920. (Said talent apparently ran in the family; Charles's brother Willard was also a cinematographer.) His earliest brush with cinema, however, came in the early '10s when he owned a Manhattan candy store on 14th Street across the way from D. W. Griffith's studio. When his sugar-dominated enterprise went under, he obtained a job with a firm that developed motion-picture film. Although it seems likely, it's not certain said pursuit led to an interest in the making of movies. Career highlights during the Silent Era include *A Doll's House*, Nazimova's eccentric version of *Salome* (both 1922), *The Phantom of the Opera*, *The Big Parade*, and Ernst Lubitsch's *Lady Windermere's Fan* (all 1925, albeit he was featured in the first two sans credit). The talkies oddly relegated Van Enger to programmers at several studios, including Universal, where he was under contract for the whole of the '40s. While there he lit W. C. Fields' absurdist *Never Give a Sucker an Even Break* (1941), *Ghost Catchers* (1944), the Abbott and Costello vehicles *The Time of Their Lives* (1946), ... *Meet Frankenstein* (1948), and ... *Meet the Killer, Boris Karloff* (1949), and the "Sherlock Holmes" entries *The Spider Woman* and ... *Faces Death* (both 1943). After leaving Big U, he'd work on *Bride of the Gorilla* (1951), *Bela Lugosi Meets a Brooklyn Gorilla* (1952), and *Magnetic Monster* (1953) before moving on to television with a few movies interspersed.

Contemporary reviewers had no appreciation of horror films at all and so couldn't discern differences between the good, the bad, and the indifferent. Thus, Beebe's effort didn't get the kind of appreciation it deserved (except from Hitchcock).

> The mortality rate in 'Night Monster' is pretty high, even for the type of chiller drama the customers of the Rialto have become accustomed to over the years at the self-styled 'house of horror.' Before this potpourri of occult mumbo-jumbo runs its tedious and fantastic course no less than eight normally healthy-looking actors wind up as corpses. Perhaps Lionel Atwill and Janet Shaw are the most fortunate of the victims, meeting their demise early in the proceedings before the audience has become inured to such violence...
> T. M. P., *New York Times*, 30 November 1942

> Night Monster, the companion shocker [ed: to *The Mummy's Tomb*] also deals with murder but it's more in the 'whodunit' style. Here again practically an entire household is done away with before the villain is

277

apprehended and shot dead. It's a fair enough mystery...

John L. Scott, *Los Angeles Times*, 11 December 1942

As usual it fell to the trades to fairly place the movie in context.

## SPINE-CHILLER WITH HIGHLY FANTASTIC PLOT SHOULD GO OVER WELL WITH SHOCKER FANS

Film-goers who get pleasure out of harvesting a crop of goose pimples will revel in 'Night Monster,' one of those fantastic melodramas that defy all fact and reason and only serve to bore people whose tastes in melodramatic entertainment are closer to reality. Devotees of spine-chillers will find the action in this film suspenseful and exciting. The way people are bumped off should be a real treat to them. Far-fetched is hardly the word for the plot... Director Ford Beebe and Author Clarence Upson Young have managed well in sustaining the interest... Charles Van Enger's camera work helps to build up the melodramatic tone of the film... Bela Lugosi and Don Porter appear to excellent advantage...

Anonymous, *Film Daily*, 20 October 1942

*Night Monster* is far more appreciated today (at least, judging by customer reviews on amazon.com) and for the final word we return to this comment by a reviewer with an appreciation of genre.

... it's hard to understand why Beebe—a specialist in serials and cowboy movies—was chosen to not only direct, but to produce the film. Yet, it would be hard to fault what he accomplishes... The story is an old-dark-house affair that finds the doctors who treated the crippled Kurt Ingston (Ralph Morgan) being killed off one by one during an ill-advised visit to their old patient. Obviously, the completely paralyzed Ingston can't be doing it, but who else would want these men dead? And what is it that prowls the night leaving pools of blood and gigantic footprints? Well, that's the mystery of the film—and it's pretty darn atmospheric about it... *Night Monster* is one of Universal's best 1940s horror pictures.

Ken Hanke, (Asheville) *Mountain Xpress*, 14 September 2010

*Night Monster* – 23 October 1942 – 73 minutes (ST)

**CAST**: Bela Lugosi as Rolf; Lionel Atwill as Dr. King; Leif Erickson as Laurie (as Leif Erikson); Irene Hervey as Dr. Lynn Harper; Ralph Morgan as Kurt Ingston; Don Porter as Dick Baldwin; Nils Asther as Agor Singh; Fay Helm as Margaret Ingston; Frank Reicher as Dr. Timmons; Doris Lloyd as Sarah Judd; Francis Pierlot as Dr. Phipps; Robert Homans as Constable Cap Beggs; Janet Shaw as Milly Carson; Eddy Waller as Jed Harmon; Cyril Delevanti as Torque

**CREDITS**: Producer: Ford Beebe; Associate Producer: Donald H. Brown; Director: Ford Beebe; Writer: Clarence Upson Young; Cinematographer: Charles Van Enger; Film Editor: Milton Carruth; Art Director: Jack Otterson; Associate Art Director: Richard H. Riedel (as Richard Riedel); Set Decoration: Russell A. Gausman (as R.A. Gausman); Associate Set Decorator: A.J. Gilmore; Costume Design: Vera West; Sound Director: Bernard B. Brown; Sound Technician: Robert Pritchard; Musical Director: Hans J. Salter (as H.J. Salter); Composers of stock music (uncredited): Richard Hageman, Charles Previn, Frank Skinner, and Hans J. Salter

*Shock Theater* Catalog No. 728: What was the terror that stalked the halls of this house of horror? What was the 'Night Monster?' See this hair-raising thriller on *Shock* over this channel (day), (date), at (time). Bela Lugosi, Lionel Atwill and Ralph Morgan head the cast in this exciting feature film, 'Night Monster'."

*- HHL*

# *Nightmare* (1942)

*Synopsis*: In London during the Blitz, gambler Dan Shayne wanders the streets, dressed in evening clothes albeit penniless and without a place to stay. His gambling house bombed out, he spent what little cash he had on a steamship ticket back to his native America, but he still has a few days to go before his departure. He gains entry to what he thinks is an empty house and is making himself a simple meal when he is interrupted by Leslie Stafford, the lady of the house. They share a sharp initial exchange, but, once she hears his story, Leslie offers him money if he will help her. He agrees and she takes him to the upstairs study where her estranged and abusive husband, Captain Stafford, sits at his desk, a knife in his back; Leslie insists she had nothing to do with the murder. Still willing to assist, Shayne calls a cab and brings Stafford's body out, telling the cabbie that his friend is passed out from drink. Shayne leaves the corpse propped up in a phone booth.

The next day, in a new set of clothes, Shayne returns to Leslie's house. At first, she rebuffs him, but then screams for his help when she goes upstairs and discovers Stafford's body has been returned to the study. She again insists she didn't kill her husband and that he uttered "SI-10" just before he died. While Shayne and Leslie ponder this mystery, Scotland Yard comes knocking. Leslie and Shayne escape in a car parked outside the house, with Leslie intending to drive to Scotland to the estate of her cousin, Lord Abbington. When they stop at an inn for the night, Leslie steals Shayne's steamship ticket. To ensure that he will complete the trip with her, she tells him that she has mailed the ticket to Lord Abbington's home.

After an encounter with a mysterious hitchhiker, they arrive at Abbington's, and Leslie reveals she's had the ticket the whole time. She also tells Shayne the car they've been driving isn't hers. Still hoping to board his ship, Shayne drives off, but stops when, while lighting a cigarette, he hears a voice speaking German coming from inside the dashboard. He then discovers a transmitter on the side of the car. We also see that the license plate is SI-10.

Shayne double backs to Abbington's estate. It turns out the Scottish lord is a Nazi agent, and the hitchhiker a German parachutist. Another parachutist, Hans, had killed Captain Stafford with the intention of pinning the blame on Leslie as the captain had discovered the spy operation. It was Hans who returned the body to the study after Shayne removed it. Shayne confronts Abbington and, after a tussle with Abbington's servants and the spy's giant wolfhounds, he escapes with Leslie, who had been locked in her room by Abbington. However, Shayne's picture is in the paper as Scotland Yard is looking for him. Soon the local police, aided by the villagers, go in search of Shayne and Leslie.

Abbington's henchmen find Leslie while Shayne is captured by the villagers who don't believe any of his story; when Abbington's car is searched, no transmitter can be found. Shayne manages to escape once again and heads for the distillery which is the headquarters of the spies. Leslie – who has already been brought there - learns that Abbington has rigged a whisky bottle to explode and intends to send many such bobby-trapped bottles on a convoy where they will be triggered to explode at sea.

While the other conspirators are elsewhere, Leslie struggles with Hans. Shayne arrives and throws Hans through a window just as Abbington and his crew rush in. Shayne holds them at bay with one of the whisky bottles, daring them to advance when they are uncertain whether that particular bottle contains the explosive or not. They back off just as Scotland Yard arrives and arrests them. It seems Scotland Yard was onto the plot from the very first. Shayne and Leslie embrace.

As is obvious from the synopsis, *Nightmare* - in spite of its much-used title and inclusion in the "Shock Theater" package - has no horror element whatsoever. It was intended as a Hitchcock-style thriller (more than one critic noticed its resemblance to *The 39 Steps*) and as a good vehicle for Universal's much publicized star, Diana Barrymore. It doesn't succeed on either count. *Nightmare* was based on the 1932 thriller, **Mystery in Kensington Gore** (released in America as **Escape**), by the prolific mystery novelist, Philip McDonald, writing under the name Martin Porlock. A number of McDonald's books were turned into movies, notably **Patrol** (which became John Ford's *The Lost Patrol*) and **The List of Adrian Messenger** (filmed as such in 1963). Obviously, there are no Nazis in **Mystery in Kensington Gore**, but the novel does feature the reappearing-corpse plot-wrinkle which made for the only arresting premise in *Nightmare*. The latter's scenarist, Dwight Taylor, claimed that he had tried for years to interest producers in the book, but - because of Taylor's identification with musicals (like *Top Hat* and *The Gay Divorcee*) - he was always turned down. When he became a producer at Universal, though, there was no longer any obstacle to filming the book. Perhaps it should be noted that *Nightmare* is Taylor's sole credit as producer.

That the film strains credulity is putting it mildly. Even though Shayne (Brian Donlevy) is supposed to be a cynical adventurer, his willingness to help Leslie dispose of the husband he assumes she has murdered makes him seem more like a *film-noir* fall guy. How on earth does Hans manage to find Stafford's body and return it unnoticed to the study? And would even the most inept of henchman - and Abbington later scolds Hans for his inefficiency - leave his keys in the car, thus providing an easy escape for the people he's trying to frame? Especially when the car contains the spies' only means of communication with their handlers? If Leslie has Shayne's ship ticket the whole time, why do we see her mail the letter supposedly containing the ticket? How is it that one moment Shayne and Leslie are hiding in a barn after their escape from Abbington, but the next, Shayne is a prisoner of the villagers? Besides the clumsiness of the transition, how exactly does Leslie end up getting captured by the bad guys instead of by that same posse? Hitchcock's thrillers have their own lapses in plausibility, but there's enough suspense and wit in his work to distract you until the closing credits. *Nightmare*'s languid pace leaves too much time for the viewer to note all the contrivances.

There's also the usual wartime propaganda. Early on in the film, Leslie tells Shayne she thinks better of him after he informs her he's headed for the States to enlist (but would he be doing so if his place hadn't burned down?). And God forbid that a Scottish laird should be a Nazi spy (of course we *know* there were no Nazi sympathizers in Britain, except perhaps for King Edward VIII), and so we are told that Abbington is actually German and was adopted when he was twelve. "I know they catch them young and train them early," snarls Shayne, even though the Nazis would not have been in power when Abbington was a boy. There's also an exchange between Shayne and Abbington wherein the turncoat laird, talking about his dogs, goes on and on about how they're carefully bred without "alien strain" and that the lessons of evolution preclude cross-breeding, but - being an American - Shayne would not understand that. (Shayne responds that mongrels sometimes take a bigger bite.) And, of course, the film is filled with lovably eccentric, funny Brits, inevitably good-natured and always quick to offer a quip or a pint. And such quaint village life! The poor constable has to go in pursuit of the escapees on a wobbly bike. However, lest

American audiences be left with the impression that our closest ally is ineffective, we find at the end that Scotland Yard was on the trail of the villains all along.

**A trio of villains – John Abbott, Ian Wolfe, and Gavin Muir – are held at bay by Diana Barrymore, Brian Donlevy, and a bottle of spirits that may be a potent potable in more ways than one.**

Director Tim Whelan began his career as a writer in the Silent Era (he scripted a number of Harold Lloyd films), but focused on directing in the '30s. Midway through the decade he moved to England where he helmed a number of films (his most notable credit was as one of the directors of the 1940 *Thief of Bagdad*). When he returned to America in 1940, his first film was the so-so thriller *The Mad Doctor* with Basil Rathbone. Detractors of *Nightmare* seemed to hold Whelan's UK sojourn against him:

> In order to get a fair slant on *Nightmare* you should know something of its director's background. The man is Tim Whelan who once wrote and directed in Hollywood. Some half dozen years ago he went to England and there continued his dual field of production. But in England, Whelan lost the Hollywood touch. He has completely lost it in *Nightmare*. It develops as slowly and leisurely as a British programmer is invariably unfolded. There is far too much talk in the early and middle chapters of *Nightmare*. A good deal of it should have been pared out, speeding up the action to the place where the 'show really gets good.'
>
> *Cleveland Plain Dealer*, 5 December 1942

Later in the critique, the reviewer refers to Whelan as "Sir Tim."

The 11 November 1942 *Variety* provided more of the same:

> Director Tim Whelan injects the English technique in presentation of the yarn, endeavoring unsuccessfully to heighten audience interest in the mystery at hand with a vague presentation .... Donlevy does much to hold what interest there is in the picture with a strong performance but Miss Barrymore is too stolid and suppressed as the mysterious girl under the weighty direction provided by Tim Whelan.

The pace of the film is indeed off, and it's surprising that Whelan, who had some experience in combining comedy and thrills, is so flat-footed in milking the humor from the material. It's not entirely his fault, though, as there is very little chemistry between Donlevy and Barrymore (even though they hit it off well during filming), which makes the light banter between them feel very strained. One can imagine Bogart getting away with calling Bacall "Butch," but it doesn't work for Donlevy and Barrymore. The whole tone of the film seems uncertain. Is the fight in the distillery supposed to be funny? With all the whiskey bottles being tossed around it seems more slapstick than suspenseful. Aside from the novelty of the reappearing corpse at the beginning - which does indeed get the film off to a lively start - the only sequence that manages some excitement is the initial confrontation between Abbington and Shayne that ends with him fleeing both the dogs and the spy's servants, all to music lifted from *Son of Dracula*.

Not all of the reviews were negative.

> While the picture is nothing big, it should give good account of itself on double feature programs. The settings and circumstances are different enough to engage the interest pretty consistently and the acting, writing and direction exceed the average.
>
> *Film Daily*, 10 November 1942

The 14 November 1942 *Harrison's* concurred: "Skillfully directed and expertly acted by the cast this combination murder mystery spy melodrama holds one engrossed from start to finish."

However, T.M.P of *The New York Times* was unimpressed:

> There is nothing like a punchy opening to make an audience sit up
> and take notice... But the principals hardly have time to get acquainted
> before the script bogs down and the suspense of the introductory
> sequence is completely dissipated through plodding direction and
> hackneyed plot developments...Miss Barrymore makes quite a chore
> out of registering fright and annoyance as the script demands.
> 4 December 1942

After praising the opening sequence of the film as something that would be
perfect for Alfred Hitchcock, Philp Scheuer of the *Los Angeles Times* expressed great
disappointment at what followed:

> But Tim Whelan is no Hitchcock. Nor is Dwight Taylor's scenario
> all that might be desired. The film has its share of plot twists and surprises
> all right; but by the time they arrive they have lost most of their impact.
> This I suspect is because Whelan doesn't 'set' for maximum cinematic
> effect; he lets us see and hear too much in each scene for our own good.
> 3 December 1942

Universal touted Diana Barrymore as "1942's most sensational personality."
Diana was the daughter of the Great Profile and writer Blanche Oelrichs. Her parents
divorced when Diana was very young, and she had little contact with her famous
father until she came to Hollywood in the early '40s after some modest success on the
stage. Universal signed her up and, after putting her in the routine flag-waver *Eagle
Squadron*, gave her the starring role in 1942's *Between Us Girls*, a project originally
intended for Deanna Durbin. In *Between Us Girls*, Barrymore played a famous actress
who masquerades as a little girl so that her mother's boyfriend won't be shocked that
his lover has a grown-up daughter (the premise plays just as foolishly as it sounds and
is actually a bit creepy). In addition to the little girl, Barrymore has to pretend to be
the girl's aunt and, on the stage, we see her as Queen Victoria and Joan of Arc. "Hobe"
of *Variety* nicely summed up the problem:

> The film not only keeps Miss Barrymore, a comparative unknown
> before the cameras almost constantly but it gives her every variety of

things to do. The result is occasionally uproarious but generally laborious, noisy and exhausting.

12 November 1942

Off-screen, Barrymore developed a reputation as a troublemaker. She was rude to Deanna Durbin when she visited the set of *Between Us Girls* and, very intoxicated, insulted Alfred Hitchcock at a party he was throwing and was promptly removed from the premises. All of 21 years old, Barrymore then married Bramwell Fletcher, 17 years her senior. Fletcher had appeared in *Svengali*, one of her father's films, and had a memorable role as the archaeologist who becomes a laughing maniac in the 1932 *The Mummy*.

**Diana Barrymore's brief sojourn at Universal was an unhappy one both for the star and the studio. Though *Nightmare* is just a mediocre spy meller and Barrymore's performance forgettable, this is still likely her best movie.**

Barrymore's performance in *Nightmare* did not get favorable notices. She seems a bit stiff and arch and her attempt at an English accent comes and goes. Universal wasn't impressed either, and Barrymore noticed that her dressing room had been downgraded for her next film. After completing *Fired Wife* and *Frontier Badmen*, both 1943, Barrymore was indignant that Universal wanted her to appear next in a Sherlock Holmes movie and, when she turned that down, an Abbott and Costello epic. The young actress told the executives she wouldn't sell the Barrymore name so cheaply: "After so brilliant an entrance was I to exit as a stooge in an Abbott and Costello comedy?"(1) The studio suspended her and when she returned to work it was in a supporting role in *Ladies Courageous* (1944), a hokey melodrama disguised as a tribute to female aviators who took over as commercial pilots so the male pilots could go to war. After that, Barrymore was finished at Universal. She returned to the stage playing opposite husband Bramwell Fletcher in a revival of *Rebecca*, but then fell into a long, sad period of alcoholism, unemployment, and scandal. She sobered up for a while and, in 1957, with Gerold Frank, wrote her autobiography, the very aptly titled **Too Much, Too Soon** (which was turned into a movie a year later). One of the book's closing lines is "I have begun to find my way." Sadly, she had not and fell off the wagon once again. In 1960 she was found dead in her apartment with liquor and pills at her bedside; she was 38 years old.

Brian Donlevy was also overly fond of the fruit of the vine, but, according to most sources, maintained his professionalism on the set. Author Derek Sculthorpe aptly summed up Donlevy's screen persona in the title of his book about him, **The Good Bad Guy**. While *Nightmare* was pretty characteristic of the sort of role Donlevy usually played, he was capable of turning toughness into sadism as he demonstrated in his performance as the brutal Foreign Legion sergeant in the 1939 *Beau Geste*. As mentioned earlier, Donlevy got on well with Diana Barrymore during the filming of *Nightmare*, and the two often had lunch in his dressing room, much to the annoyance of Bramwell Fletcher. However, according to an article in *The Pittsburgh Post-Gazette* (2 September 1942), Donlevy ran into a bit of trouble when he went AWOL from the set to do an interview on the popular radio show, "Vox Pop." He was paid $1,000 for the broadcast, but Universal docked him $1,500. Donlevy later said that *Nightmare* was his favorite movie and was the basis for the character he played in the TV show, *Dangerous Assignment*. (2) Horror/sci-fi fans probably remember him best as the abrasive no-nonsense Dr. Quatermass in *The Creeping Unknown* and *Enemy from Space*.

The only actor to get consistently good reviews for *Nightmare* was Gavin Muir (Lord Abbington). As the 14 November 1942 issue of *Showman's Trade Review* put it, "Gavin Muir turns in such a fine portrayal of the villain that one forgets to boo him." Muir appeared in supporting roles in many Broadway plays of the '20s and '30s and turned up in small parts in a number of '40s films, including several in the Sherlock Holmes series. He had an uncredited bit in *Too Much, Too Soon*, but his very last film, 1963's *Night Tide*, saw him in a good role as the murderously jealous Captain Murdock.

*Nightmare* has a good supporting cast, but they aren't always seen to best advantage. Henry Daniell is particularly wasted as Captain Stafford; he's playing a corpse for most of his screen time. However, in a flashback he gets off one good line with his usual cynical aplomb about how women, like horses, benefit from an occasional beating. Ian Wolfe, who often played butlers, here essays the varlet's valet, one whose duties entail more than answering the door and announcing dinner. At one point, he even gives Donlevy a good kick in the shins when the latter turns up at Abbington's door pretending to be a reporter. Elspeth Dudgeon, Sir Roderick in *The Old Dark House*, has a brief part as the innkeeper's wife. Hans Conreid plays the Nazi agent Hans, but doesn't seem to be taking himself seriously (nor can we). John Abbott has a couple of scenes as the hitchhiker spy.

Barely two weeks after *Nightmare* was released, Universal announced plans to do a sequel pending script approval by Brian Donlevy. It never happened but the description- "a comedy-mystery set against a wartime background" - sounded very familiar.

*Nightmare* - 13 November 1942 - 81 minutes (ST)

**CAST:** Diana Barrymore as Leslie Stafford; Brian Donlevy as Dan Shane; Henry Daniell as Captain Edgar Stafford; Eustache Wyatt as Angus; Art Shields as Sargent; Gavin Muir as Lord Abbington; Stanley Logan as Inspector Robbins; Ian Wolfe as Abbington's Butler; Hans Conreid as Hans; John Abbott as Carl; David Clyde as Jock; Elspeth Dudgeon as Angus's Wife; Harold de Becker as London Cabby; Ivan Simpson as Moneychanger; Keith Hitchcock as London Bobby; Arthur Gould-Porter as Freddy; Anita Bolster as Mrs. McDonald; Lydia Bilbrook as Mrs. Bates; Pax Walker as Gladys; Bobbie Hale as Old Gaffer; Dennis Chaldecott as Crying Child; Leonard Cary as Parker; Edwin Cooper as Superintendent; Kate Larson as Cook; Nolan Leary as Scotsman; Sven-Hugo Borg as German Voice; Sylvia Chaldecott as Cockney Woman's Voice; with Georgia Brown.

**CREDITS:** Director: Tim Whelan; Assistant Director: Joseph A. McDonough; Writer: Doug Taylor; Based on a story by Philip McDonald; Producer: Dwight Taylor; Director of Photography: George Barnes; Art Director: John Goodman; Associate: Martin Obzina; Film Editor: Frank Gross; Set Decoration: R.A. Gausman; Associate: E.R. Robinson; Gowns: Vera West; Musical Director: Charles Previn; Music: Frank Skinner; Sound Director: Bernard B. Brown; Sound Technician: Charles Carroll; Boom Operators: Bud Asher, Henry Wilkinson, Ralph Butler

***Shock Theater*** Catalog No. 727: "Settle back for action and excitement on this channel, (day), (date), at (time), when *Shock* presents the full-length feature film thriller, 'Nightmare,' starring Brian Donlevy. It's topnotch entertainment with a thrill a minute."

*- HN*

# Sherlock Holmes and the Secret Weapon (1942)

While looking to take advantage of its deal with the estate of Sir Arthur Conan Doyle, Universal planned an ambitious schedule for the release of the first three pictures: September to November of 1942. The first film, *Sherlock Holmes and the Voice of Terror*, was distributed on time, but the second was delayed, arriving in theaters in the USA late in December and in British theatres, early in January 1943. *Voice* had been intercepted by the British censor, dissatisfied with a detail that could not be removed from the footage - that the spy's true identity was that of a high official in the service of Royal Intelligence – so the studio wanted to make sure that the second film of the series wouldn't have any problems. For this reason, the writers were commissioned to insert Shakespearean texts into the mouth of Basil Rathbone and to assure that there were at least three links with Conan Doyle's work. In the opening credits, *Sherlock Holmes and the Secret Weapon* is affirmed to be an adaptation of "The Adventure of the Dancing Men," but the plot device of following the trail in the streets of London comes from the novel, **The Sign of Four**, and the persona of the old bookseller that Holmes assumes comes from the story, "The Adventure of the Empty House."

The plot begins in a rather Tyrolean (or even Carpathian) Switzerland, where a musician sporting regional dress is playing a picturesque xylophone in a tavern as Sherlock Holmes, impersonating an elderly bookseller, enters to sit at the table of two Gestapo agents. As a counter-espionage ploy, he proposes a plan to send them a scientist, Tobel, whom the emissaries of the Reich have been stalking for four months. But in truth, Holmes ends up distracting them with decoys and is able to escort the academic to a field whence, safely, he takes off in a plane bound for London. The

London that greets him has paths strewn with debris and the shadows of the sandbags that the Civil Defense put on each corner; its lights have been extinguished to bedevil the vision of the German bombers, but, as a result, nocturnal thieves have "become quite a nuisance," according to an accommodating bobby.

Tobel brings with him a calibration system that works with millimetric precision so that aerial bombs will hit their targets. After an exciting test, the High Command (led by the ubiquitous Holmes Herbert), green-lights the invention for immediate production in large numbers, but then the unthinkable arises: Tobel, a Swiss citizen, demands the right to lead the process himself and, without offering further details, leaves to begin work on his own. In an England in the midst of war, perhaps that sort of demand should not have even been presented, but the film also had a propaganda message to present, so the British had to be shown as gentlemen and their attitude toward a neutral nation as diplomatic, so the High Command accedes to the scientist's demands. As a precautionary measure, Tobel divides his invention into four parts and entrusts each part to a different scientist. Of these, we see only one: Professor Hoffner. When Tobel is kidnapped, the only clue are some hieroglyphs that he himself concocted, a succession of dancing little men that Holmes deduces have to be a part of an alphabetical system of code. In the story on which the film is based – "The Adventure of the Dancing Men" - a client brings Holmes several of these pictograms that have been appearing to him in his home night and day and that are posing a threat that frightens his wife. Based on the supposition that the most common letter in the English language is "e," Holmes slowly identifies each little man until he reconstructs what certainly were threats.

The adapters, W. Scott Darling and Edward T. Lowe, Jr., transferred an interesting turn of the screw to the screen: upon taking note of the drawings, *Watson* sits down, pencil and paper in hand, states that the little man most frequently repeated ought to be the letter "e" and starts to decode each line... until he ends up with a gibberish of unconnected words. Holmes assumes that certain initial numbers signal a certain variation in the correlative number of each letter and, upon applying his theory, reconstructs names and addresses of the three first scientists. On rushing to warn them, though, he finds them already dead and their parts of the secret bombsight stolen. Inspector Lestrade remains baffled, but when he interviews Tobel's lover, Charlotte, Holmes realizes who is behind the conspiracy and the assassinations.

It's an arch-villain, maybe more fearful than the Nazis, who enters onto the scene. It's the great Professor Moriarity (sic; see essay on *Woman in Green*), the Napoleon of Crime, enacted with punctilious frigidity by Lionel Atwill, who had earlier intervened in the Holmes universe playing Doctor Mortimer in 1939's *The Hound of the Baskervilles*. Atwill's first close-up reveals some bits of makeup on his eyelids, giving the impression of the eyes "like a snake's" mentioned by Charlotte in describing him to Holmes: "His eyes, heavy lidded, a thin film over the pupils." Holmes prepares his faithful companion for combat: "This is not a duel of intellect or with a cruel but single-minded Gestapo killer. This is our greatest problem: England is at stake and our antagonist is Professor Moriarty."

**Holmes and Professor Moriarity (Lionel Atwill): as always, engaged in struggle. The most disturbing element in the picture is the idea that Moriarity, for whatever reason, would be willing to negotiate with the Nazis over the bombsite.**

In the "B"-movie system, studios would usually assign a high budget and a fairly prominent filmmaker to the first picture of a series in order to be able to proceed with diminishing quality and investment, while resorting to journeymen filmmakers or piece-workers with each successive film. The Holmes series, though, did not adhere to these norms, as the director assigned to the second film, Roy William Neill, had by all accounts a better "pedigree" than had John Rawlins, and he was kept on for the rest of the series. Many of the commentaries on and studies of the film rightly observe that what made the Holmes series notable is the quality that was constantly maintained from picture to picture, so that the series doesn't appear to consist of "B" films. While Rawlins was noted for the almost vertiginous rhythm of his narrative process, Neill made his impression by the ease with which he created suspenseful situations at various moments, like the two clashes between Holmes and Moriarty, both with the same premise: the first is at the mercy of the second and his coterie.

In his unpublished memoirs, printed as an interview with his daughter Paula Page by Nick Utechin in *Sherlock Holmes Journal*, volume XIX (December 1988), Nigel Bruce remembered Roy William Neill as...

...a little man, very fussy about his clothes and, like myself, he always smoked a pipe. He was an extremely kind and friendly person and all his assistants and the crews who worked for him were devoted to him. Roy was an extremely able director, having a great knowledge of film technique and the use of the camera. During the many pictures w made under his direction, we found him a joy to work for. Basil and I nicknamed him 'Mousey' during our first picture and the name stuck to him from then on. We both became extremely attached to Roy Neill.

While both Holmes and Moriarity vie with each other in terms of arrogance, there is a deathless exchange that would end up being the only reference in the entire series to the character's famous affection for cocaine at seven percent. Insulting his captor, Holmes says that the methods that Moriarty has mentioned to dispose of the detective are typical of a small-minded ruffian and suggests that he be exsanguinated slowly with a catheter. Moriarity, filled with malicious pleasure, replies, almost to himself, "The needle to the last, eh, Holmes?"

"Slowly, drop by drop," answers the Master Detective, knowing himself to be trapped but using a well-thought-out strategy to gain time so that Watson and Lestrade can discover the hiding place and arrive with Scotland Yard to frustrate the professor's diabolical plans. In an obvious effort to replicate the conclusion of the previous *Voice of Terror*, Holmes delivers a final statement that seeks to breathe hope and pride into British moviegoers. Once theatre lights were turned back on, the British audiences had to return to the appalling reality of a war that, at that point, was still months away from being seen as entirely favorable to the Allies. Thus, Holmes's words ("This blessed plot, this earth, this realm, this England") were taken from Shakespeare's *Richard II*, and fittingly so, for it was a complete set of the Bard's works that Holmes pretended to offer for sale at the beginning of the picture.

*Showmen's Trade Review* (2 January 1943) explained that "although the style is a little too slow for the blood-and-thunder, cowboy-and-Indian type of fan, it is very satisfactory fare for everyone else." A publication aimed at exhibitors, *STR* suggested that they "plug this via the radio program, book stores and as other Sherlock Holmes stories... with a man, dressed as Holmes walking around town seeking things through his magnifying glass."

*Harrison's Reports* (2 January 1943), a more conservative publication, judged that the film is "Morally suitable for all," but was wrong in its synopsis, concluding that "Moriarity escapes." Was it also wrong about Charlotte, whom they identified as "Tobel's fiancée," as there was nothing very clear in the picture about the tie that linked both characters?(1) In *Motion Picture Herald* (also the 2 January 1943), William R. Weaver enumerated the film's ingredients as if it had been a recipe: "Sliding panels, trap doors, secret codes, deductions, escapes, captures and pursuits through blackouts supply the excitement." And he gave his approval of Roy William Neill's direction, which "maintains an even but leisurely pace, keeping intact the tradition of the Holmes procedure." Spinning Atwill's line ("The needle to the last, eh, Holmes?") - and showing its appeal even in the moment of its first mention - *Photoplay* (April 1943) summed up in one line the reviewer's opinion: "Give it the needle, Watson," perhaps evoking a promotional line from Fox, "Give it the needle, Mr. Showman!" from the time of the premiere and distribution of *The Hound of the Baskervilles* (1939). Perhaps it was a reminder – nothing less, surely – of a certain reference to opium in the original script that had to be withdrawn per the PCA recommendation.

Fans of Sherlock Holmes in general and of Basil Rathbone in particular may have diminished enthusiasm nowadays for *Secret Weapon* as it is one of the original titles that terrifies least and spills over most into wartime espionage. In truth, it's the most anachronistic of the first three films. First, the picture offers more scenes set in 221B Baker Street, which is specifically furnished in Victorian style as if it were a kind of time capsule of both protagonists. Then, for the presence of Moriarty, who shifts from merely being "wanted" to dominating the last third of the footage, moving the narrative away from the expected confrontation with fifth columnists or undercover spies.

Given that, from his literary debut, Sherlock Holmes had been one of the fictional characters thought to embody Britain's genius and resolve, at one point the film was to have been entitled *Sherlock Holmes Fights Back*, the name doubtless meant to inspire the average bloke to pitch in as best he could. One way in which Holmes chooses to fight is "camouflaged"; first, in the picture's opening moments, disguised as a pro-Nazi bookseller apparently seeking to kidnap the bombsight's inventor, and sometime later as the Lascar, Ram Singh, who confronts Moriarty in his den. Watson, too, joins in the fight, and while his flightiness and occasional ludicrous behavior are introduced herein, this is the last time he is seen as being savvy and perspicacious in the series. Also making his debut is Dennis Hoey as Inspector Lestrade, a role he would repeat in five more series' entries. Hoey's connection with investigative bodies would continue to please fans of '40s Universal horrors, as he also enacted Inspector Owen in 1943's *Frankenstein Meets the Wolf Man* and Inspector Pierce in *She-Wolf of London* (1946). In addition, the London-born Hoey participated in such genre favorites as *The Wandering Jew* (1933) and *Tarzan and the Leopard Woman* (1946), and such wartime paeans as *A Yank in the R.A.F.* (1941) and *They Came to Blow Up America* (1943).

Kaaren Verne - née Ingeborg Catherine Marie Rose Klinkerfuss (2) - chose the more marquee-suitable *nom du cinéma* Karen Verne for the British indie feature, *Ten Days in Paris* (1940). A year later, the Berlin-born actress was in the USA (due to the British film-making industry on leave, thanks to World War II) where her billing would vary, with her adding and subtracting a second "a" from her first name for the rest of her life. Although she was Bogie's honey in 1942's *All Through the Night*, Verne ended up marrying Peter Lorre, whom she divorced in 1950. In the mid-'40s, Verne suffered some psychological stress and attempted suicide several times. Returning to the screen in 1952, she made a brace of uncredited appearances in M-G-M productions and one for Stanley Kramer. Soon thereafter – like so many others - she moved primarily to television, with her last big-screen appearance in U-I's 1966 version of *Madame X*, the umpteenth time the eponymous Alexandre Bisson drama (from 1908) was filmed. Verne died under rather mysterious circumstances the following year, at the fairly youthful age of 49.

As opposed to Verne, who had been born in Germany and then moved (initially) to England, Henry Victor had first seen the light in Blighty and then was taken and raised in the Fatherland, which accounts for the actor's thick accent. Most famous (to us genre buffs) as the circus strongman, Hercules, in Tod Browning's 1932 classic, *Freaks*, Victor had been appearing in films to our liking since 1916 when – back in England – he appeared as male lead in silent renditions of H. Rider Haggard's *She* and Oscar Wilde's *The Picture of Dorian Gray*. Come the Sound Era's technically-evolved genre, he added vocal color and physical presence to the aforementioned Browning picture, to Karl Freund's *The Mummy* (1932; his scenes as a Saxon warrior - like those of Zita Johann's Anck-es-en-Amon's subsequent incarnations – ended up on the cutting-room floor), and to British-International's *The Living Dead* (1934; aka *The Scotland Yard Mystery*). When the skies darkened over Europe in the late '30s-early '40s, his German accent propelled him into many uncredited appearances as spies/informers/soldiers acting for the Third Reich, along with featured roles as in 1939's *Confessions of a Nazi Spy* and 1942's *Underground Agent*. In 1941, the actor combined his somewhat tenuous link to horror with his accent-driven identification with the Nazis as the villainous Dr. Miklos Sangre in Monogram's *King of the Zombies*, one of the *very* few Monogram epics ever to be nominated for an Academy Award (Best Original Score for a Dramatic Picture). Like Kaaren Verne, Victor had his career and his life cut short, dying of a brain tumor in mid-March 1945, aged 52.

As had been the case with George Zucco's Moriarty (in 20th Century-Fox's *The Adventures of Sherlock Holmes*, 1939), Lionel Atwill's professor apparently meets his end not long before Holmes's uncited quoting of the Bard's immortal words in the picture's closing moments. Not so fast, though, crowed *New York Herald Tribune* film critic, Joseph Pihodna, in the 5 January 1943 issue of that august newspaper: "There is...considerable doubt as to Moriarty's death. The chances are that Universal will see fit to bring him back." Mr. Pihodna was spot on, as the studio worked the same revivifying wonders with the Napoleon of Crime it had with its classic monsters. Come 1945's *Woman in Green*, Rathbone's Holmes would once again match wits with his most infamous foe, albeit this time, embodied by Henry Daniell.

***Sherlock Holmes and the Secret Weapon*** – 25 December 1942 – 68 minutes

**CAST**: Basil Rathbone as Sherlock Holmes; Nigel Bruce as Doctor Watson; Kaaren Verne as Charlotte Eberli; Lionel Atwill as Professor James Moriarty; William Post, Jr. as Dr. Franz Tobel; Dennis Hoey as Inspector Lestrade; Holmes Herbert as Sir Reginald Bailey; Mary Gordon as Mrs. Hudson; Harry Woods as Kurt; George Burr MacAnnan as Gottfried; Paul Fix as Mueller; Rudolph Anders as Braun; Henry Victor as Prof. Frederick Hoffner; Harold De Becker as Peg Leg; Harry Cording as Jack Brady; James Craven, Leyland Hodgson as RAF Officers; Michael Mark as George

**CREDITS**: Director: Roy William Neill; Producer: Howard Benedict; Screenplay: Edward T. Lowe, Jr., W. Scott Darling, Edmund L. Hartmann; Original Story: "The Adventure of the Dancing Men" by Sir Arthur Conan Doyle; Adaptation: Edward T. Lowe, Jr. and W. Scott Darling; Music: Frank Skinner; Musical Director: Charles Previn: Cinematography: Lester White; Film Editor: Otto Ludwig; Art Director: Jack Otterson; Set Decoration: Russell A. Gausman; Gowns: Vera West

*- DL*

# *Frankenstein Meets the Wolf Man* (1943)

First things first. We're back in Vasaria, and while Dr. Ludwig Frankenstein's old laboratory/sanatorium *is* still in evidence – at least the burned-out shell of it is – it has radically changed in appearance since the Monster screwed with the circuitry a year earlier. (Veteran Frankenstein aficionados recognize this as a circumstance to which all castles, laboratories, and old watch-towers are subject in and around Vasaria.) For the first time in the series, though, we've no Frankenstein family member who holds an M.D. degree, although Patric Knowles's character – a physician - *is* yclept "Frank."The titular surname is, however, borne by the gorgeous Ilona Massey, who is herein named "Elsa," presumably per the family tradition of naming all the distaff relatives "Elsa" after "Elizabeth" went out of fashion when James Whale took his leave. (Perhaps this is an *hommage* to the divine Miss Lanchester, who was, after all, the *Bride...*) The Monster, alternatively mute and incipiently vociferous up to this point in the series, is now *seen to be mouthing* something or another, albeit no sound is heard.. This is also the first series' film in nearly four years in which Bela Lugosi's character doesn't happen upon someone else wearing the renowned Jack P. Pierce make-up application and asphalt-spreader's boots, but wherein a "someone else" comes to discover *Bela* wearing the iconic outfit, in a sort of reverse irony.

Anyhow, just to recap for novices or *éminences grises* who – like this writer – are finding that the damnedest things have slipped their minds… After a grave-robber inadvertently sets the Wolf Man free from his tomb, Lawrence Talbot seeks medical help from Dr. Frank Mannering. When his hirsute alter-ego kills again, though, Talbot flees Cardiff and heads to central Europe, where he and Maleva the gypsy search out Dr. Frankenstein, the one man who might free Talbot from the curse of lycanthropy. The Wolf Man strikes once more in Vasaria, however, and while fleeing the understandably upset townspeople, comes upon the Frankenstein Monster, encased in ice. Talbot frees same from its icy prison in the hopes that the creature can lead him to Dr. Frankenstein's diary. This goes nowhere, but Dr. Mannering, having followed Talbot to Vasaria, decides to save Talbot and get rid of the Monster in one fell swoop. With both strapped to operating tables in the ruined laboratory, Mannering suddenly switches mental gears and – per the by now established formula - becomes determined to see the Monster at the height of its powers; he re-energizes it. The Monster breaks free – as does the Wolf Man – and both fight to the death as flood waters crash through the laboratory walls, sweeping them both away.

This is the most maddening of all the films in Universal's classic series, as it contains snippets of great writing, moments of poignancy, bits and pieces of marvelous performances, and flashes of wit and creativity, all floating haphazardly upon a vast, inert sea of the same old dreck. On the upside, we have Bela, Lionel Atwill, Lon Chaney's somewhat more seasoned portrayal of the Wolf Man, the aforementioned Miss Massey, a knockout of an opening scene, and Hans J. Salter's marvelous score. On the down side, we have Bela's new take on the Frankenstein Monster, Rex Evans, Dwight Frye, and more continuity cock-ups than you could shake a stake at. Also in evidence is about 20 seconds of the most appealing Chaney footage ever shot, the most appalling "peasant Sunday-best" costumes since the villagers' wedding scene in *Dracula's Daughter*, and some technically splendid transformations. I know as many people who heap praise on *Frankenstein Meets the Wolf Man* as I do folks who find it *meh!*; this, apparently, is the sort of film that inspires at least some type of guttural reaction.

One of the picture's many claims to notoriety is its status as the first of the studio's "Monster Rallies." As I remarked in the essay on *The Ghost of Frankenstein*, I contend that there has *never* been a Universal Frankenstein film that did not contain some sort of secondary goblin, and that the "Monster Rally" tag could be just as properly affixed to the original Karloff/Whale classic. Granted, this tongue-in cheek-hypothesis draws upon publicity blurbs used to promote the last two "serious" entries of the series, *House of Frankenstein* (1944) and *House of Dracula* (1945), but, so what? Depending upon how you read the posters, Daniel the hunchback was monster #4 or #5 in the former, and Poni Adams - for Pete's sake - was the last "monster" in the batch in the latter. As both "Houses" also made lots of noise that "Mad Doctor" was another of the ghoulies in their line-ups, it takes very little effort to see how the '31 *Frankenstein* could have made the same kind of claim, boasting three monsters!

Still, *Frankenstein Meets the Wolf Man* is the first of the pictures in which the titular antagonists ARE genuine horrors. (Honesty sidebar: with the exception of Cedric Hardwicke's Ludwig, the "mad" doctors" of the predecessors were primarily the romantic leads, Bela's Ygor had moments when you just wanted to hug him and chuck him under the chin, and Dwight Frye's whatever was – to paraphrase Ed Wood – a "monster to be pitied, a monster to be despised." So my claim in the paragraph above holds water only academically.) The press was, for the most part, taken with the idea. "Marsh," house critic for *The Cleveland Plain Dealer*, was downright enthusiastic:

> If you go for the horror picture, *Frankenstein Meets the Wolf Man* should satisfy you completely. It is one of the best horror films we have had. Universal, which created the Frankenstein monster for the screen and gave us more of it than we possibly merited, now adds its famous wolf man character to the Frankenstein screen tales, and the result is a thriller-diller... This new one is too good not to have a sequel. Wild, eerie, and utterly impossible, it does, nevertheless, carry double the usual quota of thrills.
>
> 7 May 1943

To many, the perceived weakness of the film is not that there is a surfeit of monsters, but rather that the padded shoulders of the Monster's jacket landed where they did. They feel that not only didn't Bela do himself proud in following Karloff's footsteps – as painful as that exercise might have been to him – he didn't cut the menacing mustard when it came to measuring up to Chaney's performance (in *Ghost of...*), either. Far from being the agile engine of destruction depicted by his predecessors, Bela's grotesque parades around as if he had the proverbial broomstick up his butt. Apart from one completely powerful and unsettling moment – the extreme close-up of Bela's Monster's face as he realizes that he has been super-charged again – the whole impersonation is thought by some to have been a farrago.

Still, considering the wholesale product tampering that went on, that Bela cops even *this* achievement is something of a minor miracle and is a testimony to the man's abilities. For one thing, despite the scarred and studded headpiece (Ellis Burman had molded a smaller one for Bela, one that would presumably be a tad easier to affix), the asphalt-spreader's boots, and the fact that Lugosi was a six-footer without all that stuff, much of the Monster's footage still had to be shot from below (to increases the illusion of size). He's the same height as Talbot during the Festival debacle only to

301

tower over Mannering – who's wearing a fedora – in the very next scene. When man and monster meet and prove to be of the same physical volume, you have a brawl, not a Battle of the Titans. (Still, it must be noted, that the lack of size differential didn't matter at all when Kharis had you by the throat.)

The proximity of George Robinson's lens to Bela's phiz during the table scene also lays bare the deficiencies of the Monster make-up. Granted, Pierce's first treatment had been applied to the lean face of a cinematic "D"-lister with whom very few were familiar and so there were no points of comparison to be made: The Man, the Monster, and the Make-up were as one. Heck, with Karloff identified with the role for the rest of the '30s, even the rather stark departure of the make-up in *Son* from that seen in *Bride* seems not to have struck much of a dissonant chord with the audience. But Bela assumed the role more than decade after he was all the talk in *Dracula*, and the familiar (and, of late, more rounded) contours of his face were not masked much by the iconic application. (Let us dwell only momentarily on his distinctive dimpled chin or pronounced proboscis.) Bela's managing to wring a wry and frightening expression from his Jack O'Lantern visage was an exercise in sheer artistry and was in itself more chilling than any of the purely bestial antics in which his costar had indulged in the previous picture. Still, the dread threat of the Frankenstein Monster lay less in his facial expressions than in his violent, unpredictable behavior.

Bela, of course, got the role by default. Everybody's first choice would have been Boris Karloff, but getting the creator of the part to leave behind the thrill of costarring in *Arsenic and Old Lace* – one of the biggest hits of the then-current Broadway season – would have been even more far-fetched than the idea of bringing life to any patchwork quilt of cadaver bits. Boris had gone so far as to pass on the chance of filming *Arsenic* under Frank Capra's unique direction; he stayed with the New York company so that his three Broadway costars – Jean Adair, Josephine Hull, and John Alexander – who *had* headed west to make the movie, would still have capacity houses to which to play when they returned home. If he had ceded the chance to make the movie he had really wanted to make, why would he have given the slightest thought to a project in which he no longer had any interest? I can't believe that anyone at Universal would have been foolish enough even to *ask* Karloff, but there was plenty of publicity to be had just by linking together in print the actor's name with that of his trademark character. Even had there been no *Arsenic and Old Lace*, there was just no way would Karloff have consented to sort through the pieces of the characterization after Chaney had finished with it. As far back as 1939, Boris had been unhappy with the direction in which the Monster was headed. It's believed that Karloff agreed to do *Son of Frankenstein* only

302

after he was assured that the Monster would once again be mute. And now, not only was the Monster to again raise a voice, but said voice (per the *Ghost of Frankenstein* finale) would belong to Bela Lugosi? Please!

More essays have been penned and, I suspect, more than a couple of noses figuratively bloodied over Lugosi's performance in *FMTW* than I can account for. Let's not forget that, after *Dracula*, Bela was up for the "lead" in Robert Florey's *Frankenstein*, only to discover – to his chagrin – that said "lead" was the Monster. A full account of the actor's outrage is to be had in Greg Mank's splendid *It's Alive*, but suffice to say that, upon learning that the proposed movie iteration of Shelley's gabby, philosophic Monster was limited to a few groans and snarls, that tore it for the man from Lugos. Thence, we encounter the oft-told fable of Bela's coming upon Karloff someplace and kindly (and fairly condescendingly) steering him toward James Whale. Balderdash! Nonetheless, Bela experienced no shortfall of projects in which to terrorize after he had passed on *Frankenstein*; the sluice gates of what would become known as "classic horror" had scarcely begun to open.

(The $64,000 Question: did Bela's interpretation of the Monster – committed to film at this late date only "for the money" [as Lillian Lugosi Donlevy admitted to Greg Mank] – reflect to any extent the persona he *would have* essayed back in 1931, if fate [and his own penchant for stubbornness] had not intervened? As Bela owed no loyalty to Karloff's signature role, neither did he expect anyone to be so gauche as to suggest that he "study" the Briton's movements to prepare for the undertaking. Still, the Monster was the most widely recognized grotesque in the world, and anyone donning the make-up would be reasonably expected to likewise assume the mannerisms. Bela's Monster in *Frankenstein Meets the Wolf Man* was not only a case of following in someone else's footsteps, but – literally – of wearing someone else's boots, and the radical script surgery performed on the picture prior to release did little more for Bela's performance than pull the rug out from under those already wobbly legs.

But what if Bela's rendition *had* been the first, the one from which *other* players took their cue? Take, for example, the "eyelid covers" that Karloff had astutely recommended to Jack P. Pierce after the actor opined that, after the final version of the make-up had been affixed, the Monster's eyes were still, somehow, "too normal and alive and natural." For all their being the subjects of endless discussion and the recipients of ill-aimed pin-spots, Bela's eyes were not only his most arresting feature, but were the natural entrée into an incredibly open and mobile face. In that case, would the 1931 Frankenstein Monster with mortician's wax applied to *his* eyes have downplayed them? Watching Bela's face when he delivers a line [*any* line] is like watching a tornado roll across the plains: those eyebrows - rising and falling [when one of the pair is not being cocked sardonically] - and his mouth - working visibly at forcing those totally illogical English words into some semblance of recognizable pronunciation – flank those wildly flashing eyes as they shift from avuncular benevolence to unmistakable menace. If the face of Karloff's Monster mirrored the uncertainty of his childlike emotions, Lugosi's Monster would have almost assuredly have sprung calculating and full-grown from the electrical womb, and *his* phiz would have left no doubt as to where the gangling creature was headed.)

**As would be the case with several of Universal's '40s thrillers, the least interesting (genre-wise) of the thesps received top billing, while the titular horrors were represented by outrageous artwork, and their portrayers, by "with'" status.**

A dozen years later, though, having fewer major irons in the fire than just about any other genre regular, the 60-year-old Bela was no longer as particular as he had been in the aftermath of *Dracula*. His was still a big horror name (albeit due more to Monogram than to Universal at that point), and he came cheaply. Although there was little love lost between him and the Frankenstein Monster, the bolts and the boots meant a regular paycheck for a while, and this time around, the Monster *was* to be a speaking part. In fact, since Bela had dubbed the Monster's lines in the last scene of *The Ghost of Frankenstein* – during the operation, the Monster had received Ygor's brain *and his voice!* – working the sequel would be easier, as Bela's Ygor now *was* the Monster, so he had merely to speak out as did the other actors. That changed in a heartbeat; more properly, in the few minutes it took for the production staff to sit through a screening of the scene wherein Talbot and the Monster sit by a fire and share the details of their respective woes. The fairly expository dialogue exchange between the two horrors had the production staff in stitches. The decision was made to cut the Monster's lines and reconfigure the script. Thus, for the third time in five pictures, the Monster would be mute; Ygor's voice – chillingly triumphant for a moment there at the end of *Ghost* – would be heard no longer. Scenarist Curt Siodmak – who may have been a joy as a young man but who became a mean-spirited SoB in his extreme old age – delighted more than once in laying the blame for the removal of the dialogue on Bela's delivery. As old "Pass the Buck" Siodmak explained to the boys in **Universal Horrors:**

> Lugosi couldn't talk! They had left the dialogue I wrote for the Monster in the picture when I shot it, but with Lugosi it sounded so Hungarian funny that they had to take it out!(1)

Now what kind of unmitigated nonsense is that? Was Lugosi some green, untried novice, that no one would know how he would sound on film? Since the advent of the Talkies, he had made over a dozen pictures for Universal, and a couple of dozen more for other studios, and the Universal brass were *surprised* that he sounded the way he did? Balderdash! Did those clods at the front office really believe that, arrayed in Jack Pierce's make-up and reading Curt Siodmak's prose, Bela Lugosi would sound like Ronald Coleman? Pray tell: how *would* a monster (conceived and created in the heart of Germania and who had spent four feature-length motion pictures terrorizing yokels attired in lederhosen and dirndls) speak? And for once let's insist on a little continuity in the Frankenstein series: Was it not Ygor's voice trumpeting from the Monster's throat at the end of *Ghost of...*?

Snippets of that dialogue may be found in **Universal Horrors**, more of it in Don G. Smith's essay on the film in the Midnight Marquee Press volume, **Bela Lugosi**, and the whole deleted portion in the *FMTW* entry of the **MagicImage Filmbook** series. As delineated therein, the Monster ran the gamut from being a world-class whiner – easily the equal of Larry Talbot – to seeming a quivering bundle of emotional insecurities. The tripe that good judgment removed from Chaney and Lugosi's mouths might have led Gielgud and Olivier to despair. One may make a mansion or a privy from bricks, but one must *have* bricks to do so. Bela Lugosi should not have been made to take the heat for this, an instance of Curt Siodmak's professional inadequacy. Still, inasmuch as this "inadequacy" never made it to local theaters everywhere, *Variety* (24 February 1943) had nothing but the mute Monster with which to deal, and thus scratched the Siodmak back: "Expertly contrived and carrying suspenseful chiller tenor throughout... [Curt Siodmak] delivers a good job of fantastic writing to weave the necessary thriller ingredients into the piece." And, indeed, let's give credit where credit is due.

(An odd thought. Remembering John Carradine's late-in-life claims to having turned down the *original* role of Frankenstein's Monster, one wonders whether Universal might have considered – in this universe or some alternate – making any overtures to him regarding the Monster in *Frankenstein Meets the Wolf Man*. Possessed of an awesome set of pipes, Carradine had always maintained that the role having been a mute one as the reason for his having rejected it in the first place. Now, with the script awash with some very vocal grousing from both of the title characters, the match between gaunt actor and gabby Monster would have seemed more fitting than ever. There would be no way Curt Siodmak could claim that "*Carradine* couldn't talk!" Unless he and his troupe were off somewhere, treating the Great Unwashed to a Shakespearean presentation, Long John would have been available. His film schedule for the fall of 1942 was relatively light [for him], and – as he was already on the lot in the spring of '43 for *Captive Wild Woman* – he certainly might have finagled an additional monstrous appearance with not terribly much trouble.)

Having rendered the Monster once again mute, the *FMTW* script would also tamper with his sight; *ab initio*, the Monster - who had suddenly gone blind during the previous picture's denouement – was supposed to remain sightless for the better part of the sequel. This, at least, appears to have been the plan up until that production-staff screening. In some scenes, Lugosi stumbles about, feeling his way through detritus and rubble; the poor bugger is obviously sightless. Nonetheless, when Mannering, Elsa, *et al* approach the castle ruins the morning after the Festival of the New Wine goes to hell, Bela's Monster gawks at them through a hole in the wall – he does something of an abbreviated double-take, in fact – and then he selects a good-sized log from an assortment of sticks with the meticulous care of a golfer nipping the nine-iron from his bag. This doesn't do much to support the contention that the Monster is blind. (To date we've not uncovered another Siodmak quip in which the writer accused the actor of not being able to *see* properly.) But Bela can't be let off scot-free, either. Even allowing for the debate as to the quality of his vision, his Monster stomps through Vasaria's streets with his arms held straight out (groping blindly) one moment, and then held closely against his sides (as if carved from a piece of wood) the next. This sort of thing, combined with any number of stiff-armed gestures, leads the viewer to only one conclusion: Bela chose to portray the Monster as not having elbows.

Lon Chaney does an admirable job reprising the role of "his baby." *FMTW* gives inquiring viewers their first good look at Larry Talbot as the curse comes upon him. (Save for a sequence involving gnarled and hairy feet, *The Wolf Man* allows us to peek only as Talbot is changing *back* from lupine form.) The two "Jacks" (and masters) of their respective trades – Pierce and Fulton – make the transformation scenes herein absolutely stunning. I'd venture to say that even today's jaded and world-weary genre fan – as blasé to CGI and computer "morphing" as to his chips and cheese (and for whom *The Howling* is a "vintage" film) - might raise an eyebrow at these accomplishments from the days of the dinosaurs.

Born amid terror, confusion, and superstition in the 1941 opus, Chaney's Wolf Man comes into his own here. I doubt whether any meaningful revision had been made to the make-up between pictures, so the credit for enabling us to read the fear and bewilderment on the face of the hirsute horror must go to Chaney. As riveting as his appearance had been in the earlier picture, his alter ego then had really been little more than a furry automaton; only the widening (or narrowing) of his eyes separated the stalking from the pouncing. That beast was *all* beast, displaying no emotions save for blood-lust or the thrill of the hunt, and betraying no recognition of loved ones among the prey.

In *Frankenstein Meets the Wolf Man*, the character has moved a step or two beyond that basic stage. Apparently, he can sense where his bread is buttered and can distinguish between friend and food; how else to account for his loping *away* from Maleva while the old gypsy is yodeling at the top of her lungs for him to come back? When he bursts his bonds during the closing reel, his first instinct seems to be to attack, and if his drive to kill is so strong, so foolhardy, as to consider the Frankenstein Monster as a potential victim, then his sparing Maleva *had* to be an act of the will. And if his pouncing on the Monster is to force him to drop Elsa, then he has twice differentiated between those to be ravaged and those to be bypassed. (In his next outing – *House of Frankenstein* – the Wolf Man would once again lunge at anything that moved, going so far as to kill the gypsy girl that Talbot had found so attractive. Of course, the fact that the little darling was packing heat *may* have had something to do with that.)

A neat bit of more mature characterization – almost a throwaway – takes place at Vazec's inn. While Rex Evans is snapping testily at Maria Ouspenskaya's request for directions, Chaney and Martha MacVicar are staring at each other: he, with fear, anxiety, and animal-longing in his eyes; she, with the placid and helpless gaze of a deer caught in the headlights. (Question: Might this exchange somehow tie into the conceit raised in *The Wolf Man* that the lycanthrope sees the pentagram appear on his next victim, as when said contrivance popped up on the hands of Fay Helm and Evelyn Ankers? *That* would explain Maleva's being able to just stand there and yell; her being spared was not so much a conscious decision on the Wolf Man's part as predestination. Still, there was no onscreen sign of the five-pointed star showing up anywhere on Vazec's daughter. Are we over-thinking this?) And later, after Rex Evans lugs Martha's body through the streets of Vasaria *a la* Michael Mark carrying the drowned Marilyn Harris through Goldstadt, the hirsute Chaney's face clearly shows surprise at the approaching mob and his instinctive fear of so many men, brandishing weapons. (And well might he be afraid; the townsfolk of Vasaria are no ordinary chuckleheads. Judging by the haste with which they squeeze off a shot at the distant and indistinct Wolf Man, they are either awfully casual at discovering a lycanthrope in their midst, or awfully trigger-happy for firing at a human figure while out hunting a wolf.)

Chaney's portrayal of Larry Talbot has also grown, if only by inches. The beginning of the negotiating scene between Talbot and Elsa allows Chaney a rare opportunity to allow his unaffected pleasantness come to the fore. (Along with his opening moments as "Dynamo Dan" McCormick in *Man-made monster* and the bit of time he spends fiddling with pentagram-headed canes with the lovely Evelyn Ankers in *The Wolf Man*, these fleeting seconds give us a glimpse of Chaney at his simple best. The amicable personality that is permitted briefly to emerge might well have led to a more varied career for the actor as a mainstream secondary lead had all those full moons not intervened.) Away from the light of them thar moons, Talbot is the same affable fellow he had been when flirting with Gwen Conliffe in Llanwelly. Had Larry continued along this genial tack, he probably would have wrung the much-needed concessions from the baroness.

But, no; after the briefest ray of sunlight, *Weltschmerz*. Here we go again: the same old song, with the refrain alternating between "But you must…!" and "Can't you understand!?" The dreary, one-note tone that Talbot, or Taylor, or whatever he's calling himself may be logically sound, but it's also dramatically deadening. As opposed to his father, Chaney had only a limited number of faces and expressions upon which to draw, and the sheer monotony of those incessantly whiny demands he was called upon to deliver had to be have been stultifying even to him. There may be only so many ways of getting a certain point across and, after all, this is only a slick little "B" horror movie, but was Curt Siodmak so lacking in inspiration that he could not take a character of his own creation and have him evolve beyond all that non-stop kvetching so as to win sympathy rather than cause irritation? At the end of the "Faro-La" song, Siodmak has Chaney grab Adia Kutznetzoff by the lapels, snarl in his face, and then give the whole town ten minutes to get out of town! This is growth? This is creative writing? This is the kind of rubbish that should have been tossed along with the Monster's ludicrous dialogue.

In his autobiography, **Wolf Man's Maker; Memoir of a Hollywood Writer**, Siodmak offered an interesting take on Chaney:

> Being cruelly mistreated as a child by his famous father, Lon Chaney, Sr., Lon suffered from clinical depression, which he tried to overcome by his addiction to alcohol. I knew Lon until his premature death in 1973, a tragic character who couldn't adjust himself to life. He *was* the Larry Talbot in *Frankenstein Meets the Wolf Man*, who wanted to die. In that picture, Lon played himself, which made his part frighteningly believable.(2)

Uh-huh.

Chaney aside, Lionel Atwill's lively little mayor steals the thunder from the bigger names. Never without a twinkle in his eye – and there's no doubt he's got his eye on the baroness – Atwill fills his every moment with rich, if obvious, characterization. The very act of walking out of his office speaks volumes when his pipe stem clicks audibly against his teeth; there's a spark to this man that goes beyond his jaunty stride. (And, as various sources have made it abundantly clear, there was quite a spark to old "Pinky" in real life, too.) Later, he does quite well as the town's solitary voice of reason, even as he is dwarfed physically and vocally by the corpulent Vazec of Rex Evans. (And Atwill was surely one of only three actors – the other two being Zucco and Lugosi – we can picture suggesting "making friends with the Monster" and not seem a complete ass. Thankfully, this sentiment wins over the simple [if garrulous] townspeople of Vasaria, who always and everywhere enthusiastically support each and every statement as it is made.)

Budapest-born Ilona Massey is gorgeous, picking up as she does in Evelyn Ankers' high heels. Her baroness is a bit too nonchalant much of the time, seeming no more disconcerted by the Monster's appearance at the Festival of the New Wine than she might be by finding raisins in her strudel. (This casual regard is captured best in the medium shot at the table at the Festival; a later insert finds her huddled next to Patric Knowles, with both leads widening their eyes and flaring their nostrils in pure horror.) As with Chaney, one brief vignette – wherein Elsa's expression loses its joy as she watches Talbot/Taylor wildly overreact to the words of "Faro La" – gives us the kernel of this lady. Still – other than Talbot and the Monster – Elsa is the only hold-over character from the earlier film. While she does seem to be reacting now and again with a casualness no one else in the picture seems to feel, at least her dialogue indicates that she was present during the events that occurred in *Ghost*.(3)

Patric Knowles' Dr. Mannering shifts moods more easily than Talbot sprouts hair. Blessed with the kind of medical practice that allows him to follow his patients as they wander all over Europe, Mannering is too cold to be the true hero of the piece. (A close look will reveal there *is* no "true hero" of the piece.) His time-consuming trek notwithstanding, the doctor's interest in Larry is clinical, not personal: he wants to take the lycanthrope "home" and confine him, while also making him an object of study and research. While this is certainly in sync with the scientific motivations of virtually every other of the medicos who have populated these films, Mannering is too easily led by his darker side to later betray his trust and revitalize the Monster. He has no need of Frankenstein blood in his veins or ghostly apparitions of relatives with a similar bent to get him to switch sides. Even though Machiavellian, untrustworthy, and demonstrably self-serving, he is sufficiently handsome for the predictable screenplay to allow a couple of swings with an adjustable spanner to atone for past misdeeds and to drive Elsa into his arms as the flood waters dispose of all the evidence.

Cyril Delevanti as ghoul Freddy Jolly makes a hell of an impact by underplaying his bit in the film's fabulous opening scene. Seized by Talbot's supposedly dead hand (itself hairless, but bearing pointed nails – a lovely and fairly subtle touch), Freddy forgoes the more traditional shrieking and caterwauling and turns, aghast and almost speechless, to his partner in crime. "Help me," he implores, pitifully. "Help me!" Backed by Hans J. Salter's powerful music, Delvanti's delivery raises the hair on the nape of your neck. (The graveyard scene in *FMTW* has got to be the most atmospheric introductory footage the studio produced during the decade. The multi-level interior set – the entire production was studio-bound – brings to mind, but surpasses the moody cemetery sequence that opens the 1931 *Frankenstein*. Once inside the Talbot crypt, George Robinson's eye for chiaroscuro effect becomes more evident, with the contrasts between the encroaching moon and the shadows – thick as death, themselves – entrancing. Your eyes are so busy taking in the rich detail that your ears don't mind yet another rendition of "Even a man who is pure in heart," into which everyone in Llanwelly launches at the drop of a hat.)

Maria Ouspenskaya is given less to do than in *The Wolf Man*, and she's okay. Maleva seems to have lost that mystic "aura" she had had previously; her little "The way you walked was thorny" ditty, which had worked wonders effecting transformations at convenient moments previously, is absent here. The character is so sketchily drawn in *FMTW* – she scarcely does more than get Talbot and the wagon to Vasaria – that her virtual disappearance late in the picture usually goes unnoticed by the viewer. Still, her keeping her cool in the tavern scene with Rex Evans wins her some points for good behavior. And the substantial Rex Evans *is* substantially annoying; his Vazec waddles through the picture with a chip on his shoulder (God knows, there's room for a plank) and an attitude of angry defiance aimed at just about everyone. As he never seems to want for customers despite this personality flaw, his must be the only joint in town. The sight of the phone-booth-sized Vazec eavesdropping unobtrusively on Mannering and Talbot at the festival beggars the imagination as much as the blatantly fantastic characters upsetting the citizenry. There's a tad more on Martha MacVicar (making her debut here) in the essay on *Captive Wild Woman*.

Representing Scotland Yard yet again is Dennis Hoey – Inspector Lestrade himself, except he's now investigating as "Inspector Owen." Hoey, who spent most of the early '40s appearing in a variety of roles for 20th Century-Fox, was called over to Universal every now and again to act as a comic foil to Basil Rathbone, ultimately appearing in six of the twelve "Sherlock Holmes" adventures. In an interview with Tom Weaver (4), Hoey's son, Michael – himself a film producer, writer, and two-time Emmy Award nominee – groused a bit about this:

My dad was under a non-exclusive contract to Universal, playing Lestrade. They only used in him in to or three other [non-Holmes] pictures – but they seemed to see him playing only one role, Lestrade, even though they might have called his character by another name! In *Frankenstein Meets the Wolf Man* [1943], he plays a Scotland Yard inspector and even wore the same bloody wardrobe – Lestrade's bowler hat and raincoat! Then he did a film called *She-Wolf of London* [1946] and it was the same thing, a Scotland Yard inspector, only at least he was not wearing the same clothes in *that* one. So my father was very typecast at Universal.

Opera singer Adia Kuznetzoff seems determined to enjoy himself at all costs with his *brindisi* at the festival; the singer couches his pre-recorded final high-note in a mile-wide grin that quavers not a jot despite Lon Chaney's hot breath and spittle. The ebullient Russian had made his way to Hollywood in the early '30s and – like his fellow countryman, Mischa Auer – had become familiar in pseudo-ethnic, semi-eccentric roles up and down the line. (Perhaps his most memorable appearance apart from the one under discussion here was in Laurel and Hardy's musical comedy, *Swiss Miss*, where – in the final release version – the basso sang not a note.) Kuznetzoff is the undisputed highlight of the Festival of the New Wine, a typically underwhelming Tyrolean affair (a la Universal) in which anyone not running around in circles bounces up and down in place and waves to someone else. The overriding fantasy element of the Frankenstein saga extends to the festival itself; a squeezebox player and a couple of violinists fill the air as only a 20-piece orchestra can, and who would have thought that all of those cranky and argumentative peasants spent all of their spare time rehearsing four-part harmonies?

Sadly, Frankenstein perennial Dwight Frye – for whom this would be the last credited screen appearance – doesn't make much of an impression. With Margareta (that's Miss MacVicar) lying bloody and cold only yards away, and the prospect of yet another horrific reign of terror looming, Franzec (Don Barclay, looking for all the world like Joe Kirk's renowned character, Bacciagalupe, from Abbott and Costello's TV show) sensibly asks, "Who could have done this terrible thing?" Frye's Rudi *purrs* the shattering response, "Could it have been the Monster again? Frankenstein's Monster?" with all the gut-wrenching emotion of a weary commuter mulling over his train schedule. Frye, who was due to break out of his "B"-horror rut with a substantial role in Darryl F. Zanuck's upcoming bio-pic, *Wilson*, died suddenly of a heart attack in November 1943.

There were loads of pre-production blather about Lon Chaney being set to play both monsters, about employing doubles and utilizing split-screens to help the "Master Character Creator" work his magic on *Wolf-Man Meets Frankenstein* (Yup; Chaney's "baby" was to get the titular nod over the Monster) and it turned out to be

312

nothing more than so much nonsense, despite the barrels of ink that were spilled in pressbooks and press releases issued en route to firing up the kliegs and cranking away the cameras. (Not only did the Wolf Man end up second banana, top-billing for the movie went to Ilona Massey!) If nothing else, the film's shooting schedule was too short and the studio too famously penurious to indulge in anything other than talk about such grandiose plans. Thus, among Universal horror aficionados, there's been a long-held discussion as to who doubled Bela and Lon at what point in the movie.

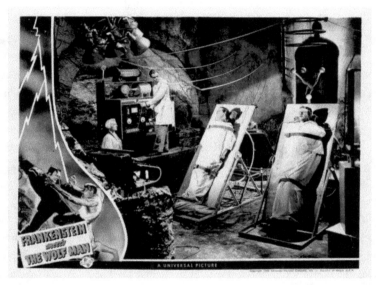

**Patric Knowles' Dr. Mannering is unique in the series, as he's the only medical type ever to have Lawrence Talbot (Lon Chaney) and the Frankenstein Monster (here, stuntman Gil Perkins) laid out on tables like an horrific smorgasbord. Ilona Massey's Baroness Frankenstein wouldn't miss this for the world.**

The late actor/producer/director/writer/genre-genius and horror-film maven Ted Newsom kindly spent time on the phone with this writer, cogitating about who did what and where and when. Ruminating over the debate as to whether Eddie Parker subbed for Lon in the climactic fight scene or whether Gil Perkins had doubled for Bela in the shot in which the Frankenstein Monster is retrieved from his icy prison, etc., - as raised and debated in more than a few printed assessments of the film over the last 35 years - Ted and I finally (and wisely) deferred to Gil Perkins's own recollections of *FMTW* (Duh!) as recorded in Tom Weaver's **It Came from Horrorwood,** wherein

Perkins said (on page 220) that Parker doubled for Chaney in the film. In the interview, Perkins had walked Weaver through the "staging of the staging" of the climactic battle some years after he and Parker had done the same for Herr Direktor:

> [Neill] just told Eddie and myself to work out a fight and let him *see* it. We worked out the thing, then we just walked through it [for Neill], went through the motions, and said 'This is what we'll do here,' 'This is what we'll do there.' He told us what he wanted, where he wanted us to start and where he wanted us to finish and what kind of a fight he wanted it to be. Apart from that, he left us pretty well alone.

Suffice it to say that Perkins insisted that it was he in the Monster get-up at all times during the picture, with Parker donning the hair and fangs for the rip-roaring finale. And yet, as Ted Newsom observed:

> The strap-bursting shot of the Monster - the sole shot in which he actually looks like Parker - has the earmarks of a reshoot. None of the lab set is visible, indicating it was made after the set was destroyed by the huge water gag.

Intriguingly, in the first version of the script – available in the **MagicImage Filmbook** on the title - it was the *Wolf Man* who burst his operating-table bonds and grabbed the nostril-flaring Elsa, only to be denied his lovely burden by the Monster. Why this reversal of roles? Had Siodmak – as screenwriter – initially posited that the Monster might have felt *indebted* in some way to Elsa and Mannering (yclept "Harley" in the first script) and that his saving the heroine from the fangs and claws of the lycanthrope would have been "pay back?" Or had Parker and Perkins taken liberties with the script and changed who did what with Ilona Massey purely for reasons of choreography and/or convenience when they walked through the scene with Roy William Neill? God only knows that both monsters were motivated to snatch up the lovely baroness – every Frankenstein Monster worth his salt had been scaring the skirts off the sundry Elizabeths and Elsas since Karloff had first snuck into Mae Clarke's bedroom back in 1931 – although the Wolf Man's interest in her was much more likely culinary.

As with most of Universal's genre thrillers, there are isolated moments in which your mind's eye ought to look the other way. The first transformation scene – arguably the best in the entire Wolf Man canon – depicts Larry metamorphosing in his hospital pajamas, but his beast subsequently scampers about those remarkably empty Cardiff streets in his standard-issue Wolf Man duds. Next morning, though, the unconscious Talbot is back in his jammies! As for the Monster, I won't fault Bela for the nasal hiss-cum-snort he chose to affect; its tepid sound is more suiting to his physically impaired character than the cavernous snarls of Karloff or Chaney; I only wish that, in doing so, he sounded less like Elsa Lanchester's Bride. And as those flood waters break through into the midst of the final battle scene, Parker's lycanthrope and Perkins's Monster are seen to be swept away, but the eagle-eyed viewer will note that the Monster in this scene is *not* balanced atop those asphalt-spreader's boots, having opted herein for sensible shoes. Obviously, questions of safety trumped issues with continuity every time.

*Harrison's Reports* (7 March 1943) started off by opining that "For those devotees who like their horror pictures strong, this will fill the bill" and concluding with "Definitely not for children"; plot summary separated the two viewpoints. Flipping that coin to its other side, the 1 March 1943 *Film Daily* didn't forbid outright the picture to the tykes, but did sort of throw a curve: "Heaven knows what so rich a diet of scariness will do to the kids." A couple of sentences later, the reviewer got down to brass tacks:

> The idea of two of the most cherished monsters of the screen carrying on in the common cause of scaring the wits out of people is something to intrigue the imagination. To say imagination runs rampant in this bit of cinematic confection is to put it mildly. Incident after incident defies all rationalization and heaps praise upon those technicians whose trickery makes such entertainment possible.

For all that talk of imagination and rationalization, though, the pronouncement that "The best performance in the film is that of Knowles" was fairly disconcerting and went unexplained.

Populated by two of the most European of Monsters, some of the more familiar faces of the "Frankenstein stock company," and at least one future "big name" in theater (the uncredited Jeff Corey), *Frankenstein Meets the Wolf Man* is an enjoyable and – in some circles – a beloved film. The silly discrepancies that pop up are easily overlooked in the light of sumptuous photography, superlative special effects, and many of the performances noted above. Nor can we neglect to applaud director Roy William Neill, who brought with him some 25 years of directorial experience and who is the subject of discussion throughout the entries on the Sherlock Holmes pictures, for helping make this – his only true Universal "horror film" – as memorable as it was and is.

And when push comes to shove, awareness of the circumstances under which Bela Lugosi was forced to work may make his Monster more of a curio to be marveled at than a classic portrayal to be revered, but, even here, Bela demonstrates how – love it or not – the Lugosi presence just cannot be ignored.

***Frankenstein Meets the Wolf Man*** – 5 March 1943 – 72 minutes (ST)

**CAST**: Ilona Massey as Baroness Elsa Frankenstein; Patric Knowles as Dr. Frank Mannering; Lon Chaney as Lawrence Talbot; Bela Lugosi as Frankenstein's Monster; Lionel Atwill as the Mayor of Vasaria; Maria Ouspenskaya as Maleva; Dennis Hoey as Inspector Owen; Don Barclay as Franzec; Rex Evans as Vazec; Dwight Frye as Rudi; Martha MacVicar as Margareta; Harry Stubbs as Guno; Doris Lloyd as Nurse; Beatrice Roberts as Varja; Adia Kuznetzoff as Festival Soloist; Torben Meyer as Erno; Jeff Corey as Gravedigger; David Clyde as Llanwelly Police Sergeant; Tom Stevenson as Ghoul; Cyril Delevanti as Freddy Jolly (Ghoul); Charles Irwin as Constable; Gil Perkins and Eddie Parker…Stunt Doubles for Bela Lugosi and Lon Chaney

**CREDITS**: Director: Roy William Neill; Producer: George Waggner; Screenplay: Curt Siodmak; Director of Photography: George Robinson, ASC; Art Director: John B. Goodman; Associate Art Director: Martin Obzina; Director of Sound: Bernard B. Brown; Technician: William Fox; Set Decorator: Russell A. Gausman; Associate: Edward R. Robinson; Film Editor: Edward Curtiss; Musical Director: Hans J. Salter; Make-up: Jack P. Pierce; Assistant Director: Melville Shyer; Special Photographic Effects: John P. Fulton: Gowns: Vera West

***Shock Theater*** Catalog No. 705: "Two of the world's most fearsome horror creatures combine their wickedness to provide a double measure of chills and thrills in the *Shock* full-length feature, 'Frankenstein Meets the Wolf Man.' See it on this channel (day), (date), at (time)…"

*– JTS*

316

# Sherlock Holmes in Washington (1943)

In his column "Product Digest" in the 3 April 1943 edition of *Motion Picture Herald*, writer "A.J." speculated that:

> If Sir Arthur Conan Doyle were alive today, he would have reason
> to congratulate the author of this exciting mystery drama for doing right
> by his characters and for contriving a plot that out-Sherlocks Sherlock
> at his pleasant best.

Behind A.J.'s overly optimistic screed, there was certainly an innate enthusiasm for maneuvering this classic British luminary into a familiar American environment. In Conan Doyle's original works, the United States is usually a source of evil, composed either of individuals belonging to secret violent societies or of more mundane, Chicago-type gangsters. In this adventure, however, America is merely the investigative theater and while the enemy will display American stylistics, he will turn out to be German and addicted to the tenets of the Third Reich.

A number of passengers show up at the steps of a twin-engine aircraft preparing to take off, and they identify themselves to the officer on duty. The first is William Easter (played by Henry Daniel, who automatically activates out innate suspicion and distrust). The second, followed closely by a swarm of anxious reporters, is Sir Henry Marchmont, evidently on a diplomatic mission and said to be carrying with him a certain secret document that would be vital for the United States. The third is Alfred Pettibone (in reality, John Grayson), a diminutive and awkward employee of a London law firm, from whose furtive gaze we intuit that he is either a spy or an agent in the service of the Allies. The travelers land in Lisbon in order to change planes and make for New York. (This transfer of passengers to an airline flying out of a neutral country followed the then-established policy, especially as the Atlantic was still infested with submarines and German pocket battleships.)

The three suspects, now in New York, board a train bound for Washington. From his unwavering gaze, it's now apparent that William Easter is plotting to snatch the documents from the diplomat, but, upon conversing with his henchmen, he deduces that Sir Henry is merely a decoy and that the timid lawyer is therefore the real messenger. Director Roy William Neill heightens this club-car sequence (a requisite in good mystery movies) with a number of characters conversing among themselves, some sequestered mice, pretty girls smoking, lots of drinking – as its details will be key in one or two reels. Predictably, everything goes black, Easter and his hit men kidnap Grayson, and it's with his disappearance that the Intelligence Service in London is put on alert and turns to Holmes, whom we surprise eating breakfast en his traditional 221B Baker Street living room. Once entrusted with the mission to locate the missing document, Holmes and Watson decide to start off, but not before deducing that the document had not been transported in its original form but rather had been photographed and reduced to microfilm. Holmes explains the logic of such technology to Watson (and, by extension, to the viewers) in a time before that gimmick became commonplace in spy movies. (In an effort to strengthen the ties that bind between allies, we are given to understand that the cricket-loving Watson is anxious to become acquainted with the American version of same; i.e. baseball. Holmes does *not* share his protégé's quickly acquired affection for the Brooklyn Dodgers.)

From the air, the camera shows us three architectural symbols of Western democracy: the Washington Monument, the Lincoln Memorial, and the Capitol. A few moments later, on the ground, we see them again via the tourist route that Holmes and Watson take upon arriving in Washington. Also becoming commonplace from here on in – perhaps a more quotidian reflection of the concord among the Allies dealing with the Axis - is cooperation among foreigners in police cinema, what with Holmes offering direction to the local police lieutenant, Lieutenant Grogan (Edmund MacDonald), when Grayson's body is found stashed in a trunk Upon realizing that Grogan is no Lestrade, he begs his pardon and explains, "You see I'm so accustomed to working quite alone at my lodgings on Baker Street that I sometimes forget the more modern scientific methods so particularly effective here in America." This paean to the American criminal detection system is eventually revealed to be overwrought when Holmes, magnifying glass in hand, heads for the forensics lab and deduces – from odd bits on the blanket in which Grayson's cadaver had been wrapped – that an antiques shop is the front for the spy ring.

We return to the club car through the testimony of George, the black porter pulling double-duty at the bar (Clarence Muse, familiar to all who love Bela Lugosi films as supporting the titan of horror as the coachman in *White Zombie* (1932) and as the butler in *The Invisible Ghost* (1941). In interviewing George, Holmes arrives at the conclusion that the ersatz lawyer had hidden the microfilm in a box of matches now in the possession of a young female passenger for whom he lit a final cigarette. (The sequence is quite engaging from the cinematographic point of view and may be said to be Hitchcockian: the matches move from hand to hand, from a soldier to a waiter, then to the sundry guests at a reception party until they inadvertently end up again with the girl.) It's clear that the girl, Nancy Partridge (Marjorie Lord), will be the next victim of the conspirators who will kidnap her before Holmes can stop them, and they do so – costumed as caterers – at the engagement party held in honor of Nancy's incipient marriage to Lieut. Peter Merriam (John Archer).

Upon falling into the hands of the kidnappers, Nancy ends up in front of the arch-villain who will lead this organization, an antiquarian named Richard Stanley; in reality, Stanley is the pseudonym of Heinrich Hinkel, a German who had earlier infiltrated United States society. (Hinkel/Stanley is incarnated by George Zucco, once again displaying his trademark fastidious tendencies for evil.) A bit later, by simply making the rounds of all of Washington's antique shops (one of the weaker bits of the internal logic of the case), Holmes finds one that is suspect, and he and Watson they end up meeting Hinkel and his henchmen.

In *Sherlock Holmes and the Secret Weapon*, Holmes mentioned the story "The Purloined Letter" and the "Poe-tic" revelation that the best place to hide something is in the sight of everyone. Per that allusion, the matchbox is now within sight, but only we audience members know that it contains the precious microfilm. The matches end up in the possession of Hinkel who, not knowing that he already has what he wants so much, uses them in his stubborn attempt to keep his pipe lit. And with this simple ruse, director Roy William Neill plays with the viewer in Hitchcockian style, creating psychological suspense through the fear that the villain will notice Nancy and Holmes's knowing glances at the matches and end up realizing that the microfilm is in no other place than his own hands.

Repeating the narrative scheme of his previous adventure, Holmes enter his nemesis's headquarters unarmed and is saved at the last minute by the arrival of Watson and the police force. Before that, in a duel of wits, Hinkel dedicates to him the arrogant turn of phrase, "It's the last strike that counts, hey, Holmes?" As in the preceding film, Neill ends with a shootout in the dusk but, on this occasion, it's staged without as much tension or excitement. The director's success lies in his moving from one sequence to another with such speed that we viewers have scarcely the time to understand the facts and clues that Holmes explains verbally to his loyal friend, let alone come to grasp the contradictions inherent in the plot.

**When Watson learns the details of the latest deduction so do we all. As the series progressed it seemed that Nigel Bruce's character seemed to regress. Here, despite his open mouth, the good doctor is up for all Holmes can give.**

A contemporary critic also perceived these flaws. Lucille Greenberg commented in *Motion Picture Daily* (26 March 1943) that "although many of the methods of creating suspense are rather obvious, they are effective." *Showmen's Trade Review* (27 March 1943) concurred with this opinion, admitting that "there is nothing startlingly new in the plot, but that's a non-essential, since the action carries along nicely and involves characters in such a way that there is a continuous thread of story interest." The 31 March 1943 issue of *Film Daily* expressed its appraisal that this Holmes was tops: "This one looks like the best of Universal's Sherlock Holmes series. Its interest is enhanced by the fact that its action transpires familiarly to us." Coincidentally, the same-dated *Variety* supported the idea that "It's one of the best to date in the Holmes series, despite the fact that Bertram Millhauser and Lynn Riggs have concocted a script that seldom ventures beyond the established formula." The critic also found it difficult to believe some logical points ("some of the magnifying glass conclusions are pulled out of a hat"), but, seeing them in context, he would conclude that they "are no longer a detriment to the sleuth sagas." *Harrisons Reports* (3 April 1943) offered an interesting observation: "The fact that the audience knows from the beginning in whose possession the document is gives the story a nice twist."

In the film's final moments, as was customary, Holmes expresses his distaste for the case but also delivers a valuable message of optimism to the viewer who, let us remember, was living World War II day by day and needed to leave the movie theater encouraged and, if he was able, willing to buy war bonds. "It is not for us to peer into the mysteries of the future," Holmes says while observing the imposing capitol from afar, "but, in the days to come, the British and American people, for their own safety and the good of all, will walk together in majesty and justice and in peace." This time it's neither Conan Doyle nor Shakespeare but rather his own prime minister, Winston Churchill, who expressed himself thus, on the 26 December 1941, in his speech before the United States Congress.

Dealing with this daring a McGuffin wasn't the only mission that Holmes appeared to have dedicated himself to during his stay in America. When *Sherlock Holmes in Washington* finished shooting, on the 5 August 1942, President Franklin D. Roosevelt – with absolute secrecy – was given membership into the "Baker Street Irregulars" (the fan club of the Great Consulting Detective, the name of which alludes to that pack of London street urchins whom Holmes would put into action every time he needed information from the streets). According to Bliss Austin's comment in "A Baker Street Folio" (Baker Street Irregulars, 1945), the membership was kept secret until the end of the conflict so that there would be no one...

> ...of little understanding who would have raised their voices in dismay if they had known that this man, President of the United States and Commander-in-Chief of its armed forces, was having inconsequential truck with Sherlock Holmes.

The Holmes who headed for the District of Columbia still sported his odd comb-over – albeit for the last time – and was neither impressed initially by the district's national monuments, nor open to sampling (as was Watson) such American institutions as chewing gum. He was, however, less civil to his sidekick than in the previous two pictures, a tendency that would be continue in subsequent movies. *In Washington* would be the first adventure in the series not directly inspired by the

Canonical stories(1) (despite the fact that Churchill's speech had some similarities to dialog in "The Adventure of the Noble Bachelor," when Holmes envisions a "same world-wide country under a flag which shall be a quartering of the Union Jack with the Stars and Stripes") and also, the last to highlight the contemporaneous updating of the character. The following films would impose a gradual and welcome return again to the quasi-Victorian terrain in which Universal felt at ease, that plot of cinematic land sharing a border with the Gothic horror that was its brand.

The secondary cast was, of course, populated by Universal's contract players (like Ian Wolfe), character actors (like Gerald Hamer), and familiar second- and third-tier thesps whose faces were much better known by audiences than their names (like Irving Mitchell.) To illustrate this last, let's consider that in the scenes at the airfield, the chief officer is played by Leyland Hodgson, a quintessential Brit who in the '40s appeared in countless "A" features from major studios although rarely with screen credit. Unlike many compatriots who only would display the true persona in a role for phlegmatic aristocrats and not for minor characters, Hodgson was versatile with respect to both types of parts. Universal turned again to him as the Talbots' butler in *The Wolf Man* (1940), the chauffeur in *The Invisible Man Returns* (1941), and as the chief of police in *The Ghost of Frankenstein* (1942). Unlike other situations, wherein the filmmakers would grant a close-up to some bit player or extra, in this case the camera takes on Hodgson from behind, leaving only a third of his profile seen, perhaps to understandably spare spectators already familiar with the face that had been present in the two previous Holmes adventures, and those for whom his face was as familiar as the ring on their finger due to military roles.

*In Washington* was Bertram Millhouser's first "Sherlock Holmes" screenplay but one: the prolific writer had adapted William Gillette's play, *Sherlock Holmes*, for Clive Brook and the Fox Film Corporation back in 1932. In addition to the film under discussion and four more series entries, the native New Yawka had worked his magic in the service of a brace of other detectives - Philo Vance (screenplay for *The Garden Murder Case*, 1936) and Nick Carter (screenplay for *Nick Carter, Master Detective*, 1939) – as well as for the French master of disguise/gentleman thief, Arsene Lupin (screenplay for *Enter Arsene Lupin*, 1944). The original story for *In Washington* was all Millhouser's idea, but he split screenplay credit with Lynn Riggs, an Oklahoman who also won half of the screenplay nod (along with John Bright) for *Sherlock Holmes and the Voice of Terror*. Perhaps inevitably, Riggs also was responsible for the original play that went on to become one of America's most beloved musicals: *Oklahoma*.

The fact that *In Washington* appears to be entirely concerned with wartime espionage might keep away fans of the fantastic and even those of "classic" Holmes, but the amusement that Neill elicits from the matchbox and the presence of two heavyweights of villainy like Zucco and Daniell provides as much interest as the first two entries in the series.

*Sherlock Holmes in Washington* – 30 April 1943 – 71 minutes

**CAST**: Basil Rathbone as Sherlock Holmes; Nigel Bruce as Dr. Watson; Marjorie Lord as Nancy Partridge; Henry Daniell as William Easter; George Zucco as Heinrich Hinkel (alias Richard Stanley); John Archer as Lieut. Pete Merriam; Gavin Muir as Agent Bart Lang; Edmund MacDonald as Lieut. Grogan; Don Terry as Howe; Bradley Page as Cady; Holmes Herbert as Mr. Ahrens; Thurston Hall as Senator Henry Babcock; Gerald Hamer as Alfred Pettibone (alias John Grayson); Gilbert Emery as Sir Henry Marchmont; Clarence Muse as George; Ian Wolfe as Antiquarian; Mary Forbes as Mrs. Pettibone, Mary Gordon as Mrs. Hudson.

**CREDITS**: Director: Roy William Neill; Associate Producer: Howard Benedict; Screenplay: Bertram Millhouser, Lynn Riggs; Original Story: Bertram Millhouser; Based on characters created by Sir Arthur Conan Doyle; Director of Photography: Les White; Film Editor: Otto Ludwig; Art Director: Jack Otterson; Associate Art Director: Martin Obzina; Music: Frank Skinner; Musical Director: Charles Previn; Set Decorator: Russell A. Gausman; Associate Set Decorator: Edward R. Robinson; Sound Director: Bernard B. Brown; Technician: James Masterson; Technical Adviser: Tom McKnight; Gowns: Vera West

*- DL*

# *Captive Wild Woman* (1943)

*Synopsis*: After a two-year expedition to Africa, wild animal trainer Fred Mason returns to the Whipple Circus with a boat-load of wild animals, including Cheela, an unusually intelligent gorilla. Mason wants to stage a spectacular animal act involving lions and tigers - natural enemies - in the same ring.

Fred's fiancee Beth brings her ill sister Dorothy to the Crestview Sanitarium in the hopes the famous Dr. Walters can cure of her glandular problems. Dr. Walters takes Dorothy on as a patient, but he has a hidden agenda that involves using Dorothy as a guinea pig in his illegal experiments. At Beth's invitation, Walters visits the circus where he is impressed by Cheela. Walters steals Cheela with the aid of a disgruntled circus worker who is then killed by the ape. Walters transfers Dorothy's unusual glandular secretions to Cheela who slowly transforms into a young woman. When Walters' nurse objects, the doctor kills her and uses part of her brain to further humanize Cheela. Walters dubs his creation Paula Dupree.

Walters visits the circus with Paula to see how she will react to Mason, who is having serious problems with his lion/tiger act. When he is nearly killed in the ring, Paula's power over the animals saves him. Mason decides to use her extraordinary abilities in the show but, as opening night approaches, Paula, jealous of Mason's love for Beth, partly reverts back to her ape form and attempts to murder Beth in her boarding house, but Beth escapes harm and Paula returns to the sanitarium.

Beth gets a frantic phone call from Dorothy and rushes to the sanitarium where she discovers exactly what Walters has been up to. When Walters tells her he intends to experiment further and use her brain as well, Beth releases Cheela, now completely in her gorilla state, from her cage. The gorilla kills Walters and heads for the circus. A

325

storm has disrupted opening night and caused chaos, but Cheela arrives just in time to save an unconscious Mason from the lions. Not understanding the situation, a policeman fatally shoots Cheela.

The 3 April 1943 edition of the *Wall Street Journal* reported that the year was seeing "the biggest boom the amusement industry has ever known. Day in and day out more people are going to the movies than ever before." The article went on to discuss just what kind of movies the public was jamming the theaters to see:

> Currently box office receipts say the public wants war pictures, musical shows and comedies. But there's a new trend in the offing. The industry suspects that the 'horror' picture is due for a major comeback. R.K.O's 'Cat People,' produced at a nominal cost has been breaking records: so movie-goers can expect an outbreak of ghosts, vampires, and others of the standard eerie thrillers.

Exhibitors subsequently reported that the public quickly tired of war movies. The fact that the war had begun to dominate every aspect of American life meant that many did not need to be reminded of the bloodshed in Europe and Asia and the uncertainty that the Allies would triumph. Exhibitors insisted that movie-goers craved escapism and of course horror films had always been good for that.

Columnist Wood Soames, writing in the 10 May 1943 edition of the *Oakland Tribune* under the headline "Horror Films Open New Bonanza," discussed the horror boom:

> Relaxation of dim out regulations has not only proved a boon to the theaters, especially those located off the main stems or less recently open to trade, but is likely to be a bonanza to the studios. Down Hollywood way, the boys have just come to the realization that Universal has been quietly making scads of money by producing a steady stream of horror movies, and because of the nature of those beasties a quantity of night shooting is required. With the dim out in effect, it was increasingly difficult to get the eerie effects needed for the delectation of the shake-and-shivers fans. These shots are best taken outdoors with artificial light illuminating the darkness. That little problem no longer confronts the producers.

Soames went on to say that "Scarcely a studio is now without at least one thriller on its list and usually with important names in the cast."

With so many men away at war, were women making up a majority of horror film attendees? A rather curious piece printed in a number of small town newspapers in December of 1943 claimed that "According to movie surveys, women are more enchanted by horror movies than men." Unfortunately, there's no indications of exactly where these surveys came from, assuming they existed at all and weren't the product of a studio flack (working for Universal, perhaps?). If women were indeed becoming fonder of horror films, some critics failed to realize it. In the 17 August 1943 review of *Phantom of the Opera*, *Film Daily* noted that "By toning down the gruesome details and playing up what light moments the subject affords, Universal has widened the film's appeal to women and those who are not out-and-out shocker fans."

Of course, when estimating audience demographics, one must also take into account children (always big horror fans), those men not serving in the war, and men and women military personnel on leave (according to one source, one-third of a typical audience was made up of service people).

Perhaps a stronger case can be made for an increased Hollywood interest in female protagonists:

> RKO today purchased 'Prodigal Women,' a recently published novel by Nancy Hale, announcing that the acquisition was part of a new studio policy calling for photoplays in which the leading characters are women. This policy has been established to combat the wartime shortage of leading men.
>
> *The New York Times*, 8 December 1942

The same piece also noted that Universal's *Captive Wild Woman* had acquired the services of John Carradine.

No doubt the success of *Cat People* inspired *Captive Wild Woman*, but the lesson Universal seems to have missed from that Val Lewton production was that audiences would respond to a horror film full of psychological nuance, ambiguity, and intelligent writing. Instead, their main take-away was that it was time for a female monster movie, and the Paula Dupree films constitute the only lady creature series in their canon.

Apparently, Universal came up with the *Captive Wild Woman* title before they had a story to attach to it (at least they didn't call it *Destiny*). In February of 1941, Universal put ads in the trade papers that their film would present a "new type of star aimed to capture the attention of novelty seekers." Sometimes the ad was accompanied by a little drawing featuring a scantily clad female and a few African tribesmen, and elsewhere it was said the star would be "the wild woman." The Big U promised exhibitors a film in which "jungle fury embodied in feminine beauty to startle and electrify your box office."

Later it was reported that Ainsworth Morgan was working on the *Wild Woman* script as a vehicle for Universal's exotic star, Maria Montez. Morgan had written the story "White Savage" which became the basis for Montez's earlier film, *South of Tahiti*, though the title *White Savage* ended up getting used for her 1943 movie (to add to the confusion, the trades sometimes muddled *White Savage* with *Captive Wild Woman*). No doubt that, had Morgan's script been produced, it would have more of the Technicolor hokum that drew Montez's fans to the theater. It's not likely Universal would have ever offered their tempestuous star a movie in which she plays an ape woman, and the idea - though not the title - was quietly dropped.

In June of 1942, it was announced that Henry Sucher, who had just written the script for *Skid Row* (which presumably became the Dead End Kids movie, *Mug Town*), was assigned the writing chores for *Captive Wild Woman*. Nonetheless, in March of 1943, *Motion Picture Herald* tells us that Universal bought the story from Ben Pivar (who is credited as producer on the film, but not as writer); several other writers were also cited as working on the screenplay. No matter whoever was guilty, Universal began touting Acquanetta, who had recently signed at the studio, as the film's first "feminine 'horror' star." An article published in the 22 December 1942 edition of *Bradford* [Pennsylvania] *Era* elaborated:

> In *Captive Wild Woman*, she will appear as both a beautiful girl and an animal-like creature. The make-up will be so complicated that the studio has already made a plaster cast of the star's whole body. Jack Pierce will practice on it to create the horror effects.

However, just a couple of weeks later, columnist Frederick Othman wrote that Universal was planning two horror films, one "Frankenstein" movie with Lon Chaney, tentatively titled (what else?) *Destiny*, but that "the other horror picture, featuring the beauteous Acquanetta, is off the schedule; she said she didn't want to be a lady ape with claws." (*Daily News*, [ Middleboro, KY], 16 January 1943). Perhaps Acquanetta did not wish to appear ridiculous to her "rival" Maria Montez. Possibly at this point,

Yvonne De Carlo's name was mentioned for the part, but in the end, Acquanetta assumed the role that is her one slim claim to fame.

In his 11 April 1943 column, Walter Winchell - apparently forgetting the 1935 *Bride of Frankenstein* - announced that "Acquanetta becomes the first feminine horrifier in films - she'll turn from a glamour gal into a lady gorilla." When the film was released, Winchell derided it: "A forlorn attempt to horrify you. The producers apparently do not know you cannot frighten audiences if they are yawning." (*Burlington Daily Times*, 15 June 1943).

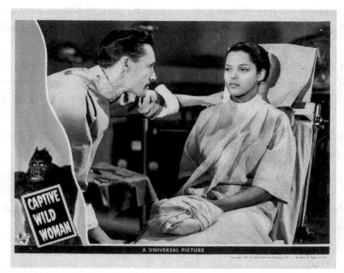

**John Carradine gives it his all whilst no doubt wishing he was doing Shakespeare in New York. Acquanetta probably had no such aspirations.**

Perhaps uncertain of both their star and how a female she-beast might go over - plus wanting to appeal to the kiddies - Universal included considerable footage from their 1933 Clyde Beatty hit, *The Big Cage*. At the beginning of *Captive Wild Woman*, Beatty is given thanks for his "cooperation in staging the thrilling animal sequences in this film." He's also mentioned in the story as the circus's first choice for the lion/tiger act, the job Fred Mason (Milburn Stone) ends up taking. When photographed from the back and wearing matching clothing, Stone easily passes for Beatty. Vince Barnett, who played "Soup Meat" in *The Big Cage*, also turns up in a similar comic role as Curly and is dressed in the same outfit as in the earlier film. The circus owner in *Captive* is named John Whipple in order to use the footage of the animal wagons that bear the name "Whipple Circus" from *The Big Cage*. All the circus scenes in *Captive* are made to parallel action from *The Big Cage*: the escape of the lion at the dock, Mason getting knocked out while in the cage, the storm at the end, and even the bit where Beatty stares down a lion (a close-up of Acquanetta is substituted). Considering the short running time of *Captive Wild Woman* (barely an hour), one could fairly describe the film as a circus movie disguised as a horror film.

Most reviewers did not realize the animal scenes were taken from a 10-year-old movie and assumed they were new, with Beatty handling the training and substituting for Stone inside the ring. However, *Variety* and *The New York Times* recognized the earlier footage, though no one had any complaints about the near-flawless matching. The first-rate quality of the old footage aided greatly in the deception.

For many modern viewers - having greater sensitivity to cruelty to animals - the lion-and-tiger-training scenes may be more shocking than any of the horror stuff. The fight between the lion and tiger ended up with the tiger getting killed, though Beatty insisted that wasn't his game plan. Such sequences didn't seem to bother many reviewers and certainly not the critic for the *New York Daily News* in his write-up of *The Big Cage*:

> Nowadays we can see those magnificent fights, which cost the Roman Emperors so much, for fifty cents. That certainly looks like progress. Let's have more and better animal fights in the future.(1)

Not everyone longed for the days of the Coliseum. British animal lovers threatened a boycott of *The Big Cage*, but Universal responded that animal welfare organizations were on the set throughout the shooting of the film and that the animals were well treated. The hapless tiger might disagree and so would Charlie the Elephant and Joe Martin the orangutan, Universal animal stars who came to bad ends.

Curly's crack that the animals won't like "meatless Tuesdays" is one of the few times that a Universal horror acknowledged what was happening in the real world (John Banning getting his draft notice in *The Mummy's Tomb* is another one). While no one at the time was aware of Dr. Mengele and the atrocious concentration camp experiments, it is possible that Dr. Walters - who is described as endeavoring three times to "improve the race" and create an army of supermen - may be meant to remind audiences of the Nazis. Then again, the fact that Walters' first name is Sigmund may possibly be a nod to the growing movie trend to treat psychiatrists as villains. Even though Walters is an endocrinologist and Dorothy's medical problem is a bit vague, he could be seen as treating her for hysteria.

The ladies definitely take center stage in *Captive Wild Woman*, with Fred Mason's heroics being confined mainly to the first reel wherein he confronts an escaped lion. Later it is Acquanetta who saves him from the wild beasts, and Cheela comes to his rescue at the finale (I was hoping the ape would carry him in her arms in true Universal monster/heroine fashion, but instead she just slings him over her shoulder like Santa's toy sack). And it's Evelyn Ankers - chic although perhaps overdressed for her planned attendance at the circus - who saves her sister, confronts Walters, and sics Cheela on him. The latter bit is the only time we see the violence on-screen (not counting the animal training): the camera turns away when Cheela kills the mean trainer, during the murder of Nurse Strand by Dr. Walters, and as Paula kills Beth's fellow boarder (Paula follows her out of the room and then runs back in and exits the through the window, a rather awkward sequence). This is in contrast to *Frankenstein Meets the Wolf Man* - often on the top of the bill with *Captive Wild Woman* - where we see the Wolf Man savagely attack the hapless constable.

While Mason claims that Cheela doesn't have a jealous bone in her body, Paula seems another matter entirely. That Paula's transformation into an animal is triggered by jealousy is somewhat of a steal from Irina's more complex situation in *Cat People*. In *Captive*, Mason seems to encourage Paula's attentions, calling her "honey" and putting his arm around her. Mason and Beth both seem to enjoy flirting as earlier Beth teases Mason about going out to dinner several times with Dr. Walters, but, in the end, they are a typical '40s movie couple. After Paula has helped Mason calm down the lions, Mason cracks to Beth, "I hope you'll be as easy to tame after we're married," a remark not likely to go over well today.

In 1942, J. Carrol Naish played an ape transformed into a man in the surprisingly brutal *Dr. Renault's Secret*; his character's devotion to his creator's daughter therein seemed more dog-like than erotic. Earlier in 1943, Bela Lugosi portrayed the title role in *The Ape Man*. His interest in the heroine in that classic was centered on her spinal fluid, which he needed in order to transform into a human. According to Hollywood at least, apes are usually better suited to males while women are "catty." Irina's alter-ego in *Cat People* is a black panther, and, of course, in *Island of Lost Souls*, we have a beautiful Panther Woman, with the gorilla being represented by the monstrous Ouran. Paula Dupree is the exception, though her make-up is not especially simian (then again one could argue that Lon Chaney's Wolf Man doesn't much resemble a wolf). Initially, her look is not too elaborate: a wig, greasepaint and some unsightly

331

yak hair. Later, as she becomes more animal-like, she sprouts additional hair, a snout, and more conspicuous fangs.

Paula's transformation into a monster is achieved very simply with a few quick dissolves, nothing like the painstaking work done to change Larry Talbot into his hairy alter-ego. The most effective bit of Paula's transformation is right at the beginning where her skin darkens (no doubt using the filter technique that was so effective in the 1932 *Dr. Jekyll and Mr. Hyde*) and this, of course, is the most controversial part of the film since it seems to connect black people and apes. This is not just a modern observation. Reviewing *Jungle Woman*, the sequel to *Captive Wild Woman*, the critic for the left-leaning newspaper *New York PM* was indignant:

> In **Mein Kampf**, Hitler calls the Negro a 'half-born ape.' *Jungle Woman* illustrates the point, changing a Hollywood glamour girl into an ape and vice versa with the Negro stage being inserted right where Hitler says.
> 16 July 1943

Like the cast of *Jungle Woman*, the reviewer seems to be experiencing a flashback to *Captive Wild Woman*, as at no time during *Jungle Woman* do we see Paula transform at all.

Other newspaper critics likewise found *Captive Wild Woman* to be tasteless, though no one mentioned the racial angle. Bosley Crowther - in an article about how horror films had gone downhill (this from someone who routinely ridiculed even the best of them of the '40s) - had a few words about the movie:

> When you think about the awesome freak pictures which were made in former years, from *The Cabinet of Dr. Caligari* to the first *Dracula* and *King Kong*, there is every good reason to grumble at the watered-down stuff of today. And there is also reason to mutter against the clinical unpleasantness of some. One doesn't expect exact science in a cock-eyed black magic film nor does one demand medical ethics from the wild-eyed practitioners of same. But at least the maniacal doctors might be prevented from talking about 'follicular cysts' which 'induce unusual amounts of secretions of the sex hormone' - which is what Mad Doctor John Carradine does in the dilly mentioned above.
> *The New York Times*, 13 June 1943

T.M.P - in *his* review in *The New York Times* - was likewise very put off by the film:

> Now there are two ways of looking at *Captive Wild Woman*. Either you decide to meet this bit of scientific hocus-pocus at its own inane level or else you are likely to get hopping mad, since there is nothing to recommend in the story or the performances. It all depends on the mood you're in. The picture as a whole is in decidedly bad taste.
> 7 June 1943

Philip K. Scheuer of the *Los Angeles Times* reviewed the film as part of its double billing with *Frankenstein Meets the Wolf Man*. His comments about the latter were tongue-in-cheek, but he called *Captive Wild Woman* "more of the same but on a trashier scale" and complained it had "the more raucous conglomeration of sounds (circus) in recent history. The affair has other repellent aspects too but the Paramount customers ate it up last night, regardless." (23 July 1943)

Glenn C. Pullen of *The Cleveland Plain Dealer* was more amused than disgusted by the film:

> If Ringling's Circus wants a new playmate for Gargantua, its prize gorilla, it can find one in the form of Acquanetta. She is the weird ape-woman of the Alhambra's latest attraction which, in turn, resembles something that might be the progeny of 'Tarzan' and 'Frankenstein' if they were mated. No, lady, Bela Lugosi isn't in it but he may turn up in the next edition of this thriller. It has all the lurid earmarks of the first chapter of a 12-part serial. Only palpitating youngsters under the age of 15 will fully appreciate its wonders... With his tongue in his cheek, John Carradine plays the demented surgeon....
> 20 August 1943

The last comment is perhaps a bit curious, given that Carradine is relatively restrained. The overacting is provided by Fay Helm (Nurse Strand) in the slightly risible scene where she takes Carradine to task for going from genius to fanatic and ignoring the inevitably fatal results of his experimenting on Dorothy. Helm works herself into a state of near hysteria: "When you took the glands from a guinea pig and grafted them to the rabbit, the guinea pig *died!* When you grafted the frog's glands into a white mouse, the frog *died!*" Carradine, by contrast, appears slightly bored by the whole tirade and seems to be suppressing a yawn or an eye roll, but endures it all patiently until the nurse threatens to go to the police and then - perhaps inspired by Curt Siodmak - he decides to relieve the lady of her cerebrum. (Though you *do* have to wonder about the wisdom of transferring the brain of the woman you've just murdered into the skull of a giant gorilla!)

The trade paper reviews were generally more favorable:

> *Captive Wild Woman* should make horror fans gurgle in sheer delight......The kids especially will respond generously to this thriller. To guarantee the picture's hold on them the authors have judiciously laid much of their story against a circus background. The circus atmosphere heightens the excitement. The youngsters will sit on the edges of their seats as Clyde Beatty, doubling for Milton Stone who plays an animal trainer in love with Evelyn Ankers, puts on a rousing act with lions and tigers...the acting is suited to a film of this nature. Carradine makes an extremely sinister villain. Acquanetta and Miss Ankers contribute considerable eye appeal.
> *Film Daily*, 10 May 1943

The 1 May 1943 reviewer for *Harrison's*, on the other hand, thought the film "too horrifying" for children and called it "another one of those implausible horror melodramas" but had no doubt it would find its audience.

The *Motion Picture Herald* (1 May 1943) was impressed, though:

> Producer Ben Pivar lifts the level of chiller-thrillers with this entry by stitching into the fabric the fantasy which gives the film its title, and a flow of legitimate excitement generated by circus sequences depicting jungle animal training supervised by Clyde Beatty. These impart to an imaginative background story a measure of realism seldom attained in horror films. Direction by Edward Dmytryk keeps the action swift and the Henry Sucher/Griffin Jay script makes the story seem plausible.

Most exhibitors were happy with the film.

"A natural exploitation film and will please generally. Animal training sequences are excellent."

*Wallace, Idaho*

"Swell animal and circus picture. A little fantastic in spots. Moved right along. Not a dull moment."

*Menno, South Dakota*

"This type of picture is all right for adults but not for children It will hold your patrons in their seats."

*Windsor, Nova Scotia*

"Not enough 'horror' and too short., yet it drew some favorable comments."

*Riversville, West Virginia*

"This picture did better than most of Universal's high -priced specials. Believe it will do business in any type theater, but best of all for action houses."

*Terre Haute, Indiana*

"Good circus picture with plenty of lions and tigers, which pleased the kids and action fans."

*Dewey, Oklahoma*

"A nice action play. Plenty of lions and thrills."

*Penacook, New Hampshire*

"This picture will scare the kids and is a little too horrible for some adults but seemed to please on our weekend double bill."

*Marshfield, Missouri*

While reviewers were enthusiastic about Acquanetta's "lulu of a figure," few thought her acting skills measured up to her curves. The comment in the 1 May 1943 issue of *Showman's Trade Review* was typical: "Acquanetta's debut finds her with little more than a blank expression, according to her role, but the boys won't mind that in view of her physical attributes." Still, *Variety* (28 April 1943) opined she made "an effective 'wild woman' though given a minimum of lines to speak." Actually, except for a few dubbed-in snarls, she doesn't speak at all, and no one at the circus seems to notice it.

*Captive Wild Woman* was not actually Acquanetta's film debut, as she had previously appeared in a bit part in *Arabian Nights* (1942) and a supporting role in

*Rhythm of the Islands* (1943). In the latter, she was billed as "Burnu Acquanetta," but dropped the first name for her subsequent appearances.

Acquanetta came to Hollywood after a successful modeling career in New York. She presented herself as being from Venezuela, claiming her father was a member of the delegation from that country, so she was promptly dubbed the "Venezuelan Volcano." When the Screen Actors Guild asked to see her passport, though, she balked, at first claiming it had been stolen. She soon gave up the pretense and admitted she had never been out of America and was actually an Arapaho Indian from Wyoming. Wags cracked she should be rechristened the "Arapaho Eruption" or the "Wyoming Wildcat."

Acquanetta's confession brought her more publicity than at any other time in her brief career, but not everyone was buying it. Columnist Paul Harrison was among the skeptics and announced that if Acquanetta's story was accurate in its details, "I am the grandmother of General de Gaulle." Harrison sat down with the actress and she told him she was born July 17, 1921 in Ozone, Wyoming, though she wasn't sure what part of the state it was in. Orphaned at three, she went to live with an Indian woman named Laura Smith and traveled with her for several years across Colorado and Oklahoma. Acquanetta was hazy about the specifics and, when Harrison pressed her, she murmured vaguely: "Always we leeved on the outskirts of town, and for awhile leeved in a geepsy camp and they sang sad songs." (The spelling is Harrison's; he said Acquanetta's accent was alternated between Spanish and French.) Smith married an Indian who didn't like Acquanetta, and the latter went to live with a nomadic couple who painted and wrote stories about Indians. When she was 14, Acquanetta ran away, worked as a waitress and - when she had saved $100 - went to New York where she learned enough Spanish to pose as a Venezuelan and began modeling. Harrison closed the interview with the actress coyly saying: "The most interesting parts of my story I cannot tell you"; the film critic then added his own comment: "This I believe." *Dunkirk* [New York] *Evening Observer*, 27 July 1942.

This is most interesting indeed as modern sources believe Acquanetta was at least part African-American; she even appeared on the 4 February 1952 cover of *Jet* magazine. She - or her agent - realized there could be no "black bombshell" in America of the '40s and thus came up with the Arapaho story. Nevertheless, Acquanetta stuck to the fabrication even in her later years, both in interviews and at her Fanex appearance.

The actress also claimed she walked out on her Universal contract, though the circumstances of this are debated. She then signed with Monogram, and the studio immediately announced several projects for her: "Voodoo Queen," "Belle of New

336

Orleans," and "Queen of the Honky-Tonks." None of these came to pass and, except for a few bit parts, her career pretty much ended with *Lost Continent* (1951), where she played opposite Caesar Romero and some stop-motion dinosaurs. Her last marriage was to Jack Ross, a businessman and car dealer, and she became a familiar figure in local Phoenix television, often appearing in commercials for her husband's agency. They were apparently a little offbeat in that Acquanetta, most fetchingly attired, delivered a little philosophy before the hard-sell, prompting one observer to label her a "Sexy Socrates." Mrs. Ross also devoted herself to philanthropy, writing poetry, and lecturing on mysticism and reincarnation.

**Acquanetta menaces Evelyn Ankers in a lobby card-cum-publicity still. In this scene in the film, the "Venezuelan Volcano" is in her Ape Woman-mode.**

No one in *Captive Wild Woman*'s supporting casting particularly stands out. Lloyd Corrigan's John Whipple is annoying with his continually nixing Fred Mason's plans and then immediately changing his mind. Paul Fix (the drunken trainer), having already suffered death at the hands of Dr. Cyclops and Red Cannon (in *Black Friday*), here meets his usual fate at the claws of Cheela. Fix - usually associated with Westerns - made out better as the marshal in TV's *The Rifleman*, where all he had to do was sit back and let his pal Lucas McCain gun down the bad guys. Martha MacVicar as Dorothy spends most of her screen time comatose on the operating table. While she can be espied (briefly) staring at Lawrence Talbot in *Frankenstein Meets the Wolf Man*,

337

her most memorable role was no doubt as Lauren Bacall's nymphomaniac sister in *The Big Sleep*.

Director Edward Dmytryk - with the help of director of photography George Robinson - brings some style to the lab scenes that anticipate his excellent work in *noir* thrillers like *Murder, My Sweet* (1944) and *Cross Fire* (1948). The aforementioned *Variety* review of *Captive Wild Woman*, while opining that much of the film was "strictly off the cobb," praised Dmytryk: "Edward Dmytryk's intelligent direction points up the numerous suspenseful episodes." The paper was not so taken with Dmytryk's only other horror film, *The Devil Commands* (1941):

> Exhibitors will have a word for *The Devil Commands* but it can't be used in polite company. Starring Boris Karloff. it's something that required just nerve to produce. To put the film on the release schedule amounts to extreme bravery.
>
> 19 February 1941

The Bible of Show Biz was also put off by the Rialto advertising the latter film as starring Boris "Arsenic" Karloff, an attempt to capitalize on Karloff's success in the current Broadway production of *Arsenic and Old Lace*. Today you would find few fans of vintage horror who would take *Captive Wild Woman* over *The Devil Commands*.

Aside from a lean, mean Carradine and a few nice directorial flourishes, the main entertainment value today of *Captive Wild Woman* is the film's trotting out the *clichés* that fans of Universal horror love like old friends: "What are those marks on her neck?" asks a puzzled detective about Paula's victim. And, of course, as Paula climbs up the side of the boarding house, we hear Hans Slater's familiar "SOMETHING is coming through the window" music. A headline for the local paper *The Daily Star* proclaims "Circus Handler Murdered by Ape!" (Right beneath that is an article titled "Youth arrested after glitter was removed from campaign sign"- perhaps that would have been the lead story that day if Cheela had not been feeling ornery.) "And there's the moral of the tale," solemnly intoned by narrator Turhan Bey at the end of the film, warning that Walters "went beyond the realm of human knowledge and tampered with things no man should touch."

An article by Dee Lowrance entitled "Shebas of Shudders" - which appeared in the 19 March 1944 edition of *The Arizona Independent Republic* - talked about the popularity of horror films and the "queens of horror" who had emerged in the '40s: Evelyn Ankers, Elyse Knox, Simone Simon, and Frances Dee. The ladies were seen

338

as doing what the ladies usually do in such films (scream and faint), and there was no suggestion that Dracula and the Wolf Man were taking second place to female monsters. Poor Paula Dupree the Ape Girl didn't even rate a mention.

Still, *Captive Wild Woman* and its star got a second go at immortality in the opera *Acquanetta*, with a score by Michael Gordon (one of the founders of the "Bang-on-a-Can" musical collective) and a libretto by Deborah Artman. According to the description of its 2010 premiere at the National Opera Center in NYC, the opera takes place during the filming of *Captive Wild Woman*:

> The mad scientist Doctor, the insistent Ape, the reluctant Brainy Woman [presumably, this is Nurse Strand], the visionary Director and the beautiful monster herself, Acquanetta, gather in this reimagining of this fateful experiment in soaring, sometimes comic and always indelible songs that capture the heightened drama of horror films... in what is ultimately a haunting meditation on the meaning of identity, transformation, stereotypes and type casting set in the heyday of Hollywood gloss.

In 2017 the opera was revised as a multi-media chamber piece described as "a one act deconstruction of the horror genre."

So... when can we expect *Rondo Hatton, the Musical?*

*Captive Wild Woman* – 11 May 1943 - 61 minutes (SoS)

**CAST:** John Carradine as Dr. Sigmund Walters; Evelyn Ankers as Beth Colman; Milburn Stone as Fred Mason; Lloyd Corrigan as John Whipple; Fay Helm as Nurse Strand; Martha Vickers (credited as MacVicar) as Dorothy Colman; Vince Barnett as Curly; Paul Fix as Gruen; Acquanetta as Paula Dupree; Turhan Bey (narration); Ed Piel, Sr. as Jake; Ray Corrigan as Cheela.

**CREDITS:** Director: Edward Dmytryk; Associate Producer: Ben Pivar; Original Story: Ted Fithian and Neal P. Varnick; Screenplay: Griffin Jay and Henry Sucher; Director of Photography: George Robinson; Editing: Milton Carruth; Art Direction: Ralph M. De Lacy; Sets: R.A. Gausman, Ira S. Webb; Costumes: Vera West; Music: Hans J. Salter; Sound: Bernard Brown, William Hedgcock

*- HN*

# *Phantom of the Opera* (1943)

Philip K. Scheuer was one of the in-house film critics at the *Los Angeles Times* for some four decades, and his critique of the picture named above – a favorite of mine - made two particularly germane points for which I am grateful. First off, he was astute enough to note that...

> Appropriately enough, a Farrar (Jane), a Galli (Rosina) and a Curci (Elvira) are included in the cast of *The* [sic] *Phantom of the Opera*. Jane Farrar, a cousin of the renowned Geraldine, makes her camera debut as Biancarolli, the second lead; the Misses Galli and Curci play maids.

As an opera buff and a former collector of '78s, I have to smile at Mr. Scheuer's name recognition; would that I had had the chance to compare assessments with him personally; still, there is some debate as to whether *Phantom's* Farrar was, in fact, kin to Opera's Farrar. The second point – about which there has been appreciative discussion by fans other than myself - the keen-eyed reviewer noticed was that, so far as Claude Rains and Susanna Foster were concerned, "Svengali to Miss Foster's Trilby, the Phantom tries by hook or by crook to make her, *his daughter* [italics mine], prima donna of the opera." Rather than burying this bit of controversial minutia over the two principals' relationship somewhere in the middle of this essay, I want to start with it.

There have been approximately 8 zillion remakes, variations, sequels, spoofs, reimaginings, or whatever on the picture's ancestral literary conceit. Film, ballet, opera, literature, television - even the Internet – all media have offered up tale after tale of an innocent mentored in some way by a grotesque figure who's either evil in purpose and by design, or who has been wildly misapprehended since the beginning of time and whose *raison d'être* can only be appreciated by a comprehensive understanding of the innocent's condition. Sheuer's mention of Svengali and Trilby can seen as a familiar illustration of same, and 1944's *The Climax* just adds another log to this fire.

There's little doubt that Universal's 1925 version remains the definitive treatment in the eyes of most of those who have seen more than a couple of takes on the theme. Sure, that picture is silent, and sure, there are lots of folks who only know of the original because they've watched the 1929 part-sound re-release (in which the Phantom remained silent, because – in the interim – Lon Chaney had signed on exclusively with M-G-M). Still, the 1925 Jewel, while not the first cinematic adaptation of the novel (1), is the production that most often comes to one's mind's eye when the subject is broached. In that film, Mary Philbin's Christine Daae is given to understand that the ultimate price for her career advancement under the tutelage of the "Angel of Music" will be her remaining at his side *pour toujours*. After some necessary exposition has unreeled, her unwise exploratory sojourn through the opera house cellars results in her being forced to choose either grasshopper or scorpion: resolve to stay with Erik – and thus save her own life and the lives of Roaul de Chagney and Ledoux of the Secret Police, who are then being roasted alive in a nearby chamber - or decide against staying and thus be responsible for the annihilation of the Paris Opera House. The 1929 re-release, though – while having added new footage, replete with dialogue and singing – cut back on the substance and tone of Erik's obsession with Christine, including a sequence in which the young singer discovers a wedding gown intended for her in the phantom's lair. She still has to choose between insect and arachnid, but the Opera Ghost's romantic yearnings have been cut w-a-y back.

In the 1943 version of the tale, there is something far less sexual but even more confidential going on between soprano and phantom. In the interest of making the story more realistic, the Taylor/Hoffenstein screenplay did not incorporate any disfigured lunatic who had escaped from Devil's Island to join the construction crew at the Gasnier project. Instead, the eponymous tragic hero would be a sacked, middle-aged musician who was deformed via an acid-hurl after having murdered someone who, said musician thought (erroneously), had stolen his concerto and – thus – his retirement income. In the first edition of the Weaver/Brunases' **Universal Horrors**, commentary (on page 362) speculates about the possibility of a genetic relationship between Daae and Claudin - "Is the girl his daughter, as most of the evidence indicates, or is she the object of affection of a much older man?" (Given the rash of accusations hurled at men of all ages in the wake of the Harvey Weinstein situation, this latter take might seem all the more likely.) Susanna Foster is quoted therein as positing that "They never could make up their minds during the whole making of the picture." Apparently – like the '25/'29 handling of its predecessor – the Universal bigwigs *could* make up their minds, albeit *after* the film had premiered.

**Created for the 1925 Chaney classic, Stage 28 – the "Phantom Stage" - saw use for any number of Universal productions. Here, awaiting Arthur Lubin's go-ahead, an audience comprised of studio extras prepares to emote with the best of them. The stage was demolished in September 2014, and the interior set was moved into storage.**

In a script entitled "'The [sic] Phantom of the Opera' by Eric Taylor and Samuel Hoffenstein" and dated 5 January 1943, it's there in black and white that – at this point in the proceedings – it was a cold, hard fact that Claudin and Daae were *pere* et *fille*, but had been separated during the singer's extreme youth. On pages 113-114 of the script, we have the following dialogue:

Anatole: "I looked up Claudin's record, found that he was born in Arles, in Provence. I knew Christine was born in Gardanne a few miles away. I went to Provence and made inquiries. I've just told you what I discovered... Tell me the rest."

Aunt (after a moment): "He deserted Christine and my sister when Christine was a baby. My sister died of a broken heart and I took the child. I led her to believe that both her parents were dead."

Anatole: "Had Claudin committed some crime?"

Aunt (shaking her head): "It was this music. My father gave him a good position in the mill at Gardanne, but music enslaved him like a drug. And because my sister wouldn't leave home to starve in a garret, he went alone."

Anatole: "You never heard from him again?"

Aunt: "Yes. He wrote – but my father very properly destroyed the letters."

Anatole: "How does Christine come by the name Daae?"

Aunt: "That is my father's name. The name Claudin was never spoken by us."

As the script bears no other notation on the title page (Continuity, Shooting, etc.), we can't assume that it was the final treatment of the theme or that it was the actual scenario for the release print. There are numerous edits within the script itself – over a dozen pages are devoted to Claudin's escape from Pleyel's office, *with* the note that shots 154-160 have been omitted - and some of the scenes outlined therein do not exist in the print that we have come to know. Nonetheless, with the movie having started production less than a month after the date printed on the script, we have to conclude that – at that early date, at any rate – it was stated right in the film (and not merely during production) that the arthritic violinist was, indeed, the father of the fresh-faced soprano. In fact, in the 28 March 1943 edition of the *Bluefield* [West Virginia] *Daily Telegraph*, Robbin Coons' syndicated column on George Waggner's taking over the picture gives the following brief plot details:

> In the new color version, the Phantom (Claude Rains) will be 'explained.' He is an embittered musician, his face horribly scarred by acid in a temperamental altercation, who haunts the caverns beneath the Paris opera house with one obsession—to promote his daughter (Susanna Foster) as leading singer. In the old film Chaney haunted those same caverns, a mishapen [sic] monster of grotesque eyes, teeth and head, a creature without a past and motivated only by a 'crush' on the leading lady. "Here," says Waggner, "we're taking time to sell the central character as a human being."

And inasmuch as the final cast crawl on post-New Millennium prints lists Barbara Everest as "Christine's Aunt" even though her character does not appear in the film, we can pretty safely assume the above exchange of dialogue had indeed been shot only to be excised following the premiere. In addition – as my colleague, Henry Nicolella, points out – on the Blu-Ray of *Phantom*, the production stills show the scene between Anatole and *la Tante*, so those jittery Universal executives made up their minds at some point before the picture's general release.

When and why, though, did Christine Daae become Christine DuBois?

In his brilliant special feature that precedes Bruce G. Hallenbeck's equally brilliant study of Hammer Films' 1962 feature, *The Phantom of the Opera* (2), Denis Meikle sums up the situation concisely.

> [...that the relationship is that of father and abandoned daughter] was established almost immediately in a telling scene in which the two of them meet backstage. But fearing the whiff of incest, the Breen Office asked for this element to be downplayed, and the revelation was removed from the film, along with some shots of Susanna Foster in dressing room *deshabille*. As ever with such diligent censorial oversight, the unintended result was worse and left Claudin looking life an aged sexual predator whose climactic ushering of Christine into his secret underground lair implied something quite different to that intended by the film's makers.

It was on the 21 May 1943 that the Breen Office ordered that "revelation" - as well as a "number of unacceptable breast shots of Christine" in her dressing room - to be cut, and yet, even as late as the 15 October of that year, there either were still 35mm prints floating about that hadn't fully eliminated clues of Claudin's paternity, or else Bosley Crowther – *The New York Times'* movie critic who seems never to have enjoyed the movies he critiqued – was much cannier than the usual ticket buyer. In his review – entitled "Nelson Eddy Much in Evidence in 'Phantom of the Opera,' Wherein Claude Rains Also Appears, at the Capitol" - Mr. Crowther explained that

> [Rains's phantom] is, in this rewritten version of the old Gaston Leroux tale, nothing more than the unsuspected father of an understudy in the opera company who tries very hard and in secret to advance his daughter's career.

The Gray Lady's movie critic may have been hard to please, but he was apparently more than willing to give innocence the benefit of the doubt in ambivalent circumstances.

Nonetheless, as Mr. Meikle writes, this censor-induced interpretation seems to have endured over the course of some seven-and-a-half decades, even making it into print in "Phantoms of the Opera: The Face Behind the Mask"(3) - the deluxe souvenir book that is still sold at performances of Andrew Lloyd Webber, Charles Hart, and Richard Stilgoe's decades-old musical hit on Broadway. In recounting the story-line of the '43 version, author John L Flynn writes of how both Christine and Claudin are called (separately) into Villeneuve's office: "As [Christine] exits [from the office], Erique is called. The two pass each other in the hall, and Claudin - enchanted by her beauty and talent - tells Christine that he is her eternal servant." As this particular enchantment is neither in the script whence came the Anatole/Christine exchange (above) nor in the film itself, we have to question Mr. Flynn's source.(4) Later - on page 36 - his uniquely subjective view becomes a whole lot tougher to understand:

> He spirits the young singer away to his underground lair and declares his undying affection, like a lovesick teen, even though he is old enough to be her father. He even resembles Christine's father (from the book), more so than the Phantom.

(Equally difficult to understand is another of Flynn's statements - in the section on "Production Notes" - where he maintains that Rains had "lost the role of the wolf man to Lon Chaney, Jr." This is the first and only mention we've *ever* found of the fairly ludicrous idea that the 50-year-old, somewhat diminutive Claude Rains might have been considered for the part of the feral - and athletic – monster in the eponymous 1941 Universal hit.)

If the existing prints of *Phantom* no longer blatantly depict Claudin as Christine's father, neither do they portray him "like a lovesick teen." What we're left with is the study of a musician whose entire adult life has been interwoven with the Paris Opera, even to the extent of his anonymously supporting a young singer whose career seems to be on hold due to the selfishness of the resident diva and the idiosyncrasies of management. Claudin is not the "Spirit of Music" who had demanded (in the '20s) Christine's love and lifelong devotion; he is, rather, the soprano's *patron*, who (whilst still gainfully employed) spends his resources funding her lessons, and who (afterwards) devotes his life to arranging her appearances, eliminating her rivals, and

– with a saw – seeking to wring concessions from the opera house administration. His leading her to his subterranean lair during the melee after the chandelier has fallen is not so that he may have his way with her, but so that she might continue her singing lessons with him at the piano. Whether or not it is spelled out onscreen, there can be no more *paternal* portrait of the "Opera Ghost" than that of Erique Claudin.

The majority of the comparisons made over the years between this version and Chaney's have greatly favored Universal's first effort. Still, some of the observations – the '43 rendition's being "opera heavy" or Rains's makeup suffering greatly against Chaney's masterpiece - are pretty ludicrous. What could be accomplished by several vignettes of onstage mime and dance during the Silent Era demanded greater attention (and lots more footage) during the War years, when movie musicals were enjoying great favor. Granted, Gounod's *Faust* fits a tale of murder, madness and monstrosities far better than than Flotow's *Martha*, but the former needed only some costumed actors, ballerinas and - if the theater screening the print was so equipped - a talent at the Wurlitzer to create the illusion. Ticket-buyers in post-*Jazz Singer* movie palaces understood that "opera" meant audible orchestrations, singing, and noise. Despite the aforementioned grousing about the quantity of *scènes musicales* in the film, one cannot deny that, to credibly create the *milieu et atmosphère* of the Paris Opera, one needs to break eggs ... *errrr...* display more than *cinq minutes* of quality on- and offstage warbling.

Thus, composer Edward Ward – he who had penned the melodic backgrounds of such thriller favorites as *The Mystery of Edwin Drood* (1935) and *Night Must Fall* (1937) – was brought aboard to create the music from the operatic scenes that would highlight Susanna Foster, Nelson Eddy and – here you go, Mr. Scheuer - Jane Farrar. *Phantom of the Opera* would mark the last of Ward's seven (7) Oscar-nominated scores, and the film's charming "Lullaby of the Bells"would prove a favorite even after the movie closed. Although credited as Musical Director here, Ward's "uncredited credits" - wherein his compositions had been snatched as underlying themes and/or ransacked as stock music - were actively compiling until the middle of the 1960s. Ironically, they included Universal-International's biography of Lon Chaney, *Man of a Thousand Faces* (1957); if only once, a shade of the studio's first Phantom and a tad of the opera that motivated its second shared screen time.

Anyhow, what with the current love affair with musicals in the cards for all to see, Universal's hand held a queen: Deanna Durbin, the 21-year-old soprano from Winnipeg, Canada who had been one of the studio's top stars. Charismatic and wildly talented, Durbin saw her first three films at Universal (*Three Smart Girls*, 1937; *One*

347

*Hundred Men and a Girl*, 1938; *Mad About Music*, 1938) become blockbusters for the studio and make big bucks at the box-office; all three pictures – in one way or another – concerned a young girl's relationship with her father, real or imaginary. When plans surfaced for an authentically operatic treatment for the *Phantom* reiteration, Durbin had a lock on the role of Christine; she and Henry Koster – her first director at Universal and by far her favorite - were seen as that winning combination that had brought not just solvency but *profit* back to the company in the mid-to-late '30s, when the first go-round for horror movies was fast collapsing. Nonetheless, by January 1943, as *Phantom of the Opera* was set to go before the cameras for the first time, the beautiful young singer – by now, the most highly-compensated female entertainer in the civilized world – was awaiting release of *The Amazing Mrs. Holliday* and was ready to embark on *Hers to Hold* – the third film in the "Three Smart Girls" trilogy that Henry Koster had begun with his young star a lustrum or so earlier.

**Nope! Not Victor Borge and Marylyn Mulvey! 'Tis Claude Rains filling in for Broderick Crawford – Universal's (but not director Arthur Lubin's) first choice – and teenager Susanna Foster filling in for the obstinate Deanna Durbin. (Lubin himself ended up "filling in" for Henry Koster.)**

But a bit of a kerfuffle had ensued, and the following paragraph from **The American Film Institute Catalog, 1941-1950** summarizes it nicely:

In October 1940, Universal announced plans to produce a sound version of Gaston Leroux's novel under the supervision of producer Joe Pasternak, starring Deanna Durbin and Broderick Crawford and directed by Henry Koster. One year later, *Hollywood Reporter* news items state that, with Durbin under suspension, Universal had decided to rewrite *Phantom of the Opera* as a comedy for the team of Bud Abbott and Lou Costello. By February 1942, however, *Hollywood Reporter* news items were reporting that Koster was once again planning a dramatic version starring Durbin. In November 1942, George Waggner took over the project, casting Lon Chaney, Jr. as 'The Phantom,' a role made famous by his father, and actor Jon Hall as the romantic lead. According to *Hollywood Reporter*, Waggner traveled to San Francisco to study a production by the San Francisco Opera Company in preparation for this film.

This passage merits a couple of comments. Per author and film historian David Wilt, the *Phantom* project had been under discussion as early as July of 1939(5), albeit this may have been a one-time item in a syndicated column, as I can find no supporting material elsewhere. As for the next step being Leroux's tragic hero meeting Abbott and Costello, that bright idea never reached the level of serious consideration, although the team's first horror-comedy, *Hold That Ghost* (1941; see essay) proved to be such a hit that it's surprising that the Phantom was about the only Universal grotesque who *didn't* cross paths with the boys when the "Meet the..." features began in 1948. And Ms. Durbin's suspension from Universal has, per various sources, been chalked up to everything ranging from her displeasure that "Universal would not give her husband, Vaughan Paul, a chance"(6) to her refusal to appear in *They Live Alone*, a feature that had been already budgeted and scheduled. On this last, another passage from **The American Film Institute Catalog** clears things up:

> On 17 Oct 1941, Durbin was suspended by the studio for her refusal to appear in *They Live Alone. HR* [*Hollywood Reporter*] later stated Durbin was continuing her suspension indefinitely, as she wanted permission to work for studios other than Universal, specifically M-G-M, where the producer of her previous Universal films, Joe Pasternak, had moved. In Dec 1941, *HR* speculated that Durbin's suspension had cost Universal over $200,000... Finally, on 30 January 1942, Durbin and Universal settled their dispute, and the actress was given story and director approval on all her films.(7)

*Phantom of the Opera* had begun production a week and a half prior to everyone coming to terms, and with the 18-year-old Susanna Foster already fitted for costumes and practicing her arias, Durbin's most tenuous connection with the picture had vanished. As top-billing was going to baritone Nelson Eddy with Ms. Foster coming in second, it became obvious to everyone that music – and not mind-numbing horror – would be the pivot on which *this* Phantom would turn. As there was/still is no specific industry award for "Fright" or some such, it behooved the studio to spend most of its budget on the film's spectacle (the art directors, together with the set decorators, took home the Academy Award for Best Production Design) as well as the sound and music so many fans of the original version thought overdone (Bernard Brown and Edward Ward were nominated for Best Sound Mixing and Best Original Musical, respectively) in order to capture the attention and win the plaudits of industry colleagues as well as the ticket-buying public.

As for the make-up, accounts abound that maintain that Rains's overarching concern for his screen image as well as sensitivity to the feelings of returning disfigured war veterans and their families played a major part in the tepid application invented by Jack P. Pierce. Masked figures of literature and legend had always felt it *de rigueur* to doff their facial coverings at the right climactic moment - unless, of course, unforeseen circumstances (or a representative of the Forces of Good) had done so first. Ergo, Claude's Claudin was up against it, despite whatever makeup treatment lie beneath the exquisitely designed mask he wore for a good part of the picture.(8) Any sort of Chaney-like, death's-head look was dispensed with at once, given the acid-tossing conceit, and although the silent phantom hadn't to so much as utter one articulate word during *his* scenes, his Technicolor descendant had to be free to assure, cajole, and threaten vocally; nothing was even momentarily considered that would muffle Rain's marvelous voice. That meant that his mouth could not be hidden or impeded in any way, *a la* the appliance borne by Herbert Lom's Professor Petrie in the 1962 Hammer incarnation.

Again, with musicals and their (usually) attendant froth gratefully embraced by wartime audiences – and this motion picture (which came in at over $1.7 million, a darned sight more than would have been allotted for a more "standard" horror fest) meant to be a treat for lovers of classical compositions as well as for fans of the novel or silent *tour de force cinématografique* – the State of the Face of the fatherly mad murderer had to be upsetting but pitiable, and not disgusting. As Denis Meikle stated in the *Little Shoppe of Horrors* piece mentioned above,

Anxiety over audience sensibilities in time of war had already prevented the chandelier from being shown crashing to earth, and the strangling of prima donna Biancarolli (Jane Farrar) had also taken place off-screen, but there remained the unmasking to be dealt with.(9)

Viewers were thus primed to accept the unmasked Claudin's face as reflecting the burns he had suffered, which extended only to the area covered by his *chic* mask. One might also say that Susanna Foster's reaction shot may have been a tad overdone – Thank you, Arthur Lubin – while, at the same time, conceding that a young, innocent Paris Opera performer, used to the presence of identical masks in the most anodyne of circumstances, would probably not have reacted in any other way. Yes, Pierce's make-up treatment falls short of Chaney's, but Chaney – as the Man of a Thousand Faces – had the liberty to design and mold his own physiognomy (and call out the film's director!) and was limited in creative vision only by the original novel. Pierce, on the other hand, was constrained time and again by the parameters of the production going on around him at the moment, and these dictated that the Phantom's phiz reflect the effects of corrosives, and not a face made appalling by time, birth, circumstance, or divine intervention. Is the treatment more disappointing to audiences than Chaney's iconic treatment? To be honest, yes. Is it, however, "in sync" with the back-story and ongoing machinations of Arthur Lubin's vision? Yes, indeed. Other than having been distributed equally across the actor's face, Pierce's conception could not have fit the screenplay – and, thus, the film – better. (The most fantastic aspect with respect to the Phantom's disfigurement herein is that Claudin – who washes the acid from his face with water from the Paris *sewer* – did not die of a massive infection within the week!)

A final thought: the 1925 version was crafted to depict Gaston Leroux's tragic hero and his domain as accurately as possible (while still trying to stay within spitting distance of budget). It's more than merely probable that – at that time – a sizable share of potential viewers were already acquainted with the novel and came to the movie to see whether Universal's imagination was as good as their own. They walked into the theater aware of Erik, the "Opera Ghost" who haunts Box Five and who communicates via notes with house personnel. They sat down knowing that he is an escaped lunatic who – horrifically ugly since birth – was made to wear a mask since his early childhood. They were impressed by his extensive underground lair, cobbled together and equipped by him, all done on the sly while he was part of the workforce designing and building the Paris Opera House. They were as shocked as Mary Philbin as they got to "feast" upon his "accursed ugliness," and his subsequent appearance as

"Red Death" at *La Balle Masquée* only reinforced his unadorned face. They – at least some of them – relished his getting his just desserts, although Chaney's capacity to touch a viewer's heart – as well as to dispense heart attacks – caused many of them leave the theater bemoaning the unfairness of the Phantom's fate.

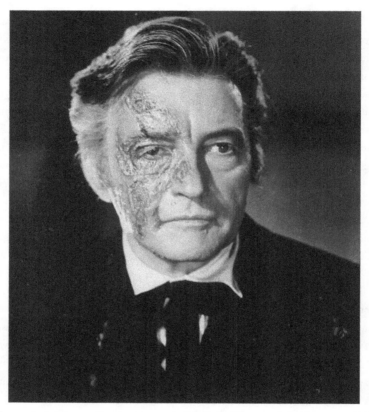

**Whereas being born a horror was part of Erik the Phantom's backstory in 1925, Erique had Phantom-dom thrust upon him via a panful of acid to the face. *Fama erat* that Jack P. Pierce was asked to "tone it down," makeup-wise, not only because of WWII-caused disfigurements, but also because Rains felt that going full-Phantom (*a la* Chaney) might negatively impact his film career.**

Nearly 20 years later, readers and lovers of literature survived and remained cognizant of the original story which – contemporaneous common sense dictated – had been "updated" and "revised" for the movies due to the medium of sound, the spectrum of color, and the absence of Lon Chaney, Sr. Following Chaney's death a decade and a bit earlier, no actor had stepped into his shoes or fiddled with his make-up kit or was hailed as the second coming of the Man of a Thousand Faces. Sure, there would always be incredibly gifted make-up artists – Universal's horror legacy had done well due to the amazing skills of Pierce, Ellis Burman, et al – but there was no single entity onstage or onscreen who could meld profound acting ability with a genius at creating all aspects of his character's physicality himself. The post-Chaney phantom would have to be played by a charismatic thespian capable of wringing emotions from his audiences, inspiring great performances from his colleagues, and – the *pièce de résistance!* - drawing equal parts pity and revulsion from his unmasking.

The second quote from **The AFI Film Catalog** (above) closes with the mention of producer George Waggner having cast Lon Chaney, Jr. as the phantom and Jon Hall as "the romantic lead." Like so many other plans for this film, the publicized casting of those roles did not pan out.

> Lon Chaney Jr. is pretty bitter at not playing his father's role in 'Phantom of the Opera.' When he first went into pictures he declared he wouldn't do anything his father had but when the 'Phantom' came along he was anxious to do it. Tells me he turned down a cook's job in the Coast Guard, expecting to get it. Now, after 'Destiny,' he'll be drafted and Claude Rains will play his father's part in 'Phantom.'(10)

This particular *Destiny* – there were quite a few other films enjoying this title whilst in pre-production, and the 1944 like-named feature is discussed elsewhere - was released as *The Wolf Man*, and both the Coast Guard job and his being drafted into the armed forces may well have been possibilities at the time, but neither came to pass. Entering films as Creighton Chaney – his birth name – not long after his father's death, the young actor was hired more for his physique than his mystique. He underwent the name change (to Lon, Jr.) and a brisk upgrade to more decent and varied roles come the mid-'30s, when he was signed on to play the title character in *The Shadow of Silk Lennox*, for Ray Kirkwood Productions. Still, it's not a little ironic that the role of Erique Claudin had first been offered to Broderick Crawford, the man who had created Lennie Small in *Of Mice and Men* on Broadway. (Crawford *did* enter the armed forces and was in uniform as *Phantom* went into production.) Lon Jr.'s performance in the Hal Roach Studios' movie version of the Steinbeck play in 1940 made *his* name synonymous with Lennie's, while his doing Universal's ongoing bidding as the "Master Character Creator" would show the movie-going public that he, too, could wear formal attire and a cape (in *Son of Dracula*) and at least appear fairly beset and conflicted in any/all of the "Inner Sanctum" pictures. Some argue that had these two experiences not *bracketed* the George Waggner production – or had Arthur Lubin not replaced Henry Koster as director - Chaney, Jr. may have had a more decent shot at the title role.

There were no auditions, *per se*, for the title role in the production. The execs were not willing to entrust their phantom to someone in a line of wannabes; rather, they considered only established thesps who had demonstrated the capacity to run the gamut between terror and consolation. In addition to Crawford, the trades and Movieland gossip columns that covered the production from its very first announcement to its preview mentioned a myriad of actors – including Caesar Romero and Charles Laughton – as being scrutinized for the part. While the three above-cited names began their film work around the same time as had Chaney – the early-to-mid '30s, although Laughton made his film debut in 1928 – each had a curriculum vitae that displayed a wide range of roles that called for a depth of vision and expression and the capacity to show a character undergo significant change. It may be argued that there could be no more radically *physical* change than Chaney's Lawrence Talbot transforming into Chaney's Wolf Man, but – for most of his career to that date – Chaney's movie roles had pretty much been limited to cowboys, sidekicks, and that brace of one-dimensional grotesques in 1941 (see essay; *Man-Made Monster*).

The role, of course, went to Claude Rains. (Per the Messrs. Weaver, Brunas and Brunas,(11) director Arthur Lubin literally could not have been clearer when he averred, "Claude Rains was my only choice, and he was wonderful.") Rains, who had escaped type-casting in the horror field after leaving Universal following 1935's *The Mystery of Edwin Drood*, had returned to the Universal fold (as it were) as Chaney, Jr's. dad – and killer – in 1941's *Destiny... errrr... The Wolf Man*. Following *Phantom*, the Clapham-born actor would cross Universal's transom only once again, as a nightclub caricaturist in 1945's *This Love of Ours*.(12) **Universal Horrors'** quote from Arthur Lubin continues to speak of Rains's perfectionist habits – prior to filming, he practiced at the piano and with the violin – and his input with respect to the unmasking scene was but another indication of the thought and feeling he put into the picture – into any of his pictures, actually. The 17 August 1943 *Film Daily* was quite effusive in its praise - "Claude Rains does excellently as the opera violinist..." - before perpetuating the myth we argued against above - "... who is secretly in love with a member of the same company." *Sigh*! *Motion Picture Daily*, published four days earlier than *Film*

*Daily,* was far less generous, adverbially - "Claude Rains does well with the role..." although reviewer Sherwin Kane maintained that the Phantom was "haunting the opera house *to advance the career* of [a] young singer" (italics mine). The afore-cited Bosley Crowther ended his critical screed by asking, "Who is afraid of a Phantom who is billed beneath [Nelson] Eddy in the cast?"

**The stylishly *nouveau* Erique Claudin goes *way* beyond reading the riot act to prima donna, Mme. Biancarolli (Jane Farrar). The soprano and her unfortunate maid become the first of the Phantom's victims, and the reign of terror at the Paris Opera is underway.**

As true as that may have been, Rains copped the acting prize, and the remaining principals – when mentioned at length at all – received some lukewarm notices. The *Film Daily* critique did offer a sentence-full of words on "Nelson Eddy and Susanna Foster [who] play the lovers who never seem to get together, thanks no little to the competition offered by Edgar Barrier, a police officer." *Motion Picture Daily* may not have writ with excessive praise about the phantom's impersonator, but did feel that "the efforts of... Nelson Eddy... and Edgar Barrier... carry action, excitement and suspense throughout the film," whilst "the singer of [Susanna] Foster, Eddy and Jane Farrar are highlights of the film." The coverage the picture received from *The Christian Science Monitor* (6 October 1943) was more... errr... *christian*, if said adjective were taken to mean "uplifting."

> Nelson Eddy, perhaps, has never appeared to greater advantage in the [sic] films than in 'The [sic] Phantom of the Opera.' He sings with authority, fire, good voice, and freedom... Edgar Barrier makes a real impression as the inspector... Miss Foster is dazzling in her blond beauty and youth and her singing is noteworthy under the demands of a score that would tax the resources of a much more experienced performer.

The 5 November 1943 *Washington Post* review opined that "it is the combined vocal brilliance of Susanna Foster, Nelson Eddy and Jane Farrar that gives 'Phantom of the Opera' its most valid claim to eminence." Critic Nelson B. Bell wrote nary a word about Ms. Foster's non-singing performance, though, and while he *did* admit that "Mr. Eddy shares with Edgar Barrier such honors as there are," the reviewer did Barrier an injustice when he spoke of the actor as a "newcomer." Barrier's movie debut had been in *Le Spectre Vert*, the French-language version of M-G-M's *The Unholy Night* (1929).(13)

Edwin Schallert, covering the picture in the 16 October 1943 number of the *Los Angeles Times*, was also effusive in his lauding the three principals' vocal talents. On other fronts...

> Miss Foster is introduced as practically a new personality in color photography, a delicate figurine, who is probably now beginning a very bright phase of her career... Edgar Barrier... [and] Nelson Eddy... together furnish some rather pleasant comedy interludes... The film yields comparatively little of acting opportunities for Eddy... I'm not sold especially on his dark wig, incidentally. (14)

Eddy – tagged as "The Singing Capon" when he costarred in features and concerts with Jeanette MacDonald ("The Iron Butterfly") – would go on to make only a brace of feature films after *Phantom*. More coverage on Edgar Barrier and Susanna Foster may be found in our essays on *Flesh and Fantasy* (1943) and *The Climax* (1944), respectively, and some of Leo Carrillo's bona fides are listed in our chapter on *Horror Island* (1941).

The one element that may have led the trades and/or syndicated columnists to announce that *Phantom of the Opera* was to be produced as an Abbott and Costello comedy was producer George Waggner (taking over from Joe Pasternak) naming Arthur Lubin as director. Waggner had produced or directed a good handful of genre titles before *Phantom*, and he receives his due in our screed on *Horror Island*. Lubin had helmed five – Count 'em: 5! - A&C comedies in a row the previous year and a half: *Buck Privates*, *In the Navy*, *Hold That Ghost*, *Keep 'Em Flying* (all four, 1941), and *Ride 'Em Cowboy* (1942). On the other hand, the native Angeleno had also guided Boris and Bela (and Stanley Ridges) through *Black Friday* the year before his Abbott & Costello tsunami. (Lubin would go on to out-do his A&C quintet by directing six – Count 'em: 6! - Francis [the Talking Mule] features between 1950 and 1955 and then spend five years helming episodes of TV's derivative talking-horse series, *Mr. Ed.*)

While dealing with an updated, color/sound rendition of a theme that every film fan to that point had associated with a mid-'20s silent/black and white classic would have been challenging even for a director more closely associated with the genre, Lubin – per the critics, at least – succeeded beyond anyone's reasonable expectations. "The direction of Arthur Lubin is aces," proclaimed *Film Daily*, and Lubin's vision included a much more mobile camera than Universal's horror arm had ever dreamed of ("The camera work of Hal Mohr and Duke Green [sic] rates raves." - *Film Daily* again); in fact, the Mohr/Greene team took home the Oscar in 1944 for Best Cinematography.

Lubin also envisioned a more comprehensive chandelier scene than the one that had gone woefully wrong in the Rupert Julian/Chaney original. Still, just as few were of a mind to voluntarily compare the Rains/Pierce climactic make-up with that of The Man of a Thousand Faces, there were those who felt the chandelier sequence could have been done more effectively. Specifically, Edwin Schallert (cited above):

> The device of cutting a huge chandelier from its moorings which was a feature of the earlier version is employed again. It makes for a dramatic climax but a somewhat empty one. The destruction does not seem overwhelming and the audience, to all appearances, is not even particularly disturbed after the crash has been duly digested. There is a phony quality to this peak event.

What had been intended as the visual climax to the '25 *Phantom*'s ever more

357

melodramatic actions two decades earlier became - per scenarists Eric Taylor and Samuel Hoffenstein, M. Lubin, and the teaming of Mohr and Greene - an unimaginable diversion created to mask the '43 Phantom's real intention: the removal of Christine to the opera house cellars. While the *viewer* is led from the auditorium to the backstage confines, the *audience* is still experiencing the aural part of the massacre; we're meant to concentrate on the kidnapping and not on the chaos. Still, as unlikely as it may seem, the chandelier scene was about the only thing that Bosley Crowther (also cited above) seemed to care for regarding the film:

> As a matter of record, this sequence is the only one in the film in which the potential excitement of the story is realized. Here the blend of monstrous violence with the wild Russian music on the stage achieves the realization of terror which is lost in the rest of the yarn.

Tuneful, colorful and more than occasionally amusing – Merci bien, Alphonse, Gaston, and the wonderfully wry Lecours of Fritz Feld – but no great shakes as a horror film, Universal's reworking of *Phantom of the Opera* remains well worth one's time. Because of the War, set redecoration was much more on the corporate mind than set construction; not only was a ton of money saved by using Chaney's old digs, but – per author Thomas M. Feramisco (15) - even the notorious *Green Hell* temple set was reshaped into Rains's new ones. Sure, it's not completely terrifying to watch Christine's old Dad jump through hoops (and scurry through sewers) to make sure she gets the breaks she deserves, but Leroux's tale – meant to touch the heartstrings as well as freeze the bone marrow – could (and *would*) do much worse. Surprisingly – although almost always regarded as a qualitative "one-up" on the rest of the decade's thrillers – the film was not part of either the "Shock Theater" or "Son of Shock" programs released to TV in the '50s. Still, thanks to the Messrs. Lubin, Waggner, Rains, Mohr, Greene, Ward, Brown, *et al* – and Technicolor - the '43 "experience" is among the most memorable of that decade's offerings at Universal.

*Phantom of the Opera* – 27 August 1943 – 92 minutes

**CAST:** Nelson Eddy as Anatole Garron; Susanna Foster as Christine DuBois; Claude Rains as Erique Claudin/The Phantom; Edgar Barrier as Inspector Raoul Daubert; Leo Carrillo as Signor Ferretti; Jane Farrar as Madame Biancarolli; Edward Bromberg as Amiot; Fritz Feld as Lecours; Frank Puglia as Villeneuve; Steven Geray as Vercheres; Barbara Everest as Christine's Aunt; Hume Cronyn as Gerard; Fritz Leiber as Franz Liszt; Nicki Andre as Madame Lorenzi; Gladys Blake as Jeanne; Elvira Curci as Yvette; Hans Herbert as Marcel; Kate Lawson as Landlady; Miles Mander as Pleyel; Rosina Galli as Celeste; Walter Stahl as Dr. LeFort; Paul Marion as Desjardines; Tudor Williams and Tony Marlow as Singers in **Martha**; Beatrice Roberts as Nurse; Marek Windheim as Renfrit; Muni Seroff, Dick Bartell, Jim Mitchell, Wheaton Chambers as Reporters; Renee Carson as Georgette; Lane Chandler and Stanley Blystone as Officers; Cyril Delavanti as Bookkeeper; John Walsh as Office Boy; Alphonse Martell as Policeman; Edward Clark as Usher; William Desmond and Hank Mann as Stagehands

**CREDITS**: Producer: George Waggner; Director: Arthur Lubin; Executive Producer: Jack Gross; Screenplay: Eric Taylor & Samuel Hoffenstein; Adaptation: John Jacoby; Based on the novel **The Phantom of the Opera** by Gaston Leroux; Directors of Photography: Hal Mohr and W. Howard Greene; Technicolor Color Director: Natalie Kalmus; Art Directors: John B. Goodman and Alexander Golitzen; Film Editor: Russell Schoengarth; Assistant Director: Charles Gould; Set Decorators: Russell A. Gausman and Ira S. Webb; Dialogue Director: Joan Hathaway; Sound Director: Bernard B. Brown; Technician: Joe Lapis; Musical Score and Direction: Edward Ward; Opera Sequences Staged by William Von Wymetal and Lester Horton; Choral Director: William Tyroler; Hair Stylist: Emily Moore; Costumes: Vera West

*-JTS*

# *Sherlock Holmes Faces Death* (1943)

A couple of decades back, Jeremy Brett, portrayer of the Great Consulting Detective on British television, revealed the secret of the success that he had in that particular moment in the Sun (said moment being prolonged throughout four series between 1984 and 1994). "I think probably the miracle that Granada Television achieved," said Brett on the program, *Daytime Live*, in 1988, "was doing the original stories... adapting literally the stories of our Doctor Watson." Indeed, the series was characterized by taking Conan Doyle's tales to the screen and producing them as closely as possible to their literary source, eschewing total fidelity only in extreme cases of budget impossibility or for dramatic reasons. Apparently one of these extreme cases had occurred in 1986 with "The Adventure of the Musgrave Ritual." During production, the text of the enigmatic ritual was changed, Watson's presence was added to certain events, and several narrative elements were altered. Fans wondered whether Granada's handling of "Musgrave" would be a *rara avis*, the one canonical story that was not so easily adapted to audiovisual language.

Without any such obligation to literary fidelity, but solely to retain a number of specific elements from the original stories, "Musgrave" was also changed by Universal to fit the requirements of the hour-and-a-quarter running time that would be allotted to the first of the character's "second season" in 1943. Screenwriter Bertram Millhauser, the same man responsible for both the original story and a share in the screenplay of *Sherlock Holmes in Washington*, now adapted a script from Gerald Geraghty, pushing the envelope with respect to the tone of the three first films in the series. If previously Holmes had confronted villainous propagandists, Nazis, or hirelings associated with them, now he would return to a Gothic environment – intentionally not that of the canon, but rather that of the cycle of horror films that was pouring enviable amounts of revenue into Universal's coffers.

Building on Geraghty's story, Millhauser added wartime references and changed details and characters so that the War would not be totally removed from the script. To do this, he discarded the text about Holmes's immutability and opted for an introduction set in "The Rat and Raven" (a not too remote Poe reference), a country tavern in which the proprietor, in lugubrious and ominous tones, tells of the wickedness of the Musgraves. In the style of *Citizen Kane*, the camera brings us across the portals of the farm and accompanies us all around the mansion, whipped by a howling blizzard, the audio of which reminds the genre-oriented audience member of the soundtrack of 1932's *The Old Dark House*. The legend reads that at midnight, just before a member of the Musgrave family is to die, the bells in the clock tower will toll 13 times. Inasmuch as this quasi-supernatural detail will remain unexplained at the end of the picture, we understand that we've witnessed the setting of a horror precedent in a series that, until that point, had not possessed any elements of the genre.

Inside the Musgrave mansion we find the familiar form of Doctor Watson, in charge of attending to officers suffering from traumas or disorders caused by their experiences in the War. The two owners of the property – Geoffrey Musgrave and his younger sister, Sally – then make their appearance, and their discussion is overheard by the butler, Brunton. A third sibling, Philip, soon adds to the discussion, and thus from the outset we're aware of the characters' interests and differences. A violent occurrence alarms everyone: Doctor Sexton, Watson's assistant in the cause, is attacked in the middle of the night and suffers a wound in the neck.

Watson returns to London and turns up at the traditional 221b Baker Street digs just as his friend is about to have breakfast. As a symbol of this new Holmes - who returns to the past whilst in the present - the character now abstains from cigarettes (which he had smoked in the previous films) preferring the pipe, and his hair has returned to the more "normal" style he had worn in the first features for Fox. After a quick exchange, the two men decide they must make for Musgrave Manor (formerly Hurlstone Towers) immediately to investigate. Upon arriving at the dismal location, they come upon both the corpse of Geoffrey Musgrave and the ineffable Inspector Lestrade, who has arrested one of the patients, Captain Vickery, because he had had a heated discussion with the deceased the previous night, certainly mere circumstantial evidence.

To carry out the famous Musgrave ritual, Sally recites mysterious verses over her brother's body before the astonished gaze not only of Holmes and Watson, but also of the staff and patients lodged at the mansion. As rampaging Nature provides a tense climax to the family cus tom, a lightning bolt shatters one of the windows and an old document is discovered. (As might be expected, all lighting artifices were concocted by Kenneth Strickfaden, the electrical magician of the classic "Frankenstein" films.) In the original story, redacted by Geraghty, the mansion resounded with mysterious noises and was loaded with centuries-old armor, in addition to a subterranean vault very much similar to the type of Egyptian sepulcher one might find in the "Kharis the Mummy" series.

While Holmes and Watson meander through the neighboring town (the set that the studio had built for the "Frankenstein" series), they come across Philip Musgrave's cadaver in the trunk of a car. Lestrade now turns his suspicions at Brunton, the butler, who, it devolves, has just disappeared. Brunton also disappears in the original story and it is the mystery concerning his whereabouts causes the aristocrat Reginald Musgrave to present the case to his school friend, Sherlock Holmes. Whereas Watson is the narrator in most of the canonical tales, in "Musgrave" Holmes himself has the job, while Watson is tasked with the introduction. In both literature and cinema, though, Brunton displays the same attributes: indiscretion and curiosity; these cause him to be sanctioned by his masters.

*Faces Death*'s Brunton is played by Halliwell Hobbes, a veteran British character actor who specialized throughout the '30s and early '40s in authoritative personages - military, academic and phlegmatic aristocratic types - only to later end up embodying butlers. The Universal classic films completist will remember him as the constable in *Dracula's Daughter* (in fact, the readers of the first volume of this work, **Of Gods and Monsters**, can see him inspecting a prop that resembles Bela Lugosi's Dracula in the still on page 263). But by the time of the War, Hobbes had already become the quintessential butler, performing said office in *The Undying Monster* (1942) for Fox, *Mr. Muggs Steps Out* (1943) for Monogram, and *Mr. Skeffington* (1944) for the brothers Warner. Universal would give him the same role in *The Invisible Man's Revenge* (1944), after which Hobbes seemed to follow in the steps of Basil Rathbone, heading to the East Coast in search of more promising roles in the challenging milieu of Broadway.

Anyhow, in addition to his excessive interest in his masters' conversations, Brunton also enjoys a drink or two, and the night before Philip disappeared was found to be inebriated. Consequently, Lestrade is led to believe that Brunton had thus committed the murder and that his absence was evidence of his guilt. But while that stolid representative of Scotland Yard is getting lost in a secret passage in the mansion, Holmes proceeds with his deductions about the secret meaning of the Musgrave ritual.

He believes it's all about a succession of chess moves, and a glance at the mansion's great hall - with its black and white tiles - confirms his theory as he realizes that the floor is a giant chess board. Using Watson, Sexton, the patients, and the staff as chess pieces, he proceeds to reconstruct that particular chess game whose last move would be the key to... that which the assassin had searched for.

This curious scene prefigured similar sequences in the television adventure of *The Man from U.N.C.L.E.: Alexander the Great Affair* (1965) and *Checkmate* (1966), and a memorable episode from the cult TV series, *The Prisoner*. It seems not to have had any cinematic precedent save for a reference in an entry in the "Philo Vance" series, *The Bishop Murder Case* (1930), with a group of assassins who follow the logic of a childish rhyme and a detective (also played by Rathbone) who asks himself if the "Bishop" - signer of every message of murder – belonged not to a cleric, but rather to a chess board. Another detail that's more than a colorful note in the satire is the presence of three of the mansion's patients, afflicted with the tics or traumas from warfare: Gerald Hamer, the lanky Vernon Downing, and the diminutive Olaf Hytten. The plot has them involved in suspicious activities, all of which end up way too risible for us to take them seriously as possible suspects.

**From an uncredited bit to making the poster AND pushing the series' leads into the background, and all in the space of four pictures! Hillary Brooke comes into her own.**

In the Holmes series, as well as in many of the movies of the period, the appearance of corpses seemed to be a taboo. In Conan Doyle's tales, one of the points of greatest interest are the descriptions of Holmes's macabre findings. In fact, in the original "Musgrave," the description of the appearance of Brunton's corpse creates an ominous atmosphere very close to horrific:

> It was the figure of a man, clad in a suit of black, who squatted down upon his hams with his forehead sunk upon the edge of the box and his two arms thrown out on each side of it. The attitude had drawn all the stagnant blood to his face, and no man could have recognized that distorted liver-coloured countenance.

A number of cadavers had appeared in the previous Holmes pictures, but the camera's vision frightens us. In *Secret Weapon*, we see the corpse of a scientist on his living room floor, but we know that a couple of others have been assassinated. As for Moriarty's death, we hear his scream during a fatal fall, but we don't see anything. In *In Washington*, a character is murdered and his body is packed in a trunk and sent to the hotel where Holmes is staying, but we never see the corpse, and react instead via Holmes's disconcerted face and those of the police who are watching him. That practice remains in force in *Faces Death*, with the discovery of the bodies of both brothers reflected in the expressions of Holmes and Watson. Later on, however, in this bizarre human chess game, the Master Detective finds Brunton, whose bloated corpse is revealed to be next to a crypt (courtesy of one of the old *Dracula* sets) by the all-seeing camera.

In the course of his solving the mystery, Holmes lays a trap for the three patients and Doctor Sexton - one of whom *must* be the murderer - and his trap, playing havoc with both the obvious and our expectations, is so well laid out that it ends up fooling us. The *Harrisons Reports* reviewer – in the 4 September 1943 number – recognized that...

> ...it holds the audience in suspense for not until the closing scenes is the identity of the murderer made known. The unraveling of the mystery is far-fetched, but is in keeping with the amazing talents of Holmes.

The appreciation of other industry press varied in accordance with their appreciation for the genre. In the 9 September 1943 *Motion Picture Daily*, Helen

McNamara decreed that "a plot with an unusual twist and unexpected climax make this a good show for the mystery devotees." In the column "Product Digest" in the 11 September 1943 *Motion Picture Herald*, Jack Cartwright considered it an "excellent Sherlock Holmes... and it measures up well with the best of the three turned out last season." Still, his assertion that "the story sticks closely to the Doyle original" revealed that he had read the tale – if indeed he ever had read it – a long time in the past.

*Photoplay* (December 1943) was satisfied with this "new" Holmes not so much for its cinematographic probity as for the fact that "at least we seem to be rid of the Nazi-spy mysteries that rendered Sherlock, part of a pre-Nazi era, a rather ridiculous figure." The influential *Variety* (8 September 1943) was categorical in that...

> ...the Sherlock Holmes series remains obviously grooved 'B' detective melodramas as emphasized by this particular Universal release... As long as there is the fingernail-biting clan buying tickets at the box office, there will always be such pictures as these. And thus the Holmes-Dr. Watson pictures remain salable.

And in the less appreciative range was found *Film Daily* (16 September 1943), which dictated in the most telegraphic of terms: "while pic is far from the best of series, it should manage to satisfy the Holmes fans." One of the reasons for this, the periodical observed, was the script: "The screenplay, which is not always to be taken seriously, is the work of Bertram Millhauser."

In the epilogue, Holmes once again recites an apothegm, but, in this case, one of his own. The secret of the Musgrave ritual is that it bestows the ownership of lands unclaimed by the crown to Sally's family, and she decides not to accept this, due to the fact that quite a few farmers are settled on her land. Her renunciation, a very wise propaganda message during a time of war and scarcity, was the timely theme that Holmes draws from history, a light dose of modernity, and social consciousness: "The old days of grab and greed are on their way out." But his conclusions, which take him fairly close to the postulates of socialism, appear to be a wink at the Soviet Union, which Hollywood, at that point, tried to show from a favorable viewpoint. "The time's coming, Watson, when we shan't be able to fill our bellies in comfort while other folks go hungry, or sleep in warm beds while others shiver in the cold."

Hillary Brooke came into her own in *Faces Death*, at least in terms of landing a role that not only saw her receive onscreen credit, but also showed that the Queens-born actress was more than just a coldly beautiful face. Entering films at a time when tall, leggy blondes made up the lion's share of aspiring young actresses, Miss Brooke briefly affected a semi-British accent, a ploy that worked out to her benefit. Later on, having dropped the professional affectation, she still possessed a husky, cultured voice that went perfectly with her height and carriage. From the film at hand, she moved on to a featured role in 20th Century Fox's *Jane Eyre*, a no-doubt "A" starring Orson Welles and Joan Fontaine. Mysteries would soon be intermingled with Westerns, *noirs*, and comedies. It wouldn't be long before the actress would cross paths with Holmes and Watson yet again (in 1945's *The Woman in Green*) and with RKO's master detective, Dr. Ordway (*The Crime Doctor's Courage*, 1945), and try to bring some semblance of normalcy when playing against Bob Hope (*Monsieur Beaucaire*, 1946), Red Skelton (*The Fuller Brush Man*, 1948), and Abbott and Costello (*Africa Screams*, 1949; ...*Meet Captain Kidd*, 1952). Come the '50s, Miss Brooke made most of her rent appearing on TV, but she still warmed the heart of genre lovers by gracing two '50s William Cameron Menzies science-fiction treasures: *Invaders from Mars* – a film designed to scare the living hell out of little kids – and *The Maze* (both 1953). Our Miss Brooke retired from the industry in 1960 and retired to Greener Pastures in 1999.

From this point forward, the series would be both directed and produced by Roy William Neill; starting with *The Scarlet Claw*, Howard Benedict would occasionally surface as the (usually uncredited) Executive Producer May we assume that one of Neill's first proclamations as producer was that Rathbone be spared the raven's-wing hairdo he had worn for the first three films? Also, the keen-eyed fan may spot an impossibly young Peter Lawford lounging at the bar during the pub scene. *Faces Death* was one of the last of the Londoner's "uncredits" before his movie career began to take off.

*Sherlock Holmes Faces Death* – 17 September 1943 – 68 minutes

**CAST**: Basil Rathbone as Sherlock Holmes; Nigel Bruce as Dr. Watson; Dennis Hoey as Inspector Lestrade; Arthur Margetson as Dr. Sexton; Hillary Brooke as Sally Musgrave; Halliwell Hobbes as Alfred Brunton; Minna Phillips as Mrs. Howells; Milburn Stone as Captain Vickery; Gavin Muir as Phillip Musgrave; Gerald Hamer as Major Langford; Vernon Downing as Lieut. Clavering; Olaf Hytten as Captain MacIntosh; Frederick Worlock as Geoffrey Musgrave; Mary Gordon as Mrs. Hudson; Harold De Becker as Pub Proprietor; Eric Snowden and Peter Lawford as Sailors at Bar

**CREDITS**: Director: Roy William Neill; Producer: Roy William Neill; Screenplay: Bertram Millhauser; Based on the story "The Musgrave Ritual" by Arthur Conan Doyle; Music: Frank Skinner; Musical Director: H.J. Salter; Photography: Charles Van Enger; Film Editor: Fred Feitshans; Art Directors: John B. Goodman, Harold MacArthur; Set Decoration: Russell A. Gausman, Edward R. Robinson; Gowns: Vera West

*- DL*

# Flesh and Fantasy (1943)

*Synopsis*: At their gentleman's club, Mr. Doakes (Robert Benchley) tells his friend Davis (David Hoffman) that he's been very disturbed by a fortune teller's prediction and a strange dream. Davis suggests Doakes consult three tales of the supernatural to rest his mind.

The first story is set during Mardi Gras. Henrietta (Betty Field), an ill-tempered, unattractive, and lonely woman, contemplates suicide. A bearded stranger (Edgar Barrier) persuades her to come with him to a costume shop where she dons the mask of a beautiful woman. The stranger tells her she must return the mask by midnight. During the revelries, Henriette runs across Michael (Robert Cummings), a poor student she has loved secretly from afar. Michael is despondent and considering ditching his law career to go to sea, but Henrietta convinces him otherwise and they have a romantic evening together. Michael is sure that Henrietta is beautiful under the mask, but Henrietta fears he will be disillusioned. She returns to the costume shop at midnight and, to her astonishment, she is beautiful even without the mask.

In the second story, set in London, American lawyer, Marshall Tyler (Edward G. Robinson) attends a fashionable dinner party during which psychic Septimus Podgers (Thomas Mitchell), reads the palms of the guests. He is uncannily accurate and Tyler, though a skeptic, insists Podgers read his palm, too. The fortune teller does so and then refuses to tell Tyler what he has seen. In a private session later, Podgers tells the lawyer that his palm indicates that he will commit murder. Tyler becomes obsessed by the conviction that Podgers is right and even puts off his engagement to his beloved Rowena (Anna Lee). Certain that he must kill *someone*, Tyler makes two attempts to commit murder, but fails both times. However, he has a chance encounter on London Bridge with Podgers and ends up throttling the fortune teller and throwing him into the water. His crime is seen by a policeman and, after a chase that ends in the circus, Tyler is arrested.

At that very circus, tightrope walker Paul Gaspar (Charles Boyer) does a dangerous act without a net. Later he has a dream wherein he sees a beautiful woman screaming as he falls. This leads to a loss of nerve on his part, and he contemplates doing a less risky act when the circus moves to New York. On the ship taking them there, Paul meets Joan (Barbara Stanwyck), the very woman he has been dreaming about. She has a secret, but they fall in love. Gaspar has another dream in which he sees Joan getting arrested. They arrive in New York and Gaspar, his confidence restored, does his usual act successfully. Joan is actually part of a gang of thieves, and the police are waiting for her after the performance. She parts with Gaspar without telling him the truth, but both are certain they will be reunited.

Doakes is seemingly convinced that free will overrides superstition, but he nevertheless avoids walking under a ladder at the club.

> There is a divinity that shapes our ends,
> Rough hew them how we will.
> - *Hamlet*

"The main theme of the film is that man is powerless against the overwhelming forces of nature, both real and imaginary." - Julien Duvivier on *Flesh and Fantasy*

*Flesh and Fantasy* is no doubt the most unique film to emerge from Universal's horror factory of the '40s. It's dripping with *noir*-ish atmosphere, full of striking imagery, and backed by an innovative musical score. In place of the usual competent journeymen and outright hacks Universal employed to helm their monster epics, this film was done by internationally famous director, Julien Duvivier, and featured a very high-powered and popular cast. Instead of mummies shambling through the swamp, you have a more cerebral approach to the supernatural, one that suggests "there are such things," but it's how the characters respond to those possibilities that provides the suspense. It *should* be a great movie. However, in spite of a strong second episode, it doesn't quite come across and is, in the end, rather unsatisfying. Duvivier claimed he wanted the viewers to think as well as be entertained, but the film's themes are muddled.

In spite of the Grand Guignol, there was very little interest in horror in the French cinema of the '20s and '30s. There was no French version of **The Phantom of the Opera**, though other works by Gaston Leroux went before the camera (**Mystery**

**of the Yellow Room, Perfume of the Woman in Black, Balaoo).** There were certainly fantasy (Georges Méliès, René Clair) and science fiction films like *L'inhumaine, La Cité Foudroyée,* and Abel Gance's *The End of the World,* but the French largely seemed content to leave the macabre to Berlin and Hollywood.

The one exception was Julien Duvivier who told an interviewer late in life that "I've always been obsessed by the fantastic, the supernatural, the unusual." Early in the '20s, Duvivier directed two shorts dealing with the uncanny, *The Reincarnation of Serge Renaudier* and, in Germany, *The Sinister Guest,* based on E.T.A. Hoffmann's tale of hypnotism and the black arts. Duvivier subsequently graduated to features and chose a wide variety of subjects, from thrillers (*The Mystery of the Eiffel Tower*) to dramas about social change (*Au bonheur des dames*) and the travails of childhood (*Poil de carotte,* which he remade as a talkie), as well as religious themes (*The Marvelous Life of Thérèse Martin;* the Jesuit-educated Duvivier often returned to the subject of religion throughout his career).

Like many other French directors, Duvivier did not welcome the coming of sound, but it was in the '30s that he made his most important films, including *David Golder* (featuring his frequent star, Harry Baur, as a ruthless Jewish financier) (1) and *Pépé le Moko* (a tale of the Casbah with Jean Gabin - the American version, *Algiers,* starred Duvivier's friend, Charles Boyer). Duvivier also helmed a film that could be considered borderline horror, *Moon over Morocco* (1931), wherein five Frenchmen traveling in Morocco are cursed by a witch doctor who claims they will all die before the next full moon. The curse seems to come true as three of the men perish in the exact order predicted by the sorcerer, but aisle-seat detectives will figure out what's going on long before does the hero, the fifth man.(2)

In 1936, Duviver directed a remake of the Paul Wegener classic *The Golem,* but the result was a slow and stolid film with many scenes dissipating without any dramatic tension and a Golem who - when he finally does get into the action at the last reel - seems more like Maciste than the monster of Jewish lore. Nonetheless, the sets were imaginative and the film certainly presented a warm, sympathetic picture of the Jewish community. Considering what was happening in Germany at the time, the film could even be seen as a anti-Nazi parable. In 1939 Duviver did a new version of the 1920 Swedish fantasy *The Phantom Carriage,* but again he fell far short of the original in spite of good performances and occasional macabre imagery. Like *The Golem,* this old legend worked much better in the less realistic silent medium; sound largely kills it with the fantastic at odds with the grim picture of poverty.

In 1937 Duvivier directed *Un Carnet de Bal,* a movie which could be considered his first "portmanteau," a genre he particularly liked and would go back to frequently. The story concerns the recently widowed Christine, who runs across her dance card for the first ball she attended as a youth and decides to visit all her former suitors. Two of them have died, and the ones who are still alive have not fared well; indeed, entering King Tut's tomb might have been safer than signing up for a dance with Christine. The episodic nature of the story allows the film to become a showcase for France's greatest actors (Harry Baur, Fernandel, Louis Jouvet, Pierre Blanchar, Raimu) and brought Duvivier increased recognition among American film critics.

In 1940 Duvivier, his wife, and his son fled Nazi-occupied France via Portugal and from there to the United States. His first film was *Lydia;* some would say this was a reworking of *Un carnet de bal*. It was not a critical or box office success. In 1942 20th Century-Fox made plans to do *Tales of Manhattan*, an anthology film with a big-name cast and a different director to helm each episode. The studio originally wanted Duvivier to do just one segment, but Charles Boyer convinced Duvivier (and Fox) that he should direct the whole movie. The story concerned a cursed coat that is passed from person to person and eventually ends up on a scarecrow. Even though receipts for the film weren't in, Boyer and Duvivier used its presumed success to pitch Universal on an anthology of supernatural tales, perhaps on the lines of German silent classics like *Waxworks* and *Eerie Tales*. According to an interview Duvivier did for the 6 September 1942 issue of *The New York Times*:

> This is the idea we told to Universal officials and, although it may sound vague in the telling they were, nevertheless, enthusiastic. They asked me how much it would cost. I said I did not know. They asked if it would run over the $900,000 that *Tales of Manhattan* had cost. I said it would. They asked me how much. I said I did not know. Then they said 'We have confidence in you. We know you will make a great picture. And if there's anything you need, let us know.'

This all sounds extraordinarily accommodating for a budget-minded studio like Universal but, in any event, the film went forward with Boyer and Duvivier acting as co- producers. Duvivier and Boyer could not decide on a title, and from 1942 to 1943, they vacillated between *For All We Know* and *Flesh and Fantasy* before finally deciding on the latter (though at least one critic complained it was a crummy title.)

In the summer of 1942, Duvivier started filming on what was originally to be the film's first story, an adaptation of Oscar Wilde's **The Crime of Lord Arthur Saville,**

372

with Edward G. Robinson. In the aforementioned *New York Times* article, the writer mentions that the second episode - with Boyer and Barbara Stanwyck - was based on a story by Brander Matthews(3), but it clearly was not. Duvivier then adds to the confusion:

> The fourth and final sequence shows the forces of the past at work in men's lives. It is a comedy sequence based on *The Crime of Lord Savil* (sic) by Oscar Wilde which tells of the love affair of two ghosts, one a woman hater, the other a man hater.

This is certainly not a description of Wilde's story, but it is something like Brander Matthews' comic spook tale, "The Rival Ghosts." Did Duvivier originally intend the Matthews' story to end the film? If so it would have been even more out of place than the golf story in *Dead of Night*, another horror anthology. The director's command of English was tenuous, and it's possible we're dealing with some misunderstandings here. Also, noted in passing is that one of Matthews' books was titled **Tales of Fantasy and Fact,** possibly an inspiration for the film's final title.

Boyer did not enjoy his time as a producer. He had a two-picture contract with Universal, but *Flesh and Fantasy* proved to be the only film he made for them, though he later produced the TV series, *Four Star Playhouse*. There does not seem to have been a lot of pre-planning; they started filming one segment at a time without even casting the entire picture, and the movie was over a year in production. Boyer's first headache came when cameraman Stanley Cortez left after doing the photography for the Edward G. Robinson segment and was replaced by Paul Ivano. Supposedly Cortez had to honor a prior commitment to David Selznick, but Cortez worked very slowly, perhaps too slowly for Boyer and Duvivier. Then, during the Boyer/Stanwyck segment, Duvivier fell ill. Publicity for the film claimed Stanwyck took that time off without expecting to be paid. She might have been glad for the break as conditions in Stage 28 - the "Phantom" set - were sweltering and her character had to wear a mink coat.

Boyer's woes increased when they came to what was planned to be the third episode of the film. This concerned a drifter named Cliff who happens across a farm run by a beautiful blind girl and her father. The setting is enchanting, and the girl otherworldly in her connection to Nature, but Cliff sees only dollar signs when he discovers how profitable the farm is. He kills the girl's father and attempts to rape her, but she flees. The forces of Nature - represented by winds, trees, and swirling dust -

protect her, and they hurl her would-be assailant into the river where he drowns. Boyer borrowed John Garfield from Warner Bros., but the actor took one look at the script and refused to play the part, explaining his position in the 29 November 1942 edition of *The New York Times:*

> Mr. Garfield said that he will not appear in any picture which he regards as unimportant in relationship to the war. The actor had been promised to Universal on a three-week loan-out by Warner Bros., and the latter studio suspended him without salary when he refused to report to Universal. Garfield explained that all his pictures 'must have something to do with reality and what is going on.' Otherwise, they seem so unimportant there's no point in working at all. *Flesh and Fantasy*, he said is a 'mystic' photo-play laid in 1932 and he thinks it has no bearing on the world as it is.

Universal responded - quite correctly in view of what exhibitors were saying - that theaters would soon be empty if studios made only war pictures.

Charles Boyer, after telling Louella Parsons that the world needs films with a spiritual dimension more than ever, had a different explanation for Garfield's turning down the part:

> Julien Duvivier, my co-producer and director, and I were, of course, upset that John Garfield refused to play the very bad boy in the last sequence. John felt it would be wrong for him to play a role that shows him as a thoroughly unscrupulous character, particularly in these times when the world needs a message of good men, not bad ones... Personally, I have a feeling we are making too many war stories yet it is impossible to ignore the terrific adjustment of life taking place at this moment.
>
> *Waterloo Sunday Courier*, 28 February 1943

Garfield portrayed tough guys and later the occasional anti-hero (*The Postman Always Rings Twice*), but he may have understandably been worried about his image playing a role that had him trying to assault a blind teenager after killing her father *and* her little dog. Garfield spent his suspension selling war bonds, and apparently got over his aversion to fantasy as in the following year he played in *Between Two Worlds*, a tale of the afterlife.

Alan Curtis took over the role of Cliff with Gloria Jean was cast as the heroine. This episode was to lead to the final story, the Betty Field/Robert Cummings segment. By the time the film was released, the stories had been shuffled around and now the movie was to begin with the Gloria Jean tale, followed by Field/Cummings, then the Edward G. Robinson episode and closing with Boyer/Stanwyck. Even though preview audiences reacted favorably to the Gloria Jean story, the studio cut it, seeing as it would have made the film run over two hours, an epic length by Universal standards. The episode was later expanded and turn into a feature, *Destiny* (see essay).

**The almost unrecognizable Betty Field looks like a witch while playing the ill-tempered and bitter Henrietta in the picture's first story. Field did notable work onstage, but in film she is perhaps best remembered for her role as Mae in the 1939 classic, *Of Mice and Men*.**

Duvivier was asked if the episodes in *Flesh and Fantasy* would have a link like the coat that provides the connection in *Tales of Manhattan*. The director responded that "They will have something stronger. They have an idea to hold them together." However, Duvivier or Boyer (or more likely Universal) must have had second thoughts about this and added the Robert Benchley framing device, with Benchley doing his usual Joe Doakes routine that he popularized in a number of shorts. David Hoffman, perhaps grateful for having a chance to get his head out of the globe in the "Inner Sanctum" series, turns up here with huge glasses and a toothy grin, coming off like some sort of crazed geek. "Are you trying to sell me insurance?" Benchley asks at one point. It's as good an explanation as any for Hoffman's overzealous insistence on inflicting the stories on Benchley. The scenes are more frivolous than funny, and they don't bother to tell you specifically what Benchley's dilemma is or how the tales help him resolve it.

The first story gets off to a bizarre start as demons hover around a body that has been found in the canal. We soon discover that it's Mardi Gras and the devils are people in costume. The body is presumably that of Cliff, and this would have provided the tie-in to the Gloria Jean segment; without that episode, the suggestion of damnation is lessened. While some speculate the man was a suicide, an elderly bystander tells the story of a man who was haunted by something no one else could see. The poor wretch finally died and the terrible expression on his face resembled that of the person dredged out of the water. This might have made for a better story than the one we see.

It's after this grim beginning that we meet Betty Field's Henrietta. She's a dressmaker, which is perhaps an allusion to "Cinderella," especially as Henrietta dons a beautiful dress, attends a gala, and must return by midnight. Field, just back from maternity leave, was an underused and underrated actress who specialized in off-beat roles like Alma in *Victory* and the tragic Cassie in *King's Row*. Though not unattractive, she was the first to admit she was not beautiful, although she had a winsome, sad quality that certainly made up for it. Here Field is shot to look as drab as possible courtesy of an unbecoming hair-do, a lack of make-up, and low- key lighting. In her early scenes, Field also speaks in a shrill, harsh tone that adds to the unpleasant, shrewish impression. Robert Cummings, on leave from his wartime job as a squadron commander for the Civil Air Patrol, is adequate as Michael, but neither his performance nor the way the character is written really nails down exactly what his problem is.

Boyer originally had hoped to get Walter Huston for the part of the old man, but Huston was busy filming *The North Star* so Universal cast Edgar Barrier instead. Publicity for the film claimed he would be portraying a 105-year-old Civil War veteran, but nothing like that is suggested in the finished film, wherein Barrier's character has a rather sinister billing as "the other." His part is never really explained - though nothing else in the story is, either - and he appears to be just a benign spirit (who turns out to be wearing a mask). He also provides some unnecessary narration. The costume shop has a nice magical feel to it - a bit like Geppetto's workshop in *Pinocchio* - and there's a good moment where Field takes the beautiful mask off the bust to reveal a scowling face underneath.

In *The Enchanted Cottage*, a homely woman and a disfigured war veteran fall in love and come to see each other as beautiful even though the rest of the world perceives the reality, not their shared illusion. However, here Field - in true fairy tale fashion - literally transforms at the ending, the metamorphosis being the result of one unselfish night during which she restores Michael's faith in himself. Something more bittersweet might have worked better. There really doesn't seem to be any thematic link to the other stories though; had the Gloria Jean segment remained, Henrietta could be seen as a contrast to Cliff who, faced with a purity he cannot grasp, returns evil for good. In any case, one would have to agree with the redoubtable Mr. Doakes: "It's a pretty story, but I don't quite get the tie-up."

In Oscar Wilde's **Lord Arthur Saville's Crime,** the main character is young, titled - and entitled - in contrast to Edward G. Robinson's middle-aged American lawyer. The big difference between the film and the story is that Wilde has his character get away with the murder and be none the worse for it, though he is always uneasy when anyone mentions a chieromantist (palm reader). Obviously, that would never do for an American film. Also, in the story, Podgers' readings, while startlingly accurate, are not as remarkable as those in the film. He *could* just be a clever conman who has done his homework on his subjects and makes some good guesses. And what better way to pique someone's curiosity (and pick their pockets) than pretending to see something too terrible in his hand to even speak of? In the film his readings are so on the money that it would be near impossible to doubt him. At one point, he warns Tyler to stay away from White Chapel on his way home; Tyler ignores this advice and is nearly killed when his car is caught in a cross fire between police and crooks. Following that is a particularly effective sequence wherein Tyler wanders through the seedy district in a near daze and even sees an ominous pavement drawing depicting a hanged man dangling in front of a full moon.

As played by Thomas Mitchell, Podgers comes off as a sinister figure masquerading as a harmless eccentric. Podgers' room could be a magician's lair: strange charts looming out of the black, an Expressionistic skylight looking down on the gloomy garret, and a bevy of cats prowling and purring. The roar of a nearby train punctuates Podgers' revelation to Tyler and, as the lawyer exits, a cloud of steam floats through the doorway and surrounds him.

Perhaps Duvivier was influenced by *The Student of Prague*; Tyler continually perceives his reflection as a kind of doppelganger, an evil twin who urges him to get the murder over with. He shows up in mirrors, shop windows, and even in the lawyer's glasses, smirking and cajoling. Perhaps surprisingly, it's never suggested that it's his

377

betrothed he could end up killing if he doesn't commit his predestined crime. His attempt to poison Lady Hardwicke is treated humorously. When he gives the old lady the "medicine," he assures her that she won't need more than one dose and then tells her "Good-bye" in a manner reminiscent of Bela Lugosi in *The Devil Bat.* In the story, Lord Saville befriends an anarchist and obtains a bomb from him which he then sends hidden in a clock to a long-winded clergyman he feels no one will miss, but the bomb is a dud. In the movie, Tyler, having heard the good reverend expound on how death is "the great liberator," takes more direct action and attempts to brain the dean with a mallet, but then loses his nerve.

The climax on London Bridge is particularly effective with its surrounding mists, the lights of the circus in the background below, and the sharp, ominous sound of Podgers's footsteps as he walks inadvertently to his doom. Tyler's final line is chilling - "I'm not a murderer. It was written in my hand" - and Robinson's delivery of it has just the right amount of madness and desperation. The episode is an expert combination of suspense and black humor (one critic opined that the satire would go over the heads of many viewers).

*Flesh and Fantasy* was not Edward G. Robinson's only encounter with the psychic world; he played the leader of a gang of fake spiritualists in *The Hole in the Wall* (1929) and the real thing in *The Night Has a Thousand Eyes* (1948).

Most would agree that the third story is the weakest of the lot, but it at least has a thematic connection to the Robinson segment. Tyler comes to see himself as a pawn of a fate he cannot escape and thus absolves himself of responsibility for his own actions. Gaspar is unnerved by his dream of falling, but in the end refuses to give in to fear and the idea that his accident is inevitable. When he meets Joan, he begins to think he has misinterpreted the dream, that its main point was a glimpse of the woman he was meant to love. His fall could just indicate that their romance will face some obstacles. His dream of Joan getting arrested also turns out to be true, even though it doesn't happen exactly as predicted. In both cases though, Duvivier seems to come down solidly on the reality of supernatural occurrences, but scorns the notion that one should become obsessed with them. They may well be true, but you have to go one living your own life regardless. The story also suggests the mystical notion that Gaspar and Joan are predestined to find each other and be lovers. The thief who reforms because of love is a tiresome *cliché*, and the romance is not very compelling. Moreover, Gaspar is decidedly incurious as to where Joan is going at the end.

Duvivier works up some tension for the scene where Gaspar loses his nerve on the high wire, but the finale, where he overcomes his fear, seems oddly perfunctory.

Grace McDonald, an up-and-coming Universal starlet, has an uncredited bit as Gaspar's assistant. Apparently, Acquanetta was to undertake a similar role and could certainly have been quite decorative in the part but, in the end, she was not used. Clarence Muse's scenes as Gaspar's helper, Jeff, are brief, and bring a little humor to the action. At least his part didn't draw pickets, a situation that occurred when African-Americans objected to the last story of *Tales of Manhattan* wherein the black community is depicted in very stereotypical terms.

**Lawyer Edward G. Robinson is cross-examined by his evil self in the picture's black-comedy second act.**

Alexander Tansman's music - so different from the Universal horror scores fans are familiar with - is powerful and haunting, particularly as the opening credits roll and it is played over eerie shots (negative film?) of trees and mist. Tansman's music becomes serene for the end credits when the same forest is seen at sunrise. Tansman was a Polish refugee who pursued a successful career in France before fleeing when the Nazis took over. He also did the score for Duvivier's 1932 version of *Poil de carotte*.

*Flesh and Fantasy* premiered in Cincinnati. According to the trades, Universal subsequently spent $250,000 promoting the film. Many of the ads for the movie emphasized the all-star cast, but there was plenty of the usual hokum, including the hiring of Hungarian psychic and hypnotist, Franz Julius Polger, to read the minds of movie patrons who had just seen *Flesh and Fantasy*. Polger would then write their thoughts on a blackboard. "Thrilling" and "A unique picture" were some of the responses; apparently, Dr. Polger didn't waste chalk on anyone who might have thought, "It stunk."

Also piquing public interest in the film was Betty Field playing in a radio adaptation of her segment on *The Kate Smith Hour*. Later Boyer and Robinson also did radio versions of their episodes.

Newspaper reviewers were appreciative of the film's attempt at novelty, but were not always impressed with the results.

> Take the picture by and large and it is unsatisfying. Vaguely expressed is the idea is the idea that dreams and fortunetellers presage happenings in the lives of men and that there are unseen forces of considerable power governing their destinies. What actually happens during the sequences is not always what the individual characters anticipate what will happen from their forebodings. It is a rather nebulous set of motifs that are presented in the film. These will find some observers, who like the occult, going all out for the picture but the majority, perhaps, not so easily won over. 'Flesh and Fantasy,' however, will not fail to evoke discussion.
>
> Edwin Schallert, *The Los Angeles Times*, 10 December 1943.

The reviewer for the 12 November 1943 edition of the *The Christian Science Monitor* was more impressed:

> A departure from customary patterns of motion picture entertainment... All the stories illustrate the lesson that man can and should cast fear out of his consciousness. An element of mysticism enters all the stories but, as no attempt has been made to explain the premonitions, none will be offered here. Rather these stories should be accepted for what they are worth as entertainment and as general character lessons set forth in fiction form.

T.M.P of the 18 November 1943 edition of *The New York Times* had mixed feeling about the film:

> If your interest in dreams and the predictions of fortune-tellers is as indifferent as this observer's, then chances are you will regard

this three -episode Universal film as just so much palaver. For at its best, notwithstanding its novelty, "Flesh and Fantasy" is an uneven entertainment….All the aforementioned performers and some others in lesser roles give competent, if not outstanding characterizations. It is in the film's conception and script its shortcomings lie. Still it is, as they say, "different." And even if the stories do not come off as well as they might, there is a great deal to be said for the picture's variety.

A film of this nature necessarily is lacking in conventional form and dramatic unity. It does not however want for romantic and dramatic interest, flashes of humor and occasional passages of great and moving beauty… The production is one that lends itself to the mood of the moment, attaining "atmospheric" effects that are by turns fantastic, eerie, and startlingly realistic. Duvivier's direction is beyond cavil-as it usually is.

Nelson B. Bell, *The Washington Post*, 14 January, 1944

Most of the trade paper reviews were favorable, but the 22 September 1943 issue of *The Exhibitor* questioned the picture's appeal, saying that "While this has a number of well-known film personalities it may tend to leave audiences for the most part with a depressed and empty feeling." Likewise, Walt Livingstone of *Motion Picture Daily* (17 September 1943) had doubts about viewer response: "Art with a capital "A" and of dubious entertainment value… Audiences must supply the answer as to whether they want motion pictures of this type."

However, Walt of *Variety* (22 September 1943) was onboard:

This is a decidedly novel and unusual picture… Duvivier directs in careful style. Injecting European style of piloting with concentration on incidents that build up into prominence and withal holding to a steady and generally suspenseful pace. Production, mounting and technical contributions are of A caliber, including both photography and background music.

The 17 September 1943 *Film Daily* was likewise positive:

The picture deals with a subject that will strongly attract the mature minds. For those who will find the thought-provoking aspects of the story and the mystic and psychic implications a bit above their taste and their thinking there is a high -powered cast to draw them and sustain their interest. With the film offering something both to lure intelligent persons and mental laggards there is little cause to worry about the box office performance of "Flesh and Fantasy" which has been told with a strong sense of irony and a touch of the macabre.

While *Flesh and Fantasy* was a hit in the big cities, small town reaction was a different story:

> "One of the poorest pictures of the year." (Loveland, Ohio)
>
> "Business was fair but audience reaction was mixed. As a finished production this picture was creditable but we would not care to book another similar one." (Scotia, California)
>
> "When people heard about this they clamored to see it but once they saw it they didn't care for it. Everybody says the first two stories were good but the one with Charles Boyer was no good. Not as good as everyone thought it would be." (Heart Mountain, Wyoming)
>
> "Here's probably the worst Sunday feature I have run. Passing remarks were not good, had a few walkouts." (Randolph, Nebraska)
>
> "Although the weather was very bad with snow and sleet this picture did the lowest Sunday-Monday gross in this theater for the past seven years. Form your own conclusions. It had no box office power for this small town." (Marshfield, Missouri)
>
> "Wow, what a shellacking we took with on this. We had the poorest business in months and many walked out." (Hay Springs, Nebraska)
>
> "Only a fair show. No high profits on it." (Jarvis, Ontario, Canada)

There were fewer "mental laggards" South of the Border where the film was a big hit and won an enthusiastic response from the Mexican Film Journalist Association.

Duvivier returned to France after the war and faced some criticism for leaving during the Occupation. While his very best work may have been behind him, he still helmed a number of notable films, including the excellent thriller, *Panique*, and the light-hearted *Don Camillo* series that pitted a parish priest against his village's Communist mayor. Many would say Duvivier did not get the respect he deserved as the French New Wave came to dominate the cinema, and its advocates failed to put him in the same league with such other greats as René Clair and Jean Renoir. Duvivier did two other films in the portmanteau vein, *Under the Paris Sky* (1951) and *The Devil and the Ten Commandments* (1962), as well as a wicked satire of film-making, *Holiday for Henrietta* (1952). One of his last movies was an adaptation of John Dickson Carr's complex thriller, **The Burning Court**. Admirers of the novel - and there were many - did not feel the film did the book justice. The movie - kind of an old dark house mystery - is indeed hard to follow, and Duvivier's direction does not demonstrate his usual imagination though there are a few eerie moments.

Fans of Universal horror rarely have much to say about *Flesh and Fantasy*. There's none of the trashy fun that can be found in many of the studio's "B"-movies of the '40s and some consider the film only borderline horror. The movie sets its sights higher than most of its shambling brethren, but it is all the more disappointing for not living up completely to its lofty goals.

***Flesh and Fantasy*** - 29 October 1943 - 94 minutes

**CAST**: Framing story: Robert Benchley as Doakes; David Hoffmann as Davis; 1st Episode: Betty Field as Henrietta; Robert Cummings as Michael; Marjorie Lord as Justine; Edgar Barrier as the Other; Charles Halton as the Mask Shop Proprietor; Eddie Acuff as the Policeman; Clinton Rosemond as the Old Black Man; Paul Bryan as Harlequin; George Lewis as Harlequin; Peter Lawford as Pierrot; Lord Chandler as Satan; Gil Patrick as Death; Jacqueline Dalya, Sandra Morgan, Phil Warren, Carla Vernell ; 2nd episode: Edward G. Robinson as Marshall Tyler; Thomas Mitchell as Septimus Podgers; Anna Lee as Rowena; Dame May Whitty as Lady Pamela Hardwick; C. Aubrey Smith as the Dean of Chichester; Leyland Hodges as Policeman; Edward Fielding as Sir Thomas; Heather Thatcher as Lady Flora; Mary Forbes as Lady Thomas; Ian Wolfe as Librarian; Harold de Becker, Anita Bolster; Ferdinand Munier, Lawrence Grossmith, Constance Purdy, Doris Lloyd, Harry Stubbs, Olaf Hytten, Paul Scott, Jack Gardner, Bruce Lester, Geoffrey Steele; 3rd episode: Charles Boyer as Gaspar; Barbara Stanwyck as Joan; Charles Winninger as King Lamar; Clarence Muse as Jeff; Grace McDonald as Gaspar's Assistant; June Lang as Angel; Con Colleano (subbing for Boyer on the high wire), Marcel Dallio, Frank Arnold, Lane Chandler, Frank Mitchell, Jerry Maren, Janette Fern, Beatrice Barrette, Nedra Sanders, Nolan Leary.

**CREDITS**: Director: Julien Duviver; Producers: Charles Boyer, Julien Duvivier; Writers: Ernest Pascal, Samuel Hoffenstein, Ellis St. Joseph; Photographers: Stanley Cortez, Paul Ivano; Art Directors: John Goodman, Richard Riedel, Robert Boyle; Film Editor: Arthur Hilton; Set Decorators: Russell A. Gausman, E.R. Robinson; Costumes: Edith Head, Vera West; Music: Alexander Tansman (score), Charles Previn (Musical Director); Sound: Bernard Brown, Joe Lapis; Make-up: Jack Pierce; Assistant Directors: Joseph A. McDonough, Seward Webb; Dialogue Director: Don Brodie

*- HN*

# *Son of Dracula* (1943)

Early on in the '30s, Universal was populated in part by a seemingly endless supply of nightmare-inducing critters. The imagination of Victorian-Age authors initially provided the studio with the lion's share of same, and for a while – regardless of whether they issued from the crypt, off the operating table, or via hypodermic injection – said grotesques fascinated the ticket-buying public by their very novelty. While capturing the hearts and minds of Depression-Era audiences was undeniably important to the Laemmles and their corporate kith, capturing their box office revenue was primo, so the time quickly came when follow-up misadventures for the most profitable of "classic" monsters needed to be planned. Actually, this sort of thing had been plotted at length a few years earlier, when – on paper, at any rate - Lon Chaney Sr. was being maneuvered into reprising his role as the Erik, the disfigured Opera Ghost, in *Return of the Phantom*. It wasn't for a lack of trying that the idea went nowhere; it was that Chaney went somewhere else – M-G-M – and Universal has to be satisfied with a part-talkie re-release of its 1925 cash cow.

Nonetheless, plans were made for other well-liked horrors to reappear, their climactic comeuppances first time 'round be damned. Junior Laemmle announced that one of his very first projects as head of his own production unit would be *The Return of Frankenstein*. That famed and fearsome surname had belonged to Colin Clive's character but had been appropriated by the masses to refer to the Monster. Thus, the title was ultimately changed to the no-less-coy *Bride of Frankenstein* as, with both Clive and Karloff in the sequel, it was bloody obvious to either school of proprietary nomenclature that "Frankenstein" had returned. (Come decade's end, the argument as to exactly who was the *Son* of Frankenstein would pick up where *Bride* had left off:

385

sure, Basil Rathbone's Wolf bore the name Colin Clive's Henry/Heinrich had lugged about with him for two pictures, but could this be Karloff's "original" Monster? *That* Monster had been scarred, disheveled, ragged, and blown to bits at the end of the 1935 entry. *This* Monster was hale and hearty, boasted a full head of hair, wore a fleece, and hung out with his homeboy. Tell me again about this "Son" of Frankenstein...?)

In 1940, the first of the aforementioned "nightmare-inducing critters" back in through the lobby doors and unto the screen again was the Invisible Man. For the title of his second "appearance," the massively non-creative and profoundly over-used noun *Return* was retained rather than rejected, but in circumstances that were substantially misleading. Given that the wearer of the gauze and goggles on the bounce was not the chap who started the fashion in the first place, the picture ought well to have been *An Invisible Man Returns*. Still, no one complained. (A couple of years down the road, the second Chaney/Kharis venture would be announced as *The Mummy Returns*; prior to release, it was retitled *The Mummy's Ghost*, a move that impacted the quality of the film not at all, but at least rid it of the titular dreariness to which the studio's horror arm was prone.)

And when it was determined that certain of those original characters weren't quite set to reemerge to appreciative applause themselves, their relatives appeared from nowhere to fill the void. There was no misguided confusion *a la* Frankenstein's heir over Dracula's daughter, even if the sudden appearance of that statuesque blood-relative gave some pause for thought regarding the count who had mesmerized viewers five years earlier. Had there been *any* indication in the '31 film that the man from Transylvania had indulged in any such extracurricular activities of the flesh – even via an *en passant* mention during his back-story, so painstakingly related by the first of the talkies' Dr. Van Helsings - the Hays Office would have quickly put the kibosh on the scene in a Carfax-Abbey minute. Audiences were given no inkling as to the identity of the mother of the Countess Zaleska (nee Dracula), but it really didn't matter: what intrigued viewers was the prospect of viewing the machinations of the daughter of *Dracula*, and not of the sweetums of Lady Someone-or-Another who let that fateful caress on the neck back when take her *way* too far.

As the decades passed, other horrific offspring came to our attention – per the14 July 1945 edition of *Motion Picture Herald*, "PRC has purchased two original stories, 'The Mummy's Daughter' and 'Prison Farm'," but nothing came of the title of interest to us - and while their paternity may have been up there in the picture's name, uncertainty followed onscreen. In 1951, for example, we learned that Dr. Jekyll had had a son, but it took another six years before it came out that the old boy had had a daughter as well. Given the circumstances featured in that brace of semi-biographical films, might we not suggest that both were much more likely to have been sired by Mr. Hyde? And while 1958 turned out to be the *annus natalis* of *Frankenstein's Daughter* – the first of many, if subsequent TV and movie credits are to be believed – it was also our first inkling that the Monster had been spreading a great deal more than dread over the years. What the Fabulous Fifties did *not* bring us was news of *Kharis's Kid* or *Little Critters from the Black Lagoon* or even *Womb of the Wolf Woman*. (An innate moral sense precluded any canoodling between the Invisible Man and his leading lady of the moment: how would she know he was about to put the move on her?)

"Keep looking in my eyes! When you awaken, you will have no recollection of ever having worn a shirt and tie today!" Count Alucard (Chaney) seems to about to use a kung-fu maneuver on an exhausted Frank Stanley (Robert Paige).

Television and direct-to-video productions would make clear the sheer volume of progeny sired by the Monster and the Vampire King over the centuries, but it was back in November of 1943 that the world first found out that Countess Zaleska had a brother; by a different mother, perhaps, but with the same sperm donor. I found this out personally via an ad for *Son of Dracula* in *TV Guide* in 1957, and my seven-year-old self couldn't wait. The Count had always held a particular fascination for me: his comparatively ordinary appearance belied incredible powers, and I found it both intriguing and frightening that he could wander amidst normal men without being spotted for what he was. I had also enjoyed Bela Lugosi very much – neither I nor any of the other members of our monster club had ever seen anybody quite like him.

Well, the TV screening came and went, and while I was tickled to death that the "son" of Dracula was apparently the Count, himself, I was as confused as hell as to why the movie had such a specious title in the first place. Some 60 years later, with more than a score of viewings under my belt, I'm still perplexed. The best that I can come up with goes like this: although the original film was over a dozen years old by 1943, and despite his having appeared in the interim in lots of movies for lots of other studios, Bela Lugosi was indelibly associated by the public with the role of Dracula. From time to time the actor still trod the boards with the Deane-Balderston play, much of the publicity he received in conjunction with other of his films, plays, and/or personal appearances reinforced his identity as "The Dracula Man," and it was plain fact that many of the mannerisms Bela took with him from one picture to another had first been seen (and not just in embryonic form, either) in his portrayal of the thirsty Count. For most interested ticket-buyers, Bela Lugosi *was* Dracula, and Universal knew it.

Not that Universal liked it much. By 1943, the friction over the moody Hungarian's *Frankenstein* debacle was ancient history; nobody gave a rat's ass that Bela had inconvenienced Junior Laemmle back in 1931. This time, the company was cheesed about his *Frankenstein Meets the Wolf Man* debacle. The studio brass felt that the aging actor's performance as the Monster had caused setbacks in filming and had incurred additional expense. Needing a scapegoat to cover any damage done by execrable writing to an interesting concept, Universal unloaded on Bela, and artist and studio parted company. His receiving consideration in re: the revival of his signature role was therefore out of the question; it would take a virtually new organization – Universal-International – to bring Bela's Count (and a welcome sense of equilibrium) back to the San Fernando Valley five years after *Son*. The studio's "classic image" of Dracula would find its Alpha and Omega in the proud figure of Bela Blasko, the Man from Lugos.

Even had there not been hard feelings all around, Lugosi could not have accommodated *Son*'s shooting schedule, as he was involved with *Return of the Vampire*, Columbia's answer to both *Dracula* and *The Wolf Man*. This happy circumstance gave Universal an out when Lugosiphiles and Dracula purists railed about the questionable casting of the title character in the new vampire movie: Mr. Lugosi is just not available. Equally useful (and equally ludicrous) would be the insistence that while the titular vampire may have shopped at the same haberdasher, he was Count Alucard, and not you-know-who. By the time the truth came out, the ticket-buyer's quarter was in a Wells Fargo truck, headed for Universal City. (Shot in the summer of '43, *Return of the Vampire* wasn't released until early 1944, as Columbia didn't want to compete for the vampiric box-office-take with *Son of Dracula*, released in November.)

Chaney is Count Alucard, a vampire bearing the absolute easiest anagram in the world for his real name, and he has been invited to visit Dark Oaks, a somewhere-in-the-South sort-of-plantation owned by the dark lioness, Katherine Caldwell. When Alucard doesn't show up for the party being held in his honor, Katherine's boyfriend, Frank Stanley – who, along with the cranky Dr. Brewster, had been sent to fetch the nobleman – return to Dark Oaks, but scarcely has the party begun when Katherine's dad is discovered dead in his bedroom. Within moments of screen time, Alucard shows up, Brewster doesn't take long to play the backwards-name-game, and – apparently up on his vampiric lore – makes contact with Professor Lazlo, who makes a living fighting off bloodsuckers. Not long thereafter, Frank is shocked – shocked! – to discover that Katherine (aka Kay) and Alucard have been married. He is *so* shocked he lets loose with his pistol at Alucard but manages to kill only Kay.

He is *more* shocked the next day, when – heading over to turn himself in – he hears Brewster tell of having spoken with Kay *after* the fusillade had hit the fan. Still, Frank's arrested for murder when the sheriff finds Kay in repose in her family's crypt. Brewster consults Lazlo, who then spells out the plot twist – Kay has allowed herself to be vampirized so as to vampirize Frank so that the two of them can live forever. Damned if Lazlo isn't spot on! That night, bat-Kay floats in through Frank's cell window (she obviously hasn't learned the mist-thing yet), sucks some of his blood, then awakens him and virtually affirms everything Lazlo had said. Frank somehow escapes, heads to the brush near the old drainage tunnel and gets a fire going in the count's casket. Alucard returns, a fight breaks out, but – providentially – the sun rises and Frank's romantic rival is reduced to bone. Franks hies back to the Dark Oaks attic – wherein Kay and casket are now stored – and, slipping a wedding ring on her finger, sets *her* alight, as well. Lazlo, Brewster, the sheriff and Frank watch as the cleansing fire makes all things right once again.

Let's not waste more than a moment to wonder how the sheriff's catching Frank burning his ex-fiancée's corpse will somehow mitigate those murder charges, shall we? This sort of thing is called willful suspension of belief, legal-style.

There's little doubt that *Son of Dracula* was conceived with Lon Chaney in mind pretty much from the start or that it was to prove the last of the studio's classic grotesques which the "Master Character Creator" would portray. (Chaney "created" only one of the nightmares with whom he became associated – the Wolf Man; the boots, bandages, and patent-leather pumps he slipped on later had been broken in by the previous decade's "Master Character Creators.") From comments made by Reginald Le Borg and others to Tom Weaver and others, it would appear that the suave, passionate, and coldly menacing Dracula was a dream role for Chaney. Never happy with heavy-make-up assignments (although justifiably proud and fiercely protective of his hirsute "baby"), the actor continually wondered why he wasn't cast in "bigger" pictures in which he got (or at least got close to) the girl and was allowed to display a romantic touch. Had he taken a closer look at the *SoD* script, the "romantic" elements therein might have made the junior Chaney long for his yak hair and Fuller's earth.

The entire story of *Son* is a clever reversal on the cinematic Dracula myth up to that point. Whereas Lugosi kept a harem of the undead and had established women as his prey of choice, Chaney's Count is virtually a kept man – imported, exploited, and sold down the river – who seems to favor attacking old, crippled men and little boys. While Bela's vampire had sailed into England on his own initiative and had proudly operated under his own name and title, Lon's is dragged into the deep South in some bogus baggage and inexplicably bears an easily uncovered alias. The original Dracula had been the psychic and physical master of his brides; the retread is little more than just another schmo who thinks he's in the saddle but is being galloped into the ground. Things can't get much more pathetic for the Count than for him to boast that "I am now master of this house!" when he's being forced to bed down in the brush besides an old drainage tunnel.

And when it comes to placing Dracula in charge, some of the film's visuals are as hapless as its dialogue. The scene wherein Kay drives her undead honey to the justice of the peace was obviously meant to be unsettling because of its incongruity. The sight of the two hustling arm-in-arm up to the judge's door, though, plays much more like the woeful results of a Sadie Hawkins' Day chase than the precision unfolding of the canny plans of the King of the Vampires. And as for the incongruous "Alucard and the shovel" vignette: just why is he wasting his time digging? Kay doesn't need a box of native earth; a swoon in any direction for some thousand miles around will put her in contact with all the soil she could ever need. Anyhow, sticking her in the family crypt or parking her in the attic bedroom seems to satisfy all the union requirements.

And as the Count certainly can't use any good old USA loam for himself – forget that he already has a casket-full in the bushes, somewhere - why all the exertion? A few minutes with "Alucard" and you wonder how he managed to make it through the past week, let alone the centuries granted him by Stoker.

For all the baloney, *Son of Dracula* is a visually beautiful film. Director Robert Siodmak's steady hand, coupled with George Robinson's practiced eye, stirs up an ever-swirling series of chiaroscuro images. Light and darkness play off each other here in an almost stylistic throwback to the '30s; the palette is reminiscent of James Whale and John Mescall in *Bride of Frankenstein*, or of Edward Ulmer and Mescall in *The Black Cat*. (Siodmak had co-directed *Menschen am Sonntag* with Ulmer for Ufa in 1929.) If no one could figure out how to rob the vampire of his shadow under Hollywood cinematic lighting conditions, Siodmak milked that shadow – and others – for all they were worth. The picture constantly moves; even talking-head sequences unreel against backgrounds of wispy smoke or mobile shadow-play. And, as if echoing the dramatic reversal of the kinky plot line, Siodmak chose to film many of Dracula's (and Kay's, once she is undead) advances from behind while covering most retreats head-on. In his autobiography, **Wolf Man's Maker**, Curt Siodmak relates how it was he who got his brother Robert the director's job on *Son of Dracula*.

> Writing B picture screenplays for Universal and worried about Robert's career, I practically forced my producer, Jack Gross, to give Robert the director's job on my screenplay *Son of Dracula*. As soon as he got the assignment, the power of the sibling competition made him replace me with yet another writer, Eric Taylor.(1)

Picking up his telling of the tale again later in the book, Siodmak reveals not only his brother's gratitude, but some of Lon Chaney's more bizarre behaviors:

> ...Lon was wrongly cast. Bela Lugosi should have played the part. Lon was on his worst behavior. His pet peeve was the then-reigning studio queen, Maria Montez. One night, Lon, in a drunken bout, threw feces at the bungalow shingle with Maria's name on it. In an alcoholic spell during shooting, he broke a vase over Robert's head. But Robert, always attracted to eccentric people, found Lon's behavior amusing. He was used to high-strung actors.(2)

Elsewhere - in a caption under a publicity still from the film in the photo section, Siodmak lauds his brother's artful technique, but goes a bit overboard when he claims that Robert's "employment of light and shadow [created] a new style in motion pictures." Despite such praise, the Siodmak brothers never worked together in motion pictures.

With a couple of exceptions, the special effects are grand. Good old John Fulton, having already spanned the cosmos and conquered invisibility, succeeds in having the decidedly substantial Chaney metamorphose in and out of unearthly mist and into an oversized bat. (The bat, however, conspires to change perspective from scene to scene. When it flaps its way down the hall en route to the Colonel's jugular vein, it clears the sides of the alcove by mere inches; in the cemetery, while about to nuzzle the unconscious Frank Stanley, it's measurably less impressive. Equally unimpressive is the fact that the keen-eyed viewer can catch Alucard's mirror'd reflection once that *grandísimo* specimen has changed back into the Count. For all this kvetching, this was the first time a vampire had transformed into a bat or from mist onscreen, and we hereby raise a glass to Mr. Fulton!) Chaney's appearance at the swamp, though, is the stuff of which nightmares are made. In studied succession, his casket merges from under the surface; the mist emitted takes the form of the implacable Alucard, and – with the silence of said tomb – the earth-box bears its master to the nearby shore. Major points here, as throughout, to Hans J. Salter's exciting score, to John Goodman and Martin Obzina's superb art direction, and to Russell A. Gausman and Edward R. Robinson's exhaustive attention to detail.

Midway through its second great horror cycle, Universal was still paying lip-service to the minutiae of the vampire mythos it had brought to the screen in 1931. As Alucard had already been invited to Dark Oaks by Kay, there is no need for the maudlin manservant to ask him to enter. Later, though – unless some speedy, off-screen snookery has been effected – no one utters the words which allow him to invade Dr. Brewster's digs. (And why doesn't vampire-bat-Kay need to be invited into Frank's jail cell?) Another note of contention is the cemetery scene, which seems to indicate that there is little problem with the Count alighting on hallowed ground; still, it may be persuasively argued that he lands on *Frank* and not on the ground itself. Then, too, the chilling marks of the vampire on little Tommy's nicks are dismissed rather peremptorily via a pair of iodine-rendered crosses; such facile treatment foreshadowed the day when fearsome bloodsuckers would be held at bay by crossed swords (*The Fearless Vampire Killers*, 1967), crossed candlesticks (*Horror of Dracula*, 1958), a cross-shaped coat-hanger (in *Tempi Duri per I Vampiri*, 1958), or even crossed arms (*Dr. Terror's House of Horrors*, 1964).

Although dressed to the nines (his white vest front *does* appear to belong to someone at least six inches shorter than he), Chaney can't pass muster and deliver the goods as Alucard or Dracula or whomever. If critics of his performance in *The Ghost of Frankenstein* lamented that the actor failed to present the Monster as possessed of anything other than inhuman strength, how much more would pertinent would that observation be when directed at the multi-dimensional Dracula? The Chaney Count is undeniably a powerhouse, but a wily, silver-tongued devil? A juggernaut in battle, perhaps, but a past-master of cunning and intrigue? Lon's Alucard is most assuredly a supremely capable foot-soldier, but not for a moment is he credible as a princely leader of great armies.

As much as must have cherished the opportunity to wear the soup-and-fish and sport that dapper little mustache, Chaney had to know that the inevitability of the forthcoming comparisons was up there with death and taxes. Following Lugosi's in the part of Dracula was more akin to stepping into Karloff's boots as the Monster than shuffling along in Tom Tyler's wake as Kharis. The Frankenstein Monster had displayed pathos and an offbeat charisma via the undeniably substantial talent of the mild-mannered Karloff. Lugosi, on the other hand, was a vivid, eccentric personality who had imbued the Count with his own hubris. Neither so innately capable as the former, nor as stylishly *recherché* as the latter, Chaney brought little to the role save for his willingness to follow Siodmak's direction to the letter. Taking all this into consideration, it's almost impossible to go into *Son of Dracula* without rooting for Chaney, and, to a certain extent, the big guy comes through. Alucard may not be able to knock back a timeless quote with anything like panache – Eric Taylor's script, albeit clever, didn't deliver much that *was* timeless – but he can toss the ostensible hero through the French doors with the flick of a wrist. And Lon's Count can *move*; there's no way *he'd* take 20 minutes to stride across the foyer toting someone's suitcase. One can even overlook his occasional wide-eyed stare or tendency at scary-face-making in light of the chiseled look of sheer, cold hatred with which he sends Frank Stanley stumbling out into the night air. Sadly, the spell is broken the moment he opens his mouth.

Lenny Smalls' classic questions apart, dialogue would never be Chaney's forte. While nobody but nobody would deny the "Master Character Creator" total ownership of the Wolf Man, there are those who would have much preferred that the dual role had been split and that someone else had mouthed the Larry Talbot half.

Nonetheless, as one-dimensional as his Monster or his Mummy may have been, the sheer physicality of the roles brought out the best in Chaney; bereft of the power of speech, both creatures were simple engines of violence, and "simple" and "engine of violence" were what Chaney did well. In contrast, virtually all of his contrived "Inner Sanctum" parts – requiring as they did the capacity to deliver one's convoluted thoughts coherently while convincingly furrowing one's brow in deep cogitation – resulted time and again in a portrait not of a genius in turmoil, but of a pretentious clod whose fear at being found out has just become the least of his worries.

**Lon Chaney visits Susanna Foster on the set of _Phantom of the Opera_. Denied on this occasion the chance to sport a mask as had his Dad, later in the year Junior would at least don an opera cloak and follow in the footsteps of his _character's_ Dad... sort of.**

To be fair – and as noted above – the Count hasn't a single memorable/quotable thing to say this time around. (The juiciest bit in the piece goes to Queen Zimba, the Swamp Witch, whose "I see you marrying a corpse, living in a grave..." snags the brass ring and would even be featured prominently on the Realart rerelease posters.)

Many of the '31 Lugosi-isms – which are still being bandied about today – had either been purloined outright from the Stoker novel or adapted from the Deane-Balderston play. Eric Taylor's screenplay for *Son of Dracula* was based on an original story by Curt Siodmak, and its chief strength is its novel inversion of the saga's more traditional elements. The stuff Lon was required to voice ranges from a stylistic lack of credibility (his referring to his homeland in his flat, mid-Western accent leads one to imagine Alucard pining for Kansas City) to the completely ludicrous (his literally being relegated to the refuse heap after delivering the arrogant "Master of the House" bit). Chaney's cadence is as careful as his pronunciation is meticulous, and he tries his damnedest to create the impression that Dark Oaks has a genuine foreigner in its midst. The turgid dialogue works against him, though, and his vampire seems less a glib and multi-lingual aristocrat than a smug bully who has memorized a series of all-purpose threats.

Evelyn Ankers isn't around long enough to do more than raise her eyebrows, but Robert Paige does one hell of a job as Frank Stanley. Figuring mightily in the economics of reversal outlined above, Frank is the opposite of any hero that horror pictures had depicted to that point. Your typical stick of handsome human furniture at the picture's outset, Frank quickly degenerates into a less-than-admirable (but highly realistic) figure who's not above casually dismissing Queen Zimba's death, throwing tantrums, spying on his girlfriend, or even trying to shoot down in cold blood an unarmed rival who had earlier bested him physically. Unlike other granite-jawed pretty boys out of stock, Frank can't size up the situation at hand in an instant and do the noble or heroic thing. He's frantic, dazed, and beside himself for most of the film's second half, and only 1943 movie convention allows us to predict that this blight of vampirism will be eradicated before the end titles hit the screen. This catharsis doesn't seem to do Frank much good, though, and *Son* effectively pulls a 180 on the genre's requisite happy endings by focusing on his numbed and shattered figure as the love of his life goes up in flames.

Ankers' sparse role in the proceedings gave her a well-earned break from being the perennial target of menace, but that left it to Louise Albritton to put to rest any conventions horror-film heroines might have enjoyed to that point. While in some alternate universe Kay's motivation (eternal life and love with the man she claims to adore) might be considered almost preternaturally noble, her machinations might also lead to her being seen as a conniving, heartless bitch. Sure, Alucard/Dracula is a monstrous icon of evil who is well deserving of the fate that awaits him, but, as delineated in the Eric Taylor treatment, he is also the shadowed remnant of an aristocrat who, we assume, is looking to abjure the trappings of the nobility, settle down with the little woman, and man the graveyard shift just like every other working...*errrr*...stiff. Watching Dracula being led down the primrose path emotionally and intellectually is hard enough, but having him outsmarted by one who, per cinematic-horror tradition, would fall victim without so much as a fight... by one who, per cinematic-horror tradition, would rely upon the astuteness and resolve of others almost by default... by one, who... Oh, Stuff and Nonsense!... *by a woman* must have struck hard some chords that usually went untouched in viewers of the era. Ms. Albritton abjures the usual damsel-in-distress conceit, and makes it clear that the failure of her scheme lay not with her meticulous planning or intestinal fortitude, but with Frank's perceived "weakness," even if said "weakness" was, in fact, his moral compass. Kay Caldwell may not be at all admirable, but Louise Albritton is wonderful.

With the miscasting of the Son of the Man of a Thousand Faces as the ersatz son of the man who turned out to be himself, *Son of Dracula* is one of the best of Universal's '40s genre offerings. Penalizing a movie for not being what it might have been had another played the lead is a useless passion; the film we have is the film we have, and it's a damned good one. Methinks it would have been even better had it eliminated J. Edward Bromberg's haughty Professor Lazlo. A coke-bottle-glasses-wearing Van Helsing clone, Lazlo is really unnecessary at this point, especially in a picture that delights in turning the same-old inside out. Sure, he explains that vampires can float about as a cloud of mist, but, as Alucard demonstrates this twice, what *have* we learned? Why must we also be forced to sit through *two* explanations of Kay's master plan? Couldn't the scenarist have left the dramatic unfolding to the vampiress and had Lazlo actually reveal something we might have wondered about? Like why didn't Kay's dad – old Colonel Caldwell – mosey back into the parlor looking for blood the night after *he* was bitten? What *would* have also been interesting to hear would be the definitive reason as to why vampires react so to the cross, but NOOOO! By 1943 – after anyone interested in the Dracula mythos would have definitely seen both the original film and the subsequent tale of the Countess - this know-it-all from elsewhere is a superfluous weight who drags the picture's pace to crawl whenever he's onscreen.

Although Chaney's effort is apparent and Louise Albritton's "heroine" is the genre's most Machiavellian ever, *Son of Dracula* remains a provocative and entertaining foray into the always popular world of the undead.

*Son of Dracula* – 5 November 1943 – 78 minutes (ST)

**CAST:** Lon Chaney as Count Alucard/Count Dracula; Louise Albritton as Katherine Caldwell; Robert Paige as Frank Stanley; Evelyn Ankers as Claire Caldwell; Frank Craven as Dr. Harry Brewster; J. Edward Bromberg as Professor Lazlo; Samuel S. Hinds as Judge Simmons; Adeline de Walt Reynolds as Queen Zimba; George Irving as Colonel Caldwell; Etta McDaniel as Sarah; Patrick Moriarty as Sheriff Dawes; Walter Sande as Matt; Cyril Delevanti as Dr. Peters; Joan Blair as Mrs. Land; Charles Bates as Tommy Land; Jess Lee Brooks as Steven; Sam McDaniel as Andy; Charles Moore as Matthew; Robert Dudley as Jonathan Kirby; Emmett Moore as Servant; Jack Rockwell as Deputy Sheriff; George Meeker as Part Guest, with Ben Erway, Robert Hill

**CREDITS**: Producer: Ford Beebe; Director: Robert Siodmak; Associate Producer: Donald H. Brown; Executive Producer: Jack Gross; Screenplay: Eric Taylor; Original Story: Curt Siodmak; Director of Photography: George Robinson; Film Editor: Saul A. Goodkind; Art Directors: John B. Goodman and Martin Obzina; Musical Director: Hans J. Salter; Set Directors: Russell A. Gausman and Edward R. Robinson; Assistant Director: Melville Shyer; Sound Director: Bernard B. Brown; Technician: Charles Carroll; Special Effects: John P. Fulton; Make-Up: Jack P. Pierce; Gowns: Vera West

*Shock Theater* Catalog No. 736: "Alucard or Dracula? It doesn't matter which way you look at it when *Shock* brings to your screen 'Son of Dracula' (day), at (time) on channel... You won't want to miss Lon Chaney and Louise Albritton in this chill-drama about that famous vampire. It's a feature film premiere."

*- JTS*

# *The Mad Ghoul* (1943)

*Synopsis*: Chemistry professor Dr. Alfred Morris has been able to recreate a deadly gas used by the Mayans in their rituals. Anyone who inhales the gas enters into a zombie-like "death in life" (or "life in death") trance that can only be broken with a combination of herbs and a human heart taken from a living person or one recently deceased. Morris is infatuated with Isabel, a singer who is engaged to Ted Allison, a skilled surgeon who is also Morris's assistant. When Isabel confides in Morris that she no longer loves Ted, Morris convinces himself that it is he Isabel really loves. Morris exposes Ted to the gas, and he is instantly transformed into a corpse-like creature with no will of his own.

A grave is robbed to extract a human heart so that Ted might be returned to normal, but he is left with no clear recollection of what has happened. Ted periodically lapses into his monster state, so Morris and he must continue to rifle graves, confounding the police while generating some sensational news stories. They are forced to murder a couple of living donors as well: a caretaker who interrupts them and reporter Ken McClure, whose trap for the ghouls backfires.

Morris discovers that Isabel is actually in love with her pianist, Eric Iverson, and sends Ted out to murder him and then commit suicide. However, Ted has finally caught on to what Morris has been doing to him and tricks the doctor into entering the lab after he's turned on the gas. Morris frantically tries to get Ted's help in procuring another heart, but Ted, now transformed into the monster, can only follow Morris's last command. Ted is shot dead by the police when he attempts to kill Eric during one of Isabel's concert performances, and a note of explanation is found in his pocket. Dr. Morris perishes from his own evil experiment while desperately trying to dig up another grave.

399

Audiences going to see *The Mad Ghoul* likely had little idea of what sort of monster to expect. In Eastern mythology and lore, a ghoul is a corpse-eating demon; the word itself is from an English translation of an "Arabian Nights" tale. Unlike the vampire, the ghoul did not engender any significant literature, and the word came to be synonymous with "grave-robber." In the movies, grave-robbers were either after loot (*Frankenstein Meets the Wolf Man*), in search of the corpses needed for experiments (*Frankenstein* et al), or intent on selling the bodies as cadavers (all those Burke and Hare variations). The first time the word "ghoul" was heard on the screen was likely in 1932's *White Zombie*, but it's doubtful that anyone recognized it as such since it was enunciated by Joseph Cawthorn - that film's Yiddish Van Helsing - who pronounced "ghouls" as "goils." In 1933's *The Ghoul*, made in England, the word is never used at all, but audiences no doubt assumed that the title referred to the creepy, monstrous Egyptologist played by Boris Karloff. Some have objected, saying "ghoul" must be a reference to those characters out to steal the dead man's diamond, but since Karloff is early on in the story called a "tomb-robber," he seems to qualify. No American reviewer discussing *The Mad Ghoul* made any reference to the 1933 film though it was revived from time to time in the late '30s and early '40s. Eventually, the word was used to describe any graveyard-dwelling fiend (like the Crypt Keeper), regardless of its diet. *The Mad Ghoul* at least moves closer to the original legends by having Ted "feeding" on a body part, even though it's turned into a serum rather than being consumed directly.

*The Mad Ghoul* was sometimes attacked for being too grisly, but there is nary a drop of blood to be had onscreen. There are shots of Ted's scalpel gleaming in the night, but the camera moves away when he begins the latest cardiectomy; still, it occasionally lingers on close-ups of Ted as he goes about his business. We're left uncertain as to whether the caretaker - having been bopped on the head with a stick - is still alive as Ted begins, but presumably Ken McClure is dead after being throttled by Dr. Morris. And although Ted's medical kit is in evidence, there is no sign of any container meant to hold the heart; that was either an oversight or an attempt to placate the censor. Early on in the film, when Morris spills Ted's drink, the close-up of the stained rug is doubtless meant to foreshadow the gore to come. This is all pretty mild when compared to Mexico's *El signo de la muerte* (*The Sign of Death*, 1939) - a bizarre combination of comedy *a la* Cantinflas and horror centered on a modern-day Aztec cult – where, in one scene, a topless maiden is sacrificed on the altar and we see the knife cut into her chest. Obviously, nothing like that would have been allowed by Mr. Breen, but *Mad Ghoul* does contain a shot of a Mayan drawing depicting a bloody human sacrifice.

400

**David Bruce and George Zucco on the prowl. Which is the title character?**

In February 1943, *Motion Picture Herald* reported that Universal had purchased the original story, "Mystery of the Mad Ghoul," from Hans Kraly; to be honest, the subject matter was not quite Kraly's forte. Kraly was Ernst Lubitsch's main collaborator on a number of important films, including *The Patriot* (1929) for which Kraly won an Academy Award for Best Writer. Unfortunately, in the early '30s, he and Lubitsch had a major falling out. Separated from her husband, Helene - the beautiful Mrs. Lubitsch – began keeping company with Kraly, and Ernst accused his friend of betrayal (there was even a scuffle between them on the dance floor at a nightclub). While Helene did not end up marrying Kraly, Lubitsch still never forgave him and, according to some sources, actively worked to sabotage his former friend's career. Whether that's true or not, Kraly's career did falter after Lubitsch severed ties with him; nonetheless, the occasional bright spot - like receiving the Academy Award nomination for best original story for Deanna Durbin's *One Hundred Men and a Girl* (1937) – was still to be had. Sadly, *The Mad Ghoul* - hardly an appropriate swan song - was to be his final credit. Kraly dropped out of the movie industry and died alone and in obscurity in 1950, surrounded by the books in his three-room library.

It's not known just what Kraly's inspiration was for such an uncharacteristic story as *The Mad Ghoul*. Prior to *Mad Ghoul*, the closest the writer had come to scripting a horror film was *The Eyes of the Mummy Ma* (1918). Another collaboration with Lubitsch, the picture stars Emil Jannings as a murderous caretaker of the tombs who schemes to frighten tourists away from the sacred sites. Perhaps Kraly had been thinking of his native Germany, wherein an evil genius was then hypnotizing young men to commit murder and to march mindlessly to their doom. More likely, Kraly had recalled *The Cabinet of Dr. Caligari* and *its* sinister doctor who sent out his knife-wielding somnambulist/slave, Cesare, in search of victims. In light of this, it was probably not coincidental that David Bruce's make-up as the mad ghoul was not unlike that of Conrad Veidt as Cesare. An article on the film in Missouri's *Hattiesburg American* (10 June 1943) mentions Kraly's past connection with Lubitsch and quotes Kraly as saying, "Sophisticated comedy used to shock moviegoers. Now I find that in order to shock them you've got to give them the horrors. I am frightening even myself." This sounds less like something you'd expect to hear from the scenarist of *The Duchess of Buffalo* and *Forbidden Paradise* and more like hokum from Universal's publicity department. In any case, *Mad Ghoul*'s final screenplay was the work of two Universal veterans, Brenda Weisberg and Paul Gangelin.

Despite these veterans' best efforts, it's unclear as to what use the fatal gas would have had either for the Mayans or modern science. A gas that immobilizes sacrificial victims to make them compliant when led to the altar makes sense, but one that just produces temporary "walking" catalepsy - requiring a heart to cure - would seem to have little value. Furthermore, there would be no practical use for it in the modern world, either, even though at one point Dr. Morris raves that Ted will be famous as the subject of this great experiment. It seems unlikely the professor would be able to write it up for *Scientific American* given the criminality that's part of the procedure.

As usual, the police - here represented by Milburn Stone long before his beloved Doc Adams on *Gunsmoke*, and Charles McGraw, right on the cusp of his tough-guy career - are firm of jaw but totally clueless. "What's this all about?" asks Stone, motioning to the ghoul's dead body. What movie-going kid growing up in the '30s and '40s would have aspired to be a cop based on the ongoing ineptitude of the onscreen police? Naturally, it is the fast-talking reporter - here played by Robert Armstrong, an expert at rapid-fire verbiage - who knows the score, and of course no newsroom would be complete without a gruff editor who never opens his mouth except to shout: a typical Addison Richards performance. That Armstrong doesn't bring the villains to justice is probably the film's only deviation from cliché.

Like Hans Kraly, director James B. Hogan was not a specialist in horror, although he did helm one of Universal's oddest films of the era, *The Strange Death of Adolf Hitler*. In the '10s, Hogan had been a professional baseball player, but after a stint in the Army Signal Corp - which sent him to places as disparate as the Philippines and Siberia - he got into the movies as an assistant to director Allan Dwan, most famous for his work with Douglas Fairbanks and Gloria Swanson. Hogan was soon directing solo, but by the '30s he was firmly ensconced in "B"-movies with only the occasional "A," like *The Ebb Tide*. The lower-berth adventures of Bulldog Drummond and Ellery Queen became Hogan's stock-in-trade, as did the stray straight-crime film, like *Queen of the Mob*.

In June 1943, Universal announced that Hogan had been signed to a long-term contract as producer/director, but on the 5 November, Hogan suffered a heart attack at his home. The responding paramedics had just finished spending a futile hour attempting to revive Lou Costello's baby, who had drowned; they had no better luck with Hogan. *The Mad Ghoul* was released just a week later.

It's evident that Hogan's direction occasionally falters, but he was working on a tight shooting-schedule (beginning the 13 May and ending a couple of weeks later) and with a budget clearly less than that of *Son of Dracula*, the feature *Mad Ghoul* was meant to support. While *SoD* has some nifty vampire into bat/mist special effects, Ted's transformation into the mad ghoul is achieved by the camera turning away as he is about to change and then turning back to him once he's the monster, a bit reminiscent of Stanley Ridges morphing from professor to gangster in *Black Friday*. *Motion Picture Daily* (4 November 1943) opined that *Mad Ghoul* "dissipates punch through the too oft repeated transitions of a handsome young medical student to a ghoulish figure and back again." It's not exactly clear just what triggers Ted's transformation, but presumably it's the emotional turmoil of his unrequited love for Isabel. Likewise, the scene depicting Ted's first attempt to kill Eric in a dark alley (that seems to run the length of a couple of a city blocks) is clumsily done. Isabel turns up and screams (at what exactly?) and Ted, though supposedly just an automaton mindlessly following orders, abandons his mission and is chauffeured away by Dr. Morris. The climax at the concert hall – where the two policemen dressed in formal wear plug away at the ghoul - seems perfunctory. It's followed by some clunky dialogue between the cops and Isabel and Eric and, surprisingly, there's not even a shot of poor Ted returned to his true self. Hogan does make up for it in the grim final scene where Morris - no longer unflappable and changing into a ghoul himself - frantically digs at a fresh grave while Ted's last words to Morris echo ominously: "There's only you and me…and death!" Plant that in your victory garden!

Columnist Robbin Coons visited the set of *The Mad Ghoul* and reported the following (which appeared in a number of papers, including the 10 June 1943 edition of the *Big Spring* [Texas] *Daily Herald*):

> 'I prefer light comedy roles,' said David Bruce. The first role he drew in Hollywood was that of an innocent man electrocuted in *The Man Who Talked Too Much*. Today he was a pleasant sight continuing on his career of 'light comedy.' He looked green and his reddish-brown hair was pulled down, caveman style, over his green forehead. His face was a wrinkled map of horror thanks to spirit gum and molded clay and make-up man Jack Pierce, who added the final touch by rimming his eyes with crimson paint to make the white look like mottled Easter eggs. David Bruce from Kankakee, Ill., who once survived three days on cough drops during a jobless period in New York, spends three hours daily getting his make-up on, without benefit of cough drops. George Zucco, the mad scientist and real heavy of the piece, suffers not at all. He just looks evilly and hypnotically at heroine Evelyn Ankers and, when his own gas gets him in the end, he dies without aid from make-up man Pierce. This a relief to Zucco and especially to Pierce, who is getting a little irked with his monster parade.

Apparently, Coons was not present for the shooting of Zucco's last scene in which the evil doctor does indeed have some wrinkles and scars on his face as he becomes a monster and then expires.

Coons also visited with Robert Armstrong during the filming of the sequence wherein he tries to trap the ghouls. "I'm mighty glad to be doing something funny and light again," the actor said, referring not to any risible aspects of *The Mad Ghoul*, but rather to his recent spate of villain roles. Coons pointed out to him that the somber mortuary setting did not seem conducive to mirth. "What I mean," Armstrong explained, "is that I have some funny moments. I'm a crime reporter out on this ghoul case. This is where I get finished off and for once the audience will be sorry."

Whether viewers were sad or not to witness McClure's fate, that particular sequence is probably the film's best, with the camera gliding across the mortuary and David Bruce's shambling ghoul groping through the shadows. There is also a good deal of black humor in the scene: the undertaker so worried about the coffin getting damaged, the gun-toting journalist pretending to be a corpse, and Zucco's acid deadpan delivery of "The reports of your death seem to have been greatly exaggerated" as McClure sits up in the casket.

**Ted begins to realize what his mentor, Dr. Morris, has done to him. An older man dominating a younger one for some evil purpose became a recurrent plot device in later films by Herman Cohen (*I Was a Teenage Werewolf*, *Horrors of the Black Museum*, etc.)**

The 13 December 1943 *Washington Post* commented that *The Mad Ghoul* offers "an innovation in corpse operas - Miss Ankers sings three songs." *Motion Picture Daily* found Ankers' performance "very acceptable except for attempts to have her sing what might otherwise be excellent concert numbers." The trade-paper scribe was presumably unaware that Universal had gone back on its promise to Ankers that she could do her own singing and obliged her to lip-sync stock recordings done by pop singer Lillian Cornell. To add insult to injury, the studio's publicity department announced during the film's release that "Miss Ankers sings for the first time on the screen."

In 1943, Evelyn Ankers received quite a bit of attention as Universal's "scream queen," and of course the publicity department kept the silly stories coming, including one in which David Bruce in his monster make-up chases Evelyn all over the cemetery set. He never actually menaces her at all in the film, but the stills department provided the usual the beauty and the beast numbers. Occasionally, though, Ankers was given a break from questions about her lung capacity; a *Screenland* article gushed about her domestic bliss with husband Richard Denning.

David Bruce delivers just the right combination of pathos and menace and he's even able to make lines like "Am I alive or dead?" sound credible. Bruce's film career never gained any traction; as his daughter Amanda McBroom sang in "Errol Flynn" - her plaintive, heartbreaking tribute to her father - "Luck kisses some and passes others by." Bruce was under contract first to Warner's and then to Universal, but he usually stayed in the supporting cast "only four or five names down below Errol Flynn." Universal failed to renew his contract after the war so Bruce found himself supporting, not Errol Flynn, but Jungle Jim, in films like *Pygmy Island.* There are flashes of neurotic intensity under Bruce's "College Joe" good looks, and I wonder how he would have done as one of the psychos in Hitchcock's *Rope.* Bruce retired in 1956, but was planning a return to film some 20 years later when he died of a heart attack. *The Mad Ghoul* remains his best- remembered role.

Hedda Hopper hoped *The Mad Ghoul* would be Turhan Bey's breakthrough film:

> Turhan Bey, Turkish Valentino who supported Maria Montez and Jon Hall in two pictures gets a starring role in 'The Mad Ghoul' with that delightful Irishman Jimmy Hogan putting him through his paces. I suppose 'the ghoul' is a combination of 'Frankenstein,' 'Cat People' and Boris Karloff - only Turhan is sexier.
>     8 May 1943

Given the fact that, in *Mad Ghoul,* Bey has little to do other than comfort Evelyn Ankers and pretend to play the piano, it's hard to understand Hopper's expectations. Bey did go on to star in an "A"-film, but unfortunately it was *Dragon Seed*, wherein Katherine Hepburn and other Caucasian actors impersonated Chinese peasants to great critical disdain. Before long, Bey was back to doing pictures like 1953's *Prisoners of the Casbah.*

The 23 October 1943 *Motion Picture Herald* reviewer described *Mad Ghoul* as "well done but just that. Zucco's performance is the only one which will command audience attention." Indeed it does, and it is no doubt Zucco's best mad scientist role and surely one of his most cold-blooded characters. Early in the film, Ted - who, like most assistants to evil geniuses, hasn't gotten the memo - begins to fret that their experiment will result in something evil, only to have Dr. Morris reply, "I'm a scientist; there is no good or evil, only truth and falsehood." If Bela Lugosi had said that line, no doubt he would have imbued it with - in the words of Carlos Clarens - "cornball demented poetry," but Zucco's (relatively) restrained reading makes it seem like less of a *cliché* and all the more chilling. Later, when Ted first inhales the gas, Morris sits at the piano in the living room, calmly playing the same romantic ballad that Isabel played the night before. Learning that Isabel doesn't love him, he reacts without emotion: "We see what we want to see most of the time. Even I, a scientist, have such moments of weakness." Disappointment in love draws no tender feeling from him, only regret that he has made an error. Of course, he's in lust - not in love - with Isabel, which marks the difference between him and Ted. Morris's scientific objectivity ultimately does fail him when his own life is at stake and he realizes that he's doomed.

The trades found *The Mad Ghoul* to be unexceptional but okay for its intended audience:

> Calculated to satisfy most horror addicts, the overwork of the ghoul here is not likely to entertain any other trade...the Jekyll-Hyde situation is weak and creates little belief in possibility.
> *Showman's Trade Review* (6 November 1943)

> A routine horror program melodrama...the theme has been done many times and this version offers little in way of originality... Discriminating audiences will probably find it tiring.
> *Harrison's Reports* (18 December 1943)

> *The Mad Ghoul* is apparently a page from *Phantom of the Opera* with a little but not sufficiently different twist... David Bruce delivers an excellent performance.
> *Motion Picture Daily* (4 November 1943)

Not surprisingly, Bosley Crowther mocked the film under the heading "Ghoul Daze":

> Most of the ghouls we've met in horror films have been more or less scatterbrained so there's really nothing out of the ordinary about the one which came clomping and google-eying to the Rialto yesterday.... We would call him a definitely a second-rate ghoul. And if anyone is privileged to be crazy it's us poor folks who have to look at such things."
> *The New York Times*, 11 December 1943

Crowther routinely made horror films the butt of his sophomoric humor, and lest anyone think it was only monster movies that amused him, let it be known that he found the Val Lewton films just as risible. Nevertheless, perhaps his mockery was preferable to the attitude of his colleague on the Grey Lady "T.M.P." who, in his review of *I Walked with a Zombie*, seemed to be suggesting that horror films needed a more rigorous form of censorship. After calling that movie "dull and disgusting," the critic went on to say:

> If the Hays Office feels it has a duty to protect the morals of movie-goers by protesting the use of such expressions as 'hell' and 'damn' in purposeful dramas like *In Which We Serve* and *We are the Marines*, then how much more important is it to safeguard the youth of the land from the sort of stuff and nonsense that their minds will absorb from viewing *I Walked with a Zombie*.
> 22 April 1943

**The pistol-packing ghoul is out-gunned by policemen Milburn Stone and Charles McGraw as Evelyn Ankers and a rather smug Turhan Bey look on.**

No doubt T.M.P. would have approved the Chicago censor's decision to label *Son of Dracula* as being "for adults only" and yet ban co-feature *Mad Ghoul* entirely. The reason given was *Ghoul*'s "excessive gruesomeness," but I wonder if "incitement to crime" - so beloved a rationale of the New York censor - was the reason. After all, no one would be inspired to turn into a bat after watching *Son of Dracula*, but grave desecration could give ideas to would-be vandals. In any case, a few cuts were made in *Ghoul*, the police censors of the Windy City then passed it, and the double-horror-bill went on to do smash business. The double- bill also did exceptionally well at the Hawaiian Theater in Los Angeles, where it broke a number of records.

On the 7 June 1943, *The New York Times* printed an announcement from Universal:

Universal is planning a picture for its 'horror' series which will include all the weird characters from the several subjects of this order made previously at the studio. The film, to be titled 'Chamber of Horrors', will revive the monsters from the former films 'Dracula,' 'Frankenstein,' 'The Wolfman' [sic], 'The Invisible Man' and 'The Mad Ghoul.' Curt Siodmak, who wrote several of the earlier 'horror' stories, is writing the screenplay and George Waggner will produce it. The picture will have an extended budget and, according to the studio, an effort will be made to engage the players who portrayed the menaces in these films for this studio described 'super-horror picture.'

Subsequent articles stated that David Bruce would reprise his role in *The Mad Ghoul*, a somewhat surprising statement given that the movie had just finished shooting and would not be released until several months later. "Chamber of Horrors" eventually became *House of Frankenstein*, minus the mad ghoul and the invisible man.

*The Mad Ghoul* was reissued in 1948 and was frequently billed with *Frankenstein Meets the Wolf Man*, an appropriate choice given the latter opens with a grave-robbing sequence.

*The Mad Ghoul* - 12 November 1943 - 65 minutes (ST)

CAST: David Bruce as Ted Allison; Evelyn Ankers as Isabel Lewis; George Zucco as Dr. Alfred Morris; Robert Armstrong as Ken McClure; Turhan Bey as Eric Iverson; Milburn Stone as Macklin; Andrew Toombs as Eagan; Rose Hobart as Della; Addison Richards as Gavigan; Charles McGraw as Garrity; Gus Glassmire as the Caretaker; with Gene O'Donnell, Isabel La Mal, Lew Kelly, William Ruhl, and Hans Herbert.

CREDITS: Director: James Hogan; Producer: Benjamin Pivar; Screenplay: Brenda Weisberg, Paul Gangelin; Original Story: Hans Kraly; Director of Photography: Milton Krasner; Art Directors: John B. Goodman, Martin Obzina; Film Editor: Milton Carruth; Set Decorators: R.A. Gausman, A.J. Gilmore; Make-up: Jack Pierce;

Costumes: Vera West; Music: H.J. Slater; Sound: Bernard B. Brown, Jess Moulin.

***Shock Theater*** Catalog No. 715: "For spine-tingling thrills tune into this channel (day) at (time) when *Shock* presents the full-length feature film, 'The Mad Ghoul.' George Zucco plays a crazed scientist who brews a poison that terrorizes a nation. It's exciting entertainment so don't miss it. Tune in (day), at (time)."

*- HN*

# *Calling Dr. Death* (1943)

*Synopsis*: Dr. Mark Steele is a renowned neurologist who frequently uses hypnotism in his treatments. He is unhappily married to the beautiful but cruel Maria who despises him, but who enjoys the prestige of being married to a famous doctor. Steele and his nurse Stella have a mutual attraction, but Steele doesn't see a way out of his marriage to Maria. One Saturday night, while brooding over the situation, Steele drives aimlessly around and then blacks out. He awakens on Monday in his office with no memory of the past 48 hours. The police arrive to inform him that Maria has been found dead in their country lodge, beaten with a poker and disfigured by acid.

Inspector Gregg, the detective in charge of the murder case, suspects Steele but then arrests Robert Duval, an architect who was having an affair with Maria. Though Stella tries to convince him otherwise, Steele can't be certain that he didn't murder Maria during his blackout. Making matters worse, Gregg continually needles Steele, trying to make him confess. Greg, with Stella assisting, tries self-hypnosis, but even that doesn't resolve things. Duval has been found guilty of Maria's murder and has been sentenced to death. Steele becomes increasingly frantic as the time for Duval's execution moves closer.

When a mysterious fire in his office destroys all his records, Steele begins to suspect Stella. He hypnotizes her, and the truth comes out: Duval, with Stella's connivance, had been borrowing money from Maria to cover his gambling debts. When Duval had a change of heart and insisted they return all the money, Stella, madly in love with Steele, killed Maria. Gregg overhears her confession and both Steele and Duval are cleared, but Gregg tells Steele he never really suspected him in the first place.

"Inner Sanctum" is today undoubtedly the least-liked horror series ground out by Universal in the '40s. Though Universal's publicity department initially promised that each picture would have a supernatural element, they were mostly weak psychological mysteries/whodunits with only an occasional nod to the paranormal. "Inspired" by the popular radio show, *Inner Sanctum Mystery* (1941-1952), the films had far more in common with Columbia's "Whistler" series (also a take-off on a radio program), wherein Richard Dix played either hero or villain in a half-dozen *noir*-ish thrillers which - unlike Universal's "Inner Sanctum" - hold up very well today.

"Inner Sanctum" initially saw print as a series of paperback books published by Simon and Schuster in 1930, and though, at first, all genres were encompassed, by 1936 we were dealing strictly with mysteries. The eponymous radio show took the series into "Grand Guignol" territory - not unlike pulp horror or the later EC comics - and the stress was on the lurid and ironic, though there was the occasional adaptation of a classic by Poe or de Maupassant. Horror specialists like Boris Karloff and Peter Lorre sometimes turned up, and the 4 April 1943 show, *Ring of Doom*, starred Lon Chaney, Jr. Publicity for the show said that Chaney essayed a role something like Lenny, the slow-witted character Chaney had played in *Of Mice and Men*; oddly enough, there was no mention of *The Wolf Man* or other of his horror roles. Like many of the *Inner Sanctum* radio shows, neither broadcast nor script survives.

The 17 May 1943 edition of *The New York Times* announced that Universal had bought the "Inner Sanctum" trademark to increase its "horror output." As the studio did not buy the rights to the stories themselves – as presented in either the books or the radio show - each film was to be an original work and would star the team of Lon Chaney and Gale Sondergaard (who had just signed up with Universal). The very next day, the trades reported that the studio had purchased an original story by Edward Dein that later became the basis for his screenplay for *Calling Dr. Death*, the first of the new "Inner Sanctum" series.

Though promoted as horror films - and usually playing at *the* "Grand Guignol" movie theater, New York City's Rialto - the series did not have to contend with some of the usual expenses associated with such pictures. Since there were no monsters - unless you count "The Mind" - there was no need for elaborate make-up or special effects. The settings were cheap, nondescript, and modern, dispensing with Tyrolean villages or crumbling old castles. And, as the horror content was very mild, an added bonus was to be had in that there was little trouble with Mr. Breen's office. No doubt the producers never even considered depicting the type of mayhem in which the radio program specialized - the latter could get away with sounds effects evoking a man being eaten alive by leeches - but film censors were not likely to allow even the suggestion of such a thing. To top it all off, the "Inner Sanctum" films would avoid the British "H" category (no children admitted); instead, they'd be awarded the "A" rating (children could be admitted, but only with adults), potentially increasing their viewership in Old Blighty.

Gale Sondergaard inexplicably vanished from the series (though not everyone got the memo; she turned up occasionally in ads for *Calling Dr. Death*), but there still remained the "Master Character Creator," Lon Chaney, Jr. Chaney was no doubt delighted that he could avoid the gruesome and painful make-ups that had become his stock-in-trade, and while he may have played a Lenny-like character on the radio *Inner Sanctum*, in the movies there was no trace of the tragic giant. Instead, he was to portray a series of well-groomed and -tailored professional men *and* be the love interest of a bevy of attractive actresses. Lon was perhaps reminded of his early days, when - as Creighton Chaney - he was occasionally mentioned as a new Clark Gable, pretty heady stuff for a former meter reader and plumbing salesman. Nonetheless, even back then there were intimations of things to come, as seen by this item from the March 1932 *Hollywood Times*: "Who is Lon Chaney's successor? It may be Chaney's only son Creighton who just signed with RKO. He will make his talkie debut in a horror story by Edgar Wallace." Elsewhere it was written that Creighton would appear in *The Most Dangerous Game*, but that too failed to materialize. Creighton had many lean years ahead of him in Westerns and serials before he became Lon Chaney, Jr. and - finally - just Lon Chaney.

The elder Chaney was most famous for his grotesque, heavily made-up characters, but his "straight" roles in films like *Tell It to the Marines* and *While the City Sleeps* were also popular with the public. Universal did not come up with anything comparable for the younger Chaney, and his performances in the "Inner Sanctum" films are as monotonous as the series. (To be fair, his work in *High Noon* and *The Defiant Ones* is memorable, but these were supporting roles in Stanley Kramer productions.) Perhaps the problem was that Chaney, Jr. simply wasn't an interesting enough actor to carry an entire series. Richard Dix, by the '40s, was sometimes a rather stolid leading man, but he was versatile enough to give the "Whistler" movies some pizzazz. Chaney certainly *tries* in *Calling Dr. Death*, but he seldom convinces. Of course, the script sometimes works against him: When he begins to awaken a young female patient under hypnosis, you expect him to snap his fingers, but instead he slaps her face! Clearly the brilliant neurologist lacks a gentle bedside manner. Later when *he* is in a trance, Stella (Patricia

Morison) seems about to do the same thing, but then abruptly snaps her fingers, pretty polite for an acid-throwing murderess.

It should be noted that not everyone disparages Lon's "Inner Sanctum" performances, including Chaney biographer Don G. Smith:

> Those who blindly see Chaney's Dr. Steele as a miscast Lennie fail to appreciate the actor's fine performance. Again, director Le Borg gets Chaney's best acting which is enough to lift *Calling Dr. Death* at least to the upper levels of average, if not a little higher.(1)

One of the most tiresome features of the series is the frequent use of stream-of-consciousness monologues going on inside Chaney's head. Critics in the '40s didn't like them, either, calling them "artificial and distracting," or opining that "what suspense is attained occasionally is dissipated by Mr. Chaney's sepulchral voice." Presumably, this device was meant to remind viewers of the radio show, but more often than not Chaney's narration is about as spooky as a whispered TV-golf-commentary on the ninth hole. Nor is there any emphasis on the sound effects, another way the radio series could have been represented.

**David Bruce and Patricia Morrison in what's certainly the best sequence in the film and probably the entire series: the hypnotically induced confession.**

414

Likewise, the radio program's famous creaking door - or anything comparable - is nowhere to be heard. And while the radio show was introduced by Raymond (Brown), whose ghoulish mirth foreshadowed Zacherley and other TV horror hosts of later years, the movies – largely humorless – offer a disembodied head floating in a crystal ball. Just before the opening credits, the head - played by David Hoffman - ominously intones the following: "This is the Inner Sanctum - a strange fantastic world controlled by a mass of living, pulsating flesh - the mind! It destroys...distorts... creates... monsters. Yes, even you - without knowing - can commit murder!" This recitation more or less fits *Calling Dr. Death*, but rather than shoot new introductions for the rest of the series, Universal tried to save a buck or two by playing the same clip for all the other films (except for *Pillow of Death*, the last of the series).

For all that, *Calling Dr. Death* got good reviews in the trade papers:

Helen McNamara, in the 13 December 1943 edition of *Motion Picture Daily*, wrote: "Not as gruesome as the title would imply but it is a rousing good picture for devotees of the heavy mystery drama."

*Motion Picture Herald* (18 December 1943) compared the film to the radio series:

> There is the same inconclusive psychiatric speculations, the same utter absorption by their characters in their personal lives and mental aberrations, the same dependence upon dialogue, and there is that disembodied voice, 'Raymond.' [?] There is also the lengthy use of inner-thought soliloquies; in this instance they are those of Lon Chaney, caught in a peculiar mess indeed... Associate producer Ben Pivar and director Reginald Le Borg give some care to this and almost succeed in tying together all the threads.

*Harrison's* concurred:

> A good program murder mystery melodrama. It should be a treat for followers of this type of entertainment, for the identity of the murderer is concealed so well that when it is finally divulged it is a complete surprise...there is no comedy, but this is to the picture's benefit, since comedy, unless done well, might have been out of place. Not edifying for children.
>
> 18 December 1943

Hobe, on record in the 15 December 1943 issue of The Bible of Show Biz, was a little less enthusiastic: "Reasonably compact and compelling yarn told in semi-radio style with a smattering of pseudo-scientific mumbo-jumbo. It's an okay programmer for whodunit fans."

Newspaper reviews, while guarded, were still better than those that would be received by subsequent films the series.

> This is heady fare for the Rialto patrons after their recent treatment to a succession of good, crude horror dramas. But if you can carefully avoid any skeptical analysis of the picture's scientific premises, you can find yourself satisfactorily immersed in a tightly knit whodunit contest... Chaney does a workmanlike job... the great performance of the picture is from J. Carol [sic] Naish who hovers in the background as a master detective with an air of being inescapable...
>
> Alton Cook, *NY World Telegram*, 14 February 1944

> Lon Chaney seems a bit uneasy in a role which makes him recognizably flesh and blood... good enough for everyday consumption and is likely to encourage an appreciative following. Had director Reginald Le Borg been as masterful with his cast as he was with the script *Calling Dr. Death* could have been a most promising introduction to Universal's new Inner Sanctum series. Even so the first of the chiller-thriller is plenty good enough.
>
> Dorothy Masters, *NY Daily News*, 12 February 1944

> Mildly interesting but not thrilling...it has a dreary habit of talking itself out of promising situations....However, despite its scientific gimmicks the intrigue in *Calling Dr. Death* ends with its title.
>
> A.W., *The New York Times*, 12 February 1944

While the picture's title might to modern ears suggest a bio of Dr. Jack Kevorkian, '40s audiences no doubt recognized it as a take-off on M-G-M's *Calling Dr. Kildare* (1939) and *Calling Dr. Gillespie* (1942).

Though *Calling Dr. Death* is a whodunit, the list of suspects is pretty small once you discount the Lonster. When Mrs. Duval turns up in a wheelchair to chat with Steele, flags immediately go up for the detectives on the aisle seat: we've been there before in films like *Night Monster* and *House of Mystery*. But when the poor lady disappears after one tearful scene, we're left with only one serious suspect: Stella, the devoted nurse. Patricia Morison gives a rather odd performance as Stella, and she appears so strange and neurotic that hypnosis scarcely seems necessary to ferret out her guilt. Her motives seem rather mixed: are we dealing with greed or passion? Why doesn't poor Mr. Duval tell the police about her? And it takes only one quick, rather casual phone call from Lt. Morris to get an imminent execution called off; I think I prefer the melodramatic race to the gallows in the last reel of *Intolerance*. And why do they turn back the clocks to help convince Stella that Duval has been executed? ("No more Duval," intones Chaney after crooning what seems like a '40s version of Johnny Cash's "25 Minutes to Go"). It's not like she's conscience-stricken over the fate of her former partner. And why exactly does Steele get amnesia? It *is* "convenient but improbable," to quote a line from the script. We see him driving recklessly and then slamming on the brakes as a train roars by, but he does so without hitting his head, the favorite *cliché* regarding amnesia victims in detective fiction and bad movies. There's also an inexplicable line when Steele wakes up in the office and tells Stella that he had to have his shoes tied by Bryant (the butler). When did *this* happen? And wouldn't you imagine that the very first question Gregg would ask Steele when he arrives on the murder scene would be about his whereabouts at the time of the murder? For all the pop-psych yakety-yak, the script doesn't consider the notion that Stella is doing what Steele subconsciously wants her to do: get rid of his she-devil of a wife. Early on in the film, Maria ridicules the notion that her husband might be driven to murder her. "You haven't the courage!" she snarls. Right after that there's a somewhat clumsy scene showing Steele entering his wife's room, apparently with violence on his mind. A screaming cockatoo (flying in from *Mad Love* or *Citizen Kane*?) awakens Maria and Steele withdraws. A more astute script would recognize Steele's complicity in Stella's crime, endorsing Maria's view that Steele has the desire but not the intestinal fortitude to get rid of her. He needs someone else to do it for him, and what better person than a woman infatuated with him?

Porfiry Petrovich from **Crime and Punishment** is the literary prototype of Inspector Morris and all movie detectives like him. Like Petrovich, Morris works on Steele's conscience and plays mind-games with him to drive him to confess. But then, at the very end of the film, all this is thrown out when we discover Morris didn't believe Steele is guilty, but - for some inexplicable reason - thought Steele could lead him to the real culprit. The detective then philosophizes about his job: "I start with death. I look for life. I find it and I've got to destroy it." Not exactly Dostoevsky. Nevertheless,

J. Carrol Naish's sardonic underplaying of the relentless detective is easily the best performance in the film, though good support is provided by two underrated and underused Universal actors, David Bruce (Duval) and Fay Helm (Mrs. Duval). As usual, Ramsey Ames (Maria) is ravishing, but barely competent.

If *Calling Dr. Death* is at all watchable, it's due mainly to Reginald Le Borg who gives Edward Dein's mediocre script far more style than it deserves. Modern commentators often mention Le Borg's use of the subjective camera taking Chaney's point of view when he arrives at the murder scene at the lodge. It hardly ranks with the most famous (at that point) POV scene - the opening sequence of the 1931 *Dr. Jekyll and Mr. Hyde* - and Le Borg unwisely interrupts the flow of the action twice rather than use one continuous camera shot to take Chaney into the bedroom where his wife's body lies. Nevertheless, Le Borg gets points for trying to shake things up a bit instead of doing what's easiest and quickest. Some of Le Borg's shots are more artfully composed than is usual for a "B"-movie, and particularly arresting is the scene where Steele is waiting for Duval to be brought in. Chaney, back to the camera, is in the foreground, and we see Duval being led down an endless corridor to meet with the doctor. It's an almost Expressionist shot and a nice foreshadowing of Stella's hypnotically-induced vision, wherein she replaces Duval on his march to the death chamber.

The whole climatic sequence is cleverly handled and is easily the film's high point. As Steele starts to hypnotize Stella, the camera is slightly off-kilter, and they are shot from a low angle. Le Borg cuts back and forth between Stella, the sequins on her dress gleaming, and Steele's shiny pocket watch, swinging back and forth like a pendulum. The subsequent montage sequence - of course, John Fulton's special effects, Virgil Miller's camerawork, and Norman Cerf's editing are essential here - is especially tense and bizarre. The bit where the buildings tilt forward as though trying to trap Stella is like something out of Murnau's *Phantom*. There are nice minor touches as well: the close-up of the button vibrating on the rug after being torn from Steele's coat at the murder scene and the lights flickering at the end of Steele visit to Duval's cell. (Of course it's a *cliché* - movie audiences knew that the flickering doesn't indicate the warden hasn't paid the power bill, but rather that a prisoner has just been executed; still, it's effective that it's just thrown away rather than explained.)

In a number of later interviews, Le Borg complained about being remembered as a horror director although he had done a variety of films (though one might be hard-pressed to name even one of them) in all genres. His personal favorite was *San Diego, I Love You* (1944), a comedy about a wacky inventor (Edward Everett Horton) and his spunky daughter (Louise Albritton). It's mildly amusing and pleasant enough, but it's the sort of film you've forgotten by the time the end credits have crawled by. Genre fans should still give it a look, though, if only to see that Louise Albritton is practically unrecognizable if *Son of Dracula* is the only one of her films that you've seen. In any case, *San Diego, I Love You* did not perform well enough at the box-office to save Le Borg from horror movies.

Born in Vienna, Le Borg originally pursued a career as a banker and stockbroker, but after the crash of '29 turned to music and theater. Having directed the musical sequences in a number of '30s films and helmed many musical shorts, he signed on with Universal since they were willing to let him direct features. According to **The Films of Reginald Le Borg** by Wheeler Winston Dixon, Le Borg chaffed at being assigned to Universal's "B"-unit and was continually lobbying the studio for better projects while disparaging the films he was forced to direct. Because of his attitude, Universal did not renew his contract in the mid-'40s; he then found himself on Poverty Row, dealing with Joe Palooka and Little Iodine. In the '50s, his only notable films were again in the horror genre, *The Black Sleep* and *Voodoo Island*. Neither of them was very good, but 1963's *Diary of a Madman*, based on Guy de Maupassant's **The Horla**, was an improvement. Le Borg did some television work, but by the end of his film career was again directing horror movies, though with budgets so low that they might have made him nostalgic for his days at Universal.

You can't escape your destiny.

***Calling Dr. Death*** - 17 December 1943 - 63 minutes (ST)

**CAST**: Lon Chaney as Dr. Mark Steele; Patricia Morison as Stella; J. Carrol Naish as Inspector Gregg; David Bruce as Robert Duval; Ramsey Ames as Maria Steele; Fay Helm as Mrs. Duval; Holmes Herbert as Bryant; Alec Craig as the Night Watchman; Frederick Giermann as Marion's Father; Lisa Golm as Marion's Mother; Charles Wagenheim as the Coroner; Mary Hale as Marion; George Eldridge as the District Attorney; John Elliot as the Priest; David Hoffman as the Inner Sanctum Head; Paul Phillips, Rex Lease, Perc Launders, Jack Rockwell, Keith Ferguson, Norman Rainey, Charles Moore, Earle Hodgins, Frank Marlowe, Jack C. Smith, Al Ferguson, Robert Hill.

**CREDITS**: Director: Reginald Le Borg; Associate Producer: Ben Pivar; Screenplay: Edward Dein; Photography: Virgil Miller; Art Directors: John Goodman, Ralph De

Lacy; Film Editor: Norman A. Cerf; Set Decorators: Russell Gausman, A.J. Gilmore; Costumes: Vera West; Music: Paul Sawtell; Sound: Bernard E. Brown, William Hedgcock; Visual Effects: John P. Fulton

***Shock Theater*** Catalog No. 694: "Murder runs amuck [sic] as a madman rules with hypnotic horror. See the *Shock* feature film presentation 'Calling Dr. Death,' starring Lon Chaney on this channel (day) at (time). If you are a mystery lover, you won't want to miss this spine-tingler! See 'Calling Dr. Death'!"

*- HN*

# *The Spider Woman* (1944)

In *Sherlock Holmes Faces Death*, we established a kind of series rule about the appearance of corpses on the screen that, evidently, is shattered in the first few minutes of *The Spider Woman*. There's a the quick succession of bold sequences which, we think, ought to have been quickly spotted by the PCA. In the stillness of the night, the camera is parked on the window of a building from which, suddenly, someone throws himself through the shattering glass; another view reveals a second suicide, his gun still in his hand, on the floor of his bedroom. While the press christens the wave as "the pajama suicides," from above we witness a third wretch hurling himself from a high building into the void while a scream freezes our blood, and a pair of police are entering a bathroom where yet another poor soul, immobile, lies on the floor, his eyes staring sightless into the abyss.

Without a doubt, one of the advantages of tagging your production as a "B"-film – as may be seen in the differences between Tyrone Power's classic Zorro and the Zorros who rode out in Republic's serials – is the censor's disdain for this class of pictures.

Whilst in a stream in Scotland where he and Watson have gone off together to fish, a disheartened Holmes acknowledges: "The pleasures of the chase are no longer for me. I'm through with crime, now and forever." Admitting that he has experienced dizziness that might be a symptom of a cerebrovascular disease, he then appears to faint, falls, and is carried away by the water. Some psychologist or dabbler in the condition might diagnose this as a case of egomania, since he's chiefly deceiving his faithful old friend here, but Holmes fakes his death on the presumption that the criminal world (and also Scotland Yard) is anticipating his demise. Back in London,

421

Lestrade, Watson, and Mrs. Hudson mourn their absent friend who, once the newspapers report on his death, returns disguised as a crotchety postman, speaking ill of Holmes (or, perhaps, of himself). When an angry Watson impulsively takes a punch at him, Holmes reveals himself; upon reflection, we see that this episode demonstrates another of Holmes's psychotic traits: putting the good doctor through this needless test of loyalty.

**Raghni Singh looks on admiringly as Adrea Spedding apparently takes a selfie. It doesn't take long, though, before the Spider Woman sees through Holmes's disguise.**

One of the delights for the readers of the original Holmesian literature is that Conan Doyle alludes to untold past cases as if they were occurring at that moment. The script here uses that approach – which could be one of the requirements for the construction of universes – when Watson mentions "the strange death of ex-president Murillo," or "the case of the giant rat of Sumatra." En route to one of his investigations, Holmes mentions "the devil's-foot root" - discussed in the story "The Adventure of the Devil's Foot" (1910) – as belonging to "His Last Bow," and Watson remembers it as "the Cornish Horror." Thus, too, some of the narrative details found in *The Spider Woman* come from diverse canonical stories: the dwarf hit-man Obongo is the successor to Tonga, the footman of Jonathan Small in **The Sign of [the] Four**; Holmes' faked death comes from "The Final Problem"; his reappearance, from "The

Adventure of the Empty House"; the use of an animal as a deadly weapon from "The Adventure of the Speckled Band"; and the presence of a child with a mania for trapping insects from "The Adventure of the Copper Beeches."

In this fashion, drawing on elements from hither, thither, and yon, Bertram Millhauser constructed an entertaining plot and provided numerous humorous touches whose narrative speed is directly in proportion to the various factors that disturb the internal logic of characters and situations. In his analysis of press reports on the suicides, Holmes deduces immediately that they are assassinations due to the fact that no victim has left behind a suicide note, a rather evident – and even blatant - detail ignored by the police. Moreover, Holmes states that the brains behind this wave of death must be a woman: "Definitely a female Moriarty. Clever, ruthless, and above all, cautious." Disguising himself as an Indian recently arrived at the Islands, Holmes comes to a casino where he immediately attracts the attention of this mysterious villainess, Adrea Spedding (Gale Sondergaard), who quickly suggests that he purchase a life insurance policy and thus obtain a monetary advance to help him recuperate from a bad streak in roulette.

One of the attractions of this story is the intellectual parity of Holmes and Spedding. Both the master detective and we, the viewers, know that she is the brains of this criminal organization, even while there is no visible evidence to incriminate her. Alone together in her apartment, each realizes the imposture of the other, starting off a game that will have a number of tension-filled rounds. In one of these, Holmes, settling into his room for the night, is visited by a gigantic tarantula which slips in through the ventilation grill. This "Lycosa Carnivora" (per the identification made by an authority on the subject [Arthur Hohl]), would obviously be the murderer's "weapon," although at that moment it's not clear who or what introduces the arachnid into the ventilation ducts. The first two encounters between detective and murderess are carried out as a sort of delicious dialectic ballet, with each one winning a partial victory. The first win, the obtaining of the lady's fingerprints, goes to Holmes, while Spedding - in seeing through her foe's disguise – cops the second. Charles Van Enger's camera frames both from a distance, as if we were viewing action under the proscenium arch (which we are, conceptually). Later, during a visit to Holmes' own flat, she tells her rival she is aware of his plans. She is accompanied by her supposed nephew (Teddy Infuhr) who – apparently the sort of boy who hunts flies while running barefoot through the farm - strikes Holmes as being the means used to convey the deadly spiders to their victims. Nevertheless, appearances are deceiving, and all this ends up being part of what is almost a mortal attack on the Baker Street duo.

After regrouping their forces, Holmes and Watson head to the countryside where they encounter another henchman of the fearsome Spider Woman and discover a small model of a skeleton. Contrary to the expectations of those who regard Watson as being something of a fool, this time it is the good doctor who recognizes - due to its molars and thoracic capacity - that this is *not* the skeleton of a child. This gives Holmes the clue he needs to deduce that what they're searching for is a pygmy from Africa. In their search they will come across an amusement fair, the proper environment in which to have their third – and final – encounter with Adrea. In a tension-filled sequence done in the best Hitchcockian style, the Great Consulting Detective becomes trapped behind a shooting-gallery target, with Watson himself about to be the executioner of his friend.

September of 1943 marked the point at which the outlook of the Second World War began to lean negatively for the Axis and its partners. There would still be two more years of struggle and the sacrifice of countless more lives, but the hope of victory soon to come had already relieved scenarists of the necessity of introducing forced elements of propaganda into their scripts. *The Spider Woman* – or *Sherlock Holmes in Peril,* as it was first known at the beginning of shooting in May of 1943 – seemed not only to avoid bellicose propaganda but also, at least for a few moments, to omit any passing reference to a war bring waged in Europe or any other part of the world. Still, this would turn up in the last reel, in the form of images of Hitler, Mussolini, and Hirohito as targets in the shooting gallery of the amusement fair, confronting the spectators with a humorous reminder of the archvillains who were threatening the freedom and structure of the world.

www.IMDb.com reports that Sylvia Andrew and Marie de Becker played two charwomen whose scenes were eliminated from the final film as being superfluous. The same ought to have been done with the two or three matrimonial sequences featuring Stanley Logan and Lydia Bilbrook, whose comments on the news they hear on the radio not only add nothing to the plot, but also cause a loss of interest and a pause in the narrative flow. Might there have been some subplot related to the War with those two charwomen and, between the conclusion of the filming (in June 1943) and the picture's premiere (January 1944), their footage was discarded and replaced by the wedding/radio scenes? Speculation, and nothing more.

In her review in the 6 January 1944 *Motion Picture Daily*, Helen McNamara stuck this Holmesian opus firmly in the horror genre with her first sentence:

*Spider Woman* ... will send chills down the spines of the most hardened of mystery fans; it will play havoc with the nerves of those unaccustomed to Holmes' methods and 'elementary' deductions, but it will doubtless be a pleasant form of nervous prostration, for this is one of the best of the Holmes adventures.

*Showmen's Trade Guide* (8 January 1944) described the film as "a skillfully concocted yarn... Holmes' hairbreadth escapes are carefully spaced to maintain a goodly pace of suspense." As did the rest of the trade media, *Variety* (12 January 1944) chiefly praised Rathbone and Bruce, but, in referring to Gale Sondergaard, commented that she "as Adrea Spedding, does a bewitching job." The 13 January 1944 *Film Daily* observed that "a touch of horror makes this one of the best of the Sherlock Holmes series of melodramas." For W.R.W. of *Motion Picture Herald* (15 January 1944), *Spider Woman* was "best of the series, in part because the screenplay by Bertram Millhauser provides solid material with which to work and in part because of Gale Sondergaard's performance as 'the spider woman' of the title." And the mere mention of the following mattered and was significant for its presence: "The place is London, the period is now, but there is no war or reference to war in the film."

Without beating around the bush, *The Independent Film Journal* (22 January 1944) considered the picture "easily the topper of the Universal series of chiller mysteries." As a sign of the times (and of his personal ingenuity), the reviewer confessed that "although death stalks more freely and there are more heroics in the situations, there seems to be less corn and somehow more credibility than usually seen in the formula." After offering praise to Rathbone, he observed that "Nigel Bruce's Dr. Watson sparkles a bit brighter – perhaps because of more restraint and less huff-puff dynamics" and that "Gale Sondergaard's portrayal as the titular menace is outstanding in its beauty and charm as well as being a convincing performance." *Photoplay* (April 1944) – with its perennially enjoyable tone – observed that "huge spiders and Hitler's face [where's the difference?] lend a creepy, crawling air to the affair," automatically creating a huge expectation on the part of every lover of horror.

The critics and the contemporaneous cinematographic studies had taken the term "Spider Woman" from Janey Place and her femininist essay, "Women in Film Noir," published in the eponymous book (1) to christen the *femme fatale*, that siren whose song would lure the hero (usually a detective or a hustler) to his destruction in the *Noir* cycle of the '40s and '50s. For Ms. Place, the "Spider Woman" would be the diametric opposite of the innocent and virginal woman who must fight against the norms of a patriarchal system. Despite her appearance, Adrea Spedding is perfectly in sync with the traits of the "Spider Woman." Although Sherlock Holmes himself classifies her as a *femme fatale*, *The Spider Woman* contains no other element – not even a secondary factor – that allows it to be considered as a *Film Noir*, while there are numerous reasons to regard it as a horror film, or – more specifically – as a black comedy.

Amanda J. Field, in her **Wartime Films of Sherlock Holmes**, brings her great appreciation for the film as a hinge in the evolution of character across the period. Field observes that, during the first four films of the series, the dramatic tension ranges "between past and present," with Holmes and Watson living in a time capsule left over from the Victorian Era. But with *The Spider Woman*, "this tension… becomes gender-based, echoing that which exists between Holmes and his female adversary." Nowadays, under the rule the ideology of genres, it would be impossible for Holmes to deduce that the "pajama suicides" were the work of a woman "because the method, whatever it is, is peculiarly subtle and cruel"; said statement is as relevant nowadays as an antique postcard. "Feline, not canine," remarks Holmes, thus assigning to this woman a mammalian symbolism whose immediate precedent might well be Jacques Tourneur's magnum opus, *Cat People* (1942).

**Arthur Hohl happily signed on for a brief turn in *The Spider Woman*. In her absence, his Adam Gilflower is left to do business with Basil Rathbone's Spider Man.**

Field presents two interesting aspects of Adrea Spedding: the link with her stepbrother and her wardrobe. First off, we see Adrea in a modern, totally luxurious apartment, reclining on a sofa while boasting of her system of collecting the policies of the victims whom she forces into suicide. At her side, her henchman Norman (Vernon Downing) celebrates the evil genius of his mistress and lights her cigarette. During pre-production, a letter from the PCA to Universal warned that this might suggest the idea that this secondary character was effeminate or submissive, so the dialogue made it clear that there was a fraternal relationship between the two: they would be half-siblings. And regarding her wardrobe, it's striking to observe how, in the casino as she hunts for victims, she is dressed in a black suit with designs of claws, or when, going to visit Holmes and Watson, she is enveloped in animal skins and wearing a curious hat with a decoration like a quite virile masculine member. This ancestor of what today would be called "phallic women" covers her face with a lace-like fabric that resembles a spider's naturally generated cobweb. But it will be at the amusement fair, the venue wherein the dramatic climax takes place, that we end up perceiving this phallic woman as the leader of a kind of freak society, with her dwarf (Angelo Rossitto), her *castrato*, the strongman on duty (Harry Cording) who carries the dwarf about in a suitcase, a pair of gypsies, and even a mute child who hops about instead of walking...

It will be with this entry that the Holmes series definitively aligns itself to Universal's "monstrous" schedule; indeed, it will hold its own with the thrillers imbued with the horrific ambiance that would emanate from the rest of the studio's series. In his book on the Great Consulting Detective (2), Jim Harmon affirms that, before an ever-increasingly intense boom in the "hard-boiled school of Dashiell Hammett, Humphrey Bogart, [and] John Huston," the Sherlock Holmes films "were going against the trend of the times." Beginning with *The Spider Woman*, "all [the films] suggested [with some accuracy] the horror picture." But it would be Holmes, rather than monsters (which Universal and the public understood to be representations of "Otherness"), who kept returning to the "Woman," a little like the character of Irene Adler as imagined by Conan Doyle, although adapted to the taste and fashion of the time.

Adrea Spedding is not the demonization of the Woman, but rather, a "female Moriarty," per Holmes' own words. And as such, the scenarist reiterates the formula with which Holmes had defeated the Moriarty of Lionel Atwill: going in person to the villain's lair, allowing himself to be trapped, and trying to gain time by challenging his foe to contrive a death that would be worthy of his intelligence. As opposed to Moriarty, though - who fell into the void to his death - the denouement of *The Spider Woman* allows the defeated archvillainess to survive and to be arrested without being handcuffed, being led off by Lestrade, the two of them smiling, arm in arm... although, as genre veterans, we have that certain feeling that, at any moment, she will befuddle her captor and escape.

427

To a certain extent, Gale Songergaard emulated Adrea Spedding in real life, being castigated for her arachnid-like daring to violate the rules of the system. Throughout the War years, Gale remained hostage to Universal. The studio tried to change her into a homegrown Judith Anderson, watching over mansions in an array of roles ranging from housekeeper (*The Black Cat*, 1941 and *The Time of Their Lives*, 1946) to the creator of discord among her own relatives in *Christmas Holiday* (1944). At times – like here – she would be the principal villain; at other times, she might be the victim - as in *The Invisible Man's Revenge* or *The Climax* (both 1944). Nevertheless, the thing that would end up stopping her career cold and exiling her from the industry would be that feverish maelstrom called McCarthyism which wasn't able to forgive her her marriage to Herbert J. Biberman, one of the "Hollywood Ten."

With *The Spider Woman*, the series abjured the custom of having Sherlock Holmes' name in every title. Referred to initially as *Sherlock Holmes in Peril*, the film was renamed *Sherlock Holmes and the Spider Woman*, and as such was reviewed by *The Hollywood Reporter*. In the end, the studio decided on the shorter version, perhaps to give Ms. Sondergaard's character her turn in the spotlight. As with the sundry adventures of "*The*" Invisible Man, *The Spider Woman* would return, and although Ms. Sondergaard would once again play the role, neither she nor the 1946 iteration of the character would be *this* Spider Woman.

*The Spider Woman* – 21 January 1944 – 63 minutes

**CAST**: Basil Rathbone as Sherlock Holmes; Nigel Bruce as Dr. Watson; Gale Sondergaard as Adrea Spedding; Dennis Hoey as Inspector Lestrade; Vernon Downing as Norman Locke; Alec Craig as Radlik; Arthur Hohl as Dr. Adam Gilflower; Mary Gordon as Mrs. Hudson; Angelo Rossitto as Obongo; Teddy Infuhr as Larry

**CREDITS**: Producer and Director: Roy William Neill; Screenplay: Bertram Millhauser; Based on a story by Sir Arthur Conan Doyle; Musical Director: H.J. Salter; Photography: Charles Van Enger; Film Editor: William Austin; Art Directors: John B. Goodman and Martn Obzina; Sound Director: Bernard B. Brown; Technician: Paul Neal; Set Decoration: Russell A. Gausman and Edward Ray Robinson; Gowns: Vera West

*- DL*

# *Weird Woman* (1944)

*Synopsis:* Sociology Professor Norman Reed returns to Monroe College after a sabbatical during which he wrote an acclaimed book on superstition and married Paula, daughter of a scholar on the South Sea Island where Reed did his research. Paula was actually raised by Laraua, a priestess of a cult devoted to the goddess Kahuna Ana-Ana and shares many of her foster mother's beliefs.

Norman and Paula are welcomed to the University community, but not everyone is enthusiastic about them, particularly Ilona, the college librarian who had an affair with Norman and is determined to rekindle the flame. Professor Millard Sawtelle is Norman's rival for the chairmanship of the Sociology Department, and while he is painfully mild-mannered, his ambitious wife, Evelyn, is determined that he will win the job.

Ilona begins plotting against Norman and Paula with the hope of driving Paula away. Norman discovers that Paula has been visiting the local cemetery at night and conducting rituals to advance Norman's career and keep him from harm. Appalled, he insists on her burning all her charms.

Margaret, a student, is infatuated with Norman, but she has a jealous boyfriend, the mentally unstable David Jennings. Ilona encourages Margaret's relationship with Norman and plants seeds of doubt in David's mind. She also discovers that Dr. Sawtelle had plagiarized a former student's unpublished thesis for his own book. Ilona lies and tells Sawtelle that Norman is aware of the deception and will likely report him. Unable to face the disgrace - and his wife's wrath - Sawtelle shoots himself. Evelyn, influenced by Ilona, accuses the Reeds of murder.

When Margaret reveals her love for Norman, he brusquely dismisses her and,

429

she accuses him of acting inappropriately with her. This draws the attentions of college officials and leads to an angry confrontation between Norman and Jennings. The chairmanship of the department is given to an outsider, and Norman begins to wonder if his run of bad luck is somehow related to Paula withdrawing her magical protection. Things get even worse when Jennings threatens Norman with a gun and is accidentally shot during their struggle. He later dies, and Norman faces the possibility of a manslaughter charge.

Adding to Paula's increasing hysteria are phone calls with someone on the other end playing a tape of the death chant from the islands. Norman discovers that Ilona is behind it and Evelyn is helping her. Norman convinces Evelyn that Ilona is responsible for her husband's death, and they come up with a plot of their own. Evelyn tells Ilona that she dreamt of a "woman who lied" and how she ended up strangled after 13 days. She came downstairs to discover a doll with a cord around its neck and nails in its head. Ilona becomes convinced that she will indeed die after the time is up and, just before midnight on the last day, she pleads with Evelyn to dispose of the doll, admitting that she is responsible for all the tragedies. Norman, Paula, Margaret, and Dean of Women, Grace Gunnison, step out from the next room and confront Ilona who attempts to flee out the window. She is entangled in vines and strangled to death, making Evelyn's phony prophecy a reality.

*Weird Woman* is the second - and probably the best - of Universal's undistinguished "Inner Sanctum" series. It benefits from a strong cast, good direction, and provocative source material - namely the novel, **Conjure Wife**, by Fritz Leiber, Jr. Granted, the film is something of a travesty of the novel and is more concerned with bitchcraft than witchcraft, but even so the strength of Leiber's premise is enough to make the movie modestly entertaining. Invariably, it suffers in comparison with *Night of the Eagle* (aka *Burn, Witch, Burn*), the 1962 adaptation that some fans consider a classic horror film in the same league as *Night of the Demon*. This is debatable, but there's no doubt *Eagle* is far superior to the Universal film and much closer to Leiber's book. (1)

Leiber, Jr. was a bit player in Hollywood before turning to writing. In contrast, his father had been an important Shakespearean actor and, while his movie career was nowhere near as significant as his theater work, the elder Leiber turns up in a number of conspicuous film roles: Franz Liszt in the '43 *Phantom of the Opera*, the grumpy old nobleman who thinks the earth is flat in the '39 *Hunchback of Notre Dame*, and the mysterious stranger in the 1948 *Inner Sanctum* - which has no connection to the Universal series. Leiber, Jr.'s **Conjure Wife** first saw print in the April 1943 edition of the pulp magazine, *Unknown Worlds*. The novel was reprinted in 1952 as part of the Omnibus, **Witches Three** (the other stories in the book were "There Shall Be No Darkness" by James Blish and **The Blue Star** by Fletcher Pratt). The review in *The New York Times* on the 14 December 1952 labeled **Conjure Wife** a "comedy-melodrama":

The basis of this is that all the faculty wives at a certain small college are practicing witches, using spells to gain advancements for their husbands. This of course is one of those ideas of which you say 'Why I never thought of that before but it's obviously perfectly true.' There is real excitement when the heroine, at her husband's insistence, tries to break out of her eerie covenant and the rest gang up on her.

**Conjure Wife** has been reprinted a number of times, and Leiber, Jr. went on to become a major writer of fantasy and science fiction, but this first book is not among his best. Norman, the sociologist-professor hero, is extremely unlikable - supercilious, condescending, and insufferable: academia at its worst. Even at the ending, after he's witnessed all sorts of bizarre happenings, he's still on the fence as to whether the supernatural is at work ("I don't know" is his closing line). Even Scully from *The X-Files* wouldn't have been such a hard sell. And the problem is one never really gets away from Norman, having to suffer through his opinions on everything from sexual mores to college life. There are long passages in which he speculates on the nature of science, math, and magic, and whether there's actually a connection. This may be an example, perhaps like **The Godfather**, where a mediocre book yielded material for an outstanding film. And it should be noted that *Night of the Eagle*'s scariest moment - the pursuit of Norman through the empty campus by the stone eagle come to life - isn't even in the book, which goes in a far different direction for the finale, with the oldest witch attempting to switch bodies with the heroine via soul transference. Actually, the film version closest to the novel may be the 1980 *Witches' Brew*, a flat-footed comedy that preserves the soul-switching climax (with Lana Turner, in her last film, ideally cast as the older witch).(2)

Since this is the pre-feminist '40s, the ladies of **Conjure Wife** are using their powers to advance their husbands' careers rather than their own. There are stabs at satire in the book when Norman wonders just what is up with the female sex. World War II was raging and many men were in the army, leaving the ladies to keep the home-fires burning, but what exactly were they cooking over those fires? Are women in general - not just the college witches - part of an underground cult, passing their secrets on to their daughters and leaving their men in the dark to foolishly believe that they, in fact, are really in charge? It was medieval misogyny - the suspicion of the feminine slant to healing/herbalism/midwifery - that sent so many women to the stake. Leiber, though, was no John Updike, and **Conjure Wife** is no *The Witches of Eastwick.* It *is* perhaps more like *I Married a Witch* (1942), though not as charming.

The trade papers in 1943 announced that Universal had purchased eight stories in September, including "Sherlock Holmes and the Woman Smuggler" and **Conjure Wife**. *Motion Picture Daily* (13 December 1943) wrote that Oliver Drake, better known for Westerns, would direct *Conjure Wife*, but this is an error as shooting had already commenced on the movie with Reginald Le Borg as director. In the final film, which wrapped on the 29 December, Drake is credited as Associate Producer. Along the way, the title was changed to *Weird Woman*; this bemused some reviewers who weren't sure whether the title referred to Paula, Ilona, or Evelyn, all of whom would qualify. Perhaps the title should have been pluralized. The budget for the film was $150,000, then typical for a Universal "B."

**Professor Chaney gets more of a workout than he bargained for after struggling with murderously jealous Phil Brown.**

W. Scott Darling, who did the adaptation of **Conjure Wife**, was a writer known mostly for Silent Era comedy, but in fact had tackled a wide variety of subjects from the '30s on, though mostly in low-budget films. There is little (intentional) humor in *Weird Woman* (and many would say the same about Darling's Laurel and Hardy films like *The Big Noise* and *The Bullfighters*), and what there is stems mainly from Elizabeth Risdon's performance as the sardonic Dean of Women. Perhaps the main problem for Darling and scenarist Brenda Weisberg was that, rather than do a straightforward adaptation, they had to try to make the story fit smoothly into the Procrustean bed of the "Inner Sanctum" series. This meant that anything supernatural could be nothing more than an aside, and the plot would have to be in the mystery/melodrama category.

The film begins on a nicely *noir*-ish note as Paula nervously walks down a dimly-lit street with leaves blowing all about. She hides briefly from a passerby, but then continues on her way and doesn't see Evelyn (Elizabeth Russell) watching her like a specter from an upper window. All too soon we are in Norman's study, caught in the stream-of-consciousness of good Professor Chaney. Since there was no monster make-up or special effects to tout, Universal's publicity department stressed Chaney's vocal intonations. After mentioning that young Lon was following in the tradition of his father by becoming a star of horror pictures, the flacks "quoted" Chaney, Jr. expounding on how he made his line delivery in the voice-overs particularly spooky:

> Projecting the voice of the supernatural, I use a trick of ventriloquism taught to me by my father. Control of the larynx produces a smothered, faintly metallic tone which sounds as though it were emanating from a mysterious loudspeaker.
> *The North Adams* [Massachusetts] *Transcript*, 27 May 1944

And here we thought he was just whispering!

While Chaney might make a believable shop teacher, it's a little hard to accept him as a sociology professor, particularly one described as a "mental giant" and "dynamic." "Oh, for Pete's sake!" as the great intellectual exclaims at one point. We are also supposed to believe that he is catnip to the ladies even though he's not particularly nice to them. Albeit he has had an affair with Ilona, Norman doesn't even tell her that he's gotten married, preferring to spring that surprise at a party she's holding in his honor. When she persists in her attentions, Norman growls that he hasn't asked for or welcomed such devotion. While it's obvious that Margaret has a crush on him, Norman initially pays no attention, but then snarls at the naïve co-ed for her "romantic twaddle." And he pretty much treats Paula like a child; their relationship is reminiscent of Desi and Lucy. Clearly, tact and diplomacy are not Norman's strong points.

The flashback to the islands is likely the film's worst sequence. If the sight of the Lonster in a pith helmet isn't risible enough, the native dancing is about as convincingly primitive as "tropic night" at the Copacabana or, as one critic put it, the hoofing that led to "the death of burlesque in these parts." Nonetheless, it could have been worse:

according to the AFI entry on *Weird Woman*, producers originally planned to include two musical numbers by Paul Paige and his Hawaiian Orchestra. A good sociologist/ anthropologist would certainly respect native taboos, but Norman seems to think that takes second place to flirting with Paula and gets injured by the tribes-people. That and the subsequent scene of Norman recuperating in a hut are clumsily handled.

It's not even clear what point there is to the "Dance of Death." Presumably, someone is getting prayed to death, but who? And why? In Polynesian religion, "Kahuna Anaana" isn't a god at all, but rather, it's the term for a sorcerer. The script - and particularly the publicity - confuses Polynesia with Haiti.

Some taglines: "Murder Strikes with the Velvet Claws of Voodoo!"

"Red Lips whispering Black Magic, Soft arms killing with a Voodoo Curse!"

"With the heat of jungle drums in her heart a modern voodoo temptress strikes terror to a large city with her black magic!"

I want to see *that* movie, but, unfortunately, it's the not the one we have. Perhaps, the voodoo angle was meant to capitalize on the success of *I Walked with a Zombie*. In *Conjure Wife*, the title character learns about superstitions in the Deep American South where Norman is doing his research, while in *Night of the Eagle*, which is set in England, the locale is switched to Jamaica. By contrast, in *Weird Woman*, Paula isn't a modern woman enticed by the world of magic, but rather an islander raised in that environment (of course, she's white, so that disposes of the miscegenation issue). This is reminiscent of 1935's *Black Moon*, wherein the female protagonist reverts to the rituals and practices of her childhood upbringing on a voodoo island. (Her husband, a bit less understanding than Professor Lon, shoots her at the end.)

In publicity stills for the film, Anne Gwynne as Paula sometimes strikes an exotic, sexy pose, lying cat-like on her stomach or standing with fingers drawn back in a claw-like manner. This might be meant to remind viewers of Simone Simon in *The Cat People* (1943) or perhaps even Hedy Lamarr's Tondelayo in *White Cargo* (1942). One critic cracked that Gwynne's performance in *Woman* consisted primarily of "looking startled," but that's a bit unfair given that Gwynne makes Paula a likable and sympathetic character who really needs the comfort and protection of her religion in a largely unfriendly new world far from the simplicity of her island life. And if the negative depiction of the academia in book and film seems exaggerated, a friend who teaches sociology at a small college tells me that bitter rivalry, factionalism, and betrayal are largely the norm even in a department with only a few faculty members.

Part of the problem with maintaining any kind of suspense in the film is that we know from the get-go that Ilona is responsible for all the trouble, and we're obliged

434

to wait patiently for the rest of the characters to stumble on to the truth. At Professor Sawtelle's funeral, Dean of Women Grace Gunnison remarks to Ilona that "there's something about your smile right now that makes me think of Jack the Ripper." Margaret also comments on Ilona's jealousy, but nobody seems to draw the obvious conclusion. The script might have generated a little more tension had there been some mystery about exactly what's going on.

**The poster emphasizes island exotica, but the sequence in the film itself – thankfully – is quite brief.**

Then and now, some have criticized Evelyn Ankers's performance, saying she's miscast as a villainess. (Ankers would later play a jewel thief in the Sherlock Holmes thriller, *The Pearl of Death,* but that part would be nothing like Ilona, the she-devil librarian.) Ankers *did* go to the dark side another time, portraying a woman out to murder her wealthy twin in the radio program *Obsession,* but she wasn't comfortable playing a baddie. One could speculate that Elizabeth Russell might have been a better choice - one can certainly see her as the "bad" witch in *Night of the Eagle* - but her emphatic style would be so attention-getting here that her villainy would be immediately apparent even to characters as oblivious as these. Russell's Evelyn is so intense and wound up, coiled like a cobra, that, as one critic opined, it seems as if she's about to bite you at any moment, making Ankers - the real villainess - quite mild and bland by comparison. Nevertheless, Russell - while she may not be the source of all the evil - portrays a very unsympathetic character whose ambitions for her husband make Lady Macbeth seem like Mother Theresa. We can see why poor, downtrodden Millard Sawtelle (played with cringing self-effacement by Ralph Morgan) might prefer the bang of his gun to the bark of his spouse's voice. This is likely the movie's best scene. Norman has just burned Paula's charms and, as her medallion explodes in the crackling fire, we hear the gunshot from Sawtelle's house. After they rush next door, closeups of Russell walking toward the camera to accuse them alternate with shots of their horrified reaction, a very effective bit of direction.

The story goes very wrong with the plot against Ilona, and this is typical of the sloppy and careless writing that plagues the entire series. Why in the name of Hecate should Ilona give any credence to Evelyn's dream? Surely, the doll turning up on the floor would arouse suspicion on Ilona's part as to how it happened to end up there. There's no indication that Ilona thinks Paula put it there or even that she believes in Paula's magic; though Ilona has earlier accused Paula of witchcraft, she clearly knows it's a lie. That Ilona might develop a guilty conscience could be made credible, but the script doesn't bother and instead has Ilona see increasingly sinister signs that her doom is approaching. (Especially silly is the poster announcing that a play called "The Lady Lies" will close in seven days.) That Ilona should meet her death *exactly* in the manner and time described in Evelyn's phony dream seems preposterously coincidental. And, typical of the movies, the characters stand around watching her dangle from the vines rather than extricating her and seeing if she might still be alive.

Jim O'Connor, reviewer for the *New York Journal-American* was dismissive:

The Weird Woman today is today brewing her broth of deviltry at the Rialto Theater but passersby in Times Square seem unaware of it. The audience in the theater at yesterday's premiere of this bogey-woman also seemed unaware of the terrible danger in all the hocus-pocus doings on the screen. In fact, some of the onlookers laughed at it.

1 April 1944

Alton Cook of the *New York World-Telegram* was equally unimpressed:

Lon Chaney continues his career of going nuts in various ways... He stands around looking very concerned and hearing voices... All in all, it is quite an ordeal for Lon Chaney and except for the people who have a specialized taste for this sort of thing, it is going to be quite an ordeal for the audience.

21 March 1944

*The New York Times'* Bosley Crowther - not surprisingly - laughed the whole thing off: "Weird, isn't it? And boy is it dull!" (1 April, 1944)

Outside of the Big Apple, a kinder word could sometimes be found:

It is better than the first [of the series] partly because it relies less on the device of representing people's thoughts in eerie whispers. It has an acceptable plot worked out with some skill and develops an interesting, spooky atmosphere...It is frankly bizarre, but the chief conflict is between reason and superstition, with reason, oddly enough for a movie melodrama, coming out ahead...Lon Chaney is surprisingly effective... Miss Ankers displays unexpected competence as the wicked daughter of civilization.

*The Baltimore Sun*, 10 April 1944

The trade paper reviews, while mostly lukewarm, were a bit more mixed:

It's a standard dual supporter and okay for the secondary and nabe crowd. Picture hits slow pace in early reels to establish characters and foundation for the series of mysterious events, after which it gains momentum and fairly fast clip through directorial efforts of Reginald Le Borg. Chaney, Miss Gwynne and Miss Ankers combine adequately for the three leads. Support is okay.

*Variety*, 5 April 1944

437

A routine program fare for the horror fan... Lon Chaney is here in another Inner Sanctum mystery, again looking bewildered. And well he might be, for the story is inferior to the radio program upon which it is in some measure patterned.

*Motion Picture Herald,* 8 April 1944

A minor program mystery melodrama is far-fetched and lacks excitement. Even the most ardent admirers of this type of entertainment may find it but mildly interesting. Slow-moving, with little comedy to relieve the tension.

*Harrison's Reports,* 8 April 1944

This weirdie has many moments of high suspense and scary scenes. However, it also has a long period in the middle when there is more talk than action and when the talk slows the film to a walk and draws the teeth out of the moments of excitement. It starts out well, slows down and then gradually accelerates to a tense and pulsating climax.... Direction by Reginald Le Borg develops many eerie moments and maintains the players in character throughout, no small job when there are so many different types with real parts to do.

*Showman's Trade Review,* 8 April 1944

The 6 April 1944 *Motion Picture Daily* was more succinct than most: "Lon Chaney delivers a thoroughly creditable performance... Reginald Le Borg directed suspensefully." One person who wasn't impressed with Le Borg's direction was actor Phil Brown. Brown, edgy and convincingly neurotic as the jealous college-boy Jennings, was interviewed by Anthony Slide in 1999:

He [Le Borg] was a real hack. He just had the advantage of being terribly European and having an accent. I know he's a cult. I was absolutely amazed when I read in recent years articles in some esoteric London newspapers of a Reginald Le Borg festival. I nearly fell off my chair. The pictures he made were just crap. They really were... Technically I think he knew what he was doing, how to work the camera and all. (3)

Brown was involved in left-wing theater in New York and continued along those lines with the Actors' Lab when he moved to Los Angeles. He was briefly under contract to M-G-M in the early '40s, but that was interrupted by a brief stint in the army and Brown ended up as a contract player at Universal. After the war Brown went to England where he had what was likely his best role, that of the victim of Robert Newton's jealous husband in *Obsession* (1948, released in the US as *The Hidden Room*). Back in America, Brown turned to directing but, shortly after his first effort, *The Harlem Globetrotters* (1951), he found himself blacklisted by Hollywood for his part in the Actors' Lab. He returned to England where he acted and directed primarily in television. In 1977 he was cast as Luke Skywalker's Uncle Owen in *Star Wars* and found that small role brought him the fame that had eluded him most of his career.

In 2008, writer-director Billy Ray (*Breach, The Hunger Games, Shattered Glass*) announced his intention to do a new adaptation of **Conjure Wife,** but the project seems to have been sucked into development limbo.

*Weird Woman* - 14 April 1944 - 63 minutes (ST)

**CAST:** Lon Chaney as Professor Norman Reed; Anne Gwynne as Paula Reed; Evelyn Ankers as Ilona Carr; Ralph Morgan as Professor Millard Sawtelle; Elizabeth Russell as Evelyn Sawtelle; Elisabeth Risdon as Grace Gunnison; Lois Collier as Margaret Mercer; Harry Hayden as Professor Septimus Carr; Phil Brown as David Jennings; Jackie Lou Harden as Student; Gertrude Astor as Party Guest; Hanna Kaapa as Laraua; Charles Hamilton as the Carpenter; Gertrude Astor, Edmund Mortimer, Larry Steers as Party Guests.

**CREDITS:** Director: Reginald Le Borg; Screenplay: Brenda Weisberg; Based on the 1943 novel *Conjure Wife* by Fritz Leiber, Jr.; Adaptation: W. Scott Darling; Producer: Oliver Drake; Photography: Virgil Miller; Art Directors: John B. Goodman; Richard Reidel; Film Editor: Milton Carruth; Set Decoration: R.A. Gausman & A.J. Gilmore; Costumes: Vera West; Music: Paul Sawtell; Sound: Bernard B. Brown, William Hedgcock; Special Effects: John P. Fulton.

*Shock Theater* Catalog No. 741: "Lon Chaney plays a college professor and Anne Gwynne is his glamorous wife in 'Weird Woman,' coming your way on *Shock* on this channel, (day), at (time). Don't miss this thrilling feature film of superstition and voodoo on a tropic island. It's exciting from beginning to end."

*- HN*

# *The Scarlet Claw* (1944)

In 1973, Victor Erice – Basque filmmaker and ostensibly very much removed from both Sherlock Holmes and Universal Pictures - premiered *El espiritu de la colmena*, a story set in the ill-fated days of the Spanish Civil War. The film's affectionate tie to the Frankenstein Monster is well known to many horror fans, having been formidably edited by Criterion into DVD format under the title *The Spirit of the Beehive*. Not so well known, *La morte rouge* (2006) is a 32-minute-long short subject that Erice directed (and also narrated) as a trip back to his own childhood via the magical evenings spent in the Kursaal cinema, the meeting place of the San Sebastian Society during the '40s. In one of their rooms – one night in January 1946 – the five-year-old attended the screening of the first movie that the filmmaker saw in his life, its sinister villain following after him in his dreams as well as in anxiety-filled nightly vigils. That character would be the mysterious assassin in *The Scarlet Claw*.

The plot of *Claw* unfolds near Quebec, in a dingy inn filled with working-class men, all of whom become timorous upon hearing the nocturnal peal of the local church bells. In an interesting contrast, a public official assumes there's some supernatural cause while the legitimate intermediary between God and man seeks a more logical explanation. Thus, the village postman, Potts (Gerald Hamer), suggests that the bells have been rung by a ghost, while Father Pierre, the parish priest (George Kirby), ventures that there is a perfectly logical explanation for their tolling at that hour. In order to prove it, he's moved to do what none of his neighbors will: go himself to the church. On arriving, he discovers that a woman (Gertrude Astor) has nearly been beheaded and has fallen with her hand clinging to the bell-rope, indicating that perhaps she used the bells to call for help.

The action moves to a hotel in Quebec, where a meeting of the Royal Canadian Occult Society is being held, presided over by Lord Penrose (Paul Cavanagh) - a fervent believer in the World Beyond - about which he debates with two hard and fast skeptics, Holmes and Watson. As evidence of his beliefs, Lord Penrose speaks of the strange mutilations of sheep that have occurred in a nearby locale, La Mort Rouge, where the aristocrat has his mansion. Quite soon after, upon learning that his wife – the Lady Penrose - was the woman murdered at the church, he ends the session and sets out for the site. The next day, a letter arrives at the hotel for Holmes; it is from Lady Penrose who, before she died, had sent it off to him, asking for help. Despite the animosity of Lord Penrose – who is convinced that his wife had been killed by a monstrous specter – Holmes decides to head over to La Mort Rouge with the intention of confronting the assassin.

Shortly after arriving, Holmes meets the suspects. Drake, the mansion's butler (Ian Wolfe); a fearful Judge Brisson (Miles Mander); and innkeeper Emile Journet (Arthur Hohl): all are questioned and dismissed by the detective. Still, Holmes continues to seek out clues between the living and the dead. "The dead can tell us many things, Sergeant," he says to the local chef of police (David Clyde, older brother of comedian Andy Clyde). From his examination of the victim's cadaver, he discovers that the murderer used a five-pronged garden weeder as his weapon, leading to the supposition that the attacker was not a wild animal, or a monster, as the superstitious townspeople believe. (It's noteworthy that the skeptical priest from the opening sequence doesn't subsequently appear; just a little loose end in the script that doesn't account for much.) One of the clues – a fragment of a portrait of Lady Penrose from her days as actress Lillian Gentry (the aforementioned Gertrude Astor had been part of the Silent Cinema, so it would not be unreasonable to suppose this portrait was one of her own from that era) – leads Holmes to deduce that the murderer was committed by an old, affronted lover of hers – Alastair Ramson - presumably hiding out in the village. Still, with his also being an actor, perhaps he's not so hidden and is actually one of the habitues of the inn.

The next victim is the judge – who had sentenced Ramson to prison - literally entrenched behind bars and bolts in his cabin, attended to solely by a housekeeper (Victoria Horne, in the first credited role of her career and, later, the wife of Jack Oakie). The camera's panning across the set (a move that director Roy William Neill used from the first reel, in the scenes set in the inn or in the sequence wherein Holmes is being stalked by a phosphorescent man in the midst of a misty moor) is what will provide the tension to the following murder. As Holmes arrives at the cabin to warn the judge to take extreme measures to safeguard his life, the camera roams about the exterior and we watch as the housekeeper closes the windows, one by one. Now inside, we see the judge and, on the second floor and furrowed by shadows, the housekeeper who is seen from behind. But it's not her, but the murderer - dressed as a woman - whose hand we see in detail dealing the fatal blow with the murderous weapon. In this way, without displaying a single drop of blood, the set-up shapes the despair and helplessness shared by Holmes, waiting outside and unable to stop the crime.

But the terrifying atmosphere is not restricted to a single scene, as Neill intends that all surfaces are wrapped in shadows, or that they allow us to distinguish only an illuminated profile of each character. At times the camera pans through interiors where two individuals are conversing against backgrounds splashed with absolute black, suggesting that danger is imminent and that the murderer may be lurking about any of these blackened corners. The story takes place almost entirely at night and moments of supposed daylight also are furrowed by darkness, attributed to the fog on the Dartmoor heath. (It's curious that, at the beginning of the footage, Watson, in one of his notable allusions to past cases, mentions the "Hound of the Baskervilles," perhaps an attempt at guiding the subconscious and the memory of the viewers thematically.) In a moment, the bells begin tolling again and the villagers take it as an evil note that exacerbates the feeling of danger shared by each of the potential victims, the sort of para-psychological traits found in the spiritualistic universe of Conan Doyle. It is remarkable (due to the ingenuity of both Edmund L. Hartman's script and the director) that in spite of knowing the murderer's name, the plot keeps sustaining the mystery due to our not knowing what appearance he may adopt. The sum of all these parts does form an appreciable whole, and *The Scarlet Claw* possesses more horror-film atmosphere than mystery although, perhaps, what might make it the most macabre entry in the series is its ominous conclusion.

The innkeeper, at first also a suspect, ends up being the potential third – and final – victim of the psychopath. Moved by a quip by Holmes ("You can't run away from yourself!"), Journet – a former prison guard who had interacted with Ramson - decides to leave his hiding place upon finding out that Ramson had killed his daughter, Marie (Kay Harding, a 20-year-old Universal starlet who had appeared in *Weird Woman and* was the heroine in *The Mummy's Curse* her credited appearance in *Scarlet Claw* would elicit a number of mentions praising her beauty in the industry press; even so, her career never really took off). Despite the seriousness of the matter, the scene in which Holmes reveals the death of the girl is played in a curious setting. Journet has his back to the camera signaling pain and distress, keeping his face hidden and denying the

443

actor a great opportunity to demonstrate his dramatic range. The innkeeper agrees to leave his sanctuary and to offer himself as bait so that Holmes and the police might capture the murderer. That won't happen, however, in any environment other than the moor. Seeing himself surrounded by his own stalkers, the killer - who is none other than the mailman, Potts – desperately hurls himself the man he intends to kill, but it turns out to be Holmes, in disguise. Potts/Ramson is then confronted by Journet, who kills him with his own murder weapon: the small gardener's rake. The end to the affair will be death by hand, an outcome unusual for the time and also for the series (wherein the villains ended up either falling from a height to their death (as did Lionel Atwill) or being arrested (like Gale Sondergaard or George Zucco). The only certainty was that it would never be Sherlock Holmes's hand that was dirtied by their blood.

**Better late than never? Holmes and Watson *finally* make it to La Morte Rouge, in response to the plea of Lady Penrose (Gertrude Astor), who has been fearing for her life.**

Despite various current critiques and studies pointing out that the denouement is somewhat anticlimactic, if we view the last few minutes understanding the context of that moment in time, the bit of comedy had with Watson tripping down the stairs and the fast cut to the car bringing the pair back to the big city help lessen the bitter taste of that judgment. When Holmes begins his final speech about Canada, we know that it will be one of his usual rhetorical pieces dealing with the war effort. Save for a trio

444

of officers who walk across the background in the first scenes of that hotel in Quebec, the war is completely absent from the film; thus, in the last frames our hero will end up quoting a famous harangue by Winston Churchill, in which he praises Canada as as much a loyal and willful ally of the United States as of the United Kingdom.

Welshman Gerald Hamer – who would also appear in series entries with The Saint (*The Saint Strikes Back*), Bulldog Drummond (*Bulldog Drummond's Bride*, both 1939), and Arsène Lupin (*Enter Arsène Lupin*, 1944) - graced five of the Rathbone/ Bruce features. In *Scarlet Claw*, Hamer enjoyed his best role(s) in the series but, sadly, after his next appearance (in *Pursuit to Algiers*, 1945), he would find his cinematic career winding down to a number of disjointed, uncredited appearances. His *Scarlet Claw* colleague, Englishman Paul Cavanaugh, was also familiar face in the Holmes series, with three titles – *The House of Fear* and *The Woman in Green* (both 1945) in addition to the film under discussion – notched on *his* belt. Both gentlemen made their life debuts during the late Victorian Age, and then won their first fame on the legitimate stage. There's more on Mr. Cavanagh in our essay on *The Strange Case of Doctor Rx*.

Notwithstanding the fact that the film was usually paired with another for double features, some print critics of the time highlighted the values of *The Scarlet Claw*. The column "The Box Office Slant" in the 29 April 1944 *Showmen's Trade Review* established an interesting artistic rank for the two actors: "Basil Rathbone and Nigel Bruce have fallen into the characters of Sherlock Holmes and Dr. Watson so perfectly that one no longer thinks in terms of a good acting role well done. They are characters in life." With many fewer words, *Motion Picture Daily* (2 May 1944) described the actors' imprint as "the deft touch." *Film Daily* (6 June 1944) classified the film as a "gripping meller"; nevertheless, it made a slight distinction between the two protagonists that, incredibly, remains a current topic of conversation among fans and scholars:

> Rathbone perfectly mirrors Holmes's sharp attributes, but there has been a compromise in the case of Bruce, who is left to carry a comedy role which is too extreme, just for the sake of providing a contrast here and there to otherwise stark happenings. Bruce, being an excellent trouper, proves right for the role. But it is a departure from the Watson of Doyle.

*Variety* (24 May 1944), which dedicated only a brief column to the film, described another dilemma that is still commented on today:

Universal has resorted to original stories to continue the Sherlock Holmes series, but it is very apparent that they don't measure up to the Conan Doyle plots, despite the presence of psychic phenomena, apparitions and premonitions, with the result that the entire thing wears thin.

A particular "failing" that one finds in the film is the rather poor depiction of Holmes's legendary gift for deduction. Potts/Ramson's talent for disguise – at one point, he is accoutered as the seaman, Jack Tanner – leaves the Great Consulting Detective ever one step behind. Holmes fails to prevent the murder of Judge Brisson – he cannot be held responsible for young Marie Journet's death – and it is only by impersonating innkeeper Journet, whom he *has* deduced is next in line, that he manages to disclose the wily killer. Not Sherlock's finest hour (and 14 minutes). Nor does the film do much to posit Dr. Watson's intellectual standing - The critic at the *New York Herald Tribune* opined that the film "puts a clown's cap again on Dr. Watson" - but this tendency had first been observed in *Sherlock Holmes Faces Death*. Another "failing" in the opinion of many fans of the series is the fact that this is the first entry in which not an instant is spent at 221b Baker Street.

Per Michael Hoey's excellent book on the series (and – in part – on his dad's participation in same):

> Universal... put out the following press release: 'Paul Gangelin and Brenda Weisberg have been assigned by Universal to do a screenplay on *Sherlock Holmes vs. Moriarity* [sic], which will be the third and last on Universal's "Sherlock Holmes" series for 1943-1944.' (1)

While this script, Mr. Hoey recounts, wasn't used at this point, following a great deal of revision, it – and its appalling use of "Professor Moriar*i*ty" - would see the carbon arc as *The Woman in Green* in 1945. Also yclept *Sherlock Holmes in Canada* in pre-production (2), its ultimate release as *The Scarlet Claw* inadvertently (or not) supported the custom initiated with *The Spider Woman* of omitting the Great Consulting Detective's name from the title.

Basque filmmaker Victor Erice reveals in *La morte rouge* that his search for the eponymous region on maps and topography was fruitless "surely because it only existed in the imagination of the screenwriters of *The Scarlet Claw*, the first motion picture that I remember having ever seen." After seeing it and declaring to have been somewhat traumatized by the discovery that the killer was the gregarious and charismatic postman – the assumed identity of an actor – the five-year-old Victor Erice asked himself, "What was an actor?" He was someone who, through beards, wigs, and shaves, was able to assume the visage and identity of everyone. "And if Potts could be everyone," deduced the narrator, "at the same time, everyone could be Potts." This explained his fear about "the evil Potts," later transferred for a long time to the postmen of his native Spain and today, decades having passed, converted into a tribute to the magic of a class "B" film, concocted by its authors with the imprint of a genre and a time.

*The Scarlet Claw* – 26 May 1944 – 74 minutes

**CAST**: Basil Rathbone as Sherlock Holmes; Nigel Bruce as Doctor Watson; Gerald Hamer as Potts/Tanner/Ramson; Paul Cavanaugh as Lord Penrose; Arthur Hohl as Emile Journet; Miles Mander as Judge Brisson; Kay Harding as Marie Journet; David Clyde as Sgt. Thompson; Ian Wolfe as Drake; Victoria Horne as Nora; George Kirby as Father Pierre; Gertrude Astor as Lady Penrose; Norbert Muller as Bellhop at the Quebec Hotel; Eric Wilton as the Night Clerk at the Quebec Hotel; Charles Francis as Sir John; William Desmond, Eric Mayne, Brandon Beach, Count Stefanelli as Members of the Occult Society; Olaf Hytten as the Day Clerk at the Quebec Hotel; with: Horace B. Carpenter, Bobby Hale, Bobby Burns, Ted Billings, Frank Austin, Jack Kenny, John C. McCallum, Phil Schumacher, George Sowards, Jack Tornek as Villagers in Pub; Harry Allen as Bill Taylor

**CREDITS**: Produced and Directed by Roy William Neill; Executive Producer: Howard Benedict; Screenplay: Edmund L. Hartmann & Roy William Neill; Based on a story by Paul Gangelin and Brenda Weisberg; Music and Musical Director: Paul Sawtell; Photography: George Robinson; Film Editor: Paul Landres; Art Directors: Ralph M. DeLacy and John B. Goodman; Set Decoration: Russell A. Gausman and Ira S. Webb; Makeup: Jack P. Pierce; Visual Effects: John P. Fulton; Camera Operator: Eddie Cohen; Sound Director: Bernard B. Brown; Technician: Robert Pritchard
- *DL*

# *The Invisible Man's Revenge* (1944)

*Synopsis:* Robert Griffin arrives in England from Cape Town after escaping from a mental hospital there and killing three orderlies. Griffin just recently regained his memory after five years of amnesia and goes to seek his former business partners, Sir Jasper Herrick and his wife, Irene. They are shocked to see Griffin when he arrives at their Shortlands estate, having believed him dead after suffering a head injury during their search for diamonds in Africa. Griffin doesn't buy that and insists on his share of the diamond mine they had discovered. When told that most of the profits had been lost through bad investments, Griffin demands that the Herricks sign over Shortlands to him. Griffin is also interested in daughter, Julie Herrick, who is engaged to Mark Foster, a reporter. When Griffin passes out after having a drink, Sir Jasper - realizing that their former friend is now dangerously paranoid - carries him out of the house, but only after Irene steals their original agreement about the mine from Griffin's pocket.

Griffin is taken in by penniless cobbler Herbert Higgins, who then tries to blackmail the Herricks, but the scheme backfires and Sir Jasper's friend, chief constable Sir Frederick Travers, runs Griffin out of the district. Wandering about in the rain, Griffin is given shelter by Dr. Drury, an eccentric scientist who has successfully experimented in turning animals - including his dog, Brutus – invisible. Griffin volunteers to be a human subject, and the doctor's drug does indeed render him invisible.

Using Higgins's cottage as his base of operations, Griffin proceeds to terrify and harass Sir Jasper and Irene. Soon, stories of an invisible man wandering around the countryside attract Mark Foster's interest. In the interim, knowing he can never woo Julie in his current state, Griffin returns to Dr. Drury and asks to be made visible.

449

Although Drury has returned his dog to a state of visibility, the doctor tells Griffin that *his* having the condition reversed would require the complete draining of another person's blood and this, Drury refuses to do. Griffin overpowers Drury and uses the lab equipment to transfuse the doctor's blood to himself. Becoming visible again, he sets the cottage on fire, but Brutus escapes the conflagration.

Griffin returns to Shortlands and insists that Sir Jasper pass him off as his friend, Martin Field. When, after a short while, Griffin starts to become invisible again, he lures Foster down to the wine cellar, knocks him unconscious, and starts to transfuse his blood. Part way through the process, though, Sir Jasper and Sir Frederick break down the door. Brutus gets in before they do, however, and kills his master's murderer, saving Foster.

In the summer of 1943, the trade papers announced that Claude Rains and Gale Sondergaard would star in *The Invisible Man's Revenge* for Universal. It's hard to believe that Universal seriously expected that Rains – by then a major star - would be willing to reprise his first very first starring role in a "B"-movie sequel, so perhaps his name was just floated to arouse a little interest in the project; come the new year, Rains was no longer mentioned. The 1 January 1944 edition of *The New York Times* then reported that *The Invisible Man's Revenge* would start production in three weeks, would star Sondergaard, Leon Errol, and Edgar Barrier, and would be based on a story by Clyde Bruckman. Bruckman was a gag writer at Universal and, in his palmier days, had been Buster Keaton's right-hand man on films like *The General* and *Our Hospitality*. Was there some thought to doing the film as an out-and-out comedy? If Bruckman really did contribute to the movie, he wasn't credited, and the script was done by another Silent Era veteran, Bertram Millhauser, who had written for Pearl White and Cecil B. De Mille.

The 2 January 1944 edition of *Showman's Trade Review* announced that the film would start production on the 10 January and would star Jon Hall, with Alan Curtis and Evelyn Ankers providing the love interest, and that "Gale Sondergaard and Edgar Barrier are set for more sinister roles." By the time the cameras had started rolling, Barrier had left Universal and his part (Sir Jasper) was done by Lester Matthews, the bland hero of *WereWolf of London* and *The Raven*.

Griffin's back story is a little confusing and full of loose ends. How did he survive in the jungle after his injury and make his way to Cape Town? Did he become a psychotic before or after regaining his memory? One would think, since he had his contract with the Herricks in his pocket, it wouldn't have taken five years to figure out who he was.

450

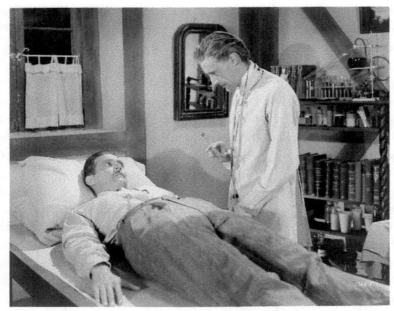

**While John Carradine played many a crackpot scientist, it was rare for Jon Hall
to appear as a villain, although he did so again in his very last film, *Beach Girls and
the Monster* (1965), which he directed, as well.**

The script can't seem to make up its mind whether the Herricks are innocent
victims or cheats out to save their reputation (the comment about "more sinister roles"
would suggest the latter). There's little ambiguity in the synopsis Universal submitted
to the Library of Congress on the 24 January 1944: "Irene drugs Griffin and, after
destroying the agreement that Griffin carries, the Herricks drop his body in the
river." The film considerably softens the Herricks, but the way the scene leading to
Griffin's collapse is set up, it would seem obvious that Irene has drugged his drink
(though would she just happen to have the makings of a Mickey Finn in her liquor
cabinet?) and then enlisted her husband as a reluctant co-conspirator. Her comment
that Griffin passing out from just one drink proves he's mentally ill is laughable. When
Irene takes the contract from the unconscious Griffin's pocket, it looks as though she's
going to burn it but, when Jasper seems shocked, she tells him they will keep it for
Griffin until his mental state improves. How running him out of town will help with
that is anyone's guess, but it will remove the possibility of a scandal if Griffin presses
his story. They don't dump Griffin in the river either; still groggy, he falls into the

water on his own. The Herricks don't come off as being very nice people, but the story in its current form tries to mitigate that, perhaps reasoning that you can't make the heroine's parents out-and-out villains and render the psychotic Griffin sympathetic. Interestingly enough, the Catholic Legion of Decency gave the film an "objectionable in part for all" rating because "there is no retribution for crime." Since Griffin getting torn to pieces by a dog would seem like retribution enough, does the rating refer to the Herricks getting off scot-free? Strangely, Sondergaard's Irene turns as invisible as Griffin after the scene where the madman frightens her; we never see her again after that, though her character is referred to once or twice. She's not even in the last scene, nor is Lester Matthews.

There's also the class war tension lying underneath the situation. The Herricks are snobs; Jasper isn't sure Julie should marry Foster since he has no money, but he relents when Irene reminds him that the reporter is from one of England's best families. The Herricks' high position in society allows them to treat Griffin and Higgins as nobodies and guarantees the legal establishment will back them up. Dr. Drury helps cajole Griffin into submitting to his risky experiment by reminding him just where he stands in relation to his high-born friends. Having encouraged Griffin's resentment and paranoia, should Drury have really been surprised when the Invisible Man preferred his mission of vengeance to being the doctor's prime exhibit? You would also think that Drury's success in rendering animals invisible would be enough to insure his scientific immortality even without a human subject.

Critics doubted that H.G. Wells' would have even recognized his story from this film version. However, the movie does overcome one objection Wells had had to the 1933 classic, namely the notion that it was the drug that rendered Griffin insane and turned him into a monster. In the book, he's an awful person from the get go, and turning invisible just gives him the opportunity to be more awful. Unlike the first film and its sequel, *The Invisible Man Returns*, here the drug is irrelevant to Griffin's mental state. Also, Griffin's relationship with Herbert seems a reworking of the book's episodes involving the tramp, Marvel, who is forced by the Invisible Man to become his helper.

The idea that a blood transfusion can return Griffin to normal provided the *Deus ex machina* for *The Invisible Man Returns,* but here it used for gruesome effect, and having Griffin revert to invisibility against his will and in need of an antidote is a bit like *Dr. Jekyll and Mr. Hyde.* It also gives Griffin a chance to make a crack about Dracula, but he conducts the transfusion procedure without even knowing whether his blood type will match his victim's (Hey, didn't anybody remember the end of *The*

*Ghost of Frankenstein?*). In addition to all this, we note that he's an extremely quick study as a phlebotomist. Still, as one critic put it, "the yarn was not intended for submission to analysis."

Most reviewers had high praise for Leon Errol's performance as Herbert, with Alton Cook of *The New York World Telegram* writing that his comedy was "several grades above the mirth that is usually provided for these horror affairs." The one naysayer was the scribe for *Film Daily* who opined that "Leon Errol's brand of comedy seems out of place in a picture like this." Errol was supposed to play an Irishman (Barney O'Dea), but became the Cockney Herbert Higgins in the final version. Errol was actually Australian and several times in the film utters "Struth," Down-Under slang for "God's Truth." Errol had become quite famous for his "rubber legs" routine in his glory days on Broadway and in vaudeville in the '10s and '20s. Things went a bit awry though during a performance in one of his greatest hits, *Louie the 14th* when he broke both ankles and had to go to Vienna for treatment. Errol had no such problem in *The Invisible Man's Revenge* and doesn't do much physical shtick here, but he still manages to be memorably funny. When the shyster lawyer Herbert has enlisted against the Herricks withdraws and nervously announces "I wash my hands of this," Errol snorts "You and Pontius Pilate." Herbert's timid request that the Invisible Man wear a bag over his head rather than sit "headless" at the breakfast table is also a good moment, as is the dart game wherein the Invisible Man "throws" the darts for Herbert who then lords his victory over his rival and the astonished pub patrons.

Jon Hall, who had himself dematerialized earlier to fight the Axis in *Invisible Agent,* here has a rare villainous role and handles it very well. *Variety* described Hall as doing a "bang-up" job as Griffin, and other reviewers likewise thought he was far more effective in this film than in his Maria Montez epics. Hall's intense performance suggests a man barely in control of himself and always on the verge of boiling over into complete mania. Hall also makes us feel his fear of Brutus, who functions a bit like Captain Hook's relentless crocodile.

Hall might well have wished himself invisible later in 1944 during a fracas in the apartment of band leader Tommy Dorsey, who thought the actor was getting a little too familiar with his wife. Hall suffered wounds that required 60 stitches to close, including a disfiguring gash across the nose. Hall said the stab wounds were inflicted by Alan Smiley, described as a "sportsman" in the papers; however, the actor subsequently asked that the whole thing be dropped. Perhaps that was a wise move, given the fact that Smiley was pals with notorious gangster Bugsy Siegel. Nevertheless, Dorsey, his wife, and Smiley were all indicted, but witnesses changed their testimony or had lapses of memory, and charges were dismissed. Doctors were able to repair Hall's nose sufficiently so he did not have to worry about his close-ups with Babette the Chimp in his subsequent TV hit, *Ramar of the Jungle*.

I suspect John Carradine's performance as Dr. Drury may have been tongue-in-cheek. He has the usual mad-scientist speech in which he proclaims his discoveries will put him on the same level as Archimedes, Galileo, and Darwin, but he comes off as being more of a crackpot than a genius. Lionel Atwill has very similar dialogue in *Man-made monster*, but the glint in his eye and his zealous delivery convince you that he's the real deal, however absurd his goals. Carradine sounds more like a street-corner crank. His best moment comes when he slyly persuades Griffin to become his subject by telling him that Brutus, when he was turned invisible, was able to take vengeance on the high-bred dogs who had been bullying him.

*The Invisible Man's Revenge* is far from Bertram Millhauser's best writing (*The Suspect* likely takes that honor). Aside from some of the inconsistencies and lapses in logic mentioned earlier, Millhauser goes into *cliché* overdrive via Sir Frederick in the last scenes: "Judgment was passed on him by a higher court than ours." "He probed too deeply into forbidden places." "What a man earns he gets. Nature has a strange way of paying him back in his own coin." What? No "He tampered in God's domain?"

Millhauser talked about thrillers and horror films to Philip K. Scheuer in the 5 November 1944 edition of the *Los Angeles Times*. Even though he himself had written a number of "Sherlock Holmes" movies for Universal, Millhauser expressed doubt that the screen had ever done a good mystery or detective story:

What you get in the movies is a horror story, not a deductive work. Horror films arouse apprehension; you wait-for the terrible, the grisly, the unseen to appear; you are subjected to a sharp series of emotional shocks in picture form. And that's all. Hitchcock is a master of that sort of thing. Take the scene in 'Foreign Correspondent' where Joel McCrea gets his coat caught. It was an emotional experience that had nothing much to do with anything in the story. But it was sufficient unto itself. Every scene in the picture was like that. Put them all together and they spelt nothing... only a great horror film.

It [*Trent's Last Case*] is a remarkable example of the best in detective story writing-reason and logic above the neck. Yet every element in is inimical to motion pictures; their appeal, whether you like it or not, is entirely below the neck. As for reason and logic you can just take them and drop them down the drain. People are interested in the 'what' of what happens, not the 'why.'

Millhauser also complained about too much talk on the screen but expressed optimism that "The 'see' pictures are gradually replacing the 'say' pictures and the horror film is helping them do it." Ford Beebe's direction of *Invisible Man's Revenge* is quick and efficient although, since this is the fifth "invisible" picture, the novelty has worn off. Still, the special effects, fairly modest here because of the "B"-budget, occasionally amuse (the invisible dog eating a sandwich) or startle (the invisible Griffin splashing water on his face to terrify the Herricks). Beebe was a veteran serial director and was lured over from Columbia to Universal in the mid-'30s with just that task in mind. However, by the end of the decade, Universal was seeing only a very marginal profit from the serials and downgraded them. This occasionally frustrated Beebe:

> I recall one occasion sitting in the projection room with about 15 of the high brass looking at the previous days rushes. We sat through a lot of mediocre film that we would never have let get by in our serials. Then when our serial stuff came on, the whole gang left en masse. For a moment I thought of blocking their exit and insisting they stay to see some REAL film. [The footage] was from *Buck Rogers*. It showed the demolition of the throne room of Saturn chiseled out of solid rock beneath a mountain. We had occupied a full stage and by means of a glass shot we had made the throne room look immense. When it was destroyed by ray-gun, walls caved in, pillars toppled and mobs ran about trying to escape. And they didn't even bother looking at it because by then serials weren't bringing in any revenue worth mentioning. (1)

Universal then put Beebe in their "B"-movie unit, assigning him to direct *Night Monster*. The studio was understandably pleased with this atmospheric and creepy little gem, and when George Waggner was called away from *Son of Dracula* to manage *Phantom of the Opera*, Beebe took his place as producer; he also did some second-unit directing on this one as well as fashioning the continuity from Eric Taylor's story. In June 1944, *Motion Picture Herald* announced that Beebe would produce a Lon Chaney film, *Dracula Meets the Wolf Man* - intended as a follow-up to *Frankenstein Meets the Wolf Man* - but *The Invisible Man's Revenge* proved to be his last horror film for the studio.

JON HALL in *THE INVISIBLE MAN'S REVENGE*
John Carradine

with
ALAN CURTIS
GALE SONDERGAARD

Original Screenplay by BERTRAM MILLHAUSER
Suggested by "The Invisible Man" by H. G. WELLS

**Lester Matthew is terrorized by his invisible nemesis. Earlier in his career, Matthews had had to contend with Henry Hull in *Werewolf of London* and with Bela Lugosi's Dr. Vollin in *The Raven*.**

Reviews for *The Invisible Man's Revenge* varied:

> "Preposterous shocker that has comic moments but becomes dubious when it turns gruesome."
> *Christian Science Monitor* 26 July 1944

A rather involved story, this picture will satisfy the lovers of suspense and melodrama. It is for adults as it concerns the crack brain adventures of a maniac and its main theme is murder. Leon Errol's impersonation of a Cockney is the outstanding character of the play. His comedy adds many laughs to the morbidity of the proceedings. Jon Hall and John Carradine present convincing characterizations. Ford Beebe's direction keeps the action moving and the suspense at a high pitch throughout.
*Showman's Trade Review,* 3 June 1944

Some of the earlier variations of H.G. Wells' Invisible Man idea were filmed with an idea that the story should make good sense. That policy has been abandoned this time for a session with the mad scientist... A proper Rialto quota of creeps and lively excitement is provided and that is the sole idea of the venture.

Alton Cook, *New York World Telegram*, 9 June 1944

Fifth in the invisible man series is fast-moving but preposterous yet has the saving grace of being intelligently performed and directed so for the duals it should more than hold its own... Leon Errol reaps plenty of laughs from his cockney role and John Carradine clicks as the daffy prof.

Donn, *Variety*, 7 June 1944

Unfortunately, trick photography is not sufficient to maintain a whole film and this one reveals quite plainly that you don't see much when you see an invisible man.

Bosley Crowther, *The New York Times*, 10 June 1944

Hall doesn't come up to the first Invisible Man, Claude Rains, who did his stint back in 1933 but for a guy who plays out half his role minus a head, he's pretty good.

John L. Scott, *Los Angeles Times*, 15 September 1944

Illogical but packs horror interest.. Hall at least meets all the requirements of the script with plenty of theatrics. The invisible premise is rather cleverly justified but the plot goes as fantastic as such themes usually do and no follow through action is qualified.

*The Independent Film Journal*, 10 June 1944

A good melodramatic idea that has inspired no more than a pedestrian thriller... The tricks have been done too often before by the camera to make them effective in themselves.

Howard Barnes, *NY Herald-Tribune*, 10 June 1944

It has been produced well enough and has enough novelty, excitement and even comedy to satisfy melodrama-loving audiences. Although the mechanical tricks may lack novelty to those who have seen any of the previous pictures, it is, nevertheless effective.

*Harrison's Reports,* 10 June 1944

While *The Invisible Man's Revenge* hardly compares with James Whale's masterpiece, it's a respectable "B"-thriller that delivers the expected goods. And, as always, it's a pleasure to see Universal's stock company in action. We have Ian Wolfe as the shyster, Skelton Knaggs as a helpful villager, Halliwell Hobbes announcing the latest unwelcome guest as the loyal butler, and there's Constable Billy Bevan, still at his post and looking none the worse for wear after his encounter with Dracula's Daughter. 'Struth.

*The Invisible Man's Revenge* - 9 June 1944 - 78 minutes (SoS)

**CAST:** Jon Hall as Robert Griffin; Leon Errol as Herbert Higgins; John Carradine as Dr. Drury; Alan Curtis as Mark Foster; Evelyn Ankers as Julie Herrick; Lester Matthews as Sir Jasper Herrick; Leyland Hodgson as Sir Frederick Travers; Halliwell Hobbes as Cleghorn; Doris Lloyd as Maud; Ian Wolf as Jim Feeney; Billy Bevan as Sergeant; Grey Shadow as Himself (Brutus); Cyril Delvanti as Malty Bill; Leonard Carey as Constable; Skelton Knaggs as Al Prouty; Yorke Sherwood as Jim Yarrow; Tom P. Dillon as Towle; Guy Kingsford as Bill; Jim Aubrey as Wedderburn; Arthur Gold-Porter as Tom Meadow; Lillian Bronson as Norma; Janna deLoos as Nellie.

**CREDITS:** Director: Ford Beebe; Writer: Bertram Millhauser; Producers: Ford Beebe, Howard Benedict; Photography: Milton Krasner; Editor: Saul A. Goodkind; Art Directors: John Goodman, Harold MacArthur; Set Decorators: Russell A. Gausman, A.J. Gilmore; Costumes: Vera West; Music: H.J. Salter; Sound: Bernard Brown, William Hedgcock; Visual Effects: John P. Fulton; Assistant Director: Fred Frank

*- HN*

# *Ghost Catchers* (1944)

*Synopsis*: Colonel Marshall and his two daughters Susanna and Melinda move into an old brownstone in New York to prepare for Melinda's debut at Carnegie Hall. Strange noises during the night convince them that the house is haunted. Susanna rushes next door for assistance and finds herself in a nightclub where Olsen and Johnson are performing. The two comics finish their act and then try to assist the Marshalls, who are becoming increasingly worried about the mysterious ruckus and the appearance of messages warning of trouble.

Olsen and Johnson learn that the house is likely haunted by Wilbur, a wealthy *bon vivant* who threw a New Year's Party there in 1900 and accidentally fell to his death before the festivities ended. The comics become convinced that restaging the party will exorcise Wilbur. On the second attempt, they seem to have succeeded and the ghost flees the house waving a white flag.

However, the mysterious happenings continue. Susanna finds the body of Diggs the caretaker hanging in the closet. While she is out summoning the police, her father, sister and then Olsen and Johnson disappear. It turns out that a criminal gang, some of them wearing animal disguises, have found valuable cases of liquor in the basement and are trying to scare off the Marshalls so they can smuggle out the booty. They are led by a man wearing an eerie mask. The gangsters wall up the Colonel, Melinda, and Olsen and Johnson, but Wilbur the friendly ghost appears and helps them escape. Police, summoned by Wilbur, arrive and capture the gang, but their leader is still at large. Olsen and Johnson set a trap for him at the night club. It succeeds and the masked man is revealed to be Jerry, the head waiter at the club.

459

"For the first time Olsen and Johnson have a story, not just a lot of funny props. It's whimsey, not whamsey." Chic Johnson on *Ghost Catchers*.

As the above synopsis indicates, the story provides only the thinnest of excuses to showcase the two comics and a heavy dose of musical numbers. Still, when compared with Olsen and Johnson's previous two films for Universal - *Hellzapoppin'* and *Crazy House* - the movie is positively plot-driven.

John Sigvard "Ole" Olsen and Harold Ogden 'Chic" Johnson got together as a team in 1914, billing themselves - perhaps optimistically - as "Two Likable Lads Loaded with Laughs." When they failed to win any bookings, they reputedly marched into a night club, camped out at the piano, and did their shtick while completely ignoring the official on-stage act to the astonishment of the performers and the delight of the audience. This was beginning of a very successful career in Vaudeville followed by stints on Broadway and on radio. The team likewise did a few movies in the '30s, but these were pretty conventional. Unlike Bud and Lou, Laurel and Hardy, or the Marx Brothers, Olsen and Johnson did not have strong individual personalities (though Johnson had a distinctive silly giggle). It was the endless string of rapid-fire gags and the things happening around them that drew the laughs.

Olsen and Johnson's biggest hit was their 1938 zany stage-show, *Hellzapoppin*, supposedly launched with a mere $16,000. The play - if it could be called that - was absolute craziness, a "Looney Tune" with flesh-and-blood actors. And, as demonic little Anthony said in *Twilight Zone: The Movie*, "In cartoons anything can happen." Richard Poe of *The Washington Post* (14 April 1942) summed it up nicely:

> It's a loud slam bang-bang riot that makes no sense whatsoever and manages to be uproariously funny. It's about as delicate as a 40-ton tank. Its inmates, beg pardon participants, work like 77 furies armed with props that include wash basins, mops, ladders, bananas, beer bottles, bags of flour, eggs, cigars and what have you... The gags may be as corny as a mid-summer field but they're there in such profusion that they get laughs they haven't gotten since cavemen started drawing funny pictures on the walls of their Neolithic caves.

Brooks Atkinson of *The New York Times* described the show as a "demented vaudeville brawl" that was "loud, low and funny." Still, the critics were divided. "There are people who will laugh at anything," sniffed *The Christian Science Monitor*, but - *Vox populi, vox Dei* - the show ran three years on Broadway and amassed over nine million dollars world-wide.

The film version followed in 1942 (adding an apostrophe to the end of the title), and Universal insisted on some sort of story-line, so Olsen and Johnson came up with a corny romantic plot that they made fun of as it was unfolding. Nonetheless, critics thought the zaniness of a live performance - with its frequent involvement of the audience - really couldn't be reproduced on film. Seen today, in this post *Laugh-In* era, the movie only occasionally amuses. Of course, when the viewer has a full catapult of gags aimed at him, it's not surprising that every so often one finds its target.

As Gary Don Rhodes points out in his **The Birth of the American Horror Film**, cinematic ghosts are practically as old as the movies; still, genuinely frightening spooks were rare. Either the ghosts were benign, or - more often than not - played for laughs. Characters pretending to be ghosts as a joke or in order to disguise some criminal purpose were also common. The latter was the case in the first full-length American ghost story, *The Ghost Breaker* (1914; remade in 1922 and – as *The Ghost Breakers* - 1940), wherein crooks posed as ghosts in a "haunted" castle to cover their search for treasure. Comedy continued to be the accent on "ghost" films - be they shorts or features - throughout the '20s and '30s. By the time of *Ghost Catchers*, it had become increasingly difficult to extract laughs from all the old haunted house gags. *Ghost Catchers* seem to realize this and has Olsen and Johnson making a couple of remarks on the very similar *Hold that Ghost* with Abbott and Costello, claiming that it was unbelievable, particularly the moving candle gimmick which *Ghost Catchers* then goes on to repeat (the cartoon shown under the credits is also taken from *Hold that Ghost*). *Ghost Catchers* does *Hold that Ghost* one better by tossing in a real spook along with the fake ones.

There are a couple of oddball references to Edgar Allan Poe in the film, as when Olsen and Johnson and the rest of the gang begin their song to exorcise Wilbur starting with "Once upon a midnight dreary" and ending with "Quoth the raven 'Nevermore'." The protagonists getting walled up alive is right out of "The Cask of Amontillado," but in spite of a sinister shot of a pair of eyes looking at the victims before the last brick is laid, the scene isn't played for thrills. In fact, the movie - perhaps mindful that there would many kids in the audience - seems to go out of it way to avoid anything scary. At the very beginning of the film, Charles Van Enger's camera moves in for a close-up of a shutter creaking closed followed by some ominous music, but that's pretty much the only concession to Universal's horror style. Instead of shrieks or moans, we hear tap dancing and the clip-clop of horses to represent the spooks. The bogus ghosts are dressed as a bear and a horse (no point in asking why), and thus are not likely to tingle any spines. Nonetheless, the mask worn by the boss is genuinely weird (one

461

reviewer said it reminded him of Pruneface from "Dick Tracy," while another thought it reminiscent of Frankenstein's Monster); it's a little bit like Preston Foster in his synthetic-flesh guise from *Doctor X*. The scene where Susanna finds Diggs hanging in the closet is about a hoary an old dark house *cliché* as you can disinter, but it's still surprisingly grim, given the film's overall reluctance to mingle chills with the laughs.

**The one genuinely spooky element of the film, the mask, is applied by Jack Pierce to – of all people – Leo Carrillo. Oh, Pancho!**

Modern viewers are sometimes impatient with all the music in these vintage comedies. Is there anybody out there who doesn't wish the Marx Brothers had dropped a couple of sandbags on Kitty Carlisle and Allan Jones doing their "Alone" duet in *A Night at the Opera*? In *Ghost Catchers*, though, the tunes are less annoying, since interrupting Olsen and Johnson's hijinks is sometimes a welcome relief. The songs are pretty hokey ("You came, you saw, you conquered me" warbles Morton Downey), but the jitterbug exorcism sequence is lively and fun. The romantic angle, another contrived time-waster that has marred many a '40s comedy, is played straight here (unlike in *Hellzapoppin'*). Will bandleader Kirby Grant and Susanna (Martha O'Driscoll) get together in spite of the interference of jealous singer, Virginia Bennett? Is there ever any doubt? However exasperating these musical and romantic interludes may seem today, audiences of yesteryear apparently liked them, and producers insisted on them.

The picture is mainly for admirers of Olsen and Johnson, but others might get a laugh or two out of it. The scene where the villains are temporarily subdued as Olsen and Johnson pretend to mourn over fallen Old Paint (the horsehead) reminded me a bit of Cleavon Little's escaping from the townspeople by holding himself hostage in *Blazing Saddles*. A couple of the criminal gang are midgets and, when the comics mention Snow White, the little people shout in exasperation how they're sick of hearing about her. Occasionally one or two of the team's off-color comments do strike home. Director Eddie Kline wrote and directed scores of classic comedies (*Million Dollar Legs* is my favorite), but here he can't do much more than turn on the camera and hope letting the boys do their thing will be enough.

In the supporting cast, only Walter Catlett as the Southern-fried colonel stands out. A scowling Lon Chaney is seen but briefly as the crook in the bear outfit, while Andy Devine and Leo Carillo are likewise wasted. Sweet Gloria Jean - who turned 18 during filming - sings a couple of tunes. In the words of *The New York Times* critic, Martha O'Driscoll is "asked to look beautiful and does so with the greatest of ease." In the first scene at the night club, she is tossed all over the place, strapped into an electric chair and then dropped through a trap door down a chute into the street. After all that, it was likely a welcome relief to appear opposite gentleman bloodsucker, John Carradine, in *House of Dracula*.

Some New York critics felt the zany magic of Olsen and Johnson still worked, but whether they loved or hated the film, they all filed reviews on the 31 May 1944:

> Olsen and Johnson seemed to have learned after two unfettered film flights that not even such bounding genius as theirs can long endure without rhyme, reason and a certain attention to production. Hence *Ghost Catchers* has all these... Olsen and

Johnson direct the pell-mell task of exorcising this ghost gallery with imagination and dispatch.

John T. McManus, *NY Newspaper PM*

*Ghost Catchers* is a series of fantastic gags. The stars will sacrifice any attempt at plot if there is a chance for a gag. The film does have a plot, one much better forgotten. It usually is forgotten popping up now and then just to point up the latest gag. The comedy is rough-and-tumble, the laughs frequent. Nothing makes any sense.

Eileen Creelman, *New York Sun*

Dorothy Masters – in *The New York Daily News* - saw a satire of Universal beneath all the lunacy:

What with talking animals, mysterious gremlins and an amiable apparition of the Gay Nineties meandering through, *Ghost Catchers* takes a playful nip at the hand that feeds the box office. A double nip actually since the studio has burlesqued a couple of coffer-swellers, the who-dun-it and the horror film by outlandish distortion of most standard appurtenances plus a few not previously in the books.

Other reviewers thought the comedy duo's frenetic style was grating and didn't work on film:

A tedious lot of hocus-pocus. The trouble would seem to be an excess of helter-skelter doings for Olsen and Johnson just pop up here and there, pulling rabbits out of the air and dropping through trapdoors without rhyme or reason.

TMP, *The New York Times*

As usual they are clowns rather than comedians. The slapstick is laid on with a heavy hand as visual gags of the most obvious type are substituted for clever lines and situations. The trap doors, exploding props, zany costumes and trick photography give the actors a lively time of it but they don't add up to an amusing screenplay.

Otis L. Guernsey, Jr., *New York Herald Tribune*

These two, unexcelled at throwing a theater into happy bedlam, leave a movie audience singularly unmoved. Their latest is another in their succession of misses. It is a collection of familiar haunted house comedy ideas, the very ones that have been serving this comedian and that one well for years. They don't work nearly as well for Chic and Ole. Their talent runs to boisterous life of the party spirit spread out over a whole theater and that doesn't come through from the movie screen. They can't throw things and they are limited on sheer volume when they start shooting and yelling.

Alton Cook, *New York World Telegram*

(We can be grateful that Chic and Ole didn't discover 3-D or Smell-O-Vision.)

There was not a lot of enthusiasm for the film in the trade press:

If any pains went into the making of this Olsen-Johnson picture the results show little evidence of it. The film is a slipshod, disjointed affair that gets the few laughs it does only at the expenditure of considerable effort. Only the very young will respond with any degree of joyousness to the sort of stuff contained in this production... Persons who are allergic to corn will be left cold by the comics' antics.

*Film Daily*, 8 June 1944

It does not however rise above program quality. Like the previous pictures this one depends for its laughs on the typical buffoonery of these two comedians who run through their bag of nonsensical tricks with varying degrees of success. At times they are quite funny but for the most part their antics provoke no more than a grin. The musical numbers which are dragged in by the ear are fairly entertaining.

*Harrison's Reports*, 10 June 1944

Still, Sten (in the 31 May 1944 edition of *Variety*) was a believer:

A tuneful screwy production, brief and zippy. Grooved on the top rung for duals, it is money in the bank. Edmund L. Hartmann's production cuts corners at every turn; the film being showcased is not too expensive but has substantial settings. Eddie Cline, an old -time comedian himself, pilots the cast in capable fashion, his direction being responsible for the fast pace. Considering everything, much credit must go to film editor Arthur Hilton, who probably kept the midnight lamps burning separating the wheat from the chaff in this one. All in all, another "rent payer" from Universal.

Olsen and Johnson went on to do one more movie for Universal, *See My Lawyer*, before returning to the stage and later television. While moderately successful, they were never able to duplicate the hubbub caused by *Hellzapoppin*, the "legitimate" production. One reviewer had even thought the play would achieve legendary status and that, in years to come, kids would ask their grandparents what it was like to attend a live performance of the lunacy. However, it was very much a phenomenon of its time, and later attempts to revive the show - one with Soupy Sales and another with Jerry Lewis and Lynn Redgrave - failed miserably.

Still, no one thought *Ghost Catchers* was worth a second look.

*Ghost Catchers* - 16 June 1944 - 69 minutes

**CAST**: Ole Olsen and Chick Johnson as Olsen and Johnson; Gloria Jean as Melinda; Martha O'Driscoll as Susanna; Leo Carrillo as Jerry; Andy Devine as Horsehead; Lon Chaney, Jr. as Bear; Kirby Grant as Clay; Walter Catlett as Col. Marshall; Ella May Morse as Virginia; Jack Norton as Wilbur; Henry Armetta as Signatelli; Walter Kingsford as Chambers; Alec Craig as Diggs; Belle Mitchell as Mrs. Signatelli; with Morton Downey, Tom Dugan, Ralph Peters, William "Wee Willie" Davis, Frank Mitchell, Sammy Stein, Tor Johnson, Al Mirkin, Harry Monty, Billy Curtis, Kay Harding, Bess Flowers

**CREDITS**: Director: Eddie Cline; Assistant Director: Howard Christie; Producer: Edward L. Hartmann; Writer: Edward L. Hartmann; Photography: Charles Van Enger; Art Directors: John Goodman, Richard H. Riedel; Film Editor: Arthur Hilton; Costumes: Vera West; Music: Edward Ward; Sound: Bernard B. Brown, Joe Lapis; Visual Effects: John P. Fulton; Dance: Louis Da Pron

*- HN*

# *Jungle Woman* (1944)

*Synopsis:* The death of the mysterious Paula Dupree results in an inquest during which Dr. Fletcher, head of a local sanitarium once run by the late Dr. Walters, admits that he killed her. Fletcher, feeling that his story will not be understood by people who are not scientists, reluctantly testifies. Fletcher had attended a circus disrupted by a fierce storm during which Cheela, an extremely intelligent ape, had been shot while rescuing her trainer Fred Mason from a cage-full of panicky lions. Though the ape had been pronounced dead, Fletcher brought the body to his lab and discovered she was still alive. However, shortly thereafter the ape broke out of her confinement and vanished.

On the night Cheela disappeared, Paula Dupree turned up, wandering around the grounds in a daze. Assuming she needed psychiatric care, Fletcher admitted her as a patient. Paula promptly became infatuated with Bob, fiancé of Fletcher's daughter, Joan. The couple now finds themselves stalked by Paula, who is extremely jealous of Joan and has superhuman strength. Willie, Fletcher's simple-minded helper, is sweet on Paula, but he is found dead, torn to pieces as are some animals on the grounds. Doing further research, Fletcher comes to the conclusion that Paula and Cheela are one and the same, the transformation due to Walters' work in glandular experiments.

Having already made one attempt on Joan's life, Paula follows her to her cottage with the intention of finishing the job. Fletcher arrives in time to prevent this and during the struggle with Paula, the doctor accidentally gives her a fatal dose of the tranquilizer he had prepared to knock her out.

The district attorney is very skeptical of Fletcher's story, but agrees to let the jury go to the morgue and view Paula's body. Everyone is shocked to discover that the corpse is that of an ape woman. The revelation confirms Fletcher's story and he is exonerated.

*Jungle Woman*, the first sequel to *Captive Wild Woman*, is perhaps the cheapest Universal horror of the '40s, and it looks it. Like its predecessor, it incorporates footage from the 1933 *Big Cage* (again with a special acknowledgment to its star, Clyde Beatty) and then proceeds to use scenes from *Captive Wild Woman* as well to serve as flashbacks. The inquest setting makes it easy to talk about various happenings without actually showing any of them. No need to hire Ray Corrigan and his ape suit for the day to impersonate Cheela escaping from the lab when Dr. Fletcher can just blather on about it instead. In fact, there's no need for a lab set at all. Paula's savaging the farm animals and a dog as well as their destroying their cages is related by George the caretaker who claims that he's never heard anything like it since "the destruction of Vienna" (Huh? When was that exactly?). No reason to hire John P. Fulton to work his magic on transformation scenes as there aren't any. Jack Pierce didn't have to put in any extra hours on this job as the Ape Woman is only shown once in the new footage, and then she's dead on a slab, and might well have been played a dummy rather than Acquanetta. (Please - no cracks on how anyone could tell the difference).

In interviews many years later, director Reginald Le Borg - who admitted *Jungle Woman* was his worst film - claimed that not showing the Ape Woman was done purposely, not to save money, but in order to bring the film more in line with the subtler approach of *The Cat People*. Le Borg claimed showing the Ape Woman early on would have dissipated what little suspense there was in the script of *Jungle Woman*. That might make a little more sense were it not for the fact that the monster is shown very clearly in the flashbacks to *Captive Wild Woman*. One would think the big reveal would work better in the climactic scene where the Ape Woman attacks Fletcher. Instead this is shown in silhouette and is actually a repeat of the footage from the beginning of the film. The sole difference between the two is that there's only music in the first scene, while growls and snarls are dubbed in when the footage is repeated.

Perhaps to make up for the scarcity of ape woman sightings, Paula is given the strength of a gorilla even in her human form, which - of course - makes her transformation into a monster unnecessary. I guess we are supposed to assume she's the creature when she kills Willie and the animals, but there's not even an attempt at consistency. In *Captive Wild Woman*, the metamorphosis occurs when Paula is in a jealous rage, but here we're only absolutely sure she changes once, at the attack on Dr. Fletcher. Moments before, she was stalking Joan and was very much in human form going in for the kill, so why the sudden transformation for the assault on the doctor?

Unlike *Captive Wild Woman* - where Cheela is just a very smart ape - here she is given a bizarre back story. Fred Mason visits Dr. Fletcher and tells him that when he was in Africa looking for animals to bring back to the circus, he heard stories of a scientist trying to turn people into beasts. Fletcher agrees that "there have been many efforts in that direction" (!), and Mason goes on to say that rumor had it that Cheela was the result of one of these experiments. This means that Cheela was originally a woman who was turned into an ape by a mad scientist (perhaps working for Monogram Pictures) and then back into a human by Dr. Walters! If this was some sort of loopy attempt to placate anti-evolution groups it didn't completely work, as the Catholic Legion of Decency gave the film a "B"-rating ("objectionable in part for all") because "the subject of this fantasy indicates some acceptance of the possibility of changing through science an ape into a human being." On the other hand, the liberal New York newspaper *PM* denounced the movie for other reasons, accusing Universal of promoting Hitlerian race ideas with films like *Captive Wild Woman* and *Jungle Woman*.

*Jungle Woman* commenced filming on the 15 February 1944 and, no doubt because of the economies, wrapped a little earlier than usual. Perhaps for that reason, Reginald Le Borg claimed he a played a little joke on the last day of shooting:

> Well I finished the picture on a Friday afternoon and I wanted to have some fun. I dressed up and put a little hair here like a beard and dark glasses. And the scene was finished and lit where the man comes in and says 'I want to see the body' and the keeper of the morgue takes the slab and puts it out and they all look at it and see. So I came in dressed up at the morgue keeper. And I let the actor come in and say the lines. And I said 'I'm the only one who knows where the body is buried.' And I took the make-up off and there was a big laugh and they filmed it. The next day the rushes appeared and one of the executives wants to see me and he says 'What do you know? We saw what you filmed there. What body's buried?' They thought I knew something about Universal executives! (1)

Assuming there's any truth at all to this story, the bean counters at penny-pinching Universal were probably more upset about time and money spent filming a gag rather than any potential scandal involving their executives.

There are a couple of acceptable bits of business in *Jungle Captive*. The scene wherein Paula overturns the canoe, hurling Bob and Joan into the water, is well led up to it, with a sinister *Jaws*-like phantom presence slowly following the boat and its blissfully unaware lovers. Not that the scene really makes any sense. An underwater ape (Acqua-netta?) seems a bit unlikely. Paula stalking Joan in the closing scenes hardly ranks with similar moments from *Cat People* or *The Leopard Man*, but it's fairly tense and made more so by the jungle noises and bird screeches on the sound track. That's certainly the best part of Paul Sawtell's music, which is otherwise largely a pastiche of themes taken from Hans Salter and Frank Skinner for other Universal horrors.

*Jungle Captive* enshrines what might be J. Carrol Naish's worst performance. His Dr. Fletcher behaves like the victim of a concussion, slightly dazed and barely connecting to the events around him. In the scene where Joan and Bob tell him how they were nearly killed, Naish reacts as though they were reading a weather report predicting rain. Perhaps he was distracted by having just won one of his best roles, Charlie Martin in *A Medal for Benny*. Akim Tamiroff, who had also been up for the part, visited the set of *Jungle Woman* to congratulate his friend and rival.

**While playing one of his numerous gangster roles in 1938's *King of Alcatraz*, J. Carrol Naish attended a criminal trial and told interviewers "I believe in being real. Literally real. That's why I'm here." Said belief probably didn't do much for the great character actor (once described as a "one-man United Nations") here. Still, Acquanetta stretches her acting chops and manages a few sexy pouts.**

Evelyn Ankers is given top billing for the film, but she's barely in it. Milburn Stone's Fred Mason is given just a little more screen time. Universal signed Stone to a contract after his work in *Gung Ho!* (1943), but in April of 1944, Hedda Hopper reported that Stone had asked for a leave of absence from the studio in order to go back to his hometown of Burton, Kansas, and run for mayor. Apparently, his stab at politics didn't work out, but he continued to have a friendly connection to his hometown for the rest of his career, especially during his *Gunsmoke* days. Acquanetta is slightly more animated than in her other films, though her dialogue delivery is as mechanical as ever: When she introduces herself to Bob ("Hello, my name is Paula"), she sounds like a talking doll. Later she sulks and pouts and behaves like a moody teenage girl about to throw a tantrum (perhaps almost as frightening as transforming into a monster). This was Acquanetta's last film at Universal. On 9 March 1944, it was announced that she *might* star in a horror-musical titled *Night Life* to be produced by Frank Gross, but nothing further was heard of this. Later in 1944, she made plans to sign at Monogram, and in December the trades reported that she would do a movie called *Jungle Queen* for that studio (oddly enough, *Jungle Queen* was the working title of *Jungle Woman*), but nothing materialized. It's sometimes said that she was exploited, but considering her lack of acting ability, she was lucky to have any kind of film career, even this minor one.

Supporting performances in *Jungle Woman* are adequate. Lois Collier, who was infatuated with Lon Chaney in *Weird Woman,* here has a more age-appropriate love interest, although she's obliged to act as jealous as Paula. Collier also has one good (possibly topical) crack: when she finds Bob alone in his room with Paula she asks "Is this the latest in closed door diplomacy?" Douglas Dumbrille plays the district attorney with an appropriate smirk on his face as he listens to Fletcher's tall tale, while Samuel S. Hinds as the coroner invokes his usual humane and sympathetic authority figure.

If Christian Rub's voice as George the caretaker sounds familiar, it's probably because he did the voice of Gepetto in Disney's *Pinocchio* as well as the modeling for the character. Rub (pronounced Rube) hailed from Bavaria and was a child actor on the stage in Germany and Austria. Later he joined the Imperial Theater in Vienna, and then moved to America. Rub usually played kindly father (or grandfather) types in films of the '30s and '40s, and though they were usually supporting roles, they were often singled out for praise by reviewers. His stage work was a bit more varied, and he won excellent reviews playing Kringelein in a LA production of *Grand Hotel* with Olga Baclanova and Ian Keith.

New York reviews of *Jungle Woman* were brief, dismissive and mocking:

Apparently Universal couldn't leave bad enough alone when it turned out a little nuisance called 'Captive Wild Woman' about a year ago. And now it has repeated the transgression in virtually identical form in a picture called Jungle Woman and again it is cloaking the whole thing in a blather of scientific bunk. Even those old shots of Clyde Beatty and his trained 'cats' are used again. What's Universal doing to us? Trying to make monkeys of us all?

Bosley Crowther, *The New York Times*, 15 July 1944

"Pseudo-scientific stuff and nonsense," wrote Otis Guernsey in the 15 July 1944 edition of the *New York Herald Tribune*.

Acquanetta plays the role of the ape woman with a stilted air while other members of the cast go through their parts with assurance trying to give the absurd story a semblance of reality.

Kate Cameron, *New York Daily News*, 15 July 1944

*Variety* pronounced the film "ok for the dualers" while *Motion Picture Herald* found that the film "ranks well with others of its ilk."

The 24 June edition of *Showman's Trade Review* showed some enthusiasm:

Acquanetta plays a fascinating but baleful lead. It is the longest bit of dramatic work that she has done and proves her to have tremendous possibilities both as an actress and as a glamorous personality. Production by Will Cowan is remarkable for getting so much out of the budget and into the film.

*Harrison's Reports*, no fan of horror pictures, liked the film because it *wasn't* scary:

The picture is void of the gruesomeness of its predecessor in that it does not show the transformation from woman to ape; it conveys that impression, as well as the ape's vicious acts, by indirection. But what it lacks in horridness it more than makes up for in suspense which is sustained effectively all the way through.

1 July 1944

An exhibitor is Shelby, Missouri agreed...

> The picture is a little off the beaten track of the usual horror picture and pleased well at the box office. Will do better if exploited as an extraordinary mystery. The spook-type picture is no good here but this has a different angle, not so many super-duper-horror scenes that scare the kids

...while a theater owner in New Paltz, New York thought otherwise:

> This is a frightening picture and I would advise you to keep it clear of dates when children attend as it will send them to the homes of their parents scared to death. Played with *National Barn Dance*.

And an exhibitor in Rivesville, West Virginia was not thinking about the kiddies when he opined:

> A very good horror show. Has plenty of leg art which attracts more attention than the other exploitation possibilities of the feature.

Perhaps Willy, Dr. Fletcher's slow-witted but occasionally insightful helper, should have the last word: "Awwww, it's a gyp!"

***Jungle Woman*** - 7 July 1944 - 60 minutes

**CAST:** Evelyn Ankers as Beth; J. Carrol Naish as Dr. Fletcher; Samuel S. Hinds as the Coroner; Lois Collier as Joan Fletcher; Milburn Stone as Fred Mason; Douglass Dumbrille as District Attorney; Richard Davis as Bob Whitney; Nana Bryant as Miss Gray; Pierre Watkin as Dr. Meredith; Christian Rub as George; Alec Craig as Caretaker; Edward Hyans as Willie; Tom Keene as Joe, the Fingerprint Man; and Acquanetta as Paula Dupree; Jurors: Charles Marsh, Edward Clarke, Diane Carroll, Nolan Leary; Heinie Conklin, Beatrice Roberts; Wilson Benge as the Court Stenographer; Kernan Cripps as Policeman

**CREDITS**: Director: Reginald Le Borg; Producers: Ben Pivar, Will Cowan; Original Story: Henry Sucher; Screenplay: Bernard Schubert, Henry Sucher, Edward Dein;

Dialogue Director: Emory Harger; Director of Photography: Jack MacKenzie; Art Directors: John B. Goodman, Abraham Grossman; Film Editor: Ray Snyder; Set Decorators: Russell A. Gausman, E.R. Robinson; Costumes: Vera West; Music: Paul Sawtell; Sound: Bernard B. Brown, Jess Moulin

- *HN*

# *The Mummy's Ghost* (1944)

With this, the third flick featuring that bandaged bad boy, Kharis, we are finally
introduced to the Princess Ananka, who – up to this point – has been nothing more
than a box of remains shunted off to a corner of the screen. Although 'twas the
princess who indirectly gave Kharis his millennia-old mission (and provided decent
salaries and benefits for those medallion-wearing high priests), we never got a good
look at Her Royal Highness, even in the flashback footage that occupied so much of
the previous two episodes. True, thanks to the unbelievable ineptitude of the latest
of the high priests, Ananka's mummified cadaver herein collapses into a heap of dust
although her soul almost instantaneously finds a new home in the body of Amina
Mansouri, and... *Wow!* The old girl could scarcely have done better. Bearing all this is
mind, we hypothesize that the elements of the title *The Mummy's Ghost* now refer to
the princess and no longer to Kharis. (Upon hearing our theory, a friend of ours – who
will remain nameless – subsequently opined, "*The Mummy's Curse*, then, refers to a
recurring physical condition that happens to female mummies every 30 years, no?")

Ahem!

George Zucco's high priest – who had been plugged several times at pointblank
range and then cascaded down one hell of a set of stone steps in *The Mummy's Hand*
– is still around (despite having died for the second time at the outset of *Tomb*). After
the picture opens with a strangely familiar long-shot of old George climbing those
Mayan steps to enter the Temple of Karnak (from *Hand*, but of course), we marvel as
it is John Carradine who crosses the transom into the Temple of Arkam. Carradine

as Yousef Bey – for some unknown reason, it is enormously important to high priest Andoheb that Bey is the son of a certain Abdul Marek – is Max-Factored to beat the band and is sporting one of the shabbiest fezzes to ever grace the head of a high priest of Karnak... *errrr*... Arkam. Andoheb's recapping of the series' mythos must have had more than a few fans scratching their fezzes, as – this time 'round – the princess Ananka was a "priestess initiate of Arkam" and Kharis has been demoted from "a prince of the royal house" to "a young man." Even though their love was "forbidden" and Ananka's soul was thus "accursed forever," Kharis was buried with her; (thank Amon Ra – whose anger can shatter the world! - that none of the Karnak/Arkam staff thought to question *that* arrangement). But just as Andoheb warms to the familiar tale - "30 years ago" he starts off - we cut to Frank Reicher's Professor Norman, who finishes the story to the most mature-looking college kids in cinematic history.

Norman – teaching at Mapleton University in the early 1970s (I reckon via rapid mathematical calculation) – speaks from firsthand experience about Kharis and such, only to have a quick cut take us back to Andoheb, who is tossing some tana leaves into one of the many sacred braziers to be found on Arkam property. Not only does this gratuitous destruction of otherwise extinct flora purely for demonstration purposes seem an enormous waste, but also we discover that only the nine-leaves-during-the-cycle-of-the-full-moon ritual need be observed at this point. Apparently, the three-leaves-to-keep-his-heart-beating application is no longer *de rigueur*; in fact, as Andoheb maintains, just set nine leaves afire and – no matter where he's at – Kharis "will know and come for the fluid." Voila! This newly-added artistic license quickens the pace of both the mummy *and* the story as a whole! If, somehow, Kharis is lurking in the vicinity (Andoheb bothers not at all to reveal the range within which the ancient Egyptian *can* sniff out the scent), he will home in on the steeping brew and have one for the road. (We have to wonder whether these latest addenda and alterations were the contributions of screenwriter Brenda Weisberg, herself an addition to the team of Griffin Jay and Henry Sucher, scenarists of *The Mummy's Tomb*.) Anyhow, later that evening, Norman cracks some hieroglyphics at home, brews up nine tana leaves, and is strangled for his trouble by Kharis, who – again - happened to be sauntering through the neighborhood when he... well, he just *knew*.

Found unconscious by the murder scene is Amina, Egyptian girlfriend of Tom, the alpha male of the *cough! cough!* college students we saw sitting through Prof. Norman's lecture and, thus, the hero of the piece. Amina, who earlier had demonstrated how she gets all weird every time the word "Egypt" is mentioned, had followed Kharis whilst in a semi-conscious state, and she now has both a strange mark on her right wrist and a "gray, skunk-like streak in her otherwise dark hair."(1) Following Norton's murder, everyone notices the mold on Norton's neck but not the gray streak in the exchange-student's hair, so we're not at all surprised when Sheriff Elwood pieces together a theory that Amina might know something about the murder. Meanwhile, Yousef Bey has arrived in Mapleton, has put the tana-leaf kettle on, and – in an obvious *hommage* to *The Mummy's Tomb* – Kharis's shadow again passes a jalopy (populated by Tom & Amina), and dispatches yet another man with a dog. High Priest and Mummy make for the Scripps Museum to rescue Ananka and bring her home, but Bey (admittedly a novice at this sort of thing) mucks up the incantation-of-the-moment and Ananka's bandages fall flat at Kharis's touch. At that very moment, Amina awakens with a shriek, and we're off on the Road to Reincarnation! Back at the museum, Kharis – quite justifiably miffed – goes on a rampage and, in a sort of foreshadowing of a very similar moment in *The Mummy's Curse* – ends up killing an elderly caretaker who happens to wander onto the scene.

**When Ananka's remains go "Poof!," the Mummy's wrath falls upon the Scripps Museum night guard (Oscar O'Shea).** *Fama est* **the old boy had earlier announced to museum coworkers he was set to retire in a week, thus establishing yet another cinematic convention.**

Bey and Kharis return to their hideout (a mining shack on stilts! It couldn't have been Chaney who demanded that there be an epic climbing sequence in every mummy pic, could it?) and a shaft of unearthly light leads them to believe that Ananka's soul is on the other end. Kharis follows the light, snatches up Amina (who has fainted on the front lawn, yet again) & lugs her back to the shack, whereupon Bey's divinely-influenced testosterone takes over and the high priest puts the move (as it were) on the unconscious soul-host. Justifiably miffed once more, Kharis knocks Bey out the window and carries Amina/Ananka into the swamp, not noticing that she is deteriorating rapidly in his arms. As Tom and a myriad of others watch, both Kharis and his now virtually decrepit "priestess initiate" sink beneath the surface of the crud.

The title card of *The Mummy's Ghost* bears a 1943 copyright date, even though the picture wasn't officially released until the 7 July 1944. The delay didn't reflect a production gone wild, or budget overruns, or problems with Reginald Le Borg - who was making his directorial debut in the Mummy realm - or anything like that. The delay occurred because Acquanetta – the Wyoming-born "Venezuelan Volcano" per the Universal BS Department - who had been signed to play the role of Ms. Mansouri, went and took a Brody during the first day of filming and was subsequently replaced by the lovely Ramsay Ames, a studio contractee who had just made her second appearance with Olsen and Johnson (and third with Lon Chaney) in *Ghost Catchers* (1944). *Universal Horrors* (2) goes into detail about the incident, but the upshot of whatever happened was that the gorgeous contract player was now to enact the fleshly receptacle for the spiritual side of the Princess Ananka.

Miss Ames, who had started her career with a Rhumba band ("The Tropicanans") was of such beauty that she apparently caused stuntmen to suffer "more injuries running on rooftops to get a better look at Ramsay walking across the [Republic] back-lot than were hurt performing dangerous action sequences in the studio's Westerns."(3) The New York native (born either Phillips Ames, Ramsay Phillips, Rita Rebecca Phillips, or Rita Rebecca Phillips Ames, depending upon the source one consults) does an adequate job as the unlucky Amina, although she does spend most of her onscreen time either unconscious, in a trance, or objecting to just about anything her boyfriend might suggest. It's incredible that no one comments on the gray streak that has nestled all of a sudden in Amina's hair – were one's friends more oblivious or less judgmental back in the '40s? (*errrrr....* '70s)? Anyhow, this was Ames's last run-in with the genre, unless one counts her appearances in the Republic serial, *The Black Widow*, or in PRC's *Philo Vance Returns* (both 1947).

The actress is not terribly well served professionally by the shift in emphasis from

Kharis's choking anyone even mildly aware of Ananka to the princess being a life-force on the move. While *any* movement away from the ceaseless brewing/shuffling/throttling would be appreciated, having Bey and Kharis both wildly surprised by the sudden reincarnation might have had more dramatic weight if the two hadn't almost immediately thereafter discovered the landing-place of the princess's soul, and hadn't even the dullest in the audience seen it coming from afar. Why – other than the fact that Amina is apparently the *only* female Egyptian within thousands of miles – is Ananka's reincarnation so predictable and instantaneous? A 60-minute running time, of course. Then why the insistence on squandering the limited running-time on yet another interaction between Zucco, the current high-priest wannabe, and those damned tana tea-party recipes? Why not some sort of summary of ancient Egyptian beliefs about spiritual rebirth? If the Karnak/Arkam Pooh-Bahs are so interchangeable that we're in essence watching Zucco *play* Carradine on the massive stone steps, do we really need waste any fraction of the film's hour on establishing Bey's bloodline or an endless series of wide-eyed invocations?

Like so many of his contemporaries, Robert Lowery began his film work in a series of pictures in which he received no onscreen credit. His "uncredits" petered out (for the most part) by the time the '30s waned, and prior to taking the romantic lead in *The Mummy's Ghost*, he sampled the genre waters in *Revenge of the Zombies* (costarring future adversary, John Carradine); subsequently, he'd step again into the Universal horror morass with 1946's *House of Horrors*. Sci-fi serial fans will remember Lowery from Columbia's *The Monster and the Ape* (1945), as well as for his performance as the Caped Crusader in that studio's 1949 chapterplay, *Batman and Robin*. Folks who grew up during the '50s – like moi – will undoubtedly associate the actor with his role as Big Tim Champion in the TV series, *Circus Boy*. (The title character was, of course, played by Mickey Dolenz, who, a decade later, would once again be part of a TV series named for denizens from the circus: *The Monkees*.)

Lowery is quite competent as Tom Hervey, even with the 30-year-old thesp a bit long in the tooth (in real life) for a college boy and a bit thick (per the scenario) for a hero. He *does* rather foolhardily run up to duke it out with Kharis, so he gets points for spunk, but he suffers the most awkward denouement in '40s Universal films (or is at least tied with Robert Paige's more pro-active Frank Stanley, as per the final moments of 1943's *Son of Dracula*), left to stand by helplessly as his erstwhile honey goes all mummy on him in the swamp. With an implacable air of defiant uncertainty on his face for most of the picture, Lowery's juvenile somehow seems less involved in the goings-on around him than were his predecessors in the series.

479

Kharis can hardly believe his good eye: Ananka (Ramsay Ames) never looked so good. Yousef Bey, meanwhile, ponders whether this latest iteration of the Mummy's Honey is up for grabs. (*He'll* be grabbed – but good! - a bit later.) Note the reversal of Kharis's eyes and hand stump between the scene and the border art.

Long John Carradine – like Lon Chaney, Jr. - is a horror-genre cottage-industry all by himself. That distinctive face of his was flashed on screens everywhere in more than 350 pictures during a movie career that spanned six-and-a-half decades and that offered a range of possibilities from his meddling (and uncredited!) hunter in 1935's *Bride of Frankenstein* to his Baron Latos (whom are we kidding?) in the *House of Frankenstein* to his being top-billed as the eponymous *Cosmic Man* (1959), although he is actually in that film for under a reel or so. Prior to getting into "the pitchers," John – a protege of John Barrymore – would wander the streets in a cape and with an attitude, "challenging" passersby to come to the theater and be caught up in matters Shakespearean (or Ibsensian, or...). His distinctive voice a definite plus to the genre – which demanded that the most outrageous of conceits be dealt with realistically – Carradine brought an unshakable sense of credulity to the most outrageous of themes. Here, he succeeds George Zucco and Turhan Bey - and anticipated both Peter Coe and Martin Kosleck - in making the hokiest of backstories into a (somewhat palatable) mixture of "Why not?" and "Things could be worse." Other than when indulging in the formulaic abandonment of his sacred trust so that he might put the moves on the skirt – admittedly more brazen here than in earlier series' entries, inasmuch as said skirt is worn by the reborn Ananka – Yousef Bey is pretty much a non-stop font of ritual invocations. If not for that beam of light – a *deus ex machina* if ever there was one – the picture would have stalled following the razing of the museum's holdings. Still, *The Mummy's Ghost* is hardly the most ridiculous of the Mummy series on account of Mr. Carradine.

Nor on account of Mr. Chaney, whose bona fides are found hither, thither, and yon within the covers of this book. Lon was battling both ennui and alcoholism by the time this second take (for him) came his way, and – if anything – this variation at least offered him a break from seeking violent redress because of sacrilegious slights done to Ananka once she was again safely in his arms... except for the quicksand, of course, and Bey's uninhibited lust. Perhaps the scene in which he knocks the stuffing out of the Egyptian exhibit at the Scripps Museum was a visual metaphor for his frustrations with the severe limitations of the role of Kharis. Well, he may have been comforted knowing there were still "Inner Sanctum" entries to be filmed, opportunities for the Oklahoma City-born actor to display his cerebral side to his following.

Tied with *Tomb* as the shortest of the Mummy series, *Ghost* suffers not only for its brevity being witless, but also for it's lowering the bar, continuity-wise, from the level displayed in *Tomb*. Despite three newspapers being displayed in the requisite headline eructation, there is no mention on the front pages of the War. The answer, of course, is that some 30 years have passed since said conflict embroiled the world (according to "mummy-time"), but why does not one of the Mapleton dailies bear a date? Piaget once opined that "One can be intelligent without being particularly logical," but it's doubtful he came out with that after sitting through *The Mummy's Ghost*. After three Kharis flicks, we must assume that the Scripps Museum situated in downtown Mapleton may not be affiliated with the Scripps Institute in either La Jolla, California, or in Jupiter, Florida. One bit of wit – indeed, brief – is the scene in which Oscar O'Shea's museum watchman is espied listening to the radio; the blurb featured at that moment is blather about "Doctor X, the Mad Doctor of Market Street!"

Still, illogic rules. Professor Norman brews nine tana leaves, Kharis arrives, and – instead of giving the old darling a grateful thumbs-up - immediately strangles his latest meal-ticket. So much for gratitude. Might there not be a momentary respite from throttling whilst the gauze-wrapped "young man" considers that that elderly academic might well be the *only* source of tana-leaf relief in the state of Massachusetts? (Watch Chaney drop his shoulders a foot after the deed has been done; "Whew! I could sure use a drink after *that!*") And although Norman had earlier told his wife he's got to do the tana-leaf thing on the spot because "tomorrow night the moon will not be full," it *is*, somehow, as it is the night after and every night subsequently until the picture ends. Surely, in the wake of the Mapleton mummy massacre as depicted in *Tomb*, the populace would have severely cut back on the amount of baggage Egyptian émigrés could unload in town, and that explains why the boys from Arkam have to repair to the museum to take advantage of the necessary doohickeys and accouterments.

This was Reginald Le Borg's first and only shot at providing some sort of guidance to the Mummy mishegas, although the Austrian-born director would experience a more dapper Chaney using his hands to mesmerize or massage, rather than to murder, in *Calling Dr. Death, Weird Woman,* and *Dead Man's Eyes.* Associate Producer Ben Pivar had hired Le Borg to helm the "Inner Sanctum" series after the director had shown he had the wherewithal to handle feature-length materials per *The Mummy's Ghost.* (Le Borg's entree into the wonderful world of film had been via 30 or so musical shorts he led from 1936 until 1943, first for M-G-M ["mini-musicals"] and, finally, for Universal.) And while there are moments in *Ghost* in which the shambling Chaney was photographed from below or from the side in a more-than-usually-creative fashion, these brief "highlights" are counterbalanced by inadequate day-for-night shooting and the flattest of flat lighting (chiefly in the Scripps Museum scene), so it's hard to argue that we've somehow come out on top. Following 1945's *Honeymoon Ahead,* Le Borg left Universal after a dispute over the quality of the material he was assigned, and headed over to Monogram and Poverty Row for a run of films largely based on the funny papers (the "Joe Palooka" series, "Little Iodine") or the adventures of the Bowery Boys.

It's not at all certain whether ticket-buyers for *Ghost* were chiefly those who were "once bitten" by the Freund/Karloff 1933 original, those who found the Cabanne/ Tyler 1940 "original" more to their liking (what with a title character who did not metamorphose into someone else and who literally took things into his own hands), or those who liked the genre in general and would plop down two bits to see almost anything that smacked of other-worldly. As has been noted here and in other published recounts of the series, were it not for the reincarnation business – as quickly and as unexpectedly as that occurs and as poorly explained as it is *in medias res - Ghost* might be considered an almost incident-for-incident remake of *The Mummy's Tomb.* No one is really given a moment to shine, and that includes the lovely Ramsay Ames, whose capacity either to walk whilst staring into space or to collapse into a heap can only be judged unfavorably when compared to Acquanetta, for whom those disciplines came as second nature.

482

If we had to settle for Mapleton's free press for the goings-on in the film, let us repair to several representatives of the Big Apple's journalism for opinion. For starters, Otis L. Guernsey, Jr. - surely not the first name that comes to mind when we consider movie criticism – made the following conclusion in the 1 July 1944 edition of the *New York Herald Tribune*:

> There is no extra subtlety or imagination to make the average film-goer rush to see 'The Mummy's Ghost'; but those who are fond of excursions into the cinematic supernatural will find little fault with it.

From the *New York Journal-American* – which saw print that same day – we have Rose Pelswick's opinion:

> On the other hand, or rather over at the Rialto Theater which brought us 'The Mummy's Ghost' yesterday, the accent is on juvenile bogey-man stuff. Lon Chaney, featuring a mud-pack make-up, gallumphs about in the role of a 3,000-year-old Egyptian who strangles a couple of innocent bystanders and then kidnaps a college glamour girl who turns out to be a 3,000-year-old Egyptian princess. It's all very silly.

As Bosley Crowther was busy criticizing other films elsewhere, so shall we pass on the Gray Lady's viewpoint and hie over to that of the *New York Daily News*, wherein reviewer Dorothy Masters writ *her* screed (also on the 1 July).

While it was only two years ago that this same Lon Chaney mummy presumably perished in flames for a weird little number called 'The Mummy's Tomb,' power of the tana leaves (plus an understandable interest in box office) prompts a return engagement... Ramsay Ames is too pretty a leading lady to deserve the cruel fate in store for her, and Robert Lowery too nice a guy to see his fiancée disintegrate before his eyes, but they play their roles in good style. John Carradine performs well as secondary menace in support of Lon Chaney's Kharis.

If nothing else, at least George Zucco could finally slap Lon Chaney on the shoulder at the wrap and tell him, good-naturedly, "You're on your on from here on in, kid!"

*The Mummy's Ghost* – 7 July 1944 – 60 minutes (ST)

**CAST**: Lon Chaney, Jr. as Kharis; John Carradine as Yousef Bey; Robert Lowery as Tom Hervey; Ramsay Ames as Amina Mansouri; Barton MacLane as Inspector Walgreen; George Zucco as the High Priest; Frank Reicher as Professor Norman; Harry Shannon as Sheriff Elwood; Emmett Vogan as the Coroner; Lester Sharpe as Dr. Ayad; Claire Whitney as Ella Norman; Oscar O'Shea as the Night Watchman; Jack C. Smith & Jack Rockwell as Deputies; Carl Vernell as Student; Dorothy Vaughan as Ada Blade; Mira McKinney as Martha Evans; Steve Barclay as Harrison; Eddy Waller as Ben Evans; Bess Flowers, Caroline Cooke & Fay Holderness as Women; Anthony Warde as Detective; Pietro Sosso as the Priest; Martha MacVicar as the Female Student; Ivan Triesault as Guide; David Bruce (voice) as Radio Actor

**CREDITS**: Associate Producer: Ben Pivar; Executive Producer: Joseph Gershenson; Director: Reginald Le Borg; Screenplay: Griffin Jay, Henry Sucher & Brenda Weisberg; Original Story: Griffin Jay & Henry Sucher; Director of Photography: William Sickner; Art Directors: John B. Goodman & Abraham Grossman; Film Editor: Saul A. Goodkind; Musical Director: Hans J. Salter; Sound Director: Bernard B. Brown; Technician: Jess Moulin; Set Decorators: Russell A. Gausman & L.R. Smith; Assistant Director: Melville Shyer: Make-up: Jack P. Pierce; Gowns: Vera West

***Shock Theater*** Catalog No. 719: "A stolen coffin and a reincarnated princess make 'The Mummy's Ghost' one of the top thrillers on *Shock*. See this exciting feature film starring Lon Chaney, John Carradine and Robert Lowery on this channel (day), at (time)."

*–JTS*

## *The Pearl of Death* (1944)

Hannibal Lecter, a sort of end-of-the-Millennium technological Moriarty, is confronted in *Hannibal* (2001) - one of his cinematic saga entries- by a rival to his intellect: the vicious and disfigured Mason Verger, with whom he establishes a love-hate link. In one of the climactic sequences, Verger - in a wheelchair and accompanied by his personal physician, Dr. Cordell (Zeljko Ivanek) - is about to execute Lecter. But he makes the mistake of allowing him to speak and, via a Holmesian-type of observation that escapes the viewer for most of the footage (Verger has been psychologically abusing his doctor), a couple of words directed at the core of this silent conflict are enough to assure that it is Verger who dies and that his executioner is the doctor, royally fed up with his patient. This conceit, save for space and time, is the one that introduces *The Pearl of Death*, the second film in the 1944 entries in Universal's "Sherlock Holmes" series.

Aboard a steamer that is about to anchor at Dover, James Goodram (Holmes Herbert), the emissary of a British museum, suffers the theft of an invaluable jewel, the Borgia pearl. Its new owner, Naomi Drake (Evelyn Ankers, in her second and last appearance in a Universal "Holmes"), is being followed by an elderly vicar who, via a happy mix of ingenuity and a bit of luck, manages to get hold of the pearl. The vicar, of course, is Holmes in one of his disguises, and his success allows him to return the piece to the museum. Francis Digby (Charles Francis), the director of the institution, boasts of having an inviolable security system, a complex network of cables that sound alarms and activate sliding panels in case of the removal of an *objet d'art*. "Electricity," ventures Holmes, "the High Priest of false security," just before

485

momentarily disconnecting the system's feed in order to demonstrate its fallibility. Unbeknownst to him, though, is that - at that precise moment - arch-criminal Giles Conover (Miles Mander), having infiltrated the museum dressed as a maintenance man, steals the pearl, making a hasty escape.

Captured and led before Holmes and the forces of law and order, Conover no longer has the pearl on him. Although Lestrade (Dennis Hoey) locks him up, without further evidence he will not be able to keep Conover behind bars for more than a couple of days. The problem of finding and recovering the valuable piece becomes urgent when the city begins to be battered with a series of murders. Every victim is found with his back broken and surrounded by a pile of broken porcelain dishes, cups, and bric-a-brac. Holmes links these deaths with the missing pearl and the viewer, starting with the ties between Naomi and Conover, realizes that the murders are the work of a criminal society whose killer turns out to be an abominable creature. The "Hoxton Creeper" is first alluded to in conversations between both characters and then suggested on a secondary visual plane, in which he is hidden by shadows or meticulously framed so that only his hand is seen. We also "see" the monster through the feelings he provokes in other characters. Conover's chauffeur (Eric Wilton, who seemed to have sauntered through Universal specializing in butlers, chauffeurs, and hotel concierges) anxiously converses with his boss about his back-seat passenger – the murderer - being either unable or unwilling to turn around and see what's what for himself. The lovely Miss Drake – a white-gloved thief – doesn't like the idea of the killer's proximity and begs Conover not to insist that she sit in front of him. By only showing the Creeper at a distance or via selective framing and through these carefully worded statements, Universal insinuated that its creature was competing head to head with RKO's psychological horrors (*a la* Val Lewton) and the Russian émigré's technique of suggesting a monster without showing it

With Rondo Hatton playing the bestial psychopathic murderer, it's a trifle odd to find Harry Cording in a non-malefic role; (we remember him best as Bela Lugosi's brutal servant in 1934's *The Black Cat*). Cording had become accustomed to playing the arch-villain's henchman in Universal's "Holmes" series, doing the heavy work for Moriarty in *SH and the Secret Weapon* and for Adrea Spedding in *The Spider Woman*. Now, bearded and with his hair combed like a Parisian artist, Cording plays a charismatic craftsman at a sculptors' workshop who supplies valuable information to the detective. It devolves that, during his brief flight, Conover had entered said shop and had hidden the pearl in one of six busts of Napoleon that were sold to a dealer. Holmes, of course, arrives at a similar theory through "pure deductive reasoning,"

486

and discovers the shop wherein each one of the victims had acquired a bust; he then determines just what it is that the killer is so anxiously seeking. Upon speaking with the owner (Ian Wolfe, who, in order to put some distance to his antiquarian in *Sherlock Holmes in Washington*, dons an Hebraic coif and adopts some gestures proper to that community), Holmes notes that the young employee who accompanies him is Naomi. Holmes succeeds in intercepting the phone call from Naomi to Conover, and in doing so obtains the name and address of the last remaining owner of the bust in which, presumably, is hidden the Borgia pearl.

**Thankfully – for the sake of the rest of the Universal franchise – that's a production assistant within throttling distance of Holmes, and not Rondo Hatton's "Hoxton Creeper."**

In minute 42 of the footage, an ominous shadow slips through a curtain and begins to advance; a spooked cat jumps up, and one of composer Paul Sawtell's thematic passages suggests we are in the presence of a threatening personage. The hither-to mystery film now changes genre: for the first time we see the "Hoxton Creeper," played by Mr. Hatton, although still without the benefit of close-ups. His first "appearance" was limited to the outline of his square-ish body; later, in the back seat of Conover's car, we have the shadow of his uneven profile; later still, he's standing behind his boss with his back to the camera, thickset (via platforms and stuffing), and always accompanied by his ominous musical theme. In this scene, we've a three-man dramatic denouement, with Holmes confronted by Conover and his monster, in search of the bust. Aware that the Creeper has certain feelings for Naomi, the detective raises his voice and lies that Drake has killed Watson and will be hanged for the crime, with all this due to Conover. This simple fabrication enrages the giant, who turns on his boss and breaks his back. When he then turns on Holmes, the detective does not hesitate to shoot him, lest he suffer the same fate. We've an electrifying ending in which physical action follows an element of psychological manipulation, and all without the the comic relief now expected of Watson or some propagandizing speech on Holmes's part to spoil it.

Nonetheless, during the sequence in which he was being held at gunpoint by Conover, Holmes had countered with some dialectical stilettos. "It has been said that imitation is the sincerest form of flattery," the detective ventured, perhaps using his customary tactic of distracting his foe in order to give Watson and Lestrade time to arrive with the forces of law and order. In their must-have **Universal Horrors**, Tom Weaver and the Brunas brothers make an interesting point regarding "imitation." Before he was hired by Universal, Howard Benedict – who would be associate producer or executive producer for eight of the 12 Rathbone/Bruce "Sherlock Holmes" films, but *not* for *The Pearl of Death* - was a producer at RKO for several of the entries in the "Falcon" series, which had starred George Sanders. Benedict's last "Falcon" assignment – 1942's *The Falcon Takes Over* – featured a character and a behavioral pattern that hadn't been created by Michael Arlen, the literary sire of the Falcon, but, rather, was taken from Raymond Chandler's novel, **Farewell, My Lovely** (the RKO film's credit crawl *does* cite Chandler). In *Takes Over*, Ward Bond plays Moose Malloy, the dangerous ex-convict who goes about breaking the necks of the film's cast while searching for his former girlfriend. Given the parallels to the Creeper, his SOP, and his fatal attraction to the blonde Naomi Drake, the authors of **Universal Horrors** argue that *The Pearl of Death* would seem quite the narrative equivalent of Chandler's plot scheme. In fact, while *Pearl* was being released, RKO was preparing an official cinematic rendition of the novel – entitled *Murder, My Sweet*, that would be in theaters in December 1944. All things being equal, it's safe to assume that Universal was not going to risk imitating *that* script. Besides, it is Moose himself who seeks to hire The Falcon/Philip Marlowe to search after his lost beauty, distancing him – at least dialogue-wise – from the brief, mute presence of the Creeper.

"Symbols of greed and cruelty," detective declares to doctor, having recovered the pearl and after the danger has passed, "and lust for power that have set men at each others' throats down through the centuries." Here, Holmes's discourse acquires an interesting, reflexive tone far removed from propaganda... "and the struggle will go on, Watson, for a pearl, a kingdom, perhaps even world domination, til the greed and cruelty have burned out of every last one of us." In that diatribe might scenarist Bertram Millhauser be speaking out against both the pettiness of the human race and the bloodshed that still had not ended? Might the subtle disappointment that inspired these words be predicting the fact that the armistice, not so very far off, would initiate still another conflict that, while not a war, would nonetheless be entitled "The Cold War?" And, finally, how did this piece of socio-political criticism escape the notice of the fervent applicants of censorship even in times of war?

**"Someone's sneakin' 'round the corner..." and it *ain't* Mack the Knife. Regardless of whether he portrayed The Creeper, Moloch the Brute, or just plain old Mario, Rondo Hatton's brief career at Universal raised him to semi-iconic status.**

*Film Daily* (28 August 1944) placed the film "among the best of the Sherlock Holmes series... [a] real treat for melodrama fans," specifying that "in every way, *Pearl of Death* is a superior melodrama." In total accord with Universal's monsters, the review pointed out that "the excitement is heightened by an air of horror that hangs over the story." In its revised review, *Variety* (30 August 1944) remarked that "Rathbone and Bruce are okay in their familiar roles, Mander is good as the criminal with aide from Evelyn Ankers as accomplice. Balance of cast has brief footage individually." Huh? The noteworthy omission of mention of Rondo Hatton contrasts with the opinion of the 2 September 1944 *Motion Picture Herald*, which alluded to the "thief's accomplice, a grisly, half-witted creature played by Rondo Hatton," a description which seems to have come from the earlier critique in *Motion Picture Daily* (29 August 1944) wherein the character was also termed a "half-witted creature." *Harrison's Reports* (2 September 1944) on the other hand, referred to the Creeper as "an inhuman monster" and "a half-witted giant." Easing off a bit, the 26 August 1944 *Showmen's Trade Review* commented that "there are enough murders to please the most bloodthirsty action fan, but without the visual spilling of blood." Still, in this case, the reviewer was obviously drawn to the character of the Creeper who "when revealed that he is really a gruesome-looking fellow, vies with Karloff in his best make-up."

What is surely the highlight of this film from Roy William Neill and script from Bertram Millhauser is the psychological manipulation that Holmes pulls off based on two words lifted from a phone conversation. When all is said and done, imitation as a sign of flattery underlies the fascinating duality between two privileged intellects who may be Holmes and Conover in *The Pearl of Death*, but – in the retrospective allowed us by the great history of the cinema – are also Holmes and Lecter.

*The Pearl of Death* – 22 September 1944 – 69 minutes

**CAST**: Basil Rathbone as Sherlock Holmes; Nigel Bruce as Doctor Watson; Dennis Hoey as Inspector Lestrade; Evelyn Ankers as Naomi Drake; Miles Mander as Giles Conover; Ian Wolfe as Amos Hodder; Charles Francis as Francis Digby; Holmes Herbert as James Goodram; Richard Nugent as Bates; Mary Gordon as Mrs. Hudson; Rondo Hatton as the Hoxton Creeper; Arthur Stenning, Wilson Benge as Stewards; Leyland Hodgson as Customs Officer; Eric Wilton as Conover's Chauffeur; Charles Knight as Bearded Man in Museum; Billy Bevan as Constable; Harold De Becker as Restaurant Owner; Leslie Denison as Sgt. Murdock; Lillian Bronson as Housekeeper; Audrey Manners as Mrs. Carey; Connie Leon as Ellen Carey; J.W. Austin as Sgt. Bleeker; Arthur Mulliner as Thomas Sandeford; Harry Cording as George Gelder; Al Ferguson, Colin Kenny as Guards; John Merkyl as Dr. Julian Boncourt

**CREDITS**: Producer and Director: Roy William Neill; Screenplay: Bertram Millhauser; Based on "The Adventure of the Six Napoleons" by Sir Arthur Conan Doyle; Music and Musical Director: Paul Sawtell; Photography: Virgil Miller; Film Editor: Ray Snyder; Art Directors: John B. Goodman and Martin Obzina; Set Decoration: Russell A. Gausman and Edward R. Robinson; Gowns: Vera West; Assistant Director: Melville Shyer

*- DL*

# *The Climax* (1944)

Cicero might have averred that "it goes without saying" that a film entitled *The Climax* would nowadays portend, if not a dramatic denouement, the promise of a more lascivious wrap. The dramatic climax that impacted the film under discussion here was taken from Edward Locke's eponymous play, which premiered in 1909.(1) The British-born actor, author, and playwright had expatriated to the States whilst still in his salad days and had quickly established a name for himself with *The Climax* and later, with *The Case of Becky*.(2)

The former work is the tale of a lovely young Italian opera singer whose voice totally disappears (courtesy of the destructive power of a throat spray administered by a jealous doctor) only to have it rebound – better than ever – when she breaks into song whilst in church on the wedding day she didn't want. (She's about to marry said doctor... It *is* a rather improbable story...) Thus, the titular climax in the play is the warbling of the "Song of the Soul," the salvific music (written by the young lady's *true* love) that causes the wicked medico to hie from the church mid-ceremony, leaving the young composer and his honey in each other's arms. Said song was popular enough to be sold – in sheet-music form – during and for sometime after the play's initial theatrical run. The *latter* work is a distaff variation on Robert Louis Stevenson's novella, [The] *Strange Case of Dr. Jekyll and Mr. Hyde*, wherein the charming Dorothy becomes the snarling Becky due to one Professor Balzamo, evil hypnotist extraordinaire, who engages in villainy such as this purely to ... *well*... show that he can!

Anyhow, even as Universal's accounting department was still tallying receipts for its 1943 Technicolor hit, *Phantom of the Opera*, Universal's projects department had decided that there were few better ways to keep the money flowing than to construct a sequel to the tale of the madman and the soprano and her lover and the opera and so forth and so on. First cast members set to be (re)- signed were Susanna Foster and Nelson Eddy; as the teenage warbler from the Windy City and the Singing Capon had been billed over the gentleman playing the title character in the first effort, it made sense to nail them down right away here, in the second. Foster was good to go, but Eddy would prove to be unavailable; it remains unclear to this day whether stage productions or the siren song of PRC's *Knickerbocker Holiday* lured him away. Claude Rains, meanwhile, had escaped Universal's tendency to cast him only in horror roles for the second (and last) time, signing on at Warner Bros. for better billing and another chance to work with Humphrey Bogart (in *Passage to Marseille*).

A kerfuffle in terms of plot and characterization then arose almost immediately. Following its *original* foray into the depths of the Paris Opera in 1925, Universal had also begun planning a sequel. While Lon Chaney's iconic Erik, the Opera Ghost, had in no way, shape, or form ever been portrayed as immortal (*a la* Frankenstein's Monster) or as undead (*a la* Dracula or Im-Ho-Tep, the Mummy), and while the denouement of the silent classic had pretty much left little doubt as to Erik's fate, the creative minds were thinking as quickly as the financial minds were doing algorithms. No matter who was paid to do what, it hadn't taken Universal long at all to begin laying out a follow-up. As we noted in our essay on the 1943 *Phantom of the Opera*, the sequel to that classic treatment ended up as a part-sound reworking of same, as Chaney had hied to another studio. In fact, per film historian George Turner, things might have ended up the same way even had Irving Thalberg not lured the Man of a Thousand Faces to M-G-M:

> Universal announced in April 1929 its plans to produce *The Return of the Phantom*, a sequel wherein the leading players of the original would recreate their roles 'in dialogue, recorded on Movietone.' It was evident to everybody concerned that the public would accept no other Phantom than Chaney, who made it clear that he had no intention of attempting such a chore. Like Charles Chaplin, he believed his kind of characterization was suited only to pantomime and that the hated 'talkies' would soon pass from public favor. So much for *The Return*. (3)

No Phantom, no sequel.(4) Much in the same way, the dramatic resonance needed to bring Erique Claudin back to what passed for life after having the opera house cellar's ceiling fall on him was deemed impossible to come by. Once again, no

Phantom, no aftermath.(5) At this late date, we cannot begin to imagine the studio's begging its original choice as Phantom – Broderick Crawford – to assume the mantle on the bounce, as it were, and we're not at all certain that – a few years after winning fame as the pathetic and misshapen Quasimodo at RKO – Charles Laughton would have jumped at the chance to be the pathetic and deformed Erique Claudin, especially as a "designated phantom." While audiences may have bought anyone wearing the bolts and the boots as that season's Monster or whoever the new chap was in cape and tailcoat as the latest iteration of the thirsty count, both horrors had slipped from their iconic days to being little more than members of some dreadful brotherhood meeting in some frat house or another for a little fun. The two opera phantoms, on the other hand, were outliers – each had but one terrific telling-of-the-tale, and neither would be saddled with a Son, a Daughter, or a number of "guest appearances" in monster-rally "B's."

So, the proposed follow-up quickly became a re-imagining: the picture's resident lunatic would still obsessed with music, albeit only insofar as he could eradicate glorious melodies and snuff out incredible voices. Stage 28 would be rechristened the "Royal Theatre," what had been the Paris Opera would be relocated to the heart of Vienna, and the semi-resident murderer would be – literally – a "mad doctor." There would be no references to "Box 5" - that locale went unmentioned in the '43 version and was sorely missed by many a fan of Leroux and Chaney – no meandering about the opera house's nether regions, "lakes," or what-have-you, and no nonsense about acid, masks, or chandeliers. Musical genius would not be found to be personified by any "Angel"; if anything, the art that had come to be known as "God's gift" would elicit the diabolical from the protagonist.

Thus...

Dr. Frederick Hohner is the official physician of the Royal Theatre. It devolves that – some ten years earlier than the opening scene at hand – he had strangled Marcellina, the house's *diva* and his *amore*, rather than have her sing for the king. Jealousy, it turns out, is w-a-y more powerful a propellant than love. Returning to the "present day," we see that Jarmila Vadek – the current high-toned leading lady – refuses to perform, citing her discomfort with Amato Roselli, her frequent co-star. When everyone worth mentioning – including Dr. Hohner – hears Jarmila's understudy, Angela Klatt, singing in her dressing room, there's an epiphany: we have found the latest, greatest soprano! Angela is a sensation and, when it's decided to revive the opera – "The Magic Voice" - that Marcellina had made her own, Dr. Hohner visits her and hypnotizes her, commanding her to sing for no one save him!

In addition to his hypnotic powers, Hohner utilizes an "atomizer" which keeps Angela infused with a quasi-medical concoction that prevents her from singing her best. The soprano's boyfriend, Franz Munzer, unable to understand what has happened to his heartthrob's high C, works night and day to discover the cause. When a command performance for the young king is arranged, Angela finally come into her own. She is magnificent, and it is not long thereafter that Hohner – closeted with the astoundingly well-kept remains of the late Marcellina – is burned to a crisp.

For all those keeping track, the elements from the 1930 *Climax* that survived incorporation into the re-imagining of *Phantom of the Opera* include the evil medico's use of some sort of throat spray/infuser to further his cause; the serendipity that marks the return of vocal magnificence to both Adella (the heroine of Universal's first shot at this story line) and the unfortunate Angela; and the parallel course run by both 1930's (and – in the case of Locke's original play – 1909's) "The Song of the Soul" and 1944's "The Magic Voice" as the treatments that restored that which God had giveneth and a wicked doctor had taken away. Still, it must be noted that – in the earlier, pre-Code *Climax* – Dr. Gardoni (the Dr. Hohner counterpart) got off easy; as he had killed no one, he needed only to flee the church wherein Adella had rediscovered her voice in order to even the score.

*The Climax* is a hard film to like – or dislike(!?) The elements that had made 1943's *Phantom of the Opera* so popular – and we're not just talking Technicolor here – would resound yet again in audiences looking (and listening) for the sort of musical/horror trope the earlier picture had wrought. Fans of classical music could revel somewhat in the fact that the '44 re-imagining also featured Jane Farrar - possible blood relation to Geraldine Farrar - as well as the undeniable talent of the lovely Miss Foster. *Phantom* producer George Waggner – here producer *and* director - brought familiarity to fans of the earlier picture, although some of the tracking techniques and camera angles may have been reminiscent of Arthur Lubin, who was reassigned to *Ali Baba and the Forty Thieves* late in the day. Even the "Phantom Stage," constructed for the '25 original and used as the backdrop for any number of pictures since (although, apparently, not for the 1930 *Climax*), gave viewers an "Aftertaste of the Opera."

Erstwhile Christine DuBois, Susanna Foster, enjoyed top billing here, but whereas said position would be unique during her '40s career, apart from her film debut in 1939's *The Great Victor Herbert* and the 1992 remake of *Detour* (her swan song), the lovely Windy City soprano was never billed lower than second. While *Phantom of the Opera* may have been her career apex, one can only wonder whether she might have run a parallel track – in non-singing roles – had she not turned down the lead in M-G-M's *National Velvet* as it *was* a non-singing role. (The part went to a certain young Elizabeth Taylor – who did not sing, of course, but who had experience working alongside adorable animals [1943's *The Courage of Lassie*] – and the rest is herstory.) Per the lads at **Universal Horrors**, Miss Foster felt that "working with Karloff was like working with a slab of ice."(6) Still it was the steady diminution of the quality of the parts she was assigned that led her to say *adieu* to the studio – and to film work, for decades – following *That Night with You*, in 1945.

New(er) elements still were considered to be old(er) friends. Turhan Bey – the Vienna-born dreamboat affectionately known as "Turkish Delight" – had been featured in Universal pictures since 1941's *Raiders of the Desert*, and he had been signed along with director Lubin for the *Ali Baba* feature in late 1943. The actor, who was accustomed to being onscreen the female magnet he was in real life, found his role to be unique for him, as his Franz Munzer devolved into a combination of gifted composer and 13-year-old boy. Gale Sondergaard (see: *The Black Cat*) – almost always something of a sinister presence – pays for her benevolent tendencies herein by ending up on the wrong end of Karloff's strangling arm. Curt Siodmak (see: *The Wolf Man*) shared the screenplay honors with Lynn Starling (responsible for the scenario of the 1939 remake of *The Cat and the Canary*) and, yet again, psychosis was the ink that filled the Siodmak pen. New Yawka Thomas Gomez had made his film debut as the heavy in 1942's *Sherlock Holmes and the Voice of Terror*. Although Gomez had been otherwise occupied for Claude Rains' *Phantom*, he managed to make it into the featured cast for Ella Raines' *Phantom Lady* the year after that.

Balanced on the border were a couple of personalities whose futures would not be enmeshed with Universal horrors, but whose presence in 1944 augured greater things to come. George Dolenz – like Turhan Bey, also born abroad (Italy, in Dolenz's case) – might have marked *The Climax* as his only genre effort, were it not for *Scared Stiff*, the Dean Martin-Jerry Lewis zombie-imbued musical from 1953. Come 1956, and Dolenz became a big star on the small screen, playing Edmond Dantes in Hal Roach's TV series, *The Count of Monte Cristo*. George's TV fame was subsequently "inherited" by his son, Mickey, who not only starred as *Circus Boy*, but was one of The Monkees. In a similar capacity – albeit due more to his history and not to his future – was Scotty Beckett, whose early success as one of Hal Roach's "Our Gang" led to featured roles in such prestigious films as *Anthony Adverse* (1936) and *Marie Antoinette* (1938). With over 100 film credits to his name – his portrayal of "Winky" in TV's *Rocky Jones, Space Ranger* comes closest to appealing to such as us – his later years saw him descend into multiple marriages, drug use, and an early death; he passed away due to an overdose at age 39.

*Susanna* FOSTER
*Turhan* BEY
*Boris* KARLOFF *in*

# The CLIMAX

IN TECHNICOLOR

with
GALE SONDERGAARD
JUNE VINCENT    THOMAS GOMEZ
GEORGE DOLENZ    JANE FARRAR
LUDWIG STOSSEL

Screen Play by Curt Siodmak and Lynn Starling    Adapted by Curt Siodmak from the Play by Edward Locke
Produced and Directed by GEORGE WAGGNER    A UNIVERSAL PICTURE

**Considering that this is the first – and mayhaps only picture - in which Boris Karloff found himself impeccably accoutered and waist-deep in beautiful women, one might think he would crack a smile, no? (Was it his getting third billing?)**

Quite a few of the supporting thesps were also either carry-overs from the Silent Era or familiar faces to Universal fans, but the most familiar of all was enjoying his first appearance for the Fellowship of the Revolving Globe since 1940's *Black Friday*.

Boris Karloff's face – among the most recognized in '30s and '40s filmdom – had been rid of extreme makeup treatments (iconic or otherwise; Mr. Wong always excepted) since 1939's *Son of Frankenstein*; what also had been excepted was Karloff's participation in any Universal feature since *Son*. Always looking to diversify – yet, like his contemporary, Bela Lugosi, somewhat saddled with typecasting for most of the decade-and-a half since he first wore the boots and bolts of the Frankenstein Monster – Karloff had spent the early '40s moving among Columbia, RKO, and Monogram. His return to the House that Carl Built was to have been a cause for celebration – *The Climax* was his first Technicolor outing – but later that same year he was relegated once again to bxw mad-doctor status for the studio's *House of Frankenstein*. As would be the case in *House*, Karloff's character here wears no expression other than one signaling anger and/or outrage, but the derivative screenplay demands nothing more. To be certain, one did not venture out to a Boris Karloff film expecting to see the last-reel heroics left to the gentle Briton, but even his Monster had managed a slight smile now and again.

While it did pale a tad in comparison with the previous year's opera "celebration," *The Climax* was anything but....*errrr*....anti-climactic. (In an effort to give credit where it is due, let me point out that *The New York Times*'s movie critic Bosley Crowther used that wordplay in his review on the 14 December 1944, wherein – surprisingly – for once, he did not condemn a genre film out of hand):

> The brooding malevolence of [Boris] Karloff and the vocal displays of Susanna Foster as the singer have their entertaining points. Miss Foster throws a very lusty larynx into the singing of such pseudo-opera airs as Edward Ward and George Waggner have concocted seemingly from classical scores... Thomas Gomez, Gale Sondergaard and Jane Ferrar are properly 'hammy' in their roles. As a matter of fact, if you'll take this film as flim-flam, you may find it rather crude but colorful fun.

A few weeks earlier, Nelson B. Bell had used his reviewer's perch at *The Washington Post* to declare that the picture was "a familiar story smothered in opulence."

> The unfolding of the tale on the screen follows familiar lines. It compounds a considerable degree of suspense and in its climactic holocaust piles up so many thrills one wonders whether Universal had it in mind to make a delightful melodious musical starring Susanna Foster, or a frank and unequivocal 'horror picture' starring Boris Karloff in a succession of his well-known deviltries. In the mind of the spectator, this will be what might be denominated a fielder's choice.(7)

Mr. Bell's tendency to employ polysyllabic and/or archaic vocabulary is somewhat understandable when one realizes that under all that linguistic weight lies little more than persiflage. (*Ouch!*) Having dismissed Turhan Bey's performance pretty much on racial lines ("Maybe it is he should confine his efforts to Oriental costume parts that utilize peculiarly exotic talents to better advantage") and then having opined that the picture's narrative thrust pretty much depends upon the viewer's predisposition (above), he concludes... actually, to be completely honest, he *pre*cludes:

> The thing is just too splendiferous to be true and in carrying itself to such lengths of garish display, it seems to me, largely vitiates any rational appeal it might otherwise exert in the direction of sympathies and emotions.

The opinion ventured by *Harrison's Reports* (30 September 1944) didn't require a college degree for comprehension.

> As entertainment... it is only fair, not only because of its far-fetched story, but also because of the stagey situations. And the players, with the exception of Boris Karloff, who is properly sinister as the demented physician, do not help matters much their performances are wooden...

*The Showman's Trade Review*, published the same day as *Harrison's*, reduced its analysis down to two perspectives: that of the audience and that of the exhibitor:

> Audience Slant (Adult): Superbly presented entertainment with all the elements for an enthusiastic reception from any audience: lavish production, enchanting color, fine performances, deft direction.
>
> Box-Office Slant: A money picture with ever opportunity for showmanship. Its appeal can be slanted to fit the needs of any situation.

We can only hope that situational slant is not akin to *The Washington Post*'s "fielder's choice."

The November 1944 issue of *Photoplay* didn't waste much ink on the film: "We don't care how elaborately they dressed the sets, lighted the affair with technicolor, or cast the leading roles, it's still a B picture." Nonetheless, when it came to addressing the two (usually) villainous actors in the piece, it was a whole different ballgame: "Gale

Sondergaard was swell; Boris Karloff (who is a doll, just a doll in Technicolor) plays the ever-loving madman." This briefest of critiques closed with the summation of the reviewer's opinion: "Boo, you big bad old picture!"

It's probably true that *The Climax* – despite Universal's monetary commitment and fans' hemi-demi-semi acquaintanceship to similar plots – is not among the first- or second- or possibly third-tier Karloff features that genre aficionados sit through. Word of mouth (or, more likely nowadays, word of blog) has relegated the picture to almost carbon-copy status with respect to the previous year's treatment of music and mayhem. One might wonder whether Karloff's perpetual scowl or snarl reflected his contractual obligation to step into someone else's patent-leather shoes, much the way (it has been argued) that Bela's hissy-fit-prone Monster was the product of his assuming a role that he had been offered first – and had refused. The film's Technicolor rendition drew much of the attention at first – God knows that Universal wasn't in any position to toss cash away blindly – but that aspect of the film (and others) soon diminished as color (and even Technicolor) became not only a mitzvah, but also a reasonable expectation. Still, the combination of Foster's vocal talent, Karloff's being Karloff, and the admitted splendor of the production values does offer the interested viewer an experience second to one.

*The Climax* – 20 October 1944 – 86 minutes

**CAST**: Boris Karloff as Dr. Frederick Hohner; Susanna Foster as Angela Klatt; Turhan Bey as Franz Munzer; Gales Sondergaard as Luise; Thomas Gomez as Count Seebruck; June Vincent as Marcellina; George Dolenz as Amato Roselli; Ludwig Stossel as Carl Bauman; Jane Farrar as Jarmila Vadek; Erno Vardebes as Brunn; Lotte Stein as Mama Hinzl; Scotty Beckett as King; William Edmunds as Leon; Maxwell Hayes as King's Aide; Dorothy Lawrence as Miss Metzger; Cyril Delevanti as Sweeper; Rex Lease, Geroge Eldredge as Reporters; Roy Darmour as Secretary; Polly Bailey as Cleaning Woman; Ernie Adams as Old Man; Genevieve Bell as Dowager; Francis Ford as Man; with Grace Cunard, Maurice Costello, William Desmond, Stuart Holmes, Eddie Polo, Jack Richardson, Ann Cornwall, Harry Mayo,Gertrude Astor, Helen Gibson, Fred Curtis

**CREDITS**: Executive Producer: Joseph Gershenson; Producer & Director: George Waggner; Screenplay by Curt Siodmak and Lynn Starling; Adapted by Curt Siodmak; Based on the eponymous play by Edward Locke; Director of Photography: Hal

Mohr & W. Howard Greene; Technicolor Color Director: Natalie Kalmus; Associate Technicolor Director: William Fritzsche; Musical Score & Direction: Edward Ward; Librettos: George Waggner; Operettas Staged by: Lester Horton; Vocal Director: William Tyroler; Orchestration: Harold Zweifel; Art Directors: John B. Goodman & Alexander Golitzen; Sound Director: Bernard B. Brown; Technician: William Fox; Set Decorators: Russell A. Gausman & Ira S. Webb; Film Editor: Russell Schoengarth; Dialogue Director: Gene Lewis; Makeup: Jack P. Pierce; Costumes: Vera West; Assistant Directors: Charles S. Gould & Harry O. Jones; Special Effects: John P. Fulton

*-JTS*

# *Dead Man's Eyes* (1944)

*Synopsis*: Artist Dave Stuart is on the verge of success; he's convinced that his portrait of the model, Tanya, will make his career and enable him to marry his fiancée, Heather, daughter of the wealthy Stanley Hayden. His world is shattered when Tanya, who's in love with him, accidentally reshuffles the bottles on his shelf, and Dave washes his eyes with acid rather than eyewash. Dave is blinded and his physician, Dr. Welles, can offer only the remote hope that a cornea transplant will restore his sight, but donors are scarce and the operation problematic.

Dave is comforted by Heather, Tanya, and his friend, the psychiatrist Dr. Bittaker, who is in love with Tanya. Full of self-pity and seeking solace in alcohol, Dave breaks off his engagement with Heather by telling her the lie that he is really in love with Tanya. Hayden, who has always despised Tanya, visits Dave and tells him he has willed him his own eyes to be transplanted after his death. The two quarrel, but Bittaker urges Dave to visit Hayden – who has been like a father to Dave - and reconcile. Later Heather enters the family home and finds Dave standing over her father's bludgeoned corpse, blood on his hands. Heather immediately concludes that Dave murdered her father though later she begins to harbor some doubt.

Captain Drury, the detective investigating the case, is suspicious of Dave but has another suspect: Heather's jealous suitor, Nick. The eye operation on Dave goes ahead as planned but, when the bandages are taken off, Dave still can't see. Dave has found a threaded nail in his pocket and remembers that he took it off the floor next to Hayden's body and feels that it is the key to the murder. Suspicious of Tanya, he tells her about it. That night Tanya telephones Heather to say she knows who the killer is but, before she can tell her, she is struck down by a mysterious intruder.

Bittaker visits Dave who accuses him of both murders. Knowing that Tanya would never leave Dave while he was blind, Bittaker killed Hayden so the eye transplant could go ahead. Tanya discovered that the threaded nail was from Bittaker's ornate walking stick, so he murdered her as well. ("You loved her, but you loved life more," says Dave). Bittaker attempts to bludgeon Dave, but the artist has actually regained his sight and thwarts the psychiatrist. Drury has been listening the whole time and arrests Bittaker. Dave is reunited with Heather and tells her that, though initially he was still blind after the operation, his sight gradually came back and he pretended to be blind to catch the real killer.

> I was dialogue director for Lon Chaney. I had just received the script. It was probably *Dead Man's Eyes* which I wasn't in. I came on the stage the first day, and as I walked in from the outdoors, the whole stage was empty except for Chaney sitting way in the opposite side talking to somebody. And as I walked across I said in a very loud voice: 'Look Chaney, who the fuck wrote this hunk of shit?' Chaney turned casually, indicating the man he had been talking to and said 'Well, meet the author.' Well, what could I say? I think it's a hunk of shit and I'm sorry. I'm sorry for you and I'm sorry for all of us. (1)

The hapless author in question was Dwight V. Babcock, and *Dead Man's Eyes* was both his first script for Universal and the only one for which he received sole credit (or blame). Whatever one's opinion of the film, Babcock was no amateur. He had spent years writing detective fiction for the pulps, notably *Black Mask* magazine, which had also boasted the work of authors like Dashiell Hammett, Erle Stanley Gardner, and Raymond Chandler to name a few of its most famous alumni. *Black Mask* scribes who went on to write horror movies include Curt Siodmak *(The Wolf Man*; his early version of **Donovan's Brain**, appeared in *Black Mask*), Eric Taylor (*The Ghost of Frankenstein*, the 1943 *Phantom of the Opera*), Peter Ruric (the 1934 *Black Cat*), and John K. Butler (*The Vampire's Ghost*) (2). Babcock graduated from short stories to detective novels, including several featuring Hannah Van Doren (called "the Gorgeous Ghoul" in the book of the same name) - a writer specializing in true crime - and her companion Joe Kirby, car salesman turned amateur sleuth. Reviews on the tome were generally good, although critic Issac Anderson complained that the characters did as much drinking as detecting.(3) Babcock had no experience writing scripts when he signed on at Universal, albeit one of his stories, "Hide Out," had been purchased by Monogram in

1937; it was never filmed. The writer apparently preferred the steady paycheck to be had working for the movies (and later television) to the vagaries of the market in the literary world, as he did very little fiction writing after signing up at Universal.

One wag suggested that *Dead Man's Eyes* should have been titled *The Cornea Murder Case*. Cornea transplants were not unknown in the '30s and '40s, but were still uncommon enough to get the occasional mention in the news. One wonders if Babcock saw the article "Blind Widow Aided by Dead Man's Eye" in the 27 February 1944 edition of *The New York Times*. Or maybe the 4 March 1938 issue of the *Los Angeles Times*, which featured an item titled "Mother to Give Up Own Eye so Son May See." Babcock had no medical background - he was a piano tuner and grape-juice salesman before turning to writing - but he did his homework, and the scene wherein the principals discuss transplants has the most intelligent and believable dialogue in the entire film. Interestingly, old moneybags Hayden suggests paying someone for their cornea. That grisly notion - never mentioned again in the film - would get some play in the *Night Gallery* episode, "Eyes."

This being an "Inner Sanctum" tale - the third in the series - the possibility of the supernatural plays no serious part, and the fact that Chaney sees with the eyes of a murder victim is not really a factor. The old myth that the final image that someone sees before dying can be captured (as in *The Invisible Ray*) is not trotted out, and - except for the offbeat idea of someone being murdered for their eyes - the film unreels as a conventional whodunit... and it's not terribly difficult to figure out the *who*. "If Dad Hayden were dead" mutters Chaney to himself at one point, but his Dave is not really a viable suspect. There's Tanya (Acquanetta), of course, but, in a rather improbable scene, she steals the eyes meant for Dave because she wants him to remain blind and dependent on her. That being the case, she would hardly have wanted to kill Hayden in spite of his dislike of her (Bittaker manages to secretly return the eyes in time in another unbelievable moment). Then there's the much-rejected suitor, Nick, who's repeatedly told to "Get out!", but he's a drunken weakling played by George Meeker, who made a career out of portraying spineless heels (though, to be fair, he *did* turn out to be the "surprise" killer in 1933's *Night of Terror*). That leaves only Dr. Bittaker, who carries a walking stick with a big silver handle (that would have done Lawrence Talbot proud in *The Wolf Man*). The stick is so conspicuous that you might suspect Babcock or director Reginald Le Borg is trying to lead the audience astray, but since Bittaker is everyone's friend and has no obvious motive, he *has* to be the culprit.

Played by Paul Kelly, a tough guy onscreen and off-, Bittaker is not a psychotic, although he brings sufficient menace to his final scene where he's revealed as the killer.

His mooning over Tanya is a bit less convincing: "She's as quiet and shy as a child and yet there's something primitive and passionate about her." Can he really be talking about the zombie-like Acquanetta? When Bittaker declares his love for her, her response is a prolonged "Yoooooouuuuuu?" delivered in her usual flat and monotone style. After Leo G. Carroll's Dr. Murchison - the head of a mental institution - was revealed as the killer in Hitchcock's *Spellbound* (1945), Hollywood's suspicion of psychiatry resulted in a number of sinister shrinks, a conceit that is anticipated here. Bittaker's air of calm after being arrested causes Captain Drury (well played by Thomas Gomez) to proclaim, "He wouldn't be the first one who's gone mad studying the processes of the mind... It's people like you that have caused me to stay clear of this book psychology." Bittaker is the more restrained predecessor of Hannibal Lecter.

**Even whilst about to be clubbed to death, Acquanetta displays her usual emotion.**

Blindness has also played the occasional role in horror. Usually it's the heroine who is blind, but her disability allows the revelation of her beloved's inner goodness - not his monstrous appearance - in films like *The Man Who Laughs* and *The Face Behind the Mask*, although Jane Adams is a bit less perceptive about Rondo Hatton in *The Brute Man* (co-authored by Babcock). O.P. Heggie's blindness in *Bride of Frankenstein* allows him to perceive the Monster as a lonely soul in need of a friend instead of as the "fiend who's been murdering half the countryside." Sometimes, there's a blind menace like Jake, Bela Lugosi's murderous henchman in *Dark Eyes of London*. And occasionally blindness can be used to generate terror: sightless heroine Audrey Hepburn outwits a trio of criminals in *Wait Until Dark*, while blind Mia Farrow has to contend with a serial killer in *See No Evil*. In *Dead Man's Eyes*, Reginald Le Borg's direction does little to suggest the fear and helplessness of suddenly becoming blind. When Chaney washes his eyes with acid, the screen grows blurry for a moment and then is followed by darkness. After that, it's up to Chaney to convey the horror and tragedy of an artist who can no longer see. He tries (*Variety* opined that his was the only solid performance in the film), but all his whining and self-pity is depressingly reminiscent of his Larry Talbot in the "Wolf Man" series. There's no scene showing Dave regaining his sight, presumably because Babcock was intrigued by the notion of a blind man trying to solve a murder, so he decided to briefly work that angle.

Edward Arnold had already played a blind detective in *Eyes in the Night* (1942) and later did a sequel entitled *The Hidden Eye* (1945), while Van Johnson did some sightless sleuthing in *23 Paces to Baker Street* (1956) and James Franciscus donned dark glasses for TV's *Longstreet*. But, of course, Dave can't remain blind for the rest of the movie, so Babcock does have him regain his sight (off-camera). In Jules Verne's novel, **Michael Strogoff**, the title character feigns blindness - after narrowly averting the real thing - in order to safely cross dangerous territory, but how does Dave's pretending to be blind in the concluding scenes help solve the murder case? The whole solution hinges on the loose-nail thread. The scene where Dave secretly enters Hayden's house to see if any of the walking sticks there might be missing a nail is a bit of a cheat, since Dave is still acting like he's blind though no one is watching (except for the audience, assuming they're still awake). However, in his subsequent scuffle with Nick, it's evident that he can see. Possibly, the finale, where Dave sees Bittaker in the mirror, is meant to be the big reveal - like the climatic sword fight in *Michael Strogoff* - but, if that's the case, it's spoiled by the lack of consistency leading up to it.

Blind artists who have their sight restored also turn up in the movies every so often. In F.W. Murnau's *Der Gang in die Nacht* (*The Walk in the Night*, 1920), an operation enables a blind painter (Conrad Veidt) to see again, but tragedy results. In *Augen der Liebe* (*Eyes of Love*, shot in 1942-43, but not released until 1951), a sculptor blinded in an accident likewise gets the lights turned back on via surgery, but pretends to be sightless because of a romantic complication, proving that melodramatic contrivance wasn't exclusive to Dwight Babcock's work.

Critics in the Big Apple had little good to say about *Dead Man's Eyes* and seemed especially annoyed by Acquanetta:

*Dead Man's Eyes* is officially billed as 'horror picture.' Casual inspection would seem to indicate the sole horror in this Universal production is that so much manpower and, to a much lesser degree, thought energy has been burned up in this concentration of outright insipidity... The acting, if indeed that's what one would call those gyrations and speeches by Lon Chaney, Jean Parker et al, was apparently hampered by the significant absence of anything to act about. All of this is brought to a high point of ineptness by a sloe-eyed lady known as Acquanetta who seems to have run a talent for inarticulateness into professional recognition.

*The New York Times*, 11 October 1944

In *Dead Man's Eyes* there is no more than a half-hearted attempt to effect a melodramatic unity. Characters skulk around hospital corridors and cabarets in atrocious lighting... The proceedings add up to one big yawn. The direction might have been handled by a script girl.

Howard Barnes, *New York Herald Tribune*, 7 October 1944

The mystery is well worked out on the screen by the scenario but unfortunately the acting of some of the members of the cast is so inept and stilted and the direction lacking... Acquanetta walks through her role like a somnambulist.

Kate Cameron, *New York Daily* News, 7 October 1944

*Dead Man's Eyes* might well have come off as an intriguing shocker were it not for those less than mediocre performances. Situations that should be torrid are tepid-and you can't really blame the script this time....Her [Acquanetta] lines are ostensibly dramatic; her delivery of them is something on the order of a six-year old reading a first grade primer... It all makes for some pretty tall figuring – and occasionally it is grim and goose-fleshy in effect. Too bad director Reginald Le Borg couldn't have assembled a more proficient cast. Of the lot Kelly, the polished performer, and Thomas Gomez in a small detective's role, acquit themselves credibly.

Irene Thirrer, *New York* Post, 7 October 1944

The film didn't wow them on the West Coast either. It played on a double bill with *The Invisible Man's Revenge* at the Hawaii Theater, which, like the Rialto, specialized in showing horror films. In the 15 September 1944 edition of the *Los Angeles* Times, reviewer John Scott did a proper though unenthusiastic write-up of *Revenge*, but I'm not sure he actually sat through *Dead Man's* Eyes, which he described as "psychological or something" with a "great sufficiency" of dialogue.

Nor was there a lot of love for the film in the trades, albeit it did earn one good write-up in the 16 September 1944 number of the generally easy-to-please *Showman's Trade Review*:

> This satisfactory mystery yarn is certain to keep customers guessing. While there are some slow spots because of the rather pat dialogue and overdrawn dramatics, the story manages to keep the interest keyed for a solution... The title is also an exploitation asset for theaters that thrive on horror films. This is not a horror film in the true sense of the word, but it will lend itself to that type of selling where it would be more advantageous without serious misrepresentation.

The 18 September 1944 edition of *Motion Picture Daily* wasn't buying:

> Although it treats of the unusual theme of transplanting a dead man's cornea to a blind man to restore his sight, *Dead Man's Eyes* rarely achieves that air of suspense and excitement that are requisites of the mystery film, being hobbled by inept dialogue that makes the film drag interminably. A troupe of earnest players strains unsuccessfully to overcome the stretches of hackneyed dialogue. The bizarre theme may afford an opportunity for strong exploitation.

*Variety's* "Sten" was among the naysayers, opining in his 13 September 1944 review that the picture was "filled with stilted dialogue, lacking action and suffering from poor performances by most of the cast."

Dwight Babcock stayed at Universal for only a short time, but a number of the scenarios he worked on were produced over the next two years, including *House of Horrors, She-Wolf of London*, and the last of the "Inner Sanctum" series, *Pillow of Death*. After some time at Republic - and before turning to the Boob Tube - Babcock freelanced on a number of bottom-of-the-barrel productions, among them something entitled *Jungle Moon Men*. The latter was likely not as polished as *Dead Man's Eyes*, but probably a lot more entertaining.

*Dead Man's Eyes* - 10 November 1944 - 64 minutes (ST)

**CAST**: Lon Chaney as Dave Stuart; Jean Parker as Heather Hayden; Paul Kelly as Alan Bittaker; George Meeker as Nick; Thomas Gomez as Captain Drury; Acquanetta as Tanya; Jonathan Hale as Dr. Welles; Edward Fielding as Stanley Hayden; Pierre Watkin as Attorney; Eddie Dunn as Policeman; with John Elliot, Allen Fox, David Hoffman, Rex Lease, Leslie K. O'Pace, Beatrice Roberts

**CREDITS**: Director: Reginald Le Borg; Producers: Will Cowan, Ben Pivar; Original Screenplay: Dwight V. Babcock; Dialogue Directors: Stacey Keach, Sr., Phil Brown; Cinematography: Paul Ivano; Music: Paul Sawtell, Frank Skinner, Ralph Freed; Film Editing: Milton Carruth; Art Direction: John B. Goodman, Martin Obzina; Set Decoration: Russell A. Gausman, Leigh Smith; Costumes: Vera West; Assistant Director: Seward Webb; Visual Effects: John P. Fulton

*Shock Theater* Catalog No. 699: "A killer feels safe until he discovers that his victim's eyes have condemned him to death... the most amazing story in the annals of crime. Don't miss the *Shock Theater* feature film, 'Dead Man's Eyes,' telecast on this channel (day), at (time)."

*- HN*

# *Murder in the Blue Room* (1944)

*Synopsis*: Larry Dearden is in a kind of lopsided love relationship with Nan Strickland, and he offers to sleep in the Blue Room – a reportedly haunted chamber wherein Nan's dad had been found murdered 20 years earlier – in order to both impress his girl and to put the lie to the room's notorious reputation. But, come the dawn, Larry has disappeared! Everyone is aghast and that includes Nan, mystery novelist Steve Randall, Nan's mom, her step-dad Frank Baldridge, and Dr. Carroll, the family physician.

Steve is of a mind that Dr. Carroll and/or Edwards, the butler, is/are involved in both Larry's disappearance and Sam Kirkland's murder. (His mentioning her step-dad in the same breath with his two suspects gets Steve in Dutch with Nan, so we cognoscenti of the genre can safely eliminate Mr. Kirkland from consideration.) Steve then spends the night in the Blue Room; when the morning rolls 'round again, *he* has vanished, but what's left of Larry Dearden has turned up, shot through the heart, plop on the bed. Police Inspector McDonald and his men nose around and get a darned sight farther than do most "B"-movie cops, actually showing up at the right place at the right time to watch the guilty party – Dr. Carroll – expire.

Steve, of course, not only survived his night in the Blue Room, but had done some behind-the-scenes sleuthing. It devolves that Larry was Sam Kirkland's illegitimate son, a fact which Dr. Carroll had revealed (separately) to both Larry and Nan, but with which the unscrupulous physician had blackmailed Sam Kirkland 20 years earlier. When Sam decided that he would no longer pay for Dr. Carroll's silence, he was murdered and left within the locked confines of the Blue Room. The doctor then murdered Larry to keep him from putting two and two together, and only Steve's discovering the chamber's secret passages and Larry's corpse – together with his crafty, mystery-writer's mind – allowed him to solve the puzzle.

511

In 1944, Universal released 14 features of interest to folks such as us, and fully 10 of them were series' films of varied design and execution. Of the autonomous remainders, one (*Ghost Catchers*) was the latest of Olsen and Johnson's zany musical comedies, one (*The Climax*) was a helter-skelter reinterpretation of the studio's 1930 effort of the same name mixed with essence of *Phantom of the Opera*, and one (*Destiny*) was fashioned to a large extent from unused footage from an earlier movie (*Flesh and Fantasy*). The last of the batch was *Murder in the Blue Room*, the studio's second remake of a film itself not quite 12 years old (1933's *Secret of the Blue Room*), an English-language take on the original German Tonfilm (sound film), *Das Geheimnis des blauen Zimmers*, produced and released the year before *Secret*. (Everything was more or less based on the short story of the same name [in German, *natürlich*] written by Erich Philippi, the pen name utilized by author/screenwriter Arnold Lippschütz.) If the film at hand doesn't quite measure up to Universal's 1933 "original," it's profoundly preferable to the anemic and somewhat obnoxious *The Missing Guest* (1938).

The genre-familiar reader will note that the chief difference between *Guest* and the picture we are scrutinizing herein lies in the fact that Larry himself kills Carroll in the earlier film. Particulars of the story which had been glossed over in a more cavalier fashion in the 1938 iteration receive more attention here, and the lovely Anne Gwynne is head and shoulders more personable than Constance Cummings had been as "Steve." Lest anyone feel that the pictures are dissimilar only in these matters, I ask his/her indulgence whilst I proceed to cast an eye on The Three Jazzybelles.

Tom Weaver and Michael and John Brunas aver (in their must-have **Universal Horrors**) that *Murder in the Blue Room* was originally intended to be a vehicle for the Ritz Brothers, somewhat along the lines of the team's 20th Century Fox comedy-meller, *The Gorilla* (1939). The Ritzes – whose greatest fame came from their acrobatic musical hijinks in nightclubs and cabarets – had become weary unto death with that studio's endless succession of "B"-movie malarkey and had raised hell over that hoary tale of apes and old, dark houses. Nonetheless, they were obligated not only for that film, but also had to finish out their contract at Fox with 1939's *Pack Up Your Troubles*. Moving over to Universal, they (as well as Olsen and Johnson) came to be regarded as *secondary* funnymen to box-office kings, Abbott and Costello, and their limited output – four features within as many years, with time off for club work – reflected what was left of their limited interest in motion pictures. Following the path they had taken at Fox, the Ritz Brothers bailed out of Universal after the release of 1943's optimistically-titled, *Never a Dull Moment*.

With the brothers off the *Blue Room* project, associate producer Frank Gross brought in a trio of talented singing comediennes – Grace McDonald, Betty Kean, and June Preisser – who happened also to be rather capable dancers. The three young women added more than just running time to the film by contributing several enjoyable (if now dated) musical interludes and a spate of amusing (even if then, vintage) quips, while indulging in a kind of low-brow silliness that kept one's attention from flagging in the odd moments between murders and disappearances. The Jazzybelles – ostensibly old chums and ex-performance partners of Nan Strickland – stumble onto clues, uncover the role the butler plays in the proceedings ("Edwards! What would your mother say about this?"), and happen upon that secret passage that leads from the Blue Room. Their glib camaraderie keeping them from growing tedious, while the three demonstrate the vocal style of the Andrews Sisters, the rubber-legged buffoonery of Joan Davis, and the acrobatic ability of – Hey! Why not? – the Ritz Brothers.

An interesting fact that has nothing to do with *Murder*'s atmosphere or horror content is that the Mlles. Preisser, McDonald, and Kean represented one of the only female comedy teams to hit the screen before the Millennium. There had been slews of comediennes from the silent days on up, but each of those women had either worked solo or had been teamed with a male partner. The only exception seems to have been the series of Hal Roach Studios' shorts made in the early to mid-'30s with Thelma Todd and either ZaSu Pitts or Patsy Kelly. Despite moments of brilliance, the Roach two-reelers were uneven, with the distaff teammates only occasionally successful in trying to adapt an historically male-oriented style of comedy to their own gifts. For all their so-so reception, the shorts would probably have continued for a while longer, but for Miss Todd's mysterious death on the 16 December, 1935.

As far as I'm concerned, the *joie de vivre* and the screwball performance art of The Three Jazzybelles give *Murder in the Blue Room* whatever excitement and energy it has. The trio has an undeniable chemistry and exudes an appeal that audiences most likely would have taken to, had they been given the opportunity to follow the women in anything resembling a series. The studio didn't spot the profitable possibilities, though; each of the ladies would continue to appear in musical pictures as she had in the past (e.g. Miss McDonald in *Behind the Eight Ball* [with the Ritz Brothers!], Miss Preisser in *Babes on Swing Street*, and Miss Kean in *Sing a Jingle* – notable titles, all.) Of the trio, Miss McDonald held the title for most appearances in a Universal genre picture, as, apart from the picture under discussion, she had an uncredited bit in 1943's *Flesh and Fantasy*, only to be fourth-billed in *Destiny*, a year later. (The lady also holds the crown for holding her own vs. the studio's resident comedy teams; in addition to dealing with the Ritzes in *Eight Ball*, she mugged with Abbott and Costello in *It Ain't*

*Hay* and did another uncredited bit opposite Olsen and Johnson in *Crazy House* [both 1943].)

Comediennes (and comedians) aside, *Murder in the Blue Room* offers the kernel of the 1933 "original," updated to an unmistakably '40s milieu. Moving at a faster pace than either of its predecessors, the picture pulsates with a boogie-woogie undercurrent that was almost a necessity of life in 1944. Most wartime films relied heavily on action to draw in the crowds, and this energy was not (as it is nowadays) always interpreted in terms of sex and/or violence, but, rather, through music, dance, and rapid-fire dialogue. It was the rare "B"-film that could butt heads with a more sophisticated "A" picture in terms of studied characterization or overly complex plot development as short running times demanded stories that moved, and very few "B's" could afford to be leisurely or cerebral.

**Just as had Laurel and Hardy and the Marx Brothers in several of their films, the Three Jazzybelles (l-r: Grace McDonald, Betty Kean, June Preisser) share a bed to add atmosphere and shake a leg to imbue an otherwise *meh* picture with song and dance.**

This limitation did not preclude creative cinematography, and few of *Murder*'s contemporary competitors could hold their own either with more moneyed films or with this pleasant Universal "B" in that category; George Robinson's contributions succeeded in wringing whatever shadows they could from Leslie Goodwin's rather too-lighthearted vision. Larry Dearden's dramatic entrance, for example (he is the only guest garbed in a weird and somewhat frightening costume), is preceded by an intriguing point-of-view shot, involving both car and mansion doors. This kind of cinematic "hook" helped to get increasingly blasé audiences involved and even anxious for the story to unfold, as well as set up a visual foundation for everything from the concept of "haunted" rooms to the disappointing appearances of the film's one genuine ghost. The most creative use of lighting in the picture, nevertheless, is also the most obvious: the shadows cast on the wall behind the Jazzybelles as they *entertain* poor Edwards into submission are a reverse-action hoot.

The musical numbers – some three songs and dances by Kean, Preisser, and McDonald, and the dubbed "One Starry Night," mouthed by Anne Gwynne (vocal by Martha Tilton) – are painless, enjoyable, and quintessentially '40s, but do absolutely nothing to advance the plot. (Apart from contemporary "prestige" pictures – solemn, no-nonsense productions, fraught with meaning – virtually every wartime film [including at least a handful focused on the war itself] had its musical moments. Swing swung into most of the then-"present day" features, singing cowboys warbled with reckless abandon, and even horror pictures sometimes took a breather while the gypsies, villagers, or whoever strutted their stuff. The vocalists may not have always been top-notch, nor their songs all prize winners, but the inclusion of a musical number or two usually meant some excruciatingly minor bit of extrapolation wouldn't be repeated more than once. In fact, even with the running time devoted to the songs and dances, *Murder in the Blue Room* clocks in at some seven minutes less than the painfully protracted *The Missing Guest*.)

This was Donald Cook's only chiller at Universal. Most of the bland leading man's other studio appearances (and there weren't many) were in comedies in support of Abbott and Costello, Lee Tracy, Jack Oakie, Donald O'Connor, and Pinky Lee [!] Cook isn't bad here, but he does seem a little long in the tooth for spring chicken, Anne Gwynne. Considering that the grandfather's clock in the Blue Room evidently swings open at the strike of three every morning, his character can't even take too much credit for having discovered the secret through elementary deductions. Still, his Steve Randall sums things up neatly and succinctly and doubtless earns the typical Hollywood reward of marriage to the heroine.

Top-billed Anne Gwynne became a Universal mainstay during the '40s, and the lovely Texan returns time and again in these pages. *Black Friday* marked the first of her Universal thriller-features, but she had had one of those infamous "uncredited bits" in her genre debut in the studio's epic chapterplay, *The Green Hornet*, earlier in 1940. Cheesehead John Litel had over 200 film appearances between the time he left Wisconsin for Hollywood – the move interrupted by the actor's service during World War I *in the French army* – and a handful (including *Sealed Lips, Mystery of Marie Roget*, and *Invisible Agent*) will be of interest to readers of this volume. The Illinois-born Ian Wolfe had more than *three hundred* separate moments on the screen in his career, which spanned nearly 60 years! His, too, was a name (and a face) that added presence (and panache) to many of the pictures discussed herein.

In this, its third iteration in English, the "Blue Room" lost quite a bit of its grandeur and stature; heck, even the supposedly supernatural chamber's host body had been downgraded from the Castle Helldorf of the 1933 original to "the old Kirkland place" in 1944. And while there *is* that ghost, he is but a derby-wearing comic effect, frightening no one except for the Jazzybelles, and with musical nuances all his own. Apparently haunted rooms had by this time become somewhat *passé*, and it seems that the *frissons* of an earlier era now had to be either larger than life (tough to accomplish a short time after D-Day) or comedy-coated to be appreciated. (For credits mavens, it should be noted that *Murder in the Blue Room* marked the debut of screen writer I.A.L. Diamond – born in Romania and raised in Brooklyn – who would go on to greatness [and an Oscar for 1960's *The Apartment*] as the long-time collaborator of the legendary Billy Wilder. Sharing the screenplay credit with Diamond was Stanley Davis, himself only three pictures removed from his debut; Davis's future was not as celebrated as Diamond's, although he did make something of a name for himself in the early days of television, with contributions to series like *The Millionaire, Topper*, and *The Colgate Comedy Hour*.)

Reviews on *Murder* were quite mixed, and the opinions seemed to depend largely upon whether or not the reviewer was taken with the antics of the Jazzybelles. Per *The Film Daily* (8 November 1944):

> The comedy overshadows the melodramatic content to the point of making the plot more or less inconsequential. Audiences will enjoy the film for its laughs more than for any other reason. Although not listed among the top players, the trio of Grace McDonald, Betty Kean and June Preisser steals the film, being responsible for most of the entertainment and all of the laughs.

On the other hand, Bosley Crowther used his column inch in the 28 October 1944 issue of *The New York Times* to kvetch:

> This one has nothing more to offer than Grace McDonald, June Preisser and Betty Kean behaving as one might imagine the Andrews [Sisters] characters might behave in a haunted house. And if that warning isn't enough to scare you out of going to see it, go ahead – and squirm.

The 16 November 1944 *Motion Picture Daily* begged to differ:

> Universal is pretty much justified in calling this 'The Merriest of Musical Mysteries.' The combination of murder, mystery and music here is riotously funny. The cast, with a better-than-average story, good gags and clever musical routines, apparently enjoyed the shenanigans to the utmost This looks like a real winner, apparently unanticipated.

The 28 October 1944 *Harrison's Reports*, though, wasn't having any of *that*:

> This combination of murder mystery melodrama, comedy, and music, is a mediocre program entertainment. There is mystery surrounding the murder, but the story is so inane that it fails to hold the spectator's attention. Moreover, the comedy situations fall flat because they are forced. The musical interpolations are dragged in by the ear, but even so they are a welcome relief from the rest of the proceedings.

Thankfully, *Harrison's* did find the picture to be "unobjectionable morally."

If Erich Philippi's story of mystery and murder is to your liking and you're looking for a movie version that is long on atmosphere and short on BS, *Secret of the Blue Room* is for you. If you don't mind the odd break for some frenetic '40s swing, and if good-natured silliness won't detract from your appreciation of that same tale, *Murder* will probably fill the bill. (Being hard-pressed to sync whatever virtues there may be to *The Missing Guest* with my own proclivities, I'm passing on taking those recommendations further.) There's not a thrill to be had in *Murder*, so it's disconcerting for an old horror buff to recommend the comic relief over the genre content, but that's where it stands. *Murder in the Blue Room* is an fun take on a tale originally spun in another time and place, but its cinematic evolution – somewhat parallel to the journey that Frankenstein's Monster took from the 1931 classic chiller to its 1948 run-in with Chick and Wilbur – was marked by enjoyable (if atmospherically disparate) ends that bracketed a middling middle.

*Murder in the Blue Room* – 1 December 1944 – 61 minutes

**CAST**: Anne Gwynne as Nan Kirkland; Donald Cook as Steve Randall; John Litel as Frank Baldridge; Grace McDonald as Peggy; Betty Kean as Betty; June Preisser as Jerry; Regis Toomey as Inspector McDonald; Nella Walker as Linda Baldridge; Andrew Tombes as Dr. Carroll; Ian Wolfe as Edwards; Emmett Vogan as Hannagan; Bill Williams [here, as Bill MacWilliams] as Larry Dearden; Frank Marlowe as Curtin; following were uncredited onscreen: Grace Hayle as the Dowager; Alice Draper, Victoria Horne as Maids; Milton Parsons as the Driver; Jack Garner as the Booking Agent; Robert Cherry as the Ghost

**CREDITS**: Director: Leslie Goodwins; Associate Producer: Frank Gross; Screenplay by I.A.L. Diamond and Stanley Davis; Based on the story "Das Geheimnis des blauen Zimmers" by Erich Philippi; Director of Photography: George Robinson; Camera Operator: Eddie Cohen; Assistant Cameraman: Phil Lathrop; Musical Director: Sam Freed, Jr.; Art Directors: John B. Goodman and Harold H. MacArthur; Sound Director: Bernard B. Brown; Sound Technician: Charles Carroll; Set Decorators: Russell A. Gausman and Edward R. Robinson; Film Editor: Charles Maynard; Dance Director: Carlos Romero; Gowns by Vera West; Assistant Director: Fred Frank; Dialogue Director: Howard Banks; Special Photographic Effects: John P. Fulton; Songs – "The Boogie Woogie Boogie Man" by Milton Rosen and Everett Carter; "One Starry Night" by Dave Franklin and Don George – vocal by Martha Tilton; "A-Do-Dee-Doo-Doo" by Lew Porter, F.J. Tableporter, and Ted Erdody

*-JTS*

# *House of Frankenstein* (1944)

In *She's Alive*, the David Skal documentary made to accompany the DVD release of *Bride of Frankenstein*, Sara Karloff relates that her father demurred subsequent boots-and-bolts appearances after his third round because he felt the Monster's story could not be expanded upon any further (farther? Is there anything further, father?). He was wise in his generation as subsequent series entries repeated in various ways *Son of Frankenstein*'s idea that the Monster was sick and needed attention from some delusional, if not outright wacko, medico. He doesn't appear particularly ill in *Ghost of Frankenstein* (1942), having survived the sulfur pit and having received that revivifying jolt of "ligh-tah-nink," but his pal Ygor insists to the contrary (while simultaneously declaring that the Monster is somehow now more dangerous than ever). In *Frankenstein Meets the Wolf Man* (1943), he appears to be nearly blind (post-production tampering omitted any mention of same, although he was definitely sightless at the end of *Ghost*) until Dr. Mannering shoots him full of voltage. Here, despite being the eponymous Monster of the well-publicized group of five, he is comatose for most of the film. (For that matter, the titular edifice is visited only briefly – but then, *House of Dr. Niemann* probably wouldn't have done spit at the box office and *The Devil's Brood* – reportedly one of the shooting titles, along with *Destiny* and *Chamber of Horrors* – while catchy, doesn't cast the sort of box-office magic as does any title including the word "Frankenstein.")

But if the scribes at Big U were running out of ideas for the Monster, they weren't doing much better for Count Dracula or the Wolf Man. The Count – if he truly *is* the Count (more on that later) – fixates on a young woman and has a mere one night of "unlife" before succumbing to the rays of the sun, while Larry Talbot is again a passive crybaby, seeking scientific attention that will either remove his lupine curse or grant him lasting death, just as he was doing in the series' previous chapter. The notion of an insufficiently hinged scientist seeking revenge on those he feels have wronged him was hardly a new one, given the clutch of PRC titles helmed by Sam Newfield and starring George Zucco, who appears here in what is essentially a cameo. Then, too, the subplot of the hunchbacked sidekick falling for a Gypsy dancing girl – Is a hunchback really to be considered a monster? – is lifted from *The Hunchback of Notre Dame*. (It bears noting that Edward T. Lowe, who scripted this potboiler, also wrote the scenario for the 1923 *Hunchback*). The freshest idea here was to combine the studio's star trio into a monster rally (Kharis the mummy was reportedly considered for inclusion, along with the Ape Woman and the Mad Ghoul, but was ditched early on) – a notion that has its roots in *Frankenstein Meets the Wolf Man*. Stuffing the cast with genre *stars* was, at any rate, a new angle.

Universal may have wanted to give the impression that this production was returning its horrors to "A" status, but the cast is the only area that seems to have received the sort of budgetary attention that the studio hadn't lavished on its genre efforts in a while. While Lon Chaney, Lionel Atwill, George Zucco, and John Carradine may not have been expensive commodities (Chaney was under long-term contract – the exact status of the others is unknown, but they were not Universal contract players), they'd never been all gathered together in a single Universal production. Boris Karloff was fresh off his success in Broadway's *Arsenic and Old Lace* and more valuable than he ever had been before he had departed Tinseltown, his abilities now proven on the Great White Way. (He would continue alternating film and stage for a couple decades, later adding the role of Captain Hook in *Peter Pan* to his CV.) J. Carroll Naish – who gets special "and" billing herein – was not yet associated with horror (albeit thanks to Universal and PRC he soon would be) and was somewhat of an "A"-lister, at least as far as character actors are concerned. Still, his appearance in Columbia's *Batman* serial at about the same time suggests a career in trouble. Then - speaking of respected character actors - there's Sig Ruman. How did he end up here?

Universal also allotted some extra cash (the film was budgeted at $354,000) for composer Paul Dessau (1894-1979), who introduced some fresh ideas on scoring for the studio's horrors. Dessau was on Universal's staff but briefly, but, in the year following *House*, he also worked on *The Woman in Green* and *The Strange Affair of Uncle Harry*. Dessau would soon move among various musical venues, and this resulted in orchestral works, operas, and incidental music for the theater; he frequently collaborated with Berthold Brecht, most notably on *Mother Courage and Her Children*. His first film scores were heard in 1926, accompanying the German releases of four Walt Disney cartoons. The Hamburg-born Dessau departed Germany for France in 1933, possibly sensing the changing political landscape in his native land; his collaborators and the subjects of many of his works showed distinctly Marxist leanings. With the outbreak of World War II in 1939, he decamped again, and this time he made for the USA, ending up at Universal City after some time spent in Manhattan. By 1946 he was at PRC, working with Edgar Ulmer on *The Wife of Monte Cristo*; the balance of his film scoring in Hollywood would be for low-budget, independent producers. Given his probable politics, he was likely only a step or two ahead of HUAC when he returned to his homeland in 1948.

**Now will you give me my chalk!?**

Curiously, *House*'s score is credited onscreen to Hans J. Salter and marks one of the few times he would receive such a designation during the run of Universal's '40s horrors. Ironically, his contribution seems to be the re-use (or "Salterizing") of cues from previous films: the music for the ice cavern scene and the theme underlying the calmer wagon rides had served similar duty in *Frankenstein Meets the Wolf Man;* other familiar cues show up here and there. Nonetheless, the title music here *is* brand new and contains several passages that sound too *avant-garde* for Salter, whose sensibilities were firmly Romantic. The shrieking brass that accompanies Niemann's attack on the prison guard and the off-kilter music for the Lampini horror exhibit scarcely sound like Salter, either. Dessau's work, however, seems to end with the culmination of the Dracula segment; the music for Ilonka's dance – original (at least to a Universal horror) and amusingly titled, "Gypsy Tantrums" – is the work of Charles Previn.

The film's opening shot (which begins under the credits) quite cleverly establishes the linking story as the wagons for Professor Lampini's Chamber of Horrors strive to make their way past Neustadt Prison, wherein are confined Dr. Niemann (Karloff) and his friend, Daniel (Naish). Niemann is given what is surely the lamest opening line ever for any Universal villain: as he throttles a prison guard, he snarls "Now will you give me my chalk?" (Why, with the guard at his mercy, does he not demand the keys?) We soon realize that Niemann is quite the looniest of all Universal mad medicos – possibly the looniest in film history – because he's delivering an illustrated lecture to Daniel on transplanting a man's brain into a dog's skull. (We will find out later that said procedure is not theoretical; Niemann has done it, though where he found a pooch with sufficient cranial capacity is anyone's guess.) The doctor states that his brother had worked for Frankenstein and had passed along all his secrets; yet, for some reason, Niemann needs to locate the late scientist's notebooks. A convenient lightning bolt does significant damage to the hoosegow (the convenience of lightning bolts in the "Frankenstein" series was established in *Ghost of...*) , and the two jailbirds escape, hitching a ride with Lampini. (As the off-kilter Lampini - quite his most eccentric performance - Zucco seems to be channeling W. C. Fields.) They repay the favor by murdering him and his driver so that Niemann can visit his old enemy, Mayor Hussman (Ruman), and exact vengeance.

Impersonating Lampini's brother, Niemann shows off his horrors to an audience that includes the former burgomaster, his grandson Carl, Carl's new wife, Rita (Peter Coe and Anne Gwynne), and the local police inspector (Atwill). Hussman so aggravates Niemann that the doctor removes the stake from the show's star attraction. (Does he do so to stab Hussman? The motive isn't at all clear, but the action is quite deliberate.) The knock-kneed skeleton that Lampini had claimed to belong to Count Dracula (Carradine) – and which Lampini... *errrr*... had borrowed from the cellar of Castle Dracula – becomes corporeal once again. The revived (and fully clothed – ah, magic!) vampire vows to do whatever Niemann proposes (disposing of Hussman, of course), in return for a guarantee that his coffin be protected. Introducing himself as Baron Latos, he ingratiates his way into the old man's household and drains the blood from him. But he also develops a fixation on the old gent's granddaughter-in-law and absconds with her, albeit pursued by a posse led by her husband and the police

522

inspector. Niemann and Daniel take off, thinking the police are after them but, on realizing the vampire is the target, Daniel tosses his coffin off their wagon. (Niemann thus early demonstrates that loyalty is a one-way street with him.) Latos' carriage crashes, and he is unable to make it quite back into his coffin before the rays of the sun reduce him once again to a skeleton. Dracula's ring – part of the vampire's supernatural seduction – slides off the young woman's hand, and she and her husband embrace. Fade out and on to the film's second half.

   -- A brief sidebar to explore an idea this writer first proposed in an exchange of letters with Don Mankowski (and which idea Mankowski found sacrilegious) in the pages of the late, lamented *Cult Movies* magazine: Tod Browning's *Dracula* (1931) closes with the titular count being staked in Whitby and later burnt to ashes in *Dracula's Daughter* (1936), said pyre also being located in Britain. In *Son of Dracula* (1942), Count Alucard – as he calls himself – simply appears undead and well with no explanation. At the movie's conclusion, the sunrise melts him away, an ending for a vampire from which there is no coming back (at least not until the Hammer renaissance). Baron Latos is first introduced as a staked skeleton found in the basement of Castle Dracula, not Carfax Abbey (from which he was taken and burnt in any case). Now, if we are really to pay attention to continuity – which clearly the scribes at Universal weren't by this point – these cannot all be the same vampire. Consider, too, that Alucard is duped by a woman in a *Double Indemnity*-like plot (two years before Billy Wilder's film) to commit a murder that has her gain an inheritance and the undead condition she desires, after which she plans to have the man she really loves dispose of the vampire. Not only do we find it difficult to swallow the notion of the King of the Vampires being hornswoggled by a mere *noir femme fatale*, but his demeanor is more in line with a mobster than with the suave creature who terrified Transylvania and preyed on London.

   Latos is so obsessed with a young woman he's just encountered that he brings about his own demise. Why doesn't he abandon the carriage and her by transforming into a bat - as we've seen him do earlier - and flap off to the safety of the Lampini wagons? (And while we're at it, what happened to the exquisite bat puppet from *Son*? The itsy-bitsy one here is from hunger and looks particularly lame – more like a winged Tribble – as a shadow on the wall.) Again, ask yourself: Is this the behavior of the King of the Vampires who had survived for five centuries? This guy can't make it through a single night. My suggestion is that Count Alucard really *is* the son of Dracula; the dialogue of the movie identifies him as such, as does the title (after all, Drac had had a daughter and no one has ever suggested she was really the Count in drag). Baron Latos is just that – another vampire who took up residence in the count's castle after his departure to Britain, appropriating his coffin and ring – or rings; he apparently has several, as witnessed in the next *House*.

Just saying ---

Niemann and Daniel next arrive in the village of Frankenstein to search for the late scientist's notebooks – talk about continuity issues! The ruined Vasaria castle of Ludwig Frankenstein and the breached dam that put paid (temporarily of course) to the Monster and the Wolf Man have been transported lock, stock, and broken battlements to the village where Wolf von Frankenstein took up temporary residence and revived his father's creation. (Is that clear?) The continental drift that moved Kharis and Ananka from New England to Cajun country pales in comparison to this transfer of real estate and infrastructure, both slightly the worse for wear. Daniel becomes smitten by a chunky gypsy dancer (Elena Verdugo) with the unfortunate moniker of Ilonka and saves her from being whipped. In searching the castle ruins, Niemann and Daniel stumble on the bodies of the Monster (Glenn Strange) and the Wolf Man (Chaney), frozen in blocks of ice. (Stills show us that the aged and infirm Bela Lugosi was actually behind the ice for *Frankenstein Meets the Wolf Man* – though unaccountably substituted for in the actual filming. Here, Glenn Strange – former stuntman and bit player, and presumably more fit and healthy than the sexagenarian from Lugos - is doubled by a dummy of the Monster in the ice.) Both creatures are thawed because they might reveal the location of the notebooks. After his usual round of kvetching about being alive again (and talk about lame opening lines! How about the mouthful of "Why have you freed me from the ice that imprisoned the beast within me?"), Talbot takes Niemann to a secret compartment that is neither the one in *Ghost of Frankenstein* nor ... *Meets the Wolf Man*. (Besides, wasn't the much-vaunted journal last seen being studied by Frank Mannering? Wouldn't it have been swept away by the flood waters? Just how many of these damned diaries in how many hidden caches were there anyway?)

The party heads off for Visaria (not to be confused we suppose with Vasaria, where Ludwig lived, unless of course this is another case of careless continuity). A bit of light dusting (cue montage) and Niemann's old lab is ready for use again. Conveniently, it includes one of those oversize massage tables to accommodate the Monster and, even more conveniently, a glass dome that fits right over it so that the Monster's damaged tissues can be restored with steam. Intriguingly, Niemann's equipment consists of precisely the same gizmos we've seen in previous "Frankenstein" films (not to mention *Man-made monster* and any other U horror infested with inadequately hinged M.D.s), apparently ordered from that medical supply company whose catalog boasted a basic Mad-Doctor-Laboratory package. While the Monster is being pressure cooked – and a complaining Talbot is being put off because Niemann has yet to figure out how to combine his techniques with Frankenstein's... or so he says – the doctor and his assistant go into the village and abduct Strauss and Ullman (Frank Reicher and Michael Mark), whose testimony helped convict him 15 years earlier. Niemann plans to give Strauss the brain of the Wolf Man and transfer Ullman's brain into the Monster; we later learn this latter brain will be given to Talbot (for whom Niemann had promised to *build* a new brain). Daniel, however covets Talbot's body as a new home for *his* grey matter, thinking it will make Ilonka love him. As some writer noted somewhere once (we've tried tracking down the remembered quip, to give credit where credit is due, with no success), the brain-switching here gets so fast and furious you need a scorecard. Credit (or blame) brain operation-obsessed Curt Siodmak, who supplied the story on which Lowe's script was based.

Meanwhile Talbot has succumbed to the full moon (a sign of the film's cheese-paring is that the transformation is shown merely by human footprints in the dirt changing to wolf paws rather than the familiar facial lap dissolve, and a pan to the lycanthrope loping off into the night.) The corpse of Larry's victim, added to the disappearance of Strauss and Ullman, incites the townspeople into forming a torch-bearing vigilante party (cue stock shots from the original *Frankenstein*) to hunt down the beast responsible. Ilonka, in the meantime, has been told of Larry's secret and, with the knowledge that a werewolf can only be killed by a silver bullet (which we already knew) fired by one who loves him enough to understand (which is a new wrinkle), hammers some of her jewelry into a projectile and loads it into a pistol. That night Niemann brings the Monster back to full power - though it remains strapped to the table - using both his own equipment and stock-shots from Whale's films. (Curiously, a dummy again stands in for Strange for part of the process – the camera even gliding in for a semi-close-up that reveals the chicanery; oddly enough, said dummy resembles Chaney's monster more than Strange's.) Niemann finally declares himself to be ready for Talbot (presumably this means brain switching and not brain building, but who the hell knows?). Larry, however, is preoccupied staring in the mirror and watching himself become more hirsute (the only proper transformation scene in the flick). He crashes through the French doors – or, rather, through the closed one, choosing to ignore the one that's wide open – and attacks Ilonka; who shoots him. They both expire. Losing "the only thing I ever loved" infuriates Daniel, who assaults Niemann and snaps his back, prompting the Monster to break free of his restraints and toss

Daniel from a high window and to his death. (Dubbed in here is Karloff's scream – on discovering Ygor's corpse - from *Son of Frankenstein*.) Just then the townspeople arrive, having been alerted by the flashing lights of Niemann's equipment (why didn't he think to put up curtains?). The mob uses torches ("He can't stand fire," declares the mayor of the Monster, though how he knows that is a puzzlement) to drive the Monster out of the castle and into some quicksand, which seems to be just beyond the front yard. (Location. Location. Location.) As he is carrying the crippled Niemann - whose "Don't go that way" pleas go unheeded - they both sink below the glop, and the film ends with all the principals dead, save for the married couple and the police inspector from the first segment. It is Universal's answer, in its frenzied finale, to a Jacobean tragedy.

Now, from the abundance of snarky observations in the above precis, the reader might infer that this writer doesn't think much of *House of Frankenstein*. On the contrary it's one of my favorites. We'll grant that, after Whale departed the series (and Universal departed him), none of the subsequent installments might have been considered as "art" (some might make a case for *Son*, but this writer can't go that far). Quickly dropped to "B" status when Universal realized it could still turn a pretty penny on its horrors without spending big bucks, the series was encumbered by a monolithic turn by Chaney as the Monster in *Ghost* (he *might* have been hampered by Jack Pierce's fake eyelids entirely obscuring his eyes, an actor's most important tool) and by post-production tampering that most likely damaged ...*Meets the Wolf Man* (it certainly damaged Lugosi's performance). *House*, however, might be regarded as "pure fun" *because of* rather than *in spite of its* loopiness and sheer disdain for continuity with respect to earlier entries. (Even more disdain would follow.)

Some have criticized it for playing out like an anthology film, glued together by the characters of Niemann and Daniel. Dracula – or, rather, Latos – comes and goes before the Wolf Man and the Monster even enter the picture, and the latter lies inert throughout the former's portion of the story, becoming ambulatory only in the final few minutes of the movie. This is certainly a flaw in a film whose trailer promised "Monster Battling Monster," a smack-down that never transpires. (One wonders if the producers, who had pondered Chaney's playing both title roles in *Frankenstein Meets the Wolf Man*, ever contemplated the same possibility here. Actually, the script's structure would have allowed his playing *all three* with no camera trickery.) It is undoubtedly a flaw that the Monster has almost nothing to do given its comparatively rich (if formulaic) story-lines in the preceding non-Whale films. While the story-lines involving Dracula (if indeed it was he) and the Wolf Man would be somewhat better integrated in the next *House* (though they never properly meet up), the Monster would fare no better than there. What's truly sad is the realization that - even with the integration of the horrors' actions, the return of Bela Lugosi to his iconic role, and the gift of significant screen time (again) to the Monster - it would still fall to Abbott & Costello to serve the trio reasonably well.

*House* is a film of scattered rewards, mostly in the "Latos" section. We first learn (in a Universal film) that being staked through the heart is not necessarily the end of a vampire. Indeed, the removal of the thing will restore his "undeadness," an idea already presented two years earlier in Columbia's *Return of the Vampire*; as noted previously, Universal wasn't above borrowing from other studios. The scene wherein Latos seals his seduction of Rita by placing his ring on her finger - and it shrinks to fit her digit - is a lovely fairy-tale touch worthy of Jean Cocteau. (It slides off again when the count perishes). The young woman's locked bedroom door gliding open so she can join him has an eerie romanticism, and the nighttime forest scenes are richly atmospheric (though whether this is due to the director, the cinematographer, or the scenic designer is open to debate).

The Wolf Man's segment is the same old-same old, but there is, however, a moment - just a moment - therein that pegs the film as something more than mere entertainment. On meeting the ever-truculent Talbot for the first time, the chatty and flirtatious Ilonka tries to draw him out, asking his name. "Lawrence," he tersely replies. "They call you Larry?" she asks. "They used to," he replies. Taken together, the line itself, Chaney's doleful delivery of it, and the ineffable sadness in his eyes, give 1940's Universal horror a poignant and – yes – a *human* moment rare in its output. It is especially notable in a film that – like most of its co-participants - is otherwise chiefly by the numbers. But given that, other than the familiar sets (not that many, surprisingly), familiar music, familiar players, etc., there is little else to challenge the little gray cells of series fans, and that may well be what fans of this era of U horrors found/find appealing.

Karloff, Chaney, Zucco, Gwynne, Carradine, Coe, Reicher, and Atwill are all dealt with elsewhere in this volume (it must be noted, however that Coe gives an ingratiating performance here, contrasted to his dour interpretation in *The Mummy's Curse*, and that Atwill herein is positively jovial in a non-evil role). New to the party is Elena Verdugo (1925-2017), whose first film appearance was at the age of six. Nine years would pass before she was again before the camera, and she was still a teenager in this, her introduction to horror. The following year's *The Frozen Ghost* would be her only other genre credit. Beginning in 1952, her *Curriculum Vitae* is dominated by television, with recurring roles on several series, including her famously playing Nurse Consuelo Lopez for seven years to *Marcus Welby, M.D.*, arguably her best remembered part.

German-born Sig Ruman (born Siegfried Carl Alban Rumann, 1884-1967) was indeed capable of impressive dramatic performances, but he is likely best known as a foil to the Marx Brothers in *A Night at the Opera* (1935), *A Day at the Races* (1937) and (in a dual role) *A Night in Casablanca* (1946). His comedic turn in *To Be or Not to Be* (1942) and his playing the duplicitous guard in *Stalag 17* (1953) are also worthy of mention. Ruman's genre credits are slim, but they include Rene Clair's comic fantasy *It Happened Tomorrow* (the same year as *House*), and *Houdini* (1953) on the large screen, and episodes of *One Step Beyond*, *The Addams Family*, and *The Man from U.N.C.L.E.* on the small.

Sometimes it seems as though Michael Mark (born Morris Schulman, 1886-1975) pops up in every Universal horror film. Born in the then Russian Empire (now Belarus) town of Mogileb, he emigrated to the U.S.A. in 1910 and started working in films in 1928. His first turn in horror is his most notable: the father of the doomed Little Maria in James Whale's *Frankenstein* (1931); it is also one of his largest roles in the studio's chillers. In mostly uncredited appearances, he binds Julie Bishop for sacrifice in Edgar G. Ulmer's *The Black Cat* (1934) before heading off to other studios for bits in *Mad Love*, *The Black Room*, and *The Last Days of Pompeii* the following year. Back at Universal, he had a decent enough role as a town councilman in Rowland V. Lee's *Son of Frankenstein* before playing an uncredited servant in *Tower of London* (both 1939), followed by *The House of Seven Gables*, chapters 5-10 of *Flash Gordon Conquers the Universe*, the guy who sells John Banning the potsherd in *The Mummy's Hand* (all 1940), and *The Ghost of Frankenstein* and *Sherlock Holmes and the Secret Weapon* (both 1942 and both uncredited). He would not return to genre again until 1953's *Phantom from Space*, followed by *Attack of the Puppet People* (1958), *The Wasp Woman* (in another sizable role as the chemist who develops the wasp jelly extract), and *Return of the Fly* (both 1959).

At six foot six inches (yipe!), Glenn Strange (born George Glenn Strange, 1899-1973) was physically the most imposing Frankenstein Monster of all at Universal, while reportedly possessing a face Jack Pierce thought ideal for the character. The thick soles on the boots took him to nigh seven feet; more's the pity then that here and in the next *House* he'd be recumbent for most of his screen time. After stints as a rancher, deputy sheriff, and rodeo performer, he entered films courtesy of musical interludes in Westerns with his cousin, Taylor McPeters (aka Cactus Jack). His first actual role (though uncredited) was as one of Ming's soldiers in the original *Flash Gordon* serial (1935). Billing and roles improved, as he went about playing heavies in a slew of "B" westerns. His first monster role was as the Oshkosh B'Gosh-clad werewolf, Petro, in *The Mad Monster* (1942); he followed that with another Sam Newfield/ George Zucco thriller, *The Black Raven*, a year later, and yet another Newfield opus - this time with J. Carrol Naish instead of Zucco - *The Monster Maker* (1944), before stepping into the Monster's asphalt-spreader boots. One more creep role, "Atlas the Monster" in *Master Minds* (1949) with the Bowery Boys, completes his horror resume. In 1961 he assumed the role of Sam the bartender on *Gunsmoke*, for which he is best remembered and which he'd play for 12 years until shortly before his death.

In keeping with his "and…" onscreen credit, we come at last to J. Carroll Naish (born Joseph Patrick Carrol Naish, 1896-1973), considered one of the most versatile character actors in film. He logged in his first of 225 celluloid appearances in 1925 with his first genre credit, *The Return of the Terror* (1935); the following year's *Charlie Chan at the Circus* was as close as he'd get until 1942 and *Dr. Renault's Secret* (with George Zucco in a rare plum role that wasn't at PRC). By the next year, he was Dr. Daka in the first *Batman* serial and made the first of his "Inner Sanctum" appearances, in *Calling Dr. Death*. Once a supporting player in mostly "A" projects, he was more often than not now in lesser productions, and *The Monster Maker* (at PRC!) and *Jungle Woman* (both 1944) followed – both before *House*. Afterward there was another "Inner Sanctum," *Strange Confession* (1945, a remake of *The Man Who Reclaimed His Head*, 1934), then *The Beast with Five Fingers* (1946), and, eventually on to television work that would dominate his resume. *Life with Luigi* and *The New Adventures of Charlie Chan* were popular series that gave him a chance to display his ethnic impersonations as the eponymous characters, while one-shots on *I Dream of Jeannie* and *The Man from U.N.C.L.E.* took him back to genre territory. His final role was in the ghastly *Dracula vs. Frankenstein* (1971). As Daniel, he goes from cold-blooded killer to a whiner more annoying than Larry Talbot (no mean feat), and by the time the Monster tosses him through a window to his presumed death, some viewers might opine it happens none too soon. On the plus side we note his subtle, wordless byplay with Karloff in Lampini's wagon.

By the time he directed this monster rally, Erle C. Kenton (Erle Cauthorn Kenton, 1896-1980) was no stranger to horror, though his forte was comedies (he started out in Mack Sennett shorts and was one of the original Keystone Kops). Additionally, he took on any behind-the- scenes work at the Fun Factory that was available – not bad training for a director - and by 1919, Sennett was letting him hoist the megaphone.

529

In the comedy category, he directed W. C. Fields in *You're Telling Me* (1934) and Abbott and Costello in several features, including *Who Done It?*, after moving to Universal. Early in his Paramount tenure, he helmed the decidedly kinky - and, in its menagerie of half-humans - downright creepy *Island of Lost Souls* (1932), which shows that Kenton was paying some attention to the films of Rouben Mamoulian – or at least a study of that director's 1931 *Dr. Jekyll and Mr. Hyde*. He'd lay off the horrors until moving to Universal, but once there his assignments included *The Ghost of Frankenstein* (1942) prior to *House* and *House of Dracula* (1945) and *The Cat Creeps* (1946) afterward. Indisputably a"B"-list director, after the dismantling of the studio system, Kenton found his paychecks to be had from television from 1952 on.

*The New York Times* on 10 December, 1944, ran what was essentially a puff piece purporting to be an on-set visit by Edward J. Eustace. entitled "A Witch's Sabbath." Its second paragraph begins:

> There was Boris Karloff, with nothing on his face, for a wonder, but a long white beard, Lon Chaney, made up like a wolf man that girls forget; John Carradine, artificially whitened to seem in need or a red corpuscle cocktail in his vampire role as Count Dracula; J. Carroll Naish with a big buckram hunch tied on the back of his neck, and Glenn Strange sporting a green stucco face and two big metal studs sticking out of his neck as the Frankenstein monster.

Now ask yourself... On which particular shooting day did all these actors – in those makeups – need to be on set? (And Anne Gwynne and Elena Verdugo are on hand as well!) Karloff doffs the crepe spinach before he meets up with any of the monsters for starters, and the penny-pinchers at Big U were hardly going to pay for actors to show up on days they weren't needed. What's particularly odd about this softball bit of reportage (or should it perhaps be labeled fiction?) is that the *Times'* reviewers were almost invariably dismissive (to put it mildly) of all horror films. Indeed, when A. H. Weiler critiqued it six days later, he equated the film's monsters to "a baseball team with nine Babe Ruths, only this grisly congress doesn't hit hard; it merely has speed and a change of pace. As such, then, it is bound to garner as many chuckles as it does chills." Well at least we had learned (or did we?) from Eustace such tidbits of info as that Karloff drinks a quart of milk a day, and that Strange is wearing the same suit created for Karloff, but that it had to be taken *in* a bit. (Really?)

**Karloff and Glenn Strange and the usual torch-bearing villagers at the film's climax. Per the *NY Journal-American*: "One by one the monsters are disposed of and the finish finds Frankenstein's pet and the mad doctor sinking into the quicksand. But we'll probably be told in the next installment that they were rescued in the nick of time by the Invisible Man." (16 December 1944)**

And if the reportage was somewhat whimsical (one detects the fine hand of Universal's publicity department), reviewers weren't taking the studio's Christmas box (paired with *The Mummy's Curse*) very seriously as evidenced by the *Times'* critique above and the excerpt below:

> It was quite a party yesterday at the Hollywood Blvd. emporium of eerie movies, with the Wolf Man, Frankenstein's monster, Dracula, a mad doctor, and a hunchback brightening up the holiday season. True to tradition, all the monsters are liquidated before the finale, and the last cheery shot shows the mad medico, who has brought the characters to life, and the Frankenstein monster sinking out of sight in quicksand... The story needs no recounting. It is sufficient to say that all the characters except Dracula meet in an old castle and the fun begins.
>
> John L. Scott, *Los Angeles Times*, 23 December 1944

In the trades, opinion was divided, though more willing to deal with the production on its own terms. *Variety* - in its 20 December 1944 edition - said *House* was "a solid entry for the attention of the horror addicts" and opined Naish was "particularly well cast," while *Harrison's Reports* of 23 December declared it was...

> only a mild horror picture, more ludicrous than terrifying. The whole thing is a hash of the fantastic doings of these characters in previous pictures and, since they do exactly what is expected of them, the spectator is neither shocked nor chilled.

For contemporary estimates of the film's merits – or lack thereof – we must mostly turn to the internet.

> Marking Karloff's return to the Frankenstein series (albeit as a mad scientist), House of Frankenstein also features an excellent turn by John Carradine as Dracula (the look on his face when he surprises the Bürgermeister one evening will send chills down your spine). Chaney Jr. is his reliable self as Talbot / the Wolf Man, and Karloff steps into the role of the mad scientist quite nicely. There's even a brief appearance by Lionel Atwill as a police inspector. The truly stand-out performance, though, is delivered by J. Carrol Naish, whose Daniel falls in love with Ilonka, only to be cast aside when she develops feeling for Talbot. Story-wise, the House of Frankenstein doesn't make a lot of sense, and gets a little confusing at times (I completely lost track of which brain was going to be transplanted into which body). But if it's classic monsters you want, look no further than this film.
>
> Dave Becker, 2500 Movie Challenge

> Time to forget the artistic vision of James Whale's first two films in the Universal Frankenstein cycle, to overlook the depth, pathos, wit and creativity that made both Frankenstein (1931) and Bride of Frankenstein (1935) such genre transcending masterpieces. By the time Universal gave the green light to The House of Frankenstein (1944), the series had degenerated to a pale shadow of its gothic, melodramatic past – though, unbelievably enough, worse was still to come, in the eventual form of Abbott & Costello Meet Frankenstein (1948).
>
> Abraham, *A Wasted Life*

*House of Frankenstein* is a kid's dream 'Monster-Mash' type film. Not only do you get Frankenstein (who doesn't show up until near the end of the movie), but you get Dracula and the Wolf Man (plus as the poster indicates 'The Hunchback' and "The Mad Scientist')... unfortunately, it isn't very good...

The film makes no effort to bring [its] two halves together and it feels like a sheer marketing ploy to make money.

JPRoscoe, *Basement Rejects*

House of Frankenstein is brisk, nostalgic entertainment. As contrived as it may be, much fun is packed into its brief 70 minutes. It's a delight to see Boris Karloff back in the lineup, and J. Carrol Naish is especially good as the love-struck Daniel. John Carradine plays Dracula for the first of several times here, and, while he's no Bela Lugosi, he presents an interesting and more restrained take on the evil character.

Jien Lozowskiy, *DVD Drive-In*

The late Ken Hanke was one of the few newspaper critics with a love of the old horror films. On the occasion of a local revival showing of the film he offered the (hugely redacted) following:

*House of Frankenstein* has the advantage of having Boris Karloff, but the downside of having J. Carroll Naish—not to mention no clear idea how to bring its monsters together but it does have its moments;; a lot of fun and an OK end to the studio's glory days. The smartest thing Universal did was send Frankenstein Meets the Wolf Man director Roy William Neill back to his Sherlock Holmes films (at which he was good), and brought back Erle C. Kenton from Ghost of Frankenstein (1942). Kenton brings some real zip to the proceedings—maybe a little too much sometimes—and more atmosphere than he brought to the strangely high-key lighting of Ghost. Getting Edward T. Lowe to write the scripts instead of Curt Siodmak was also a big help, though he was stuck with Siodmak's storyline for House of Frankenstein, which likely accounts for its non-integrated narrative. That said, most of the individual components are nicely scripted...

It also has a terrific little role for George Zucco as Prof. Bruno Lampini, who gets killed off far too early. But it does have Karloff. It's not Karloff at his best, but neither is it Karloff at his walk-through-it worst. Instead, what we get here is Karloff in his rarely seen over-the-top mode... it becomes one of Karloff's nastiest and least sympathetic characters.

Ken Hanke, 17 January, 2012, *Asheville* (NC) *Mountain Express*


*House of Frankenstein* - 15 December 1944 - 71 minutes (SoS)


**CAST**: Boris Karloff as Doctor Niemann, Lon Chaney as Larry Talbot, J. Carrol Naish as Daniel, John Carradine as Dracula aka Baron Latos, Anne Gwynne as Rita Hussman, Peter Coe as Carl Hussman, Lionel Atwill as Inspector Arnz, George Zucco as Professor Bruno Lampini, Elena Verdugo as lonka, Sig Ruman as Hussman, William Edmunds as Fejos, Charles Miller as Burgomaster Toberman, Philip Van Zandt as Inspector Muller, Julius Tannen as Hertz, Hans Herbert as Meier, Dick Dickinson as Borg, George Lynn as Inspector Gerlach, Michael Mark as Frederick Strauss, Olaf Hytten as Hoffman, Frank Reicher as Ullman, Brandon Hurst as Dr. Geissler, Glenn Strange as The Monster; following are uncredited: Edmund Cobb as Coachman; Gino Corrado as Man in Audience at Dracula Exhibit; Joe Kirk as Schwartz; Belle Mitchell as Urla - Gypsy Woman; Anne G. Sterling as Gypsy Girl; Charles Wagenheim as Jailer

**CREDITS**: Producer: Paul Malvern; Director: Erle C. Kenton; Writing Credits: Edward T. Lowe Jr. (screenplay –as Edward T. Lowe), Curt Siodmak (story): Music – Hans J. Salter (as H.J. Salter, musical score), Paul Dessau (uncredited); Director of Photography :George Robinson; Film Editing: Philip Cahn; Art Direction: John B. Goodman, Martin Obzina; Set Decoration: Russell A. Gausman, A.J. Gilmore; Costume Design: Vera West (gowns); Makeup Artist: Jack P. Pierce (uncredited); Second Unit Director/Assistant Director: William Tummel; Sound Department: Bernard B. Brown (sound director), William Hedgcock (sound technician); Visual Effects: John P. Fulton (special photography); Stunts: Billy Jones, Carey Loftin,

Gil Perkins (all uncredited); Music Department: Hans J. Salter (musical director, as H.J. Salter), Charles Previn, Frank Skinner (composers: stock music, uncredited) - *HHL*

# *Destiny* (1944)

*Synopsis*: The police pursue two bank robbers, Cliff Banks and Sam Baker, but both get away. Via flashbacks we learn Cliff's hard luck story. In LA, he fell for a singer, Phyllis, and she introduced him to Sam who got him involved in a payroll robbery. Cliff subsequently had some good fortune at the racetrack and was even able to return his share of the stolen loot. However, when he sees the police are still looking for him, he entrusts the rest of his money to Phyllis. She leaves town with it, and Cliff ends up doing a three- year stretch. When he gets out, he gets a job and is determined to go straight, but meets Sam again who hitches a ride into town with him and promptly robs a bank, forcing Cliff into the role of getaway driver.

After getting double-crossed by Marie, a roadhouse owner who temporarily gives him shelter, Cliff finds himself at a farm owned by Clem and his blind daughter, Jane. Jane has an extraordinary affinity with nature; animals, bees, even plants are drawn to her. Cliff, who distrusts all women, is skeptical of her purity, but nonetheless impressed by her. He steals some money and a necklace from a drawer, but then confesses it to Jane. She urges him to stay on with them.

That night Cliff has a dream wherein he kills Clem and attempts to assault Jane who flees. He goes after her, but a fierce storm suddenly arises and wind and rain lash out at Cliff. Jane runs to the river and Cliff, still in pursuit, falls in and drowns. Frightened by this dark vision, Cliff tells Jane he must leave. However, Clem accidentally shoots himself, and Jane begs Cliff to help her take her badly wounded father into town. Cliff is reluctant knowing that the police are still after him, but he finally agrees and is arrested. However, Sam has also been arrested and admits to the authorities that Cliff was not really in on the bank robbery. Cliff is exonerated and will go on to live with Jane and Clem on the farm.

*Destiny* started life as the first segment of Julien Duvivier's 1943 anthology film *Flesh and Fantasy* (see essay). The episode ended with Cliff's death by drowning and was linked to the second segment (with Robert Cummings and Betty Field) by the discovery of Cliff's body in the canal. In spite of very positive audience reaction to the story, Universal cut the segment out after the preview, thinking that it would have made *Flesh and Fantasy* too long. It had been an expensive and somewhat frustrating experience for the studio, and they were not about to write the whole episode off. They paid Duviver and co-producer Charles Boyer for the rights to the footage which was then expanded to feature length (a very short feature at barely 65 minutes) with Roy Chanslor(1) writing the screenplay and Reginald Le Borg directing.

Films started by one director and finished by another often provide unsolvable puzzles for film historians trying to determine who did what. The classic example is perhaps *Merry-Go-Round* which was begun by Erich von Stroheim who was subsequently fired and replaced by the mediocre Rupert Julian. *Destiny* provides far less of a challenge. Duvivier's footage begins with Cliff waking up at the farmhouse and ends with his drowning, but it is argued that Duvivier must have shot something depicting Cliff's travels just prior to arriving at the farm as he couldn't have opened the segment as abruptly as it stands now. One source says the story is supposedly set in 1932; possibly the Depression background is meant to explain why Cliff is on the road. No doubt this footage would have been very brief, but, perhaps because there was some problem matching it to the revised story, it wasn't used. The only intrusion into the Duvivier footage are shots of Cliff experiencing the whole thing as a nightmare. The first part of the film and the happy fade-out all come from Chanslor and Le Borg.

Naturally, there are big stylistic differences between the sundry sources as well. Even though *Destiny* seems to fit into the *film noir* category, there aren't the mean streets and shadowy alleys usually associated with that genre. Most of Le Borg's film takes place outdoors and on the road; it's also shot in a very nondescript manner, much like a "B"-action film. Duvivier's footage (and Paul Ivano's camerawork) is – understandably - more carefully composed. There's a strikingly lit shot in the farmhouse in which Alan Curtis looks down on Gloria Jean from the top of the stairs; she's a small figure far below, and the beams of the farmhouse are prominent above both her and Curtis.

The farm setting has a fairy-tale quality to its look. Per the AFI, the producers originally planned to shoot the sequence in the Malibu Lake area, but fire destroyed the proposed location; thus, the scenes were all shot on an indoor set. Warren Garin commented on the result in the April 1943 edition of *Home Movies*:

Four process screens used for background projection were recently used by Universal for a single shot in 'Flesh and Fantasy.' This is a record number of process screens ever to be used in Hollywood and the result is amazing. The setting is of a mountain bisected by a waterfall. Two screens, one on either side, carry projections of the distant mountains. Two more screens, one on top of the other, are in the middle and the waterfall with a rushing stream at its base, is projected on them. In all four background projectors were used. Chief difficulty was getting lighting to match all four screens; synchronization of the four projectors with a camera was also a problem but successfully overcome by cinematographers John Fulton and John Boles. (2)

During production, the film was alternately known as *The Fugitive* and *Faith* before Universal decided on *Destiny* – a working title often used for the studio's monster epics, like *The Wolf Man*. The final title is no doubt intended as a link to *Flesh and Fantasy* where questions of free will and predestination are the core of the movie. *Destiny* gives lip service to those concepts; double-crossing dame Phyllis warbles "I'll see you in my dreams" twice, and later Cliff tells her he has had a horrible nightmare about the security guard who was injured during the hold-up. (There's a nice bit of editing linking the sound of the guard blowing his whistle to the hiss of the radiator in Cliff's room). When Phyllis dismisses his concerns with "Dreams can't hurt you," Cliff relates how he had a nightmare about his mother when he was kid, and she was killed in an accident the very next day.

Disposing of the climax of the Duvivier footage as a nightmare indicates the schizophrenic nature of the film as far as Cliff's character is concerned. Cliff of *Destiny* isn't a bad guy; he's just unlucky and too cynical for his own good. Why would a basically decent sort like Cliff dream of becoming a murderer and would-be rapist? Actually, it's because that's just what he is in Duvivier's original film. The problem begins in the scene between Jane and Cliff in the deserted church. Hearing how profitable the farm is gets Cliff thinking about the possibilities of taking it over. When he falls to his knees to repent, he's clearly playing a game to win Jane's favor and stay on at the farm. (One does wonder, though, why Jane - with her second sight - doesn't see him for the rat he is). Are we supposed to think *Destiny*'s Cliff is sincere even though Alan Curtis here plays the part for the opposite effect? Duvivier had told of a vicious character who learns the hard way not to fool with Mother Nature (or her acolyte), while Le Borg's Cliff is a flawed person redeemed by love, a hoary *cliché* right out of the Silent Era. "Life is like a bank account," the warden tells Cliff; "You can't take anything out unless you put something in," a line Cliff repeats when his one good deed has drawn interest. One reviewer snickered at that bit of wisdom while another pronounced a good philosophy to live by.

In spite of Duvivier's Catholic proclivities, Jane does not seem like a traditional saint; dowsing and coziness with nature are not qualities associated with orthodoxy. Jane's favorite place is a *ruined* church, one where lovers inscribe their names on the wall for good luck. True, there's a statue of the Virgin Mary there, but mother goddesses were common in the ancient world. Jane's blindness hearkens back to Greek mythology and sightless seers like Tiresias (who at one time was transformed into a woman). It's the forces of Nature - not God - which are protecting their blind priestess and striking down her enemy. Jane is pretty much a Vestal Virgin of the boondocks.

**A poster that conveys absolutely nothing about what kind of picture is being advertised, perhaps illustrating Universal's inability to categorize this hybrid film. Note that, although Gloria Jean is the top-billed star, *femme fatale* Vivian Austin is given more prominence.**

Originally, Duvivier had wanted John Garfield and Theresa Wright of *Shadow of a Doubt* fame to play Cliff and Jane, but Garfield refused (as discussed in our *Flesh and Fantasy* essay) and Wright declined as well, citing exhaustion and even turning down

Universal's offer of $50,000 for one week's work.(3) The little-known Alan Curtis, who had just signed with Universal, replaced Garfield. Some 60 other actresses were tested for Jane before it was decided to use Gloria Jean, who was already under contract. Jean had debuted in *The Under Pup* (1939), and the powers-that-were obviously had hopes for the little girl with the pretty voice to become another Deanna Durbin, Universal's singing superstar; however, Gloria Jean ended up being used only in programmers, leaving the high-ticket items to Durbin. Jean later heard that Durbin, wary of any kind of rivalry, had used her influence at the studio to make sure Jean did not make any classy Technicolor films. Nevertheless, the little song bird was popular with audiences and critics alike.

Prior to *Destiny*, my one encounter with Gloria Jean was her annoying and unwelcome presence in W.C. Field's bizarre *Never Give a Sucker an Even Break* (1941; as Pauline Kael wrote, "And you can't just close your eyes because she *sings*). Her performance here, though, seems natural and unaffected, never cloying in spite of the sweetness of her character, and her panic and terror during the "nightmare" where Cliff attacks her is unnervingly convincing. According to publicity, Gloria Jean did not have an easy time on the set. In the script, the bees on the farm may have loved Jane, but they felt no such affection for Gloria Jean, and she was stung several times. Alan Curtis inadvertently broke one of her ribs during the assault scene, and she ended up with eye trouble as well, according to writer Harrison Carroll:

> Universal starlet Gloria Jean is paying a heavy price for her role as the blind girl in 'Destiny.' The unblinking stare with which she was obliged to sustain for abnormal intervals resulted in eye-strain that was aggravated in her last film 'Easy to Look at.' Result is she must wear dark glasses and stay away from the camera for a month and she'll probably have to wear tinted glasses for a year
>
> *Evening Independent* (Massillon, Ohio), 3 January 1945

No doubt Jean would have found all this worthwhile had her sequence stayed in *Flesh and Fantasy*, and she told Edwin Schallert in the 23 January 1944 edition of the *Los Angeles Times* that while her five-year career had its ups and downs, she was crushed about what happened with what was touted as her dramatic debut:

> But I've loved every bit of my experiences during those five years, even the heartbreaks. The 'Flesh and Fantasy' one was the worst because

that part I played really meant a lot to me. It was the first time I've ever done real drama....But now they plan to develop it into a full-length picture so that probably proves, as I've learned that these things generally work out for the best. But it did seem like a tragedy when I became a face on the cutting room floor temporarily.

Her comments were optimistic. She had gone from playing a prominent dramatic role in a prestigious all-star production to starring in a throwaway "B"-movie that created little impression. And while Reginald Le Borg was apparently satisfied with *Destiny*, neither Alan Curtis or Gloria Jean was impressed with the final results, as Gloria recalled for her biography:

> [Curtis said] 'I don't know about this. They should have kept this in *Flesh and Fantasy*. I'm not sure this is going to come off.' He was not happy with director Reginald Le Borg. Le Borg was a lovely man but he *did not* have what Duvivier had. He did the best he could. I saw the difference and it was just glaring. Le Borg kind of threw everything away and Duvivier took everything dead serious. (4)

Le Borg's film gets off to a lively start by literally cutting to the chase, with the police in hot pursuit of Cliff and Sam. The excitement is heightened by Cliff's leap from a bridge into the river (courtesy of footage from Hitchcock's *Saboteur*). The flashbacks are well done, with Grace McDonald and Minna Gombell contributing good performances in small roles, but Cliff is such a chump and Phyllis such an obvious bad girl, I couldn't help thinking of *femme fatale* Sean Young's line to Armand Assante in *Fatal Instinct* (1993): "You're stupid; I like that in a man." It's also rather unlikely that a treacherous scoundrel like Sam would willingly exonerate Cliff.

Some critics were aware that *Destiny's* origins were to be found in *Flesh and Fantasy*, but the New York critics were united in disliking the hybrid final product. After calling *Destiny* a "half-baked thriller," Otis Guernsey, in the Feb 3 1945 edition of *The New York Herald Tribune*, did note one worthwhile sequence:

> There is a very good scene in which Cliff runs amok and scares the good people out into the storm that rages over the countryside but this one moment of suspense turns out to be a hoax. Gloria Jean turns in a first -class performance...Frank Craven has the usual assignment as her

father. Their hard work is generally in vain in 'Destiny.' The script has a little bit of charm and a whisper of menace but not enough of either to make an effective motion picture.

On the 3 February 1945, the *New York Post*'s Irene Thirer opined:

> Reginald Le Borg directed in the typical 10-20-30 thriller fashion—and if you want to get 'way back into the atmosphere of the corny silent cinema, 'Destiny' is your dish. Don't take it too hard though.

And consider the *New York World Telegram*'s Alton Cook, who shared the following in the 2 February 1945 edition:

> After seeing 'Destiny' which is full of birds and bees I came out of the place feeling as though I had been walking in honey. They don't have beehives in the lobby of the Rialto so I know I was wrong. [After mentioning *Flesh and Fantasy*, the critic went on to observe that] The old sequence was salvaged and padded recently. In the first instance, the idea was to show how a small gesture might change a whole life. When they had a collection of episodes about such gestures, the picture didn't have nearly as tough going as it does now with the whole story depending on one kindly act by a blind girl.
>
> Seeing the picture 'Destiny' at the Rialto Theater, home of crime and horror, is like having an ice cream soda with whipped cream in a saloon. [After noting the film began as a sequence in *Destiny*, the reviewer commented that] It was understandable that it was left out. Since Universal revamped and lengthened the plot, the result is a melodrama with too little suspense and too much sentiment.
>
> Wanda Hale *New York Daily News*, 3 February 1945

Bosley Crowther, in the 3 February 1945 review in *The New York Times*, was equally (and unsurprisingly) unimpressed.

> Gloria Jean plays the little lady in a way so sweet and sublime that she makes Snow White look like a burglar, and Alan Curtis plays the lad with a scowl and a sneer so acid that it virtually corrodes the screen.

543

Frank Craven, by some strange misfortune, is trapped briefly in this silly mime. This we are happy to mention is a 'Destiny' which others need not face.

Some of the trades had good things to say about *Destiny*, among them the reviewer for the 12 September 1944 edition of *Harrison's Reports*:

> An unusually interesting program picture....The action varies from fast moving gangster melodrama to the idyllic atmosphere of a backwoods farm. Alan Curtis and Gloria Jean are exceptionally good. Some of the sequences are deeply appealing, while others are extremely suspensive. A dream sequence, in which Curtis' criminal tendencies get the best of him, is very effective.
>
> Old fashioned story should have strong sentimental appeal for most women. An unashamedly sentimental film 'Destiny' is a drama of the old school that will bring a measure of entertainment to those who are touched at the mere mention of a tear. The picture possesses melodramatic overtones that may succeed in luring the meller devotes... Director Reginald Le Borg finds himself in the position of having to change from tender to melodramatic mood time and again.
>
> *Film Daily*, 21 December 1944

> A logically told dramatic story with fine performances places this picture well above-the average among program offerings. In fact, it is strong enough to top in many situations in spite of its lack of names; for once word of mouth spreads, the returns will probably force it into the top spot. It is the type of picture that comes unexpectedly to the theatergoer who goes in to see the top feature and its message will remain long after the original draw picture is forgotten... Reginald Le Borg deserves laurels for the understanding way in which he interpreted the characters and situations.
>
> *Showman's Trade Review*, 9 December 1944

"Walt," in the 13 December 1944 number of *Variety*, was impressed with the salvage job:

544

Overall result displays an excellent job of recouping otherwise lost footage and production costs….Reginald Le Borg's direction of the added footage hits a fast pace and adequately ties to the episode originally made by Julien Duvivier.

However, Charles Ryweck of *Motion Picture Daily* found the movie bewildering and hard to follow:

Fault seems to lie with Roy Chansler's and Ernest Pascal's screenplay. Inept script. Reginald Le Borg's direction does manage to extract several suspenseful sequences, outstanding of which is a dream sequence conveying a strong sense of realism. The parts are more interesting than the whole as the sharp break in mood militates against the film. Photography by George Robinson and Paul Ivano is notably successful in the latter part where their cameras are permitted to roam over beautiful countryside.

7 December 1944

Seemingly forgetting *Destiny*, Universal publicity announced that Gloria Jean would be making her dramatic debut in *Fairy Tale Murder*. The title was subsequently changed to *The River Gang*, but under any name it got bad reviews with *Variety* describing it as "corny" and bound to disappoint Gloria Jean's fans. It was her last film for Universal. Her agent, Eddie Sherman, who had also represented Abbott and Costello, convinced Jean to go on a two-year personal tour, but when she returned to Hollywood, she found she was already a has-been. During her childhood and teen years, producers and actors had treated her deferentially, but now that she was an adult and desperate for work, she was shocked to discover that the casting couch came to the forefront. She made a few more "B"-movies and then took a job as a hostess in a West Side restaurant before settling in to a happier career at Redken, a cosmetics company.

Would Gloria Jean's career have been any different if *Flesh and Fantasy* had remained intact? Hard to say, but *Destiny* ended up pleasing no one. No doubt her fans were puzzled to find that half the film was over before her first appearance, and those moviegoers looking for blood and thunder found instead a mild *film noir* that morphed into a fable about redemption. Maybe the warden was right, and you can't take anything out unless you put something in.

*Destiny* - 22 December 1944 - 65 minutes

**CAST:** Gloria Jean as Jane; Alan Cutis as Cliff Banks; Frank Craven as Clem; Grace McDonald as Betty; Vivian Austin as Phyllis; Frank Fenton as Sam Baker; Minna Gombell as Marie; Selmer Jackson as Warden; Lew Wood as Guard; Perc Launders as Officer.

**CREDITS:** Directors: Julien Duvivier (uncredited), Reginald Le Borg; Assistant Director: Seward Webb; Associate Producer: Roy William Neill; Producers: Charles Boyer (uncredited), Julien Duvivier (uncredited), Howard Benedict; Writers: Roy Chanslor, Ernest Pascal, Jean-Levy Strauss (story idea, uncredited); Directors of Photography: George Robinson, Paul Ivano; Art Directors: John Goodman, Abraham Grossman, Richard H. Riedel; Film Editor: Paul Landres; Set Decorators: Russell, A. Gausman, Victor Gangelin; Costumes: Vera West; Music: Frank Skinner, Alexander Tansman; Sound: Bernard Brown, William Hedgcock; Visual Effects: John P.Fulton, Willis R. Cooke

*- HN*

# *The Mummy's Curse* (1944)

Somewhere in the Book of Ecclesiastes, it is written that "There is no new thing under the Sun." Other than the intriguingly Kabuki-like sequence involving said Sun and the Princess Ananka, the same may be said about *The Mummy's Curse.*

This, the last installment of the interminable-seeming saga of Kharis and his squeeze hasn't much to offer in the way of novelty, save for the following: 1) The quarter-century that passed since the action in *The Mummy's Ghost* has apparently allowed the Earth's tectonic plates to shift to the extent that the Massachusetts swampland has expanded to embrace the Louisiana bayous; 2) The name of the latest in the line the top-shelf graduates of Arkam University - Karnak U. apparently having gone the way of Trump University - Ilzor Zandaab (fodder for merriment) demonstrates that even the picture's authors needed relief from the series' tedium(1); 3) Dr. Zandaab does *not* lustfully pursue the skirt, as had his predecessors. 4) But Dr. Zandaab *does* have a henchman, and the henchman *does* fulfill the saga's lustful-pursuit requirement. 5) Forget all-encompassing conflagration; all it takes to destroy once and for all a patented Universal grotesque is a collapsing roof.(2) 6) The climactic shot of the mummified Princess Ananka is indisputable proof that, when performed by the gods and not left to their flunkies, Egyptian embalming does not produce loose ends or unsightly sagging. 7) The picture opens with a snappy, upbeat song ("Hey, you!") sung by Tante Berthe, owner of the eponymous cafe where every non-American secondary- and tertiary-cast member hangs when not protesting the rumored presence of The Mummy or gabbing with his peers in a veritable panoply of Cajun-accent approximations. 8) Addison Richards' character does not even once yell out 'Jumpin' Butterballs!"

Despite these specks of gold amidst the mud, saying that inspiration flagged with respect to virtually every aspect of *The Mummy's Curse* is being *nth*-degree charitable. The same-old, same-old – angry/vengeful Kharis, innocent/woeful Ananka, devoted/ *über*-testeronic high priests, elderly/wrong-place-at-the-wrong-time victims, simplistic/incessant tana-leaf distributions – had become achingly over-familiar in less than a lustrum while any novelty whatsoever was to be had only through the sacrifice of logic and continuity. Sure, we weren't where we thought we'd be, back when Kharis's biggest worry was about yet another ladder or staircase to climb (what with his bad leg and all), but... come on! A half-year had passed since *Ghost*'s premiere, so what difference should a few hundred cinematic months or miles make? Formulaic pictures follow their formula per the formula: Showing the known-known is less demanding on viewers and less expensive for producers than gambling on introducing the unknown-known into the mix.

The common element in all of these films (other than the balderdash) is Lon Chaney, Jr., albeit – per film historian, William K. Everson - even that was not a given. Referring to the three *Mummy's Hand* sequels, Everson opined... "The three subsequent entries to the series... all *allegedly* [italics mine] with Lon Chaney, Jr., were increasingly less effective each time out."(3) Since the Messrs. Weaver, Brunas and Brunas have averred that "Chaney walked off with an easy $8000 for his uninspired performance"(4), we will cheerfully attribute Kharis's lackluster performance to the man credited for it. Nonetheless, both in this epic and its immediate predecessor (*The Mummy's Ghost*), The Mummy's Abs are more noteworthy than they were in *Tomb*, wherein it seemed obvious that – labonza-wise – Chaney's Kharis was a tad heftier than Tyler's. Had Chaney been encouraged to "shape up" following *Tomb* so that the array of business suits (the Inner Sanctums), formal wear (*Son of Dracula*), and whatever one might call his garb in *The Ghost of Frankenstein* would not hang poorly on a husky frame? Who can say for sure?

Plot-wise, in the act of draining the swamp (*Ouch!*), Ragheb – a secret ally of the Scripps Museum's Dr. Ilzor Zandaab – has discovered the mummy of Kharis, and with the help of some fellow workers (whom he then killed) has moved same to an enormous abandoned monastery on a hill in the swamp. He and Ilzor revive Kharis, who immediately throttles the "self-appointed" old caretaker of the place. A bit later, the Princess Ananka – whose burial plot has been uncovered by a piece of heavy machinery – claws her way out into the sun and, following a dip in a nearby pond, emerges gorgeous and coiffured to beat the band. Soon thereafter, she is discovered wandering about the weeds by Cajun Joe, who brings her to Tante Berthe's where

548

Tante is killed by Kharis for getting in his way as Ananka – apparently not recognizing her honey after 3000 years – makes good her escape. Later, after Kharis has strangled a couple more of the secondary cast (including Cajun Joe), he snatches up Ananka and makes for the monastery, where Dr. Z spoons some tana-leaf fluid into her mouth, a move that ultimately re-mummifies her (sort of). Ragheb, having lured Betty Walsh – niece of and secretary to Pat Walsh, who is the foreman or something of the entire project - to the monastery for licentious reasons, kills Zandaab and then is chased into a cell by Kharis after which the roof collapses, Dr. Halsey (Zandaab's American colleague) walks off into the sunset with his arm around Betty, and the film ends. This time round, we argue that the "Curse" in the title makes reference to the last conscious eructation allowed Ananka after she'd had that bloody tana-leaf fluid dribbled onto her lips.

Other than appreciating the aforementioned sequence in which Virginia Christine actually makes us believe that the princess has been restored to life and loveliness courtesy of Ra – Sun God and cousin of Amon-Ra (whose anger can shatter the world!!) - commenting cogently on *The Mummy's Curse* is both nigh impossible and embarrassing, even for us. (Please do see **Universal Horrors** for a wonderful accounting by Ms. Christine of the trials and tribulations that this scene entailed.)

Continuity – *The Curse of the Mummy Series* – is so poorly followed that even though the tana-leaf monologues are recited yet again (by Peter Coe, whose frequent staring off into space throughout the picture signals either Ilzor's great focus on divine command or Coe's yearning to be somewhere else) and repeated (by toady Ragheb), they prove to be manifestly wrong. Having donned sacred robes, lit the sacred brazier, and opened the (obviously sacred) copper tin of tana leaves – just prior to the traditional flashbacks to Tom Tyler's flashbacks to Boris Karloff (only about 3 minutes worth, a damned sight less than Harold Young felt was necessary to bring *Mummy's Tomb* viewers up to speed) – the Egyptians start in. Ilzor reminds the ticket-buyers that Kharis requires "three leaves each night in the cycle of the full moon to keep his heart beating," despite Andoheb and Yousef Bey's having steadfastly ignored that part of the blarney in *The Mummy's Ghost*, and Ragheb – having just handed over three leaves to his boss, who will somehow obtain "fluid" from same – repeating the formula. Ilzor then adds that Kharis needs "Nine leaves each night to give him life and movement," and Ragheb goes along for the ride. First-grade math would seem to indicate that the Mummy would be getting a dozen leaves worth of fluid thusly, and we all remember that George Zucco (or was it Eduardo Cianelli?) had nearly gone apoplectic when warning Turhan Bey (or was it George Zucco?) against overfluiding Kharis. No matter; Kharis is on the receiving end of only three leaves worth of juice here, yet it's enough to give him sufficient "life and movement" to get him out of his sarcophagus and over to the old caretaker's neck in the twinkling of an eye! (In compensation for his early demise, the old caretaker – played by Silent-Era star of stage and screen, William Farnum – is given some of the goofiest dialogue in movies not written by Edward D. Wood or Tommy Wiseau: "In a room beneath the chapel, I found the bodies of freshly murdered men. Never has this happened before!")

Other bits of familiarity that may lead one to contempt: the sundry backwoods (back*bayou*?) shrubbery that Kharis has been condemned to shuffle through for all eternity is, of course, the same backlot shrubbery that appeared (uncredited) as Mapleton and the Giza suburbs, while that abandoned monastery – laden with more iron bars than Rikers Island – is festooned with numerous remnants of the departed clergy, as well as enough Egyptian paraphernalia to pass for the Scripps Museum itself. (How many rowboats worth of sacred hardware did Ragheb and his late coworkers lug up those equally familiar, Mayan-like steps, and whence, exactly, came all of it?) Also somewhat reminiscent of earlier chapters in this saga is the High Priest's knack for being precisely on the mark whenever a plot-advancing line is spoken. (As with the inescapable latent horniness for the female juvenile lead, this quality is evident in Ragheb - not Ilzor - who comes across the newly lovelified Ananka as she's moaning the name "Kharis" in the midst of the ferns. Inasmuch as Ragheb briefly survives Dr. Z – whom he had earlier addressed as "Master" with Dwight-Frye-level pandering – we might wonder whether, had the box-office take been higher than it turned out to be, Martin Kosleck would have inherited the robe and role for *The Mummy's Sequel*, Number Five.)

Performance-wise, Chaney gives a Chaney-esque take on Kharis, the one Universal grotesque (other than his "baby," the Wolf Man) he was to repeat, but the only variations in level, quality, and/or interpretation we could note were: a) Kharis – semi-blackened in *Tomb* – has apparently been bleached by exposure to the cleansing properties of the atmosphere/earth of the United States of America, and b) the mask (fashioned yet again by the wondrous Jack P. Pierce) that saved the Messrs. Pierce and Chaney from spending more time together than either of them could have wanted saw Chaney's good eye stand out like a sore thumb. Lon, whose non-Kharis Universal roles during this period saw him attired in actual clothing rather than swathed in gauze, must have regarded his participation in the Mummy series as a necessary evil. Nonetheless, given that his impersonations of the sundry geniuses upon whom the various "Inner Sanctum" films turned were scarcely more credible than his mute depiction of this "Prince of the Royal House," we'll either give him a bye here or the fish-eye for his later appearances.

Virginia Christine – wife of the wonderfully eccentric Fritz Feld – does a splendid job as Ananka, whether slowly navigating her way back to full loveliness under the merciless (but revivifying) rays of the Louisiana sun, or more quickly fleeing from the embrace of the remnant of her former beau in an assortment of venues. Both the lads at **Universal Horrors** and Thomas Reeder, author of **Stop Yellin': Ben Pivar and the Horror, Mystery and Action-Adventure Films of His Universal B-Unit,** are effusive in their praise of Christine's exquisite mime. The actress, whose greatest fame would come from hawking coffee to a couple of decades worth of couch potatoes, made her genre debut here and her genre *adieu* in the studio's *House of Horrors* (1946) wherein she was less successful in evading the grasp of Rondo Hatton. Still, the Iowa-born actress spent the last 30 or so years of her non-Folgers career chiefly on the small-screen; she retired from the industry in the early '80s and passed away in Los Angeles in July 1996.

Peter Coe, whose Ilzor Zandaab seems to have brought only one suit of clothing with him from the Land of the Nile, was an oft-married (*eight times*, maintaineth wwwIMDb.com) émigré from Dubrovnik who managed – in only his second credited screen appearance – to land third billing (behind Maria Montez and Jon Hall) in Universal's Technicolor romp, *Gypsy Wildcat* (1944). Of greater interest than that to fans such as us is his presence in *House of Frankenstein* that same year. As mentioned above, Coe's turn as the series' only chaste high priest lit few fires (sacred braziers excluded), but we're of a mind to place the blame for Ilzor's frequent gazes into a higher realm on director Leslie Goodwins than the actor himself. Aficionados of Edward D. Wood, Jr. will doubtless recall that it was to Coe's North Hollywood apartment that the infamous filmmaker repaired after he and his wife, Kathy, were evicted from their own Yucca Street flat days before Woods' death. In an interview conducted by another pal of Wood, Conrad Brooks, in issue number eight of *Cult Movies* magazine, Coe admitted as to how he – as a stage actor – had become physically ill ("I was sick! I vomited. I was shocked.") when asked by Universal to do a screen test. More germane, perhaps, was his recollection of his *Curse* co-star – and personal friend – Lon Chaney, Jr.

Brooks: "Did Chaney drink much on the set?"

Coe: "Yeah. As a matter of fact, he tried to get me to drink on the set of *The Mummy's Curse.* I told him: 'You're the fucking mummy in this, all you've got to do is grunt. I've got to memorize three pages of dialogue for one scene!' "

In light of this, perhaps we've been too hard on Ilzor. Like Virginia Christine, Coe retired from acting some years before his death – not long after this interview was held – in 1993.

Martin Kosleck, like Coe, emigrated from Europe, but under much more dire conditions: the press reported that he was fleeing the Nazis. A comprehensive treatment on Mr. Kosleck and his career may be found in our essay on *The Frozen Ghost*.

Leslie Goodwins – yet another import from the other side of the Atlantic (he was born and bred in London) – spent most of his early Hollywood career directing comedy shorts and "Mexican Spitfire" features. *Murder in the Blue Room* and *The Mummy's Curse* comprise the alpha and omega of his genre movies; even his switch over to the boob tube for last 20 or so years of his professional life added but two hemi-demi-semi-genre titles to his CV: he directed nine episodes of *Topper* in the mid-'50s and 19 episodes of *My Favorite Martian* in the mid-'60s. Texan Dennis Moore spent most of his movie/TV career in oaters, although he was a cop (uncredited) in Bela's *Voodoo Man*, a radio announcer (uncredited) in *The Frozen Ghost*, and as close as one can get to being one of the principal cast without actually doing anything in *The Mummy's Curse*. Polish-born Kurt Katch spent his cinematic salad days in German silent films (he was in *Die Mexikanerin* with Conrad Veidt in 1919), having (like Veidt and so many others) found himself in the dramatic debt of Max Reinhardt and having (like Veidt, etc.) escaped Hitler and his ilk once the handwriting was on the wall in Germany. Katch – like Kosleck – was typecast as monocle'd Nazi officers and such a dozen times for every chance he had to play a Halugu Khan in *Ali Baba and the Forty Thieves* or a Cajun Joe in *Curse*.

Other than *Dead Man's Eyes* (1944), *Curse* was writer Dwight V. Babcock's entree into the world of '40s Universal horror, and his name – and more of his professional resume – will be found in later chapters. For Leon Abrams - Babcock's partner-in-crime here – *Curse* was his only genre misfortune.

Jack P. Pierce was once again in charge of wrapping up (or was it "zipping up?") the Screen's Master Character Creator and, as noted above, Chaney's good eye is all-too-obviously cradled under a layer of rubber. If the role no longer presented a challenge to the actor, it's pretty obvious the make-up assignment no longer brought out the best in Pierce. Chaney would, of course, twice again portray a mummy –

actually, a werewolf interred as a mummy – in 1960's *La casa del terror*, a Mexican comedy starring South-of-the-Border favorite, Tin Tan, and then in 1964's *The Face of the Screaming Werewolf*, a Jerry Warren bastardization born of footage edited from *Casa* and 1957's *La Momia Azteca*, a Cinematográfica Calderón production that featured another mummy (and another backstory) entirely. Chaney's mummy also turned up – this time, anticipated and quite welcome, given the advance publicity – in an enormously enjoyable 1962 episode of *Route 66* entitled "Lizard's Leg and Owlet's Wing." "Leg and Wing" also featured Chaney in a brace of other make-ups (as a variation of his father's Quasimodo and his own Wolf Man) and Boris Karloff as *his* baby, the Frankenstein Monster. Peter Lorre, who co-starred with the horror-film icons but could neither fall back on a signature "monster" role nor on a dad made famous by the judicious application of Max Factor, did not wear any reworkings of classic appurtenances, but appeared mainly as "Mr. Retep," head of the "Society for the Preservation of Gerenuks." We can only suppose that Chaney did not grouse too much about assuming an ersatz-Kharis look for the CBS viewers.

"Okay, Ilzor. Make it a double!" Even though this is probably his first shot of the day, Kharis seems somewhat overwhelmed by the current batch of tana-leaf juice. Peter Coe (l) longs to be elsewhere, Martin Kosleck eyes Chaney's good eye disapprovingly, and the border art here is almost identical with that of *The Mummy's Ghost*.

553

As might be expected, *Curse* didn't *Wow!* them so much as *Why?* them. Bert McCord, earning his keep in the 31 March 1945 edition of the *New York Herald Tribune*, felt that things could only get better:

There's action but no excitement in 'The Mummy's Curse,' the latest Universal horror. which opened yesterday at the Rialto. It would seem impossible to punctuate a film with stabbing, strangulation, swathed mummies stalking through the night and buried Egyptian maidens digging their way out of Louisiana swampland without creating a shudder or two. But there it s, and it will be at the Rialto until such time as the management can book an attraction.

On that same day, *The New York Post*'s Archer Winsten admitted that he had found a saving grace down in the bayou:

There is, though, one bit of fancy that has its own charm. Out of the mud track of a passing bulldozer, you see a hand and then an arm emerge. Lo! It's a female mummy, the onetime girl of Chaney, somewhat the worse for dirt after all those years. She staggers off to the nearest pool and, when she comes out, she'd remind you of anything but a mummy. You will be safe in assuming that there has never been a mummy half as well built or a quarter as good looking. Just for the record, her name is Virginia Christine.

The day before the Messrs. McCord and Winsten made things clear, Alton Cook – over at the *New York World-Telegram* – wrote not of the bloody venue or the lovely Virginia, but, rather, of the best possible circumstances in which to view the film: "Take a boresome neighbor whom you hope never will speak to you again. This will do it."

Well, for all the quirks the picture offers (in the flashback, Ananka's father is referred to as A-men-O-phis, whilst Ananka – in checking out the threads-per-square-inch on Kharis's wrappings – calls her dad A-MEN-o-phis); for all the poorly thought-out bits (Zandaab to Kharis, who has just been resurrected in a Louisiana monastery: "You know your destination!"); for all the unlikely non-Egyptian nomenclature (not longer after the viewer is informed that there's a worker yclept "Ulysses," we hear Addison Richards order a minion to go "Wake up Achilles and some of the boys!)... *The Mummy's Curse* isn't so much bad as it is painful. Did no one (in any sort of responsible position) care? With the sun high in the Louisiana sky long after quitting time (i.e. during the *summer*), Cajun Joe (his name sort of indicates he's a native, no?) offers Ananka his *coat*! Did no one – I'm targeting camera operator William Dodds here, if not Director of Photography Virgil Miller (if not Leslie Goodwins, himself!) – not notice that Chaney looks positively *cross-eyed* whilst schlumping over to accept a ladle-full of tana-leaf cocktail from Coe the first time Kharis is spotted standing "erect?"

God bless us all, said Cajun Joe (to no one in particular)...

*The Mummy's Curse* – 22 December 1944 – 62 minutes (SoS)

**CAST:** Lon Chaney as Kharis; Peter Coe as Dr. Ilzor Zandaab; Virginia Christine as Ananka; Kay Harding as Betty Walsh; Dennis Moore as Dr. James Halsey; Martin Kosleck as Ragheb; Kurt Katch as Cajun Joe; Addison Richards as Pat Walsh; Holmes Herbert as Dr. Cooper; Charles Stevens as Achilles; William Farnum as Michael, the Caretaker; Napoleon Simpson as Goobie; Ann Codee as Tante Berthe; Herbert Haywood as Hill; Nina Bara as Cajun Girl; Eddie Abdo as Pierre; Tony Santoro as Ulysses; Eddie Parker, Bob Pepper as Chaney's doubles; Carey Loftin, Teddy Mangean as Stuntmen; with Heenan Elliott, Budd Buster, Al Ferguson

**CREDITS**: Director: Leslie Goodwins; Associate Producer: Oliver Drake; Executive Producer: Ben Pivar; Screenplay: Bernard L. Schubert; Original Story and Adaptation: Leon Abrams, Dwight V. Babcock, Bernard L. Schubert, T.H. Richmond; Director of Photography: Virgil Miller; Camera Operator: William Dodds; Special Photographic Effects: John P. Fulton; Film Editor: John B. Goodman and Martin Obzina; Musical Director: Paul Sawtell; Song "Hey, You": Music: Oliver Drake; Lyrics: Frank Orth; Set Decoration: Russell B. Gausman and Victor A. Gangelin; Sound Director: Bernard B. Brown; Technician: Robert Pritchard; Properties: Eddie Smith and Eddie Case; Make-up: Jack P. Pierce; Gowns: Vera West
- *JTS*

# *The House of Fear* (1945)

In his essay on *The Black Doll* (1938) – the most supernatural of the "Crime Club" mini-thrillers that John Soister covered in the first volume of this work – we became familiar with the term "tontine": a joint financial agreement wherein the participants contribute equally to the sum that will be awarded to the last survivor. With the passage of time and innumerable movies, that conceit would be filed away alongside the genre *cliché* that the butler always did it. The French cinema had its own version with *Le dernier des six* (1941), a Georges Lacombe mystery that went unreleased in the United States. "The Last One of the Six" is a tontine-related case solved by Inspector Wens, a character found in the thrillers of Belgian author, Stanislas André Steeman; before Lacombe's take on the novel, the British cinema had adapted same to the screen as *The Riverside Murder* (1935), a trifle that never reached American screens, either. (1) Having judged that enough time had passed since Pierre Fresnay's detective had worked toward his solution, Roy Chanslor - the scenarist of this particular Sherlock Holmes adventure - revisited the idea of the deaths that increase the patrimony of the survivors for *The House of Fear*.

Holmes and Watson meet with an insurance agent (Gavin Muir, whom we had already heard as the BBC announcer in *Voice of Terror* and whom we later saw as the police inspector in *In Washington* and as one of the Musgraves in *Faces Death*; despite his appearance and his proper British phrasing, Muir was a native of Chicago). Two men who had died - albeit in accidental circumstances – had been living in seclusion in one of those old mansions next to some Scotch loch, punished by the wind and marked by the gossip from the neighboring town. Named Drearcliff, it is a large old house that accommodates the exclusive club of the Good Comrades, seven old gentlemen who had withdrawn from city life to share evenings devoted to reading, tobacco, and – ultimately – camaraderie. Nonetheless, a troubling fact has gained the attention of the insurance man: at dinnertime, each of the dead men had received an envelope containing orange seeds as a mournful warning.

Although Holmes and Watson insinuate themselves in Drearcliff - all the better to investigate the case where it has taken place – the delivery and receipt of orange pips continue as before (the number of pips dwindling each time, reflecting the number of surviving members), and the good comrades keep on dying. Each cadaver is found to be unrecognizable: one has been burned black, the next almost vaporized, the third, dismembered. Of course, the camera doesn't highlight these – we've not a single disturbing image – so we learn about each of these macabre findings through the characters' dialogue. In a curious – albeit happy – case of jurisdictional synchrony, the police official who comes to solve the case if the dear Inspector Lestrade, but even his presence doesn't seem to intimidate the murderer, who ends up decimating the Good Comrades.

Not all of the deaths, though, are of club members. A shopkeeper possessed of certain information valuable to the police is killed with his own daughter a witness to the event. (Said daughter was played by Florette Hillier, an unknown starlet to whom Universal was obviously giving the opportunity to show off her talent, as they would Jackie Lou Harding in *The Scarlet Claw*.) This time the corpse is recognizable by everyone, and the method of murder, a totally purposeful bullet. Nonetheless, Holmes detects a pattern among so many pips and corpses and, after making sure that the grave of one of the murdered men is, in fact, empty, finally discovers the key to the mystery. While virtually every other cinematic treatment of tontines has one of the beneficiaries liquidating the others, in *The House of Fear* we have a reversal: one innocent member and many guilty parties. Despite this original narrative stance (not terribly logical, to be sure), the contemporary critics were not totally won over in the face of the weakness here of the mysterious framework that Holmes would show off in all his films.

"SHHH!" wrote someone in the June 1945 issue of *Photoplay*: "Here come Sherlock and Watson again." Following that pronouncement, the scribe took but two lines to advise of the duo's comings and goings: "It's the fact that they don't get to live it up at all that brings our favorite sleuths into this mediocre film that doesn't matter a gosh darn anyway." At least the review concluded with a Holmesian aphorism: "Quick, Watson! A better picture!" The 24 March 1945 *Boxoffice* was likewise merciless with respect to the latest treatment:

Sherlock Holmes detects in his best prescribed manner and his stooge, Dr. Watson, harrumphs and grumbles all over the place, but the picture fails to attain the high degree of surprise and tempo that characterized the many predecessors in the series.

*Motion Picture Daily* (20 March 1945) also detected some difficulties because "a superfluity of clues and suspects baffles even this 'human bloodhound'."

As might be expected, there *were* disparate professional opinions:

[The picture is] a typical specimen in the Universal series, maintaining its customary high level of dialogue and logically flowing sequences. One shortcoming, however, lies in the film's lack of realism. As the weird murders and obscure goings-on are flashed upon the screen, they seem no more emotionally gripping than a disassembled jig-saw puzzle.

*Motion Picture Herald*, 24 March 1945

On the other hand, *Film Daily* (which bore the previous day's date) predicted that "the Sherlock Holmes fans should have for themselves a grand time, for the film is among the best of the series, being loaded with action, suspense, and unalloyed villainy." A month or so later, *Film Bulletin* (16 April 1945) would foretell the same future for the pictures, albeit with slightly different words, maintaining that *The House of Fear* "will fully satisfy in action spots and make a good supporting dualler in the neighborhoods," while observing that "there is no romance to distract one's attention from the gruesome happenings." The 21 March 1945 *Variety* was a good deal more succinct, pronouncing the film "better than average."

The picture was certainly at least a step below its three immediate predecessors in terms of horrific content and internal logic. What was the ultimate goal of the Good Comrades, after each faked his own death and then hid out waiting for the club's leader to collect on everyone's policies? Did they intend to make an attempt on his life, while stealing the accumulated funds before leaving the country? Or was the scenarist trying to take the characters into areas more proper to other genres? Although conceding an entirely horrific character to the previous films, *House of Fear* makes no pretense at being a horror film – or even a mystery – but, rather, a black comedy. No sooner have our heroes arrived at the gloomy (and *so* aptly-named) Drearcliff, then the frames of the camera begin to subtly twist, perhaps as a tacit indication of this generic shift.

Later, in the customary bit of comedy reserved for Nigel Bruce's Watson – whose responsibility for the films' comic relief has been (and is) a controversial topic among fans of the series – director Neill allows more time than usual to tracing his steps across the parlors, staircases, or bedrooms of the castle during the nightly vigils Holmes has entrusted to him. Ultimately, when Sergeant Bleeker (Leslie Denison) informs his superior of the discovery of one of the Comrades (Harry Cording) - or, better said - of his headless and limbless torso, Holmes consults the officer about the appearance of the corpse and those mutilations. When Bleeker assumes that the neatness of the lacerations must be the work of a surgeon, the director inserts a fade and the scene moves to a close-up of a turkey being meticulously carved by Doctor Merrivale (Paul Cavanagh), another of the suspects. This transition would be too patent for a mystery film in which the viewers are working to deduce the murderer's identity, but not for a black comedy wherein the macabre details are blatantly obvious and the motives of the characters are nothing if not weak with respect to reality and logic.

Noting the stolid nature of the gentlemen at the club and their opposites and seeing the vast contrast between the virility of Cording's character and the wildly nervous and hysterical edge to Holmes Herbert's comrade, has us assuming a repressed homosexual community. Their secluded lives and near-total isolation from the rest of the world - mainly from women (other than their housekeeper, Sally Shepherd's laconic character) – stir up suggestive undertones with respect to this. The solution to the mystery and the criminal method (the substitution of cadavers of those who recently died in the village for the supposedly murdered comrades) certainly portrays the good comrades as remarkable necrophiliacs.

Another noteworthy contrast has the last of the survivors – whom Lestrade sends off to pose as a potential murderer – be the most feminine in the lodge, Bruce Alastair (Aubrey Mather). When the secret passage wherein those assumed dead hide while waiting to collect on the insurance policies is discovered, we note that Alastair ends up being the only one of the comrades not in on the conspiracy. In this subtext, his apparent homosexuality doesn't put him on the receiving end of any sort of onus or penalty, as one would expect in other films from that time (especially those set in a Victorian milieu), but, more fittingly, he comes into his own in the last reel. On the return to London, Holmes and the insurance company representative agree that the reward for the solution to the crime would go to that good – and gay – comrade.

**Watson is captured and nearly killed by the "Good Comrades," members of a unique gentlemen's club consisting of scoundrels who are anything but gentlemen. Thankfully, the good doctor is saved by the "Best Comrade" a man could ever have.**

In none of the myriad histories of the series at Universal does anyone raise the prospect of there being a projected set of themes to the pictures that remained. First off, there was no anticipated length to the series: with Universal – as with all of the major studios in LaLaLand at that point – the box-office take ruled all. So long as a string of features centered on a family, topic, character, etc. that was bringing in the gelt, said string would lengthen. For example, fast forward to the very early '50s, when the now Universal-International had okayed a series based on a mule who could communicate with Donald O'Connor! Windy City-native O'Connor, one of the iconic trio of stars of M-G-M's astounding musical comedy, *Singin' in the Rain*, would find the picture that brought him everlasting fame bracketed by 1951's *Francis Goes to the Races* and 1952's *Francis Goes to West Point*. The talking mule continued to chatter until 1955, and at that point both Francis and Donald bid farewell to the House that Carl Had Built Quite a While Earlier. All this to point out that neither Basil Rathbone nor Nigel Bruce had any inkling of how long the roles they had made their own would remain theirs. Still, it's interesting to observe how – after *The House*

561

*of Fear* turned on a conceit that featured a cast that was 99.44% male – the series took a hard-right turn and started to highlight the distaff side of villainy.

One of the more blah elements of the film is its title. The screenplay is credited as being based on Arthur Conan Doyle's "The Five Orange Pips," a short story which first saw the ink-of-page in the November 1891 edition of *The Strand Magazine*. The original tale – which contained narrative ties to the Ku Klux Klan – was reported to have been up there among Sir Arthur's dozen favorite S.H. yarns. The story takes place in Horsham, in West Sussex, and albeit several of the Horshamites (Horshamians?) find themselves on the wrong side of the grass fairly quickly, there is not the subtlest wisp of tontines anywhere about. As noted above, the last time tontines had made any sort of effort to power a plot was in Harold Buckley's screenplay for Universal's "Crime Club" series entry, *The Black Doll*, seven years earlier. (After Holmes and Watson dealt with the situation at hand, the next motion picture that was extravagantly involved with tontines was Salamander Film's 1966 farce, *The Wrong Box* [suggested by screeds from Robert Louis Stevenson and Lloyd Osbourne] which featured Michael Caine, Peter Cook, Dudley Moore, and Peter Sellers. When one also considers that he scenarists for the British comedy were Americans Burt [*A Funny Thing Happened on the Way to the Forum*] Shevelove and Larry [*Forum, M\*A\*S\*H*] Gelbart, it became quite evident that no one was taking tontines seriously any longer...)

Now, had the production staff at Universal insisted that the picture bear the name of Conan Doyle's 7th-favorite short story, some confusion might have arisen among potential ticket-buyers as to whether the plot centered on rationing of citrus fruit during what would turn out to be the final months of the War. Thus, *The House of Fear*... a title that not only dispelled any notions of food shortages, but also was far and away much more effective than using the name of the local of the pseudo-murders – "Drearcliff" – was employed to entice the curious into the theaters. Still, Universal was just then making far too many trips to that particular well: the studio's '40s genre renaissance had already chalked up visits to *The House of the Seven Gables* and the *House of Frankenstein*, with tours of the *House of Dracula* and the *House of Horrors* to be had within a year or so down the road. Worse still, the previous decade had ended with a meller set in a theater, and said theater then being referred to as *The House of Fear*! That earlier *House of Fear* may have had nothing to do with tontines (we're stating yet again that the "Crime Club" entry from '38 took that theme out of play for a while, if only to demonstrate how repetition is *not* the soul of wit), but was based on a couple of disparate works, including Thomas F. Fallon's play, *The Last Warning*, and a novel by Charles Wadsworth Camp, *The House of Fear*. (2)

562

Compounding the felony is the fact that – at the end of the previous decade (we're talking the '20s now) - Stuttgart-born director Paul Leni had produced Universal's first (and much better) stake on *The House of Fear*, although Leni's landmark version – a Universal "Super Jewel" - was entitled *The Last Warning*. The part-sound picture, which also attributed its source material to Camp's novel and Fallon's play, was released on the 6 January 1929. Then, via either an altogether remarkable coincidence or some absolutely devilish cunning, on the 6 January 1939, a decade to the day later, Universal released *The Last Warning* – not a remake of Leni's last film, but an entry in the "Crime Club" series, based on Jonathan Latimer's novel, *The Dead Don't Care*. To make a long short story shorter – unless, of course, *we* no longer care – it would definitely take Sherlock Holmes to unravel this mess of Houses of Fearful Warnings.

*The House of Fear* – 16 March 1945 – 69 minutes

**CAST**: Basil Rathbone as Sherlock Holmes; Nigel Bruce as Doctor Watson; Dennis Hoey as Inspector Lestrade; Aubrey Mather as Bruce Alastair; Paul Cavanagh as Dr. Simon Merrivale; Holmes Herbert as Alan Cosgrave; Harry Cording as Captain John Simpson; Sally Shepherd as Mrs. Monteith; Gavin Muir as Insurance Agent; Florette Hillier as Alison MacGregor; David Clyde as Alex MacGregor; Following are uncredited: Cyril Delevanti as Stanley Raeburn; Wilson Benge as Guy Davies; Richard Alexander as Ralph King; David Thursby as Sergeant; Doris Lloyd as Bessie; Alec Craig as Angus; Leslie Denison as Sergeant Beeker; Bobby Hale as Pub Patron; Hobart Cavanaugh (extra).

**CREDITS**: Director: Roy William Neill; Producer: Roy William Neill; Screenplay: Roy Chanslor; Based on the story "The Adventure of the Five Orange Pips" by Sir Arthur Conan Doyle; Musical Director: Paul Sawtell; Director of Photography: Virgil Miller; Camera Operator: Edward Cohen; Film Editor: Saul A. Goodkin; Director of Sound: Bernard B. Brown; Technician: William Hedgcock; Art Directors: John B. Goodman and Eugene Lourie; Set Decoration: Russell A. Gausman and Edward R. Robinson; Assistant Directors: Melville Shyer and Mort Singer, Jr.; Dialogue Director: Ray Kessler

*- DL*

# *That's the Spirit* (1945)

*Synopsis*: In turn-of-the-century (20th Century, that is) New York, Libby Cawthorne and her cousin, Patience – daughter and niece, respectively, of Jasper Cawthorne, a rich banker – sneak into the Majestic Theatre to witness a Vaudeville show for the first time. The girls have to do so on the sly, as Cawthorne – who runs his home like a petty tyrant - regards show business as horrific and has, in fact, just fired a dressmaker used by the girls and his wife, Abigail, because the seamstress also makes costumes and clothing for "show people." After the show, Libby and singer Steve "Slim" Gogarty find themselves attracted to each other and this quickly blossoms into love, a condition which will certainly not please the grouchy banker, who insists that the two get married to cover any indecent behavior they may have indulged in while alone together. Wildly attracted to each other, they do marry, and Steve carries Libby over the threshold of their hotel room, only to trip and fall awkwardly, his new bride by his side on the floor. This is witnessed by a wraith-like woman – late called "The Dark Lady" - who moves on.

Cut to the maternity ward, where Steve paces while Martin Wilde – owner of the Majestic Theatre – predicts the child will be a girl. "I got a boy, you got a girl, later on they get married and carry on our business." Moments later, two nurses confer over "complications," and the Dark Lady is seen walking toward Libby's room in the maternity ward. Steve prays, "If anything is going to happen, let it happen to me." Steve walks off with the Dark Lady, as the nurse reappears, announcing "It's all right now... a beautiful girl." Cut to newspaper headline: "Steve Gogarty Called by Death. Friends Mourn Passing of Prominent Showman."

Cut to the heavenly realm. Steve walks up to the complaint desk, kvetching not so much about his having died as about how he was taken from this life. "Jasper saw the Dark Lady and he didn't know who she was. He thought I just walked out on Libby with another woman." Steve is told he has to wait 18 years – a probationary period – before anything can be done. Those years pass, and Steve – watching from the clouds as his 17-year-old daughter Sheila sings and dances (and Jasper Cawthorne cruelly reminds Libby that Steve "walked out on her" with another woman) - is finally given a "seven-day pass" to return to Earth and straighten things out. Invisible and inaudible to everyone, Steve listens as Cawthorne launches into a dreadful rendition of "Evening Star" in front of a resigned audience of senior citizens. Taking a flute from his pocket, Steve plays a few notes, causing the entire crowd to break into dance (to Cawthorne's amazement). Going up to his daughter's bedroom, Steve is pleased to note that Sheila *can* see and hear him. In telling Sheila he knows where she belongs, Steve takes her over to the Majestic Theatre. Bilson the maid – having discovered Sheila "missing" when bringing up the teenager's midnight snack – caterwauls and Libby says she might just know where her daughter is...

At the theater, Martin Wilde Jr. is dancing up a storm, preparing for a performance the following day. Sheila needs very little encouragement from her father to introduce herself to Martin Jr., - he tells her that, before she was born, their fathers planned on their marrying someday - and before long, the two are dancing together with all the panache of Fred and Ginger. Cut to Cawthorne's house, and both Libby and Sheila are laughing as they enter. Libby tells her father that Sheila will lead her own life, no longer needing non-stop criticism from him. Next day, while dress rehearsal (featuring Martin Jr. and Sheila) is going on at the theater, Cawthorne tells Martin Sr. that Martin's loan note has been bought by Cawthorne from the bank. Understanding the unspoken threat, Martin Sr. tells Sheila she hasn't the talent to entertain professionally. As Cawthorne and Martin Sr. walk to the attorney's office to settle affairs, Steve – following them – plays his flute. The music impacts the men, who begin to jump over fire hydrants, play hopscotch, and get involved with kids playing baseball. When they end up back at the Cawthorne house, it is announced that Libby is very ill, and she and her father head for Florida to seek medical care. As they board their train, we see the Dark Lady follow them.

At the Majestic Theatre, the show is on, with Sheila back in as Martin Jr.'s co-star, thanks to a huge check from Abigail, Cawthorne's wife. As Cawthorne leaves the railroad station on his return, he sees a sign for "Manhattan Frolics" with Sheila Gogarty receiving top billing. He heads to the police station to get some ops to close down the show, but when they arrive at the theater, the combination of his granddaughter's talent and the announcement by his family members that they can no longer tolerate his puritanical ways leads Cawthorne to come to his senses. Just then a telegram is delivered; Libby has died. As the show continues, Libby's spirit joins that of her husband's and they walk off into eternity as the closing words to the show's top song are heard: "You're with me no matter where you are."

From time to time, the entertainment media seek not only to entertain, to educate, or to edify, but also to console. As we cobbled together this tome, television's *Madame Secretary* – a weekly dramatic series dealing with Tía Leoni's capacity to avoid the most egregious of potential national disasters as head of the Department of State – has included any number of iffy situations imposed/initiated/encouraged in "real life" by the current administration, perhaps with an eye to showing that it takes experience, intelligence, and compassion to deal with deplorable circumstances. One emerges from almost any episode of the show reassured and relieved that political horrors *can* be taken care of when one strives to understand action/reaction, behavior, ideology, and the sundry philosophies of life. Or of death.

Following the Great War, there were numerous plays written and motion pictures produced that dealt with life-after-death; not as a possibility or a desperate hope, but as a positive reality. Death then was very much in the air – and on the ground and at sea – as an estimated 16+ million soldiers and civilians died during the hostilities. In addition, apart from the war casualties, countless others – chiefly Armenians and Assyrians – were victims of genocide perpetrated by the Ottoman Empire, while the influenza pandemic of 1918 did in millions more throughout the world. It has been argued that the aggregate of such mind-boggling disasters – whether induced by mankind or mismanaged by mankind – led to the "birth" of Expressionism in Germany. Cultural historian Siegfried Kracauer hypothesized that it was the unbridled chaos of the Great War, the profoundly discriminate destruction of entire peoples, and the worldwide helplessness felt during the pandemic that ultimately led to the obsessive drive for order that would mark the rise of the Nazis. As quoted by film historians Olaf Brill and Gary D. Rhodes, Kracauer saw the Weimar Era - from late 1918 to early 1933 – as "The German soul, haunted by the alternative images of tyrannic rule and instinct-governed chaos, threatened by doom on either side, tossed about in gloomy space like the phantom ship in *Nosferatu*."(1) Still, as reflected in the German cinema of that Era, Death onscreen - frequently portrayed as bizarre and/ or picturesque entities by Expressionist *auteurs* – represented not the *end* of life, but the conduit to existence *after* life. The conclusion reached via many representations was that Death – no matter how grotesquely (or preternaturally beautifully) depicted

– served at the pleasure of a Higher Being, with the underlying message of comfort to be found in the Roman Catholic Missal, "Life has changed, not ended."

Still, in the recovering Fatherland, a number of filmmakers sought to explain such catastrophic ends of war while heartening those who had suffered losses because of them. Joe May's three-part *Veritas Vincit* (*Truth Wins*, 1918), for example, paralleled the relationship between truth and falsehood with that of life and death, with the film's third part – set in a European country just prior to the outbreak of the Great War – seeing Mia May (Joe's *frau*) triumph over deceit (and, subsequently, Death) thanks to veracity and a magic ring. (A year earlier, in *Hilde Warren und der Tod* – *Hilde Warren and Death* – Joe had the personified Death tenaciously offering himself to Mia as a solution to her problems in the course of the film.) Fritz Lang's *Der müde Tod* (*The Weary Death*, 1920) has Lil Dagover seek to bargain with Death to allow her lover to return with her to the land of the living, but after three failures (due to the actions of others), she chooses to offer her life for that of a child and is reunited with her lover in the afterlife. Per these films and others, Death – and *not* a Deity - *is* the Master of the Afterlife, and one's existence continues therein.

Abel Gance's *J'accuse* (1919) offered the French cinema's take on war and deceit and Death, as the picture heads to its conclusion via a scene of dead soldiers rising from the ground and heading to their homes as their living relatives ponder whether they have been worthy of the military men's sacrifices. In other climes, the legitimate theater led the way along a similar path, as Sutton Vane's *Outward Bound* premiered on Broadway in 1923, while Italian playwright Alberto Casella's 1924 masterpiece, *La Morte in Vacanza*, would play in the USA as *Death Takes a Holiday* come 1929; both plays would be filmed before the mid-'30s. In 1920, Goldwyn Pictures had produced *Earthbound*, in which the spirit of a man murdered by a cuckolded husband spends his afterlife trying to be a positive influence on the folks with whom he had acted dishonorably. There are many other examples that may be cited, but the stage and screen not only created visual media designed to explain and comfort the legions of people who had lost friends and family due to one tragedy or another, but also served to reflect the reawakening of interest in what had been popularly known as "spiritualism."

Spiritualism saw [an] incredible resurgence after World War I. Most credit this to the fact that families were really introduced to the wholesale slaughter of loved ones in a way they had never seen before... Now, thanks to Spiritualism, their lost loved ones were no longer lost at all. They could be communicated with and contacted as if they were still alive. Spiritualism managed to fill a huge void for the everyday person, who

568

now had something to cling to and a belief that their friends and family members had gone on to a better place. (2)

During and after World War II, though, matters were quite different. Although the horror of international warfare had not diminished in the least, the awareness that mankind had managed to survive appalling conflicts some 20 years earlier – and would undoubtedly do so again – caused something of a shift in entertainment and informational media coverage. The unspeakable had been dealt with once already - that line had been crossed - and the unthinkable was now to be thought of differently. Battle plans, troop movements, enemy engagements, episodes of espionage, and the like consumed the lion's share of coverage throughout the world. Truth and deceit were now the provenance of spies, concessions were made and bargaining was carried out with corporeal entities, and the incredible loss of life was treated as statistical data instead of wholesale tragedy.

And the movies went along with it.

**Libby Cawthorne (June Vincent) and Steve Gogarty (Jack Oakie) fall for each other...hard. Not long after their wedding, a problem with Libby's pregnancy will cause Steve to offer himself up to "the Dark Lady."**

On the face of it, *That's the Spirit* is a fairly dreary musical dealing with a *secular* afterlife. Given Buster Keaton's unimpressive turn as the head of Heaven's Complaint Department – and the assigning of what appears to be a bellboy to lead Steve off to "Quarantine" - we're left to assume that life after death is as bureaucratic and legalistic as the path we take prior to our demise. As a huge fan of the Great Stone Face, I find it not only disconcerting that one of my comic idols was given zilch in terms of material with which to work – why hire an iconic funnyman to mouth lines that might be better suited to a department-store flunky? - but also insulting that the film didn't see the need to have Steve confront one of cinematic tradition's more important celestial entities. Why couldn't Buster have received a pre-production promotion? In Columbia's *Here Comes Mr. Jordan* (1941), the title character was an angelic elite; in M-G-M's *A Guy Named Joe* (1943), said guy was directed this way and that by "the General"; and in 1945, Jack Benny was commanded to see that *The Horn Blows at Midnight* by "the Deputy Chief of the Department of Small Planet Management."

Sure, what with the plethora of post-demise-adventure movies that were cranked out during and after the Second World War – Ciceronian paralipsis allows us to omit mention of other such pictures, like *Heaven Can Wait* (1943) or *It's a Wonderful Life* (1946) – both the film's conceit (Steve must be granted a visitor's pass to earth so that he might explain his walking out with the "Dark Lady") *and* the nature of the aforementioned accommodating character seem distinctly second-rate. Nonetheless, *That's the Spirit* contrives to exhibit the same basic elements displayed by its fellow '40s features in a totally non-religious milieu. There are no angels, *a la Wonderful Life* or *Horn Blows*; no devils, *a la Heaven Can Wait*; not even the suggestion of superior officers at or near the head of the chain of command, *a la Guy Named Joe*. Just a desk jockey with whom one can register a grievance.

Nonetheless, the lack of religious overtones regarding the action and passion of Death herein is firmly in keeping with the rather mundane nature of the plot and players. Jack Oakie's Steve Gogarty is a rotund, amiable entertainer whose act – "The Man with the Flute" - centers on his being able to cause the sudden appearance/ disappearance of his fellow actors by playing a few notes on his pipe. Although the instantaneous movements of these folks onscreen is due to a camera trick that could not be possible onstage, the idea that Steve's "magic flute" can thus impact the motion and direction – dare we imply "the lives?" - of folks foreshadows sequences later in the film that lead to the denouement.

If we stop to consider the role that musical instruments have played in international myths and fables, we can more readily understand the underlying link between magic and desire. "Joshua Fit the Battle of Jericho" was more than just an African-American spiritual; in the Old Testament, 'twas the tale of the overthrow of that city – its walls "came a tumblin' down" - due in the main to the priests marching seven times 'round the walls on the seventh day and then letting loose with their rams' horns. Jack Benny's Athaneal in *The Horn Blows at Midnight* is looking to emulate the performance of the seven angels blowing their trumpets seven times (following the breaking of the seventh seal) and thus causing the events outlined in Revelations 8-11. (Fear not! 'Tis not the right moment to discuss the mystical power of the number 7 in Freemasonry, myth, and/or religion.) (3) Taking the size of the magic mouthpiece down a bit, we can do worse than recall the flute belonging to *Der Rattenfänger von Hameln*, or the pipes and bells played by Papageno in Mozart's *Der Zauberflöte*. If Congreve held that "Music hath charms to soothe a savage breast," countless millions of people looking for some sort of structure in an unforgiving world came to believe that certain music, certain words, certain instruments (the devil apparently favored the violin), certain appurtenances (rings, sticks, statues) would help bring order out of chaos. Through manipulation of unknown forces, one's wants may be satisfied, and that, in essence, is what magic – and prayer - is all about.

Steve's flute is merely one trick out of many whilst the entertainer is alive, but it is awarded genuine preternatural power once he has offered himself up for Libby and their baby. In the theater, his tooting a few notes supposedly causes the space/time continuum to be disrupted, an effect that sees the audience witnessing the routine merely applaud and not be driven into disbelieving convulsions.(4) (Inasmuch as the film in no way, shape or form was presented as occurring during the war that was still raging, there was no subplot involving Armed Forces officials scheming to mass-produce Steve's flute for use in battle.) In the afterlife, his tooting a few notes causes Cawthorne and Wilde Sr. to revert emotionally to their childhood. While this sequence makes for some cute displays of juvenile behavior on the part of Lockhart and Devine, we seek dramatic justification. Is this the effect *intended* by Steve, or is it just something decreed by whatever powers there be (other than the complaint manager)? How does magically coercing the two men into playing hopscotch and such satisfy Steve's wants and needs? It is at the theater itself that Sheila, Martin Jr. and the collective redressing by Cawthorne's family work the "magic" that forces the erstwhile dictator to understand that everyone has the right to live his/her own life.

From there, we have to ask whether it is a sense of caprice in the afterlife that leads to the flute being empowered thus. The Dark Lady – Death, herself? Or merely his/her lackey? - is apparently rather capricious: she veers off her original course (to

Libby's room in the maternity ward) due solely to Steve's quiet plea in the hospital, and we have to wonder why she would opt to show herself following the fall at the transom. Is she there to measure the extent of the injury and then carry off whichever party does not survive the accident? Or is she there to *cause* a death, as she apparently does in the hospital hallway? Inasmuch as the film offers no supernatural hierarchy, we have little material with which to conjecture. Between her unwelcome and occasionally happenstance presence and the unforeseen effects of Steve's flute (Did he think the flute would make the two older gents just up and disappear, as it did to his costars at the Majestic?), we have the pun-ish kernel of the picture: "spirit," both as Steve's nonphysical side and as the animating principle that keeps him pushing to change outcomes. If nothing else, it's due to the high spirits of the hero's spirit that injects a spirit of youthful joy into the resident grouch.

Jack Oakie is hardly a name associated with horror; comedies, musicals, and college romps were the chubby comedian's stock-in-trade. The closest he came to a real thriller was the 1937 comedy-mystery *Super Sleuth*, wherein he played a movie star and self-proclaimed "crime buster" stalked by house-of-horrors proprietor and arch criminal, Eduardo Cianelli; the film was later remade as *Genius at Work*. Oakie's name was also fairly removed from subtlety, but he was a master of the double and triple take, a veteran scene-stealer, and a vocal critic of low-key performances. (He claimed to have watched Jean Gabin and Robert Mitchum underplaying each other in a scene "until the director started yelling, 'Start acting, somebody!'")

Oakie had worked on Wall Street – one theory to the Missouri-born actor's substantial loss of hearing was his proximity to midst of the Wall Street bombing that happened on the 16 September 1920 – before playing in the amateur theatricals that infected him with the acting bug. He made his professional stage debut as a member of the chorus – not bad for a functionally deaf performer – in George M. Cohan's *Little Nellie Kelly* in 1922. (Oakie apparently lost little of his stock market savvy, as he later became one of Hollywood's richest actors; he cracked that he had had stock in General Electric "when it was General Candle.") After more stints on Broadway and in Vaudeville, he moved to LaLaLand in the late '20s. He appeared in a few silents before his talkie debut in *The Dummy* (1929), and soon after followed a Paramount contract *and* a starring role contract *and* a starring role in *The Social Lion* (1930). Oakie was modest about his success, telling an interviewer for the *Los Angeles Times*:

I happened into this business at exactly the right time. Pictures were on the verge of a big change. The handsome chaps had been having things all their own way all the time and the public was ready to give some of the rest of us a chance, just for the change of diet. Sound was just around the corner and when it arrived my real opportunity came. Anyone in this racket who thinks he has the world by the ear with a downhill pull is just crazy. I may be here today and gone tomorrow.

These latter words seemed prophetic when the actor returned from an extended vacation in Europe only to find that producers had drunk of the waters of forgetfulness and behaved as though they had never heard of him. Luckily, Charlie Chaplin subsequently gave him one of his best roles, parodying Benito Mussolini in 1940's *The Great Dictator*; this led to Oakie's only Academy Award nomination. His film career was back on track, and he had plenty of radio work on his schedule, too; nevertheless, he found himself increasingly cast in supporting roles. Television provided more opportunities, as it did with many "fading" stars from earlier decades, but his movie appearances became fewer and fewer. Illness forced him out of Frank Capra's *A Pocketful of Miracles* (1961; he was replaced by Thomas Mitchell) and he subsequently went into a comfortable semi-retirement with his wife, Victoria Horne. Horne had a supporting part in *That's the Spirit* (as Libby's cousin, Patience) and, after Oakie's passing in 1978, she devoted herself to keeping his memory alive in the public eye.

Andy Devine's horror credits barely surpass Oakie's, but he did appear in Olsen and Johnson's *Ghost Catchers*, as well as in *A Dangerous Game* (see essays on both). An athlete in his younger days, Devine played football while at Santa Clara University. During his sophomore year, his father died and the young man dropped out of school and made for Alaska, where he worked in a lighthouse before going to Los Angeles to play semi-pro football. This didn't work so well financially, according to an interview Devine gave to Lupton Wilkinson for the 9 October 1938 edition of the *Los Angeles Times*. In 1926, a friend suggested that the husky Devine try out for a role in *The Collegians*, a series of two-reel comedies helmed by Wesley Ruggles over at Universal Pictures. Devine – an uncredited extra – rubbed shoulders with an older Walter Brennan (also an uncredited extra) for a number of episodes before seeking out (and finding) more extra work, and he was soon making $60 a week, no small sum for that era. The coming of sound, however, put a crimp in Devine's modest career, as his raspy, squeaky voice – the result of a childhood accident – was thought to be unusable given the new technology. Per the Wilkinson interview:

Because Andy's personality is one of the most likable in Hollywood, friends soon created a new job. In *Stark Mad* he appeared as a sailor. He didn't speak, of course, but he carried the microphone. It was strapped to his broad beam. If Louise Fazenda spoke to H.B. Warner, the sailor stood at attention, facing Warner and three quarters turned toward Louise. Mechanical improvements soon make a human mike carrier unnecessary.

573

After working as a lifeguard and in construction, Devine found that his unique voice, perhaps not suited for Shakespeare, made people laugh, and he clicked as football player, Truck McCall, in Universal's *The Spirit of Notre Dame* (1933) (5). Devine had no problem finding work after that and although he did an occasional dramatic role – like the young cowboy sentenced to hang in 1932's *Law and Order* – comic supporting roles became his bread-and-butter. He won a long-term contract at Universal and there found his true calling as sidekick to hero Richard Arlen in a series of low-budget adventure films. Later he did the same on television as Jingles P. Jones to Guy Madison's Wild Bill Hickock in the eponymous TV series ("Hey, Wild Bill! Wait for me!" became a familiar cry to a generation of kids growing up in the '50s) and also hosted the popular kid's program, *Andy's Gang*.

While plagued with health problems during his later years, Devine had a strong marriage to Dorothy House, an actress he had met on the set of *Doctor Bull* (1933). His 70th birthday party was attended by 1000 guests, including former co-stars John Wayne and Claire Dodd. "It's been a helluva life," Devine said on that occasion. "I can't think of anything I'd want to change, though maybe I should have passed on *Yellowstone*" (a 1936 turkey). The actor's favorite role was Danny in the 1936 production of *A Star Is Born*.

Gene Lockhart, a native of Ontario, Canada, was no more usually associated with the horror/sci-fi genres than were his colleagues Oakie and Devine. In fact, had he not played Bob Cratchit (with his real-life wife, Kathleen, and daughter, June, helping fill out the family) in the 1938 *A Christmas Carol*, or appeared as the judge charged with determining whether Edmund Gwenn was the legitimate article in *Miracle on 34th Street* (1947), *That's the Spirit* would have been "That's All She Wrote," genre-wise. Lockhart played a wide variety of characters onscreen; he was nominated for Best Supporting Actor for his role as the perfidious "Regis" in 1937's *Algiers*, yet was also the forthright Stephen Douglas in *Abe Lincoln in Illinois* (1940) and the Starkeeper in *Carousel* (1956). On stage, he essayed the role of Uncle Sid in Eugene O'Neill's *Ah, Wilderness!* (1933) and replaced Lee J. Cobb as Willy Loman in Arthur Miller's *Death of a Salesman* in 1949. Here Lockhart's Cawthorne is initially a tyrant, and his "Damascus experience," as it were, comes late in the proceedings and is rather abrupt. Still, the Canadian thesp does a great job of keeping the audience's loyalties firmly on the side of the right.

**At long last, Abigail Cawthorne (Edith Barrett) stands up to her husband (Gene Lockhart) and insists on her family's right to enjoy life. Martin Wilde (Andy Devine) agrees, if only because his son is in love with Abigail's daughter. Oh, and because everyone has fallen under the benevolent influence of the spirit of Slim Gogarty (Jack Oakie).**

Sprightly Peggy Ryan – a splendid singer and dancer and, with a fairly prominent proboscis, much closer to the "girl next door" look adored by fans rather than the "drop dead gorgeous" physiognomy preferred by critics - had started off in films in 1937. (We're opting to skip the 1930 Warners' short, *The Wedding of Jack and Jill*, wherein Ryan – as Jill - was backed by the Gumm Sisters, including the soon-to-be renamed Judy Garland.)   Not much to look at, but one hell of a terpsichorean, Ryan was soon paired with Donald O'Connor as Universal's answer to the team of Mickey Rooney and the aforementioned Ms. Gumm. As Sheila Gogarty, Ryan spearheads the behavioral revolution against her granddad's Puritanical demands, and her opening dance number with Johnny Coy (as Martin Wilde, Jr.) takes one's breath away.

Among the *That's the Spirit* supporting cast, Arthur Treacher goes through his trademark butler bit, while the Cawthorne maid is played by none other than Irene Ryan, most famous as Granny in *The Beverly Hillbillies*. Also on view is Edith Barrett, who fared better, role-wise, in *I Walked with a Zombie*, *The Ghost Ship*, and Robert Stevenson's *Jane Eyre* (all 1943). Marriage-wise, she found life with Vincent Price a

575

damned sight better than her onscreen relationship with Gene Lockhart. Among the numerous uncredited folks to be spotted were *Wizard of Oz* veteran, Jerry Marin; Lou Costello's stooge, Bobby Barber; and ubiquitous character people, Dorothy Christy, Wheaton Chambers, Harry Semels, Eddie Dunn, Lloyd Ingraham, and Fred Kelsey... to name but a few.

*That's the Spirit* was perhaps typical of director Charles Lamont's work although that year it was overshadowed by his bizarre Technicolor extravaganza, *Salome Where She Danced*; "It must be seen to be believed," one critic opined, "and then it can't be, but it amuses." No matter, the film was a big hit for Universal that year, with the studio's new star – Yvonne De Carlo – getting the overwhelming share of the publicity. Lamont had started his career as an actor in the Silent Era, but he soon switched to directing and helmed dozens of two-reel comedies, including the "Big Boy" series starring child actor, Malcolm Sebastian. (Lamont is also credited with having discovered Shirley Temple and Baby Sandy.) The St. Petersburg (Russia!)-born Lamont was just as prolific during the Sound Era and is best remembered for his nine Abbott and Costello films. Ironically, he directed all of the team's horror spoofs, save for their best: *Abbott and Costello Meet Frankenstein*. Besides working with Bud and Lou, the director helmed the "Ma and Pa Kettle" series, and – fittingly – his last film was the 1956 *Francis in the Haunted House*.

*Spirit* was received with mild acquiescence by most of the trade and popular press. *The Christian Science Monitor* (27 July 1945) felt "For chief attraction [sic], it has Peggy Ryan (Sheila) and Johnny Coy (Martin) in eccentric dances." As for spirit, "Jack Oakie is blandly amusing as Steve, and, with the aid of trick photography, carries off numerous 'supernatural' doing [sic] with gusto." *Variety*'s Char found that "The spirit angle provides many interesting and amusing moments in between the various song and dance numbers," an observation that succinctly put the film's sundry elements into perspective. As for the rest of the *dramatis personae*...

> [Sheila] Ryan dominates all scenes in which she appears and scores strongly in her new song and dance numbers. Oakie, now plenty corpulent, fits into the proceedings nicely while the girl he marries, Miss Vincent, is a highly sympathetic and appealing type. Lockhart, the straightforward banker, is also well cast. Others all giving good performances include Arthur Treacher, a butler; Irene Ryan, house maid; Miss Horn, part of the Lockhart household and Andy Devine, now also pretty obese, who is the operator of the majestic theater.
>
> 16 May 1945

The 28 May 1945 edition of *Film Bulletin* summed up best the aggregate critical opinion:

> The earthbound spirit theme has again been employed in engaging fashion in *That's the Spirit*, an entertaining programmer which audience approval may boost into the 'sleeper' class.... Laid in the 1890's and early 1900's, the story starts slowly and the sequences laid in a stuffy-Victorian-minded household contain several dull spots. However, Director Charles Lamont has injected a generous quantity of down-to-earth (literally) in the latter half of the film which also contains most of the pleasing and nicely-staged song-and-dance interludes... The trick photography is well done and helps to keep the laughs coming.

In an effort to be true to its title, we have to acknowledge that *That's the Spirit* is indeed *spirited*, but not at all *spiritual*. The afterlife apart, the lesson of the dramatic narrative seems to be that one must loosen up if one is to appreciate *joie de vivre* and that there's more to life (and afterlife) than dwelling on either or both philosophically.

*That's the Spirit* – 1 June 1945 – 87 minutes

**CAST**: Jack Oakie as Steve Gogarty; Peggy Ryan as Sheila Gogarty; June Vincent as Libby Cawthorne Gogarty; Gene Lockhart as Jasper Cawthorne; Johnny Coy as Martin Wilde, Jr.; Andy Devine as Martin Wilde; Arthur Treacher as Masters; Irene Ryan as Bilson; Buster Keaton as L.M.; Victoria Horne as Patience; Edith Barrett as Abigail Cawthorne; Rex Story as Specialty; Jerry Maren, Billy Curtis as Specialty Midgets; Karen Randle as The Dark Lady; Harry Tyler, Billy Newell, Jack Shutta, Fred Kelsey as Detectives; Jack Roper as Ticket Taker; Virginia Brissac as Miss Preble; Charles Sullivan and Sid Troy as Men; Monty Collins as Bellhop; Dorothy Christy as Nurse; Eddie Dunn, Ed Gargan as Policemen; Mary Forbes as Woman; Mabel Forrest, Genevieve Bell, Herbert Evans, Lloyd Ingram, Nelson McDowell as Guests; Wheaton Chambers as Doctor; Herbert Heywood as Doorman; Bobby Barber as Butcher; Lou Wood as Assistant Dance Director; Brooks Benedict as Assistant Stage Manager, with Teddy Infuhr, Charles Teske, Eddie Cutler, Gloria Marlen, Mary McLeod

**CREDITS:** Director: Charles Lamont; Producers: Michael Fessier, Ernest Pagano; Original Screenplay: Michael Fessier, Ernest Pagano; Director of Photography: Charles Van Enger; Art Directors: John B. Goodman, Richard H. Riedel; Sound Director: Bernard B. Brown; Technician: Charles Carroll; Set Decorators: Russell A, Gausman, Andrew J. Gilmore; Film Editor: Fred R. Feitshans, Jr.; Gowns: Vera West; Dialogue Director: Monty Collins; Assistant Director: William Tummel; Special Photography: John P. Fulton; Musical Score and Direction: Hans J. Salter; Dance Ensembles Staged by Carlos Romero; Peggy Ryan-Johnny Coy Musical Numbers Staged by Louis DePron; Songs: "No Matter Where You Are," "Evenin' Star" by Jack Brooks, Hans J. Salter; "Fella with a Flute," "Oh, Oh, Oh" by Sidney Miller, Inez James: "Nola" by Felix Arndt; "How Come You Do Me Like You Do?" by Roy Bergere, Gene Austin; "Baby, Won't You Please Come Home?" by Clarence Williams, Charles Warfield; "Bugle Call Rag" by J. Hubert Blake, Carey Morgan; "Ja-Da" by Bob Carleton; "Do You Ever Think of Me?" by Earl Burnett, John Cooper, Harry D. Kerr

*- JTS/HN*

578

# *The Frozen Ghost* (1945)

*Synopsis*: Gregor the Great is a mentalist with a popular radio show. Gregor himself is not psychic, but when he hypnotizes his assistant Maura - to whom he is engaged - she displays telepathic powers. One night during a performance, a drunken skeptic in the audience insists on being hypnotized. When Gregor obliges, the intoxicated man promptly drops dead, causing Gregor - who had angrily wished him dead - to believe he is somehow responsible. Inspector Brant informs Gregor that the man had a bad heart and his death was surely an accident, but Gregor insists on blaming himself and even breaks off his engagement to Maura.

At the suggestion of George Keene, his business manager, Gregor goes to stay at the wax museum owned by Madame Monet and help out there. Both Monet and her niece Nina fall in love with Gregor, much to the annoyance of Rudi Poldan, the museum's eccentric curator who is infatuated with Nina.

Madame Monet collapses during an argument with Gregor, who subsequently blacks out. He recovers with no memory of what happened, but is horrified to discover that Monet has disappeared and then Nina also goes missing, all of which make Gregor fear his psychic powers have turned deadly again. However, that is not the case for, in reality, Keene and Rudi are conspiring against him in the hopes of having him declared insane and gain control of his fortune. Both Monet and Nina are in a state of suspended animation brought on by a drug administered by Rudi, who was once a plastic surgeon. However, Monet dies and a panicked Keene insists that Rudi dispose of both Monet and Nina by throwing them into the furnace.

Not entirely convinced of his own guilt, Gregor finds Maura and brings her to the museum to put her into a trance under which she reveals Keene's scheme right in the presence of the treacherous business manager. Keene tries to escape, but runs right into Inspector Brant who has been listening outside the door. Gregor saves Nina and, in the melee, Rudi stumbles backwards into the furnace.

Some fans of vintage horror consider *The Frozen Ghost* to be the low point of the unloved "Inner Sanctum" series, but it is actually the only one of the six films to be a bona fide horror movie. In spite of its cheat title, the movie has a gloomy wax museum with its crazed curator (is there any other kind?), a psychic phenomenon that is real and not rationalized away at the ending, and even a sub-plot about a drug that can produce suspended animation. Sadly, these elements don't really jell, and illogic is rampant even for a picture of this type. The fault may well lie with too many writers - perhaps sometimes working at cross purposes - trying to tie everything together.

Apparently, Universal's original plan was to release *The Frozen Ghost* as the third "Inner Sanctum" and to shoot it back to back with *Dead Man's Eyes*, both films to be directed by Reginald Le Borg. The Big U bought the original story that became *Frozen Ghost* from Harrison Carter (1) in October of 1943 and assigned him to do the screenplay as well. However, while working on the adaptation, Carter, who had been ill for some time, suffered a fatal heart attack. *Dead Man's Eyes* went before the cameras first with Le Borg at the helm, but he subsequently left the series while *Frozen Ghost* remained in limbo.

Somewhere along the line, Henry Sucher (*The Mummy's Tomb*) and Bernard Schubert worked on the script. Schubert had been, in the words of Grace Kingsley, "a more or less noted playwright" (2) whose work included *Fish Gotta Swim*, *Soft Coal* (which was actually staged in Germany by Max Reinhardt), and the reform school drama *The Kid Himself* (which got execrable reviews). Schubert came to Hollywood in the '30s to work on Richard Dix movies for RKO Radio Pictures. His one notable horror credit from that era was the screenplay for *Mark of the Vampire*, a film every bit as muddled as *The Frozen Ghost*. Schubert would go on to be a successful radio/TV producer in the '50s, but at Universal worked on such forgettable fare as *Jungle Woman* and *The Mummy's Curse*.

The May 1944 issue of *Showman's Trade Review* noted that writer Luci Ward - whose specialty was actually Westerns - had been hired to "unfreeze" *The Frozen Ghost*. Production finally started on the 19 June 1944 with Harold Young directing. Young had been a film editor in the '20s but, while working on Alexander Korda's *The Scarlet Pimpernel* in 1934, he was promoted to director after Korda fired Rowland Brown early on during the shooting; no doubt much of the film was handled mainly by Korda, but he allowed Young to receive sole credit as director. Nonetheless, Young may have reached his level of incompetence then, as all that awaited him back in Hollywood was the likes of *Machine Gun Mama, Song of the Sarong, The Frozen Ghost,* and a short-lived attempt to run his own production company.

Universal kept *The Frozen Ghost* on... errr... ice for an entire year after shooting, finally releasing it on the 29 June 1945, co-billed with *The Jungle Captive* (also directed by Young, in case anyone is thinking of staging a Harold Young retrospective).

The film starts out promisingly enough, with Paul Ivano keeping his camera at a sinister tilt during Gregor's act and then cutting to audience reaction, including an amusing bit of business with a couple of bobbysoxers who wonder if Maura can read their minds, causing Maura to utter from the stage, "Yes, provided there are some traces of mental activity." Things quickly go wrong when Arthur Hohl - usually a much better actor - hams it up shamelessly as the drunken spectator. During the alternating close-ups between Chaney and Hohl, one can't help but notice that both men have identical moles right alongside their noses. This battle of the moles might be less distracting had Chaney been able to manage a proper hypnotic glare but, as *Son of Dracula* proved, the Lonster was no Bela Lugosi. He does manage a few twitches which, of course, became his main acting device in the later *Indestructible Man*.

The script never gives any kind of convincing rationale for Gregor believing he really has the evil eye and can will someone dead. An actor like Conrad Veidt, even without proper motivation from the story, might have been able to suggest a man obsessed, but Chaney seems more perturbed than driven. He was whiny in *Dead Man's Eyes*, but here he acts like an irritable guy with a chip on his shoulder. And we're supposed to believe that lovely Evelyn Ankers, sophisticated beauty Tala Birell, and winsome teenager Elena Verdugo are all gaga for him? It must be the mole.

Things pick up a bit at the wax museum, though no one seems wonder why the wealthy Gregor - who presumably could to travel anywhere to get away from it all - would opt to sojourn in such a cheerless environment. (We're never told where his fortune came from, though it certainly could not have been from his act.) We're informed that he makes a wow of a tour guide, but - perhaps wisely - we never see him in action; nor, for that matter, are there ever any customers at all at Madame Monet's establishment. Creepy wax museums in the movies have been around since 1914 and Maurice Tourneur's *Figures de cire*, wherein a man unwisely agrees to spend a night in a wax museum (a situation repeated in 1936's *Midnight at the Wax Museum*). Tourneur returned to the subject again in *While Paris Sleeps* (1923), with Jack McDonald playing the torture obsessed curator, and Tourneur even had people locked in a wax museum for a sequence in his horse-racing epic, *The Whip* (1917). Wax museums also turn up in Paul Leni's *Waxworks* (1924), Richard Oswald's *Unholy Tales* (1932), and, of course - with Lionel Atwill as the maddest curator of them all - in *Mystery of the Wax Museum* (1933), not to mention the latter's remake *House of Wax* and *The New Exhibit*, one of the scariest episodes of *The Twilight Zone*.

Compared to some of the films mentioned above, Madame Monet's waxworks are pretty tame. Cameraman Paul Ivano tries to spook things up with some low-key lighting, but the museum still looks a department store with mannequins playing dress-up. And even though Rudi Poldan is said to be an expert researcher, we see an exhibit showing Marie Antoinette losing her head to the executioner's ax rather than to Madame Guillotine. So much for being true to history.

Since the picture contains no ghost – frozen or otherwise – the poster settles for a
noir-ish look.

Rudi and Keene's plan to drive Gregor crazy would make a little more sense if Madame Monet were in on it. As it stands now, the conspiracy works to the extent that it does because Monet faints at exactly the right moment, with Gregor conveniently blacking out an instant later (an embarrassingly lazy bit of writing). If Rudi and Keene were able to predict all this in advance, *they* must be the ones with psychic power and should have formed their own stage act. And since it is Maura who will inherit Gregor's fortune (we are told this early in the film), why does Keene think he has any chance of getting power-of-attorney over the mental mentalist?

Even though Nina comes off as a sweet simpleton, you would think even she would quickly exit the building after Rudi follows her around, tossing knives in her direction. Rudi also hurls a knife at Gregor when he comes to investigate. It adds some action to the film, but there doesn't seem to be any kind of logical motivation unless to suggest that, in addition to his careers as plastic surgeon and sculptor, Rudi worked in a circus as well.

The detectives in the "Inner Sanctum" films really serve no purpose in the plot other than to harass the innocent hero and to listen behind a door when the guilty party confesses or the plot is unraveled. Brant, played by sleazeball-and villain-specialist Douglass Dumbrille, seems particularly clueless. He saunters around the museum quoting - and misquoting - Shakespeare and doesn't notice that Madame Monet is lying there right under his nose "disguised" as the Lady Macbeth waxwork, something that doesn't escape even the naïve Nina. Brant also provides some very lame comedy at the very end.

Playing a supporting role in a "B"-movie must have given Tala Birell a wistful flashback to her earlier career at Universal in the '30s, when she was touted as "the new Garbo" (one of many). In spite of all the publicity build-up, Universal wasn't quite sure what to do with the Romanian-born actress who had achieved some success on the German stage. At one point they considered starring her in a version of *She*, but she ended up making only two movies: *Nagana*, a jungle film, and *The Lost Battalion*, a remake of a German war movie that cannibalized much of the original's footage. After that Birell freelanced and occasionally won good roles (*Bringing up Baby, Crime and Punishment*) before drifting into poverty row purgatory in the '40s.

In her 19 June 1944 column for the *Los Angeles Times*, Hedda Hopper noted that Evelyn Ankers and Grace McDonald are "pretty fed up with the roles they've been getting at Universal." Perhaps it's no coincidence that June 19th was the first day of shooting for *The Frozen Ghost*. Ankers delivers her usual professional performance in a thankless role. Pregnant at the time time, with the connivance of cast and crew she kept that fact from Universal who would have fired her had they known.

Elena Verdugo in later interviews admitted her performance as Nina in *The Frozen Ghost* was pretty bad, but she hadn't had much acting experience at the time (she'd been trained as a dancer) and, of course, received little help from the script or direction. She shows none of the charm she displayed in *House of Frankenstein* and might have been better cast as one of the bobbysoxers in the first scene.

Milburn Stone, usually a down-to-earth, realistic good guy, makes for an acceptable "surprise" villain here and has one very good moment where he panics, thinking they've killed Madame Monet and are now facing a murder rap. That scene has a little frisson: we hear Nina's heartbeats as Rudy checks her out with a stethoscope, but then ominous silence when he does the same to Madame Monet.

If *The Frozen Ghost* is at all watchable today, it's due primarily to Martin Kosleck's Rudi. The character is given an interesting back-story as a disgraced plastic surgeon (one of his patients "took off her bandages too soon") and, like all crazed curators, he spends a lot of time talking to his wax creations. Kosleck has a subtle, smoldering style that can suggest either madness or genius, and he uses it to very good effect here.

The entry on Kosleck in the IMDB is laughably inaccurate; it depicts Kosleck as an anti-Nazi activist in the '30s and under death sentence by the Gestapo who pursue him across Europe. While this might make for a good movie - and even sounds like a '40s propaganda film - Kosleck left Germany before the Nazis came to power and seems to have been pretty much apolitical, later claiming that the Nazis were clownish and that no one took them seriously at the time. Kosleck had done work on the German stage and had small roles in a couple of films, but his career in the Fatherland, just barely underway, was hardly noteworthy. He spent time in Italy (later claiming he learned English by listening to his grandmother's phonograph records) before going to America in 1932. Of course, being Jewish and gay, he no doubt would have departed Germany anyway.

In America, Kosleck relied on his friends Marlene Dietrich (he had acted with her in *The Taming of the Shrew* in Germany) and Hans Heinrich von Twardowski, an actor known for his work in Expressionist films (*The Cabinet of Dr. Caligari, Genuine. From Morn to Midnight*) and who was also a left-leaning stage director. Kosleck had a talent for art which initially drew more attention than his acting credentials. In an interview for the 29 May 1939 issue of *The Washington Post*, Kosleck elaborated for interviewer Frederick C. Othman:

> And it wasn't long before I got an offer from Fox Studios to paint some elaborate murals. I had never done anything like that before and I was scared. But I did my best and they complimented me on my work. So that was a good start. I kept on painting all kinds of pictures and kept selling them. I got $300 each for them... I had a one-man exhibition at a New York art gallery. It didn't do so well until Albert Einstein came to see it and gave out an interview complimenting me far beyond my work as an artist. But that started the ball rolling and it was the thing to do in New York to see my exhibition.

In addition to portraits and serious work, Kosleck also became well known for his caricatures of Hollywood celebrities, depicting the stars in exaggerated poses and spoofing their fan magazines' pictures. Kosleck drew Greta Garbo with a pot on her head and Clark Gable, dressed as an aviator, taking flight with just his ears.

Kosleck did not neglect acting and did some notable work at the famous Pasadena Playhouse, beginning with *Macbeth* (starring Irving Pichel), and he drew particularly good notices portraying the saintly Alyosha in a production of *The Brothers Karamazov*. Still, it was his performance as Shylock's servant Gobbo in von Twardowski's New York production of *The Merchant of Venice* (in modern dress and with an emphasis on anti-Semitism) that brought him to the attention of Warner Bros. and his casting as Dr. Goebbels in their *Confessions of a Nazi Spy* in 1939.

Fearing retaliation against his family (still in Germany), Kosleck played Hitler's propaganda minister using the moniker Nicolai Yashkin (a name suggested by Marlene Dietrich). His performance as the dour, relentless fanatic was duly noted by the critics. (3) It also drew the attention of Dr. Goebbels, who mentioned the film in his diary and did not seem put off by Kosleck's interpretation. Kosleck subsequently signed with Warner Bros using his real name.

**Mad sculptor Martin Kosleck shows off his creations to Tala Birell, Milburn Stone, and Lon Chaney.**

Anti-Nazi feeling was on the rise in Hollywood in the late '30s and of course America's entry into the war meant that Kosleck was assured of steady work as a bad guy in the service of *der Führer*. However, his favorite villain role was as Basil Rathbone's partner in crime in 1940's *The Mad Doctor*, wherein Rathbone marries wealthy women for their money and then murders them with Kosleck's help. Modern commentators think that, flying under the radar of the Production Code, the two are meant to be partners in more ways than one. Occasionally, Kosleck would play a sympathetic role (a Polish partisan in *Manila Calling*, the artist in Universal's dismal *She-Wolf of London*) and even did an heroic turn as Edmond Dantes in *The Wife of Monte-Cristo* (one critic who liked Kosleck's performance opined he was too short to be a leading man; Kosleck himself hated the film).

In the late '40s Kosleck married Eleonora von Mendelssohn, a noted actress with whom Kosleck appeared in a Broadway revival of *The Madwoman of Chaillot*. Von Mendelssohn, who had been married three times prior to Kosleck, was a descendant of the composer Felix Mendelssohn and the goddaughter of tragedian Eleonora Duse, as well as coming from a family that owned numerous art treasures. The marriage was not a happy one. In January of 1951, Kosleck fell three stories from their New York apartment. He claimed it was an accident, but his male lover, actor Christopher Drake, had just left Kosleck and was watching from below, causing later speculation that the two had quarreled and Kosleck was on the ledge as a suicide gesture. In any case, he was very seriously injured. Barely a month later, von Twardowski found von Mendelssohn dead in her room with an ether-soaked bandage over her mouth and a bottle of sleeping pills nearby. The actress, who had chronic insomnia, sometimes used ether to help her sleep. Whether her death was suicide or an accident is not known; however, in his diary (published many years later), von Mendelssohn's friend Leo Lehrman speculated that Kosleck - whom he called a "horrible man" - may have killed his wife with the connivance of Drake. Lehrman might have taken the plot of *The Mad Doctor* a little too seriously as *The New York Times* reported that Kosleck was still in the hospital at the time and was never even initially informed of his wife's death.

Kosleck recovered and the rest of his life, at least publicly, was drama-free. He did some stage work and still appeared steadily in the movies and on television, although usually his parts on the big screen were small. One exception was his starring role as a mad scientist in the gory sci-fi cheapie, *The Flesh Eaters* (1964), which also featured Christopher Drake as the captain who gets eaten up by the title creatures. Ill health forced Kosleck into retirement, but he lived to be 89. Drake was with him at the end.

New York film critics hated *The Frozen Ghost* though they were at least able to have fun with the title:

> 'The Frozen Ghost' will leave you stone cold but not from fear. An Inner Sanctum mystery, it might have been good reading in book form, but on the screen, its obviousness strips it of suspense and it is handicapped by performances that are too bad to be called hammy... The wax museum fails as a spine-chilling device... There is no ghost, there is no mystery and there is no suspense.
>
> Wanda Hale, *The New York Daily* News, 28 July 1945

> When an uninspired cast is coupled with an uninteresting plot, the result is bound to add up to unexciting film fare... The film doesn't have a ghost of a chance.
>
> J.R.L. *The New York Times*, 28 July 1945

> The theory behind 'The Frozen Ghost' must be that if a ghost gives you the shivers, a frozen one will turn you into an icicle of terror. That is, if you pay attention to the title and don't notice there's no ghost. Since nothing at all in the picture is believable, there's no point in subjecting it to close scrutiny. You either sit there with your mouth hanging open or you wonder why you didn't stay home.
>
> Acher Winsten, *New York Post*, 28 July 1945

> It's impossible to find anything favorable to say about 'The Frozen Ghost.' After sitting through it, the only thought that arises is just what a frozen ghost would look like after it is thawed out. And that reflection is prompted solely by the title which has virtually nothing to do with the film itself... It is difficult to decide who was the more indifferent, the actors on the screen or the people in the theater.
>
> Bert McCord, *New York Herald Tribune*, 28 July 1945

Critic Alton Cook of *The New York World Telegram* wondered if he was calling horror movies by their proper name:

During a conversation about mysteries and horror movies, a friend of mine referred to them as 'dark pictures' (everything photographed in the dark) and was surprised that I never had heard of that term used by everyone she knew... The devotees of 'dark pictures' are fortunate in having the Rialto. They don't have to hunt around for their specialty... Even on the low standards that 'dark pictures' set, this thing is on the minus side. This is a very lazy piece of story writing that would pass only with the 'dark picture' people.

27 July 1945

Outside the Sour Apple, critics were much kinder to *The Frozen Ghost.*

Lon Chaney, without the benefit of gargoyle face or twisted limbs and indeed playing a hero role shows you that he's a fine actor... The whole thing is rather spine-tingling. Martin Kosleck does a fine, sinister job as the waxworks crook, and Evelyn Ankers is just too lovely as the heroine.

G.K. *Los Angeles Times,* 20 September 1945

"Sten" in the 13 June 1945 edition of *Variety,* after commenting how the plot gets more involved by the minute when the action switches to the wax museum, commented that:

the climax is surprising enough to please whodunit fans... Chaney give a forthright performance as do Evelyn Ankers as his vis-à-vis, and Milburn Stone as his business agent. Remainder of cast aids in giving suspense to the proceedings.

Other trade paper reviews were also favorable:

The latest Inner Sanctum mystery is another psychological thriller replete with eerie backgrounds and completely fantastic happenings. With Lon Chaney (minus weird make-up) coupled with a sure-fire title to attract avid horror fans, 'The Frozen Ghost' should do well with houses that cater to that kind of audience...Lon Chaney gives a generally competent performance but Martin Kosleck is outstanding as a sadistic-minded waxworks employee. Tala Birell is also effective but Elena Verdugo adds an amateurish note as a sweet-faced maiden who is almost tossed into the furnace.

*Independent Exhibitors Film Bulletin*, 23 June 1945

Susceptible folk are provided with ample opportunity to work themselves into a nervous stew. Some of the screen's most favored melodramatic devices have been drawn upon in an attempt to keep the audience on tenterhooks.

*Film Daily*, 18 June 1945

The followers of psychological murder melodramas should find this program to their liking though the story is far-fetched, it is mystifying and has considerable suspense. The mood of the story is one of brooding terror, with no comedy to relieve the tension.

*Harrison's Reports*, 26 May 1945

R.I. of *Motion Picture Herald* (16 June 1945) had some reservations:

Here's a film that has a good idea for a murder story. But somehow this Inner Sanctum mystery lost its direction during filming and as a consequence the audience is going to have difficulty telling whether the story is an out-and-out murder story or one with spirit world overtones... Harold Young's direction has brought a lot of chilling atmosphere into the story and Evelyn Ankers as the principal blonde interest easily keeps up the romantic side of the film

I would rate *The Frozen Ghost* as the second best "Inner Sanctum," right after *Weird Woman*. But that's not saying a whole lot.

*The Frozen Ghost* - 29 June 1945 - 61 minutes (ST)

**CAST**: Lon Chaney as Alex Gregor (Gregor the Great); Evelyn Ankers as Maura Daniel; Milburn Stone as George Keene; Douglas Dumbrille as Inspector Brant; Martin Kosleck as Rudi Poldan; Elena Verdugo as Nina Courdreau; Tala Birell as

Madame (Valerie) Monet; Arthur Hohl as the Skeptic; Dennis Moore as Announcer; Leyland Hodgson as Doctor; David Hoffman as Inner Sanctum (4)

**CREDITS**: Director: Harold Young(5); Original Story: Henry Sucher and Harrison Carter; Adaptation: Henry Sucher; Screenplay: Bernard Schubert and Luci Ward; Producers: Ben Pivar and Will Cowan; Dialogue Director: Edward Dein; Photography: Paul Ivano; Art Direction: John B. Goodman and Abraham Grossman; Film Editor: Fred R. Feitshans, Jr.; Set Decoration: John B. Goodman and Ray L. Jeffers; Costumes: Vera West; Music: H.J. Salter; Sound: Bernard Brown, William Hedgcock, Edwin L. Wetzel, Paul Neal

*Shock Theater* Catalog No. 706: "After the patient of a hypnotist dies while under his spell, a series of baffling crimes take [sic] place in the *Shock Theater* feature length presentation, 'The Frozen Ghost,' starring Lon Chaney on this channel (day) at (time)."

*- HN*

# *The Jungle Captive (1945)*

*Synopsis*: Dr. Stendahl is experimenting with reviving the dead using small animals as his subjects. Stendahl is much admired by his assistants, Ann and Don, but they fail to realize the medico's utter ruthlessness. Stendahl decides Paula Dupree, the notorious Ape Woman, could be brought back to life with his technique: a combination of electrical stimuli and blood transfusions. Stendahl sends Moloch, his slow-witted henchman, to steal her body from the morgue and bring it to the doctor's country home. Moloch succeeds but kills an attendant in the process. Police detective Harrigan investigates the murder and questions Don and Ann.

Stendahl lures Ann to his lair and uses some of her blood to revive the Ape Woman. The doctor uses glandular transfusions from Ann to change the monster to her human form, but Paula seems not to have any capacity for self-awareness or thought, so Stendahl decides to transplant Ann's brain to stabilize her. Don arrives at the house, but he's promptly overpowered and tied up by Moloch. Moloch has fallen in love with Ann and, when he realizes the operation will kill her, he turns on Stendahl, who shoots him. As Stendahl prepares to operate, Paula transforms back into the Ape Woman, who then strangles the doctor. The monster attempts to kill Ann but is shot dead by Harrigan (who has been suspicious of Stendahl all along).

> "Don't be a fool! You're a scientist, not a sentimentalist!"
> - Dr. Stendahl (Otto Kruger) to Moloch (Rondo Hatton)

Many full moons ago, I would spend my Saturday afternoons watching vintage horror on "Monster Movie Matinee," hosted by Dr. E. Nick Witty with his companion,

591

Epal. Dr. Witty was never shown; you would see his hand and hear his mellifluous voice, silky and sinister, always directed at his grisly and somewhat benighted assistant. Watching *The Jungle Captive* brought back memories of the Doc and Epal; I kept expecting a commercial, then an exchange between Stendahl and Moloch followed by a return to "today's feature." The loopy interplay between the mad doctor and his henchman pretty much provide the main pleasure of *The Jungle Captive*. One particularly memorable exchange:

> Stendahl (after wearily collapsing into his chair after a hard day at the lab): "All this only proves half a theory."
> Moloch: "What's a 'half a theory'?"
> Stendahl: "So far we've only brought life back to this hybrid. If she could be transformed into a woman, then I'd have brought life to a human."
> Moloch: "So why don'tcha do it?"

Later, after Moloch has killed Dr. Fletcher and has stolen his notes on Paula, Stendahl asks his helper why he finds it necessary to commit murder doing these errands.

> Moloch: "Well, he came in and switched on the light."
> Stendahl: "Oh, I see. You certainly left that office in a shambles."
> Moloch: "I dun all right, huh?"

The third episode of the adventures of Paula Dupree, ape lady, is better than its dull predecessor, *Jungle Woman*, and is at least no worse than the first of the series, *Captive Wild Woman*. The latter title is better directed than *The Jungle Captive*, but happily we're spared here from sitting through large chunks of *The Big Cage* that padded out the first two films. *Jungle Captive* pretty much encapsulates Universal '40s "B"-horror: a mad doctor and his murderous henchman, a well-equipped laboratory, a Jack Pierce monster, howling dogs, an isolated old house, nosy cops, and a very perfunctory romance. And, of course, there's the inevitable lab montage showing the progress of the experiment, though the moving clock-hands to indicate the passage of time is overused to the point of being comical. None of this adds up to a good film, but at least it moves along quickly.

**A moment of uncertainty for Hatton's Moloch the Brute: menace Amelita Ward? or get in a bit of stretching?**

The movie gets off to a busy start with Moloch stealing the Ape Woman's body, but his actions really don't make much sense. Why does Moloch – after killing the attendant – call the ambulance people to pick up the Ape Woman? He already has a vehicle in which to transport her cadaver. Then, after tossing his lab smock into the ambulance, he drives it over a cliff. The smock – which improbably survives the resultant conflagration – seems to have been written in just to provide a clue to the police. This seems like a rather glaring mistake, even for an inept minion like Moloch.

Perhaps the biggest howler, though, is Stendahl's motive for trying to revive the Ape Woman instead of using a real person: he has moral qualms about experimenting on human beings! When Ann points out the obvious inconsistency in the scientist's willingness to kill people in order to further his aims, Stendahl just shrugs it off. Intentionally amusing (presumably) is the doctor's expecting Ann – half in a stupor from being drained of her blood – to share his enthusiasm for the project: "*We* did it! She's alive!" Ann, who showed considerably more interest when Stendahl had revived a rabbit, is understandably less keen on being a participant in Paula's resurrection.

One critic wrote that Otto Kruger should be "ashamed" for playing such a corny part, echoing the earlier remarks of a reviewer of *Dracula's Daughter* (wherein Kruger played the hero) who opined that such a good actor was probably embarrassed by the supernatural shenanigans. Other critics described Kruger's performance as Stendahl as "conscientious," but G.K. - in the 20 September 1945 edition of the *Los Angeles Times* – went a bit further:

Producers seem to have learned that they must have actors, even for their thrillers, and Otto Kruger comes under that heading. Even the absurdities of this one in which Dr. Otto changes an ape that had been a girl back into a girl becomes faintly believable whenever he is around.

Kruger's underplaying is even able to make lines like "I need you, Ann. I need your blood" less risible than they sound. Maybe he's doing it for the Fat Lady, but he's wholly serious in giving a polished, professional performance even with *Jungle Captive*'s ridiculous story. The actor's ability to deliver lines in a realistic manner go back to his earliest days on the stage as the following anecdote – taken from the 11 September 1974 edition of the *Los Angeles Times* – illustrates:

The 5-foot-7-inch player was appearing on Broadway in George M. Cohan's *Young America* when matinee idol William Simpson reared back on his heels, rolled his eyes and bellowed to the gallery 'Where is Annie tonight?' Mr. Kruger dusted some imaginary lint off his sleeve, stifled a yawn and replied in a normal speaking voice: 'She's outside.' Simpson was so flabbergasted at such an unorthodox delivery that he left the script and, wringing his hands, shouted at the young actor 'What did you say?' Mr. Kruger casually stuck a hand in his pocket, jingled some coins and again said in a matter-of-fact manner: 'She's outside.' At that point Cohan, who was watching the play from an orchestra seat, burst into laughter.

"Very soon after that," Mr. Kruger recalled during an interview in the 1960s, "the idea spread – that actors could talk like people, and all of them began doing it."

Otto Kruger was a major player on the Great White Way in the 1920s and had a big hit spoofing John Barrymore in *The Royal Family of Broadway* for 1,400 performances, but he played the leading man as often as he did the *farceur*. Kruger's film career did not amount to much during the Silent Era, his first film being the 1917 comedy short, *Oh, Pop*, but he had been involved in films even before that. In 1905 he was providing piano accompaniment at a nickelodeon when the manager suggested that he and another worker stand behind the screen and synchronize sound effects props with the action onscreen. Kruger claimed the practice worked very well, and that "we even used our voices for shouts and a few words now and then. Thus, you might say it was the first talking picture." (1)

In 1933 Kruger was put under contract by M-G-M and starred with Lee Tracy and Mae Clarke in *No Hands on the Clock*. Kruger did well during his time at M-G-M and had a variety of good roles: the German-American teacher who becomes a victim of relentless prejudice during World War I and turns to spying in *Ever My Heart* (1933); the detective who frames his wife's lover for murder in *Crime Doctor*; Dr. Livesey in *Treasure Island* (the latter two, 1934). Nonetheless, by the late '30s, the actor was freelancing and willing to appear thereafter in low-budget but offbeat films like *Mercy Island* (1941), *Hitler's Children* (1943), and *Woman Who Came Back* (1945). He alternated these bread-and-butter chores with bigger films, like Hitchcock's *Saboteur* (1942) and *The Great John L* (1945). He returned to Broadway from time to time, playing the German commander in John Steinbeck's *The Moon Is Down* (Cedric Hardwicke essayed the role in the film version) and the acid-tongued critic (and killer), Waldo Lydecker, in *Laura*. The advent of television kept the actor very busy indeed, and he was frequently to be seen on *Perry Mason*. Kruger's last genre effort was 1958's *The Colossus of New York*, wherein he plays a scientist who transfers his dead son's brain into a giant robot, the sort of endeavor that probably brought back memories to Kruger of *The Jungle Captive*.

Kruger does have one bad moment in *Captive*: when the Ape Woman grabs him, he utters a cartoonish "Ahhhhhhhh!" Not to be outdone, the monster (Vicki Lane), after being shot, emits a whole series of grunts and groans before collapsing. The whole scene is less Universal horror than *The Carol Burnett Show*.

Vicki Lane looks fetching in a low-cut top, but has little to do in the film other than act dazed in what was actually the biggest role in her very brief movie career, though she later achieved some success as a jazz singer. Lane took over the Ape Woman role from Acquanetta who, in later years, enjoyed deriding her successor by quoting critic Bert McCord's description of Lane's version of the monster as "looking like an oversized woodchuck with a hangover."

Rondo Hatton garnered some notice playing the Hoxton Creeper in the Sherlock Holmes adventure, *The Pearl of Death*. Still, that film is very canny in not showing the Creeper until the climax. Prior to that, the Creeper is frequently – and fearfully – mentioned by the other characters (co-conspirator Evelyn Ankers shudders when told the Creeper is asking about her), and his shadow is sometimes shown. This makes for a suspenseful build-up to his actual appearance. *The New York Herald Tribune*'s review of that picture singled out Hatton, saying: "If he goes to the right Hollywood parties with the right people, Boris Karloff had better look to his horrors."

Whether Hatton whooped it up at parties or not, Universal took this opinion seriously and, with *The Jungle Captive*, began building Hatton up as horror star.

595

Unwisely, instead of the chilling – and mute – cameo in *The Pearl of Death*, Hatton is on view throughout *Captive*, and he has dialogue which he delivers with all the aplomb of Tor Johnson. *The Independent Film Bulletin* opined that Hatton was "a perfect type to 'scare the daylights' out of susceptible fans," but the *Los Angeles Times* review noted that the actor "drew only giggles from the kids in the audience." More on the unfortunate Hatton – whose deformed features were the result of the glandular disease, acromegaly - can be found in our essays on *House of Horrors* and *The Brute Man*.

**Ape-woman Vicki Lane is "chastised" by Otto Kruger's Dr. Stendahl. Referred to as *Mister* Stendahl for much of the film, Kruger's character hardly inspires confidence when he's caught reading a book on brain surgery. *Not* a good sign for all potential patients.**

Phil Brown and Amelita Ward are saddled with the vapid roles of the young lovers. Brown scowls a lot – understandably – and, like David Bruce (whom he resembles slightly), he might have made a good villain had he been given the opportunity. Betty Bryant, who came to audience attention in *40,000 Horsemen* (1940; the first Australian motion picture to make an impression in America), was originally cast as Ann, but was replaced during filming. (2) Not everyone got the memo, and her name still turned up in some ads for *Captive*. Amelita Ward had a very minor film career and later married Leo Gorcey (of "Bowery Boys" fame), perhaps an even worse fate than being stuck in the picture under discussion. Jerome Cowan brings his usual cynical persona to the part of Harrigan.

New York critics had a good time poking fun at the film:

> This claptrap is played with unvarying emphasis on commotion... In a spare moment one of these mad scientists might try to find an injection to bring life to such pictures as this one.
> Alton Cook, *New York World Telegram*, 7 June 1945

> And what happens to that girl when the doc decides to use her as an unwilling blood donor and later prepare to transplant her brain shouldn't even happen to the producers of this film – or should it? Vicki Lane plays the brainless woman with monosyllabic finesse and in her dual role of primitive savage, she grunts and growls as though she thought the whole business to be as stupid as it actually is.
> J.R.I, *The New York Times*, 7 July 1945

> I have come to the unalterable conviction that I just don't like motion pictures in which a fanatical doctor dis-inters werewolves, wolf-men, troglodytes and the like to bring them back to life with dire results to countless innocent victims. In the language of The Two Black Crows, 'even if they were good, I wouldn't like them.' But there's no danger of that in the case of *Jungle Captive*.
> Bert McCord, *The New York Herald Tribune*, 7 July 1945

The reviewer for the 16 June 1945 edition of *Showmen's Trade Review* was equally unimpressed:

> Neither better nor worse than the usual horror picture, this will serve suitably for double bill programs. Produced inexpensively and directed as though the director wanted to complete a distasteful job just as quickly as possible, the entertainment merit will be discerned only by audiences addicted to this form of fantastic fare. The acting is just about as good as the material with which the actors have been provided which is not saying too much. Just fair entertainment, even for the horror fans.

The 16 June 1945 *Harrison's Reports* found the picture

> Gruesome and repulsive. Like most horror stories, this one is too far-fetched and most of what transpires has been done many times but it does succeed in generating considerable suspense.

However, "Sten" of *Variety* had a few kind words for the film:

> Universal didn't pull any punches in trying to build this chiller into one of the starkest mellers of the year. Pic was made on an obviously low budget but has a mad sadistic theme. Acting by all members of the cast is just average, Kruger's suave performance standing out. Settings and camerawork as well as direction and screenplay endeavor to keep the viewers in the thrilling mood upon which the story is based and rather successfully, too.
> 13 June 1945

The saga of Universal's only female monster of the '40s finally came to an end. No one was sorry.

*The Jungle Captive* – 29 June 1945 – 64 minutes (SoS)

**CAST**: Otto Kruger as Dr. Stendahl; Amelita Ward as Ann; Phil Brown as Don; Jerome Cowan as Harrigan; Rondo Hatton as Moloch; Eddie Acuff as Bill; Ernie Adams as Jim; Charles Wagenheim as Fred; Ernie Chandler as Motorcycle Cop; Jack Overman as Detective; Vicki Lane as the Ape Woman

**CREDITS**: Director: Harold Young; Dialogue Director: Willard Holland; Producer: Morton B. Cox; Original Story and Screenplay: Dwight V. Babcock; Screenplay: M. Coates Webster; Music: Paul Sawtell; Cinematography: Maury Gertsman; Film Editor: Fred Feltshans, Jr.; Art Directors: Robert Clatworthy John B. Goodman; Set Decoration: Russell A. Gausman, A.J. Gilmore; Make-up: Jack P. Pierce; Assistant Director: Charles Gould; Costumes: Vera West; Sound: Bernard B. Brown, Robert Pritchard

*– HN*

# *The Woman in Green* (1945)

A story in *off* (a modality that began to come into vogue with the rise of *Film Noir* - here we have a forerunner from the Holmes series going ahead of its time) places us in contemporary London, but with a murderer who reflects the Victorian world. Following a bit of official narrative on the "Finger Murders," the CID director (the diminutive Alec Harford) - meeting with his staff - compares the killer to Jack the Ripper and outlines how he has committed three violent, bloody crimes, mutilating each victim and carrying off a piece of the corpse – a finger – as if it were a souvenir. The narrator intervenes as we move to a scene in which a young woman is walking through a dark alley. We may not be able to make her out, but the imminent victim is the uncredited Kay Harding, whom Universal had fired after giving her the heroine's role in *The Mummy's Curse* (1944) and whom the fans of the Holmes series may have recognized as the innocent young lass in *The Scarlet Claw*. At the moment of the murder (suggested by shadows), the narrator turns out to be Inspector Gregson (whom every reader of the canon identifies as the officer of the law who intervenes in the novel **A Study in Scarlet**, the first appearance of the soon-to-be immortal partners). Gregson will turn to Holmes for advice on dealing with this grotesque business. These initial sequences – which take the first four minutes of footage here – will offer a different way of establishing the case, instead of the frequent conceit of the arrival of visitors to 221b Baker Street and their oral recitations (at times alternating with flashbacks) that was becoming the norm for the series.

We are then introduced to the distinguished Sir George Fenwick (Paul Cavanagh, in his third and last role in the series) who, after flirting with the provocative Lydia Marlow (Hillary Brooke, also in her third and last appearance), comes to in a boarding-house on the same street where the fifth murder of the severed fingers occurs. He returns to Lydia's apartment where another distinguished gentleman (Henry Daniell) – albeit one given to evil – makes an appearance and hints at his intention to blackmail the disconcerted aristocrat. Immediately thereafter, Fenwick's daughter (Eve Amber, a minor Universal starlet to whom director Roy William Neill would grant some remarkable close-ups) arrives (*now*) at the Baker Street flat to ask Holmes's help. The previous night, her father had buried a receptacle containing a severed finger in the garden. Upon rushing up to the nobleman's house – accompanied by Scotland Yard – they find him dead. If, to this point, the camera had spared us our seeing loose digits, now it puts Sir George's cadaver on display. Holmes observes that one hand has been closed up into a fist and – upon opening it to discover what it's hiding – the crackling noise of *rigor mortis* is heard; this, we believe, was a gift directly meant for horror fans.

This detail may have been compensation for the fact that one of the original ideas of scenarist Bertram Millhauser could not be filmed: that the murderer's victims were *not* young women, but rather girls between eight and nine years old. The Breen Office believed that it saw in this plot issue a risk for the public morality and sensibility, but the problem was quickly resolved by aging the victims by a decade or more. The new script conformed with the censors' opinions and guaranteed a green light to start filming; nevertheless, there remained loose ends: one of Moriarity's [sic] minions – Dr. Simnell (an uncredited Percival Vivian) – carried into a scene a picturesque doll that, we suppose, was to be used to attract potential victims *a la* the classic *M* of Peter Lorre.

It doesn't take long for the detective to perceive the killer's motive - "I smell the faint, sweet odor of blackmail" - and, after an additional pair of deductions, to announce the identity of the villain: "If my assumptions are correct," says Holmes, "this little scheme has behind it the most brilliant and ruthless intellect the world has ever known." In a curious and untrue utterance, Watson replies that it couldn't be Moriarity, as "he was hanged in Montevideo... over a year ago."

A telephone call summons Watson, and he's out the door. Thus, our cinematic *cliché*: the reason for removing the character from the flat so that Moriarity can pay a "friendly" warning visit: "Mr. Holmes, I should strongly advise you to drop this case." In this way, our hero is to concentrate more on the blackmail than on the murders, or on the means that Moriarity uses to lead his potential victims to the scenes of the crime, or how he plants the incriminating evidence (the fingers), thus forgetting a bit not only the series of murders, but also the murderer himself. Nevertheless, we can suspect the aforementioned Dr. Simnell, not only for his delicate speech and affected mannerisms, but also because of an ingenious dialogue exchange with Moriarity, suffering from an annoying splinter in his finger. "Nasty things, splinters," replies Simnell, "most trying. One can't be too careful, but I'll get it out for you. I have the very instrument to help you," he says, as he opens his bag of medical instruments and brandishes a scalpel. "Sharp enough to split a hair," says Simnell, displaying a smile as delicate as his speech. Unmoved, Moriarity order him to put his tools away. The doctor insists they're instruments, and not tools, but – no matter which – his subtlety on the part of the scenarist allows us to know the murderer's identity.

**Dr. Simnell (Percival Vivian) appears to enjoy poking Holmes's neck with a "medical instrument," while Professor Moriarity (Henry Daniell) and Lydia Marlow search his face for signs of shamming. Thankfully, the Great Consulting Detective had anticipated same and had taken a dose or two of "Dr. Watson's Amazing Cure-All," which rendered Holmes impervious to hypnotism and his nervous system, to random stabbing.**

It would be an attack that provides the crucial clue to Holmes: a soldier discharged due to physical ineptitude fires at the detective from the building opposite. He hits his target, of course, but it turns out to be a bust of Julius Caesar and not the detective, who opines that "prominent men have prominent noses." Both episodes, taken from canonical tales (the interlude with "Moriarity" from "The Final Problem" and the attack by Colonel Moran from "The Adventure of the Empty House") demonstrate an interesting resource for the scenarists, fusing elements from different stories into a new plot. The denouement featuring Moriarity falling into space reminds us of earlier incursions – like that of Lionel Atwill (the series' first "Moriarity") in *Secret Weapon* (1943) and George Zucco (as 20th Century-Fox's Moriarty) in 1939's *The Adventures of Sherlock Holmes* – both of which offered the professor a similar fate, perhaps due to the character's bad karma. And with respect to Holmes, hypnotized and led to walk along a high ledge, an interesting precedent would be the "B"-offering from Monogram – Phil Rosen's *Charlie Chan in Black Magic* (1944) – in which a medium hypnotizes the Hawaiian bloodhound (here incarnated by Sidney Toler) and likewise takes him to the rooftop of a building.

There's a clever moment and a couple of hiccups in evidence to the more attentive viewer. In the first scenes, when Lydia takes Sir George to her apartment, the camera gives us a panoramic view of the rooftop where the maid is smoking and taking in some fresh air while she leans on a loose brick that barely stays in place. At the picture's climax, when Holmes takes his dangerous walk out on the heights, director Neill shoots a close-up of that very brick, as it causes the detective a momentary loss of balance. Less clever are the framing errors that occur in several scenes: the camera's shadow is seen on Watson's back when he and Holmes enter Sir George's library to inspect the corpse. Later, a boom is seen when the faithful doctor walks along Baker Street and is confronted by a street vendor. Lastly, the camera shows us the source of the water Lydia uses to hypnotize her victims; when the focus is on it, the characters reflected thereon ought to appear backwards, as if it were a mirror, but no. This happens during the hypnotizing of Sir George and again, later, during that of Holmes.

To a large extent, contemporary criticism was rather positive, although undoubtedly lacking in superlatives. *Film Daily* (19 June 1945) classified it as "[an] acceptable, swift-moving melodrama," while lauding it with the most tepid of praise: "Lovers of melodrama will derive much enjoyment from *The Woman in Green*." Sten, called upon to review the film for the 20 June 1945 edition of *Variety*, was apparently no great fan of the series, as he observed that "[the] acting by the entire cast is fairly substantial. Production and direction is in the familiar light-budget whodunit groove, along with the settings and camerawork." Gotta love that "substantial acting," though.

Still, T.M.P. wasted little ink on the picture in the 16 June 1945 issue of *The New York Times*: "A Hollywood script writer named Bertram Millhauser takes full responsibility for what transpires on the screen of the Rialto, and it's just as well, for Sir Arthur never perpetrated a disappointment such as 'The Woman in Green.'." The *New York World-Telegram*'s Alton Cook beat T.M.P. to the punch by 24 hours: "If you have never seen one of [the Holmes films], this one is worth a try on an idle evening. Or if you have seen any of the series, don't be surprised if you find yourself wondering whether you haven't already seen this one."

*Showmen's Trade Review* (23 June 1945) opined that "the story has been cleverly contrived and has plausibility, suspense and a satisfying culmination. It is well produced and directed." *Film Bulletin*, which hit the streets a month later, remarked that the picture "has suspense, a neatly contrived plot and better-than-usual characterizations as well as mystery." One of the critic's comments is a bit unusual and might be appreciated only after seeing a colorized version of the film: "Although she is not photographed in Technicolor, Hillary Brooke adds pulchritude and charm as the woman of the title." Technicolor might also have helped to illustrate – if not explain – what was to be gained by dressing Lydia Marlow in green.

Another point for consideration was the adjustment to the spelling and *nouveau* pronunciation of Holmes's great nemesis, Professor Moriarty [sic]. Possessed of a surname that reeked of Ireland in his literary appearances, the professor retained that name – *Moriarty* – in virtually every film in which he was raising the bar for the rest of Sherlock's foes. From his cinematic debut (in William Gillette's recently rediscovered *Sherlock Holmes*, 1916) wherein he was portrayed by French actor, Ernest Maupain; through his subsequent participation in two identically-entitled features, whether opposite John Barrymore (Gustav von Seyffertiz, 1922) or Clive Brook (Ernest Torrence, 1932); through *three* challenges for Arthur Wontner's Great Consulting Detective: *Sherlock Holmes' Fatal Hour* (1931; as Professor *Robert* Moriarty, played by Norman McKinnell), and – impersonated by the Welsh thesp, Lyn Harding – in *The Triumph of Sherlock Holmes* (1935) and *Murder at the Baskervilles* (1937). *Zounds!* Even when confronting Basil Rathbone's iteration of the man from Baker Street (in 1939's *The Adventures of Sherlock Holmes*), George Zucco's archvillain was yclept Moriarty! Was the ungainly change due to Universal's legal department – somehow fearful of a lawsuit? - or was it an uncaught typo in the final script of *Sherlock Holmes and the Secret Weapon*, which went on to remain uncaught in the film at hand? - or, most suspect of all, was the dialogue director from Brooklyn? Another Holmesian mystery! (1)

The ninth offering in the series, *The Woman in Green* would mark the end of horror as a predominant element in the generic makeup of the series entries, which looked to embrace new narrative resources, like *Film Noir* and its attendant *femme fatale,* and psychoanalysis implicitly achieved through hypnotism. Modern times were coming, and the anachronism of a Victorian detective solving cases - at first linked to the fearsome Axis powers, then to horrific scenes or characters, and later to "Woman," either as the evil genius (as in *The Spider Woman)* or the secondary villain, as in the film at hand – slowly lost its appeal to the viewer. The series had already lost a great deal of appeal for Basil Rathbone, who would end up being "married" to his character, the only one not allowed to display the creativity needed to change or the freedom to take on interpretive challenges. To be honest: The cases, the adversaries, and the milieu could vary – these were shaped by genre-based, narrative trends – but Holmes always had to keep on being Holmes.

*The Woman in Green* – 27 July 1945 – 68 Minutes

**CAST**: Basil Rathbone as Sherlock Holmes; Nigel Bruce as Doctor Watson; Hillary Brooke as Lydia Marlow; Henry Daniell as Prof. James Moriarity [sic]; Paul Cavanagh as Sir George Fenwick; Matthew Boulton as Inspector Gregson; Eve Amber as Maude Fenwick; Frederic Worlock as Dr. Onslow; Coulter Irwin as Corporal Williams; Sally Shepherd as Crandon; Mary Gordon as Mrs. Hudson; Alec Harford as CID Commissioner; Boyd Irwin as CID Officer; Jackie Lou Harding as 4th Victim; Ivo Henderson as Constable; Leslie Denison as Vincent, Pembroke House's Barman; William H. O'Brien as Waiter; Olaf Hytten as Norris, Fenwick's Butler; Harold De Becker as Street Seller; Percival Vivian as Dr. Simnell; Arthur Stenning as Mesmer Club Butler; John Burton as Waring; Tony Ellis as Carter; Violet Seton as Nurse; Eric Mayne and Count Stefenelli as Members of Mesmer Club; Colin Hunter and Kermit Maynard as Detectives.

**CREDITS**: Director and Producer: Roy William Neill; Executive Producer: Howard Benedict; Screenplay: Bertram Millhauser; Musical Director: Mark Levant; Photography: Virgil Miller; Film Editing: Edward Curtiss; Art Director: John B. Goodman and Martin Obzina; Set Decoration: Russell A. Gausman and Ted von Hemert; Director of Sound: Bernard B. Brown; Gowns: Vera West; Dialogue Director: Raymond Kessler; Special Photography: John P. Fulton; Assistant Director: Melville Shyer.

*–DL*

# *Strange Confession* (1945)

*Synopsis*: In the middle of the night, a very distraught Jeff Carter calls on Brandon, an old college acquaintance who is now a famous criminal lawyer. Carter begs Brandon to listen to his story, but the lawyer is reluctant until Jeff shows him what's inside the satchel that he has brought with him.

Jeff is a brilliant and idealistic chemist whose work has made millions for his ungrateful boss, Roger Graham, who is quick to claim credit for Jeff's discoveries. Jeff's salary is so low that he, his wife Mary, and their little son Tommy can barely make ends meet. Mary chides Jeff for not standing up for himself, and Jeff does draw the line when Graham wants to market Zymurgine, the anti-influenza drug Jeff is working on, before he has completed his experiments. Jeff quits and, because Graham has had him blackballed at other labs, he can only find work as a pharmacist.

After a year, Graham offers Jeff his old job back at a much bigger salary and with the freedom to pursue his work unhindered. Jeff is reluctant, but Mary persuades him it is the right thing to do. Jeff is close to perfecting Zymurgine, but needs a mold found only in South America to clinch the deal. Stevens, Graham's assistant, secretly copies Jeff's notes. Graham, who is attracted to Mary, agrees to let Jeff and his helper Dave go to South America. Mary, not aware of Graham's true intentions, allows him to take her out a few times.

Jeff's work in South America proves successful but, in the meantime, Graham markets Zymurgine using Jeff's old, incomplete formula. An influenza epidemic breaks out and Tommy, stricken with the disease, dies when Zymurgine proves ineffective. Discovering that Graham has released the drug prematurely, Jeff heads back to America having telegraphed Mary as to what's going on. Armed with a gun,

Mary accepts Graham's invitation to his apartment. He wrests the pistol away from her, but then Jeff enters and is wounded by Graham. The chemist then kills and beheads his treacherous boss with a bolo knife as Mary faints.

The police and Mary arrive at Brandon's home just as Jeff starts to pass out from his wound. Brandon assures Mary that he will do everything he can to help Jeff.

*Strange Confession* is certainly an atypical entry in the "Inner Sanctum" series. It's not a mystery, and there are no horror overtones. Even the annoying stream-of-consciousness device characteristic of the series is missing. The film is pretty much a straightforward drama with some social criticism and one grisly touch.

The story is based on Jean Bart's 1932 play, *The Man Who Reclaimed His Head*, which Universal had previously filmed in 1934.(1) Apparently there was some question as to whether Universal had retained the rights to do another version, and both the film and the Library of Congress copyright entry tried to fudge the matter by crediting the story to a *composition* ("Fourth grade, perhaps?" cracked *The New York Times'* critic) by Jean Bart. Given the fact that, earlier in 1945, Universal was slapped with a lawsuit by Harold Lloyd over copyright infringement, one would think the studio would tread carefully, but perhaps they figured no one would notice that one of their "B"-movies had revised the plot of a previous work. Initially, no one did, but then the film was reissued in 1953 under the title *The Missing Head*. An exhibitor with a sense of humor in Hamilton, Ohio, doubled it with *The Vanishing Body* (the reissue title of the 1934 *The Black Cat*), but lawyers for the Jean Bart estate were not amused. They objected both to the liberties Universal had taken with the story and their questionable right to do a second film based on the play. Universal withdrew the movie and did not include it in their later "Shock Theater" television package. Nonetheless, the film did not disappear completely, and eye-straining, multi-generation VHS copies circulated among collectors in the '80s and '90s. In 1997 Universal cleared up the rights issue and released *Strange Confession* to video along with the other "Inner Sanctum" titles.

Bart's play was one of many post-World War I dramas that espoused pacifism, pointing out that the War to End All Wars did no such thing and might well have been spurred on by the self-interest of munitions manufacturers. In the title role of the drama, Claude Rains played Paul Verin, a brilliant writer and pacifist who happens to be deformed. He stays in the shadows and ghost-writes anti-war speeches for a publisher with political ambitions. Ultimately, in order to further his own career, his boss betrays him, gives in to the merchants of death, and supports the march to war. After serving in the trenches, Verin gets his revenge and beheads the publisher who had also been pursuing Verin's wife; (pacifists can certainly turn very violent; note the finale of the play and film version of *High Treason*). The play lasted barely a month on Broadway, but Universal went ahead with a film version anyway, as it offered a plum follow-up role for Claude Rains after his triumph in *The Invisible Man*. The film eliminated the character's deformity (critics thought it was a bit too grotesque, a Lon Chaney turn) but otherwise stayed faithful to the play.

*Strange Confession's* borrowings from the play are obvious. Of course, a straight remake of the original would have been out of the question anyway. The Allies had just won World War II - the just war - and no one was likely to buy into the notion that the arms industry - and not idealism - had prompted America's entry into the conflict. And, naturally, it goes without mention that war scenes would have been far too elaborate and costly for a "B"-movie.

**Lon Chaney – the idealist – unwisely puts his trust in J. Carrol Naish – the treacherous.**

Scenarist M. Coates Webster substituted the pharmaceutical industry for the munitions business. This was an astute move; in 1937, the drug company Massengill had marketed an antibiotic elixir called "Sulfanilamide" that resulted in 100 deaths. It turned out the drug company had not done the usual animal testing before releasing the drug, and their head pharmacist - facing trial - had killed himself. The mass poisonings lead to the creation of the Food and Drug Administration. While *Strange Confession's* audiences might not have recalled the details of the scandal, it no doubt left

607

them with a predisposition to mistrust big pharmacy. In addition to that, there was a 1943-1944 influenza epidemic that, while not nearly as terrible as previous epidemics, claimed its share of lives. These tragedies would have lent some topicality to a bigger, more prestigious film, but were not noted by critics for *Strange Confession*. The script also takes a jab at Madison Avenue: "You can sell almost anything if you advertise it enough," snorts a pharmacist after noting that everyone is buying Zymurgine even though its effectiveness has not been established.

This picture of Chaney seems to have been lifted from *Dead Man's Eyes*.

M. Coates Webb had been an actor and a novelist, but had enjoyed success in neither profession before settling into screenwriting. His work for Universal - which includes *Jungle Captive* and *The Brute Man* - was far from distinguished. He seems to get the science right for *Strange Confession*, but the drama is lacking, a flaw not helped by the sluggish pace and John Hoffman's by-the-numbers direction. The family scenes border on the maudlin, especially the Christmas Eve dinner sequence wherein the Carters - poor but happy - sit down to a modest meal amidst equally humble surroundings; I half expected Tiny Tim to limp through the door.

The film begins on an intriguing note as Chaney lurks in the shadows with his satchel and avoids the police, but that's as *noir*-ish as it gets, the mood quickly dissolving into the visually commonplace. The story might have had a little more *frisson* if Mary's character had a harder edge, but she's no Lady Macbeth, and her attempts to get her husband to stop being a doormat seem quite reasonable. We know she's virtuous and will be not seduced by Graham's wining and dining her - nor does she even seem slightly aware of his motives - but that means the scenes where he takes out her are repetitive and rather pointless since there's no dramatic tension whatsoever. Things are a little livelier over in South America, but that's chiefly due to the presence of likable wiseacre Lloyd Bridges (Dave) and a very cute monkey. The scenes leading up to the climax seems hasty. We see headlines about Zymurgine being revealed as a fraud, but Graham, returning from out of town, seems singularly unconcerned, while Jeff's making it back from South America just at the moment when Mary confronts Graham is contrived even for a melodrama. And why does it take the police so long to get to get to Brandon's house when he's told his butler to call them even before Jeff sits down to tell his story?

In *Night Must Fall* (1937), a woman is decapitated and it's obvious that her likely murderer, Robert Montgomery, is concealing her head in a hatbox. The audience is teased with the possibility of seeing exactly what's in there, even though the head is never actually shown. *Strange Confession* shows little interest in its satchel, which is practically forgotten until we see a cop cart away it at the end. When *Strange Confession* played at New York's horror emporium - The Rialto Theater - Alton Cook, in the 7 November 1945 issue of *The New York Telegram*, expressed mock indignation at the film's reticence:

> The makers of this picture were chickenhearted at the finish though, showing a complete lack of confidence in the fortitude of Rialto patrons' stomachs. To climax the story Lon Chaney cuts off a man's head and the audience is not allowed so much as one teeny glimpse at either the severing or the bloody head. Unless that omission leaves you feeling cheated this picture should give a proper Rialto quota of excitement and creeps. Quite a while has passed since the Rialto connoisseurs of the revolting have seen a head cut off and I can't help feeling what a shame it is that this opportunity was muffed. The gang takes such relish in these innocent little pleasures!

Lon Chaney's performance in *Strange Confession* is his best in the entire series. He makes Jeff's idealism and honesty completely convincing, and he brings warmth to his scenes as a family man making the best of a bad economic situation. Perhaps Chaney brought his own experience to bear for those sequences. When he married his wife Patsy in 1937, he was a struggling actor and could only afford a six-dollar ring. Eight years later his fortunes had greatly improved, and he had a second wedding ceremony with Patsy, this one considerably more lavish than the first and followed by a honeymoon in Mexico. In *Strange Confession*, Chaney is less persuasive when he goes mad; he just seems distracted much as he is waking up after a blackout in other "Inner Sanctum" films.

Brenda Joyce looks just as fetching wearing an apron and doing the dishes as she did swinging through the trees in several Tarzan movies. J. Carrol Naish cleverly underplays Graham; butter wouldn't melt in his mouth, but his good manners and quiet tone belie his true ruthless nature. Milburn Stone as Stevens has only a few brief scenes, while Addison Richards, uncharacteristically gentle and grave, plays the doctor who gives poor Mary the bad news about little Tommy.

Not surprisingly, *The New York Times'* T.M.P was unimpressed:

> A curiously unstimulating melodrama. There's no excuse for the dullness of events leading up to the gory finale. Moreover, the acting of the principals is incredibly unprofessional.
>
> 8 November 1945

Writing on the same day as her Grey Lady counterpart, Dorothy Masters of *Daily News* was more positive:

> Characters are disarmingly human in *Strange Confession*. Even Lon Chaney appears sans make-up... There's a little too much domesticity in the film for thriller fans plus a pokey introduction but suspense is moderately good. Good performances from all the principals.

You would think after four prior "Inner Sanctum" films, no one should have been too surprised that Chaney doesn't play a monster.

As usual, Grace Kingsley of the *Los Angeles Times* was enthusiastic about Chaney and wrote in the 19 October 1945 edition: "Lon Chaney impresses more and more as a fine actor who could essay any dramatic role. In *Strange Confession* the impression is deepened."

Alton Cook, however, was not a fan:

Lon Chaney is ponderously and heroically wrestling with those uncontrollable emotions of his once more in *Strange Confession*. This one sets him to gurgling and moaning and kicking up a neurotic rumpus on a level with all his others.

Other Big Apple critics were equally indifferent:

A poorly motivated domestic tragedy with a touch of melodrama added as an afterthought... His life history is a rather shallow variation on the theme that business executives in the sordid economic world sometimes exploit professional talent. There can be very little objection to murdering bosses who send their employees off to South America for such secret purposes but this moral lesson can hardly make up for the general lack of sense and excitement...

Otis L. Guernsey, Jr., *New York Herald*, 8 November 1945

It isn't nearly as eerie as a couple of its predecessors; that is goose-pimply only in a conventional manner. Scenarist M. Coates Webb hasn't done any heavy, unearthly dreaming up for this story...Lon Chaney, looking constantly harassed as usual, is the keen minded chemist.

Irene Thirer, *New York Post*, 9 November 1945

On the 21 December 1945, *Film Daily* called the film "a good programmer with an absorbing and unusual story," but other trades dismissed it as run-of-the-mill:

This picture features a 13-year- old South American ringtail monkey. And not bad this monk. The rest of the cast, headed by Lon Chaney, turn in performances that are routine albeit quite as natural as Bebe's and under fairly able direction by John Hoffman manage to produce a mystery item that should do fairly.

"Char," *Variety*, 14 November 1945

This murder melodrama does not rate anything higher than ordinary program fare. Since the picture is being billed as an 'Inner Sanctum Mystery' this may help attract patrons but there is nothing mysterious about the proceedings; the spectator is aware at all times of what's going on. The story is, in fact, an unconvincing mixture of melodrama and domestic tragedy, slow in action and lacking in suspense. The one redeeming feature are the performances of the players, but even their efforts are insufficient to hold one's interest throughout.

*Harrison's Reports*, 17 November 1945

*Harrison's*, by the way, was the only publication to realize *Strange Confession* was a remake of *The Man Who Reclaimed His Head*; this in an article complaining about so many remakes and how Hollywood should come up with some fresh material instead. *Strange Confession* seems to bolster their case, but the film certainly gets points for doing something different, and it's even a bit relevant given today's opioid crisis and skepticism about "Big Pharma."

Unfortunately, different does not add up to good.

**Strange Confession** - 6 October 1945 - 62 minutes

**CAST**: Lon Chaney as Jeff Carter; Brenda Joyce as Mary; J. Carrol Naish as Roger Graham; Milburn Stone as Stevens; Lloyd Bridges as Dave; Addison Richards as Dr. Williams; Mary Gordon as Mrs. O'Connor; George Chandler as Harper; Gregor Muradian as Tommy; Wilton Graf as Brandon; Francis McDonald as Hernandez; Jack Norton as Border; Christian Rub as Mr. Moore; Ian Wolfe as Frederick; David Hoffman as Inner Sanctum

**CREDITS**: Director: John Hoffman; Producer: Ben Pivar; Scenario: M. Coates Webster; Dialogue Director: Willard Holland; Assistant Directors: Seward Webb, Harry Jones; Photography: Maurie Gertsman; Art Directors: John Goodman, Abraham Grossman; Film Editor: Russell Schoengarth; Set Decoration: Russell A. Gausman, A.J. Gilmore; Costumes: Vera West; Music: Frank Skinner; Sound: Bernard Brown, Jess Moulin; Based on the 1932 play *The Man Who Reclaimed His Head* by Jean Bart

*- HN*

# *Pursuit to Algiers* (1945)

Prince Nikolas is a young aristocrat of Rovenia (an imaginary country supposedly located in one of the stranger Balkans that are accessed by the capital of Algeria) who has been educated in an English public school ("a wise move, very sound," according to Watson). His father, His Highness King Stefan, has fallen victim to a fatal attack ("a great loss to the whole democratic world" - and this time it is Holmes who is opining). In the name of the world's democracies and going against the wishes of his personal physician – who would prefer to take him fishing in Scotland – Holmes agrees to provide bodyguard service and to escort the prince back to his homeland. While the details of the mission are revealed with hyper-clever aplomb by the customers and staff of a fairly nondescript pub – ultimately the detective is led to a meeting with the Rovenian prime minister (Frederick Worlock) - Holmes is absent for a decent part of the drama. Watson assumes the role of decoy boarding a steamer - the *SS Friesland*, bearing the Swedish flag - while his partner decides to accompany the prince home on an airplane. Nevertheless, after a few minutes of footage have been run through the gate, it devolves that although the plane *has* been shot down, all is well (on the *SS Friesland*, at least), given that Holmes had also earlier boarded the steamer, together with His Highness, whom they pass off as the nephew of the good doctor. (Watson, unaware of the dual deception, is at first quite disconcerted.)

Before long, beautiful singer Sheila Woodbury (Marjorie Riordan, a Warners' starlet on loan to Universal) enters the scene, as do two men with a penchant for loudly conversing about royal bodies and sinister plans (John Abbott and Gerald Hamer). It will ultimately turn out that the gentlemen had every right to parlay in that fashion, their being archaeologists and all. Three more exceptional personages will be added to the list of suspects before the anchor is raised in Lisbon, and they will prove to be worthy of misgiving: Martin Kosleck's shifty Mirko; the apparently in-charge Gregor of Rex Evans; and the giant Gubec, played by herculean Wee Willie Davis, filling in as the thuggish type usually played by Harry Cording. We might also pause to note the mature presence of a Mrs. Agatha Dunham (Rosalind Ivan, whose real-life nickname was "Ivan the Terrible"), in whose bag Watson espies a small pistol. Yet another character - Sanford, the steward in charge of the bar (Morton Lowery) - will pass before the camera whilst bearing a cagey demeanor so many times that Watson begins to regard him with quizzical eye.

That this plot, which might have simply been a whodunit, isn't one is due to the fact that nobody does anything; at least, there is no murder onboard. Early on, Holmes notices that the cream in Nikolas's coffee appears to have curdled, a tip-off that someone has introduced "cyanic acid" into the cup. Later, Martin Kosleck's knife-hurling Mirko fails in his attempt on Holmes's life, and the detective fractures his hand with the porthole. "These porthole covers are notoriously treacherous," Holmes comments from the interior of his cabin, as he allows Mirko to gingerly withdraw his broken hand. The following morning, Watson, apparently the only physician on board, mentions at breakfast that he had attended to the now-incapacitated Mirko during the night: "He's got a nasty fracture. Took me over an hour to set." Still later - and without much effort - Holmes frustrates another attempt at Nikolas, for whom the devilish trio has prepared an explosive device in a party favor. While the quoted dialogue and the ongoing verbal exchanges between Holmes and Gregor do provide some ironic humor, they lessen the tension and weaken the menacing aspect of the characters. Due to this, they seem less like villains and more like three unruly schoolboys causing Holmes, nostalgically, to recall an adversary who truly was a worthy rival: "the late professor Moriarty was a virtuoso on the bassoon." Nonetheless, the picture's climax - with Watson's nephew in a small cabin at the mercy of his captors – offers little more than minimal tension and, by relegating the wicked trio to an off-screen fate, echoes – however distantly – the same type of outcome seen in 1939's *The Hound of the Baskervilles.*

One of the picture's more striking features is its having Watson, for the first and only time in the series, showing off his baritone register by singing the ballad "Loch Lomond" while being accompanied on the piano by Miss Woodbury. Likewise, in an effective wink to Conan Doyle's readership, the doctor also alludes to one of the many cases that went forever unwritten, that of the Giant Rat of Sumatra. And, serving as a litmus test of resigned acceptance for the most stalwart of Holmesians, the Great Consulting Detective receives a quite feminine kiss - courtesy of the lovely Miss Woodbury - after setting things aright for her. This kiss would be "the first in both written and celluloid fiction," according to Tom Weaver in **Universal Horrors**, his citation taken from a written promotional article by Roy William Neill himself in 1945. *Pursuit to Algiers* would also gain a bit of notoriety for being the second series' entry not to allow so much as a glimpse of 221b Baker Street.

**Gubec (Wee Willie Davis) has Holmes just where he wants him, as brains-of-the-outfit, Gregor (Rex Evans) flashes a pistol, just in case. Missing from the photo: Mirko, the sicarius (Martin Kosleck), and John H. Watson, MD.**

Also of note – if only because *Algiers* marks the first time we have witnessed such an array of talents/emotions on the good doctor's part – are Watson's various reactions to the women with whom he rubs elbows. In the film's first moments, while with Holmes at the fairly sordid fish-and-chips place, he sits near a solitary woman (Dorothy Kellogg) whose gestures and comments make us guess that the profession she plies may well be the oldest in the world; Watson is obviously in agreement with us. Later, aboard the steamboat, he approaches Miss Woodbury in a most friendly manner, and he continues to interact with her throughout the picture in a quite paternal manner. Lastly, he's quick to resist the advances of Mrs. Dunham, a mature and – as we have already noted – armed woman whom we supposed to be a widow

615

and, therefore, potentially again on the hunt for men of a certain age. It's a matter of record that – with a brace of definite exceptions (Irene Adler, Mary Marston) and a bit of unproven braggadocio on Watson's part (his claiming, in **The Sign of Four**, "an experience of women which extends over many nations and three separate continents") - the partners against crime were not drawn as being overly attracted to the opposite sex. Still, from the time of Conan Doyle's writing, through their many and varied cinematic interpretations, and – for the most part – up until today, most fans of Holmes and Watson have not been inclined to accept that detective and doctor possessed the capacity *to attract* the opposite sex. *Pursuit to Algiers* certainly gives those particular character fibers a good stretching.

The 26 October 1945 edition of *Film Daily* took it easy on the picture: "It is far from being one of the best of the Sherlock Holmes series." (The critique in the 31 October 1945 issue of *The Exhibitor* begged to differ: "One of the better entries in the Sherlock Holmes series... Suspense is handled nicely and several songs are included.") A bit more caustically, the March 1946 *Photoplay* asked itself: "How far away can they get from the original Sherlock Holmes story and still have Basil Rathbone and Nigel Bruce around?" before shrugging at the inevitability of the story's outcome: "So, of course, you know everything turned out as it should." *Harrison's Reports* (27 October 1945) gave it a thumbs down, classifying the film as:

> ...below par for the series. It is mild program fare at best, but it will probably get by with non-discriminating mystery fans...the action bogs down frequently because of excessive dialogue.

*Variety*'s critique - which shared a publication date with *The Exhibitor* - navigated a midway point between praise and regret: "[The] latest Sherlock Holmes from Universal will not disappoint albeit slightly below par for the course." A little tougher to agree with is the review's opinion that "suspense is maintained until last footage."

Still, one may find quite interesting the opinion of a certain Nick Raspa – a movie house owner in Riverside, West Virginia - whose professional opinion was put on record in the *Motion Picture Herald*'s column "What the Picture Did for *Me*" in its 12 October 1946 issue:

> Here is a good little mystery. As a matter of fact, it is all mystery. This is the trouble with these Holmes pictures. They don't give the people a chance to find the killer. Holmes is the only one who knows. This is the reason why this series doesn't appeal to my patrons.

Mr. Raspa's argument leaks a bit of water, as – in this entry, at least – there *is* no killer, the villains are as obvious in their presence and intent as the Marx Brothers, and we are *told* (rather than shown) that they have been apprehended and that Watson's nephew is safe. The greatest bit of sidearm snookery herein is the revelation that Prince Nikolas had been parading throughout the picture disguised as Sanford, the steward! Yes, Holmes *is* the only chap to be aware of the double-substitute, but the viewer's learning of this through the application of his own deductive powers – the core of Mr. Raspa's complaint - would have done nothing but lessen the impact of the film's only "mystery."

*Pursuit to Algiers* may well have been a letdown for those hopeful for another "canonical" tale, or a more engaging trail of clues, or – at the very least – a more obvious tie-in to the War the Allies were fighting. Some have argued that it represents the nadir of the series. Still, in the 21st Century, no stalwart aficionado of the Great Consulting Detective would shove it off to the side.

***Pursuit to Algiers*** – 26 October 1945 – 65 minutes

**CAST**: Basil Rathbone as Sherlock Holmes; Nigel Bruce as Doctor Watson; Marjorie Riordan as Sheila Woodbury; Rosalind Ivan as Agatha Dunham, Morton Lowry as Sanford; Leslie Vincent as Nikolas; Martin Kosleck as Mirko; Rex Evans as Gregor; John Abbott as Jodri; Gerald Hamer as Kingston; Wee Willie Davis as Gubec; Frederic Worlock as Prime Minister; Olaf Hytten as Simpson; Alan Edmiston as Passerby with Newspaper; James Craven as Anton Petzval (Customer in Soho Oyster House); Tom Dillon as Matthias Cherney (Owner of Soho Oyster House); Dorothy Kellogg as Woman in Soho Oyster House; Eric Mayne as Customer in Soho Oyster House; Sven Hugo Borg as Capt. Johansson; Ashley Cowan as Steward; George Leigh as Reginald "Reggie" Dane; Cap Somers as Dock Worker; Wilson Benge as Mr. Arnold (a Clergyman); Ernst Brengt as Passenger; Gregory Gaye as Ravez; John Dutra as Sailor; Curt Furburg, Charles Millsfield, Sam Savitsky, James Carlisle, Sayre Dearing as Aides

**CREDITS**: Director and Producer: Roy William Neill; Executive Producer: Howard Benedict; Screenplay: Leonard Lee; Musical Director: Edgar Fairchild; Photography: Paul Ivano; Film Editing: Saul A. Goodkin; Art Director: John B. Goodman and Martin Obzina; Set Decoration: Russell A. Gausman and Ralph Sylos; Director of Sound: Bernard B. Brown; Gowns: Vera West; Director of Make-Up: Jack P. Pierce; Dialogue Director: Raymond Kessler; Assistant Director: Seward Webb.
- *DL*

# *House of Dracula* (1945)

*Synopsis*: Baron Latos (as he is "known to the outside world") pays a 5:00am call on Dr. Franz Edelmann, seeking a cure for his "affliction." Stating that he is Count Dracula – and presenting as proof a coffin with the Dracula crest that had been mysteriously stashed in the doctor's locked basement – he tells the skeptical medico he is weary of eternal life and seeks to regain a mortal existence. From a sample of the Baron's blood, the doctor speculates that an antitoxin might be prepared return the walking undead to a state of motionless death. Meantime he prescribes a series of transfusions of his own blood into the vampire. On the occasion of the first procedure, Latos renews his acquaintance with nurse Miliza Morelle; as we first saw the Baron peering in her bedroom window, some suspicion arises as to the count's motives. Does he wish to be human again so he can woo her? or is the whole thing a ruse to insert himself into her circle? (The question, by the way, is never truly resolved.)

Larry Talbot (aka the Wolf Man) also arrives (*quelle coincidence!*) and demands to see the doctor immediately; when he's told it's not possible (said transfusion being in progress), he races out and demands to be incarcerated in the town jail. Edelmann is summoned by Police Inspector Holtz and, along with Miliza, they witness Talbot's transformation from man to beast just after the doctor has told the prisoner such a thing was not physically possible. Delivered into the doctor's care the next morning, he is told that his "curse" is due to pressure on the brain that causes him to physically become what he emotionally fears. The doctor is working with a mold that, when distilled, can soften bone; with the pressure relieved, Talbot will be cured. There is not sufficient quantity readily available for an immediate procedure, however, and so, with his familiar cry that he can't go through his full-moon horror again, Talbot hurls himself off a cliff. (Visaria has a very interesting topography that includes quicksand bogs and seaside cliffs.)

Edelmann has himself lowered down to a cave entrance and discovers a) Talbot very much alive, b) the perfect environment for growing the mold at a more rapid rate and, as an added bonus, c) the body of the Frankenstein Monster and the skeleton of Dr. Niemann, the mire they sank into in the preceding film having somehow oozed them to a location under Edelmann's house. To pass time until Talbot's operation, the doctor decides to revive the monster – "Frankenstein's challenge to science" – but gets talked out of it by his hunchbacked nurse, Nina, whose deformity is also to be rectified by the mold essence. Meanwhile Latos' motives become apparent (or he has grown impatient) when Edelmann discovers him attempting to hypnotize Miliza. The doctor temporarily deters this by calling the Baron in for another transfusion, but the vampire pulls a switcheroo and injects the doctor with his blood. Edelmann, Nina, and Talbot quash Latos' abduction of Miliza, sending him scurrying for his casket. Edelmann drags the coffin into sunlight and Latos disintegrates... again.

But the doctor now has spells where he turns into a fiend and again tries to revivify the Monster – only to be interrupted again by nosy Nina. For no good reason he kills his handyman, Siegfried. Pursued back to his castle by a mob, he manages to change back before answering the door. Suspicion falls on Talbot, but the doctor assures Holst that the possibly erstwhile lycanthrope could not have left his room post-operation. Evidence then comes to light the doctor has killed Siegfried, and a mob that includes Siegfried's brother, Steinmuhl, heads for the castle, where Talbot is stepping into the full moonlight without experiencing a hirsute transformation. Edelmann scurries off to the lab and has time to bring the Monster to full power and murder Nina – callously tossing her corpse through a trapdoor – before everyone bursts in. He pushes Holtz into some equipment that electrocutes the inspector before the doctor is shot by Talbot. The frenzied finale culminates with the Monster creating no mayhem except for his stumbling into chemicals that explode and set fire to the place. Frantic *fini* to a very busy 67 minutes.

Having found some (or, at any rate, enough) measure of success with *House of Frankenstein*, the powers that be promptly ordered up more of the same and to assure sameness even assigned some of the same personnel. Trade papers early in 1945 reported that *HoD* would have a $750,000 budget (supposedly twice that of *House of Frankenstein*) and would star Karloff and J. Carrol Naish in addition to Lon Chaney, John Carradine, et al. Obviously little of that came to pass. Chaney as the Wolf Man, Carradine as Baron Latos, and Glenn Strange as Frankenstein's Monster returned,

620

along with Lionel Atwill as a different police inspector, while writer Edward T. Lowe, Jr., director Erle C. Kenton, and cinematographer George Robinson took up their familiar positions behind the cameras. Karloff and Naish were *in absentia*. The basic plot – or plots, if you will – have scarcely changed, though there are some new wrinkles. Latos is still fixated on a single woman to his ultimate undoing; only the timeline is more extended this time round. Talbot is still seeking a cure to his condition; only this time he *does* get cured. *And* gets the girl! Latos neither gets a cure nor the girl, and neither he nor the Wolf Man claim a single victim. (In the latter case, the Production Code would not have allowed Talbot a happy ending had he killed anyone.)

**This Belgian one-sheet displays artwork that's a bit more expressionistic than Universal's usual domestic treatments. Sadly, Poni Adams' hunchback didn't make the cut.**

621

Both Latos and Talbot simply show up without even a lame attempt at explaining how they survived their respective demises in the preceding opus. Perhaps in Talbot's case – he had to be killed by silver wielded by "someone who loves him enough to care" – either Ilonka's love or her jewelry was not as pure as was necessary. We had already seen Talbot revived by the light of the silvery moon once before; possibly his corpse was just left lying in Dr. Niemann's yard, and a month later, *voila*! As to Latos' resurrection… we haven't a clue.

And, of course, the Monster spends nearly the entire film lying comatose on a massage table before becoming vertical for a few climactic moments – and even then a significant portion of his running-amok footage is cribbed from *The Ghost of Frankenstein*! This creep, too, claims not a single victim; all the murders in this entry are at the hands of Dr. Edelmann. Admittedly most of the body count in the previous film was courtesy of the hunchback, Daniel - albeit instructed by Niemann - but at least the vampire, the Wolf Man, and the Monster (inadvertently for the last) each killed *somebody*.

Also returning is the lab equipment; the same collection of Strickfaden gizmos with which Universal had been dressing its sets since *Son of Frankenstein*. Perhaps, as we are still in Visaria, in this case the stuff was acquired from Dr. Niemann's estate sale rather than from Acme's basic mad doctor package.

Even Universal couldn't just repeat the previous entry entirely (or simply reference earlier films in their respective series), so the result might be described as resembling the old wedding dictum: something old, something new, something borrowed, something blue. Obviously a new mad doctor and hunchback had to be found to add to the line-up of "monsters" – Dr. Niemann and Daniel having been put paid to (the former rather decisively) – but this doctor is not very mad (at least not initially) and the hunchback is scarcely monstrous, no matter what the posters and trailer might otherwise maintain. Nina is entirely kindhearted – even if she's somewhat prone to sticking her nose into spots where it would have been wiser not to do so.

If Nina is fairly new to the series' fans' understanding, a great part of Dr. Edelmann's split personality is borrowed from Robert Louis Stevenson's novella, "Strange Case of Dr Jekyll and Mr. Hyde," which M-G-M had released just a couple years earlier. *HoD* even nabs a scene wherein the evil personality, pursued by a mob, flees into his house's rear entrance and opens the front door as his good self. (The effect is somewhat diminished as the same trick had been used earlier when Nina disturbs Edelmann who is then juicing up the Monster; director Kenton builds and prolongs the suspense in this sequence masterfully.) This had been cribbed by M-G-M (as was a good deal else) from Rouben Mamoulian's 1931 Paramount film. Also appropriated from Mamoulian's production by Kenton was the effect of Hyde's shadow growing larger and larger on a wall as he runs away from outraged citizenry. (Kenton had already pinched this effect in his 1932 *Island of Lost Souls*, but, as both films shared the same cameraman - Karl Struss - it may have been Struss's idea and not Mamoulian's. No matter who conceived the image, Kenton makes healthy use of it here. Edelmann's large shadow also threatens to engulf Nina as she stands inside the laboratory door, interrupting yet again his attempt to revive the Monster.

While we're on the subject of cinematography, let's note that Kenton and Robinson's collaboration here is far more impressive than the relatively prosaic approach they brought to the preceding monster rally. The camera glides about the spacious laboratory and the magnificent main hall of Dr. Edelmann's castle (wonder from what film *that* was left over?), and interesting angles are found in both sets, particularly on the splendidly intricate staircase of the latter. And as there was never a master shot of the venue, we can never quite grasp the geography of the place and the result (intentionally or not) is quite disorienting. In the lab, Miliza and Nina are often photographed through shelving – indeed, Nina is often seen solitary in footage involving her; in an absolutely gorgeous shot, Miliza descends the lab stairs, her lighting coming through shelves of bottles and beakers, their outlines thrown against her and the wall. Possibly the growing number of *noir* films had pushed the pair to revert to a more German Expressionistic approach than before. If nothing else, this *House* is a visually luscious one; it is one of the things that makes it superior to its predecessor.

Also an improvement is a better integration of the star trio's stories, even if they interact only barely. Talbot is introduced shortly after Latos' arrival, and the Monster is discovered not long afterward. Talbot "meets" Latos for a nanosecond before the Baron's demise and encounters the revived Monster just long enough to topple a shelving unit of chemicals, prompting the final conflagration that is lifted from *The Ghost of Frankenstein*... meaning Chaney kills himself. But this re-purposed footage may not be Chaney's only appearance as the Monster in this movie. Edelmann has a dream sequence (another sequence possibly inspired by M-G-M's Jekyll/Hyde effort) wherein he first imagines himself doing good – correcting Nina's spinal deformity – and then unleashing the Monster to run amok. Strange is used in a snippet or two here, but a lot of this is footage taken from *Bride of Frankenstein*, the only film is which the Monster goes on a proper rampage. Except... there is one shot of Edelmann leering over a recumbent Monster that is clearly not the craggy-faced Strange, but that certainly resembles the fuller-faced Chaney. It doesn't appear to be a trick shot combining the doctor with an image from *Ghost of...*, so just what do we have here? Chaney back in the Monster makeup for a day because Strange was curiously unavailable? Your supposition is as good as ours.

Also "borrowed" is Latos' attempted seduction of Miliza at the piano as she plays the "Moonlight Sonata" (or, more accurately, the Piano Sonata No. 14 in C minor 'Quasi una fantasia', Op. 27, No. 2) and it transforms into something quite modern (but hardly eerie, save maybe to audiences of the time). This may be the only original scoring in the film (we're uncertain about some other music in the Latos section) – everything else is the cues that are quite familiar by now – and as IMDb lists the Musical Director Edgar Fairchild with "Music" as well, this is likely his contribution. The idea, of course, hails from *Dracula's Daughter* (1936), wherein Sandor urges Countess Zaleska back to the dark side. Here it also echoes Latos' seduction via signet ring in the previous *House*. It's a game attempt and certainly atmospheric but, again, not as effective as either of its inspirations.

Under the "something new" category we can list many of the actors supporting the unholy trio. Martha O'Driscoll (1922-1998) who plays Miliza (pronounced Ma-LIT-sa) Morelle had, in common with numerous "B"-product beauties of the studio era, a brief and altogether unremarkable 12-year stay in Tinseltown. She was discovered in a community theater production by Fred Astaire's frequent choreographer, Hermes Pan, and for the latter half of the 1930s played small, sometimes uncredited bits; she also managed to raise her profile by nabbing some advertising gigs. O'Driscoll's first sizable role was as Daisy Mae in the dreadful adaptation of Al Capp's *Li'Abner* (1940). Once at Universal, she appeared in a variety of films, including *Ghost Catchers* (see essay), before becoming the Wolf Man's girlfriend. Two years after *House of Dracula* – and turned loose by Universal - she made her final film, *Carnegie Hall*, one of Edgar G. Ulmer's rare "A"-budget projects. She married a prominent Chicago businessman and became active in many of that city's civic projects, including the Sarah Siddons Society; yes, there really *is* one, although the fictional organization in Joseph L. Mankiewicz's *All About Eve* was the inspiration.

Jane Adams (née Betty Jean Bierce, 1918-2014) could have studied violin on a scholarship to Juilliard, but opted instead to take acting lessons at the Pasadena Playhouse. She began her career in radio, making her first film appearances (billed as "Poni" Adams) in 1942, and she followed *House* with genre credits in the Universal serial, *Lost City of the Jungle*, and *The Brute Man* (both 1946), the latter feature handed off from Universal to PRC when the studio decided to drop "B"-product. These was followed by *Tarzan's Magic Fountain* at RKO, *Batman and Robin* (playing Vicki Vale) at Columbia, and *Master Minds* (with the Bowery Boys) at Monogram (all 1949). With her career clearly going nowhere, it was probably with some relief that she retired following her second marriage. Adams did resume her industry activity with some television work, including an episode of *Adventures of Superman*, while her husband was deployed in Korea.

As Steinmuhl, the role that would have normally gone to Dwight Frye had he not shuffled off his mortal coil two years earlier, we have Skelton Knaggs (born Skelton Barnaby Knaggs – yes, Virginia, it really *was* his birth name – 1911-1955) on temporary leave from RKO, where he did most of his best-remembered work. After some time in the legitimate theater, he started working in British quota quickies in 1936, but moved up to prestige projects such as Michael Powell's *The Spy in Black* (1939, in support of Conrad Veidt), before jumping the pond and landing that same year in Victor Haplerin's *Torture Ship*, along with Lyle Talbot, Irving Pichel, and Julie Bishop, at PRC. He is uncredited as Finn, the mute who narrates (in voice-over) Val Lewton's *The Ghost Ship* (Mark Robson, 1943) as he is in *The Lodger*, *The Scarlet Claw*, *The Invisible Man's Revenge* (all 1944), *The Picture of Dorian Gray*, and *Isle of the Dead* (both 1945). He remained at Universal after *HoD* for *Terror by Night* and then hied off to Columbia for a "Crime Doctor" entry before returning to RKO, reuniting with Lewton and Robson for *Bedlam* (1946) and then appearing in two "Dick Tracy" entries, ... *vs Cueball* (also 1946) and ... *Meets Gruesome* (1947), where he was once again in support of Boris Karloff.

After joining Adams to encounter the Bowery Boys (the ultimate horror, according to some), he began alternating television with (mostly uncredited) film work. Two episodes of the *Dick Tracy* show and several of *Boston Blackie* are his genre and nigh-genre credits on the cathode-ray tube. His final two films before his death (at the age of 43 from cirrhosis of the liver) were *Son of Sinbad* and Fritz Lang's *Moonfleet* (both 1955). Knaggs' gaunt face is so familiar in films of the 1940s that it's a bit of a shock to realize how rarely he received an onscreen credit. *House of Dracula* is one of those rare times, and his Steinmuhl is either an example of very bad acting or a masterful portrayal of the kind of kvetching, self-important dimwit we have all come to know too well (and who, by the way, is always right in his assumptions). Both opinions have been expressed; we lean toward the latter while also noting that a liberal application of alcohol may have informed his performance.

Ludwig Stössel (1883-1973) is just possibly best remembered as the image of "That little ole winemaker, me" in a long-running series of commercials in the 1960s;

(his was the image only, as he was dubbed by Jim Backus!). Stössel began performing on Austrian and German stages when he was 17 years of age, and he made his first film in Germany in 1926. He then emigrated to Britain in 1940 (not before adding Fritz Lang's 1933 *Das Testament des Dr. Mabuse* to his many German film credits), and then on to Hollywood that same year. While he gave many memorable performances in "A" films – such as Mr. Leuchtag ("What watch?" "Such watch!") in *Casablanca* (Michael Curtiz, 1942) – his genre credits are few. He played Turhan Bey's uncle in *The Climax*, was a member of the featured cast in Edgar G. Ulmer's *Bluebeard* (both 1944), and appeared in Byron Haskin's *From the Earth to the Moon* (1958) on the big screen. As was the case with many character actors, he found much of his work in television beginning in the 1950s; his genre credits there included two episodes of *Science Fiction Theater* and the infamous failed pilot, *Tales of Frankenstein*.

**Onslow Stevens tussles with Lon Chaney's Wolf Man, but it's John Carradine's Dracula he needs to watch out for. Stevens' vigorous performance as the Jekyll/Hyde medico is one of the film's strong points.**

But chief amongst the newbies - in fact, the real star of the show - is Onslow Stevens (born Onslow Ford Stevenson, 1902-1977), though he wasn't precisely a stranger to the genre or even to Universal, for that matter. Back in 1933, he'd appeared in Kurt Neumann's *Secret of the Blue Room* – not exactly a horror, but included in the "Shock Theater" package – the studio's serial, *The Vanishing Shadow* (1934), which would be rejiggered into the 1939 serial *The Phantom Creeps* starring Bela Lugosi, and the based-on-a-true-story "horror," *Life Returns* (1935), with Valerie Hobson. (To be fair this was a Universal release, not actually one of their own productions.) In 1941 he appeared in the shamefully underrated *The Monster and the Girl* (directed by Stuart Heisler) with George Zucco in one of his plummier roles, but afterwards in no other horrors until his masterful turn as Dr. Edelmann. The kindly persona we encounter at the beginning of the picture may not seem like much of a turn, but when his evil self takes control, the madness radiating from his eyes is truly scary – and let's face it, the Universal horrors of the 1940s had little that was actually frightening; Stevens' tense scene in the wagon with Stössel is the high point of the movie.

On a purely technical level his timing in the scene where he watches his reflection fade away, matching his movements perfectly with matted in footage he cannot actually see, is immaculate. (This might be the time to mention another mirror scene beautifully pulled off by John Fulton and his crew: the scene with a reflection-less Baron Latos enticing Miliza into the garden. And Latos' bat-to-man transformations are an improvement over the previous film.) Stevens also appears to be doing a fair amount of his own stunt work while being lowered into the seaside cave and whilst running about Visaria after murdering Seigfried. More genre would follow with *Angel on my Shoulder* (1946), *Night Has a Thousand Eyes*, *The Creeper* (both 1948), *Them!* (1954), and his final film, the Robert Bloch-scripted *The Couch* (1960). At the risk of seeming like a broken record, Stevens' work was increasingly in television as the 1950s waxed, but none of his appearances were in genre fare. It is reported that during this period alcoholism impinged on his ability to work. His death came from pneumonia following a broken hip that seems to have resulted from mistreatment in a nursing home.

Of our returning principals, Carradine, Chaney, Atwill, and Strange are all dealt with elsewhere in this book. Chaney was released from Universal after completing work on this film (making reports that the studio planned to do it all over yet again questionable). The studio had likely tired of his heavy drinking and the problematic behavior that resulted. Indeed, he looks quite haggard here except when carefully lit; any and all traces of leading man's looks are gone, if he ever had any (opinions vary). Chaney would freelance with reasonable success in an assortment of comedies and dramas thereafter. Lionel Atwill was probably already quite ill and would pass away a few months after completing this feature. He died of lung cancer while in the midst of shooting the Universal serial, *Lost City of the Jungle*. Carradine "… in a woeful frame of mind and a fearsome blue make-up…" told King Features syndicated writer Harrison Carroll, in a column dated the 19 October 1945, that he was appearing in the "hunk of junk" yclept *House of Dracula* because he was a "victim of alimony." Still, Carroll notes, "John says that about everything but Shakespeare, so don't let it keep you from seeing the picture, which will have a lot of thrills and chills." Carroll's piece confirms our supposition that it was Fairchild who took Beethoven and "... warp(ed) it to the desired effect." For some reason he refers to the composer as "Cookie" Fairchild.

As to "something blue," well, the Code was still in effect so the closest we get is a very chaste clinch between Miliza and Larry after the full moon doesn't have its usual deleterious effect.

One thing that distinguishes the Universal horrors of the 1940s (the World War II years) from the Laemmle-era productions (essentially the Depression years), is that here the monsters are usually under the control of someone else; it may be a mad doctor or a broken necked blacksmith or the high priest of an obscure cult, but they are rarely self-determining. Even Count Alucard is manipulated, albeit unbeknownst to him, as is Latos, to an extent following Niemann's agenda in the initial *House*; of the studio's recurring characters, only the Wolf Man lacks an evil master. In something of a transition to the studio's genre productions of the 1950s – termed science fiction, but rarely more than good, old-fashioned monster movies with some scientific (or, rather, pseudo-scientific) trappings – the emphasis of the Standard Capital years is increasingly on science of one kind or another. In *The Wolf Man*, Larry Talbot is told that his belief he changes into an animal is all in his mind, something that is repeated by Dr. Frank Mannering in the sequel; it reappears here and his cure is effected by a cranial operation that ends the belief becoming a reality. So much for his lycanthropic condition being caused by the bite of another werewolf. Similarly, a scientific cure is attempted on Baron Latos – a cure which might have been successful for all we know if he hadn't terminated it – courtesy of an antitoxin prepared from his own peculiar blood. But the shift from supernatural to scientific and from free agent to minion goes somewhat deeper and is best expressed by R. H. W. Dillard in his book, **Horror Films**, wherein he examines in detail a half-dozen features from various eras.

> The early horror films, those made in Germany between 1913 and 1931 and the major American horror films of the 1930s, were openly metaphysical in their concerns, even when those concerns were also social and political... all of these films, along with Carl Dreyer's *Vampyr*, were fully committed to an exploration of essential human nature, or what it means to be an individual human being, free in a complex and mysterious world to choose between an understanding of that world which is creative or decreative, to choose, in other words, between the darkness or the light.

> The films of the 1940s, which were mainly American, reduced the

range of that parabolic    quest from the spirit to the flesh, from the metaphysical to the psychological... the films of the 1940s defined the human being primarily as a physical as opposed to spiritual being. The human psyche was no longer capable of the metaphysical yearning and force of a Henry Frankenstein, but rather became the victim of mental aberration, which should be cured... *The Wolf Man* (is) cast in the terms of a Freudian psychological understanding, and in... *Son of Dracula*, Kay's morbid psychology which predisposes her to vampirism is more truly the heart of the film than Count Alucard... Even Frankenstein's monster is reduced to a medical problem in his film appearances from *Son of Frankenstein* to *House of Dracula*, and in the latter of those films Larry Talbot is finally cured of his lycanthropic problems by an operation on his skull. (1)

Reviews of the time did not probe as deeply as Dillard – no one would see these films as more than entertaining junk for many decades – and, as usual, the trades were more disposed to treat the production as entertainment aimed at a specific demographic, even though they weren't appreciably more impressed.

Universal has reassembled its old hobgoblin league... and a ghoulish time maybe had by all hardy souls who venture into the Rialto these days... Frankenstein's monster is resurrected briefly, only to be destroyed again when the evil house goes up in flames. But don't worry, folks, you can count on Universal pulling the monster from the embers just as soon as they cool off. Frankenstein's little boy doesn't die easily.

And, unfortunately, neither does this kind of cinematic nightmare.
T. M. P., *The New York Times*, 22 December 1945

These strange and weird characters cause thrills and chills... This film fulfills the requirements for a satisfactory motion picture... The musical background in the typical eerie vein... adds to the strangeness of the atmosphere."
Unsigned, *Motion Picture Herald*, 8 December 1945

WITH ITS GALAXY OF MONSTERS THIS ONE PROMISES A FEAST FOR LOVERS OF HORROR FILMS
... a horror picture to end horror pictures... All the prized stock situations so dear to the creators of shockers have been dumped into

the footage to make a Roman holiday for those who have a taste for this sort of entertainment... Erle C. Kenton's direction is ordinary while Paul Malvern, working under Executive Producer Joe Gershenson, has produced the film in a haphazard manner.

Unsigned, *Film Daily*, 3 December 1945

The passing decades add perspective, and we think the late Ken Hanke's assessment is a fairer and more perceptive one.

>...actually one of the studio's more interesting 1940s efforts... *House of Dracula* is better integrated, and altogether more atmospheric and effective (than *House of Frankenstein*) – with a terrific performance from Onslow Stevens... a distinct improvement in almost every way— despite the fact that it has even less budget... the structure is tighter, but there's a trade-off there, since there's never even any attempt at an explanation of just how Dracula and Larry Talbot have come back from their seemingly pretty final deaths in the last film. They're just there... The only monster whose presence is explained is the Frankenstein Monster, who— somewhat absurdly—has floated on an underground flow of mud to a cave underneath Edelman's castle... The whole Wolf Man angle is much more interesting this round, even if it's light on mayhem. That was probably somewhat dictated by the production code, since it was impossible to give old Larry a happy ending if he killed anyone. (Those killings in earlier movies apparently don't matter.) ... the big improvement lies in Larry becoming less of a gloomy Gus as a werewolf looking at the prospect of being cured from his curse. At least here he manages to keep the dreariness of the character at bay for most of the picture...There's no denying that *House of Dracula* has flaws all its own, but it's hardly the worst thing Universal brought out in the 1940s—and it's blessed with the kind of simple studio artistry that would very soon be a thing of the past.

Ken Hanke, *Ashville Mountain Xpress*, 17 January 2012

Perhaps it's an impression formed by hindsight – it was surely not intentional – but there's an air of finality to *House of Dracula*. It isn't just because the Wolf Man is cured of his monthly curse – the studio could have found a way around that if they chose (or maybe they'd just take the easy way out and ignore the ending of this film, too) – but having run out of ideas for individual tales of their star monsters, they'd quickly squeezed all the juice out of the monster rally approach. What next? What possibly could be done next? Another inadequately hinged physician who, in serendipitous fashion, becomes acquainted with the threesome and happens to be entangled with a hunchback and provides the connective plot tissue for the monsters to trudge through their familiar storylines yet again? Perhaps Kharis would be added to the mix (as was reportedly initially planned for the first *House*) and everyone would show up in Egypt... or Mapleton... or to wherever the Scripps Museum has relocated? Perhaps a *House of the Wolf Man* would have resembled the plot of *Abbott & Costello Meet Frankenstein* without the supposed comedy, but still with Count Dracula seeking to have the Monster revived for some nefarious purpose and with Larry Talbot as a lupine hero. (The comedians' vehicle *does* essentially follow the template of the *House* films and acts as an unofficial sequel.)

Beyond the plot content, there's the lack of the familiar Jimmy McHugh fanfare under the chrome globe, with its revolving lucite letters (one of the greatest, if not the greatest, movie studio logos of all time). Consider that the title music – Frank Skinner's overture for *Son of Frankenstein* – begins under the logo, thus starting the film off as it did in *Son*, which was made before the logo was introduced. Of course, that music had been repurposed to a few other productions along over the years, but the effect here is of things having come full circle. And there are no end credits, which had been a staple of Universal films since the silent days. Was this cast not worth repeating? The familiar supporting cast faces, aside from Atwill – Michael Mark, Harry Cording, Doris Lloyd, et al – are missing. Universal is supposed to have kept a list of which of its contract players were to be cast in its horror movies, but they're not to be found here. And, of course, there's no Evelyn Ankers, no Anne Gwynne (imagine *them* as Miliza and Nina). There would be a few more horrors before Universal decided to shut down all "B" production, but this feels very much like the end of the line.

It certainly was for the creepy three.

*Sic transit gloria mundi.*

*House of Dracula* - 7 December 1945 - 67 minutes

**CAST:** Lon Chaney Jr. (Lawrence Talbot / The Wolf Man (as Lon Chaney), John Carradine (Dracula / Baron Latos), Martha O'Driscoll (Miliza Morelle), Lionel Atwill (Police Inspector Holtz), Onslow Stevens (Dr. Franz Edelmann), Jane Adams (Nina), Ludwig Stössel (Siegfried – as Ludwig Stossel), Glenn Strange (The Frankenstein Monster), Skelton Knaggs (Steinmuhl). The following are all uncredited: Joseph E. Bernard as Brahms – Coroner; Fred Cordova as Gendarme; Carey Harrison as Gendarme; Boris Karloff as Frankenstein Monster in dream sequence, archive footage; Gregory Marshall as Johannes; Jane Nigh as Villager, unconfirmed; Dick Dickinson, Robert Robinson, Harry Lamont, Anne G. Sterling, Ruth Sterling as Villagers

**CREDITS**: Executive Producer – Joseph Gershenson (as Joe Gershenson), Producer – Paul Malvern, Music – William Lava and William Fairchild (uncredited), Director of Photography – George Robinson, Film Editing – Russell F. Schoengarth (as Russell Schoengarth), Art Direction – John B. Goodman and Martin Obzina, Set Decoration – Russell A. Gausman and Arthur D. Leddy, Costume Design – Vera West (Gowns), Makeup Department – Carmen Dirigo (Hair Stylist), Jack P. Pierce (Makeup Artist), Second Unit Director or Assistant Director – Ralph Slosser, Assistant Director – William Tummel (uncredited), Sound Department – Bernard B. Brown (Director of Sound), Jess Moulin (Sound Technician), Visual Effects - John P. Fulton (Special Photography), Stunts – Carey Loftin (stunt double Onslow Stevens, uncredited), Music Department – Edgar Fairchild (Musical Director), Paul Dessau, Charles Henderson, Charles Previn, Hans J. Salter, Paul Sawtell, Frank Skinner (composers stock music, uncredited), stand-in: Lon Chaney Jr. – Walter De Palma (uncredited)

*- HHL*

# *Pillow of Death* (1945)

*Synopsis*: Lawyer Wayne Fletcher and his secretary Donna Kincaid are in love, but Fletcher is married. He promises Donna that he will divorce his wife Vivian. Donna lives with her eccentric and wealthy aunt Belle and Belle's brother Sam. Belle is a believer in spiritualism and often consults Julian Julian, a medium. Belle disapproves of her niece's relationship with Fletcher and tries to break them up. Next-door neighbor Bruce Malone, who is smitten with Donna and often spies on her, sneaks into the Kincaid home via a passageway that is connected to his house.

Vivian is found smothered to death, and while police captain McCracken suspects Fletcher, he has no proof. Julian conducts a seance during which the voice of Vivian accuses her husband of murder. Fletcher dismisses the whole thing as a fraud cooked up by Bruce and Julian, and it is later discovered that Julian was once a ventriloquist.

In rapid succession, both Sam and Belle are found dead, smothered by a pillow. Fletcher begins hearing Vivian's voice and discovers her tomb is empty. McCracken seems to have shifted his suspicions to Julian, but releases him from custody just in time for the medium to prevent Fletcher and Donna from being murdered by crazed Cousin Amelia, the housekeeper.

Fletcher and Donna discover Vivian's corpse in the passageway, and Bruce admits having stolen the body to try to coerce a confession out of Fletcher. Donna overhears Fletcher talking to his dead wife and learns that he is a psychopath and that he is responsible for all the murders. Urged on by Vivian's voice, Fletcher tries to kill Donna, but she is saved by McCracken and Bruce. Obeying Vivian's commands, Fletcher jumps out the window to his death. Bruce and Donna get together, and McCracken thanks Julian for his help on the case.

His help on the case? What exactly did Julian do? Audiences must certainly have been puzzled, but it's unlikely anyone stayed for a second viewing to try to figure things out. And how on earth did Bruce - a stalker and a grave robber, for God's sake - end up with Donna? Universal must have been desperate to have the usual romantic clinch end the film.

The last of the undistinguished "Inner Sanctum" series, *Pillow of Death* differs from its five predecessors in several ways. For one, the usual introduction with David Hoffman's head floating in the glass is missing. Lon Chaney, instead of being the innocent victim of some sort of frame-up, is actually guilty, a switch that a few reviewers appreciated (though the list of other possible suspects is pretty small). Usually, Chaney's inner monologues consisted of him talking to himself, but here he carries on a conversation with his dead wife, who likely represents the other part of his split personality rather than an actual ghost. If she were a real spook and were controlling his behavior, why would she urge him to kill off the Kincaid family (except perhaps for Donna)? No attempt is made to explain Fletcher's motives. It might make sense that his other self would try to free himself of his wife in order to marry Donna and likewise kill the disapproving Belle, but why smother Samuel, the cynical old coot who is sympathetic to Fletcher? Apparently, it's enough to know that Fletcher is a psychopathic killer (as Vivian's voice helpfully points out), and that's all the rationale he needs. This is sloppy writing even for a series not given to coherence and logic.

The idea of a ventriloquist using his voice-throwing abilities in a seance is admittedly unusual, but nothing comes of it. Did scenarist George Bricker perhaps consider having Julian imitate Vivian in the graveyard in order to drive Fletcher to confess? Nor is it clear whether the redundantly named medium is a genuine psychic or just a clever fraud; the film *seems* to lean towards the latter - especially given J. Edward Bromberg's performance - but such annoying ambiguities are typical of the series as a whole.

Understandably, the murders aren't shown, but they could at least have been suggested (though I imagine watching a pillow slowly moving towards the camera wouldn't have been very scary; still, they got away with something like that in *Invisible Ghost*). As it stands, very little suspense is generated. Actually, the most effective sequence is when Amelia, not wrapped too tightly to begin with but driven completely batty by the deaths of her cousins, becomes convinced that Fletcher and Donna are guilty of the murders and locks them in a closet which she prepares to turn into an improvised gas chamber. The couple realizes, much to their horror, that she could

636

easily succeed. A longer sequence would have built up more tension, but it ends too quickly here with Julian's timely intervention. And, typical of the script's lack of logic, Amelia just trots off unhindered, no one apparently minding that a dangerous lunatic is on the loose!

**Although Chaney can't bear to look, detective Wilton Graff and sexton J. Farrell MacDonald discover that the body of Lon's wife has disappeared in a particularly absurd plot development. MacDonald played in hundreds of movies, often as an Irish cop.**

The script listlessly shuffles out the usual *clichés* - an old mansion, secret passageways, a seance, a lonely graveyard, spectral voices - but with little conviction. However, to quote one critic, Jerome Ash's cinematography "gives an inconsequential item a photographic treatment of which it is not deserving."

Director George W. Fox started as an assistant director in the Silent Era, but by the '30s had moved up the ladder and subsequently helmed many Westerns. He is best remembered by fans of vintage horror for two of Bela Lugosi's Monogram Nine epics, *The Corpse Vanishes* and *Bowery at Midnight*, films that are jaw-dropping in their straight-faced craziness but very entertaining, in contrast to *Pillow of Death* which, while not much more believable, is no fun at all.

As usual for the series, Lon Chaney acts troubled and a bit lost. His performance remains much the same when he is revealed as a madman with nary a glint of murderous lunacy in his eyes. Brenda Joyce as Donna pretty much walks through her thankless role.

The supporting cast is a bit livelier.

The ill-named Belle, grumpy and frumpy, is played by Clara Blandick, whose claim to movie immortality is doubtless her Auntie Em of *Wizard of Oz* (one week's work for which she was paid $750).(1) Blandick had a distinguished Broadway career in the late '20s, but traded the Great White Way for Hollywood in the early '30s and there remained, playing in countless movies (many for M-G-M), but often uncredited. Belle has none of Auntie Em's warmth, being straight-laced and humorless; she is often the foil for her brother Samuel's jibes.

Samuel is portrayed by George Cleveland, "Gramps" of the early episodes of TV's *Lassie* and supporting or bit player in dozens of films in the '30s and '40s. Samuel is a typical Cleveland role: curmudgeonly, likable, a tad salty. He brings some much-needed humor to the dreary proceedings here and is killed off a bit too early.

Rosalind Ivan delivers the best performance of the film as loony Cousin Amelia. Ivan worked on Broadway as both as an actress and a writer/translator (adapting **The Brothers Karamazov** and **Nju** to the American stage). Her career on the boards had stalled by the '40s, but was revived with a role in *The Corn is Green* (which she repeated for the film version in 1942). In movies she's best remembered as the relentlessly shrewish wife of Charles Laughton in *The Suspect* and the equally insufferable spouse of Edward G. Robinson in *Scarlet Street*.

Oddly enough, Fletcher's wife Vivian is never shown, but her voice was provided by Victoria Horne. (The actress is not credited in the film, but several reviews list her in the cast; was she cut out after a brief appearance?) Horne was about as glamorous as Margaret Hamilton, but she might have been more believable as Chaney's spouse than the young lovelies irresistibly - and unbelievably - attracted to the Lonster in the other "Inner Sanctum" films. Horne's film career consisted of mostly uncredited bits, but she did have a good role in the whimsical *Harvey* (1950). That same year, Horne married beloved comic actor Jack Oakie. After his death in 1978, Horne dedicated herself to preserving his memory and wrote several books about his life and career.

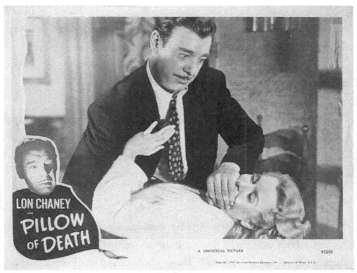

**Brenda Joyce discovers the hard way that Lon Chaney is *not* the man she though
he was.**

Not surprisingly, there was little enthusiasm for *Pillow of Death* from reviewers in
the Big Apple. T.M.P.'s comments for the 23 January 1946 edition of *The New York
Times* were typical:

> It's an old plot line Universal is pursuing with dogged earnestness
> and studied banality so perhaps the charitable act this morning would be
> to dismiss the subject without further ado. An expression of sympathy
> might however might be extended to Lon Chaney, Brenda Joyce, J.
> Edward Bromberg and Rosalind Ivan, who are certainly deserving of
> more considerate treatment from Universal.

The one exception to this was Ruth Thirer of *The New York Post* who was impressed
with the film's ability to keep the audience mystified as to the killer's identity: "Credit
Wallace Fox for this and George Bricker for making an entirely theatrical, but
nevertheless startlingly persuasive script out of Dwight V. Babcock's Inner Sanctum
original."

York of the 7 January 1946 edition of *The Independent Film Bulletin* agreed:

One of the better Inner Sanctum programmers, *Pillow of Death* will keep mystery fans guessing until the surprise denouement. It's very obvious but effectively photographed and exceptionally well- played.

The rest of the trade papers were largely indifferent.

The picture is earmarked for audiences with no defense against the melodrama virus... The story makes no pretense of being convincing.... The direction of Wallace Fox is one of the weaknesses of the picture. The acting is spotty, helping little to bring conviction to the film.

*Film* Daily, 14 September 1945

Ordinary program fare. It may serve as a supporting feature in theaters whose audiences like chilling mystery stories, regardless of whether or not they make sense. Those who demand some semblance of logic in stories will be either amused or bored by the lack of it in this tale about a psychopathic murderer.

*Harrison's Reports*, 15 December 1945

*Variety's* "Brog" liked it a bit more:

'Pillow of Death' measures up to the program murder mystery demands and is an okay supporting feature. Production mounting is adequate and direction unfolds plot of psychopathic killer in good fashion. Chaney and Miss Joyce deliver in okay fashion. Cleveland is excellent as are Clara Blandick, Rosalind Ivan, J. Edward Bromberg and Wilton Graf.

12 December 1945

Universal did not renew Lon Chaney's contract, no doubt realizing that the horror genre was petering out and they had no further use for the "master character actor" who had helped make it so popular in the war years.

***Pillow of Death*** - 14 December 1945 - 65 minutes (ST)


**CAST:** Lon Chaney as Wayne Fletcher; Brenda Joyce as Donna Kincaid; J. Edward Bromberg as Julian Julian; Rosalind Ivan as Amelia Kincaid; Clara Blandick as Belle Kincaid; George Cleveland as Samuel Kincaid; Wilton Graf as Captain McCracken; Bernard Thomas as Bruce Malone; J. Farrell McDonald as Sexton; Victoria Horne as the voice of Vivian.


**CREDITS:** Director: George W. Fox; Producer: Ben Pivar; Screenplay: George Bricker; Original Story: Dwight V. Babcock; Dialogue Director: George Bricker; Photography: Jerome Ash; Art Directors: John Goodman, Abraham Grossman; Film Editor: Edward Curtis; Set Decoration: Russell A. Gausman, Leigh Smith; Costumes: Vera West; Music: Frank Skinner; Sound: Bernard V. Brown; Jess Moulin; Visual Effects: John P. Fulton


***Shock Theater*** Catalog No. 729: "Suspense holds the stage when a demented killer terrifies a whole city as he eludes a baffled police department. See 'Pillow of Death' starring Lon Chaney, the *Shock Theater* film presentation over this channel (day), (date), at (time) for the tops in thrills see 'Pillow of Death'."


*- HN*

# *Terror by Night* (1946)

A voice-over, this time anonymous (a previous film in the series, *The Woman in Green*, began with the narration of Inspector Gregson), takes a moment to familiarize us with the "Star of Rhodesia" (the former name of the current Zimbabwe), a diamond that leads to the death of whoever possesses it. The story literally and metaphorically starts in Euston station, where Holmes is charged with escorting the latest owner of the precious stone, Lady Margaret Carstairs (Mary Forbes), so that she and it both arrive safe and sound in Edinburgh. Prior to this, a young woman (Renee Godfrey - wife of director Peter Godfrey - who would climb from uncredited roles at RKO and protagonists at Poverty Row studios to *femme fatale* here in the Universal series) arrives at a carpentry shop. She intends to place an order with the woodcraft artisan (the robust Harry Cording) for the construction of a coffin in which to transport her deceased mother to Scotland for burial.

The first reel consists of the requisite introduction of the suspects but, before we can discover much about any of them, the first victim falls dead, and we immediately understand that what we've been given is a *whodunit* that will unfold on the rails. Watson once again take the lead during the more comic moments, such as his attempt to interrogate a suspicious mathematician (Frederic Warlock) or his premature deduction regarding a neurotic passenger (Gerald Hamer, in his fifth and last appearance in the Holmes series). Despite there being a number of passengers filling the required role of red herring, we can pretty quickly guess the villain's identity. And perhaps recognizing that fans of this series are anything but naive, scenarist Frank Gruber has the Great Consulting Detective announce early on his feeling that Colonel Sebastian Moran will be the one who is after the jewel; shortly thereafter the camera reveals to us the identity of the colonel, as well as his hit man (a brief but threatening appearance by the diminutive Skelton Knaggs, in what might be a nod to the undersized Tonga of **The Sign of the Four**). Said character carries a kind of silent pistol that fires a poisoned dart, perhaps yet another tribute, this time to "The Adventure of the Empty House," wherein Moran would shoot at the young Ronald Adair with a type of silencer.

It doesn't take long before the next victim is produced, but that moment in the passenger carriage is cut off and the viewer is shunted into the luggage wagon, where Holmes discovers that the funeral casket, besides transporting its cold occupant, has a secret compartment in which the murderer was supposedly hidden. One or two stewards will suffer the consequences of a distraction or of being in the wrong place. As with the first murder, director Roy William Neill suggests each attack to the viewer via brief but precise images. In one instance, we see the body of the murderer, but not his face; in another, we see a face in the foreground, but it is that of the victim and the fatal dart is in its neck. In homing in on the discovery of the cadavers, the camera resorts to the level of a wobbling seat or the open back doors of the last carriage. In another tension-filled scene, the murderer tries to push Holmes out of the train, placing him in a very dangerous position (fairly rare for the detective, at least until Downey, Jr).

The climax contains just the right balance of mystery and narrative speed (crucial if the viewer is not to start asking questions about the internal logic of this or that action of the characters). In his final explanation as to how he succeeded in detecting the imposture of the fake inspector, in addition to his usual display of almost superhuman powers of observation, he also demonstrates a sense of humor: "I forgot to mention," he says, "that I also happen to know the real Inspector MacDonald of the Edinburgh police," the sort of reasoning that leads us to the sort of explanations typical of Don Adams' Maxwell Smart.

Scenarist Frank Gruber was a sort of pieceworker, accustomed to working on dozens of stories a month which earned him about ¾ of a cent per word. Certain elements of the story came from Conan Doyle's "The Adventure of the Empty House," but the majority of the screenplay was based on an original idea by Gruber. A nice change from previous treatments was the alteration of the intellectual and dynamic range of Watson and Lestrade: each one of their jokes and disconcerting mannerisms was permitted, but – at the same time – they were allotted a part of the responsibility in the action scenes. Showing both men to be capable here – rather than comically capricious – is something of a 180 from previous presentations. The, too, the emphasis on alternating interiors with stock footage of trains crossing the nocturnal forest at full steam or an anonymous coal-man feeding the locomotive's boilers provides, as the majority of current critics observe, that touch of vertigo that works well with the series' normally quick transitions.

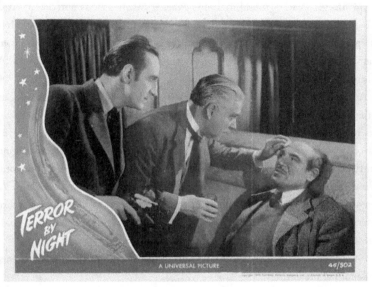

**Professor Moriarity is *in absentia* here, but his chief henchman, Colonel Sebastian Moran (Alan Mowbray), makes the cut... as does the affable Inspector Lestrade (Dennis Hoey). Tending to Lestrade's cut is Dr. Watson, as Holmes looks on.**

Some reviewers note the similarity of plot with *Pursuit to Algiers*, which took place almost entirely aboard ship. Granted, Sherlock Holmes' having agreed in the first place to accompany someone/something/*anything anywhere* leads the cognoscenti to understand immediately that, for the Great Consulting Detective, it was either that rather pedestrian task or the needle. The assumption of false identities in order to carry out (or prevent) nefarious deeds – we've Colonel Sebastian Moran riding the rails here, as opposed to Prince Nikolas getting a taste of the working man's routine on the *SS Friesland* – can be found in any number of earlier series entries, albeit it is usually Holmes who's done up in unfamiliar regalia. The supposed guilt of members of the featured cast – please refer to the pair of archaeologists glared at suspiciously in *Algiers* - is handled superlatively here: again, Nigel Bruce's inept interview of Frederic Worlock – the actor himself a leftover from the previous film - is a joy and

645

the aforementioned Gerald Hamer (and Janet Murdoch, portraying his wife) cannot help but confess to their crime: snatching a teapot!. Still, given that conventional wisdom maintains that there are but seven basic plots, the elements incorporated herein extend beyond *Terror by Night*'s immediate predecessor. The "Star of Rhodesia" has the "Borgia Pearl" - found in 1944's *Pearl of Death* – as its antecedent, as does Gruber's initial obfuscation of the murderer's face. Nonetheless, the "railroad" Holmes – as opposed to his "shipboard" self - seems to be more fully committed and is more dynamic; perhaps Gruber was looking to eclipse the previous film's premises. And, with the "body count," he succeeded.

At the film's premiere, the critics displayed a wide range of subjective appreciation for the genre. Gene Arneel, reviewer for *Motion Picture Daily*, noted the picture's debts to its forerunners: "*Terror by Night* clings closely to the general pattern of its predecessors. It is good, fairly substantial melodrama, although lacking in originality in story development." (28 January 1946) "The Sherlock Holmes series does not gain any stature with this latest offering," opined the 2 February 1946 *Showmen's Trade Review*, "for it hasn't the action and suspense one expects to find in these murder-mysteries." The anonymous reviewer concluded that "the story is too thin to hold the interest or build up suspense, and the solution a little too obvious."

Nevertheless, the reviewer at *Film Daily* (4 February 1946) appears to have seen a different picture entirely:

> Taking its place among the best of the series, *Terror by Night* enhances its suspense by limiting its locale and acquires a good measure of conviction...The picture profits from the restraint exercised in devising its melodramatics.

One critic who was entirely optimistic was writing for the 26 January 1946 edition of *Harrison's Reports:*

> Those who have enjoyed the other pictures in the series will probably enjoy also this one, for the action is pretty exciting and, for the most part, mystifying... One's interest is held pretty well, for suspicion is directed at several of the characters and it is not until the finish that the guilty person's identity is divulged.

We pause momentarily to note that the practice of directing suspicion at secondary characters is pretty much par for the series' course, and that it is highly unlikely that any viewer with more than minimal familiarity with the Rathbone/Bruce entries would be surprised by the revelation of the guilty person's identity.

*Terror by Night* marks the first – and only – series entry graced by the presence of Alan Mowbray, decorated veteran of the Great War and one of the founding members of the Screen Actors' Guild. The London-born actor found his place early on in the movies, making his debut in Michael Curtiz's comedy, *God's Gift to Women*, in 1931, and appearing regularly thereafter on screens of all sizes until his death in 1969. Mowbray's versatility saw his rather aristocratic persona involved in films of every category, and he was featured in two early sound Holmes efforts – Clive Brook's *Sherlock Holmes* (1932) and Reginald Owen's *A Study in Scarlet* (1933) – before confronting Basil Rathbone in the picture under discussion. Pretty much ubiquitous cinematically – the actor was seen in over 150 feature films in the course of his career, with only two (2) uncredited parts along the way - he did participate in a handful of pictures near and dear to our hearts: 1934's *Charlie Chan in London*, 1935's *Night Life of the Gods*, 1937's *Topper* (and the following year's *Topper Takes a Trip*), *I Wake Up Screaming* (1941), *The Phantom of 42nd Street* (1945), and 1949's *Abbott and Costello Meet the Killer, Boris Karloff*. American audiences accustomed to adjusting rabbit ears on their TV consoles in the early '50s might well remember the actor (working hard at conning those who would con others, alongside his partner, Frank Jenks) as *Colonel Humphrey Flack* for the DuMont Television Network.

As Sebastian Moran – also a colonel, albeit a damned sight more menacing – Mowbray is avuncular (at least when pretending to be Watson's old pal from school, Major Duncan Bleek), alert and helpful (offering a solution to the problem at hand), and cold-blooded (ejecting Holmes from the moving train car). It's a good performance, with a well-earned gasp when Skelton Knagg's Sands blows the whistle on the Major's... *ummmm*... the Colonel's identity shortly after making his way out of the Carstairs casket. As for Knaggs himself, please see our coverage on *House of Dracula*.

It's fitting to allow the Bible of Show Business the last word(s) on this non-canonical tale:

> This one follows the usual production pattern of the previous Sherlock Holmes mysteries from Universal. It is standard for the series and will pay off in okay style. Roy William Neill, as producer-director,

has given it a good mounting for the budget and nice pacing. Neill's direction wraps all loose ends in finale as Holmes prepares for another adventure.

It would, of course, be just a question of time for the following adventure, but none of the fans imagined that it would be the last one.

*Terror by Night* – 1 February 1946 – 60 minutes

**CAST**: Basil Rathbone as Sherlock Holmes; Nigel Bruce as Doctor Watson; Alan Mowbray as Major Duncan Bleek; Dennis Hoey as Inspector Lestrade; Renee Godfrey as Vivian Vedder; Frederic Worlock as Prof. William Kilbane; Mary Forbes as Lady Margaret Carstairs; Skelton Knaggs as Sands; Billy Bevan as Train Attendant; Geoffrey Steele as Roland Carstairs; Harry Cording as Mock Sr.; Bobby Wissler as Mock Jr.; Tom Pilkington as Baggage Car Attendant; C. Aubrey Smith and Stuart Holmes as Gentlemen at Train Station; Janet Murdoch as Mrs. Shallcross; Gerald Hamer as Alfred Shallcross; Gilbert Allen as Dining Car Steward; Leyland Hodgson and Charles Knight as Stewards.

**CREDITS**: Director and Producer: Roy William Neill; Executive Producer: Howard Benedict; Screenplay: Frank Gruber; Musical Director: Milton Rosen; Photography: Maury Gertsman; Film Editing: Saul A. Goodkind; Art Director: John B. Goodman and Abraham Grossman; Set Decoration: Russell A. Gausman and Carl J. Lawrence; Gowns: Vera West; Makeup: Jack P. Pierce; Assistant Director: Melville Shyer; Dialogue Director: Raymond Kessler.

*– DL*

# *The Spider Woman Strikes Back* (1946)

For any aspiring cinephile nowadays, the name "Arthur Lubin" is pretty much synonymous with the comedies of Abbott and Costello, the clowns who basically cleaned up Universal's debit column during the War. Still, delving into his filmography, we find that he wasn't a complete stranger to the crime mystery and horror genres, taking on such minor efforts as *Black Friday* or more ambitious projects like *Phantom of the Opera*, and getting the results that the staunchest of lovers of Universal horror still discuss.

Nonetheless, we must admit that part of this credit must be given to the screenwriter of both pictures, Eric Taylor, whom film scholar David Wilt has called to our attention due the various horror-themed screenplays the studio entrusted to this little-known screenwriter during the War years. Thus, it's not at all strange that, with both craftsmen behind the camera, the formula works yet again. *The Spider Woman Strikes Back* is a constant flow of atmospheres, ominous music, shadows entering and leaving rooms, inexplicable noises in the middle of the night, basements populated by botanical freaks, and a monstrous mute manservant who's not sure if he wants to protect or ambush the defenseless protagonist.

Jean (Brenda Joyce) arrives at the town of Domingo to take on a job as a companion to a blind woman, Zenobia Dollard (Gale Sondergaard), who lives in a home together with her mute servant, Mario (Rondo Hatton). Upon arriving, despite a cordial reception from the lady of the house, Jean feels somewhat impelled by her hostess to drink a glass of milk before going to bed. As anticipated, this drink makes her sleep deeply and, in the midst of her slumber, the strange woman enters the bedroom and extracts a measure of blood from her. This is the liquid that feeds an incredible specimen that dwells in her basement-laboratory: a plant called drochenema whose tendrils have their own power of movement. And that is not all, because the rest of the

649

specimens also require live food. Thus, the lady of the house proceeds with neurotic pleasure to give a spider to each one (it is to this ritual, we believe, the title of the film alludes).

What kind of research is the lady carrying out in this house? We can't with certainty describe a particular science, but it does lead to a notorious death-rate in the herds of various ranchers, who complain bitterly to the authorities. It is even said that a child has fallen ill from drinking milk and it's thought that some poisonous herb may be the cause of everything. One of the bits of padding, so to speak, involves the appearance of an agricultural official (Milburn Stone, fourth in the credits, higher than Rondo, despite appearing for less than five minutes). The official conveys to a drowsy Jean (a sign of anemia) some points that might explain that mortality vaccine and our heroine begins to suspect her hostess and employer. As Jean discovers that her employer is not blind as she had supposed, Mrs. Dollard reveals her motives: in the past the whole of the surrounding area belonged to her father, who lost it all gambling while his daughter was in Central America. Relegated to his mansion, she now carries out her experiments to scare off the neighboring ranchers and to lower the price per hectare so that she can recover what she considers is rightfully hers. Behind mad science and psychosis lays Capitalism. Ordering Mario to destroy all evidence of her activities, the Spider Woman discovers that she and her mute manservant are trapped in the subsequent flames.

Clearly, as the picture lasts only 59 minutes, there's not a great deal of time to develop or expound on themes. And the mention of four performers (Four! Not one, not two, but four) whose characters never appear on the screen is evidence that the film had been dramatically plundered in the cutting room. One of the things that the film does not offer (and that almost every horror film worth its weight can't avoid having) are deaths. The only living beings that die – apart from the poisoned-milk-swilling kid and the title character and her mute manservant, Mario – are those cows; no other human being succumbs on camera due to the nefarious experiments of this mad scientist... Or if there were victims, maybe they were those absent characters and - as it was either that they diverted the attention from the heroine or that the studio demanded shortening a film that it planned on sticking in a double bill - it was decided that the plot wouldn't suffer if they were removed. Even so, apart from that detail about the lack of victims, the film is a continuous terrifying experience from beginning to end.

*Showmen's Trade Review* (23 March 1946) considered it "an illogical plot, done in the stereotyped manner of most horror pictures, wastes Gale Sondergaard's talents" and, addressing the film's potential audience, observed that its being of an "adult classification, it will probably be viewed by more kids than any one else which is as it should be, for the film never rises above adolescent intelligence." Still, the film – with Zenobia feeding blood to her plants (one of which wraps a tendril around her arm, apparently in gratitude) - *is* something of a ancestor of Roger Corman's *The Little Shop of Horrors*, with which "adolescent intelligence" is forever bound.

The *Independent Exhibitors Film Bulletin* (15 April 1946) took the same approach as *Showmen's*; critic Leyendecker – although he conceded that "sophisticated patrons will laugh at its ridiculously fantastic and infantile plot" - opined that "it should do well in the action spots where Gale Sondergaard and the late Rondo Hatton, specialists in sinister roles, will lure the horror addicts." *Motion Picture Daily* (15 March 1946) classified it as "essentially for horror trade consumption." *Film Daily* (15 March 1946), perhaps the most equable of the trade media, felt that "morbidity is given its fling in this hour-long attraction whose story deals in those fantastic qualities aimed at the productions of goose-pimples without much regard of logic," although recognizing that "every horror picture must have its story notwithstanding."

Gale Sondergaard had a career filled with hills and valleys that would frighten and frustrate the most rabid roller coaster fan. Having made her cinematic debut with Claude Rains in 1936's *Anthony Adverse*, the novice from Minnesota took home the Academy's first statuette meant for a Supporting Actress. A member of New York's Theatre Guild, Sondergaard appeared onscreen with fellow-Guild-member Rains twice more in the next three years – married to him, both times – in *Juarez* and the two-reel *Sons of Liberty* (both 1939). The next decade saw her in supporting roles for various studios – she passed on playing the Wicked Witch of the West in *The Wizard of Oz* – with a strong slant towards the sinister marking most of her projects. Her film career was abruptly put on hold during the '50s as her husband, director Herbert Biberman, who had appeared before the House Un-American Activities Committee (HUAC) in the late '40s, was named as one of the "Hollywood Ten" communists by Joe McCarthy. Sondergaard, who – like the "Ten" - refused to testify against friends and acquaintances at HUAC – was blacklisted. Subsequently moving with her husband from California to New York, the actress returned to the theater later in the decade and then began TV work at the end of the '60s. Still, just after *Strikes Back*, she copped another Oscar nomination for her Lady Thiang in Fox's opulent "A," *Anna and the King of Siam*, a role pretty much atypical of her persona in most of her "B" thrillers of the '40s. There's more on the lady in our essay on *The Black Cat*.

**Best known throughout her brief film career as Jane in the last of the Johnny Weismuller Tarzan features, Brenda Joyce walked away from Tarzan – and the movies – after Lex Barker's first turn as the ape man. Sadly, due to acromegaly, Rondo Hatton was best known – if not *as* an ape man – as a Creeper, the next closest thing.**

Brenda Joyce's true claim to fame may have been her taking over as Tarzan's Jane when Maureen O'Sullivan demurred from swinging on any more vines, but by the time she first won Lord Greystoke's favor,(1) the spunky actress had already come to grips with the genre in Fox's *Whispering Ghosts* (1942), and two stints in Universal's "Inner Sanctum" series – *Strange Confession* and *Pillow of Death* (both 1945) – would follow. Kirby Grant also had a "signature role" of his own, but the title role in *Sky King* didn't cross the Montanan's path until he had pretty much abjured the big screen except for ten programmers as Corporal Rod Webb of the Canadian Mounties – partner of "Chinook, the Wonder Dog" - done for indie studios in the late '40s/early '50s. Possessed of a smooth baritone voice, Grant spent the mid-'40s at Universal where he would occasionally carry a tune on his own, especially in Olsen and Johnson or Abbott and Costello features (see: *Ghost Catchers*, 1944). Both Grant and Joyce do their jobs well here, albeit Arthur Lubin might well have opted for one or two fewer shots of Joyce wandering about the darkened corridors of the Dollard digs.

Special mention to Rondo Hatton, that actor who suffered from acromegaly and who, after short spurts as an icon in Universal thrillers, began to gain ascendancy as a star in this truculent genre until his premature death. His offering a permanent and ambiguous counterpoint to the mansion's interiors brings a needed monstrosity that even manifests a sub-theme: his fascination with the young visitor and his latent desire to possess her. On one of the nights (the film almost always takes place in shadow), his Mario surreptitiously enters the bedroom of the sleeping beauty and not only keeps touching her but also sits on the bed and leans down almost onto her face. The sudden appearance of Zenobia foils one of the most twisted scenes in the cinema at that time. Later, the mute whips up the courage to stand in front of the girl, touching her hand and even bringing his hypertrophied fingers up to her face. It's "Beauty and the Beast," months before the tireless Jean Cocteau premiered his ornate Rococo version.

*The Spider Woman Strikes Back* was the last of Hatton's films that allowed him to portray anything other than a back-breaking maniac. While a mute in the employ of a totally blind person doesn't make a great deal of sense – how might they communicate on any level save for the most basic? - the great reveal as to Zenobia's sight makes the matter moot. It's intriguing to see Mario interact with Jean as if his mistress *were* blind, though, and couldn't see/suspect the goings-on under her nose. Even if scenarist Eric Taylor had intended that Mario's clumsy attempts were meant to evoke pathos from the audience, there's no word other than "creepy" to describe the behavior. And while Mario may creep in ways that do not recall his Hoxton "relative," his being united with a "Spider Woman" (as in the case of Universal's handling of H.G. Wells's Invisible Man, apparently there is no *the* Spider Woman) – also fairly fresh from the studio's updating of Sherlock Holmes – indicated there might have been some thought about yet another derivative series on the part of the Powers That Were. Nothing came of that, of course – despite their apparent toasting in the last-reel conflagration and explosion, both Zenobia and Mario could have enjoyed Universal's own type of "immortality" had only the box-office revenues have been higher – as there's only so far one can take even hyper-villainous activity if it's ultimately based on running perceived interlopers off one's land.

Sadly, *The Spider Woman Strikes Back* was also the first of Rondo's last three films (including *House of Horrors* and *The Brute Man*, both 1946; see essays) to be released posthumously. The screen's most famous victim of acromegaly died of a heart attack on the 2 February 1946.

For the hard-and-fast Universal horror fan, it's a mitzvah to note that Paul Ivano directed the photography for *Strikes Back*. Known best as the photographer of Bela Lugosi's test footage as the Frankenstein Monster back in 1931, Ivano would progress from that point to the mid-'40s without again participating in a project designed to raise one's hackles. 1943's *Flesh and Fantasy* opened the door to the French-born cinematographer's involvement in several "Inner Sanctum" entries, 1944's *Destiny*, and the Sherlock Holmes adventure, *Pursuit to Algiers*, the following year (see essays on all); *Strikes Back* would mark the last of Ivan's genre efforts, save for the wonderfully bizarre *Captive Women* in 1952.

The picture was initially designed as a follow-up adventure of the Sondergaard Spider Woman who had crossed paths with Rathbone's Great Consulting Detective – a series was in the works – when delays and reductions(2) caused a rethinking of the concept and resulted in the 59-minute-long "B" we have today. Shot amidst his run of Abbott & Costello comedies, thrillers (*Phantom of the Opera*), fantasies (*Ali Baba and the Forty Thieves*), and costume epics (*Night in Paradise*) - and just prior to his swing into the realm of talking mules - *Strikes Back* was hardly a favorite of Arthur Lubin, who felt the assignment could have been handled as well (if not better) by one of the house staff more accustomed to dealing with lower-shelf product.

*The Spider Woman Strikes Back* – 22 March 1946 – 59 minutes (ST)

**CAST**: Gale Sondergaard as Zenobia Dollard; Brenda Joyce as Jean Kingsley; Kirby Grant as Hal Wentley; Milburn Stone as Commissioner Moore; Rondo Hatton as Mario; Hobart Cavanaugh as Bill Stapleton; Norman Leavitt as Tom; with Eva Mudge, Guy Beach, Guy Wilkerson, Horace Murphy, Hans Herbert, Bill Sundholm

**CREDITS**: Director: Arthur Lubin; Producer: Howard Welsch; Original Screenplay: Eric Taylor; Director of Photography: Paul Ivano; Camerman: William Dodds: Film Editor: Ray Snyder; Assistant Director: Fred Frank; Art Directors: John B. Goodman and Abraham Grossman; Musical Director: Milton Rosen; Set Decorators: Russell A. Gausman and Ralph Warrington; Dialogue Director: Joan Hathaway; Sound: Bernard B. Brown; Technician: Robert Pritchard; Make-up: Jack P. Pierce; Hair Stylist: Carmen Dirigo; Gowns: Vera West

*- DL*

# *House of Horrors* (1946)

*Synopsis*: Marcel de Lang, a surrealistic sculptor, has an important sale spoiled by nasty art critic Holmes Harmon. Despondent at his poverty and lack of recognition, Marcel goes to the waterfront to drown himself but instead rescues a man floundering in the water. Fascinated by the man's gargoyle of a face, Marcel takes him home and nurses him back to health. However, his new friend is actually a serial killer known as the Creeper who is believed by the police to have drowned. He agrees to pose for a bust of the "perfect Neanderthal Man."

Suspecting the true identity of his guest, Marcel tells the Creeper about Holmes Harmon, and the Creeper kills him. Police lieutenant Larry Brooks thinks artist Steve Morrow might have committed the crime since he despised the critic for his unfair reviews. An attempt to trap Morrow using another art critic backfires when the latter also falls victim to the Creeper.

Morrow's girlfriend, art critic Joan Medford, visits Marcel's studio and sneaks a peak at the bust of the Creeper while Marcel is out of the room. She also steals Marcel's sketch of his subject intending to publish it in the paper, not realizing who the model is. However, the Creeper has been watching her from hiding and informs Marcel, who sends his murderous friend after her. Stella, one of Steve's models, ends up as his victim instead. Joan returns to Marcel's studio, and the sculptor tells her the truth about the now-completed bust, informing her she will soon "meet the Creeper." However, the Creeper overhears Marcel saying he has no compunction about giving him up should he be recognized from the bust. The Creeper then kills him and destroys the bust. He goes after Joan, but Steve and Brooks save her, and the Creeper is shot.

After the release of Frank Sinatra's *None but the Brave* in 1965, Tommy Sands, who was married to Nancy Sinatra at the time, sought out and punched a movie critic who had derided his performance in the film as "hopelessly hammy." Nonetheless, the critic got in the last word; after noting his review had been written weeks before, he cracked that Sands "must be a slow reader." Luckily for the critic, Sands, though son-in-law to the Crooner - who certainly *could* be dangerous - was not pals with the Creeper.

Revenge is certainly a common theme in horror films, but singling out victims among critics of the arts was something new, and reviewers at the time of *House of Horrors* were amused at this conceit. A typical comment on this came from Theresa Loeb in the 12 July 1946 edition of *The Oakland Tribune*: "At the risk of incurring fruition of any of the film's implied threats to newspaper critics in general, the only horror in this movie is its drawn-out length."

One somewhat unusual aspect to *House of Horrors* is that the Creeper doesn't die at the ending. Noting this, reviewer Otis Guernsey remarked that "the doors for sequels are left wide open at the end since the detective, after shooting the killer, says 'We have to get this man to a hospital.' This is one door that should be closed at once."

The door did not quite close, even though another critic, John T. McManus, wrote that "*House of Horrors* is the Creeper's last crime. The character who played him - craggy-browed, broad nose, prognathous Rondo Hatton - died earlier this year."

Alas, there *was* one more crime, namely *The Brute Man*, ground out quickly just before Hatton's demise and, like *House*, released after his death. Unlike Universal's stable of monsters who could be brought back to life at the studio's whim, the Creeper was not superhuman, so the writers must have been told not to kill off the Creeper in *House* as a set-up for the sequel. Such logic usually didn't hold sway at Universal when it came to other human characters: Andoheb in *The Mummy's Hand* was riddled with bullets and fell down a long flight of stairs, but returned only slightly the worse for wear in *The Mummy's Tomb*, while Ygor, though shot repeatedly in *Son of Frankenstein*, was back for *The Ghost of Frankenstein*. The writers for *House of Horrors* needn't have bothered worrying about questions of continuity since *The Brute Man* seems to have been a prequel. Today's fans of vintage horror might argue the issue, but it's not likely any viewer in the '40s gave a hoot.

Still, *House* was supposed to be the first in a series of Creeper films, according to publicity releases like the one printed in the 14 November 1944 issue of *Film Daily*:

Ben Pivar, Universal production executive whose schedule was recently cleared of alllow- budget pictures, has been given a special assignment to develop a new set of scare characters for the studio where Frankenstein, the Wolf Man and their kin have made melodramatic history. His first creation is to be known as the Creeper and is to make its debut in a million-dollar production called *House of Horrors.*

Typical studio hoo-hah; people in the know must have snickered at the notion of Universal doing a million-dollar monster movie. Pivar likely did not have to stretch his imagination too far to come up with the Creeper; a character called the Hoxton Creeper and played by Rondo Hatton had already put in a brief appearance in the Sherlock Holmes film, *The Pearl of Death.* The Hoxton Creeper was a particularly menacing member of a criminal gang in *Pearl;* in *House,* the Creeper is a solitary serial killer who lurks around the mean streets of urban America rather than the fog-bound lanes of Old Blighty. Universal also claimed that many letters had been written to the studio asking about the *Pearl of Death* character and Rondo Hatton. The Big U released more publicity material about their new horror star:

Rondo Hatton is known in Hollywood Studio circles as 'the Brute Man.' Hatton has been  called the most fantastically visaged actor. His ponderous frame and eerie movements have added a new threat to the screen's shudder-dramas.

The publicity did not mention that Hatton came by his fantastic visage because of the acromegaly that had struck him in the 1920s. He had seen service in the Great War and had been gassed and developed the disease - which is caused by out-of-control growth hormones in the pituitary gland - after he had been pensioned off and returned to America, but whether the gassing had anything to do with his condition is arguable. Once a handsome high-school athlete, Hatton found that the disease turned his facial features rough and swollen, and (possibly) resulted in his raspy voice as well. Acromegaly was first used as a horror element in the 1942 Argentine film, *A Light in the Window,* wherein a doctor stricken with the disease experiments on human subjects in search of a cure.(1)  Later, evil scientist J. Carrol Naish uses a serum to cause acromegaly in Ralph Morgan in *The Monster Maker* (1944), and Leo G. Carroll and his co-workers fall victim to an artificially induced version of the disease in *Tarantula* (1955). Though they were all supposedly victims of acromegaly, they were monstrous in different ways, the make-up men apparently having divergent ideas about what a person suffering from the malady would look like. Hatton, unfortunately, was the real thing.

Hatton settled in Florida after the war and worked for a couple of different newspapers, *The Tampa Daily Times* and the *Tampa Tribune.* In 1930, when Henry King and his movie company arrived in the area to shoot *Hell Harbor,* Hatton went to cover the event, and King gave him a small part as a bouncer (other Tampa residents were also cast in bits). The disease had taken its toll, and Hatton looks pretty much like he did in his Universal films. In addition to his newspaper chores, Hatton acted as a publicity agent for boxing promoter Jim Downing and, in 1933, he worked doing public relations for Sun Haven Pictures, an ill-fated attempt to revive film-making in Florida. The studio made just three films, among them *Chloe, Love is Calling You*, which was a bizarre, racist mishmash of voodoo and romance.

Though Hatton loved Tampa, he struck out for Hollywood in the summer of 1937. Henry King, no doubt remembering Hatton from *Hell Harbor*, gave him the small but conspicuous role of Tyrone Power's bodyguard in his latest film, *In Old Chicago* (1939). Interviewed by phone by his old newspaper pal Bill Abbott, Hatton talked about his experience in LaLaLand in the 14 March 1938 edition of *The Tampa Tribune*:

> I was out here and barely hanging on. The studio called late one afternoon and said Mr. King wanted me. I was 12 miles away, but got there in record time on a bus with three transfers. Bob Webb - another prince and the assistant director - told me right away he had a job for me and sent me up to get the monkey suit I wear. They looked me over and told me to come back the next morning. Boy, that was a swell feeling. I was a country yokel but I got used to things and everybody was swell. They played some tricks like putting the "hot foot" on you, but we had a great time...I got a day's work yesterday in *Alexander's Ragtime Band* and I'm going back tomorrow. They're just giving me a little atmosphere part in this one. But things are looking pretty good out here. Everybody says they're getting better. I'm gonna stick around a while longer anyway and see what happens.

Hatton received a lot of fan mail from Tampa. He also arranged for an invalid war veteran and old friend to be brought via ambulance to the Tampa opening of *In Old Chicago*.

A very curious item on Hatton appeared in the July 1939 "Believe It or Not" feature which was printed in many newspapers. It displayed a photo of Hatton in his youth and a drawing of how he looked today: "Movie Actor who played Horror parts without make-up won a prize as the handsomest youth in his school days. Gassed during the Great War, he now suffers from acromegaly." However, at this point in his career, Hatton hadn't played in *any* horror films; maybe Mr. Ripley was just making a suggestion as to how Hatton could earn his living in Hollywood. Just a few years later this came to pass when Hatton signed with Universal.

Unfortunately, Hatton couldn't act. He delivers his lines like a robot reading off a cue card, and his gravelly voice is more suggestive of a thug than a mentally deranged killer. His expression never changes throughout *House of Horrors* nor in any of his films (though he does once manage a kind of evil smile in *Jungle Captive*). Still, his deadpan style does pay off in a couple of exchanges in *House*. Reading from the newspaper about the Creeper's latest female victim, Marcel (Martin Kosleck) wonders aloud as to why someone would snap the spine of a beautiful woman. "She screamed" is the Creeper's matter-of-fact response. Later, when the sculptor proclaims that the bust will finally make critics praise his talents, Hatton mutters "They'd better." Hatton's other readings often border on the comical, especially when he yells "Shaddup!" to one of his screaming victims. And later "You'd-let-the police-get me---huh?" when he realizes Marcel isn't really his friend after all.

**Rondo Hatton in his most famous pose as The Creeper.**

The Creeper's rationale for murder is never clearly spelled out. Presumably, it's a recap of Bateman's self-justification in *The Raven*: "When a man is ugly, he does ugly things." Women screaming at the sight of him apparently trigger his homicidal impulses. Being an outcast because of one's physical appearance is a common element in horror, and one thinks of Frankenstein's monster and a number of Lon Chaney roles in the Silent Era, but neither Hatton nor *House's* script are able to bring any poignancy to the character. The Creeper is basically just an ancestor of Jason and Michael Myers, nothing more than a killing machine who keeps the plot in motion with his crimes. There *should* be a certain sadness to the Creeper; even the man he thought was his friend is just using him. The monster henchman turning on his master probably goes back as far as Quasimodo sending Claude Frollo airborne off the parapets of Notre Dame and became a *cliché* in horror films, though more often than not a woman provides the impetus for the last-reel reversal.

Marcel is a sympathetic character at first, speaking soothingly to his beloved cat and lamenting his poverty and then, in a fit of despair, destroying the sculpture he has unsuccessfully tried to sell and heading for the waterfront to end it all. The two art critics who get killed are obnoxious and not more likely to garner audience sympathy than the two stuffy burghers who fall victim to Ygor's revenge via the Monster in *Son of Frankenstein*. The story might have played out more interestingly had Marcel been unaware of exactly what his Creeper pal was up to instead of consciously using him as a tool for murder. In any case, it's one of Kosleck's best performances - his very best, I'd say - and he makes the sculptor both a mad genius (we'll take Joan Medford's word for it that the bust of the Creeper is a masterpiece; I was a bit less impressed, but then, I'm not an art critic) and a vindictive, the little man finally on top and able to indulge his worst impulses and most destructive fantasies. The cat coming down the stairs as Marcel is killed and then sniffing at his body is a moving touch.

Kosleck could certainly relate to Marcel's passion for his art since he himself had won acclaim as a painter (see the profile on him in *The Frozen Ghost* essay). Kosleck did not have to deal with the negativity that greeted Marcel's sculptures, but still not everyone fully grasped his work, as indicated in this article printed in the 22 May 1939 edition of the *Middleboro* (Kentucky) *Daily News*:

In art circles he is regarded as a modern primitive. We hate to display our ignorance concerning art but the paintings of modern primitives, as exemplified by those of Kosleck, have to be explained before they can be understood at all. One of his pictures, for instance, shows a girl in a red dress flying through the air with two strange creatures soaring after her. They look like little goats. Kosleck says they are goats. His picture was entitled 'Memory of Childhood' and it shows his memory of his sister being chased by a couple of angry barnyard animals.

Perhaps it's a good thing that Holmes Harmon didn't review "Memory of Childhood." Harmon, by the way, is superbly played by Alan Napier: prissy, gleefully acid-tongued, and malicious. Napier might have made a good Waldo Lydecker in *Laura*.

Joan Medford, the film's only "nice" art critic, is played with affable assurance by Virginia Grey, though a couple of her outfits appear as though they could have been designed by Marcel had he been into fashion rather than surrealistic sculpture; at one point she wears a hat that makes her look a Mouseketeer. Grey was a child actress in the late Silent Era, playing Little Eva in Universal's *Uncle Tom's Cabin* in 1928; if the IMDB is to be believed, Rondo Hatton was also in the film in an uncredited bit as a slave. In a 1948 interview, Grey said she thought actors had it better in the Silent Era and that talkies ruined many careers; she later had sad encounters with people who had been on top of their game reduced to being prop men and grips because of the upheaval caused by sound. After a brief hiatus from acting to continuing her education and training as a dancer, Grey was soon back in front of the cameras and worked steadily for decades to come, though she never achieved major stardom. She had no pretense about her occupation and once said "I consider myself a professional who acts - not to express my soul or elevate the cinema - but entertain and paid for it."(2) As far as Grey's other genre credits go: she ran away from guys in suits pretending to be dinosaurs in *Unknown Island* (1948); was menaced by scrap-metal robots in *Target Earth* (1954); and was killed by George Barrows - Ro-Man himself - in his gorilla costume in *Black Zoo* (1963).

Robert Lowery as artist Steve Morrow (his work is apparently patterned after the pin-up drawings of Alberto Vargas) is the nominal hero, but he is given even less of a work-out than he had in *The Mummy's Ghost*. At least he gets the girl this time. Lowery was finally able to do the hero bit properly in the 1948 serial, *Batman and Robin*.

The 8 September 1945 issue of *The New York Times* announced that, in addition to starring Virginia Grey and Robert Lowery, Universal's *Murder Mansion* (the working title of *House of Horrors* and just as inapt; in Australia it was known as *The Sinister Shadow*) would feature Kent Taylor as "the principal menace." Presumably this was an error, and Taylor most likely would have played the police lieutenant Larry Brooks. Bill Goodwin, better known as a radio announcer than an actor, took the role of the good-natured detective and had a far lighter touch than the usual hard-nosed cops

661

assigned to hassle Lon Chaney or investigate ape women and ghouls. Goodwin even gets to flirt with Stella (Joan Shawlee, looking very fetching in a tennis outfit), though that doesn't end well since she won't "Stop screamin'" when confronted by the Creeper.

**Lurid poster for the film. The title is a bit of a misnomer as we assume Marcel's sculptures constitute the titular horrors.**

Director Jean Yarbrough was not exactly Orson Welles, but his modest talents for speed and efficiency were put to good use in *House* and others of its ilk for Universal, and he certainly keeps things moving. Likewise, cameraman Maury Gerstman labored primarily in the lower-berth levels (*Four Skulls of Jonathan Drake, Invisible Invaders*), but occasionally came up for air in somewhat classier productions like *City Across the River* (1949) which garnered some praise for its documentary, *Naked City*-like approach. There's a gloomy, *noir*-ish look to his work in *House*, and one moment stands out: when poor Stella answers the door expecting to see Lieut. Brooks, there's an eerie low angle shot of Hatton looking, for once, more like a caveman than a thug. It's probably the only time he actually resembles Marcel's bust.

Somewhat surprisingly, E.J.B. in the 23 Feb 1946 edition of *The New York Times* was not as scornful of *House of Horrors* as one might expect:

The moral appears to be that art critics had better be careful of whom they criticize (film critics, happily, were not mentioned). If you like this sort of thing, the picture is in the approved shuddery tradition and gets the story told quickly. Rondo Hatton is properly scary as the Creeper.

That's pretty much the highest praise the film received in the Big Apple. Among the more typical comments:

> Besides being a pretty silly hair-raising device, Universal's horror creation is not in the best of taste. The menace is a glandular and mental case, an ugly Neanderthal-featured brute of a moron called the Creeper...The Creeper is more pathetic than terrifying.
> Otis Guernsey, *New York Herald Tribune*, 23 February 1946

> Surrealistic sculpture and a creature who, sans make-up, is more revolting than Frankenstein's Monster. Eerie little opus - it was to have been one of a long line of Universal 'Creeper' shockers, starring Rondo Hatton, whose elephantine contours and foghorn voice, were enough to frighten the fiercest thriller addict... Grim item to be sure.
> Irene Thirer, *New York Post*, 23 February 1946

> The melancholy ugliness of the late Rondo Hatton helps in the gooseflesh department. You have to scare pretty easily to get any real chills out of this picture but if you happen to be not overly bright this should be very satisfactory movie fare.
> *New York World Telegram* 22 February 1946

> "It's a spine-chiller guaranteeing to scare those who scare easily."
> Wanda Hale, *New York Daily News*, 23 February 1946

The film drew no enthusiasm in the trades, either:

> The picture is not designed for impressionable youngsters but it will fill the supporting spots in most secondary duals. Whenever there is the least suspicion that action may be slowing down to a somewhat normal pace, the Creeper takes to the path of murder...There is nothing particularly outstanding about this offering. Theaters purveying this type of entertainment can use it profitably, however. There is some love interest but it doesn't matter much since the script makes death

decidedly stronger than love.

*Film Daily*, 7 May 1946

This is just another program melodrama, developed according to formula and with few surprises. Nor is it outstanding in either production values or performance. Unlike the title indicates, there is little about the proceedings to terrify one unless the fact that the murders are committed by a half-witted giant can be considered horrendous rather than unpleasant......Its appeal should be directed just to those who, regardless of story values, enjoy melodramatic action, for the second half has a few exciting scenes.

*Harrison's Reports*, 9 March 1946

And after describing the Creeper as "a grotesque looking physically powerful imbecile," Charles Franke in the 3 March 1946 issue of *Motion Picture News* added that "Jean Yarborough's direction makes the most of isolated opportunities for suspense and the performers breeze confidently through assignments that strain the acting talents of none."

*House of Horrors* is not as good as *The Pearl of Death*, but it is certainly more watchable than Rondo Hatton's other Universal horror films. It has a knowing, smoothly sinister portrayal by Martin Kosleck, sharp supporting performances, a somewhat offbeat premise, a few eerie moments, a quick pace, and an appropriately grim leitmotif for the Creeper. The main problem with enjoying the film is Hatton himself. Should you be rolling your eyes at his bad acting, feeling sorry for him because of his affliction, shaking your head at Universal for exploiting him as a "monster without make-up?" All three at once?

The premise of artists avenging themselves on their critics would turn up again in 1973's *Theater of Blood* wherein ham Shakespearean actor Vincent Price kills off his detractors using plot elements from the Bard's plays. Instead of the Creeper, he has daughter Diana Rigg as his co-conspirator.

A definite improvement.

*House of Horrors* - 29 March 1946 - 66 minutes (ST)

**CAST**: Robert Lowery as Steven Morrow; Virginia Gray as Joan Medford; Bill Goodwin as Lieut. Larry Brooks; Martin Kosleck as Marcel de Lang; Alan Napier as F. Holmes Harmon; Howard Freeman as Hal Ormiston; Joan Shawlee (aka Joan Fulton) as Stella; Virginia Christine as Streetwalker; Rondo Hatton as the Creeper; Bryon Folger as Mr. Samuels; Tom Quinn as Taxicab Driver; Jack Parker as Elevator Boy; William Newell as Detective Tomlinson; Oliver Blake as Janitor; William Ruhl as Ellis; Syd Saylor as Jones; Clifton Young as Detective; Kernan Cripps as Detective; Terry Mason as Clarence; Stephen Wade as Speed; Danny Jackson as Office Boy; Mary Field as Nora; Charles Wagenheim as Walter; Janet Shaw as Cab Driver; Perc Launders as Smith.

**CREDITS**: Directed by Jean Yarbrough; Producer: Ben Pivar; Screenplay: George Bricker; Original Story: Dwight V. Babcock; Director of Photography: Maury Gertsman; Art Directors: John Goodman, Abraham Grossman; Film Editor: Philip Cahn; Set Decorators: Russell A. Gausman, Ralph Warrington; Costumes: Vera West; Music: H.J. Salter; Sound: Bernard B. Brown, Robert Pritchard; Make-up: Jack Pierce

***Shock Theater*** Catalog No. 709: "A sinister revenge backfires and starts a chain of horror when the Creeper breaks loose preying upon a city maddened by fear. See the *Shock* feature film presentation, 'The House of Horrors' [sic], telecast on channel (day), at (time). It's the last word in thrills."

*- HN*

# *She-Wolf of London* (1946)

*She-Wolf of London* may be the most unfairly maligned of Universal's '40s horror films. It's possible that this is a reaction to the title being a bit of a cheat, but as a film it's nowhere near as bad as the best of the Paula Dupree films, which is... *errr*... *ummm*... well, we digress. The fact is that as U-horror sputtered to a stop, *She-Wolf* is actually one of the better of the later productions – but it must be admitted the bar is quite low.

There are attacks - sometimes murderous - with the victims clawed at the throat, occurring in a park near the Allenby Mansion. The first has happened before the film begins, and Scotland Yard is investigating. Young heiress Phyllis (June Lockhart) becomes convinced she is responsible due to the family curse, despite reassurances from her fiancé, Barry (Don Porter) and her aunt Martha (Sara Hayden). But how to explain that she wakes up with blood on her hands and mud on her slippers? The attacker has been described by witnesses and survivors as a woman who emits animal growls. The newspapers have stories about werewolves ("The newspapers are full of it," we are told a couple times in what may be a deliberate bit of disparagement), and detective Latham (Lloyd Corrigan) tries to convince his boss, Inspector Pierce (Dennis Hoey – did he inevitably portray police inspectors?), and anyone else who will listen for that matter, that a lycanthrope is on the prowl.

That there is no werewolf becomes obvious quite early on, and since it's impossible to believe that sweet young Lockhart – later the Mom on *Lassie* and *Lost in Space* – is a serial killer, it also soon becomes clear that Phyllis is being given the *Gaslight* treatment by way of *Devil Bat's Daughter* (a film to which this one has clear plot parallels). But as the film's title is somewhat of a cheat, it's one that some monster movie fans find unforgivable. We admit that in our youth we shared this grudge against the film, but we've since come to accept it for what it is: a compact little Gothic mystery-cum- *noir* thriller with a rather too easily perceived solution. As Phyllis is clearly innocent, the remaining possible suspects – which include some tetchy dogs that are shown leaping over the garden wall – are a pretty sparse lot, which is never a plus in a mystery.

So, whodunit? – or should that be whoozdoinit? Is it Phyllis' solicitous aunt Martha with her endless supply of glasses of warm milk? She seems very concerned about the Allenby heiress, but we learn early she's not a relative, but merely the housekeeper. Is it all an act? What about Phyllis's non-cousin, Carol (Jan Wiley)? Might she, despite affections supposedly directed elsewhere, actually want to snag sturdy fiancé Barry for herself? And let's not discount Barry; he might be colluding with Carol and doing a Norman Bates, getting all dragged up to confuse the authorities. And then there's the housekeeper (Eily Malyon) who's forever suspiciously lurking around doorways and pressing her ear to doors, eavesdropping on conversations. Why, it might even be Latham. Yeah, he gets killed off halfway through, but maybe he fakes his death. Ever see *Ten Little Indians*? Such things happen! I doubt a SPOILER ALERT would be necessary were we inclined to reveal the "surprise" ending.

*She-Wolf* may be no great shakes as a mystery, much less as a film, but it's not the steaming pile of offal some declare. Intriguingly, it is one of Universal's "garden weasel" mysteries - along with *The Mystery of Marie Roget* and *The Scarlet Claw* - wherein the murder weapon is that pronged implement commonly used for breaking up soil. Now we don't want to imply that this is the most notable thing about the film, but what's interesting is that the studio writers' fondness for the tool (not that they ever deliberately recycled ideas – oh no!). A particularly notable aspect of the film is that it features a rare instance in the Production Code era of a child being murdered – off-screen of course; Universal was not about to be *that* transgressive.

That the murderer emerges from the Allenby mansion - heavily swathed with a shawl that obscures her (or maybe his) face - is another tip-off that we should probably discount little Phyllis as the culprit. The film does pull a good trick with this, though, when on one instance it is Carol, similarly wrapped, sneaking off to an assignation with her lover (Martin Kosleck), whom Mom deems too poor to be proper husband material. That he is non-fatally attacked by the growling woman while awaiting Carol who, to plop the cherry on this parfait, shows up immediately afterward, makes her a suspect. Has she attacked him and then returned to the scene to divert suspicion? Oh, hell, why do we bother trying to lead you astray, gentle reader?

If the script is rather ho-hum, at least the cast (what there is of it) is above average. June Lockhart is quite good as a young woman who is being driven mad by the thought that she has been infected by the vaguely defined family curse and has become a murderess. That she too rapidly shifts from carefree to neurotic is the fault of the script (by George Bricker, from an idea by Dwight V. Babcock), not hers. To watch her here is reason alone to check out this little flick. Lockhart made her debut, uncredited, playing one of the Cratchit children in the 1938 *A Christmas Carol* (her dad, Gene, was Bob - a change from his usual weasel roles - and mom, Kathleen, portrayed Mrs. Cratchit). Within a few years, she was working exclusively in television, with *Lights Out* and *Science Fiction Theatre* episodes among her early credits. Lockhart would also clock in on *Voyage to the Bottom of the Sea* before joining the cast of that other Irwin Allen show - playing Maureen Robinson for three years - and gradually ceding more and more screen time to Jonathan Harris and the robot as things became increasingly ludicrous. The actress did not return to big screen genre until *Troll* (1986) – in which Boomers were startled to hear her using four-letter words - and *C.H.U.D. II* (1989). A 1986 episode of *Amazing Stories* completes her genre credits.

**Can Timmy's mom actually be some "Crazed Thing of Evil?"**

Don Porter (1912–1997) has a far less demanding task; he's simply the stalwart but ineffectual hero. But with his deep voice (he doesn't bother to feign a British accent – for that matter Lockhart doesn't trouble herself, either) and manly demeanor, he's a more convincing hero than, say, David Manners – though per typical Universal plotting, he's nowhere on the scene when his sweetie needs rescuing. And that may be what really is the most interesting thing about this little flick: It's an entirely female affair in terms of victim, villain, and rescuer. In a kind of reflection of the Rosie-the- Riveter, World-War-II years, the men play very little part in the home-front proceedings and none at all in the resolution when the killer is undone because she's a klutz. Porter, who made his screen debut in Universal's 1939 "Crime Club" entry, *Mystery of the White Room*, gets to be somewhat more proactive in *Night Monster* (1942), and for more on him and his career see the essay on that film.

Sara - sometimes billed as Sarah - Haden (1898–1988) turned in a slew of roles as grumpy spinsters and martinet schoolteachers, such as the truancy officer who's mean to treacly Shirley Temple in *Captain January* (1936) and her recurring role as Andy Hardy's Aunt Milly. Haden started her film career at RKO in 1934, but by 1935 she was at M-G-M, playing Frances Drake's devoted maid in Karl Freund's *Mad Love*. *She-Wolf* would be her next genre credit, but a year later she showed up in *The Bishop's Wife*. George Pal's *The Great Rupert* followed in 1950, about the same time her appearances were almost exclusively relegated to the small screen, whereon the closest thing to a genre credit was an appearance on *My Favorite Martian*.

At least Haden got through her stay at Universal without having to costar with Rondo Hatton. No such luck for Jan Wiley (1916–1993), who appeared with him in *The Brute Man* (1946). Wiley's first film role was a small one in *Stage Door* (1937) and that was followed by some so small - like being one of the reporters in 1941's *Citizen Kane* – that they went uncredited. That same year, Wiley put in time at Republic to make the serial *Dick Tracy vs. Crime Inc.* A year later, she was at Universal for an uncredited bit in *The Strange Case of Doctor Rx*, after which Universal loaned her to Monogram for *The Living Ghost* (1942). She moved back and forth between the two studios, often in uncredited appearances, and her final role – again uncredited – was in *The Best Years of Our Lives* (1946) for Goldwyn, the same year as *She-Wolf* and *Brute Man*. Just why she retired from the screen is unknown, but it's clear her career was going nowhere fast, veering as it did between featured and uncredited roles, and she may have just decided to hang it up. Her disappearance did, perhaps significantly, coincide with her second marriage to composer Mort Greene (most famous for the *Leave it to Beaver* theme).

670

Dennis Hoey, Martin Kosleck, and Lloyd Corrigan are dealt with elsewhere in this volume. Eily Malyon (née Eily S. Lees-Craston, 1879–1961) began appearing in films in 1931. Her genre and nigh-genre credits include *Rasputin and the Empress* (1932), *Great Expectations* (Stuart Walker, 1934), *The Florentine Dagger* (Robert Florey, 1935), *Dracula's Daughter* and Tod Browning's *The Devil Doll* (both 1936), *Night Must Fall* (1937), *The Hound of the Baskervilles, On Borrowed Time* (both 1939), *I Married a Witch*, John Brahm's *The Undying Monster* (both 1942) and *Jane Eyre* (1943). Her roles were generally small, so small she often didn't receive screen credit, but she was all but an old hand at scary stuff by the time she got to *She-Wolf*, her second-to-last film.

Director Jean Yarbrough (born Arthur Jean Wilker Yarbrough, 1900–1975) was late of PRC and Monogram where he churned out (that is the only applicable description) a slew of schlocky flicks on time and on-budget. After dozens of short subjects for RKO, he made his feature debut with the memorably loopy *The Devil Bat* (1940); a year later he was over at Monogram for *King of the Zombies* and more low-budget time-wasters. 1943 marked a move to Universal, with more generous budgets and several pictures with Abbott and Costello. (He was apparently a favorite of the duo; he also helmed a number of episodes of their TV series.) Not everyone's CV includes working with Bela Lugosi, Madame Sul-Te-Wan, Mantan Moreland, Bud & Lou, and Emil van Horn in his goofy gorilla suit. *House of Horrors* and *The Brute Man* (both 1946) bracketed *She-Wolf*. That memorable trio was followed by a move back to lesser companies and *The Creeper* (1948), *Master Minds* (1949) with The Bowery Boys, a return to A&C in *Jack and the Beanstalk* (1952), and the inevitable immersion in television – which he reportedly preferred for its swift shooting schedules. A few movies were interspersed, including the unforgettable (no matter how much you try) *Hillbillies in a Haunted House* (1967). At least, in *She-Wolf*, Yarbrough took advantage of a more generous shooting schedule and better technical facilities for some fluid camerawork (though a great many scenes are staged in master-shots and two-shots). He was also not above filching a camera set-up from Alfred Hitchcock (hint: it involves a glass of milk and a staircase).

Writer George Bricker's first genre script was for the quirky *Sh! The Octopus* (1937); that was followed by *The Mark of the Whistler* (1944), *House of Dracula* (1945; story, uncredited) and *Pillow of Death* (also 1945). Bricker (1898–1955) seems to have been a favorite of Jean Yarbrough, for whom he also wrote *Devil Bat, Law of the Jungle* (1942), *House of Horrors*, and *The Brute Man*. Dwight V. (Vincent) Babcock (1909–1979) wrote for such hard-boiled pulps as *Black Mask* before trading that market for the higher paychecks offered by Tinseltown, beginning with *Dead Man's Eyes* (1944).

671

His genre work for Universal included *The Mummy's Curse* (story and adaptation), *The Jungle Captive* (story and screenplay), *House of Dracula* (story, uncredited), *Pillow of Death* (story; all 1945), and the stories for *House of Horrors* and *Brute Man* (both 1945). He also contributed additional dialogue for *The Devil's Mask* and wrote the adaptation for *The Unknown* (both 1946), both entries in RKO's *I Love a Mystery* series. Starting with a 1949 episode of *The Lone Ranger*, he became a prolific television writer with a theatrical film - including the delirious *Jungle Moon Men* (1955) - tossed in every now and then.

For a production so carefully designed to be low-budget – a small cast, totally filmed on existing sets (the front door to the Allenby manse will be familiar), no lycanthropic transformations – it's odd that *She-Wolf* does not trot out all the comfortably familiar Universal music cues; even the familiar Jimmy McHugh fanfare is missing. The score might be mostly original (www.IMDb.com credits Frank Skinner for stock cues, although we recognized none), albeit the onscreen credit to William Lava (1911–1971) is only as "Music Director," suggesting he cobbled it together from existing cues with only a few freshly-composed transitional passages. Lava was an astonishingly prolific composer who, given the variety of studios he would work for in any given year, was apparently also an amazingly successful freelancer. His film composing career began in 1937 with the Republic serial, *Zorro Rides Again*, and most of his work for some years would be for that studio's serials: *Daredevils of the Red Circle*, *Dick Tracy's G-Men* (both 1939), and *Drums of Fu Manchu* (1940). By 1943, when he scored *The Mysterious Doctor* for Warner Bros., he was also working at Universal. His first horror credit there, however, was contributing to the "Salterized" score for *The Invisible Man's Revenge* (1944). This was followed by equally uncredited work on *The Mummy's Curse* (1944) and *House of Dracula*. Post-Universal genre work included Arch Oboler's *Five* (1951), *Phantom from Space* (1953), *Revenge of the Creature* (1955), *The Deadly Mantis* (1957), *Chamber of Horrors* (1966), and episodes of *The Twilight Zone* and *Thriller*. He also scored the long-running Joe McDoakes comedy-short series and seemingly hundreds of "Looney Tunes" (we didn't count). He passed away while midway through writing the music for the notorious *Dracula vs. Frankenstein* (1971).

Critical reaction to *She-Wolf of London* at the time was lukewarm, even from exhibitors:

Fair little mystery. These program pictures from Universal don't seem to be as good as they used to be.

S. T. Jackson, Jackson Theatre, Flomaton, AL

"Good program picture in the horror class. Business was average."

E. M. Frieburger, Paramount Theatre, Dewey, OK - as recounted in *Motion Picture Herald,* 9 April 1946

In their dealing with the picture as an "it is what it is" fashion, the trades appeared to be fairer than the dailies.

The ready-made audience – the one to which the title obviously beckons – will find the cost of admission paying off in the form of well-contrived screen thriller entertainment. There are flaws in the presentation of the murder yarn, particularly in some of the top performances, which are labored, but the plot has substance. And further in its favor is the fact that it does not go overboard with too much 'horror' stuff.

Gene Arnett, *Motion Picture Daily,* 9 April 1946

Of course, the "'horror' stuff'" is precisely what the "ready-made audience" craved – and its lack could be one more reason the film is held in low regard by horror fans

Bosley Crowther's column in the 6 April 1946 edition of *The New York Times* (in which Eily Malyon's name is misspelled "Emily") contains T.M.P.'s dismissive assessment (typical of *The Times,* but possibly justified in this case) that relates the plot and reveals the ending in the first half of its single paragraph. It then continues:

All that remains to be said now about this latest release from Universal's bottom drawer is that it certainly doesn't justify the effort expended on its behalf. June Lockhart is the girl who believes she is part werewolf and Don Porter is the nice young man who is sure she isn't.

And that is all he wrote. Makes this writer feel positively loquacious. The anonymous writer in the June 1946 *Harrison's Reports* may have thought the ending predictable, but at least he stayed mum about it.

An ordinary psychological program murder melodrama, it is boresome [sic] and long-drawn out, and it is given more to talk than to action. The plot, which has been done many times, is obvious, for the spectator is never really in doubt as to the murderer's identity...

Two of the trades spoke positively of the director's contribution (possibly the first and last time he received such praise). On the 15 May 1946, *Film Daily* opined that "Jean Yarbrough manages to stretch the film into feature footage with mild suspense and interest." The following month, the *National Board of Review* took it a bit further:

Jean Yarbrough makes of the entry a substantial spine-tingler which, though unalleviated by comedy, creates a suspenseful mood and hangs together with as much logic as can be expected.

It remained for the dailies to rain disdain on this middling murder mystery.

This is another film in the category of wolf murders... June Lockhart, appealing in the dramatic role of Phyllis Allenby, fears she is the criminal. Sara Haden, as the aunt with whom the girl lives, gives a performance which should thrill audiences... The atmosphere of strangeness is maintained throughout a weird story.

M. R. Y., *Motion Picture Herald*, 13 April 1946

**Likable Lloyd Corrigan usually made it all the way to the final reel; here, not so much.**

*Another* flick about wolf murders? There was a trend? Well, only if you count werewolf pictures. M. R. Y.'s review also reveals the ending – as does the following (now *there's* a trend) though we have, of course, omitted that section of the review.

> The spine-chilling title... gives promise of gory thrills which this slow-moving and generally unexciting programmer fails to deliver. Although cast names are decidedly weak the picture will satisfy as part of a dual horror bill (Universal is coupling it with *The Cat Creeps*) in action houses. The story, laid in the gaslit era at the turn of the century, is fairly well developed and Director Jean Yarbrough achieves some suspense merely by suggesting rather than actually showing the were-wolf murders... The only outstanding performances are those of Sara Haden, as the aunt, and Eily Malyon, as a gaunt housekeeper.
>
> YORK, *Independent Exhibitors Film Bulletin*, 29 April 1946

Other dailies were more circumspect and we particularly like the first of the following, which makes an amusing point of not spilling the beans.

> The story is so flimsy and transparent, the slightest description would reveal the whole affair, right down to the final climax. So the title will have to be all you learn here about this tale of gruesome murders in foggy London nights. In any case, you will know the whole plot within five minutes after the picture begins...
>
> Alton Cook, *New York World-Telegram*, 5 April 1946

> Apparently working on the theory that if girls could step into such previously man-held jobs as riveters and train conductors they could also handle movie monster chores, Universal presented a lady fiend known as the Spider Woman just a couple of weeks ago, and this week introduces 'The She-Wolf of London...' But Boris Karloff, Bela Lugosi and the other veteran bogiemen [sic] have no need to worry about their ratings... the Rialto has done better by its patrons than this item...
>
> Rose Peswick, *Journal American*, 6 April 1946

> A wolf-like killer makes life generally unpleasant for strollers in a London park, without accomplishing very much in the way of cinematic

terror... In spite of random maniacal evil which baffles the police, this new Universal film is a sluggish and sometimes even dull thriller...

O. L. G. Jr., *New York Herald Tribune*, 6 April 1946

Hep Rialto audiences don't believe that cute June Lockhart is a killer... The gaslit era is persuasively presented; the park murders aren't the shockingest ever – but director Jean Yarbrough has cast his characters so that lots of them look suspicious...

Irene Thirer, *New York Post*, 6 April 1946

There's nothing hubba-hubba about Rialto's 'She Wolf of London'... Most of the gory details are offscreen – in deference, no doubt, to the extremely sensitive of most horror film fans. There's a lot of malevolent atmosphere to evoke suspense, however...

Dorothy Masters, *(New York) Daily News*, 6 April 1946

The reputation of *She-Wolf of London* has not become more hubba-hubba over the years. It has a lowly 17% rating on Rotten Tomatoes.

*She-Wolf of London* – 17 May 1946 – 61 minutes (ST)

**CAST:** Don Porter as Barry Lanfield; June Lockhart as Phyllis Allenby; Sara Haden as Martha Winthrop; Jan Wiley as Carol Winthrop; Lloyd Corrigan as Detective Latham; Dennis Hoey as Inspector Pierce; Martin Kosleck as Dwight Severn; Eily Malyon as Hannah; Frederick Worlock as Constable Ernie Hobbs; following are uncredited: Clara Blandick as Mrs. McBroom; James Finlayson as Constable with Hobbs and Latham; Olaf Hytten as Constable Alfred; Warren Jackson as Constable; William H. O'Brien as Constable; Brick Sullivan as Constable; David Thursby as Constable Herbert

**CREDITS:** Producer: Ben Pivar; Director: Jean Yarbrough; Screenplay: George Bricker; Story: Dwight V. Babcock; Music: William Lava, Frank Skinner (uncredited); Cinematography: Maury Gertsman; Film Editing: Paul Landres; Art Direction: Abraham Grossman, Jack Otterson; Set Decoration: Russell A. Gausman, Leigh Smith; Costume Design: Vera West (gowns); Makeup: Jack P. Pierce; Assistant Director: Ralph Slosser; Sound Director: Bernard B. Brown

***Shock Theater*** Catalog No. 735: "Soft hands become ripping claws when a fabulous beauty turns into a crazed thing of evil. See the *Shock Theater* feature film presentation, 'She-Wolf of London,' telecast over this channel (day), (date), at (time)."

*- HHL*

# *The Cat Creeps* (1946)

*Synopsis*: Sampler, the editor of *The Morning Chronicle*, receives a strange letter from Cora Williams, an elderly eccentric who lives alone with her cat on a small island. Williams claims that the suicide of Eric Goran on the island some 15 years before was actually murder and that she has found the $200,000 that was the motive for the crime. Walter Elliot, Cora's distant relative, was under suspicion at the time. Since Elliot is running for the Senate against Sampler's brother-in-law, the editor decides it's time to stir up some bad publicity for Elliot by reviving interest in the case. He assigns his top reporter Terry Nichols to the job. Nichols is wooing Elliot's daughter Gay, but agrees to the task so that someone else won't do the expected hatchet job on Elliot. Gay is nevertheless angry at Nichols for going along with Sampler.

Elliot and Gay decide to pay a visit to Cora, accompanied by Elliot's lawyer, Tom McGalvey, his secretary Connie Palmer, and Ken Grady, a private eye who worked on the case before. Nichols and his photographer Pidge invite themselves along on the boat leaving for the island. No sooner have they arrived at Cora's old house than someone attacks the elderly lady, leaving her in a coma. The boat that brought them to the island is set aflame. Connie attends the stricken Cora and overhears her saying that the money is in "the little house," information she shares with Grady, with whom she obviously in cahoots. Cora is murdered shortly thereafter.

Kyra, a mysterious woman claiming to be Goran's daughter, turns up and warns that Cora's soul is now in the body of her cat and is seeking vengeance on her killer. Connie is terrified of cats, and Kyra uses that fear to drive her into hysteria. However, before Connie can confess what she knows, she is killed. Grady also ends up dead, impaled on a gardening pitchfork.

Universal '40s Monsters: A Critical Commentary

Gay thinks the little house might be the doll house she had as a child. McGalvey finds the house guarded by the cat but, before he can kill the feline, he is interrupted by Terry who overpowers him. McGalvey admits he killed Goran - who was a bootlegger and had amassed the $200,000 - but the lawyer was never able to discover the whereabouts of the cash. Connie and Grady knew of his crime and had been blackmailing him with that knowledge for years. Kyra turns out to be a hoofer/actress hired by Terry, and the hidden money is found in a birdhouse.

"A listless little opus that should be arrested for loitering." - Walter Winchell

Tom McGalvey is surely one of the dumbest crooks ever to disturb the dust in an old-house whodunit. He murders Goran before he knows where the money is and then, 15 years later, makes the same mistake by killing Cora before she can reveal the location of the loot. Not exactly a criminal genius. And, if he's after the money, why does he take his two blackmailers along for the ride and then strand everybody on the island by burning the boat? He does, however, earn the "Quickest-Murder-Ever" Award by dispatching Connie - off-screen with method unspecified - after Kyra turns away from her for about 10 seconds.

In the 17 September 1944 edition of *The Los Angeles Times*, critic Edwin Schallert wrote the following:

> Nothing like the tried and true-in thriller-dillers or otherwise. Universal, which released 'The Cat Creeps' in 1930, very early in the sound days, as a champion event, is planning a biggie revival of this mystery tale. Ford Beebe, who has just completed the Arsene Lupin feature for the studio, will be both associate producer and director while Gerald Geraghty who worked on the elaborate 'Frisco Sal' is developing the mystery.

*The Cat Creeps*, done in both Spanish and English versions in 1930, was a remake of Universal's 1927 hit, *The Cat and the Canary*, which was based on the eponymous John Willard play. Was Universal really planning a remake of the film in the '40s? It seems unlikely, as they had sold the rights of the play to Paramount in 1939 so that the story could be done as a Bob Hope vehicle. Universal, however, did still own the title *The Cat Creeps*, but - as pointed out by Bosley Crowther - the new film had nothing in common with the old one "except that it has the same title and is also shown on a screen."

While still in pre-production, the name Ford Beebe was touted in conjunction with the project. Beebe had scored with *Night Monster* (1942), Universal's best horror mystery of the '40s, and had done a respectable job - given the budget - on *The Invisible Man's Revenge (*1944), as well as having produced the superior *Son of Dracula*. Beebe continued to be associated with the new *Cat Creeps* throughout the remainder of 1944. The 1944 edition of *Box Office Barometer* lists Beebe as producer-director and gives the following advance synopsis: "A murder mystery in which a killer terrorizes a town but meets his match in a clever sleuth." Clearly, the story had not been nailed down yet. In 1945 the project was apparently put on hold, although Gerald Geraghty's name popped up in the trades from time to time as being assigned to write *The Cat Creeps*. Geraghty, son of pioneer screenwriter, Thomas G. Geraghty - who had done films for Doug Fairbanks and Mary Pickford - was primarily a scenarist specializing in Westerns, a genre he should have stayed with. The film did not creep before the cameras until early January of 1946 and wrapped late that month with Ford Beebe having been replaced by Erle C. Kenton.

**Lois Collier – far sexier on the poster than in the actual film – was noted for her singing voice, but she ended up making more Westerns and horror flicks than she did musicals.**

Would *The Cat Creeps* have been a better film had Beebe stayed on as director-producer? Erle C. Kenton did decent though unremarkable work on other Universal

"B" horrors: *The Ghost of Frankenstein, House of Frankenstein* (which had actually been intended for Beebe when it had the title *Dracula vs. Frankenstein*), and *House of Dracula*. Kenton's main claim to fame is, of course, *Island of Lost Souls* (1933), though one is tempted to attribute the effectiveness of that classic to Karl Struss's photography, Charles Laughton's memorably wicked portrayal of Dr. Moreau, and a virtual stampede of monstrous faces. Nonetheless, that attribution wouldn't be entirely fair as Kenton certainly does a good job building tension and creating a closed-in, claustrophobic, queasy atmosphere. It's unlikely that even a Hitchcock could have done anything much with the script of *The Cat Creeps*, but Kenton's direction is still pretty slack.

*The Cat Creeps* was paired with *She-Wolf of London*, as dismal a double-bill as one could imagine for finishing off Universal's monster tradition. Universal had revolutionized horror in the '30s by insisting "There *are* such things" as the supernatural in *Dracula*, but *Cat* and *She-Wolf* are throwbacks to the Silent Era, wherein the uncanny was usually explained away as the work of a human malefactor, a man behind the curtain. At least *She-Wolf pretends* there's something monstrous afoot until the last reel reveals otherwise, but *Cat* doesn't even make a stab at seriously suggesting the old lady has been reincarnated as a vengeful cat. Kyra has barely shown up on the scene when there's an exchange between her and Terry that indicates the two are working together. And is it even worth asking how Terry knows Connie is ailurophobic? Or why the cynical McGalvey falls for the stunt? It's not likely viewers in 1946 pondered such questions on the way to the box office to demand their money back after having been promised a horror double-bill.

The "mystery" in *The Cat Creeps* no doubt made whodunit buffs yawn with boredom. The heroine's father is hardly going to turn out to be the heavy and, since his shadow shows the killer wearing a hat, that narrows things down to McGalvey or Grady (Paul Kelly). But when the detective gets bumped off, the lawyer (played by sleaze-master, Douglass Dumbrille) becomes the only act in town. He then obligingly confesses to everything, even though there is no evidence against him and trying to throttle a cat is not a capital offense. Even the set for *The Cat Creeps* is pretty nondescript; it's just a generic old house without even a secret passageway thrown in the mix, but George Robinson's photography - more than the film deserves - distracts from the drably dressed rooms as well as provides what little spooky atmosphere there is.

Fred Brady's Terry is another reason the picture is hard to sit through. Though he's billed fourth, Brady is pretty much the star of the picture, as *Variety*'s "Wear" noted in a rave (!) review of *The Cat Creeps* that we will reference at length later: "Picture is virtually a screen test for Brady as the reporter and the personable young actor turns it into a starring vehicle for himself. He'll be heard from in the future." "Wear" was closer to Criswell than Nostradamus in that particular prediction, as Brady's film career quickly fizzled though he worked in television a lot in the '50s. Theresa Loeb of *The Oakland Tribune* was more on the money when she wrote that Brady's character should win the title of "the most unrepresentative newspaperman to date in the movies." His grating performance in *Cat* makes Brady's Terry extremely obnoxious, especially in the scene wherein he tells Gay and her pop the bad news about his new job and tries to lessen the blow by clowning around. The viewer shares Gay and Elliot's exasperation with that tactic.

Noah Beery, Jr. (Pidge) is first on the cast crawl, but he's definitely (as usual) a second banana. The running gag here is that Pidge is stopped by Terry when he's about to say the word, "outhouse." Still, though he doesn't get to duke it out with the villain, Pidge does find the missing cash and gets to flirt with Kyra. Beery's father and namesake was one of the great villains of the Silent Era, and his uncle Wallace was the "Aw, shucks!" good guy (though not so much in real life) in many major M-G-M productions. Beery, Jr. had pretty much only one acting device: a likable folksiness that made him ideal for the hero's sidekick in many a sagebrush saga. In his later years, his most conspicuous role was as James Garner's father on *The Rockford Files*.

Rose Hobart doesn't have much to do but look frightened and scream as McAlvey's cat-fearing secretary, Connie. The scene wherein Krya tries to terrify her into a confession might have worked with more build-up, but it happens too quickly and plays without any tension. At this point in her career, Hobart was trooping through similar supporting roles in "B" movies like *The Mad Ghoul* and *Soul of a Monster*, though she occasionally caught a loftier project, like *Conflict* with Humphrey Bogart, with whom Hobart had appeared on Broadway in 1933's *Our Wife*. The veteran actress had done well on the Great White Way in the '20s and, based on her performance in *Death Takes a Holiday* in 1930, Hobart was brought to Hollywood to star in *Liliom*. She was not impressed with LaLaLand: "It scared the hell out of me. I was used to the theater and in Hollywood I was treated like a horse. They wanted to look at my teeth and my legs."(1) The fact that she was willing go from a classy Paramount production like *Dr. Jekyll and Mr. Hyde* to Poverty Row potboilers like *The Shadow Laughs* likely indicates she didn't take her film career very seriously, especially as she continued to work steadily on the stage and was an active participant in the left-leaning Actors Studio.

That participation got Hobart into trouble when the Committee on Un-

American Activities started investigating Hollywood. Called before that august body of witch-hunters in 1949, Hobart refused to say whether she had ever been a communist. She was promptly blacklisted, but years later was not especially bitter about the experience: "You're only threatened when you're not able to make a livelihood but I was married [to an architect] so I was just frustrated."(2) Hobart also developed a strong interest in spirituality and metaphysics, joining the Church of Religious Science. She later did some television work, but was no longer keen on acting. Amateur filmmaker Joseph Cornell was fascinated by Hobart and, in 1936 - using a 16mm copy of Hobart's 1932 *East of Borneo* (which Hobart once described as "the schlockiest film ever") - he made a 19-minute-long, surrealistic movie composed mainly of close-ups of the actress from that picture. It was later critically acclaimed as one of cinema's greatest shorts.

**Paul Kelly glares suspiciously at Iris Clive, while Rose Hobart – whose character has a complete and all-consuming horror of cats – gives Smoky the fish-eye.**

Iris Clive as the mysterious Kyra seems to be channeling Gale Sondergaard - but not very well; I guess Kyra was a better chorus girl than actress. Clive started her career as Iris Lancaster in the '30s and was a stand-in for Joan Crawford, whom she greatly resembled. She made two films in 1934: *The Trail Beyond*, a Western with John Wayne and Noah Berry *pere et fils*, as well as *Murder at the*

*Vanities.* Though Lancaster didn't get billing for the latter film, the young chorines involved did receive their share of publicity in connection with it, particularly in an article that asked the leggy lovelies to consider whether they preferred marriage to a career. Iris answered emphatically in the negative, but in February of 1936, columnist Walter Winchell speculated that she was secretly engaged to Colin Clive; the month before, Winchell had described Iris as Clive's "bay-bee." The tormented, alcoholic actor died of lung problems in June of 1937 and – although she had not, in fact, been the "Bride of Frankenstein," Iris began to bill herself as "Iris Clive" in the '40s, appearing in a few Westerns before dropping completely from view.

Bosley Crowther was not impressed with *The Cat Creeps*, as he wrote in the 18 May 1946 issue of *The New York Times*:

> The rather remote combination of a brilliant young newspaper man with a cat with extra-sensory perception is the team which unravels the crimes in the new Universal picture *The Cat Creeps*. But that fascinating singularity is about the only thing mentionable in this film. Otherwise, it is a routine little thriller with feeble attempts at comedy. The cat gives a pretty good performance but gets mediocre support.

For the record, the cat was played by "Smoky," who had to be tempted with catnip to look away from the microphone (I wonder if they ever tried that with Clara Bow?). Publicity for the film claimed that Lois Collier was allergic to cats and thus could share no close-ups with Smoky.

The trades offered mixed reviews:

> There is nothing no or novel or especially thrilling in 'The Cat Creeps', a routine murder mystery which will get by as a filler on action dual bills…the average patron will be able to figure out the identity of the murderer before half the film's 58 minutes have elapsed. Slowly-opening doors and shadowy figures will get a few shudders but only from the youngsters or impressionable adults. Noah Berry, Jr. makes a futile attempt to get laughs with his wise-cracking lines. Vera Lewis' hawk-like features are more frightening than most of the creepy doings of the plot.
> *Independent Exhibitors Film Bulletin*, 16 June 1946

Vera Lewis may not have come back as a cat, but - according to the goofy playwright, Elinor Glyn (who had earlier coined the term "It") - the distinguished stage actress was the reincarnation of Maria Sophia, the Austrian Empress, which meant she was ideal for the role of the Princess in the movie version of Glyn's *The Only Thing* (1926). While Lewis had some starring roles in the Silent Era, most of her career in the talkies consisted of small parts as dowagers, landladies, and mothers.

The 15 April *Film Daily* felt the film was...

> handicapped by a weak screenplay and Erle C. Kenton's direction which deflates the thrill appeal by repetitious turning of doorknobs, opening of doors and shadowy effects of a figure or a cat sounding the warning note for another murder on the editor's cue sheet.

The reviewer for the 13 April *Harrison's Reports* was a little more favorable:

> A moderately entertaining program murder- mystery melodrama. The story, which goes in for wholesale murders, is interesting only mildly, for there is nothing novel in the plot or in its treatment. Even the performances are only fair, but this is probably due to the fact that the players were unable to cope with the material at hand. The action takes place in a lonely house on an isolated island and it unfolds in a routine manner, with suspicion directed at several of the characters to mystify the viewer. The manner in which the murders are solved is contrived and absurd. The stupidity of a newspaper photographer is used as the comedy relief but is not particularly comical.

*Variety's* "Wear" must have seen a different movie. After admitting the film's plot was nothing new, the writer went on to say:

> Never pretending to be anything more than a lesser feature, *The Cat Creeps* turns out to be nearly an hour of gripping mystery. Geraghty's original follows few of the familiar lines and the Edward Dein-Jerry Warner screenplay is crisp enough to fit a longer vehicle. In fact, much of the dialog and situations measure up to the A mark. Unlike many of the Sherlock-spook –chillers having animals in the plot the black cat in this plays a vital role in solving the mystery.
>
> April 10, 1946

"Wear" went on to mention "the astounding body count" (Really? Three corpses is pretty average for this type of film) and to praise the editing, camerawork, and "solid" supporting cast ("Even Lois Collier is better than usual").

The 13 April *Motion Picture Herald*, while positive, was a bit more restrained:

> Suspicion is directed impartially at all present during the proceedings, which engage interest without throwing onlookers into a dither, and the solution squares neatly with the clues. Direction by Erle C. Kenton is paced in a manner to give each point full opportunity to register, and performances are evenly weighted, one against the other for suspense.

*The Cat Creeps* played a week at the Rialto while another theater, the Ambassador, drew bigger crowds by double-billing reissues of *The Cat People* and *The Curse of the Cat People*. The notion of a cat seeming to avenge its owner's death can be traced back to Edgar Allan Poe's *The Black Cat* and has found more recent treatment in 1961's *The Shadow of the Cat* where, unlike in *The Cat Creeps*, puss-in-boots really means business.

***The Cat Creeps*** - 58 minutes -17 May 1946 (ST)

**CAST:** Noah Berry, Jr. as Pidge Lorry; Lois Collier as Gay Elliot; Paul Kelly as Ken Grady; Fred Brady as Terry Nichols; Douglass Dumbrille as Tom McGalvey; Rose Hobart as Connie Palmer; Jonathan Hale as Walter Elliot; Iris Clive (aka Iris Lancaster) as Kyra; Vera Lewis as Cora Williams; William B. Davidson as Sampler; Arthur Loft as Publisher; Jerry Jerome as Polich

**CREDITS:** Director: Earle C. Kenton; Executive Producer: Howard Welsch; Associate Producer: Will Cowan; Scenario: Edward Dein and Jerry Warner; Original Story: Gerald Geraghty; Photography: George Robinson; Art Direction: Jack Otterson, Abraham Grossman; Film Editor: Russell Schoengarth; Set Decoration: Russell A. Gausman, Theodore Offenbecker; Costumes: Vera West; Music: Paul Sawtell; Sound: Bernard B. Brown, William Hedgcock; Make-up: Jack Pierce

***Shock Theater*** Catalog No. 695 - "A nightmare of mystery takes place on an island of terror in the *Shock* feature film presentation 'The Cat Creeps,' telecast on this channel (

day), at (time). There's a thrill a minute, a shiver a second, in this story of murder on an island! Don't miss 'The Cat Creeps' (day), (time)."

*- HN*

# *Dressed to Kill* (1946)

There's a new gambit that director Roy William Neill permits himself in face of the viewers' familiarity with the Holmes series: without off-screen narration, we're in for a prologue that takes almost eight minutes of the opening footage. After a brief scene in the prison at Dartmoor, with a prisoner determined to make music boxes during his two years of incarceration, the action moves to a sumptuous London auction house and we sit through the auction of three of those boxes.

Once the event is over, a phlegmatic gentleman (Frederic Worlock, in his sixth and last appearance in the series) arrives in search of several already sold music boxes, which he's seeking "for sentimental reasons." This character, whom we later discover is Colonel Cavanaugh, consults with the auctioneer (Holmes Herbert, in his fifth series role) about the identity of the buyers. One of them is a certain Mr. Kilgore (Harry Allen). In the comments on the meager price of several shillings paid by Kilgore, the first of the dialogues reflecting the usual British sense of humor comes into play:

"Quite a drop from two pounds."

"Mr. Kilgore was a Scotsman."

It is only then – as in so many of the series' preambles – that the camera takes its accustomed place at the door of 221b Baker Street in order to head inside through its hall and climb its stairs, this time to a sweet version of "Danny Boy," apparently from Holmes's violin. The detective is seated on his sofa while Watson reads a copy of *The Strand* magazine, wherein one of his latest stories has just appeared. The sight of Holmes, going gray at his temples, and of Watson, wearing reading glasses, gives us the immediate impression of both characters in the autumn of their lives. And more… on commenting on Watson's reading about a certain "Scandal in Bohemia," Holmes acquires a nostalgic tone of voice when referring to "The Woman": Irene Adler. None of the films in the series (or the two initial features by Fox) had featured Irene Adler or had adapted that famous Conan Doyle novel, but her "title" was truly *vox populi* for the viewers who – as the screenwriters and producers appreciated – were also faithful readers.

Then Julian Emery, a distinguished gentleman who had acquired one of the music boxes at auction, arrives. (Emery was played by Edmond Breon, a Scots actor of vast experience in the fight against crime, his having portrayed Inspector Juve in the original presentation of the cinematic melodrama, Louis Feuillade's *Fantomas*.) Emery turns out to be an old friend of Watson's and, while they're conversing about an apparently unimportant event ( the removal of one of the music boxes from his personal collection), Holmes becomes highly interested in one detail: Why would the thief take a piece worth five pounds when he had within arm's distance objects worth more than 500? On the way back, Holmes tosses one of usual dialectic statements at his faithful biographer: "It's often a mistake to accept something that's true merely because it's obvious." And then he tops it all off with a famous concept that, in more or less the same words, he has been expressing in countless stories since the sixth chapter of **The Sign of Four**: "The truth is only arrived at by the painstaking process of eliminating the untrue."

A different dilemma confronts poor Emery: during a nocturnal visit by a mysterious young woman, Hilda Courtney (Patricia Morison), who admits to being interested in the box, he seeks to excuse himself: "I am a collector... and a collector buys, but never sells." Hilda's driver and hitman, Hamid (Harry Cording, seventh and last sighting in the series), nonetheless resolves the problem via an accurate stab in the back. Scotland Yard shows up later and Holmes is called at Lestrade's suggestion, which we mention because the inspector doesn't appear on this occasion, as a certain Inspector Hopkins (Carl Harbord) will take on the case. Beginning in this way, the viewers may feel a sense of familiarity with this story of villains after *objets d'art* manufactured in quantity. In *The Pearl of Death*, they were the little busts of Napoleon that disappeared from Harry Cording's workshop (both films linked argumentatively via "The Adventure of the Six Napoleons"). The fate of the older man who tries to hang on to a flirtatious life with younger women reminds us of the tragic character played by Paul Cavanagh en *The Woman in Green*. The belief that the boxes have some encrypted message takes us back to *Sherlock Holmes and the Secret Weapon*, with the technique for decoding the cipher of the "dancing men," only here pointed at the musical notations found in the melody of each box. And as for yet another conceit that's become something of a given, it's that Watson involuntarily provides the key to the correspondence between musical notes and letters. Lastly, Holmes' visit to his rival, Hilda Courtney, although not as memorable as his interlude with Adrea Spedding, will lead to the usual pattern being followed: Holmes' apparent defeat, capture and execution, from which he is saved at the last moment.

The critics received the picture with the sort of approval that, except for specific instances, it had expressed to this point. *Showmen's Trade Review* (25 May 1946) found it to be "a very good mystery; much more logical than most," praising "the fine direction of Roy William Neill" and lauding the perfect Rathbone/Bruce chemistry that "makes the picture a smooth-running bit of entertainment." More given to moderation, *Film Daily* (20 May 1946) decreed it to be "no better and no worse than the others in the series," although it agreed with the virtue that had gone observed by all of the previous reviewers: "the picture has a direction by Neill that never permits a lag in the action at any time." In a positive rapture of synthesis, *Variety* (22 May 1946) described the picture in one line: "Okay supporting film fare." Building on the narrative a bit, the Bible of Show Business then admitted: "Like most of the Universal series it is expertly put together and excellently played by a cast familiar with the technique necessary to keep Holmes fans satisfied." Far from indulging in critical pretension, *Harrison's Reports* (18 May 1946) found some narrative contradictions: "A fairly interesting Sherlock Holmes mystery melodrama, but it is spoiled somewhat by plot twists that are a bit too pat." The reviewer agreed with the rest of the specialized media, saying that the film "should satisfy the followers of this type of entertainment." *Box Office* (25 May 1946) went a little bit further, making the interesting point that "the series has gone a long way now, and on so consistently satisfactory a standard, that it is beside the point to say whether one episode is better than another."

Viewed nowadays – knowing it to be the last entry in Universal's series – most critics attribute the end of the affair to Basil Rathbone's "fatigue" with the role, a sentiment borne out by the actor in his memoirs. Nonetheless, another important factor had been the reorganization of the studio as Universal-International, whose new policy was to abjure "B"-films and serials. Did Roy William Neill have plans to continue the series in Great Britain? It's curious that for the final scene, set in the home/museum of Dr. Samuel Johnson, the director greatly concerned himself that the settings reproduce as faithfully as possible the rooms of the real museum, in Gough Square, London. (The construct also included – via some dialogue exchanged by two visitors to the museum near one of the corners of the exhibition – a couple of unmistakable winks at the British public.) The filmmaker's sudden death - he

691

had a heart attack at the end of 1946 in London, where he had gone to visit some family – had perhaps put an end to the most prolific of the detective's sound-cinema adventures.

The truth is that Rathbone continued to interpret Holmes in *The New Adventures of Sherlock Holmes*, a radio program that he made together with Nigel Bruce since October of 1939; his last take in the role was in "The Singular Affair of the Baconian Cipher," which aired on the 27 May 1946. With Nigel Bruce's Dr. Watson at his side, Tom Conway – who would also play sleuths Bulldog Drummond, the Falcon, and the Saint - stepped into the role of the Great Consulting Detective; the series aired its final segment 38 weeks later.

Despite the fact that its dramatic elements were certainly not original – even if we were to consider only the studio's other efforts in the series – *Dressed to Kill* possessed an appreciable subtext, which is dealt with comprehensively by Amanda J. Field in her **England's Secret Weapon; the Wartime Films of Sherlock Holmes** (1). Almost from its first frames, which reveal an almost antique-looking photographic panorama of the Dartmoor prison, the succession of art and antiquities galleries and antiquities and collected musical artifacts up to and including the "parishioners" of that gas-lit tavern and, of course, the final outcome in a museum... everything leads to the past. "The men," observes Ms. Field, "are shown to inhabit the Victorian Era, and women the present." Both the dress and the accouterments of Holmes and Watson seem always a tad "old-fashioned" when compared to the garb of their onscreen colleagues; it's as if the famed duo is ever fated to have one foot stuck resolutely a half-century or so in the past. As for Ms. Field's Freudian reading about Edmond Breon's toupee in front of the fox fur that Hilda's wearing... we'll be passing on that in order to encourage all of our readers to consult that valuable volume published by Middlesex University Press.

Holmes, a much larger-than-life character, transcends all epochs and eras and, as we intended postulated whilst covering the first films in the series, is "invincible and unchanging." And as the only way we are aware of to remain "unchanging" is to not give into the impositions of the present, "What better place to take refuge from dizzying attacks than that adorable room on the first floor of 221b Baker Street?

*Dressed to Kill* – 7 June 1946 – 76 minutes

**CAST**: Basil Rathbone as Sherlock Holmes; Nigel Bruce as Doctor Watson; Patricia Morison as Mrs. Hilda Courtney; Edmund Breon as Julian Emery; Frederic

Worlock as Colonel Cavanaugh; Carl Harbord as Inspector Hopkins; Patricia Cameron as Evelyn Clifford; Holmes Herbert as Ebenezer Crabtree; Harry Cording as Hamid; Leyland Hodgson as Tour Guide; Mary Gordon as Mrs. Hudson; Ian Wolfe as Commissioner of Scotland Yard; Cyril Delevanti as John Davidson; Guy Kingsford as Scotland Yard Undercover Convict; Olaf Hytten as Alfred, Auction House Bookkeeper; Alex Pollard as Crabtree Assistant; Harry Allen as Mr. Kilgore; Eric Mayne, Hans Moebus and Florence Wix as Patrons at Auction; Topsy Glyn as Kilgore Child; Tom Dillon as Detective Thompson; William H. O'Brien as Detective; Charles Hall as Taxi Cab Driver; Marjorie Bennett as Antique Shop Assistant; Boyd Irwin as Detective with X-ray Photos; Wallace Scott as Joe Cisto; Ted Billings, Bobbie Hale, Tiny Jones, Matthew McCue, Frank Mills as Pub Patrons; Sally Shepherd as Tobacconist; Lillian Bronson as Minister's Wife; Wilson Benge as Minister; Anita Sharp Bolster as Teacher; Guy Bellis as Doctor; Frank Baker as Photographer.

**CREDITS**: Director and Producer: Roy William Neill; Executive Producer: Howard Benedict; Screenplay: Leonard Lee, adapted by Frank Gruber, Musical Director: Milton Rosen, Photography: Maury Gertsman, Film Editing: Saul A. Goodkind, Art Director: Martin Obzina and Jack Otterson, Set Decoration: Russell A. Gausman and Edward R. Robinson, Gowns: Vera West, Makeup: Jack P. Pierce and Carmen Dirigo, Assistant Director: Melville Shyer and Judson Cox, Matte Artist: Russell Lawson, Dialogue Director: Raymond Kessler.

*- DL*

# *Danger Woman* (1946)

*Synopsis:* In the wake of the Nagasaki and Hiroshima devastation, we find physicist Claude Ruppert involved in seeking how to use nuclear energy for something other than catastrophic desolation: namely, for the sake of business. Pretty much against his personal ideology, Ruppert's research to date has been utilized to build weapons of mass destruction, but he feels that his new formula could be used very much in the service of mankind. Ruppert has already discussed his fears that his new discovery could easily be misappropriated for violent purposes with Dr. Albert Sears, the university Dean, as well as with June Spenser, Ruppert's secretary and confidant, who is silently suffering from unrequited love vis-à-vis her boss. Sears, having reviewed his colleague's research paper, encourages him to present same to the public, but Ruppert refuses and is viewed as intentionally stalling progress in the use of atomic energy.

Out of nowhere, Ruppert's beautiful wife, Eve – from whom the physicist has been separated for three years – reappears and asks her husband for another shot at making their marriage work. Secretary June is quite disconcerted at this, and Ruppert tells her that, although he no longer loves his wife, it's only fair to try yet again. Eve moves back in and that night, there's a car accident outside the house. The injured victim, Gerald King, is allowed to remain with the Rupperts and to recuperate in their spare bedroom after having been examined by a Doctor Carey. It later devolves that King is a spy who is working with a certain co-conspirator named Lane, and that the accident had been arranged so that he could get into Ruppert's house.

Later, Dr. Sears informs Ruppert he has been suspended, as it is assumed that he and June are having an extramarital affair. That night the Rupperts share the conjugal bed, and June – later still – advises Ruppert that his sharing of his discovery will end up with him back in the good graces of the university and society at large. When Ruppert calls Dr. Sears to tell him that he would speak at the upcoming convention, the physicist hears that his financial grant had been withdrawn. Suspecting that something is up, Dr. Sears heads over to try to talk the fellowship committee into withdrawing its withdrawal, but he is killed in yet another car accident, this one triggered by Lane's having tampered with the good doctor's auto.

Eve is approached by King, who talks her into attempting to get Ruppert to at least show her his paperwork, but, after all that has transpired, he refuses. In the interim, June has confided in Dr. Carey that it is *she* and her feeling for Ruppert that are responsible for his ill treatment by the university and his inability to find work elsewhere. Not long thereafter, Dr. Carey is also killed, and Ruppert visits Police Inspector Pepper to discuss the two killings. King threatens to blackmail Eva unless she steals the paperwork from Ruppert's safe; however, June finds Eva at the safe, and Eva – displaying a change of heart – instructs June to run and bring Ruppert back to deal with King.

After Jane has gone, Eva intends to kill the resident spy, but it is she who is killed by King and the energy papers are now tossed out the window, where henchman Lane awaits. The plan goes awry, though, as Inspector Pepper is there, also, to arrest Lane. King insists that Eve killed herself, but the discovery of Lane's fingerprints in Dr. Sears' car and on Dr. Carey's desk leads to the arrest of King for murder. The following day, Ruppert and June again are sitting in the park where June announces that it would be best if she were to get out of her boss's life until things are looking up for him again, and Ruppert agrees, vowing to "wait forever" for her.

Admittedly, that's a lot of synopsis for a fairly standard spy story, but the presence of the "energy paper" MacGuffin at least gives the film a hint of a science-fiction, even if the plot does reflect the then-current political/scientific state of affairs. The last year or so of the Second World War – before either Germany or Japan surrendered – saw the incipient introduction of war-time technology that might very well have tipped the balance of power in the favor of the Axis partners. It was during August of 1944 that *Generalfeldmarschall* Hermann Göring, the Supreme Commander of the Luftwaffe, thrilled his Führer by introducing the Arado AR 234, a jet-propelled bomber, into the skies. The aircraft, which was used primarily for reconnaissance, recorded no "kills," and only 250 or so were produced. More germane to our argument, though, was the mass production (1400+) of the Messerschmitt Me 262, the first fully operational jet-fighter/bomber in the war. While the U.K. had introduced its Gloster Meteor F.1 and

F.3 at about the same time – 'twas a British G.M. that was the first jet plane to shoot down another jet plane during the hostilities – the United States' contribution to the "product line," the Lockheed P-80 Shooting Star, was limited to four aircraft flying over Europe before the ETO was over. None saw combat.

**Four of the least engaging photographs in movie history "grace" this TC, along with the unremarkable "Ne touchez pas!" artwork containing *an* Invisible Man. We still doubt anyone was shocked by this when it premiered on TV in 1957.**

While perhaps not as horrifyingly daunting as the atomic bomb (when viewed in retrospect), the plethora of the German Messerschmitt Me 262s might have played a crucial role in the Third Reich's dominance of the air had their deployment not come as other factions of the German machine were winding down and the Allies were introducing similar aircraft of their own. Spying and defections played a rather important role in the development of such technology, and the American public – including the very large movie-going public – were quite aware of this. Tales of spies working on both sides had become commonplace fodder in movie palaces everywhere (cf: *Enemy Agent*, 1940), and *Danger Woman* was but another float in that parade. As stated above, the inclusion of a nuclear "wrinkle" in the whole cloth of the conceit may serve to give us a slight genre preference for the picture under discussion over stuff like *Enemy Agent*, but it is still the film's charter membership in the "Shock Theater" package that accounts for the discussion here.

The picture's plot-line – the familiarity of a "spy among us" apart – hinges on a couple of facets that were old when the Earth was young: coincidence and sheer lunacy. The coincidence at hand is the timely resurgence of the ravishing Eve Ruppert. Just as old Claude is caught between Scylla and Charybdis with respect to his taking his discovery out of the safe and into the public, he is once again thrown for a loop by her beauty, and the Ruppert household is once again possessed of a mistress. June's later catching Eve with her fingers in the till, as it were, was way too frequent a plot wrinkle to be tagged a "coincidence"; a "foregone conclusion" or a "hoary *cliché*" might be more precise. The addition of a virtual stranger injured in a nearby car accident is an instance of the lunatic facet, and we have to wonder whether scenarist Josef Mischel – a late-in-life immigrant from Austria-Hungary – honestly thought either that auto accidents were ten for a penny in his adopted homeland, or that it was a common American practice for private homes in the vicinity of such an occurrence to take in injured "boarders."

We also have to wonder who arrived at the release title and, more pertinently, how. With June the hopelessly smitten, good-natured, obviously patriotic American young heroine, the marquee obviously belongs to Eve. Sure, she's quite lovely, but the audience suspects that Ruppert – himself the good-natured (if a tad preoccupied), obviously patriotic American hero – would never have parted ways with her had she been decent and above-board in the first place. 'Tis within moments of screen time following her abrupt return that the woman seduces – there is no other word – her ex-ish husband, and her initial participation on the side of King and those whom he stands for indicates yet again how specious her loyalties are. She is indeed a *dangerous* woman, but we remain hard-pressed to understand the variation in titular adjective.

Released less than a year after Imperial Japan surrendered on the 15 August 1945, *Danger Woman* played up the danger of atomic energy to an audience that was at once enormously grateful for a sudden end to hostilities in the Pacific and yet understandably terrified of consequences should knowledge of the technology end up in unfriendly hands. Once again following the pattern established by *Enemy Agent* and its kith, the picture reveals that espionage is not something restricted to governmental buildings or secret meetings of high-ranking officials; it's going on next door and is carried out by those whom you regard as friends and neighbors. "Creating public awareness" may have been a tertiary side effect of revelations such as this – we currently are experiencing the same calls to vigilance in terms of abandoned parcels, suspicious packages, and "If you see something, say something"-type campaigns – but the near ubiquity of the message courtesy of "B"-level programmers such as this may have watered down the desired effect.

*Danger Woman*'s cast consists of Universal's contract players, all of whom do a totally adequate job in portraying the types outlined in the script. Don Porter – best remembered by this writer as Ann Sothern's boss in the actress's late-'50s TV series – is completely credible as the conflicted physicist with a sense of duty, and more on him may be found in our essay on *Night Monster*. Brenda Joyce is probably better remembered as successor to Maureen O'Sullivan as "Jane" in latter-'40s features in the "Tarzan" series than as "June" in *Danger Woman*, and we've a lengthier accounting of her genre credits in our chapter on *The Spider Woman Strikes Back*. As does the rest of the cast – including old hands Milburn Stone and Samuel S. Hinds – Miss Joyce personifies the qualities her character is meant to display, at least per the established formula for pics like this one.

Patricia Morison is the title character, and we're still uncertain as to whether she's meant to be a woman *of* peril or, as the denouement has it, a woman *in* peril. With a very eclectic cinematic résumé – the New York native really can't be pigeonholed as favoring one genre over another – Miss Morison very aptly portrays the beautiful woman with an indistinct past who has come to toss the adjustable spanner into the works. When her Eve switches sides suddenly as the threat of the end credits grows closer, the actress does so without indulging in the sort of theatrics that make instantaneous transformations visible to the back row. Following her role here, she appeared in quick succession in *Queen of the Amazons*, *Tarzan and the Huntress* (along with Brenda Joyce), *Song of the Thin Man* (all three, 1947), and Robin Hood epic, *The Prince of Thieves* (1948). Boy! Talk about eclectic! And, in the midst of so much cinematic fluff, the New York City native was given a shot at cinematic gold – the Academy Award – when she was signed to portray the doomed wife of Nick Bianco (Victor Mature) in Fox's *Kiss of Death* (1947). While Richard Widmark *did* win the Oscar (for Best Actor in a Supporting Role), Morison came away empty as virtually all her scenes - among them, the depiction of her rape and her suicide – were cut by the censors, with her character disappearing completely from the picture!(1)

The lovely actress also possessed quite a singing voice and played the female leads in stage productions of *The King and I*, *Kiss Me Kate*, *The Merry Widow*, and *Pal Joey* among others. Miss Morison made it to her 103rd year, passing away in LaLaLand in March of 2018.

Neither Lewis D. Collins' direction nor Maury Gertsman's photography are anything to write home about, although other of Gertsman's projects – notably 1955's

*To Hell and Back* – gave the man the opportunity he needed to make a cinematic impression.

Inasmuch as critical expectations were low, they were pretty consistently met. We can't find the citations for either of the following, but their sharing a viewpoint is undeniable. "A tight little yarn incorporating the basic elements of the eternal triangle and, at the same time, dragging in the top question of the day – the atom bomb," saith one, whilst the second avers:

> The picture has been modestly produced by Morgan B. Cox, and directed without too much pains by Lewis D. Collins, who has not been able to make the film more than mildly suspenseful... The players have given to the film no more of themselves than the script deserved."

*Harrison's Reports* likewise found the picture to be absolutely nothing special:

> An ordinary program melodrama, modestly produced. It subject matter – atomic energy, is timely, but the plot is so commonplace and so obvious that one loses interest in the outcome, since one surmises in advance just what is going to happen. Moreover, the picture lacks excitement and, since it is given more to talk than to action, it moves at a slow pace. Some of the dialogue is quite trite. The players do their best with the mediocre material given them, but they fail to overcome the plot's defects.
>
> 13 July 1946

As with those who have entered nobility due solely to accidents of birth, so does *Danger Woman* settle comfortably in these pages. Nothing special – you've seen it all done before, and, as the saying goes, you've seen it done better – but it does offer the opportunity to see some of the '40s most recognizable character actors present their wares in the comfort of our living rooms.

**Danger Woman** - 12 July 1946 – 59 minutes (ST)

**CAST:** Don Porter as Prof. Claude Ruppert; Brenda Joyce as June Spenser; Patricia Morison as Eve Ruppert; Milburn Stone as Gerald King; Samuel S. Hinds as Dr. Albert Sears; Kathleen Howard as Eddie; Griff Barnett as Dr. George Carey; Charles

D. Brown as Inspector Pepper; Ted Hecht as Lane; Leonard East as Howard; with Eddie Acuff, Douglas Carter, Ronnie Gilbert, Chuck Hamilton, Keith Richards, Howard Negley

**CREDITS**: Director: Lewis D. Collins; Producer: Morgan Cox; Story: Josef Mischel; Cinematographer: Maury Gertsman; Film Editor: Russell F. Schoengarth; Art Directors: Harold H. MacArthur, Jack Otterson; Set Decoration: Russell A. Gausman, Leigh Smith; Makeup: Carmen Dirigo, Jack P. Pierce; Assistant Director: Melville Shyer; Sound: Bernard B. Brown; Technician: Jess Moulin; Sound Mixer: Ronald Pierce; Musical Director: Paul Sawtell; Dialogue Director: Willard Holland; Gowns: Vera West

*Shock Theater* Catalog No. 697: "A gang of international thieves uses a woman's beauty to seize atomic energy secrets in 'Danger Woman.' The *Shock* full-length presentation starring Brenda Joyce and Don Porter with the shock of tomorrow's headlines: 'Danger Woman' brings you on this channel, (day) at (time). A story bursting with Fury!"

*-JTS*

# *The Time of Their Lives* (1946)

*Synopsis*: In 1780 New York, tinker Horatio Prim and his sweetheart Nora overhear Thomas Danbury conspiring to join up with Benedict Arnold and betray the revolutionary cause. While Horatio is imprisoned in a trunk by Danbury's butler, Cuthbert Greenway, Nora is kidnapped by Danbury's men, and a letter of commendation for Horatio - signed by George Washington - is taken from her and hidden in the secret cache of the traitor's clock. Danbury's fiancée, Melody Allen, frees Horatio from the trunk, but when she and the tinker head off to warn the Continental Army of Danbury's betrayal, they are shot down by the revolutionaries who, not realizing what the two had set out to do, condemn them as traitors and throw their bodies into a well, condemning them to be bound to Danbury Acres forever – or until their names are cleared. Moments later, their ghosts materialize and find it impossible to leave the grounds.

There they sit, until 1946...

Sheldon Gage has purchased the manor and is seeking to outfit it with the original accouterments had by Danbury. Together with his fiancée, June Prescott, psychiatrist Ralph Greenway (a descendant of Danbury's butler), and June's Aunt Millie, they look to bring the property back up to snuff. The ghosts of Horatio and Melody are not keen on any more newcomers and begin to haunt the house at midnight. Although the guests are disconcerted, housekeeper Emily advises them that the ghosts are from the well and – following a number of gags – holds a séance. The ghosts, pulled by the ritual into the house, hear Sheldon say that he wants to help them. The fact of the Washington letter in the clock is communicated to the table sitters – the contrite spirit of Tom Danbury briefly enters Emily's body to provide the combination to the locked drawer - but it devolves that the original clock is in a New York museum. Greenway heads off to retrieve it, in an act that he says will atone for his ancestor's sins.

Snatching the clock, Greenway is pursued back to the house by the police, who seize him before he can open the secret drawer. The presence of Horatio and Melody in the squad car prevents the cops from leaving the grounds, however, and the ghosts crash the car when the police climb out to see what's gone wrong. In the melee, the secret drawer to the clock has opened, and Sheldon reads aloud the letter from George Washington, effectively ending the curse. Melody departs for the Pearly Gates, as does Horatio, who follows the voice of his darling Nora. A final gag reveals that – even after 165 years – Horatio will have to wait a bit longer before entering heaven as it is closed for Washington's birthday.

Albeit regarded by many as one of the more "minor" of the team's efforts, *The Time of Their Lives* successfully blends elements of the true supernatural with some grand comedic bits in a way that anticipates the more operatic *Abbott and Costello Meet Frankenstein*. It's only a short step from believing in an afterlife as dictated by religion to believing in ghosts, and seances had become popular and – especially in Europe – fairly commonplace following the Great War. To counterbalance the more serious side of the plot with the sort of nimble buffoonery in which Lou Costello had very few equals took vision, and Charles Barton – who had previously helmed a slew of comedies starring such diverse *pagliacci* as Joe Besser, William Bendix, Judy Canova, Jackie Gleason, Eddie "Rochester" Anderson, and Joe E. Brown – was just the man to do so. The diminutive director (5'2", without shoes) had earlier shown (in flicks like *The Island of Doomed Men* and *The Phantom Submarine*, both 1940) that he was more than capable of sustaining tension; in fact, a glance at his earlier bona fides reveals the man's colorful and diverse palette: *Rocky Mountain Mystery* (1935, Western), *The Last Outpost* (1935, War), *Rose Bowl* (1936, Sports), *Behind Prison Gates* (1939, Crime), *Five Little Peppers at Home* (1940, Family Drama), *Two Latins from Manhattan* (1941, Musical Comedy). *The Time of Their Lives* was the first of Barton's efforts with Bud and Lou – *Dance with Me, Henry* (1956) would be his last with the team, as well as the team's final feature – and seven other ABC (Abbott, Barton, Costello) pictures were produced in between.

*The Time of Their Lives* was the second experiment (*Little Giant*, released six months earlier, was first) in having Bud and Lou not work continually opposite each other, as they had in all their previous films. Sources vary on the whys and wherefores for the move, among them the claim that the movie-going public had grown weary of the boys' routines and/or that personal relations between the two were fraying.

In Chris Costello's biography of her dad, she quotes Charlie Barton as saying that "When I started working with them and directing their films in 1946, I could sense an animosity between them."(1) With this being the director's first project with the team, it's safe to assume said "animosity" had been present for some while. No matter the reason for the move, it was perhaps a wise one, as it gave both men room to act and react outside of the parameters that had been repeatedly set during the preceding lustrum. And inasmuch as Costello spent most of the film partnered with Marjorie Reynolds – the two of them cut a wonderful swath through some top-notch special effects – the novelty of a beautiful colleague sharing the after-death experience allowed the comic a new dimension in which to work his magic.

**Everything above the title (*The Ghost Runs Away*) could be termed "stock art," but the sight of Marjorie Reynolds towering over Bud and Lou...well, THAT certainly gets one's attention!**

One might say that the special effects by Jerome Ash and D.S. Horsley were co-stars along with the boys and the glamorous Miss Reynolds. Whereas *Hold That Ghost* had featured all sorts of mechanical contraptions meant to send Costello's character into fits and audiences into convulsions, the camera magic here concentrates mostly on non-corporeal waftings, appearances and disappearances, and passages of the ethereal through the substantial. The sequence in which Horatio and Melody run through each other – with the result that each is now wearing the other's clothing – is unexpected, clever, and quite funny. The logical quibble I have occurs toward the end of the film: we're aware that neither spirit can leave the grounds because of Major Putnam's eternal curse, but we're also made aware – time and again – that both ghosts can pass through solid materials. Thus, whilst they cannot pass through the solid gates that encircle Danbury Acres, both surely ought to be able to pass through the solid police car in which Horatio is sitting. Methinks that logically (might one hope for logic in instances such as this?) the car would pass unimpeded through the gates, while Horatio is sent careering out the back. Still, let's not let overthinking stand in the way of a good gag and the plot solution.

Marjorie Reynolds' screen debut was at six years old - as an uncredited gamin - in 1923's *Trilby* (1923), when Arthur Edmund Carewe was her Svengali and a new cinematic version of the story had been/continued to be cranked out almost every year. While she graced a brace of Karloff/"Mr. Wong" programmers as the '30s and '40s came to meet and is under our scrutiny once again in our essay on *Enemy Agent* (1940), Miss Reynolds probably remains best known to duffers like myself as William Bendix's long-suffering wife in the mid-'50s TV series, *The Life of Riley*. She is splendid here, whether in acting out the fate of the unfortunate Melody Allen or in reacting to Costello's scripted antics, and an intriguing bent to her interpretation of the decidedly non-corporeal Melody is her performance of a decidedly sexy wiggle to achieve invisibility. (There's also a peculiar moment when it seems as if her long-deceased Melody is succumbing to urges of the flesh, as she approaches Horatio with something other than philosophical banter on her mind, but 'tis an oddity attributed to the script and not to the actress's interpretation.)

An appreciative addition to the resident ghosts is the presence of the always shuddery Gale Sondergaard, who conducts seances like no one else. A closer look at the Minnesota-born actress may be found in our essay on *The Black Cat*.

706

**Both John Shelton and Bud Abbott look as if they're focused on Marjorie Reynolds (whom, of course, they cannot see). Lou and Marjorie are doing the acting thing, and Binnie Barnes is an inch from making clucking noises at the romantic lead.**

By the time *The Time* hit the screen, Lou Costello had come a long way from being his partner's stooge/fall guy, either onstage or on film. While there may have been viewers who yearned for the back-and-forth with which they had grown familiar when Bud and Lou represented one united front for goodness (or, at least, for laughs), there were probably just as many – if not more – who were grateful that an overly familiar formula had been dispensed with. The comic *is* made to deal with the occasional throwback: as Horatio Prim, Costello is not only a flesh-and-blood human being (you know what I mean), but also one who actually has a romantic relationship going on. He's not the brightest candle in the window; still, he's a darn sight from being the dimmest, and the repudiation of this latter personality quirk is quite welcome. Costello demonstrates not only his zany side, but – in a very real way for the first time – a sense of pathos that had only been hinted at in previous films.

None of the other men's roles in the film amount to much more than brief sequences in which the plot parameters are established, although Bud Abbott does a nice job impersonating a couple of Greenways. John Shelton *did* act alongside other spiritual entities – bogus, all – in some early '40s efforts: *The Ghost Comes Home* (1940), *Whispering Ghosts* (1942, with Milton Berle), and *A-Haunting We Will Go* (also '42,

707

with Laurel and Hardy), before call it quits as a thespian in 1954. The Los Angeles native survived his film retirement by nearly 20 years, passing away in mid-May 1972. *The Time of Their Lives* was virtually the only genre feature in which South Carolinian Jess Barker signed up, but he was to be spotted here and there on the small screen during the '50s until the mid-'60s. Like Shelton, Barker left the cinema before leaving behind all other ills: his last role was in 1977; his last breath, in early August 2000. Robert Barrett didn't have too lengthy a role herein, but as Major Putnam he did effectively pronounce the fatal words that set things hopping, and the New York-born actor appeared in his share of genre efforts/thrillers, including 1921's *Whispering Shadows*, a post-Great War treatment of the dead trying to communicate with those they left behind; Universal's *Secret of the Blue Room* (1933); *Return of the Terror* and *The Dragon Murder Case* (both 1934); *Charlie Chan in Honolulu* (1938); *Strangler of the Swamp* (1946); and *Flight to Mars* (1951).

Lurking in the midst of the uncredited folk running hither, thither and yon is Kirk Alyn – soon to be widely acknowledged as Superman in the eponymous 1948 Columbia serial – whose film career to that point consisted of a couple of dozen screen appearances, mostly uncredited. Intriguingly, other than his two turns as the Man of Steel (let's not forget 1950's *Atom Man vs. Superman*) and his subsequent title portrayal of *Blackhawk* (Columbia, 1952), Alyn's only genre part would be yet another uncredited moment in 1951's sci-fi classic, *When Worlds Collide*.

*The Time of Their Lives* was the last "purely" Universal picture the team would make; their next offering – *Buck Privates Come Home* – was a product of the newly nascent Universal-International. While it shares a plot with countless other spirit flicks – the ghost must perform some sort of task to "move on" (here, just get your hands on the bloody clock) - *Time* benefits from Costello's talent, Charlie Barton's guidance, and Horsley and Ash's cinematic marvels.

The picture won mixed reviews, albeit the Bible of Show Business was impressed by both comedy and cinematography, while the *Hollywood Reporter* wrote (somewhat redundantly) that "Something new is being offered by Abbott and Costello, something gay and riotously brand-new." On a more local level, the *Cleveland Plain Dealer's* W. Ward Marsh opined that Bud and Lou "Are at Their Film Funniest" in the picture:

Writing as one who in the past has been able to take Abbott and Costello or, preferably, leave them strictly alone, I must confess that 'The Time of Their Lives' amused me more than have all their past screen antics.

In my always humble opinion, the film has its moments, the team's characterizations are great, and the machinations employed to support all the otherworldliness are spot on. Still, my – and many others' – favorite misadventure of the team with supernatural forces was concocted and realized a couple of years in the future.

*The Time of Their Lives* – 16 August 1946 – 82 minutes

**CAST**: Bud Abbott as Cuthbert Greenway and Dr. Ralph Greenway; Lou Costello as Horatio Prim; Marjorie Reynolds as Melody Allen; Binnie Barnes as Mrs. Prescott; John Shelton as Sheldon Gage; Jess Barker as Tom Danbury; Gale Sondergaard as Emily; Robert Barrat as Major Putnam; Donald MacBride as Lieutenant Mason; Anne Gillis as Nora; Lynn Baggett as June Prescott; William Hall as Connors; Rex Lease as Sergeant Makepeace; Harry Woolman as Motorcycle Rider; Harry Bown as Second Sergeant; Walter Baldwin as Bates; Selmer Jackson as Curator; Vernon Downing as Leigh; Boyd Irwin as Cranwell; Marjorie Eaton as Bessie; with Kirk Alyn, John Crawford, Scott Thompson, Myron Healey

**CREDITS**: Director: Charles T. Barton; Producer: Val Burton; Executive Producer: Joe Gershenson; Screenplay by Val Burton, Walter DeLeon, Bradford Ropes; Additional Dialogue: John Grant; Director of Photography: Charles Van Enger; Film Editor: Philip Cahn; Musical Score and Direction: Milton Rosen; Art Direction: Jack Otterson, Richard H. Riedel; Director of Sound: Bernard B. Brown; Technician: Jack A. Bolger, Jr.; Set Decoration: Morgan Farley; Special Photography: D.S. Horsley, Jerome Ash; Gowns: Rosemary Odell; Make-up: Jack P. Pierce; Assistant Director: Seward Webb

*–JTS*

# *The Brute Man* (1946)

*Synopsis*: A deformed serial killer dubbed the Creeper is terrorizing the town and eluding capture by the frustrated authorities. The Creeper's only friend is Helen, a blind piano teacher who doesn't realize her occasional visitor is a spine-breaking psychopath. Two of the Creeper's victims had connections to the local college and eventually the police discover the Creeper's waterfront lair where they find an old newspaper clipping of star college athlete Hal Moffat and his two friends, Clifford and Virginia. Clifford gives the cops the story: He and Hal were rivals for Virginia's affection and, after Cliff got the upper hand, Hal, in a fit of rage, hurled a test tube in chemistry class causing an explosion that disfigured him. After his recovery, he disappeared, and Virginia and Cliff married. The police place a guard at Cliff and Virginia's home.

Helen tells the Creeper that an expensive operation would restore her sight. The Creeper visits Cliff and demands Virginia's jewels. In the ensuing melee Cliff is killed and the Creeper, though shot, escapes back to Helen to give her the jewels. When Helen has them appraised, the jeweler calls the police. Helen is shocked to hear about her friend's true nature. When she tells her story to the newspapers, the Creeper, feeling she has betrayed him, sneaks into her apartment to kill her, but it's a police trap and he is captured.

It's speculated - though without any hard evidence - that Universal sold *The Brute Man* to PRC, Poverty Row's humblest studio, partly because they were embarrassed by how the film exploited the disfiguring disease of its star Rondo Hatton who had died in February of 1946, a couple of months after *The Brute Man* was filmed. (If so, they were a bit late in developing a conscience since Hatton had already done four horror films for the studio.) When PRC did a trade-press preview of the movie on the 1 October 1946, it was revealed for the first time that PRC had purchased the movie from Universal 10 weeks prior for $125,000. The studio that had produced so many entertaining - and profitable - monster movies during the war years was now Universal-International and as such had no interest in "B"-films or horror movies, going so far as to dismiss many of the company men who specialized in such productions, including *The Brute Man's* producer, Ben Pivar. Universal-International had also considered selling to PRC two "B"-Westerns, *The Vigilante's Return* and *The Michigan Kid*, but relented since the films were in Cinecolor, which made them a bit classier and more in line with the studio's new policy of doing higher-budgeted entries.(1) *The Brute Man*, drab and threadbare, certainly *looked* like something that PRC would spawn. Some of the music from Universal's classic *Son of Frankenstein* was appropriated for *The Brute Man*, but it's not likely anyone noticed.

Apparently, the PRC publicity department was not familiar with its company's new acquisition and reported to the trades in September of 1946 that *The Brute Man* would star a popular wrestler called "The Angel," who was sometimes billed as "the ugliest man who ever lived" or, more modestly, "the ugliest man in the world." (And you thought "the monster without make-up" was bad!) Theresa Loeb, film critic for *The Oakland Tribune*, wrote in her review of *House of Horrors* - to which *The Brute Man* is a kind of prequel - that Hatton reminded her of the Angel, perhaps not surprisingly as both men suffered from acromegaly.(2)

*The Brute Man* is probably no worse than *The Cat Creeps* or *She-Wolf of London*, but like those two duds, it represents the exhausted last whimper of Universal's second horror cycle, which had begun so promisingly with *Son of Frankenstein*. Though running under an hour, *The Brute Man* is padded and repetitious. Shot after shot of the Creeper lurking behind studio shrubbery alternates with stock footage of police cars on the move, redundant exchanges between the police chief and the commissioner ("I want the Creeper captured within 24 hours"), and newspaper headlines ("Waterfront Shack Tells Mute Story of Depraved Life"). Hatton delivers his usual non-performance while the rest of the cast is competent, though Jack Parker is pretty annoying as a dumb delivery boy who drops off the Creeper's groceries at his waterfront digs and then spies on him, only to be killed for his trouble, It's good though to see Peter Whitney in his slimmer days before he turned into a beefy, jowly, beetle-browed bad guy in many a Western, gangster film, and TV program. Here he plays a nice cop and probable romantic interest for Helen in the last scene.

Apparently, they had "GoFundMe" even in 1946, as he and his boss tells Helen she'll be able to have that costly sight-restoring operation after all.

**Adieu, Tom Neal! The Creeper gets into Neal's house, kills him, steals the jewels, and – although wounded – makes good his escape. Perhaps the commissioner's observation that the police force is incompetent is justified.**

While Jane Adams tries hard as Helen, she can't overcome the mawkish Hollywood sentimentality about how the blind have a second sight into someone's true character since they're not distracted by the physical. The script doesn't grasp the irony in her being so off-base. The Frankenstein Monster was more sinned against than sinning, so the Blind Hermit is right on the money in his acceptance of his strange guest in *Bride of Frankenstein*, while Gwynplaine in *The Man Who Laughs* has a beautiful soul that belies his grotesque appearance and that his adoring Dea perceives. Some of the best horror flicks make us see the humanity within the monster and the monster within ourselves (There, but for the grace of God, go I), but that really doesn't come off in the Creeper films; Hatton can't really suggest it, and the poor writing would defeat even someone who could act. The Creeper recoiling from his own reflection and smashing the mirror is as close as the film comes to trying to generate sympathy for the character.

The Creeper's motive for murder is unclear; the events in the film seem to take place long after his initial accident, so what was he doing all this time and what made him turn to spine snapping? (Maybe Universal was saving this for another prequel?) You would think Cliff would be at the top of his list, but in their scene together you get the impression he would have spared his sneaky classmate's life had he not pulled a gun on him. The scene wherein the Creeper tells the pawnbroker he'll pay him later - and then kills him when he refuses to give the Brute Man credit - is almost funny as are the shots of Hal Mofatt on the football field catching a pass thrown from stock footage of a real game. The only poignant moment in the film is likely unintentional and due to Hatton's one note performance: when the police pounce on the Creeper and drag him off, he seems unsurprised, passive, and unresisting, as though he's glad that the inevitable has finally come.

The Creeper's origins are based loosely on Hatton's own life. Hatton was a good athlete in his younger days and, as mentioned in our essay on *House of Horrors*, he was gassed during the Great War and developed acromegaly shortly thereafter. Obviously, no one in 1946 was going to depict a returning war vet as a monster, so the character becomes a hot-tempered college athlete with his strength as a football player perhaps meant to explain the Creeper's prowess as a back breaker. Moffat himself comes off as arrogant and unlikable, and his subsequent predicament is his own fault.

Trade reviews of *The Brute Man* were mixed. It found favor in the 9 November 1946 write-up of *Boxoffice Digest*:

> It is a horror chiller of the deepest dye produced and directed by workmen who know their way around this field, containing sufficient gore and shriek excitement to satisfy the most avid of fright fans, yet withal presented with a modicum of intelligence and capable playing. Hatton carries the role satisfactorily while director Jean Yarbrough throws the brunt of the acting demands to a well-chosen cast.

In the 31 October 1946 issue, the critic for *Motion Picture Daily* concurred:

> *The Brute Man* is a better than average horror film that will satisfy both horror fans and the general theater-goer. Director Jean Yarbrough has injected into this Ben Pivar production an element of what is popularly known as 'Hitchcock suspense', Rondo Hatton and Jane Adams turn in particularly effective performances.

Surely this is the first and only time that hack director Jean Yarbrough was ever compared to Hitchcock.

*Harrison's Reports* wasn't buying.

It has moments to recommend it to undiscriminating patrons who go in for this type of pictures. Others however will probably find it tiresome, for it suffers from triteness in plot and treatment... it has a suspensive situation here and there but the whole effect is artificial and 'stagey'; in fact, some of the situations and dialogue may provoke laughs instead of a serious response.

October 26 1946

The Bible of Show Biz was equally unimpressed:

A semi-horror picture...singularly unexciting meller is suitable only for lower duals. Hatton's facial features which run a close second to those of Frankenstein furnish the film's few thrills. Producer Ben Pivar, long U's keeper of the Bs has done little to make what may have been his last 'B' to stand out from similar fodder. Scripting and acting are in keeping with the quality of the production.

*Variety*, October 23, 1946

Hatton's disease was getting the better of him during filming of *The Brute Man* and resulted in a fatal heart attack on 1 February 1946. After a service in Hollywood, his body was sent to his beloved Tampa for burial by the American Legion. Had he lived, he probably would have gone back to work as an extra. It's not hard to picture him as one of Johnny Friendly's goons in *On the Waterfront*, but he would not have had the more substantial roles he enjoyed at Universal. His brief sojourn at the Monster Factory assured that the trades and papers would mention his passing, something that would not have happened had he stayed an extra. From all reports, Hatton was a kindly man, very religious and devoted to his fellow vets, especially the disabled ones. A journalist who knew him sang his praises:

As nice and gentle a person as you would want to meet. He used to be a newspaper reporter, an associate of this writer, for a number of years in Florida. He had a wide circle of friends. And a friendly faculty for enlarging the circle. Rondo's appearance which has won him fame and fortune (we hope) was an embarrassment for him in those days. He shrunk from exploiting it in pictures though given the chance in the twenties when the movie producers were flirting with Florida as a movie center. In comparatively recent years, however, he was somehow persuaded to try the Hollywood ordeal and made the grade.

H.C.S. *The* [Dubuque, Iowa] *Telegraph Herald*, 12 January 1947

We don't know how Hatton felt about the way his deformity was used by Universal. Did he yell at Ben Pivar that "I'm not a monster and people don't run screaming at the sight of me?"

Probably not. He was a sick man with limited employment prospects, and he was likely grateful for the job and the regular paycheck. There have been other actors whose faces would not win a beauty contest (Charles Laughton, Louis Wolheim) but, unlike Hatton, they could act. Hatton went before the cameras only because of his unfortunate condition. None of the title performers from *Freaks* went on to a movie career, so that makes Hatton unique.

**Though wounded, Rondo Hatton delivers the stolen jewels to Poni Adams for the operation to restore her sight. Hatton's health was declining and it's obvious in the film.**

716

"Shock Theater" insured that Hatton would haunt the Late, Late Show for years to come, but he was otherwise largely forgotten. As film books became more popular in the '60s, Hatton got an occasional, though rarely appreciative, mention. In **The Bad Guys**, William K. Everson referred to Hatton's listless acting style and how his deformed facial features, tastelessly exploited, put him in the freak category. Don Miller, in **B Movies**, was equally negative, and although he doesn't mention the Creeper series at all, he did pen a few words about *Jungle Captive*:

> Also in the cast was one Rondo Hatton, victim of a physically
> distorting disease, used by the studio for his physically repellent features.
> A real baby-scarer. Poor Hatton was not an actor and when called upon
> to recite dialogue, was hopelessly out of his depth. (3)

Even monster magazines of the '60s - like *Famous Monsters of Filmland* and *Castle of Frankenstein* - usually ignored Hatton, as did serious analysts of the horror genre like Carlos Clarens.

However, the times, they were-a-changing. Old movies became increasingly popular on college campuses; sometimes they were treated respectfully, but the notion of oldies as "camp" took hold, especially when it came to horror films. In March 1968, the following ad appeared in *The Texas Ranger*, the humor magazine put out by students at the University of Texas in Austin:

> Who combines the rugged looks of Humphrey Bogart?
> The eternal youth of Mae West?
> The sardonic wit of W.C Fields?
> The bitter rebellion of James Dean?
> Rough suavity of Clark Gable?
> Cryptic inscrutability of Marlon Brando?
> Rondo Hatton!
> Find out why this man, above all others, is the only fit person to be
> the hero of this age of disillusionment.

Students and the general public were invited to the campus to see three of Hatton's films and were no doubt bemused and amused when they discovered who Hatton really was. The *Texas Ranger's* editor was Bob Burns, and this was the beginning of his life-long interest in Rondo Hatton. The following year, Burns threw an on-campus birthday party for Hatton with a special showing of *House of Horrors* that drew 500 people. Burns went on to work in horror and sci-fi films as an actor, art director, prop man, and writer, and amassed a huge collection of memorabilia from classic and not-so-classic monster movies. And, of course, Rondo Hatton was prominently featured.

As the video age came to pass, more and more vintage fear films became readily available. Ed Wood, whose inept cheapies horror fans had hitherto scorned, suddenly became a cult figure, with video outlets like "Something Weird" dredging up his most obscure work, and one magazine dubbing his sometimes star Bela Lugosi the "King of Bad Cinema." At the same time, reviewers began taking the horror genre more seriously, and critics offered learned (and increasingly jargon-filled) analyses of everything from *Vampyr* to *The Texas Chainsaw Massacre*.

In 1991 horror fan and low-budget filmmaker Fred Olen Ray (*Dinosaur Island*, *Attack of the 60 Foot Centerfold*) did a respectful, well-researched article on Rondo Hatton for *Filmfax*. Ray came up with lots of biographical information and visited Hatton's old haunts in Tampa, though surprisingly he missed the radio interview Hatton did for *The Tampa Tribune* (see our essay on *House of Horrors*). Ray even took Hatton seriously as an actor, writing that Hatton played his role in *House of Horrors* "superbly, and in his own way, with subtlety."(4)

In 1991 *The Rocketeer*, a film adaptation of a graphic novel, featured a villain made-up (by Rick Baker) to resemble Rondo Hatton, though director Joe Johnson admitted that few people would get the reference. Four years later, the clowns at *Mystery Science Theater 3000* subjected *The Brute Man* to their brand of sophomoric humor. Meanwhile, *Cult Movies*, a magazine dedicated to the bizarre, made Hatton's image as the Creeper part of their masthead. Hatton's status as a horror icon was further confirmed in 2002, when the Classic Horror Film Board, the premiere hangout for fans of vintage horror, established the Rondo, an award for excellence in the horror field; the winners receive a small bust of Hatton as the Creeper.

While no one in the '40s complained about Universal's use of a man disfigured by illness portraying a monster, the 1977 horror film *The Sentinel* sparked some controversy when it used people with real deformities and diseases to represent the denizens of hell at its climax. In these more sensitive, post-*Elephant Man* days, a Rondo Hatton would not be possible.

*The Brute Man* - October 1946 - 58 minutes

**CAST:** Tom Neal as Clifford Scott; Jan Wiley as Virginia Rogers Scott; Jane Adams as Helen Day; Donald MacBride as Captain Donnelly; Peter Whitney as Lt. Gates; Fred Coby as Hal Moffat (flashback); JaNelle Johnson as Joan Bemis; Charles Waggenheim as the Pawnbroker; And Rondo Hatton as the Creeper; Beatrice Roberts, Oscar O'Shea, John Gallaudet, Pat McVey, Tristam Coffin, Jack Parker, Peggy Converse, Joseph Crehan, John Hamilton, Lorin Raker

**CREDITS:** Director: Jean Yarbrough; Producer: Ben Pivar; Writers: George Bricker, M. Coates Webster, Dwight V. Babcock (original story); Photography: Maury Gertsman; Art Direction: John Goodman, Abraham Grossman; Film Editor: Philip Cahn; Set Decoration: Russell A. Gausman, E.R. Robinson; Costumes: Vera West; Sound: Bernard Brown, Joe Lapis; Make-up: Jack Pierce

*- HN*

# *Abbott and Costello Meet Frankenstein* (1948)

Well, they say that all good things must come to an end.

With *Abbott and Costello Meet Frankenstein*, the classic Universal interpretations of the Monster, the Wolf Man, and the thirsty Count saw their last iteration. Happily, the latter two figures were portrayed by their creators – Chaney and Lugosi - and the actor who played the Monster here (Glenn Strange, for the third time), was coached by the only other man who had enacted the role thrice – Karloff, another "creator." This returning to the source, plus the dynamic of playing the grotesque parts "straight," gave their scenes much of the same atmosphere as had the earlier misadventures of this unholy three. The comedy, then, was all the stronger by contrast. (We will refrain from going into Abbott and Costello's bona fides here, as there is *en passant* coverage of same in our entries on *Hold That Ghost* and *The Time of Their Lives*, plus we would heartily encourage fans of the team to devote their time to the more studied accounts of same listed in the bibliography.)

In a sense, the picture was a last-gasp extension of the "Monster Rally" movies that had their genesis in *Frankenstein Meets the Wolf Man* and the fulfillment of their formula with the addition of a pseudonymous Count Dracula to the "House" entries in the mix. (As Cicero might have said, I promise not to mention my sole-Frankenstein Monster theory yet again. I also promise that this is Cicero's last stand in this book!) Continuity may have dictated that there were no grotesques left to menace Universal's top comedic team – sunlight, explosions, and a final cure for what ailed Lawrence Talbot pretty much saw to that – but, Hey! This is Universal! Final solutions were anything but final when potential box-office revenue was brought into play. A definite jolt of Strickfadden-inspired electricity saw the return of *the* Count Dracula – none

721

of this "Alucard" or "Latos" silliness – to the team, and it must be admitted up front that Bud and Lou would have drawn much less comic-oriented inspiration from John Carradine's count than was to be had from Bela's.

Chaney, of course, was a shoo-in as the Wolf Man; he was the only enactor of the role since his characters (let's not forget Lawrence Talbot!) made their debut in the 1941 sensation. As pre-production gab had included Kharis, Alucard (the "son" of Dracula), and the Invisible Man, we take a moment to ponder the potential casting. Chaney had already played every grotesque in the batch, save for the Invisible Man (Chaney's *voice* was never a major selling point), but the transparent one was already "taken." (As we mentioned in our chapter on *Frankenstein Meets the Wolf Man*, the rumor that Chaney would be playing both titular horrors there via doubling, special effects, etc. was so much blarney, so his doubling up herein was never considered.) It's beyond belief that Claude Rains – at that point in his career - would have considered for a moment flying in from Stock Grange to don the bandages and goggles again, but kudos to Universal for getting Vincent Price – who *had* portrayed an Invisible Man in that series' first sequel - to voice the film's closing line. In keeping with the insistence on "creators- portrayers," the only Kharis available for hire at that point would have been Tom Tyler, the first to enact that particular Mummy for Universal, but by 1948 the former Captain Marvel *was* suffering the latter stages of rheumatoid arthritis, and his stomping about with the urge to throttle may well have been too much to ask. And let's face it, if you've already got Dracula swooping about hither, thither, and yon, how in blazes would you expect Alucard – arguably revealed to *be* Dracula towards the end of the 1943 film – to add anything unique to the mix?

Lugosi, though, was anything but a lead-pipe cinch to be cast as as Dracula. Although the Hungarian thesp had portrayed the vampire king in the 1931 original, his relationship with the Laemmles – and with subsequent ownership of Universal – was anything but pleasant. His planned cameo in the 1936 follow-up, *Dracula's Daughter*, had been dropped, and thus the count was present therein only in effigy. The temporary "horror film ban" (due, in the main, to Joseph Breen and the Production Code Administration) then took place, but after the re-release of *Frankenstein*, *Dracula*, and *Son of Kong* at a Los Angeles itch, horror films were back, and Bela made his debut as "Ygor" in *Son of Frankenstein*. The actor was also back at Universal for a half-dozen films over the next four years, but never a once as Count Dracula.

A *sort* of title card, bereft of the usual credit/copyright info, and limited to the
identification of five characters only. Two of these (Bela and Lon) are represented
by splendid artwork, while Glenn Strange's Monster has an almost sleepy
Caribbean look to him. As for the drawings of A&C... well, we're of the opinion
that neither looks like either.

In addition to the '43 Chaney interpretation, '44 and '45 saw the cape and tails
worn by Long John Carradine, who for quite some time had claimed that he had
turned down the role of the Frankenstein Monster back at the franchise's genesis
because the character had no lines. So, too, had Lugosi. Ygor became the only
character that Bela would play more than once - other than Dracula, of course – and
the actor came to have a bit of affection for the old blacksmith: "God, he was cute,"
Bela would recall, more than once. Although virtually everything ever written in-
depth about *A&C Meet Frank* mentions agent Don Marlowe's claim that it was *he*
who got Bela his role in the picture, film historian Greg Mank put that to rest in citing
studio records showing that Bela had been cast before Marlowe got a chance to spin
his tale.(1)

Glenn Strange had his hat trick as the Frankenstein Monster herein. Although
much more at home in horse operas than in thrillers, Strange was no stranger to

monsters: he had portrayed both the titular Mad Monster opposite George Zucco in the 1942 indie programmer and the eponymous Monster Maker's henchman in the 1944 indie programmer before donning the latest iteration of Jack Pierce's masterpiece makeup for *House of Frankenstein* that same year. Speculation as to whether either of those Sigmund Neufeld masterpieces had influenced Universal to give Strange the iconic role was tossed out once and for all by the commentary by genre super-fan, film historian, and legendary collector, Bob Burns, in Universal Studios Home Video gem, *The Making of Abbott and Costello Meet Frankenstein*:

> When Jack Pierce was doing some work at Universal, at that time they were going to do *House of Frankenstein* and Karloff didn't want to play the Monster any more... Pierce was doing Glenn in a pirate picture with Yvonne DeCarlo... and he kept looking at Glenn and Glenn kept saying, 'Every day you keep looking at me.' And one day [Jack Pierce] said, 'Will you stay over tonight? I'll pay you 25 bucks. It might get you a good part in a movie.' He put paper over all the mirrors so Glenn couldn't see what was going on. He worked on him for about an hour... Glenn said, 'He did a lot of stuff to my head.' They took the papers down and he said, 'My God! I'm Boris Karloff.' Jack said the craggy face that [Glenn] had was the kind of face he has always thought about for that Monster.(2)

Lovely Lenore Aubert – despite her *nom d'écran*, not French but Austria-Hungarian - had made her genre debut in Republic's *The Catman of Paris* (1946). While she'd never again meet the likes of Dracula, the Wolf Man, or Frankenstein's Monster, she would run across Bud and Lou once more, in *Abbott and Costello Meet the Killer, Boris Karloff*, in 1949. More than the unwilling puppet of Dracula, Aubert's Sandra Mornay is the first woman to step in the scrubs of the doctors Frankenstein, Bohmer, Mannering, *et al*, and ready the Monster for yet another brain operation. Said procedure never takes place, of course – let us recall that the not-so-good doctor is tossed through a convenient window – but Mornay's presence is, in itself, at least a nod at distaff evil in the series. Given that original line-up of studio monstrosities discussed during pre-production, we might wonder why the only villainess Chick and Wilbur end up encountering in the sundry houses of horror herein would be a neurosurgeon. If there was talk of Dracula's son, why was no thought given to his daughter? Surely her presence could have been no more redundant than Alucard's.

How about the Monster's bride? Why would she not have survived the laboratory explosion along as did her intended mate at the end of what would be her only misadventure at Universal? Had Colin Clive's character used lower-shelf ingredients in constructing that other *Bride of Frankenstein*? Surely those two females – along with the Jungle Woman, if only to complete the available slate ('tis doubtful the Inner Sanctum's *Weird Woman* would have been sufficiently weird) – could have given lovely Jane Randolph a shudder more akin to her own genetic propensities.

Like Lenore Aubert, Miss Randolph's genre priors were feline-related: the Ohio native appeared in both *Cat People* (1942) and sequel *The Curse of the Cat People* (1944), both times as the same character. (Intertwined with her meanderings with cats were two films marking her mixing with the avian set: *The Falcon's Brother* [1942] and *The Falcon Strikes Back* [1944], again playing the same character in both films. Prior to all these, the lady had an uncredited bit in 1942's *The Male Animal*. Do we detect a trend here?) Not long after she survived meeting Dracula - and just about everyone else we've mentioned so far - Miss Randolph wed and moved to Spain, her cinematic career (save for yet another uncredited bit) over for good.

Character actor Frank Ferguson (the grumpy Mr. McDougal) had more credits – both big- and small-screen - than the rest of the principal cast save for Glenn Strange, with whom he was in a virtual tie. This is pretty impressive as the actor had spent most of his younger years at the Pasadena Community Playhouse and didn't make the move into the movies until he was in his late thirties. His curriculum vitae included pictures of all types, with mostly uncredited bits during his first year or two, and *Abbott and Costello Meet Frankenstein* was pretty much his only genre credit. Ferguson's McDougal is the perfect foil for Costello's shtick and his reappearance towards the end of the picture sparks yet another great comedic moment. Still, we have to wonder how he managed to survive a werewolf's bite without himself transforming into one, especially on that climactic fourth full moon in a row that led to the climax of the film. Charles Bradstreet ultimately made more of a name for himself (and more money) in real estate than in the movies. Per www.IMDb.com, the Maine-born Bradstreet appeared in only 10 films between 1946 and 1950, and seven of those were as uncredited bits. Nonetheless, with his role herein not much more than window-dressing and the male side of the requisite boy-girl business (occupied on the opposite end by Jane Randolph's Joan Raymond), Bradstreet isn't bad. And that is the quintessential example of being damned with faint praise!

Originally, the picture was to have been *The Brain of Frankenstein*, but that title seemed to augur nothing more than yet another trip to the operating table for the Monster. While a variation on that was to have been the anticipated dramatic denouement anyhow, 'twas decided to change the title to its current status as Abbott and Costello – the only entities under contract to Universal-International at the outset of the project – were still quite popular and their names on a marquee couldn't help but to boost sales.

No matter the title, it all boiled down to brains, anyhow.

The reason the Monster is subject to such dramatic mood swings – it was explained early on – is that Fritz (*quel* dunce!) destroyed the "normal" brain meant for the Monster's noggin when the Beijing Opera (playing a limited engagement next door) or somebody let loose with a third-act climactic gong and the jar hit the floor. Thus, 'twas the "abnormal" brain that found cranial shelter and the Monster would thereafter become violent and enraged if anyone so much as dare to prod him with a hot poker or take a swing at him with a blazing torch. *Bride* gave the Monster's brain a respite and focused on keeping him relaxed and happy via attending to urges emanating from a different organ. In *Son*, empirical evidence leads Wolf to the conclusion that the Monster needs brain surgery to calm him down, not realizing for a few reels that the Monster is being directed to do awful things by Ygor, a demented blacksmith bent on avenging the treatment he has received from local politicians. The neurosurgery goes nowhere, but Ygor is shot down and the Monster is kicked into a sulfur pit! The subsequent, non-Karloff series entries are more indirect in their attention to the seat of learning, and the film under discussion turns on giving the Monster the most pliant brain imaginable.

Per Bob Furmanek and Ron Palumbo(3), though, prior to any casting or shooting taking place, Bertram Millhauser – he of the "Sherlock Holmes" series' scenarios - whipped up a story that involved not cerebra, cerebella, or medullae oblongatae, but which – per the afore-cited two authors – more than casually resembled the screen treatment of *Sherlock Holmes in Washington* (1941). Soon thereafter, producer Robert Arthur turned the assignment over to Robert Lees and Frederic I. Rinaldo - who had already successfully teamed up on the screenplays for *The Invisible Woman* (1941) and a slew of Abbott and Costello features (including 1941's *Hold That Ghost*) – and John Grant, the comedy writer who might very well have been the comics' third team member. Their treatment, "The Brain of Frankenstein," was acclaimed by everyone except Costello, who called it a "piece of junk,"(4) but whose primary concern may have been the dearth of routines that he and Abbott had perfected over the years. Costello's observation *was* spot on, so their "moving candle" shtick was inserted inasmuch as it placated the comedian and... *well*... fit the picture like a glove.

With respect to the sundry grotesques teaming up, the aforementioned *Frankenstein Meets the Wolf Man* was constructed around the conceit that Lawrence Talbot had tired of murder and shedding all over the carpet and thus ventured out into woolly Germania hoping to meet Dr. Frankenstein and be cured once and for all. As for his success, well... the best laid plans of mice and monsters... Nonetheless, in 1945's *House of Frankenstein*, Talbot – still seeking a respite from hair and howling – gives Dr. Frankenstein's secret records (which he must have had tucked into his back pocket whilst wrestling with the Monster in the earlier film) to Boris Karloff's Dr. Niemann, who quickly enough decides that fixing up the Monster is of greater intrinsic worth to mankind than a Lawrence Talbot who has molted for the final time. The climax of this first *House* refreshingly eschews natural elements (fire, water) disposing of monstrous personages and provides a healing mud bath for the usual suspects. *House of Dracula* then shakes things up a bit, blending mad doctors with bloodsuckers and allowing Talbot the chance to enjoy a full moon without the requisite transformations, before yet again setting the Monster aflame before the end credits.

The story here has freight handlers Chick Young and Wilbur Grey bringing crates to McDougal's House of Horrors, where we learn that the boxes really do contain Count Dracula and the Frankenstein Monster. (As the boys unpack the first crate in the House of Horrors, the placard on a nearby stand clearly is titled "Frankenstein's Monster." When removing the tarp from the box reveals a coffin, though, Chick turns to read the placard, which now refers to Dracula.) Anyhow, Lawrence Talbot attempts to warn the boys that Dracula plans on fitting out the Monster with a new brain, but the full moon stops him from making himself clear. Dracula puts the bite on Dr. Sandra Mornay, who then is compelled to agree to implant Wilbur's brain in the Monster's head. Just before the operation can commence, the Monster tosses Dr. Mornay out a window, Talbot transforms again into the Wolf Man and chases after Dracula, and all hell breaks loose. The end of the film finds the grotesques destroyed and Chick and Wilbur in a boat, wherein they find themselves in the presence of the Invisible Man.

Having agents of the supernatural menacing purveyors of laughs was a *profoundly* established theatrical formula that had been putting backsides in seats since Thespis and friends abandoned the stage and discovered the carbon arc. Back in 1920, for example, Harold Lloyd had confronted ectoplasmic types in *Haunted Spooks*, the very best kind of spooks out there. Not to be outdone, the following year Buster Keaton ventured into a haunted house in the aptly titled *The Haunted House*. (5) Before he teamed up with Babe Hardy, Stan Laurel played both roles in *Dr. Pyckle and Mr. Pryde*

(1925), a departure from the formula in that the comic *was* the "monster." When later joined at the spiritual hip with Hardy, the pair visited the formula several times, including the two-reel *The Live Ghost, Babes in Toyland* (both 1934), and the post-Roach feature for Fox, *A Haunting We Will Go* (1942). Bob Hope notched a couple of top-shelf comic horrors for Paramount in 1939's *The Cat and the Canary* and 1940's *The Ghost Breakers*, both remakes of silent productions. And so, on and so forth.

**Far be it from us to suggest that Jack Kevan have 6'5" Glenn Strange - closer to 7', what with those asphalt-spreader's boots - to have a seat. a) We're a tad late, and b) affixing the neck bolts is probably easier if you approach same as if you were hanging a picture.**

You get the...*errrrr*...picture.

Adding to the overall atmosphere of ...*Meet Frankenstein* was Frank Skinner's wonderful musical score and the great special effects by David Horsley and Jerome Ash. The sundry transformations were as good as ever, with our top marks given to

Dracula's oozing into bat form, as seen from the rear; the smooth glide from opera cape into bat wings was almost preternatural in its effectiveness. While we admired the full-frontal take on same, the melting (if you will) of Bela's features as they melded into bat-face were more obviously a cartoon than the effect as witnessed from behind. And if we may, a couple of Dracula observations: it appears that the rather venerable count now had to adapt a certain pose – arms out, cape hanging just so – in order to transform himself into that winged critter of the night. Took a while; in fact, so much time that the Wolf Man was able to catch up with him at the end and both took that plunge off the balcony. In the count's earlier misadventures (*a la* Universal) he appeared to be able to bat-a-size himself – or vice versa – whilst on the run. Apparently aging catches up even with the deathless. Also, why did it not occur to Dracula that a better way of battling Larry the lycanthrope – much better than tossing furniture at him – would be to turn *himself* into a wolf, and so that the two could go at it *mano a mano* (or paw-a-paw, or however dueling wolf-speak would have phrased it).

Side quibble: albeit we witness what appears to be the (once again) fiery end of the Frankenstein Monster, does it not seem that the obstinate big guy needed only to have jumped a few feet to either side to have ended up in the water? Failing that, once the pier burned away, wouldn't he have plunged several feet *into* that same, fire-quenching liquid? Sure, he might have gotten singed a bit, but the Monster had been subjected to far worse time and again in the earlier entries. Yes, we know: the handwriting was on the pier for the "series," of which this was, if anything, the outlier. Still... one may conject, no?

The making of the film was not without its problems, of course, or its solutions. Initially, Costello was adamant on *not* doing the picture, as he reportedly hated the script, being much more comfortable with doing the routines he and Bud had been doing for years; a share of the profits helped Lou feel better about the endeavor. Karloff, of course, declined to appear in the film, thus frustrating any and all attempts to have all three monsters' original portrayers share the screen for the first time. Nevertheless, he did agree to help publicize it, and photos of the actor standing in line at the box office soon were ubiquitous. Jack Pierce, the makeup genius who had designed the Wolf Man and the Frankenstein Monster (*fama erat* that Lugosi had more or less waved him off for the '31 *Dracula*, preferring to do his own application) was deemed too old-fashioned and his methods too dated for the new film. Pierce's successor, Bud Westmore, "updated" the makeup procedures, using latex and foam rubber that were easier to attach and remove, with the result – Chaney's innumerable layers of hair notwithstanding – being less time in the chair and more on the set. (At this point in his career, Lugosi was in no position to ixnay Westmore, and his "older" vampire king is seen to be much paler, with a much darker set of lips, than he had appeared some dozen-and-a-half years earlier.)

The most nearly tragic occurrence during production was the attempted suicide by Lon Chaney on the 22 April. Chaney biographer G. Don Smith wrote that, following an epic verbal battle with his wife, Chaney – well known as a drinker of operatic proportion – gulped down a handful of sleeping pills and went off to die. Had it not been for the intervention of his son, Ron, who rushed his father to the hospital, the actor would have been successful in his effort.(6)

Other than that near-catastrophe, the biggest problem during shooting was Glenn Strange's injury. If I might quote the *MagicImage Filmbook* on the picture:

> When the Monster tossed Dr. Mornay through the window, she suddenly swung back into camera range, kicking and screaming like a spastic Peter Pan. Strange gallantly lunged to catch her, fell – and fractured his ankle. A great professional Strange made little of his injury, and kept working. However, after dinner that night... Strange found he couldn't get his Monster boot on, due to the fractured ankle. He finally managed, and the actor worked until 11:00pm that night, throwing barrels off the pier at the comedians. The next morning, however, Strange couldn't walk – and was unable to report for work. (7)

It looked for a while there that the production might have to be halted until Strange could literally recover his footing. Saving the day, as it were, was Lon Chaney, who offered to take on the Monster makeup and the responsibility for tossing stunt woman Helen Thurston through the window yet again. Albeit he did so sans credit, technically this marks Chaney's second onscreen appearance in the role, thus following only Karloff and Strange and being one up on Bela, who had only taken *his* turn out of financial need.

Despite the fractiousness and the fractures, *Abbott and Costello Meet Frankenstein* was a hit, earning over $3 million in worldwide revenue. The upswing was that the comedy team once again was numbered among the industry's top grossers, and their future clashes with other of the studio's monsters became inevitable (the erstwhile uncooperative Karloff would end up "meeting" them twice!). Post-release, though, not all was good in Monsterland. At the end of their chapter on the film, the Messrs.

Furmanek and Columbo quote Lon Chaney opining on the negative impact of the picture:

> I used to enjoy horror films when there was thought and sympathy involved. Then they became comedies. Abbott and Costello ruined the horror films; they made buffoons out of the monsters. (8)

It's debatable whether Chaney's observation has the majority of fan support, then or ever, if only because the scenarists, director Charlie Barton, and the actors themselves (including Lon) did the best they could to maintain the dignity and integrity of the characters. Methinks most horror aficionados appreciated the effort.

Still, I was surprised in looking over reviews for the film. *The New York Times*, for example, felt that most of the film's humor was to be found in the opening titles; its 29 July 1948 critique was headed "That One Laugh." The Grey Lady's West Coast counterpart – the *Los Angeles Times* – apparently went to a whole different ball game. As critic Philip K. Scheuer opined rather alliteratively in the 26 July 1948 edition:

> The film has been put together with enormous ingenuity. Its comic inventiveness seldom falters yet it never seriously violates the tradition of the three celebrated creatures who are its antagonists. The Monster remains the soulless automaton who doesn't know its own strength, Dracula is still batlike, batty and a bloodsucker, and the Wolf Man continues to be the loony lunar lycanthrope of yore.

Several months later, the ultra-accurate R.L.C. of *The Washington Post* (17 September 1948) was vociferous in his agreement with Mr. Scheuer (and Boris the K must have been a tad intrigued by the following comment):

> This wild charade is called 'Abbott and Costello Meet Frankenstein,' which is about as clear, if inaccurate, a title as there could be. Frankenstein's Monster is the specific character referred to, and he's as beguiling a chap as ever. Glenn Strange is playing the wheezy fellow these days and I dare say not even George Nathan could tell the difference between the Strange and Karloff readings.

R.L.C. wrapped up his thoughts with "I found it relaxing fun." When *The Christian Science Monitor* set *its* critical type for the 3 September 1948 issue, though, the result was fairly ho-hum.

Five screen celebrities appear in this week's offering at the Keith-Boston, 'Bud Abbott and Lou Costello Meet Frankenstein.' Besides the three of the title, Count Dracula and the Wolf Man are thrown in for good measure. The name is a giveaway. The picture is a combination of slapstick comedy, secret passages, and Hollywood laboratory effects. An electrical 'brain machine' which shoots sparks in at least a dozen different places at once is perhaps the most menacing thing in it.

Though apart from *The New York Times* the lion's share of the press's opinions was quite good, there were a couple of rather more thoughtful (if not totally spot-on) observations made by *The Times*'s arts commentators. On the 14 March 1948, Thomas F. Brady's column "Hollywood Digest" was headed "Old Ghoulish Friends Roam the Sets at Universal," and Mr. Brady – who obviously hadn't been a fan of the studio's previous series' entries and was working with publicity puffs from an early version of the scenario – disclosed that...

The majority of these lovable characters are concentrated in 'Abbott and Costello Meet Frankenstein," a film described by the studio as a comedy. Glenn Strange is playing both the Monster and the invisible man, since, in the first characterization, he need only be visible, and in the second, only audible... Bela Lugosi, the perpetual Dracula, disclosed last week that he is to be revived for his new appearance by one of the unwary comedians who is foolish enough to pull an oaken stake out of his heart... He will not be permitted to sink his teeth into anyone's jugular vein in the comedy, however, he explained...

A couple of months later (on the 25 July, to be exact), Mr. Brady's piece – entitled "Monster's Memories: Boris Karloff Views His Ghoulish Past and Finds He's Happier as an Indian" - gave some detail on that actor's presence in LaLaLand only days before the picture was to have its press preview.

It was disclosed to [Karloff] that the local U-I drumbeaters expect to get some shots of him staring curiously at the marquee of Loew's Criterion when 'Abbott and Costello Meets Frankenstein' opens Wednesday. He is prepared to cooperate as long as he doesn't have to see the picture. 'I'm too fond of the monster,' he said. 'I'm grateful to him for all he did for me, and I wouldn't like to watch anyone make sport of him.'

Mr. Brady's screed to that point is on target, but – as he had back in March – he went on a bit too long and got a tad, well... hypothetical:

> Indeed, the rigors of monster work, which he recalls without nostalgia, were fully demonstrated during the filming of the Abbott-Costello comedy. It took two men to do the job. Glenn Strange, who started out in the role, had to retire before the picture was finished because of illness, and Lon Chaney Jr., who had already done a stint [sic] as the Wolf Man, stepped in and completed the monster job, proving the validity of Karloff's claim that the make-up makes the monster.

(Uh-huh. If nothing else, we hereby demonstrate how researchers who restrict themselves only to consulting primary sources may nonetheless be led astray.)

**We are told that the essence of comedy is timing. Lon Chaney proves in this scene that – had he put his mind to it – he might have had a successful second career making people laugh.**

Considered nowadays to be one of the best horror comedies ever to hit the screen, *...Meet Frankenstein* open the creaky door to other meetings with a couple of other of the studio's copyrighted horrors, the Invisible Man and the Mummy. Karloff, who had filled his contractual obligation by being photographed standing in queues and glancing at posters in '48, returned in '49 to confront the team whilst donning a turban in ...*Meet the Killer, Boris Karloff*. Inasmuch as the denouement revealed that Boris Karloff was *not* the killer and because the film was neither imbued with the supernatural nor was part of the two "Shock" packages, we did not comment on same here.

Besides being a huge financial success domestically for Universal, the film enjoyed lengthy and profitable runs in overseas markets, as well.(9) Fans rejoiced at seeing Bela Lugosi as Dracula once more, and while they may have realized that the Hungarian actor and Universal had given moviegoers the iconic image of the thirsty Count – the "alpha," if you will – back in 1931, they were witnessing the "omega" here. Glenn Strange not only went three for three in this, the last big-screen view of the classic, Jack P. Pierce-concocted Monster, but his was only the third voice to be heard issuing from the Monster's lips. This would be Lon Chaney's baby's last appearance in a Universal (or Universal-International) feature film, although the "Screen's Master Character Creator" would return as a lycanthrope (stuffed inside a mummy) in the Mexican feature *La casa del terror* (1960) and in the 1962 *Route 66* episode, "Lizard's Leg and Owlet's Wing." What's more, if we include his standing in for Glenn Strange herein, Lon took *his* third turn as the Frankenstein Monster in a 1951 episode of *The Colgate Comedy Hour*.(10)

I may be going out on a limb, but methinks *Abbott and Costello Meet Frankenstein* is as equally anticipated and welcome as are any/all of the other features turning on Universal's "classic monsters." To paraphrase the PETA notice at the end of many of our latest cinematic efforts, "No Monsters were disrespected or lampooned during the shooting of this motion picture, although they all ended up dead." By far the best of the "*Abbott and Costello Meet...*" series (in my humble opinion), I found the film the perfect way to introduce my kids (decades ago!) to the Universal icons without terrifying them the way the first TV showing of the '31 *Frankenstein* did me back in 1957.

### *Abbott and Costello Meet Frankenstein* – 20 August 1948 – 83 minutes

**CAST**: Bud Abbott as Chick Young; Lou Costello as Wilbur Gray; Lon Chaney as Lawrence Talbot; Bela Lugosi as Count Dracula; Glenn Strange as the Frankenstein Monster; Vincent Price (voice) as the Invisible Man; Lenore Aubert as Sandra Mornay; Jane Randolph as Joan Raymond; Frank Ferguson as J.K. McDougal; Charles Bradstreet as Dr. Stevens; Howard Negley as Mr. Harris; with Joe Kirk, Clarence

Straight, George Barton, Charles Sklover, Paul Stader, Joe Wells, Bobby Barber, Harry Brown, Helen Spring

**CREDITS**: Director: Charles T. Barton; Producer: Robert Arthur; Original Screenplay: Robert Lees, Frederic I. Rinaldo, John Grant; Musical Score: Frank Skinner; Orchestrations: David Tamkin; Director of Photography: Charles Van Enger; Special Photography: David S. Horsley, Jerome Ash; Assistant Director: Joseph E. Kenny; Art Directors: Bernard Herzbrun, Hilyard Brown; Set Decoration: Russell A. Gausman, Oliver Emert; Film Editor: Frank Gross; Make-Up: Bud Westmore; Sound: Leslie I. Carey, Robert Pritchard; Gowns: Grace Houston; Hair Stylist: Carmen Dirigo; Animation (uncredited): Walter Lang

*- JTS*

# AFTERWORD

The great age of Universal horror commenced when strains of "Swan Lake" accompanied the "strangest love story ever told "and ended with Bud telling Lou, "There's no one to frighten us anymore." True, the Big U had its share of competition in the monster market of the '30s and '40s, but no other studio was as devoted to making its audiences spill their popcorn.

After a brief intermission in the late '30s, the monster factory cranked up with a vengeance just as America was stoking up the furnaces to fight the flesh-and-blood powers of darkness. Looked at today, after decades of a seemingly endless number of horror films - many with lavish special effects and dangling viscera - are the Universal terrors of the '40s at all frightening? No doubt when Kharis grabbed Dr. Petrie's arm, or when the Wolf Man, sporting yak hair and fangs, lunged from the fog, viewers shuddered... and not just the kiddies. Scenes like those are not likely to cause such a reaction today, but for fans of vintage horror, familiarity breeds, not contempt, but fondness.

Few of these '40s films reached the classic stature of their '30s counterparts. No one is likely to prefer Kharis to Im-ho-tep or question the superiority of the earlier tribulations of Frankenstein's Monster to Glenn Strange stomping around the lab. True, not everyone is impressed with the original *Dracula*, but will his son - if that's who he was - ever replace his old (old) man? The one exception to this opinion is 1941's *The Wolf Man*, which eclipses the earlier *Werewolf of London* in the eyes of many fans. The 1943 *Phantom of the Opera* likewise gets a bum rap, but many would rather bellow "Faro-La Faro-Le" than hum "The Lullaby of the Bells." Other than *Phantom*, the only attempt by Universal to do horror on an "A" budget was *Flesh and Fantasy*, but it's a bloodless effort, and neither Charles Boyer nor Barbara Stanwyck can substitute for Lon Chaney and Evelyn Ankers.

Today, even the humblest of Universal's '40s horror output is likely to get the Blu Ray treatment - often with commentaries and extras - and that will doubtless continue as long as Baby Boomers draw breath. While most of the books on these films are in the popular vein (like ours), there is the occasional academic treatment hoping to ferret out subtexts and sociological and political meaning to the Ape Woman and the Creeper and the like. Good luck to them, but - in the end - the only lasting importance of these films is their fun factor. They may be illogical and sometimes silly, but they are rarely dull.

Philistine that I am, I'm much more likely to spend an evening with *Frankenstein Meets the Wolf Man* than *Citizen Kane*.


- Henry Nicolella

738

# Endnotes

*Introduction*:

(1): **Frank Wisbar; The Director of Ferryman Maria, from Germany to America and Back**, McFarland, 2018.

(2): Although we dealt with *The Brute Man*, a Universal production released by another studio, we did not cover *Mr. Peabody and the Mermaid*, a 1948 Nunnally Johnson production which was merely filmed at Universal.

(3): "Fears New and Old" in **Recovering 1940s Horror Cinema**, p. 245.

(4): Ibid., p. 244.

(5): Jules Stein, as quoted in **The Films of Sherlock Holmes**, p. 85.

*The Invisible Man Returns*:

(1): p. 209

(2): p. 255.

*Black Friday*:

(1): Granted, Siodmak's screenplay for *The Invisible Man Returns* had raised the specter of megalomania, but that conceit had first been onscreen in the 1933 original.

(2): **The Immortal Count: The Life and Films of Bela Lugosi**, p. 245.

(3): Ibid., p. 279.

(4): **Lugosi: The Man Behind the Cape**, pp. 194-196.

*The House of the Seven Gables*:

(1): **Hollywood Red**, p. 159.

(2): Ibid., pp. 172-173.

(3): **The Complete Kay Francis Career Record**, p. 144.

(4): **Vincent Price; A Daughter's Biography**, chapter 15.

(5): **Hollywood Red**, p. 172.

(6): **Golden Age of B-Movies**, pp. 2-3.

*Enemy Agent*:

(1): For discussion of the serial, please see our volume, **Up from the Vault**, and for thoughts on the feature, cf. **Of Gods and Monsters**.

*The Mummy's Hand*:

(1): p. 218.

*The Invisible Woman*:

(1): See our essay on 1920's *Sherlock Holmes* in **Down from the Vault**.

(2): **Wolf Man's Maker; Memoir of a Hollywood Writer**, p. 257.

(3): Ibid.

*Cracked Nuts*:

(1): **Mantan the Funnyman; The Life and Times of Mantan Moreland**, p. 28.

(2): Ibid., p. 103.


*Hold That Ghost*:

(1): **Hold That Ghost**, pp. 71-76.

(2): **Abbott and Costello on the Home Front**, p. 27.

*A Dangerous Game*:

(1): Anyone wishing details and synopses on this series can consult Thomas Reeder's biography of Ben Pivar, **Stop Yellin'**.

(2): This was also the title of a 1948 Hal Roach comedy-mystery.

*The Wolf Man*:

(1): Chaney was billed as Chaney, Jr. in both *North to The Klondike*, which was begun before *The Wolf Man*, but released in 1942, and in 1942's 15-episode serial, *Overland Mail*. With very few exceptions, he was billed without the adjective for the rest of his career.

*The Mad Doctor of Market Street*:

(1): **The Films of Joseph H. Lewis**, p. 110.

*The Ghost of Frankenstein*:

(1): One of the many folks who have contributed to this volume – a brilliant wag with quite a sense of humor – said that "any and all of the Frankenstein films cranked out after *Son* treated continuity as 'so much crap'." Said contributor went on to suggest that – in Universal's case, at least – the opposite of "continuity" is "incontinence."

(2): p. 53.

(3): Ibid., p. 99.

*The Strange Case of Doctor Rx*:

(1): The gorilla's name here has been variously spelled Bongo, Nbongo, and Inbongo. We mention this so that we might differentiate Corrigan's simian here from his other cinematic apes, which enjoyed such names as Gege, Congo, Zamba, Simba, Goliath, Brutus, Bonzo, Nabu, Ping Pong, and Naba, (twice).

*Invisible Agent*:

(1): Benny's father was so appalled at his first viewing of the film that he walked out of the theater. Following an explanation by his son, Mr. Kubelsky reconsidered and ended up loving the film, which he viewed 46 times. See: **Seven Nights at Seven** in our bibliography. Chaplin's religious background has always prompted curiosity; please cf. "Charlie Chaplin or Israel Thornstein. A mystery even in modern times," by Jill Lawless in www.timesofisrael.com, 17 February 2012

(2): In a bizarre set of circumstances, Jennings died suddenly in January 1953, and Paramount hired on John P. Fulton as his replacement. Coincidentally, Jennings died on a golf course adjacent to Fulton's home.

(3): **Wolf Man's Maker**, p. 255-256.

*Sherlock Holmes and the Voice of Terror*:

(1): The story was first printed in *Collier's* magazine in September 1917 as "His Last Bow: The War Service of Sherlock Holmes."

(2): Reproduced in Nick Utechin's interview with Paula Page, Bruce's daughter, in *Sherlock Holmes Journal*, volume XIX (December 1988).

*Destination Unknown*:

(1): For coverage on the 1935 remake of *The Great Impersonation* – which *does* include genre elements – please see **Of Gods and Monsters**.

*The Mummy's Tomb*:

(1): **Lon Chaney, Jr.: Horror Film Star, 1906-1973**, p. 60.

*Nightmare*:

(1): **Too Much, Too Soon**, p. 215.

(2): **Brian Donlevy, the Good Bad Guy; a Bio-Filmography**, pp. 79-80.

*Sherlock Holmes and the Secret Weapon*:

(1): For what it's worth, **The AFI Catalog** identifies Charlotte as Tobel's wife.

(2): Per Gary Brumburgh's biography on www.IMDb.com. Per Steven Youngkin's biography of Peter Lorre (see bibliography), the actress was born Ingeborg Greta Katerina Marie-Rose Klinkerfuss.

*Frankenstein Meets the Wolf Man*:

(1): p. 340.

(2): p. 270.

(3): Ted Newsom, in a conversation with John Soister

(4): **A Sci-Fi Swarm and Horror Horde,** p. 80.

*Sherlock Holmes in Washington*:

(1): The website www.arthur-conan-doyle.com avers that *In Washington* was inspired by Doyle's "The Adventure of the Naval Treaty."

*Captive Wild Woman*:

(1): **The Welfare of Performing Animals,** p. 242.

*Phantom of the Opera*:

(1): Due to a proofreading mistake on my part, the chapter "Les Fântomes de Paris" in Henry Nicolella and my book, **Down from the Attic**, omitted mention of Ernst Matray's *Das Phantom der Oper* (1916), the first feature-length movie treatment. *Mea culpa* entirely, but the widespread unfamiliarity with the German-made film confirms my statement about the Universal feature's serving as the "default version" of the cinematic renditions.

(2): *Little Shoppe of Horrors* (magazine), no. 34, May 2015, p. 54.

(3): Image Publishing of New York, 1993

(4): p. 31.

(5): David Wilt, *Hardboiled in Hollywood: Five Black Mask Writers and the Movies,* p. 62

(6): *The Sunday Times* (Perth, WA), 19 October 1941

(7): **Feature Films, 1941-1950,** p. 64.

(8): Thomas R. Burman – five-time Emmy Award winner and Academy Award-nominated make-up artist – graciously answered my query and informed me that his father, Ellis Burman – and not Mr. Pierce – had created the beautiful mask worn by Rains and others in this film, as well as the silver wolf's head/pentagram-headed cane wielded by Chaney, Jr. and Rains in *The Wolf Man.*

(9): Op. Cit., p. 56.

(10): "Hedda Hopper's Hollywood," in the *Los Angeles Times*, 13 January 1943.

(11): **Universal Horrors,** p. 361.

(12): He was welcomed back across Universal-*International's* transom in 1959 for *This Earth Is Mine.*

(13): For some respectable coverage of same, please see **Up from the Vault.**

(14): Schallert's counterpart Robbin Coons – writing for syndication – quoted George Waggner as saying that for the first time "Eddy, with new dark hair and black mustache... doesn't seem to fade into M-G-M's wallpaper." (28 March 1943)

(15): **The Mummy Unwrapped**, p. 34.

*Flesh and Fantasy*:

(1): In 1950, Edward G. Robinson appeared in a British version of the same story: *Operation X*.

(2): Duvivier did a German version of the film simultaneously with the French one and featuring Anton Walbrook. The same story was also filmed in 1920. The plot is remarkably similar to that of *Black Magic* (1929). Information on the latter film can be found in **American Silent Horror, Science Fiction and Fantasy Feature Films, 1913-1929**.

(3): Matthews (1852-1929) was an educator and literary critic who was especially interested in the art of the short story.

*Son of Dracula*:

(1): p. 173.

(2): Ibid., p. 277.

*Calling Dr. Death*:

(1): **Lon Chaney, Jr.: Horror Film Star, 1906-1973**, p. 70.

*The Spider Woman*:

(1): The British Film Institute, 1978

(2): **The History of Sherlock Holmes, in Stage, Films, TV, Radio**; p. 8.

*Weird Woman*:

(1): Wheeler Winston Dixon would emphatically disagree. See his **The Films of Reginald Le Borg**.

(2): The novel was also adapted for television in 1960 for the *Moment of Fear* series. Janice Rule and Larry Blyden starred. Reputedly, Leiber thought this was the best version of his story.

(3): **Actors on Red Alert**, pp. 22-23.

*The Scarlet Claw*:

(1): **Sherlock Holmes and the Fabulous Faces**, p. 127.

(2): Ibid.

*The Invisible Man's Revenge*:

(1): *Screen Facts* magazine, No. 13, p. 39.

*Jungle Woman*:

(1): **The Films of Reginald Le Borg**, p. 48.

*The Mummy's Ghost*:

(1): **Stop Yellin'**, p. 326. Can't write a better description than that...

(2): p. 428.

(3): Per director William (*Adventures of Captain Marvel, Drums of Fu Manchu*) Whitney, as quoted in www.IMDb.com.

*The Climax*:

(1): **The Climax** was originally written – and staged – as a three-act *comedy*.

(2): For coverage of the movies' treatment of *The Case of Becky* – both the 1915 and 1921 versions – please see **American Silent Horror, Science Fiction and Fantasy Feature Films, 1913-1929**, vol 1.

(3): *American Cinematographer*, volume 63, issue 7 (1 July 1982), p. 674.

(4): As was demonstrated when Andrew Lloyd Webber's enormously triumphant musical magnum opus (which, at the time of this writing, is *still* running on Broadway, 33 years after its premiere) led to a follow-up, *Love Never Dies* (2010), sometimes even a sequel *avec un Fantôme* is no guarantee of success.

(5): We discuss elsewhere in this volume that Rains's Jack Griffin – *The* Invisible Man (according to plan and titling parameters) – never made a second onscreen appearance, but that didn't stop Universal's *The Invisible Man* from returning and subsequently having his revenge. As chaps also named Griffin figured substantially in the action of those pictures, might there not also have been a *cousin* Claudin lurking somewhere in the stalls?

(6): p. 434.

(7): 24 November, 1944.

*Dead Man's Eyes*:

(1): Phil Brown, quoted in *I Was a Monster Movie Maker*, p. 6.

(2): Career pieces on the last three - as well as Babcock - can be found in David Wilt's **Hardboiled in Hollywood.**

(3): From the *Los Angeles Times* review of **The Gorgeous Ghoul,** 2 November 1941.

*Destiny*:

(1): Chanslor's sturdier claims to fame come from his having authored the books **The Ballad of Cat Ballou** and **Johnny Guitar,** both of which were turned into celebrated films.

(2): I'm not familiar with any Universal special effects guy named John Boles.

(3): According to *Modern Screen* (Feb 1943), this offer was made before the government imposed a salary cap of $25,000.

(4): **A Little Bit of Heaven,** page 167.

*The Mummy's Curse*:

(1): I disremember his name, but some years back a commentator on the film (William K. Everson?) opined that the name was pronounced "Eels or Sanddab." I believe the same writer also observed the infinitesimal distance between "Ragheb" and "Raghead."

(2): Please see our coverage of *Phantom of the Opera* (1943).

(3): **More Classics of the Horror Film**, p. 129.

(4): **Universal Horrors**, p. 479.

*The House of Fear:*

(1): The literary source of both films was *Les Six Hommes Morts – The Six Dead Men*. Among the featured cast of *The Riverside Murder* was Ian Fleming... no; not *that* Ian Fleming, but – rather – the Australian character actor who was a familiar face to pre-Rathbone Sherlock Holmes fans. Fleming was Dr. Watson to Arthur Wontner's Holmes in *Sherlock Holmes' Fatal Hour* (1931), *Sherlock Holmes and the Missing Rembrandt* (1932), and *The Triumph of Sherlock Holmes* (1935).

(2): In several of the more renowned works devoted to the horror genre – and specifically to Universal's take on same – the novel **The House of Fear** is not mentioned; instead, Camp's source novel is referred to as **Backstage Phantom**. While it is certainly possible that *HoF* may have been reprinted somewhere as *BP*, we have yet to be able to track down a single copy of the tale that bears that title. And we've been trying.

*That's the Spirit:*

(1): **Expressionism in the Cinema**, p. 2.

(2): "History and Mystery of Spiritualism"The Haunted Museum at www.praireghosts. com/spiritualism.html

(3): Intriguingly, Mozart was a Freemason – for *seven* years! Masonry started out as a fraternity of those men who had built churches and cathedrals during the Middle Ages. Masons had no religious ties, save that one had to believe in a Supreme Being. Musical accouterments of the cathedrals constructed included pipe organs and bells. Bells were utilized at these places of worship to announce supernatural events: the tolling in the bell tower heralded the imminent start of interaction between man and God; altar boys rang bells to alert those nearby to the consecration of the host and chalice. Hence, in *It's a Wonderful Life*, no one is left unaware of Clarence's finally getting his wings.

(4): This total indifference to an undeniably impossible physical act had its parallel that same year in RKO's *The Crime Doctor's Courage*, wherein an audience in a small club witnesses a dancer disappear from the midst of her fellows in front of their eyes and, when told the dancer can "make herself invisible," barely reacts with the most tepid of applause!

(5): McCall was based on famed Notre Dame football player, George Gipper - "The Gipp" - and Devine was made to recite a variation on "Win one for the Gipper" almost a decade before Ronald Reagan made the line famous.

*The Frozen Ghost*:

(1): Obits for Carter said he had worked 25 years as a screenwriter, but if that's true, he only got credited for two other films besides *The Frozen Ghost*.

(2): *Los Angeles Times*, 20 February 1931

(3): Kosleck would play Goebbels again in *The Hitler Gang* (1944), *Hitler* (1962), and *The Last Days of Hitler*, a 1954 episode of *The Motorola Television Hour*.

(4): **The AFI Catalog** entry on *The Frozen Ghost* states that Hoffman does not appear at the beginning of the film in the print they viewed. However, he's very much there in the DVD of the film I watched and is mentioned in one of the contemporary reviews of the film.

(5): Library of Congress entry on *The Frozen Ghost* has Fred Frank listed after Young's name, but then Frank's name is crossed out. Frank functioned as an assistant director (usually uncredited) on many of the Universal classic horrors.

*The Jungle Captive*:

(1): Interview with the actor in the 14 June 1964 edition of the *Los Angeles Times*.

(2): All the bizarre details of this fiasco may be found in Weaver and the Brunases' **Universal Horrors**.

*The Woman in Green*:

(1): No matter the spelling of his name, the character himself was nowhere to be found in the 39 episodes of the 1954-1955 television series that starred Ronald Howard and Howard Marion-Crawford. Legal problem? Uncaught spelling error?

*Strange Confession*:

(1): For our coverage of the 1934 film, please see: **Of Gods and Monsters**, and/or **Claude Rains: A Comprehensive Illustrated Reference.**

*House of Dracula*:

(1): **Horror Films**, pp. 3-5.

*Pillow of Death*:

(1): **Mothers, Mammies and Old Maids**, pp. 7-8

*The Spider Woman Strikes Back*:

(1): *Tarzan and the Amazons*, 1945.

(2): **Universal Horrors** gives splendid detail about how the film was to have included other "episodes" and a larger cast; p.525.

### House of Horrors:

(1): For coverage on *Una luz en la ventana,* please see the chapter "Hispanic Horrors" in our **Down from the Attic**.

(2): *The New York Times,* 6 August 1948.

### The Cat Creeps:

(1): Interview in the *Los Angeles Times,* 11 March 1977.

(2): Ibid.

### Dressed to Kill:

(1): London: Middlesex University Press, 2009.

### Danger Woman:

(1): "Patricia Morison: Danger Woman," Gregory Mank in *Midnight Marquee* magazine, Spring 1998, p. 44.

### The Time of Their Lives:

(1): **Lou's on First,** p. 125.

### The Brute Man:

(1): *Variety,* 10/23/1946.

(2): The Angel, sometimes called the French Angel, was Maurice Tillet. He did a few bit parts in French movies and, like Hatton, died at age 51 of complications caused by the disease.

(3): p. 241.

(4): *Filmfax,* No. 26, page 59.

### Abbott and Costello Meet Frankenstein:

(1): **Karloff and Lugosi: The Story of a Haunting Collaboration,** p. 282.

(2): The video is a must-view for the genre fan and is hosted by the inestimable David Skal.

(3): **Abbott and Costello in Hollywood,** p. 165-166

(4): Ibid., p. 166.

(5): Actually, our list might well start in the very late19th century, when a short entitled – What else? - *The Haunted House* dealt with the misadventures of "Silas Hayseed" as he is confronted by a ghost and Satan himself. The list of comic/horror shorts that preceded – or even followed - Lloyd's effort is too long to include here. Please see Roy Kinnard's requisite classic, **Horror in Silent Films.**

(6): **Lon Chaney, Jr., Horror Film Star, 1906-1973,** p. 103

(7): **Abbott and Costello Meet Frankenstein,** p. 34.

(8): Op. cit., p. 175.

(9): The film was released in Spain as *Abbott y Costello contra los fantasmas* ("A&C against the Ghosts"), and *Abbott and Costello Meet the Ghosts* was an alternative release title when the film played in the U.K.

(10): Chaney also played the Frankenstein Monster – albeit not a la Universal's treatment – in the 18 January 1952 episode of television's *Tales of Tomorrow*.

# Bibliography

The American Film Institute Catalogue: Feature Films 1931-1940, 1941-1950. Berkeley, CA: University of California Press.

Bojarski, Richard. **The Films of Bela Lugosi**. Secaucus, NJ: The Citadel Press, 1980.

_____ and Kenneth Beals. **The Films of Boris Karloff**. Secaucus, NJ: The Citadel Press, 1974.

Brill, Olaf and Gary D. Rhodes. **Expressionism in the Cinema**. Edinburgh University Press, 2016.

Brunas, Michael, John Brunas, and Tom Weaver. **Universal Horrors: The Studio's Classic Films, 1931-1946**. (Second Edition) Jefferson, NC: McFarland & Company, Inc., 2007.

Cole, Lester. **Hollywood Red**. Palo Alto, CA: Ramparts Press, 1981.

Costello, Chris with Raymond Strait. **Lou's on First; The Tragic Life of Hollywood's Greatest Clown Warmly Recounted by His Youngest Child**. New York, NY: St. Martin's Griffin,1982.

Cremer, Robert. **Lugosi: The Man Behind the Cape**. Chicago, IL: Henry Regnery, 1976.

De Waal, Ronald Burt. **The International Sherlock Holmes**. Hamden, CT: Archon Books, 1981.

_____. **The World of Sherlock Holmes and Dr. Watson: A Classified and Annotated List of Materials Relating to Their Lives and Adventures**. New York, NY: Random House, 1988.

DiGiglio-Bellemare, Mario, Charlie Ellbé and Kristopher Woofter, eds. **Recovering 1940's Horror Cinema: Traces of a Lost Decade.** Lanham, MD: Lexington Books, 2014.

Dillard, R.H.W. **Horror Films.** New York, NY: Monarch Press (Simon & Schuster), 1976.

Dixon, Wheeler Winston. **The Films of Reginald LeBorg: Interviews, Essays, and Filmography.** Metuchen, NJ: The Scarecrow Press, 1992.

Druxman, Michael B. **Basil Rathbone: His Life and Films.** Cranbury, NJ: A.S. Barnes & CO., 1975.

Dundas, Zach. **The Great Detective; The Amazing Rise and Immortal Life of Sherlock Holmes.** Boston, MA: Mariner Books, 2015.

Everson, William K. **The Bad Guys: a Pictorial History of the Movie Villain.** Bethesda, MD: Carol Publishing Group, 1964.

_____. **Classics of the Horror Film.** Secaucus, NJ: The Citadel Press, 1974.

_____. **More Classics of the Horror Film.** Secaucus, NJ: Citadel Press, 1986.

Feramisco, Thomas M. **The Mummy Unwrapped.** Jefferson, NC: McFarland & Company, Inc., 2007.

Field, Amanda J. **England's Secret Weapon: The Wartime Films of Sherlock Holmes.** London: Middlesex University Press, 2009.

Furmanek, Bob and Ron Palumbo. **Abbott and Costello in Hollywood.** New York, NY: Penguin USA, 1991.

Halliwell, Leslie. **The Dead That Walk.** London: Grafton Books, 1986.

Hawthorne, Nathaniel. **The House of the Seven Gables.** Originally published in 1851. Introduction and notes by Gordon Tapper. New York, NY: Barnes and Noble, 2007.

Hayes, Paul Stuart. **The Theatrical Sherlock Holmes.** London: Hidden Tiger Books, 2012.

Hoey, Michael A. **Sherlock Holmes & the Fabulous Faces: The Universal Pictures Repertory Company.** Duncan, OK: BearManor Media, 2011.

Johnson, Tom. **Censored Screams.** Jefferson, NC: McFarland & Company, Inc., 1997.

Kear, Lynn and John Rossman. **The Complete Kay Francis Career Record.** Jefferson, NC: McFarland & Company, Inc., 2012.

Klinefelter, Walter. **Sherlock Holmes in Portrait and Profile.** New York, NY: Shocken Books, 1975.

750

Lennig, Arthur. **The Immortal Count: The Life and Films of Bela Lugosi.** Lexington, KY: The University Press of Kentucky, 2003.

Lindsay, Cynthia. **Dear Boris: The Life of William Henry Pratt a.k.a. Boris Karloff.** New York, NY: Alfred A. Knopf, 1975.

MacGillivray, Scott and Jan MacGillivray. **A Little Bit of Heaven.** Lincoln, NE: iUniverse, 2005.

Mank, Gregory William. **It's Alive!; The Classic Cinema Saga of Frankenstein.** San Diego, CA: A.S. Barnes & Company, Inc., 1981.

_____. **Karloff and Lugosi: The Story of a Haunting Collaboration.** Jefferson, NC: McFarland & Company, Inc., 1990.

_____, James T. Coughlin and Dwight D. Frye. **Dwight Frye's Last Laugh.** Baltimore, MD: Midnight Marquee Press, Inc., 1997.

McClelland, Doug. **The Golden Age of B Movies.** New York, NY: Bonanza Books, 1978.

Miller, Don. **B Movies.** New York, NY: Carol Publishing Group, 1987.

Miller, Jeffrey S. **The Horror Spoofs of Abbott and Costello.** Jefferson, NC: McFarland & Company, Inc., 2000.

Mulholland, Jim. **The Abbott and Costello Book.** New York, NY: Popular Library, 1975.

Nissen, Axel. **Mothers, Mammies and Old Maids.** Jefferson, NC: McFarland & Company, Inc., 2012.

Nollen, Scott Allen. **Sir Arthur Conan Doyle at the Cinema.** Jefferson, NC: McFarland & Company, Inc., 1996.

_____. **Abbott and Costello on the Home Front.** Jefferson, NC: McFarland & Company, Inc., 2009.

O'Brien, James. **La ciencia de Sherlock Holmes.** Grupo Planeta, Barcelona, 2013.

Palmer, Scott. **Sherlock Holmes: The Basil Rathbone Years and Other Films.** Bloomington, IN: Xlibris Corp., 2015.

Palumbo, Ron. **Hold That Ghost.** Albany, GA: BearManor Media, 2018.

Pohle, Robert W. Jr. and Douglas C. Hart. **Sherlock Holmes on the Screen.** Cranbury, NJ: A.S. Barnes and Company, 1977.

Pointer, Michael. **The Sherlock Holmes File.** London, David & Charles, 1976.

Price, Michael H. **Mantan the Funnyman; the Life and Times of Mantan Moreland.** Baltimore, MD: Midnight Marquee Press, Inc., 2006.

Price, Victoria. **Vincent Price: A Daughter's Biography.** New York, NY: Open Road Media, 2014.

Rathbone, Basil. **Basil Rathbone; In and Out of Character.** Limelight Editions, Washington, DC, 1989.

Raw, Lawrence. **Adapting Nathaniel Hawthorne to the Screen.** Lanham, MD: The Scarecrow Press, 2008.

Reeder, Thomas. **Stop Yellin': Ben Pivar and the Horror, Mystery and Action-Adventure Films of His Universal B-Unit.** Duncan, OK: BearManor Media, 2011.

Rhodes, Gary Don. **Lugosi.** Jefferson, NC: McFarland & Company, Inc., 1997.

_____, ed. **The Films of Joseph H. Lewis.** Detroit, MI: Wayne State University Press, 2012.

Riley, Philip J., ed. **Abbott and Costello Meet Frankenstein.** Hollywood, CA: MagicImage Filmbooks, 1990.

Savater, Fernando. **Misterio, emoción, y riesgo.** Madrid, 2008.

Schulthorpe, Derek. **Brian Donlevy: The Good Bad Guy; a Bio-Filmography.** Jefferson, NC: McFarland & Company, Inc. 2016.

Siodmak, Curt. **Wolf Man's Maker.** Lanham, MD: The Scarecrow Press, 1997.

Skal, David J. **The Monster Show: A Cultural History of Horror.** New York, NY: W.W. Norton & Company, 1993.

Slide, Anthony. **Actors on Red Alert; Career interviews with five actors and actresses affected by the blacklist.** Lanham, MD: The Scarecrow Press, 1999.

Smith, Don G. **Lon Chaney, Jr. Horror Film Star, 1906-1973.** Jefferson, NC: McFarland & Company, Inc., 1996.

Starrett, Vincent. **The Private Life of Sherlock Holmes.** Pickle Partners Publishing, 2016.

Steiff, Josef. **Sherlock Holmes and Philosophy; The Footprints of a Gigantic Mind.** Chicago, IL., 2011.

Steinbrunner, Chris and Norman Michaels. **The Films of Sherlock Holmes.** Secaucus, NJ: Citadel Press, 1978.

Svehla, Gary J. and Susan Svehla, eds. **Bela Lugosi.** Baltimore, MD: Midnight Marquee Press, Inc., 1995.

Thomas, Bob. **Bud & Lou: the Abbott and Costello Story.** Philadelphia, PA: J.B. Lippincott Company, 1977.

Weaver, Tom. **It Came from Horrorwood.** Jefferson, NC: McFarland & Company, Inc., 2004.

_____. **A Sci-Fi Swarm and Horror Horde: Interviews with 62 Filmmakers.** Jefferson, NC: McFarland & Company, Inc., 2010.

Wilt, David. **Hardboiled in Hollywood; Five Black Mask Writers and the Movies**. Bowling Green, KY: Bowling Green University Popular Press, 1991.

Youngkin, Steven. **The Lost One; A Life of Peter Lorre**. Lexington, KY; University of Kentucky Press, 2011.

www.thefanzine.com/vera-west-2/

vampiregothicrose.blogspot.com/p/the-mystery-of-vera-west.html

https://www.reddit.com/r/UnresolvedMysteries/comments/6cwqtx/umexplained_death_the_fortuneteller_told_me_the/

https://dressingvintage.com/blogs/dressing-vintage-blog/haute-horror-the-costumes-designed-by-vera-west

nzpetesmatteshot.blogspot.com/2010/08/wild-and-wonderful-world-of-john.html

https://filesofjerryblake.com

# Index

Numbers in **bold** indicate photographs

Abbott and Costello xvi, xvii, xxi, 2, 6, 69, 78, 97-98, 110, 124, 130-137, **133**, 158, 217, 241, 277, 287, 288, 312, 349, 357, 367, 461, 512, 513, 515, 530, 545, 576, 647, 649, 652, 671, 703-709, **705**, **707**, 721-735, **723**

Abbott, Bud 130, 137, **707**, 707, 709, 732, 734

Abbott, John 40, **284**, 289, 613, 617

*Abbott and Costello Meet Frankenstein* xvi, xvii, 6, 78, 110, 277, 532, 576, 631, 704, 721-735, **723**, **728**, **733**

*Abbott and Costello Meet the Invisible Man* 110, 124

*Abbott and Costello Meet the Killer, Boris Karloff* xvii, 277, 647, 724, 734

Abrams, Leon 552, 555

Acquanetta 68, 205, 214, 328-329, **329**, 330, 331, 333, 334, 335-337, **337**, 339, 379, 468, **470**, 471, 472, 473, 478, 482, 505, 506, **506**, 507, 508, 510, 595

*Acquanetta* (opera) 339

Adams, Jane (Poni) 300, 506, 624-625, 632, 713, 714, **716**, 719

"Adventure of the Copper Beeches, The" 423

"Adventure of the Dancing Men, The" 291, 292, 297

"Adventure of the Devil's Foot, The" 422

"Adventure of the Empty House, The" 291, 423, 601, 644

"Adventure of the Musgrave Ritual, The" 361

"Adventure of the Speckled Band, The" 423

*Adventures of Captain Marvel, The* 57

*Adventures of Champion, The* 276

*Adventures of Robin Hood, The* 121, 157

*Adventures of Sherlock Holmes, The* 237, 297, 602, 603

Adventures of Sherlock Holmes, The (radio) 238

*Adventures of Superman* 625

*Adventures of Wild Bill Hickock* 574

Affleck, Ben 49
*Africa Screams* 135, 367
*A-Haunting We Will Go* 707, 728
Albright, Hardie 175, 179, 181
Albritton, Louise 68, 256, 395, 396, 397, 419
*Ali Baba and the Forty Thieves* 205, 496, 552, 654
*All About Eve* 624
*All the Living* 179
Allan, Anthony *see* Hubbard, John
Alyn, Kirk 708, 709
Amber, Eve 600, 604
Ames, Ramsay 418, 419, 478, **480**, 482, 483, 484
Anders, Rudolph 144-145, 297
Andrews Sisters, The 131, 132, 133, 135, 136, 137, 261, 513
Ankers, Evelyn 23, 38-39, 68, 105, 106, 134, 136, 137, 147, 154, 155, 160, **185**, 195,
    197, 239, 241, **243**, 246, 308, 310, 331, 334, **337**, 338, 339, 395, 397, 404, 405-
    406, **408**, 409, 436, 437, 439, 450, 458, 470, 473, 485, 490, 581, 583, 588, 589,
    595, 631, 728
*Anna and the King of Siam* 107, 651
*Anthony Adverse* 107, 272, 497, 651
*Ape, The* 20, 219, 220
*Ape Man, The* 331
*Arabian Nights* 145, 205, 217, 335
Arlen, Michael 488
Arlen, Richard 140, 142-144, 145, 146, 574
Armstrong, Robert 43, 46, 402, 404, 409
Arnold, Edward 507
*Arsenic and Old Lace* (play) 22, 189, 302, 338, 520
Arthur, Robert 726, 735
Artman, Deborah 339
Ash, Jerome 46, 181, 637, 641, 706, 709, 728, 735
Astaire, Fred 74, 624
Asther, Nils 268, 272-273, 279
Astor, Gertrude 439, 441, 442, **444**, 447, 501
*L'Atlantide* (novel) 206
*Atom Man vs Superman* 708
Atwill, Lionel 74, 75, 76-78, 85, 86, 87, 88, **175**, 175, 176, 177, 180, 181, 182, 195,
    196, 197, 215, 216, 221, 222, 267, 270, 277, 279, 292-293, **293**, 295, 297, 300,
    309-310, 316, 427, 444, 454, 520, 522, 527, 532, 534, 582, 602, 621, 627, 631,
    632
Aubert, Lenore 724-725, 734
Auer, Mischa 120, 121, 122, 127, 135, 137, 312
*Augen der Liebe* 507

Babcock, Dwight V. 504-505, 506, 507, 509-510, 552, 555, 598, 639, 641, 665, 669,
    671, 676, 719
Baker, Rick 718

Backus, Jim 626
Balderston, John L. 50, 388, 395
"Ballad of Reading Gaol, The" (poem) 154
Barclay, Don 312, 316
Barker, Jess 708, 709
Barnett, Vince 145, 329, 339
Barrett, Edith **575**, 575-576, 577
Barrett, Robert 708
Barrier, Edgar 246, 355-356, 358, 369, 376, 383, 450
Barrymore, Diana 282, **284**, 285, 286-288, **287**, 289
Barrymore, John 65-67, **67**, 70, 71, 155, 480, 594, 603
Barton, Charles xvii, 704-705, 708, 709, 731, 735
Basch, Felix 250, 253
*Batman* (serial) 98, 520, 529
*Batman* (1966) 242
*Batman* (TV series) 7, 82, 94
*Batman and Robin* (serial) 479, 625, 661
Baur, Harry 371, 372
Beatty, Clyde 97, 329-330, 334, 468, 472
Beckett, Scotty 497, 501
Beebe, Ford 269-270, 274, 275-276, 277, 278, 279, 397, 455, 456, 458, 680, 681-682
*Behind Locked Doors* 140
Bellamy, Ralph 148, 154, 156, 160, 161, **185**, 195, 197, 226
Belmore, Lionel 189, 192, 197
Benchley, Robert 369, 375-376, 383
Benedict, Howard 238, 244, 246, 297, 323, 367, 447, 458, 488, 546, 604, 617, 648, 693
Benny, Jack 50, 226, 274, 570, 571
Benoit, Pierre 206
*Best Years of Our Lives, The* 269, 670
*Between Two Worlds* 374
*Between Us Girls* 286-287
Bey, Turhan 227, 250, 252, 253, 261-262, 264, 338, 339, 406, **408**, 409, 480, 497, 500, 501, 549, 626
Biberman, Herbert J. 46, 108, 428, 651
*Big Cage, The* 329-330, 468, 592
Birell, Tala 581, 583, **585**, 588, 589
*Bishop Murder Case, The* 106, 364
*Black Cat, The* (1934) 104, 391, 486, 504, 528, 606, 687
*Black Cat, The* (1941) 23, 92, 94, 103-117, **110**, 199, 215, 216, 428, 497, 651, 706
*Black Doll, The* 7, 111, 273, 557, 562
*Black Friday* 15-26, **19**, **22**, 30, 33, 80, 83, 95, 106, 109, 110, 158, 158, 206, 217, 337, 357, 403, 498, 515, 649
*Black Mask* 504, 671
*Black Room, The* 18, 165, 528
Blaisdell, Paul 219
Blandick, Clara 638, 640, 641, 676

*Blazing Saddles* 463
Bond, Ward 488
Bowery Boys, The 130, 482, 529, 596, 625, 671
Boyer, Charles 370, 371, 372, 373-374, 375, 376, 380, 382, 383, 384, 538, 546, 738
Boyle, John W. 253, 254
Bradstreet, Charles 725, 724
Brahm, John 150, 671
*Brain of Frankenstein, The* (working title) 725, 726
Bredell, Elwood (Woody) 51, 61, 72, 75, 83, 88, 100, 136, 137, 195, 197, 204, 210,
    223, 246
Breen, Joseph (The Breen Office) 345, 400, 412, 600, 722
Brett, Jeremy 361
Bricker, George 636, 639, 641, 665, 669, 671-672, 676, 719
*Bride of Frankenstein* 50, 84, 113, 121, 185-186, 242, 329, 385, 391, 480, 506, 519,
    532, 623, 685, 713, 725
Bright, John 239, 246, 322
Bromberg, J. Edward 230, 234, 358, 396, 397, 636, 639, 640, 641
Brook, Clive 322, 603, 647
Brooke, Hillary 241, **241**, 246, **364**, 366-367, 559, 603, 604
Brooks, Conrad 551-552
Brooks, Jean **141**, 144, 145
Brophy, Edward 71, 145
Brown, Phil **432**, 438-439, 510, 596, 598
Brown, Roland 580
Browning, Tod 55, 296, 523, 671
Bruce, David **401**, 402, 404, 405-406, 407, 409, **414**, 418, 419, 484, 596
Bruce, Nigel xvi, xx, 68, 202, 203, 237, 238, 242, 245, 246, 294, 297, **320**, 323, 367,
    425, 428, **444**, 445, 447, 488, 490, 560, 561, 563, 604, 616, 617, 645, 647, 648,
    691, 692
Bruce, Virginia 63-72, **64**, **69**, 113, 228
*Brute Man, The* xvi-xvii, xx, 97, 506, 596, 608, 624, 653, 656, 657, 670, 671, 672, 711-
    719, **713**, **716**
*Buck Rogers* (serial) 49, 276, 455
Buckley, Harold 562
Burman, Ellis 153, 301, 353, 742
Byrd, Ralph 97, 110

Cabanne, Christy 51, 57, 60, 61, 82, 140, 220, 482
*Calling Dr. Death* 97, 157, 411-420, **414**, 482, 529
Calvert, Steve 218, 219
*Captive Wild Woman* 63, 68, 97, 155, 157, 219, 257, 306, 311, 325-339, **329**, **337**, 468,
    469, 472, 592
Carlson, Richard 134, 136, 137, 140
*Carnet de Bal, Un* 371-372
Carradine, John 58, 158, 271, 306, 327, **329**, 332, 333-334, 338, 339, **451**, 454, 456,
    457, 458, 463, 475, 479, 480, 481, 483, 484, 520, 522, 527, 530, 532, 533, 534,
    620, 627, 632, 722, 723

Carrillo, Leo 92, 93, 94, 98, 100, 252, 261, 357, 358, **462**, 466

Carroll, Leo G. 506, 657

Carson, Jack 42, 46

Carter, Harrison 580, 590

Carter, Howard 50

*Casa del terror, La* 158, 553, 734

*Cat and the Canary, The* (1927) 104, 680

*Cat and the Canary, The* (1939) 92, 104, 107, 115, 134, 497, 728

*Cat Creeps, The* 530, 675, 679-688, **681**, **684**, 712

*Cat People* 144, 150, 326, 327, 331, 406, 426, 434, 468, 470, 687, 725

Catlett, Walter 92, 93, 95, 100, 463, 466

*Catman of Paris, The* 274, 724

Cavanagh, Paul 215, **216**, 216-217, 222, 442, 445, 560, 564, 599, 604, 690

Cawthorn, Joseph 400

Cerf, Norman 418, 420

*Chamber of Horrors* (working title) 409, 519

Chandler, Raymond 488, 504

Chaney, Lon (Jr.) xix, xx, 51, 53, 57, 60, 68, 74, 76, 78-80, **79**, 82, 85, 86, 87-88, 88, 89, 97, 105, 113, 126, 147, **149**, 151, 152, 153, 154, 158, 159, 160, 161, 176-177, 179, 188, 189, 191, 193-194, 195, 196, 197, 218, 255-256, **257**, 259, 260, 261, 262, **263**, 263, 264, 265, 300, 301, 302, 306, 307, 308, 309, 310, 312, **313**, 314, 315, 316, 328, 331, 346, 349, 350, 353, 354, 386, **387**, 389, 390, 391-393, 394, **394**, 395, 396, 397, 412, 413, 414, 415, 416, 417, 418, 419, 420, **432**, 433, 437, 438, 438, 439, 455, 463, 466, 471, 478, 480, 481, 482, 483, 484, 494, 504, 505, 507, 508, 510, 520, 524, 525, 526, 527, 530, 532, 534, 548, 550, 551-553, **553**, 554-555, 581, **585**, 588, 589, 590, 607, **607**, **608**, 608, 609-611, 612, 620, 623-624, **626**, 627, 632, 633, 636, **637**, 638, **639**, 639, 640, 641, 662, 721, 722, 723, 729, 730-731, 733, **733**, 734, 738, 740, 742, 748

Chaney, Lon (Sr.) xiii, 65, 78, 154, 159, 220, 273, 309, 342, 344, 347, 351, 352, 353, 357, 358, 385, 413, 494, 495, 660

Chanslor, Roy 538, 546, 557, 563, 744

Chaplin, Charlie 129, 226, 494, 573, 741

*Charge of the Light Brigade, The* 207

*Charlie Chan at the Circus* 529

*Charlie Chan in Black Magic* 602

Christie, Agatha 92, 179

Christine, Virginia 549, 551, 552, 554, 555, 665

*Chronicles of Grey House* 39

Cianelli, Eduardo 53, 54, 58, 60, 61, 258, 262, 549, 572

*Citizen Kane* 109, 153, 204, 362, 417, 670, 738

Clarence, O.B. 22

Clarke, Mae 186, 314, 595

Cleveland, George 638, 641

*Climax, The* (play) 493

*Climax, The* (1930) 494-496

*Climax, The* (1944) xix, 82, 107, 242, 262, 342, 356, 428, 493-502, **498**, 512, 626, 744

Cline, Eddie 127, 463, 465-466

Clive, Colin 53, 121, 184, 186, 189, 385-386, 685, 725
Clive, Iris 684-685, **684**, 687
Cocks, Jay 174
Coe, Peter 480, 522, 527, 534, 549, 551-552, **553**, 555
Cohan, George M. 572, 594
Cole, Lester 10, 13, 30-32, 33, 38, 39, 40
Collins, Lewis D. 699, 700, 701
"Color of Your Eyes, The" (song) 37
*Colossus of New York, The* 114, 595
Conan Doyle, Sir Arthur 202, 237, 238, 239, 244, 246, 291, 297, 317, 321, 323, 361, 365, 368, 422, 427, 428, 443, 446, 491, 562, 563, 614, 616, 644, 690
Conreid, Hans 289
Cooper, Gladys 107, 111, 115, 117
Cording, Harry 13, 39, 40, 158, 160, 197, 246, 259, 262, 264, 297, 427, 486, 490, 560, 563, 614, 631, 643, 648, 690, 693
Corrigan. Lloyd 97, 200, **201**, 204, 208, 210, 337, 339, 667, 671, **674**, 676
Corrigan, Ray ("Crash") 213, 214, 218-219, **219**, 223, 339, 468, 741
Cortez, Ricardo 111
Cortez, Stanley 105, 111, 117, 145, 167, 171, 373, 384
Costello, Lou **133**, 403, 576, 704, 707, 709, 734
Cowan, Jerome 597, 598
Cox, Morgan B. 700, 701
*Cracked Nuts* xii, 119-127, **120**, **125**, 135, 218
Crawford, Broderick 104, 105-106, 115, 116, 117, 349, 353, 354, 495
Crawford, Joan 155, 684
*Creeper, The* 97, 98, 272, 627, 671
*Crime Doctor's Courage, The* 366, 745
"Crime of Lord Arthur Saville, The" (short story) 372-373
Cromwell, Richard 44-45, 46
Crowther, Bosley 86, 195-196, 208, 332, 345, 355, 358, 407-408, 437, 457, 471-472, 483, 499, 517, 543-544, 673, 680, 685
Cummings, Robert 30, 130, 369, 375, 376, 383, 538
Curtis, Alan 375, 450, 458, 538, 539, 541, 542, 543, 544

*Danger Woman* 42, 695-701, **697**
*Dangerous Game, A* 43, 139-146, **141**, 573
Daniell, Henry 239, 246, 289, 297, 323, 600, **601**, 604
*Dark Eyes of London* 17, 22, 507
Darling, W. Scott 127, 195, 197, 255, 292, 297, 432, 439
Dastagir, Sabu 205, 227
Davis, Wee Willie 466, 614, **615**, 617
*Dead Man's Eyes* 97, 242, 482, 503-510, **506**, 552, 580, 581, **608**, 671
*Dead Ringer* 165, 276
De Carlo, Yvonne 329, 576
Dein, Edward 412, 418, 419, 473, 590, 686, 687
Delevanti, Cyril 276, 279, 310-311, 316, 397, 501, 563, 693
Denning, Richard 155, 406

Denny, Reginald 239, 242, 246
Dessau, Paul 520-521, 522, 534, 633
*Destination Unknown* 42, 247-254, **250**
*Destiny* (working title) 150, 153, 168, 327, 328, 353, 354, 519, 539
*Destiny* 274, 353, 375, 512, 513, 537-546, **540**, 654
Devine, Andy 140, **141**, 142, 144, 145, 146, 252, 261, 463, 466, 571, 573-574, 575, 576, 577, 746
Dietrich, Marlene 271, 584, 585
Dix, Richard 412, 413, 580
Dmytryk, Edward 334, 338, 339
*Dr. Renault's Secret* 219, 331, 529
*Doctor X* 77, 175, 177, 276, 462
Dodd, Claire 108, 117, 175, 180, 181, 574
Dodds, William 554, 555, 654
Dolenz, George 497, 501
Donlevy, Brian 283, **284**, 285, 288, 289, 290
*Dracula* (1931) 1, 17, 18, 30, 50, 51, 92, 104, 189, 191, 231, 237, 302, 303, 305, 332, 365, 388, 409, 523, 581, 682, 722, 729, 737
*Dracula's Daughter* 7, 63, 300, 363, 523, 593-594, 624, 671, 722
*Dressed to Kill* 276, 689-693
Dumbrille, Douglass 471, 473, 583, 589, 682, 687
Dupont, E.A. 39
Durbin, Deanna 96, 108, 286, 287, 347-350, 401, 541
Duvivier, Julien 370-373, 374, 375, 377, 378, 379, 381, 382-383, 384, 538, 539-540, 542, 545, 546, 743

Edeson, Arthur 195
Eddy, Nelson 229, 345, 347, 350, 355-356, 358, 494, 742
Eldredge, John 94, 100, 108, 117, 181
*Enemy Agent* 41-46, **44**, 249, 697, 698, 706
Erice, Victor 441, 446-447
Erickson, Leif 267, 270, **271**, 279
"Errol Flynn" (song) 406
Errol, Leon 261, 450, 453, 456, 457, 458
*Espiritu de la colmena, La* 441
Evans, Rex 13, 300, 308, 310, 311, 316, 614, **615**, 617
"Eyes" (TV episode) 505
*Eyes of Love* see *Augen der Liebe*

Fairchild, Edgar 617, 624, 628, 633
Fallon, Thomas F. 562, 563
Farnum, William 550, 555
Farrar, Jane 341, 347, 351, **355**, 356, 358, 496, 501
"Feathertop" (short story) 29
Feld, Fritz 358, 551
Ferguson, Frank 725, 734
Field, Betty 369, 375, **375**, 376-377, 380, 383, 538

Fields, W.C. 64, 68, 80, 106, 114, 123, 130, 135, 277, 522, 530, 541, 717

"Final Problem, The" (short story) 422, 601

"Five Orange Pips, The" (short story) 562, 563

Fix, Paul 26, 137, 297, 337, 339

*Flesh and Fantasy* 111, 273, 356, 369-384, **375**, **379**, 512, 513, 538, 539, 540, 541-542, 543, 545, 654, 738

Fletcher, Bramwell 287, 288

Florey, Robert 23, 199, 303, 671

Foran, Dick 39, 40, **52**, 55, 57, 59, 61, 78, 92, 93-94, 100, 151, 152, 252, 261, 264

Ford, Wallace **52**, 55, 57, 59, 59, 61, 92, 259, 261, 264

Foster, Susanna xix, 341, 343, 344, 345, 347, **348**, 350, 351, 355, 356, 358, **394**, 494, 496, 497, 499, 501

Fox, George W. 637-638, 641

Fox, Wallace 639, 640

Francis, Kay 38, 207

*Frankenstein* (1910) 29, 108,

*Frankenstein* (1931) 16, 23, 30, 51, 83, 92, 104, 149, 184, 185, 189, 193, 237, 242, 249, 260, 300, 303, 311, 400, 406, 409, 525, 528, 532, 722, 734

*Frankenstein Meets the Wolf Man* 77, 82, 113, 157, 158, 193, 195, 229, 273, 276, 296, 299-316, **304**, **313**, 331, 333, 337, 388, 400, 409, 455, 519, 520, 521, 524, 526, 533, 721, 722

Freund, Karl 24, 50, 51, 57, 97, 296, 482, 670

*Frozen Ghost, The* 155, 527, 552, 579-590, **582**, **585**, 660, 746

Frye, Dwight 185, 186, 189, 197, 300, 301, 312, 316, 550, 625

Fuller, Mary 29

Fulton, John P. **9**, 13, 26, 50, 68-69, 71, 72, 75, 88, 105, 113-114, 117, 160, 228, 230, 231, 234, 307, 316, 392, 397, 418, 420, 439, 447, 458, 466, 468, 502, 510, 518, 535, 539, 546, 555, 578, 604, 627, 633, 641, 741

Gallow, Janet Ann 194, 196, 197

Gangelin, Paul 402, 409, 446, 447

Garfield, John 95, 374, 540

Gargan, William 167, **168**, 168-169, 170, 250, **250**, 251-252, 253, 254

Gausman, Russell A. 13, 26, 40, 46, 53, 61, 72, 88, 100, 117, 127, 137, 145, 160, 171, 182, 197, 210, 223, 235, 246, 254, 265, 279, 289, 297, 316, 323, 339, 359, 368, 384, 392, 397, 409, 420, 428, 439, 447, 458, 474, 484, 491, 502, 510, 518, 534, 546, 555, 563, 578, 598, 604, 612, 617, 633, 641, 648, 654, 665, 676, 687, 693, 701, 719, 735

Geraghty, Gerald 361, 362, 363, 680, 681, 686, 687

Gertsman, Maury 598, 612, 648, 665, 676, 693, 699-700, 701, 719

*Ghost Breaker, The* (1914) 461

*Ghost Breaker, The* (1922) 461

*Ghost Breakers, The* (1940) 92, 134, 461, 728

*Ghost Catchers* 94, 129, 277, 459-466, **462**, 478, 512, 573, 624, 652

*Ghost of Frankenstein, The* 77, 82, 83, 107, 110, 113, 121, 127, 155, 156, 158, 175, 181, 183-197, **185**, **190**, **194**, 269, 273, 300, 303, 305, 322, 393, 453, 504, 519, 524, 528, 530, 533, 548, 622, 623, 656, 682

*Ghoul, The* 6, 400

*Golem, Le* (1936) 371

Gomez, Thomas 240, 242, **243**, 246, 497, 499, 501, 506, 508, 510

Goodwins, Leslie 518, 551, 552, 554, 555

Gorcey, Leo 130, 134, 596

Gordon, Mary 13, 68, 71, 170, 223, 242-243, 246, 261, 264, 297, 323, 367, 428, 490, 604, 612, 693

Gottlieb, Alex 92, 97, 99, 100, 214, 220, 223

Grant, John 137, 709, 726, 735

Grant, Kirby 463, 466, 652-653, 654

Grant, Lawrence 189, 192, 197

*Great Impersonation, The* (1942) 226, 245, 249

*Green Hell* 34, 51, 73, 358

Gwynne, Anne 23, 25, 26, 74, 104, 106, 110, 116, 117, 155, 213, 214-215, 216, **216**, **219**, 221, 222, 434, 437, 439, 512, 515-516, 518, 522, 527, 530, 534, 631

Hall, Jon xvi, 113, 205, 226-227, 228, 230, 233, 234, 261, 349, 353, 406, 450, **451**, 453-454, 456, 457, 458, 551

Hall, Thurston 68, 71, 133, 135, 137, 323

Hamer, Gerald 322, 323, 364, 367, 441, 445, 447, 613, 617, 643, 646, 648

Hamilton, Margaret **67**, 68, 71, 638

*Hamlet* (play) 65, 155, 179, 370

Harding, Kay 443, 447, 466, 555, 599

Harding, Lyn 603

Hardwicke, Sir Cedric 6, 13, 14, 188, 194, 196, 197, 227, 228, 229, 230, 234, 301, 595

Hardy, Oliver (Babe) 50, 64, 129, 130, 312, 432, 460, 708, 727-728

Harris, Marilyn 308

Hartman, Edmund L. 46, 297, 443, 447, 465, 466

Hatton, Rondo xvi, xx, 339, 486, 487, **489**, 490, 506, 551, 591, **593**, 595-596, 598, 649, 651, **652**, 653, 654, 656, 657-659, **659**, 660, 661, 662, 663, 664, 665, 670, 711-712, 713, 714, 715, 716-718, **716**, 719

Hawthorne, Nathaniel xx, 28-29, 30, 31, 32, 33, 34, 36, 39, 40

*Hellzapoppin'* 81, 83, 96, 97, 135, 170, 217, 460, 463

Helm, Fay 148, 157, 160, 267, 273, 279, 308, 333, 339, 418, 419

Herbert, Holmes 197, 234, 292, 297, 323, 419, 485, 490, 555, 560, 563, 689, 693

Herbert, Hugh 104, 106, 115, 116, 117

Hervey, Irene 250, **250**, 251, 252, 253, 254, 268, **271**, 271, 279

*Hilde Warren und der Tod* 568

Hillier, Florette 558, 563

Hinds, Samuel S. 65, 74, 75, 81, 82, 85, 88, 213, 216, **216**, 222, 397, 471, 473, 699, 700

"His Last Bow" (short story) 239, 241, 246, 422

*Hit the Road* 38-39, 134

Hitchcock, Alfred 81, 107, 112, 165, 170, 270, 275, 277, 282, 283, 286, 287, 319, 406, 424, 454, 506, 542, 595, 671, 682, 714-715

Hodgson, Leyland 13, 160, 197, **216**, 222, 246, 297, 322, 458, 490, 589, 648, 693

Hoey, Dennis 295-296, 297, 311-312, 316, 367, 428, 446, 486, 490, 563, **645**, 648, 667, 671, 676
Hoffman, David 369, 375, 383, 415, 419, 510, 589, 612, 636
Hogan, James B. 402-403, 406, 409
Hohl, Arthur 423, **426**, 428, 442, 447, 581, 589
*Hold That Ghost* 83, 109, 110, 122, 123, 129-137, **133**, 155, 274, 349, 357, 461, 706, 721, 726
Homans, Robert 274, 279
Hope, Bob 78, 92, 104, 123, 134, 367, 680, 728
Hopper, Hedda 406, 470-471, 583
Horne, Victoria 442, 447, 518, 573, 577, 638, 641
*Horror Island* 55, 82, 83, 91-101, **93**, 108, 109, 220, 357
Horsley, David (D.S.) 13, 705, 708, 709, 728, 735
*Hound of the Baskervilles, The* (novel) 237, 443
*Hound of the Baskervilles, The* (1939) 77, 242, 293, 295, 614, 671
House, Dorothy 574
*House of Dracula* 77, 158, 300, 463, 530, 562, 619-632, **621**, **626**, 647, 671, 672, 672, 682, 727
*House of Fear, The* (1939) 10, 95, 251, 271, 562, 563
*House of Fear, The* (1945) 95, 217, 273, 276, 445, 557-563, **561**
*House of Frankenstein* xii, 23, 77, 158, 186, 270, 300, 308, 409, 480, 499, 519-535, **521**, **531**, 551, 562, 583, 620, 630, 682, 724, 727
*House of Horrors* xx, 97, 275, 479, 509, 551, 562, 596, 653, 655-665, **659**, **662**, 671, 672, 712, 714, 718, 727
*House of the Seven Gables, The* 6, 7, 25, 27-40, **35**, 55, 562
Howard, Curly 135, 217
Howard, John 67, 69, **69**, 70, 71
Howard, Lewis 96, 100
Howard, Moe 126, 135, 217
Howard, Shemp 68, 71, 121, 122, 126, 127, 135, 137, 217, 222
Hubbard, John 261, 264
Hull, Henry 53, 113, 148, 152, 154
*Hunchback of Notre Dame, The* (1923) 154, 203, 520
*Hunchback of Notre Dame, The* (1939) 6, 430
Huston, Walter 376
*I Walked with a Zombie* 408, 434, 575
*Indestructible Man* 79, 581
*Inner Sanctum* xvi, xx, 43, 68, 80, 97, 242, 268, 354, 375, 394, 412-413, 414, 415, 416, 419, 430, 433, 438, 481, 482, 505, 509, 529, 550, 580, 583, 587, 588, 589, 606, 610, 611, 612, 636, 638, 639-640, 652, 654
*Invisible Agent* 69, 71, 206, 225-235, **230**, 249, 453, 516, 741
*Invisible Man, The* 2, 8, 11, 50, 69, 154, 186, 234, 242, 409, 428, 457, 607, 653, 722, 744
*Invisible Man Returns, The* 1-14, **3**, **9**, 38, 50, 63, 84, 105, 109, 217, 233, 243, 322, 386, 452, 739
*Invisible Man's Revenge, The* 10, 71, 107, 155, 273, 276, 363, 428, 449-458, **451**, **456**, 509, 625, 672, 681

*Invisible Woman, The* 63-72, **64**, **67**, **69**, 83, 109, 110, 122, 135, 205, 217, 230, 243, 726
*Island of Lost Souls* 24, 109, 144, 331, 530, 623, 682
Ivan, Rosalind 614, 617, 638, 639, 640, 641
Ivano, Paul 373, 384, 510, 538, 545, 546, 581, 582, 590, 617, 654
*J'accuse* 568

Jacoby, Michel 207, 209, 210
Jay, Griffin 51, 54, 58, 61, 151, 257, 260, 264, 334, 339, 476, 484
Jean, Gloria 375, 376, 377, 463, 466, 538, **540**, 541, 542, 543, 544, 545, 546
Johnson, Joe 718
Johnson, Noble 179, 181
Jones, Allan 130, 271, 463
Joyce, Brenda 610, 638, **639**, 639, 640, 641, 649, **652**, 652-653, 654, 699, 700, 701
Joyner, Joyzelle 207
*Jungle Captive, The* 68, 469, 470, 581, 591-598, **593**, **596**, 608, 659, 672, 717
*Jungle Woman* 68, 81, 97, 155, 332, 467-474, **470**, 529, 580, 592, 725
Karloff, Boris xiii, xv, **xv**, xvii, xviii, 1, 6, 16, 17-18, 19-20, 21, 22, 25, 26, 30, 34, 43,
    44, 50, 51, 52, 53, 57, 58, 73, 79, 84, 95, 110, 113, **120**, 121, 147, 158, 165, 177,
    186, 188-189, 191, 192, 193, 194, 196, 204-205, 220, 249, 255, 263, 277, 300,
    301, 302-304, 314, 315, 338, 385, 386, 393, 400, 406, 412, 482, 490, 497, **498**,
    498-499, 500, 501, 519, 520, 522, 526, 527, 529, 530, **531**, 532, 533, 534, 549,
    553, 595, 620, 621, 625, 632, 647, 675, 706, 721, 724, 726, 727, 729, 730, 731,
    732, 733-734
Karloff, Sara 519
Katch, Kurt 552, 555
Kellaway, Cecil 6, 7, **9**, 11, 13, 36, 40, **52**, 55, 56, 57, 59, 61, 92, 228
Kelly, Burt 26, 30, 40, 72, 109, 116, 117, 137
Kelly, Paul 505, 508, 510, 682, **684**, 687
Kenton, Erle C. 195, 197, 529-530, 533, 534, 621, 622-623, 630, 681-682, 686, 687
Kerr, Frederick 186, 187
Kerrigan, J.M. 147, 160
*King Kong* 43, 85, 179, 218, 252, 262, 270, 332
Knaggs, Skelton 458, 625, 632, 644, 647, 648
Knight, Fuzzy 92, 93, 94, 100, 253
Knowles, Patric 151, 154, 157, 160, 200, **201**, 204, 207, 210, 213, 215, 216, **216**, 221,
    222, 299, 310, **313**, 315, 316
Knox, Elyse **257**, 261, 264, 338
Korda, Alexander 155, 580
Kosleck, Martin 480, 550, 552, **553**, 555, 584-586, **585**, 588, 589, 614, **615**, 617, 659,
    660, 664, 668, 671, 676, 746
Kraly, Hans 401-402, 409
Kramer, Stanley 296, 413
Krasner, Milton 13, 40, 195, 197, 409, 458
Kruger, Otto 591, 593-595, **596**, 598
Kuznetzoff, Adia 309, 312, 316
Lacombe, Georges 557
Ladd, Alan 108-109, 117

Laemmle, Carl Jr. ("Junior") xxi, 6, 17, 49, 50, 55, 112, 114, 121, 153, 185, 269, 275, 385, 388, 628, 722
Laemmle, Carl Sr. xxi, 6, 17, 49, 55, 112, 114, 121, 153, 169, 275, 385, 628, 722
Landers, Lew (Lewis Friedlander) 43, 46, 151
Lane, Vicki 68, 595, **596**, 597, 598
Lanchester, Elsa 299, 315
Lang, Fritz 38, 95, 111, 217, 568, 625, 626
*Last Warning, The* (play) 562
*Last Warning, The* (1929) 95, 271, 563
*Last Warning, The* (1938) 140, 563
Lattimore, Jonathan 140
Laughton, Charles 24, 354, 495, 638, 682, 716
Laurel, Stan 50, 129, 130, 312, 432, 460, 708, 727-728
Laurel and Hardy 50, 64, 129, 130, 312, 432, 460, 708, 727-728
Lava, William 633, 672, 676
Le Borg, Reginald 82, 261, 390, 414, 415, 416, 418-419, 432, 437, 438, 439, 468, 469, 473, 478, 482, 484, 505, 507, 508, 510, 538, 539, 542, 543, 544, 545, 546, 580
Lees, Robert 64, 72, 109-110, 117, 137, 726, 735
Leni, Paul 95, 104, 112, 271, 563, 582
Leroux, Gaston 199, 345, 349, 351, 358, 359, 370-371, 495
Lesser, Sol 109, 253
Lewis, Joseph H. 174, 181
Lewton, Val 144, 150, 327, 408, 486, 625
*Life Returns* 270, 627
*Li'l Abner* 109, 624
Lindsay, Margaret 30, 33, 34, 35, 36, 40
Litel, John **165**, 166, **168**, 169, 170, 206, 210, 234, 516, 518
"Lizard's Leg and Owlet's Wing" (TV episode) 79, 158, 553, 734
Lloyd, Doris 158, 160, 197, 267, 273-274, 279, 316, 383, 458, 563, 631
Lloyd, Harold 123, 129, 284, 606, 727
Locke, Edward 493, 496, 501
Lockhart, Gene 231, 571, 574, **575**, 576, 577, 669
Lockhart, June 574, 667, 669, **669**, 670, 673, 674, 676
Lockhart, Kathleen 574, 669
Loftus, Cecilia 108, 117
Lorre, Peter 38, 79, 227, 229-230, 234, 296, 412, 553, 600
Lowe, Edward T., Jr. 292, 297, 520, 525, 533, 534, 621
Lowery, Robert 49, 479, 483, 484, 661, 664
Lubin, Arthur 26, 137, **343**, 351, 354, 357, 358, 359, 496, 497, 649, 653, 654
Lubitsch, Ernst 77, 277, 401-402
Lubitsch, Helene 401
Lugosi, Bela xiii, xvii, 1, 16-17, 19, 20, 22, **22**, 25, 26, 30, 34, 43, 55, 73, 77, 84, 96, 104, 107, **110**, 115, 117, 147, 148, 151, 158, 159, 160, 176, 177, 195, 196, 197, 207, 218, 220, 231, 253, 255, 263, 267, 269, 270, 273, 277, 278, 279, 299, 301, 303, 304, 305, 306, 310, 316, 319, 331, 333, 363, 378, 388-389, 390, 391, 393, 395, 406, 486, 499, 507, 524, 526, 527, 533, 581, 627, 637, 654, 671, 675, 718, 721, 722, 723, 729-730, 732, 734

Luke, Keye 234, 252, 253

MacDonald, Edmund 13, 26, 213, 217, 222, 318, 323
MacDonald, J. Farrell **637,** 641
MacRae, Henry 275
MacVicar, Martha 308, 311, 312, 316, 337, 339, 484
*Mad Doctor, The* 67, 181, 272, 284, 586
*Mad Doctor of Market Street, The* 23, 77, 108, 123, 173-182, **175, 178,** 481
*Mad Ghoul, The* 43, 76, 97, 155, 262, 399-410, **401, 405, 408,** 683
*Madame Secretary* (TV series) 567
*Magnificent Ambersons, The* 111
Malvern, Paul 181, 200, 205, 210, 534, 630, 633
Malyon, Eily 668, 671, 673, 675, 676
Mamoulian, Rouben 530, 623
*Man-Made Monster* 1, 23, 73-88, **79,** 99, 100, 147, 149, 158, 204, 216, 255, 270, 308,
    354, 454, 524
Mander, Miles 39, 40, 359, 442, 447, 486, 490
Mankiewicz, Joseph L. 624
Manners, David 670
Marin, Edwin L. 231, 232, 234
Mark, Michael 39, 40, 61, 186, 189, 197, 297, 308, 525, 528, 534, 631
Marlowe, Don 723
Massey, Ilona 229, 233, 234, 299, 300, 310, 313, **313,** 314, 316
Matthews, Brander 373, 743
Matthews, Lester 450, 452, **456,** 458
Maupain, Ernest 603
May, Joe 2, 8, 9, 10, 13, 31, 33, 34, 37, 38-39, 40, 64, 66, 72, 95, 568
May, Mia 37, 568
Mayer, Louis B. xvii, 206
McBroom, Amanda 406
McDonald, Grace 379, 383, 513, **514,** 515, 516, 517, 518, 542, 546, 583
McDonald, Philip 282, 289
McGraw, Charles 402, **408,** 409
Meeker, George 397, 505, 510
Merkel, Una 123, 127, 175, 181
*Michael Strogoff* (novel) 507
Millhauser, Bertram 320, 361, 362, 366, 368, 423, 425, 428, 450, 454, 455, 458, 489,
    490, 491, 600, 602, 604, 726
Mitchell, Thomas 369, 377, 383, 573
Montez, Maria xvi, 68, 71, 112, 200, 203, 205-206, **205,** 208, 209, 210, 227, 261, 328-
    329, 391, 406, 453, 551
Moore, Dennis 552, 555, 589
Moran, Peggy **52,** 55-56, **56,** 57, 59, 61, 92, 94, 100, 205
Moreland, Mantan 92, 124, 125-126, 127, 188, 214, 217-218, 221, 222, 671
Morgan, Ainsworth 328
Morgan, Ralph 267, 271, 272, 278, 279, 436, 439, 657
Morison, Patricia 414, 417, 419, 690, 692, 699, 700

*Mug Town* 328

Muir, Gavin **284**, 288, 289, 323, 367, 557, 563

*Mummy, The* (1932) **xv**, 51, 54, 58, 189, 287, 296

*Mummy's Curse, The* 60, 97, 443, 475, 477, 527, 531, 547-555, **553**, 580, 599, 672

*Mummy's Ghost, The* xii, 97, 270, 386, 475-484, **477**, **480**, 547, 548, 549, 661

*Mummy's Hand, The* 7, 47-61, **52**, **56**, 83, 92, 93, 94, 97, 256, 258, 263, 475, 528, 548, 656

*Mummy's Tomb, The* 55, 57, 94, 97, 243, 252, 255-265, **257**, **263**, 270, 274, 277, 330, 476, 482, 483, 549, 580, 656

*Murder in the Blue Room* 23, 206, 511-518, **514**, 552

"Mystery of Marie Roget, The" (short story) 199

*Mystery of Marie Roget, The* 83, 157, 199-211, **201**, **205**, 216, 270, 516, 668


Nagel, Anne **19**, 23, 25, 26, 71, 76, 80, 83, 85, 88, **168**, 169, 170, 181

Naish, J. Carroll 331, 416, 418, 419, 470, **470**, 473, 520, 522, 529, 530, 532, 533, 534, **607**, 610, 612, 620, 621, 657

Napier, Alan 7, 13, 38, 39, 40, 661, 664

Neill, Roy William 242, 293, 294, 295, 297, 314, 315-316, 318, 319, 320, 323, 367, 368, 428, 442, 443, 447, 490, 491, 533, 546, 560, 563, 600, 602, 604, 615, 617, 644, 647-648, 689, 691, 693

Newfield, Sam 520, 529

Nigh, William 82, 215, 220, 222, 223

*Night Monster* 77, 111, 157, 220, 221, 227, 267-279, **271**, **275**, 417, 455, 670, 681, 699

*Nightmare* 281-290, **284**, **287**

Norris, Edward 201, **205**, 206-207, 210


Oakie, Jack 442, 515, **569**, 570, 572-573, 574, **575**, 576, 577, 638

O'Connor, Donald 515, 561, 575

O'Driscoll, Martha 463, 466, 624, 632

*Of Mice and Men* 78, 105, 353, 412

Olsen and Johnson 94, 129, 135, 459-460, 461, 463-464, 465, 466, 478, 512, 514, 573, 652

O'Shea, Oscar **477**, 481, 484, 719

O'Sullivan, Maureen 652, 699

Otterson, Jack 13, 26, 36-37, 40, 46, 53, 61, 72, 88, 100, 117, 127, 137, 145, 160, 171, 182, 197, 209, 210, 223, 235, 246, 254, 265, 279, 297, 323, 676, 687, 693, 701, 709

Ouspenskaya, Maria 148, **149**, 157, 159, 160, 200-201, 204, 208, 209, 210, 308, 311, 316

Owen, Reginald 231, 237, 647


Paige, Robert 65, **387**, 395, 397, 479

Parker, Eddie 194, 195, 197, 234, 264, 313-314, 315, 316, 555

Parker, Jack 665, 712, 719

Parsons, Louella 374

*Pearl of Death, The* xx, 155, 436, 485-491, **487**, **489**, 595, 596, 646, 657, 664, 690

Perkins, Gilbert 195, **313**, 313-314, 315, 316, 535

*Phantom* 418

*Phantom, The* 57, 98, 219

*Phantom of the Opera, The* (1925) 277, 342, 349, 353, 357-358, 385, 494

*Phantom of the Opera* (1943) xix, 6, 82, 110, 155, 199, 242, 276, 327, 341-359, **343**, **348**, **352**, **355**, **394**, 430, 455, 493, 496, 497, 504, 512, 649, 654, 738

Pierce, Jack P. xix, 17, 26, 50, 57, 61, 88, 112, 152, 153, 160, 189, 197, 210, 262, 265, 299, 302, 303, 305, 307, 316, 328, 350, 351, 353, 357, 384, 397, 404, 409, 447, **462**, 468, 484, 502, 526, 528, 534, 550, 552, 555, 592, 598, 617, 633, 648, 654, 665, 676, 687, 693, 701, 709, 719, 724, 729, 734, 742

Pierlot, Francis 127, 257, 274, 277

*Pillow of Death* 97, 415, 509, 635-641, **637**, **639**, 652, 671, 672

Pivar, Ben 46, 61, 82, 96-98, 100, 109, 140, 145, 264, 328, 334, 339, 409, 415, 419, 473, 482, 484, 510, 551, 555, 590, 612, 641, 656-657, 665, 676, 712, 714, 715, 716, 719

Poe, Edgar Allan 28, 104, 115, 116, 199-200, 202-203, 208, 209, 210, 211, 319, 362, 412, 461, 687

Porter, Don 268, **271**, 272, 278, 279, 667, 670, 673, 676, 699, 700, 701

Price, Vincent **xviii**, 2, **3**, 5-6, 7, **9**, 13, 14, 30, 31, 32, 33, 34, 35, 36, 37, 38, 39, 40, 55, 63, 68, 69, 71, 96, 113, 575-576, 664, 722, 734

*Private Life of Sherlock Holmes, The* (novel) 239

*Pursuit to Algiers* 445, 613-617, **615**, 645, 654


Raines, Ella 113, 497

Rains, Claude xi, xiii, **xviii**, 2, 4, 5-6, 8, 21, 55, 63, 68, 71, 113, 147, 152, 154-155, 159, 160, 227, 341, 344, 345, 346, 347, **348**, 350, **352**, 353, 354-355, 357, 358, 450, 457, 494, 497, 606, 607, 651, 722, 742, 744

Randolph, Jane 725, 734

Rathbone, Basil xvi, xx, 38, 68, 77, 106, 116-117, 187, 194, 204, 237, 238, 242, 244, 245, 246, 284, 291, 295, 297, 311, 323, 363, 364, 367, 386, 425, **426**, 428, **444**, 445, 447, 488, 490, 561, 563, 586, 603, 604, 616, 617, 647, 648, 654, 691, 692, 745

Rawlins, John 140, 142, 145, 240, 244, 245, 246, 293

Ray, Fred Olen 718

Reicher, Frank 205, 210, 262, 264, 267, 270, 279, 476, 484, 525, 527, 534

*Return of the Vampire, The* 43, 150-151, 388-389, 527

Reynolds, Marjorie **44**, 44, 46, 705, **705**, 706, **707**, 709

Richards, Addison 169, 170, 402, 409, 547, 554, 555, 610, 612

Ridges, Stanley 16, 19, 20, 21, **22**, 25, 26, 95, 357, 403

Riggs, Lynn 239, 244, 246, 252, 254, 320, 322, 323

*Ring of Doom* (radio episode) 412

Riordan, Marjorie 613, 617

"Rival Ghosts, The" (short story) 373

Roach, Hal 70, 78, 129, 353, 497, 513, 728

Robinson, Edward G. 369, 373, 375, 377, 378, **379**, 380, 383, 392, 638, 743

Robinson, George 83, 195, 265, 302, 311, 316, 338, 339, 391, 397, 447, 514-515, 518, 534, 545, 546, 621, 623, 633, 682, 687

*Rocketeer, The* 718

Rogell, Albert S. 105, 109, 115, 117
Rogers, Buddy 206
Rosen, Phil 97, 202, 203, 207, 208, 209, 210, 602
*Route 66* (TV series) 79, 158, 553, 734
Ruman, Sig 520, 522, 528, 534
Ryan, Irene 575, 576, 577
Ryan, Peggy 575, 576, 577, 578

Salter, Hans J. 13, 26, 46, 61, 82, 84, 87, 88, 100, 117, 127, 137, 145, 153, 160, 171, 182, 195, 197, 210, 223, 235, 254, 265, 269, 279, 300, 311, 316, 339, 368, 392, 397, 428, 458, 470, 484, 521-522, 534, 535, 578, 590, 633, 665, 672
*San Diego, I Love You* 418-419
Sanders, George 32, 34, 35, 38, 40, 55, 488
Sarecky, Barney 275
Sawtell, Paul 420, 439, 447, 470, 474, 487, 491, 510, 555, 563, 598, 633, 687, 701
*Scarlet Claw, The* 202, 217, 367, 441-447, **444**, 558, 599, 625, 668
Schubert, Bernard 473, 555, 580, 590
Schulberg, Budd 157
Schumm, Hans 234, 252, 253
*Sealed Lips* 23, 163-171, **165**, **168**, 206, 243, 251, 516
Sennett, Mack 220, 529
*7th Victim, The* 144
*Shadow of a Doubt* 112, 275, 540
Shane, Martin 51
Shaw, Janet 137, 264, 267, 274-275, 277, 279, 665
*She* (1916) 296
*She* (1936) 218
*She-Wolf of London* 68, 97, 202, 204, 272, 296, 312, 509, 586, 667-677, **669**, **674**, 682, 712
*Sherlock Holmes* (play) 322
*Sherlock Holmes* (1916) 603
*Sherlock Holmes* (1922) 242
*Sherlock Holmes and the Secret Weapon* 77, 291-297, **293**, 319, 528, 603, 690
*Sherlock Holmes and the Spider Woman* xxi, 68, 107, 277, 421-428, **422**, **426**, 446, 486, 604
*Sherlock Holmes and the Voice of Terror* 83, 155, 237-246, **238**, **241**, **243**, 291, 322, 497
*Sherlock Holmes Faces Death* 241, 244, 277, 361-368, **364**, 421, 446
*Sherlock Holmes' Fatal Hour* 603
*Sherlock Holmes Fights Back* (working title) 295
*Sherlock Holmes in Peril* (working title) 424, 428
*Sherlock Holmes in Washington* 217, 317-323, **320**, 361, 487, 726
Siodmak, Kurt (Curt) 9-10, 13, 16, 18-19, 21, 23, 24, 26, 64, 66, 71, 72, 144, 147, 150, 151, 152, 158, 160, 214, 220, 231, 233, 234, 305, 306, 307, 309, 314, 316, 334, 391-393, 395, 397, 409, 497, 501, 504, 525, 533, 534, 739
Siodmak, Robert 39, 83, 113, 157, 391, 392-393, 397

Skinner, Frank 13, 37, 40, 61, 84, 88, 100, 153, 160, 210, 223, 246, 254, 279, 289, 297, 323, 368, 470, 510, 535, 546, 612, 631, 633, 641, 672, 676, 728, 735
*Son of Dracula* 65, 68, 80, 81, 113, 155, 191, 204, 276, 285, 354, 385-397, **387**, 403, 408-409, 419, 455, 479, 523, 548, 581, 629, 681
*Son of Frankenstein* 1, 17, 20, 30, 36, 76, 77, 84, 92, 104, 106, 109, 111, 121, 147, 183, 187, 191, 195, 302-303, 385-386, 498, 519, 526, 528, 622, 629, 631, 656, 660, 712, 722
Sondergaard, Gale 68, 104, 106, 107-108, 115, 117, 412, 413, 423, 425, 428, 444, 450, 452, 497, 499, 501, 649, 650, 651, 654, 684, 706, 709
*Spider Woman, The* see *Sherlock Holmes and the Spider Woman*
*Spider Woman Strikes Back, The* xxi, 95, 107, 110, 277, 428, 649-654, **652**, 699
Stanwyck, Barbara 370, 373, 375, 383, 738
Starling, Lynne 497, 501
Starrett, Vincent 239
Stevens, Onslow **626**, 626-627, 630, 632, 633
Stevenson, Robert Louis xiii, 24, 493, 562, 575, 622
Stevenson, Tom 148, 160, 316
Stone, Milburn 46, 234, 329, 330, 334, 339, 367, 402, **408**, 409, 470-471, 473, 583-584, **585**, 588, 589, 610, 612, 650, 654, 699, 700
Stössel, Ludwig 501, 625-626, 627, 632
Strange, Glenn 259, 262, 264, 524, 525, 528-529, 530, **531**, 534, 620, 623-624, 627, 632, 721, **723**, 723-724, 725, **728**, 730, 731, 732, 733, 734, 737
*Strange Case of Doctor Rx, The* 23, 77, 81, 83, 97, 122, 124, 135, 157, 204, 213-223, **216**, **219**, 243, 276, 445, 670
*Strange Confession* 97, 243, 529, 605-612, **607**, **608**, 652
*Strange Death of Adolf Hitler, The* 166, 403
Strickfaden, Kenneth 17, 83-84, 175, 363, 623
Struss, Karl 623, 682
Stuart, Donald 246, 252, 253
Sucher, Henry 257, 260, 264, 328, 334, 339, 473, 476, 484, 580, 590
Sutherland, Eddie 64, 66-67, 71, 72
Sydney, Sylvia 157

*Tales of Manhattan* 372, 375, 379
Tansman, Alexander 379, 384, 546
Taylor, Dwight 283, 286, 289
Taylor, Eric 18, 26, 110, 117, 195, 197, 255, 343, 358, 359, 391, 393, 395, 397, 455, 504, 649, 653, 654
Taylor, Ray 253, 254
Taylor, Robert 206
*Terror by Night* 625, 643-648, **645**
*That's the Spirit* 145, 565-578, **569**, **575**
*Time of Their Lives, The* 44, 134, 277, 428, 703-709, **705**, **707**, 721
*Too Much, Too Soon* (autobiography) 288
Tourneur, Jacques 150, 426
Tourneur, Maurice 581
*Tower of London* 2, 6, 7, 18, 528

Tracy, Lee 515, 594
Treacher, Arthur 575, 576, 577
Trowbridge, Charles 40, 50, **52**, 61
Tyler, Tom 50, 52, **52**, 53, 57, 59, 61, 92, 113, 253, 255, 256, 260, 262, 263, 393, 482,
    548, 549, 722

Valentine, Joseph 154, 160
Van Enger, Charles 127, 277, 278, 279, 368, 423, 428, 461, 466, 578, 709, 735
Varnick, Neil P. 257, 264, 339
Veidt, Conrad xi, 6, 37, 43, 226, 402, 507, 552, 581, 625
Verdugo, Elena 524, 527-528, 530, 534, 581, 583, 588-589
Verne, Jules 507
Verne, Kaaren 296, 297
Victor, Henry 92, 296, 297
Vinson, Helen 43, 44, 46
Vivian, Percival 600, **601**, 604
Von Mendelssohn, Eleanora 586

Waggner, George 74, 75, 76, 82, 85, 87, 88, 99, 100, 153, 154, 158, 160, 166, 167-168,
    169, 170, 171, 197, 207, 234, 316, 344, 349, 353, 354, 357, 359, 409, 455, 496,
    499, 501, 502, 742
Walker, Stuart 147, 671
Ward, Amelita **593**, 596-597, 598
Ward, Edward 347, 350, 359, 466, 499, 502
Ward, Luci 580, 590
Wegener, Paul ix, xii-xiii, 371
*Weird Woman* 23, 68, 97, 155, 272, 429-439, **432**, **435**, 443, 471, 482, 589, 725
Weisberg, Brenda 402, 409, 432-433, 439, 446, 447, 476, 484
Welles, Orson 111, 204, 367, 662
Wellman, William 143, 206
Wells, H.G. 2, 4, 8, 13, 72, 225, 234, 452, 456, 653
West, Vera 14, 26, 40, 46, 61, 72, 88, 100, 111-113, 117, 127, 137, 145, 160, 171, 182,
    197, 210, 223, **230**, 235, 246, 254, 265, 279, 289, 297, 316, 323, 339, 359, 368,
    384, 397, 410, 420, 428, 439, 458, 466, 474, 484, 491, 502, 510, 518, 534, 546,
    555, 578, 590, 598, 604, 612, 617, 633, 641, 648, 654, 665, 676, 687, 693, 701,
    719
Westmore, Bud 730, 735
Whale, James 8, 51, 63, 68, 73, 77, 80, 83, 111, 112, 149, 154, 185, 186, 187, 188, 191,
    195, 272, 273, 299, 300, 303, 391, 458, 525, 526, 528, 532
Whelan, Tim 284-285, 286, 289
Whitney, Peter 712, 719
Wilde, Oscar 154, 296, 372, 373, 377
Wilder, Billy 37, 204, 516, 523
Wiley, Jan 223, 668, 670, 676, 719
William, Warren 148, 155, 160
*Wings* 143-144, 206

*Wolf Man, The* 6, 78, 82, 84, 87, 99, 100, 105, 121, 147-161, **149**, **156**, 168, 181, 195, 204, 216, 241, 262, 270, 273, 307, 308, 311, 314, 322, 353, 354, 388, 412, 497, 504, 505, 539, 628, 629, 737, 740, 742
Wolfe, Ian **284**, 289, 322, 323, 383, 442, 447, 458, 487, 490, 516, 518, 612, 693
Woman in Green, The 68, 217, 292, 297, 367, 445, 446, 520, 599-604, **601**, 643, 690

Yarbrough, Jean 662, 665, 671, 674, 675, 676, 714-715, 719
Young, Clarence Upson 214, 220, 223, 268, 276, 278, 279
Young, Harold 264, 549, 580, 581, 589, 590, 598

Zucco, George 53, 54, 58, 59, 61, 97, 193, 218, 256, 258, 262, 264, 297, 310, 319, 323, **401**, 404-405, 406-407, 409, 410, 444, 475, 479, 480, 483, 484, 520, 522, 527, 529, 534, 549, 602, 603, 627, 724

Printed in the USA
CPSIA information can be obtained
at www.ICGtesting.com
LVHW020414030124
767934LV00005B/103

9 781629 336930